AF510161

EXAMPLES & EXPLANATIONS

Real Estate Transactions

EDITORIAL ADVISORS

Rachel E. Barkow
Charles Seligson Professor of Law
Faculty Director, Peter L. Zimroth Center on the Administration of Criminal Law
New York University School of Law

Erwin Chemerinsky
Dean and Jesse H. Choper Distinguished Professor of Law
University of California, Berkeley School of Law

Richard A. Epstein
Laurence A. Tisch Professor of Law
Director, Classical Liberal Institute
New York University School of Law
Peter and Kirsten Bedford Senior Fellow
The Hoover Institution
James Parker Hall Distinguished Service Professor of Law, Emeritus
Senior Lecturer in Law
The University of Chicago

Ronald J. Gilson
Charles J. Meyers Professor of Law and Business, Emeritus
Stanford University
Marc and Eva Stern Professor Emeritus of Law and Business
Columbia Law School

Tracey L. Meares
Walton Hale Hamilton Professor of Law
Founding Director, The Justice Collaboratory
Yale Law School

Marc L. Miller
Ralph W. Bilby Professor of Law
Dean Emeritus
James E. Rogers College of Law, University of Arizona

Richard K. Neumann, Jr.
Alexander M. Bickel Distinguished Professor of Law
Maurice A. Deane School of Law at Hofstra University

Robert H. Sitkoff
Austin Wakeman Scott Professor of Law
John L. Gray Professor of Law
Harvard Law School

David Alan Sklansky
Stanley Morrison Professor of Law
Faculty Co-Director, Stanford Criminal Justice Center
Stanford Law School

EMERITUS EDITORIAL ADVISOR

James E. Krier
Earl Warren DeLano Professor of Law Emeritus
The University of Michigan Law School

EXAMPLES & EXPLANATIONS

Real Estate Transactions

Eighth Edition

Barlow Burke

Professor of Law Emeritus and John S. Myers and Alvina Reckman Myers Scholar
Washington College of Law
American University

ASPEN PUBLISHING

Copyright © 2026 Barlow Burke.

Thank you for complying with copyright laws by not reproducing or distributing any part of this book in any form without permission. Aspen Publishing supports copyright because it encourages creativity and the sharing of knowledge and fosters a climate of fairness, progress, and innovation.

No part of this publication may be reproduced or transmitted in any form or by any means, electronic or mechanical, including photocopy, recording, or utilized by any information storage or retrieval system, without written permission from the publisher. Under no circumstances may any part of this publication be used in content generation software, systems, or tools such as those that utilize artificial intelligence processes or algorithms. For information about permissions or to request permissions online, visit us at www.AspenPublishing.com.

To contact Customer Service, e-mail customer.service@aspenpublishing.com, call 1-800-950-5259, or mail correspondence to:

Aspen Publishing
Attn: Order Department
1 Wall Street
Burlington, MA 01803

1 2 3 4 5 6 7 8 9 0

ISBN 979-8-8941-0158-3

Library of Congress Cataloging-in-Publication Data

Names: Burke, D. Barlow, 1941- author
Title: Real estate transactions / Barlow Burke, Professor of Law Emeritus and John S. Myers and Alvina Reckman Myers Scholar, Washington College of Law, American University.
Description: Eighth edition. | Burlington, MA : Aspen Publishing, 2026. | Series: Examples & explanations | Includes bibliographical references and index. | Summary: "An attorney's practice in this country is likely to present matters arising in residential purchase and sales and/or commercial transactions involving real property. In the former capacity, the real estate attorney functions amid the work of many other actors-brokers, property inspectors, surveyors, mortgage lenders, appraisers, title abstractors, and title insurance companies, to name a few of the principal ones. Succeeding chapters will deal with each of these. Often, residential work comes to the attorney's attention in mid-transaction-most significantly, after the contract of sale has been executed. Thus, often in residential sales practice, the attorney's role is limited by the contract and is limited to interpreting the contract as the executory period proceeds"—Provided by publisher.
Identifiers: LCCN 2026021425 (print) | LCCN 2026021426 (ebook) | ISBN 9798894101583 paperback | ISBN 9798894101606 epub
Subjects: LCSH: Vendors and purchasers—United States | Conveyancing—United States | Mortgages—United States | LCGFT: Study guides
Classification: LCC KF665 .B87 2024 (print) | LCC KF665 (ebook)
LC record available at https://lccn.loc.gov/2026021425
LC ebook record available at https://lccn.loc.gov/2026021426

ABOUT ASPEN PUBLISHING

Aspen Publishing is a leading provider of legal education content and digital learning solutions in the United States and globally. Our innovative products and platforms—designed based on best practices in learning science—engage students and enhance outcomes. From textbooks and audiobooks authored by renowned experts to digital platforms and products like LEAF, Connected eBooks, Connected Quizzing, PracticePerfect, and JD-Next, we empower the next generation of legal professionals with innovative, trusted, and accessible resources.

The Aspen Casebook Series, affectionately known as the "red and black" casebooks among law faculty and students, includes hundreds of highly regarded textbooks across more than 80 disciplines. These range from foundational courses like Torts and Contracts to emerging electives such as Sustainability and the Law of Policing. Our study aids, including the popular *Examples & Explanations* series, help law students master complex topics with clarity and confidence.

Aspen's expertise extends to undergraduate education with our Paralegal, Criminal Justice, and Business Law series, offering the same hallmark quality to a broader audience. JD-Next, our groundbreaking online law school prep course and admissions test, provides a realistic preview of law school, equips students with essential skills for academic success, and evaluates their readiness for legal studies.

Aspen Publishing Is Proud to Be a UWorld Company

Since 2003, UWorld has been a global leader in developing high-quality learning tools for students preparing for high-stakes exams. With a commitment to excellence, UWorld has helped millions of students in undergraduate, graduate, and professional programs in fields such as medicine, nursing, finance, and law achieve their academic and career goals.

Founded by Chandra S. Pemmasani, M.D., during his medical residency, UWorld began focusing on medical education and has since expanded into various academic fields, including law. In 2020, UWorld launched its Legal vertical, starting with its comprehensive Multistate Bar Exam (MBE®) Question Bank, followed by the acquisition of Themis Bar Review, which integrated resources to provide a complete bar exam preparation experience. In 2024, UWorld expanded its offerings by acquiring Aspen Publishing, enhancing its suite of legal education products.

Today, UWorld offers an unparalleled range of study materials that blend active learning methods with expert content, ensuring students and educators can access the most effective resources. From bar preparation to law school success, UWorld is committed to supporting the next generation of legal professionals. Learn more at uworld.com.

Summary of Contents

Contents

Preface

This book is intended to supplement law school elective courses in real estate conveyancing and transactions, mortgages and finance, and business planning and investment in real property. First-year students whose basic property course deals with real estate transactions will also find many parts of the book helpful. *Real Estate Transactions: Examples and Explanations* covers basic information needed for these courses and deals with the issues and leading cases likely to be discussed in class. It is divided into two parts: conveyancing and mortgage financing.

Real Estate Transactions: Examples and Explanations begins with simple residential transactions and proceeds to more complex commercial transactions. It discusses the various actors who play a role in these transactions and presents them chronologically in the order in which they are likely to appear. The book traces the general organization of the leading casebooks on the subject.

Explanations of the examples (or problems) are provided for your convenience. After reading the examples, I recommend that you pause to think about your answer. You will profit from considering your own explanation, and you may enjoy arguing with mine. This kind of mental engagement is the real value of a book like this.

The eight editions of this book have been prepared during very different real estate markets. Many of the additions to the current edition reflect recent changes in the marketplace, particularly in the mortgage market.

This edition retains the most valuable features of its predecessors: condensed documents of various types, abridged statutes, and, above all, example after example. New examples emphasize trends in the current market. Examples from the previous editions that proved especially instructive have been retained.

My hope is that this book will help students to understand the issues and cases that make up real estate transactions, a fascinating and basic field within the general practice of law.

Barlow Burke
January 2026

Acknowledgments

A teacher is constantly learning and relearning the subject he teaches. I am grateful, first, to the authors of the many casebooks I have used over the years, as well as the authors of the treatises I've consulted, and of the numerous law review articles and cases I read to stay current. Second, my students' comments and questions in class have proven to be a wellspring for this book. I thank them all, too numerous to mention. Third, all my research assistants over the past several decades—Julie Richmond, Catherine Brown, Les Alderman, Stephanie Quaranta, Catherine Thomas, Meryl Eschen, Michael Vila, William Weaver, Stacy Pine, and Brad Jensen—have pursued the answers to my questions with steady and patient research. Finally, Aspen Publishers has provided solid encouragement and excellent support. I thank all.

CHAPTER 1

American Conveyancing and Professional Responsibility

An attorney's practice in this country is likely to present matters arising in residential purchase and sales and/or commercial transactions involving real property. In the former capacity, the real estate attorney functions amid the work of many other actors—brokers, property inspectors, surveyors, mortgage lenders, appraisers, title abstractors, and title insurance companies, to name a few of the principal ones. Succeeding chapters will deal with each of these. Often residential work comes to the attorney's attention in mid-transaction—most significantly, after the contract of sale has been executed. Thus, often in residential sales practice, the attorney's role is limited by the contract and is limited to interpreting the contract as the executory period proceeds.

In commercial real estate transactions, the attorney's role is similar to that of an attorney in other areas of corporate or commercial practice. The attorney is interested in limiting the risks the client faces in proportion to the rewards the client expects. This entails a balancing of business and legal concerns in the context of reviewing the title of the property to be purchased, selecting a note and mortgage, and negotiating their covenants. The following documents detail the typical transaction:

1. The vendor's listing agreement and the purchaser's "buyer's broker" agreement. It is the two real estate brokers' employment contracts and defines the terms of these brokers' agency with the vendor.
2. The contract of sale. Whether the attorney helps negotiate the contract or is given it only after the fact to interpret and implement, the contract is the product of two English statutes: the Statute of

Frauds (1677), one of whose sections required that the transfer of interests in real property be written, and the Statute of Uses (1535). The latter statute validated a new form of future interests, known as executory interests. (Thus the period of time between the execution of the contract and the closing is known as the "executory period.") Americans have taken the common law contract of bargain and sale, added the idea of an executory contract as it developed in the eighteenth century, and adapted it for use in this country—that is, filled it with conditions, contingencies, and "subject to" clauses. In some regions of the country, escrow instructions implement the contract.

3. The note, along with a mortgage or deed of trust. These provide the two financing instruments—an IOU and a security agreement for the loan—necessary for either the vendor or a third-party (often institutional) lender to provide a loan to finance the purchase of the property.
4. Closing documents. The deed from the vendor to the purchaser, plus a welter of documents that (1) account for the money changing hands in the course of the transaction, (2) protect the lender from defenses to the note or mortgage, (3) protect the purchaser's title as offered by the vendor (e.g., an attorney's title opinion or a title insurance policy), or (4) indicate compliance with various state and federal consumer and regulatory statutes. Americans do not use the common law forms of conveyances. Instead we have adopted statutes authorizing the transfer of title to real property by simple forms for deeds and authorizing the recording of all documents transferring an interest in realty on public land records. The documents memorialized on the public record are available later as evidence of the history of the title transferred.

An attorney may be involved in the preparation of all of these documents, ranging from filling them out to drafting them completely. Whether in residential or commercial work, the attorney is arranging a transaction that both parties consider will work to their benefit, adjusting the risks to be commensurate to the benefits expected by the client. The work is not adversarial in the same sense that litigation is—although, as changing markets and circumstances produce new risks for the parties, it can come to that. It is when markets and circumstances change or unanticipated risks arise that professional responsibility issues also are likely to arise. Those issues are the subject of the next section.

With the Statute of Uses providing a legal mechanism for executing contracts of sale and the Statute of Frauds requiring written contracts and deeds, Americans added another new element to their conveyances—the public record, from which vendors could show title to their purchasers. The system of public records, maintained typically at the county or city level, relies on each purchaser of an interest in real property promptly recording it.

The earliest purchasers were interested in only one interest or estate in real property—the full fee simple absolute. Anything less felt reminiscent of the feudal relationships that Americans had left the Old World to escape. Thus early American legislatures enacted legal reforms to make the fee more freely alienable with regard to feudal interests: They abolished primogeniture, abolished the common law presumption for the joint tenancy with a right of survivorship in favor of the tenancy in common, and limited the common law marital estates of dower and curtesy to land seized at death—all done to make real property free of familial interests. Yet at the same time, they often viewed land as a commercial commodity, so state legislatures created restraints on the fee for commercial interests (such as mechanic's liens and new forms of mortgage liens)—interests unknown in England. Thus, our conveyancing simultaneously became both simpler and more complex.

While the public records reflected the state of the title, it yielded its answers as to what a particular vendor has to transfer with some difficulty. With the passage of time, as the records came to reflect a greater number of transfers, this difficulty became extreme. In theory, the records had to be searched on every transfer back to the sovereign—the proprietor of the colony, the king, or the state or federal land office patent. Eventually, on the mistaken notion that the Statute of Limitations on every conceivable common law writ had run after 60 years, that length of time came to be the period of search for real property titles. However, in states where land was obtained out of the public domain of the federal government (and so not subject to state statutes of limitations), title is often still searched "back to the sovereign."

Attorneys quickly acquired the skills necessary to search titles, and the law of conveyancing and title search became their domain. Of course, attorneys were not available everywhere, and where they were not, deeds drafted by laypersons often became confused. If a deed of bargain and sale (or, in New York, a deed of lease and release) was not used, the lay conveyancer and often the attorney threw in every legal verb that came to mind. Thus the vendor would "give, enfeoff, grant, convey, bargain and sell, lease and release, covenant to stand seised, assign and transfer" whatever property it was that was changing hands. This potpourri of legal verbs eventually came to mean "what I (vendor) have, I transfer it to you (purchaser)." Thus the warranty-free quitclaim deed was recognized. This type of deed is another American conveyancing invention intended to make a title more freely transferable.

A title search is necessary because every purchaser wants to know not only that the vendor is entitled to transfer the title but also that the title is "marketable"—that is, is transferred in such a state that it in turn can be transferred to a future purchaser. Even for a quitclaim deed, therefore, the law read a standard of marketable title into every contract of sale as an implied term. The title-searching attorney's job is to determine whether the vendor is eligible to transfer the title and whether there are any liens or encumbrances attached to it. The attorney's notes on these two issues are gathered together and arranged chronologically into an "abstract of title."

As attorneys did more and more title searches, they accumulated stacks of abstracts as their work product; these abstracts had value if and when they handled a later transfer of the same property. Some firms hired nonattorney employees as title searchers. Thus began the practice of having a lay abstractor search the title and an attorney review the resulting abstract and issue an opinion on the state of the title.

The next question was what to do about abstractor negligence. The possibility of an expensive and time-consuming lawsuit always loomed. Title insurance responds to this threat. Early policies were designed to substitute for a vendor's deed warranties and to provide a remedy for abstracting mistakes, as well as to protect against interests that the abstractor could not discover by searching the public records. Thus title insurance policies protected against both record and nonrecord defects. This double coverage became their great selling point. By the beginning of the twentieth century, title insurers were established as abstractors, reviewers, and insurers of titles in many large urban areas. In rural communities, attorneys and abstractors continued to do the business of conveyancing as before. Today, however, the conveyancing industry evidences three patterns for attorney participation. Attorneys function as title searchers, title reviewers, or employees of title insurance companies.

This pattern of participation still means that attorney involvement comes usually after the contract of sale is executed and the executory period underway, at a time when real estate brokers, lender mortgagees, appraisers, property inspectors, and title insurers—and, in some regions of the West, escrow agents—are also involved. Some attorneys bemoan this lateness, arguing that the provisions of the contract of sale determine what will happen during the executory period and that consequently, vendors and purchasers need legal advice while they are still able to affect the provisions of the contract.

In the twentieth century, the reform of American conveyancing patterns was statutory. One generation of statutes took; the other didn't. First, the failed effort: From the 1890s to the 1930s, more than 20 state legislatures enacted Torrens, or title registration, statutes. Under them, a title search was performed, and a certificate of title reflecting the state of the title was issued; thereafter, a transfer of the certificate, amended to reflect new less-than-fee interests, was a transfer of the title. The states enacting such laws acted with many jurisdictions around the world to implement some versions of a title registry (as opposed to a public records office). In this country, this reform did not take. For many reasons, the Torrens statutes were repealed or fell into disuse during the 1930s, and a conveyancing reform that had proved efficient for many countries around the world was here discarded. However, a title registry is still available in a few states as an alternative form of conveyancing.

The problem of title searches becoming increasingly longer and ever more mired in paper did not go away. After World War II, the process of searching title, no matter how it was conducted, needed further definition, and a second generation of statutes, less comprehensive than the Torrens acts, followed. The problem was this: As time passed, title searches covered a longer and longer period of time and involved ever more diverse types of interests. The need to shorten and simplify them was addressed by two types of state legislation. First, Marketable Record Title Acts shortened the period for the search from the 60-year, common law search to periods of 30 to 40 years. Second, statutes of various types enacted shorter statutes of limitations for encumbrances on the fee simple (particularly for old mortgage liens) and for curing defects appearing on the face of documents on the public record for a certain length of time. Attorneys supported enactment of these two types of legislation. These second-generation statutes are still with us.

PROFESSIONAL RESPONSIBILITY

Real property transactions generate a disproportionately great number of malpractice claims, perhaps in part because investigations are conducted in hindsight. Absent a client's informed consent to an alternative arrangement, attorneys representing clients must maintain the confidences and secrets of the client and exercise "independent professional judgment" on their behalf, judgment free of self-dealing and dual representation. This requires that no representation of a client be undertaken if it will be directly adverse to the interest of another client unless (1) the attorney believes reasonably that the representation otherwise prohibited will not adversely affect the relationship with the other client and (2) each client consents after consultation and disclosure of all relevant facts. *See* Am. Bar Assn., Model Rules of Profess'l Conduct (hereafter MRPC) (replacing the ABA Code of Profess'l Responsibility and the basis for every state's rules); MRPC, Rules 1.1, 1.3, 1.6, & 2.1 ("A lawyer shall exercise independent professional judgment and render candid advice"—a rule adopted in all states). Self-dealing is prohibited absolutely, and there are, moreover, reasonable arguments for abolishing dual representation outright.

The structure of a real estate transaction requires constant communication—a virtual monologue with the inexperienced client and communication about new aspects of the transaction with experienced ones, from the engagement letter forward. This is so because the transaction culminates in a closing, or the close of escrow, and a client should never experience any surprises when sitting at the closing table. In order to satisfy themselves about potential problems, levels of knowledge, and conflicts of interest in the transaction, attorneys need to assess existing representations for conflicts—their own, their partners', and their firms'—both before and after undertaking the representation. When conflicts are reasonably foreseeable, and before they arise, attorneys have a professional obligation to avoid them, even if that means withdrawing from the representations and the transactions.

Moreover, because attorneys often represent developers and mortgage lenders on a continuing basis and vendors and purchasers of property on an irregular basis, they must diligently watch for potential conflicts of interest.

Enforcement of these rules is uneven, but that is no reason to ignore their precepts. They should be incorporated into an attorney's ongoing duties. Some believe that every real estate transaction should involve two attorneys, one for the vendor and another for the purchaser, but in the many transactions in which the purchase price is not paid in cash but is instead financed by a third-party lender, at least one other party needs representation. In fact, a third-party lender seldom goes unrepresented, and indeed in some regions its attorney is often the only attorney present, handling the closing of the title as well as the lending transaction. Does an attorney violate any rule of professional responsibility by representing both parties to the transaction? Merely representing both parties, except in negotiating the contract of sale, does not violate any rule so long as the attorney meets the requirements of consultation with the clients. *See ibid.*, MRPC, Rule 1.8.

In the following short examples, assume that the attorney has checked and found no past conflicts of interests in the representations of two parties, vendor and purchaser.

Examples

EXAMPLES

Example 1a

Once hired by one party, could an attorney obtain a written consent from both parties at closing, and satisfy the MRPC, Rule 1.8?

Explanation

No. The timing shows conclusively that the parties consented too late in the transaction.

Example 1b

Could an attorney have obtained the same consent at the execution of the contract of sale?

Explanation

No again. Why? Because the rule requires that there be a consultation. Simply signing the consent form does not meet that requirement.

Example 1c

What sort of consultation is required? Suppose an attorney once hired by one party consulted with both together and explained the potential problems to them. Is that sufficient?

Explanation

Maybe not. A separate meeting with each client may be required. When a vendor is first represented, there must be a separate meeting with her to obtain her consent to multiple representation; with her consent, then a separate meeting with the purchaser is in order.

Example 1d

If the vendor and the purchaser in the prior examples proceed to close the transaction, suppose the attorney does not attend and instead sends her very competent paralegal. Is she violating the canons or encouraging the unauthorized practice of law?

Explanation

Yes to both questions in some states like South Carolina but not in most states (*see*, e.g., North Carolina Ethics Opin. 9 (02 FEO 9), issued Jan. 24, 2003 (a nonattorney assistant may identify the documents at the closing, even with no attorney present); and N.C. Gen. Stat. §84-2.1 (defining the practice of law)).

Example 1e

Suppose the vendor and purchaser ask the attorney at the closing to act as an escrow agent for a fixture on the property when the parties disagree on whether it was sold. Is this allowed?

Explanation

Sometimes. Some cases make the agent only liable to carry out the terms of the escrow, so they had better be clear and in writing. Other cases say that the agent is the fiduciary of each party to the escrow.

Example 1f

Suppose the attorney, practicing in a jurisdiction that makes the post-closing escrow agent a fiduciary of the parties, breaches a fiduciary's duty of loyalty to one of the parties. Is breach of that duty proof of malpractice?

Explanation

No, *see Dunn v. Leepson*, 830 A.2d 325 (Conn. App. Ct. 2003). First, a breach of fiduciary duty is self-proving, but malpractice, tried as a tort, requires expert testimony to establish a standard of care. Second, the ABA rules do not form a basis for civil liability; they are guidelines meant to police the profession.[1]

Real estate attorneys often say that they are expert in the processes required to complete a transaction, but that in many situations, what they know is to step down the office hallway to consult with their more specialized partners.

Example 2a

You are representing a developer in a complex real estate transaction. You see a looming tax problem for the developer that will prevent the deal from closing. You consult your firm's tax partner by e-mail. In later litigation over the transaction, is the e-mail discoverable?

Explanation

Be careful what you write in an e-mail, but many courts do recognize an intrafirm attorney-client privilege generally.

1. An issue splitting the courts is whether an attorney's ethical violation may be admissible as evidence in a malpractice action against him, and a real estate transaction gone wrong provides the leading case for inadmissibility. *See Hizey v. Carpenter*, 830 P.2d 646 (Wash. 1992), discussed at 109 Harv. L. Rev. 1102, 1104-1106 (1996) and reaffirmed as inadmissible, with an exception for a lawyer who transacts business with a client (then admissible) in *LK Operating, LLC v. Collection Grp., LLC*, 331 P.3d 1147, 1165-1167 (Wash. 2014). But *see Lazy Seven Coal Sales v. Stone & Hinds, P.C.*, 813 S.W.2d 400, 405 (Tenn. 1991) (admissible). The traditional rule is one of inadmissibility, justified as protecting attorney-client confidentiality and fostering the attorney's duty to serve clients zealously.

Example 2b

Your client in the previous example is sued by the mortgage lender in the transaction. You now discover that a partner of yours has represented the developer in the past and never ended the relationship with him. Is your e-mail discoverable?

Explanation

Yes, it is. The conflict of interest of you and your firm abrogates the attorney-client privilege. *See* Douglas R. Richmond, Law Firm Internal Investigations: Principles and Perils, 54 Syracuse L. Rev. 69 (2004). In addition, once the e-mail is disclosed, the tax partner's opinion attached to the e-mail is discoverable, too.

Example 2c

Once the partner's opinion is disclosed, is the metadata (when the e-mail was created, versions and revision history, the server where saved, comments, etc.) also discoverable?

Explanation

Perhaps. A motion to compel the forensic examination of a cell phone, computer, or other electronic device requires courts to consider two issues. First, whether the examination will reveal information relevant to the merits of a cause of action. Second, whether the result—in text messages, emails, and so forth—is proportional to the needs of the action when balanced against the device owner's interest in privacy, or here, a lawyer's duty to keep confidential information necessary to maintain the lawyer-client relationship and protect both that privileged information and his work product. Proportionality is shown in part by the movant showing the possibility that the data sought is recoverable. With such a motion pending, a protective order is appropriate to prevent tampering with the device—preserving the metadata but not ordering its production.

Mining such data presents issues of privileged communication and confidentiality. MRPC, Rules 1.4 & 1.6. State professional responsibility opinions are split on such mining. It is not unethical in some states. *See* Md. State Bar Ethics Comm'n, Op. 2007-09 (Oct. 16, 2006) and ABA Standing Comm. on Ethics and Prof. Respon., Op. 06-442 (Aug. 5, 2006). But it has been found unethical in New York and Florida. *See* e.g., Flor. Bar Prof. Ethics Comm'n, Op. 06-12 (Sept. 16, 2006). Lesson: Send e-mails as a PDF or use software that will strip out the metadata from the transmission. Generally, an attorney may be disciplined for mishandling someone else's privileged information. So consult in person with a client.

Once an attorney is found liable for professional malpractice, he may not retain the complaining client's fee when asked for its return. Disgorgement of fees is the rule everywhere. Only when the client seeks additional compensatory damages does the client need to show that the malpractice proximately caused the damages claimed. Otherwise, disgorging the fee follows the showing of a breach of professional responsibility. When an attorney is paid by the hour and a client asks for the return of the fee, cases split on whether the attorney must return only that portion of the fee charged after the malpractice or all fees charged for work before and after the malpractice occurred. If proximate cause need not be shown, the better view is that the entire fee must be returned. If the violation of the Rules occurred in the course of a lawyer's transacting business with a client, any resulting document—lease, deed, or contract—may be declared null and void.

In the following examples, we go from a single attorney to a law firm setting, as follows.

Examples

EXAMPLES

Example 3

You (Abe Abel) graduated from law school last year and are very busy practicing law in a two-person firm with Nancy Willing, an attorney with ten years of practice experience. Dick and Debbie Developer, local developers and friends of Nancy, are the sole owners of Blackacre Company, a single-asset entity that they've established to subdivide and develop a large land parcel (the Company's sole asset, acquired from Dick) in your community. Dick asks your law firm, Abel and Willing, to represent the Company in a real estate transaction in which Worldwide Realty, a large, out-of-state, national residential builder, will acquire an interest in the Company and become Developers' partner in building homes on the parcel. Will you accept the representation?

Explanation

You may, but you first need to consider three matters: your competency, your and your firm's conflicts of interest, and a letter of engagement or retainer agreement, often called the three Cs: competency, conflicts, and cash. MRPC, Rules 1.1, 1.2, 1.7, & 1.8.

The first is your competency. Attorneys duly licensed to practice law are assumed competent to handle matters brought to them. For this reason, professional rules about this matter are often statements phrased negatively: for example, an "attorney shall not handle matters that he knows or should know he is not competent to handle. . . ." This assumption holds even when an attorney's learning curve is a steep one. *See* MRPC, Rule 1.1, Comment [1]. A newly admitted attorney may be as competent as a long experienced one. *Id.* What is required is preparation that is reasonable and adequate in the circumstances. Skills, hopefully acquired in law school, not specialized knowledge, are the measure of competence. Indeed, incompetence most likely appears when an attorney proves incapable of managing his workload or the technology he uses.[2]

As you read this example, you probably thought that it would be nice for a local practice to have a national client who might bring in more future business than any local client would. In order to avoid a charge of unauthorized practice of law, the national out-of-state business will probably hire local counsel. National counsel appearing virtually may raise unauthorized practice of law issues for in-state attorneys. *See Birbrower, Montalbano, Condon, & Frank, P.C. v. Superior Court*, 949 P.2d 1 (Cal. App. Ct. 1998) (allowing such virtual representation but repealed by statute). Local counsel will have similar tempting thoughts. Your competency creates opportunities, not the other way around, so stay focused on it. For example, if you are very busy already, you have to think about how you will meet your obligation to represent a new client adequately.

The second matter to consider is whether you or your firm has any conflicts of interest. Larger firms have in-house, sometimes full-time, counsel to make decisions about this matter, but you will need to talk to Nancy Willing about it.

Example 4

In your discussion with Nancy, you learn that she once worked as an in-house counsel for Worldwide Realty and is well acquainted with Worldwide's acquisition of an interest in local developers' projects, although during her employment by Worldwide it never showed any interest in any of Dick and Debbie's projects. Is your firm disqualified from representing Dick and Debbie?

Explanation

Yes, it is. When any attorney would be required to disqualify himself under any disciplinary rule, her firm and all its partners and associates are disqualified as well. MRPC, Rules 1.10(a), 1.12(c), & 1.13(c). If the rule were not one of imputed disqualification, what's to prevent Nancy from becoming local counsel to Worldwide while you represent Dick and Debbie? That would be an impossible situation, in which the confidences of each client would be imputed to everyone in the firm. However, Nancy's prior experience may be the very reason that your client came to you and your firm

2. Technology is ever changing: An example is artificial intelligence (AI): Case citations generated by AI require checking their validity and relevance. Likewise, it is up to a lawyer to know the limits, the codes, and the metadata used in any AI search engine a lawyer employs.

about this. Nancy may know (not in a transaction-specific way, but generally) how Worldwide approaches this type of transaction as well as what's important to it, and what's not so important. Nonetheless, her duty to preserve the confidences and secrets of a former client continues after the termination of her employment, except when the relevant client information is in the public domain. MRPC, Rule 1.9, Comment [2]. Disqualification from later representation of adverse parties is intended to protect present and past clients alike. However, after its disclosure, consent to and waiver of this disqualification is possible under MRPC, Rule 1.9(a) (requiring consent only after consultation, unlikely here), 1.7(b), 1.13(g), & 1.9(a). Advance waiver of conflicts of interest is possible so long as the client was given all the advance information about the conflict that is reasonably necessary to make an informed decision about it. Under some state professional responsibility codes, screening of the matter from Nancy's participation in the work and the fees is possible, but in a two-person firm, that may be difficult in practice and create the appearance of improper conduct in any event. Further, if your own learning curve on the matter is steep, Nancy's supervision and advice may benefit you to the point where screening, even if possible, is not desirable.

So there is a lot to discuss with the client before dealing with the third matter—a retainer agreement. This agreement should be clear, defining the scope of the work and the terms of the firm's employment, including a cash retainer and other fees and charges. Many jurisdictions require that this agreement be in writing. Having it written is a prudent practice in any event.

Example 5

In the previous example, who is your client?

Explanation

Dick asked for the representation, but he and Debbie have formed Blackacre Company for the project, and so the client might be Dick individually, or the entity, the Company itself. MRPC, Rule 1.13. Dick's interests may during the transaction become adverse to the entity's. What if in the future you discover that the land parcel was purchased by Dick from a vendor who has the right to rescind the Company's purchase of its sole asset because Dick acted fraudulently? Your future representation of the Company would give you a duty to disclose your discovery to Debbie and, with the client's consent and in the case of fraud that is likely to produce substantial financial injury, to Worldwide as well. *See* MRPC, Rules 1.2(d) & 1.13, Comment [10]. Otherwise you would be assisting in the perpetuation of the fraud. Without a disclosure to Worldwide, your other option would be to withdraw from your representation of the Company, and then you would have the problem of whether your withdrawal can be explained to Worldwide—a matter on which states have different rules. To the Company's successor counsel, no explanation is required. *See* MRPC, Rule 1.6. Receiving no explanation, however, will set successor counsel on a quest to secure further waivers of confidentiality in order to protect his own professional standing. *See* MRPC, Rule 1.6(a). If successor counsel went ahead, but learned of the fraud later, after the transaction with Worldwide was closed, his duty to protect the confidences of his client would trump any duty to disclose to Worldwide. But think about it: What attorney would want to be in such a position?

Given all of the foregoing considerations, the prudent as well as the professionally responsible course of action is probably to assume that Dick is now the client and the entity Blackacre Company is the proposed client. Dick will have to consent to this new, possibly adverse, representation. Likewise, if a multiple representation is proposed for Dick, Debbie, and Blackacre Company, they will have no right to confidentiality *inter se*. All consent and waivers (of Dick, Debbie, and Worldwide) must be obtained in advance of the letter of engagement, in separate documents. Likewise, since you are presently very busy, any new professional arrangements that the firm of Abel and Willing will have to make—temporary attorneys, new associates or staff, and so forth—will have to be fully disclosed and explained to the client beforehand. *See* MRPC, Rules1.2(a) & 1.4(a)(2) (requiring an attorney to discuss with a client how a client's objectives will be met). The letter will have to define the client as "Blackacre Company, and not any or all persons (including Dick) interested in the Company." Representing the Company also may have the advantage of forestalling conflicts when you seek to represent other components of the real estate industry (that is, brokers, title insurers, etc.) in the future.

Example 6

After Dick and Debbie execute a written retainer agreement for Blackacre Company, Fred Dolittle, of the firm of Dolittle and Stahl, is retained as local counsel for Worldwide Realty. Fred is approached by the consumer fraud division of the state attorney general's office investigating the fraudulent procurement of the land parcel by Blackacre Company. May Fred speak with Dick about this matter?

Explanation

Not without notifying you first and receiving your permission. MRPC, Rule 4.2 (prohibiting communication with a person represented by counsel). Fred need not disclose to you, unless asked, why he needs to speak to Dick. If you ask why, Fred may disclose the reason; in doing so, he may not make a false statement of any fact material to his request. *See* MRPC, Rule 4.1, Comment [2]. Your representation of Blackacre Company, or your joint representation of Dick, Debbie, and Blackacre, requires your attendance. Even if your representation of Blackacre Company ended and it was unrepresented, Fred still could not proceed to meet Dick without first informing him that he represents Worldwide and is not a disinterested party. *See* MRPC, Rule 4.3. At the start of the meeting, advise Dick anew that you still represent Blackacre either solely or jointly and that at some point during the meeting its interest and his may become adverse, at which point you should advise Dick to retain independent counsel before proceeding.

Example 7

Blackacre Company's development of its residential subdivision proceeds on time and on budget until the first houses are about to be conveyed to their contract purchasers. Then an environmental law violation is discovered. It will cost $500 per house to fix. The purchasers are unrepresented by counsel. What should you do?

Explanation

Even if you are sure that the contracts allocate the risk of this violation to the purchasers, your letting them close their transactions is imprudent. They are not your clients, but generally you may be liable to a nonclient if the client intended that your work benefit the nonclient and you know or should know that he will rely on your work. The duty of due care that then arises applies only when it does not interfere with the attorney's obligations to the client. *See Schlegel v. Barney & Graham, LLC*, 536 P.3d 231, 464-467 (Wyo. 2023) (giving a multifactor test for determining an attorney's duty to third parties) and *Perez v. Stern*, 777 N.W.2d 545 (Neb. 2010) (giving a multifactor test at 550-551 and collecting cases on this issue at n. 15). Reasonable arguments may be made that this rule applies to these purchasers. Blackacre Company by contract means to convey a benefit on them—the houses—and they are unrepresented at meetings with you (their closings). The very events (the closings) will, after they are all over, become evidence of reliance. One way to handle this is to think how you would behave if any of them showed up with an attorney to represent them: Early, preclosing disclosure of the problem, and a proposal to share the costs of fixing the violation, seem in order. Proceeding otherwise may even harm your client, subjecting its subdivision to litigation, so there is a good argument that your preexisting duty to Blackacre Company will not be breached by such a disclosure and proposal. Liability of attorneys to nonclients runs counter to many of the traditions of our adversary system, so state rules vary—and should be checked.

CHAPTER 2

Real Estate Brokers

The first person any prospective vendor of real property is likely to consult is a real estate broker. Today a broker is likely to specialize in selling particular types of property—residential or commercial, sales or rentals, and so forth. An agreement to employ a broker is called a listing agreement. A short form of such an agreement appears a little later in this chapter. It is often promulgated in a standard format by the local trade group representing brokerage firms. In most jurisdictions, this agreement must be in writing, either because the jurisdiction's Statute of Frauds applies or because of a special statute or regulation in the law governing brokers.

For his services, the listing broker receives a commission computed as a percentage of the selling price of the property. Because the broker is employed by the vendor, he is usually considered to be the agent of the vendor in the subsequent transaction; but most purchasers also hire their own broker (aka the buyer's broker), either to search for property of a specific type or to represent her during the course of a transaction. A buyer's broker generally has a written employment agreement too, stipulating the compensation that he or she will be paid if and when the search for a property to purchase is successful.

In addition, each party to a commercial lease often hires a broker to oversee lease negotiations. In this chapter, we will deal with the broker's role in the purchase and sale of real property.

An agent or broker usually employs associate agents or brokers, often known as salespersons, who may do most of the actual selling, often for a set percentage of the commission.

Often the listing broker is not the selling broker or salesperson, which sometimes causes the unrepresented prospective purchaser to think that the selling broker, salesperson, or firm is working for her. Not so. The selling broker is typically the subagent of the listing broker, and the selling salesperson is the subagent of the selling broker. Confusing perhaps for the purchaser, but think of it this way: The vendor is the principal, the listing broker is her agent, the selling broker is the subagent of the listing broker, and so on until the final contact is made, by the ultimate sub-subagent of the vendor, with the purchaser. These relationships form a chain of agency and subagency reaching to the purchaser, who is (legally) on her own. For purchasers, one cannot lay too much stress on those last three words—on her own. Hopefully, too, she is on her guard, warily evaluating the words of the broker or salesperson presenting properties and describing their features. Some commentators have found this arrangement misleading when viewed from a purchaser's perspective.

When a prospective purchaser is represented by a broker, the buyer's broker agreement may by its terms break the chain of subagents discussed in the previous paragraph. However, because the prevalence of buyer brokers' agreements is more recent than that chain, and because that chain is most used in tort suits for misrepresentation of the physical condition of property, the issue of whether the contract relationship between buyers' brokers and purchasers affects this chain, is an open one.

Examples

Example 1

O, the owner of Blackacre, is anxious to sell this choice parcel of real property. Real estate broker B tells her that P is interested in purchasing it and that B would be happy to have a listing for it.[1] "Forget it," says the owner, who nonetheless does not forget what B said about P. The owner negotiates directly with P for the sale of Blackacre and then executes a contract of sale to transfer Blackacre to her. Can B recover anything for the information that he gave the owner?

Explanation

Only if the owner and B had a prior relationship of mutual trust and confidence or if the owner expressed a desire to help the blurting broker in his business would B have even a chance of a recovery. There is no basis for an implied contract, and no written one exists either. In some jurisdictions,

1. In the examples in this chapter, O or V (for vendor) will be the listing owner, B the broker, and P a prospective purchaser.

the special statute of frauds for listing agreements would also be a bar to B's recovery. The lesson is that B should obtain a listing of the property before blurting out the information that is the broker's stock in trade.

THE LISTING AGREEMENT

A listing agreement is the real estate broker's employment contract. It is typically in writing. Indeed, in most states, a writing may be required either by a special-purpose statute of frauds for such agreements or by regulation of the state regulatory agency in charge of broker licensing and supervision. With such requirements in force, it is also likely to appear on a standard and preprinted form issued by the local brokerage board or trade group. It must usually identify the parties, the listed property, the commencement and termination dates, the sales price, and the commission. Consider the following, quite typical document.

LISTING AGREEMENT

I, Victor Vendor, agree to *employ the services* of _______________, a real estate broker duly licensed in the State of _______________, to list my real *property known as* _______________ with him, and to permit him to *sell* that property.

This listing *begins* on __________, _____, *and ends* at midnight
date year

on __________, _____. During this period, I promise to accept offers to
date year

sell the property for a *total price* of $_______________, payable as follows:

____

I agree to pay a commission of 6 *percent* of the total selling price when the property is sold by *the undersigned, or any other broker*.

This agreement is executed on _______________, ____________, at
date year

_______________, _______________.
city state

______________________, ______________________

Broker Vendor-Owner

Employ the services? What does that refer to? More particularly, what is it that the broker is promising to do? We know that the owner is promising a commission for whatever it is, but what is it? At a minimum the broker is making a promise to expend reasonable effort, in good faith, to procure an offer meeting the prospective vendor's terms. Beyond that, the listing agreements one typically sees are not specific. This raises the question of whether, at the listing's inception, it is a unilateral or bilateral contract. If it is the former, it is not binding on either party until the effort is expended—a *de minimis* effort won't do.

Listing agreements generally provide few details about the broker's efforts. In some instances—and from the broker's hopeful perspective—a phone call will line up a purchaser. In others, a month of open house Sundays won't do the job. In other words, the broker is playing the odds, hoping that over the whole of her accumulated inventory of unsold, listed properties, some will sell each month. Perhaps the services required of the broker should be spelled out in a listing agreement. A broker can be required to put a "for sale" sign on the property, advertise its availability for purchase, show the property at agreed times, and even accept a deposit (or earnest money) or a down payment in an agreed amount. Some of these things the broker will want to do anyway without being required to do so. A "for sale" sign, for example, really advertises the broker's firm—the more of them appearing around town, the better for the firm. Even though the broker will want to do most of these things, some things a vendor may want to do: holding the deposit, for example. Is it a good idea to let the broker do that?

Property known as? What if the blank following this phrase is left empty and Owner O, standing in front of his house, signs an otherwise valid listing agreement with broker B, saying, "Sell my house for me." O points to the house, but B knows that O means to sell his farm. B has actual authority to sell the farm, but may also have apparent authority, stemming from his expressive conduct, to sell the house. This being so, filling in the blank is necessary under the law of agency. See Restatement (3d), Agency, § 1.03, Illustration 3, & § 3.03 (2006). How should the blank be filled in? A legal description of the property is not needed. This is a contract for personal services. It is not a contract or a conveyance of real property, so the legal description is not necessary. A street address will do. Simply because a legal description is not necessary, however, does not mean that it is not good practice to use one. This agreement is the first of many documents needed to generate a closing of the title. The use of a full description here might flesh out the intent of later documents or more formally be incorporated by reference into them. Each of these documents might then be construed together to establish a conveyance of the property. Unless it is agreed otherwise, it is presumed that a fee simple absolute in the title will be sold and that the listing vendor warrants that he has good title.

Sell? This cannot mean literally that the broker is given the authority, via a power of attorney, to convey the property in the name of the owner. No, no—in early cases, in which brokers actually argued this, the courts rejected this notion. The prevailing view is that the word "sell" here means that the listing broker may market the listed property, but may not force either vendor or purchaser to close when either refuses to go forward with the transaction. The word here gives neither actual nor apparent authority to either broker to do that. However, this lack of authority does not mean that the vendor may not be liable for the commission. Thus several issues arise: Is the property "sold" if a binding contract of sale is executed? Can the legal doctrine of equitable conversion be applied to it? Or is it sold when the title is conveyed, at the closing? In this one simple word lurks the problem of timing the broker's right to a commission. A bit of drafting advice: Make sure the timing is clear!

In most jurisdictions, if the offer meets the terms of the listing agreement, the making of the offer is the time at which the commission becomes due so long as the broker has procured the purchaser and the latter is ready, willing, and (financially) able to purchase. There is no need for a contract of sale. But is this the common meaning of the word "sell"? *See Tristram's Landing, Inc. v. Wait*, *infra*, this chapter, holding that because a contract of sale had conditional language, it was not considered a sale.

Begins . . . and ends? That's it!? When the listing ends, it's over? What about the vendor who accepts a qualified offer the next day? What about the vendor who holds off accepting the offer in the expectation of not having to pay the commission? How should this problem be handled? As written, this agreement may stand as an invitation to vendor fraud. So most listing agreements provide that the listing is effective if the property is sold within (say) six months after the termination date to someone the broker introduced to the vendor during the listing period. This provision is known as an extension period provision. This period may end earlier than the specified time if the property is relisted with another broker.

Total price? Inclusive of the commission? Of any mortgage on the property? Again, clarify these matters. A price "net to the vendor" improves this listing, but again, this phrase might mean "net to the vendor after paying any capital gains tax due on the proceeds taken from the closing." Since the payment of such taxes is strictly a matter for the vendor after the closing, this last interpretation is unlikely and would be rejected by a court.

Six percent? The percentage is seldom preprinted on a brokerage board standard form. It is something that the listing broker hastens to supply. Consent agreements in several price-fixing antitrust actions brought by the federal government in the 1970s prevent preprinting of the percentage. Some judicial opinions have inferred that a "usual and customary" fee is intended when this portion of the agreement is left blank. Negotiation over the fee is possible but, as an empirical matter, is seldom undertaken.

The rationale for pegging the commission at a percentage of the purchase and sale price is that brokers will then have an incentive to sell a listed property at the highest price available. Holding broker effort constant, this rationale makes sense, but brokers are also interested in housing inventory turnover—and this interest may mean increasing the turnovers at a price below the highest possible price.

The undersigned, or any other broker? What type of listing is this anyway? Consider the section that follows.

The Types of Listing Agreements

Listing agreements typically fall into one of three main types: (1) the **open listing**, (2) the **exclusive agency listing**, and (3) the **exclusive right to sell**. *See Real Estate Listing Service, Inc. v. Conn. Real Est. Comm'n*, 425 S.E.2d 581, 584 (Conn. 1979). An open listing is a broker's authority to procure an offer but reserves the owner's right to sell the property herself or to authorize other brokers to procure offers too. An exclusive agency listing is again a broker's authority to procure an offer, but it denies the owner the right to deal in a similar way with other brokers without paying the first broker the agreed-on commission. An exclusive right-to-sell listing has the same effect as an exclusive agency but, in addition, denies the owner the right to sell the property herself without incurring liability for the commission. Each of these three types of listings increases the number of situations that entitle the broker to collect a commission and, concomitantly, restricts the number of situations that assign the owner liability for the same. Because the exclusive right-to-sell listing is the most commonly used, a broker with such a listing may do little to sell a property but nonetheless be entitled to a commission.

There are other types of listings as well: The net listing is one. Here the broker agrees to accept as his commission any portion of the purchase price over an agreed-on figure. A considerable number of states have prohibited this type of listing.

The following problems will help you sort out the three main types of listings.

Examples

Example 2

Bill, a licensed real estate broker, hears that Peter is interested in purchasing Sam's residence. He tells Sam this and obtains Sam's signature on the following agreement, dated in January this year:

BROKER'S AGREEMENT

I agree to pay *Bill*, broker, a commission of 5% of the selling price of the following property, *my residence at 1234 Big Shot Way, Potomac, MD* if and when this property is sold by me to *Peter*.

____

Sam, Owner

Is this agreement a valid listing?

Explanation

No. It sets neither a listing price for the property nor a termination date for the listing, as required by many state regulatory statutes and regulations for brokers. A listing agreement is not merely an agreement to pay a commission; it is an employment contract for personal services.

Example 3

In the letter agreement in the previous problem, what if the body of the letter states:

> I agree to list the property below with Bill, broker, on an open listing basis for a period of ninety days from the date of this letter, and pay Bill any of the net proceeds over $5,000,000 of the selling price of the following property [thereafter the letter continues as above].

Explanation

This letter contains a termination date and arguably also contains a listing price. A 90-day listing period allows computation of a termination date measured from the date of execution. A 60- to 90-day period is standard for most listings. If the broker wants more time, the listing might be for (say) 180 days, but terminable by either party on (say) 15 days' written notice. This would give the listing's effectiveness an outer limit—fulfilling the purpose of regulations requiring a termination date—but makes it subject to termination sooner. The change in the structure of the commission creates what the brokerage trade calls a "net listing." But the amount of the commission may be uncertain: There may be difficulties in defining what deductions the vendor may use to calculate the net proceeds of the sale, and so the agreement may still lack a material term. In addition, a net listing creates some conflicts of interest between the broker and the listing vendor. The broker may be less willing to discuss the fair market value of the property with the vendor and the broker is working for himself, rather than as the vendor's agent, on any sale over the stipulated price. To the extent that the broker is self-dealing, he is violating a long-standing principle of agency law. For such reasons, net listings are prohibited by the regulatory statutes governing brokers in many states.

Example 4

Assuming the agreement in the previous two problems is a valid listing, will Bill recover if the property is sold to Peter?

Explanation

No. A further issue is whether Bill expended any effort to procure the sale of the property to Peter. If the answer is no, then the further issue is whether the regulatory code for brokers requires that he do so. Many codes will require the expenditure of broker effort as a precondition to any entitlement to a commission. Assuming that it is valid as a listing, this is an open listing, and so if more than one broker claims the commission, the issue of effort and which broker procured the sale will be all important.

Example 5a

V lists her property with real estate brokers B1, B2, and B3 for sale at \$100,000. B1 produces a customer at that price; B2 produces a customer at \$110,000. V refuses to execute a contract of sale with B1's customer but does so with B2's customer. That latter customer suffers financial losses and cannot close the transaction. B3 then produces a customer at \$95,000. V executes a contract with B3's customer and closes this transaction. All three brokers invoice V for a commission. What type of listing is involved here? And whom should V pay? (This problem comes from Casner & Leach, Property 700 (3d ed. 1984).)

Explanation

Because the type of listing is not identified, the listing is presumed to be an open one. As to whom V should pay, the answer is all three: B1 because she first produces a customer satisfying the known terms of the listing. B1 is the only broker with whom V initially has a duty to deal, but V goes on and signs a contract with B2's customer. The contract is the best evidence that B2's customer is a presumptively suitable purchaser, which entitles B2 to his commission. B3's customer has the same status, only more so: that customer closes the transaction.

Example 5b

Would your answer change if B1 did not hold a real estate broker's license and instead is a salesperson?

Explanation

Yes. A broker's license is a precondition to filing suit for a commission. Further, salespersons hold licenses that contain a condition—that is, they generally cannot sue for a commission on their own behalf; rather, the broker who supervises the salespersons must sue on their behalf.

Example 5c

Would your answer change if B2 had agreed to share his commission with B4, an unlicensed broker?

Explanation

Yes, in many states. Agreeing to share a commission with an unlicensed person is grounds for denying the commission entirely, even to a properly licensed broker.

Example 5d

Would your answer change if B3's customer proposed that V syndicate the property and sell the resulting limited partnership shares in it to the customer?

Explanation

Yes. A limited partnership interest is personal property, not real property. A broker may only deal in realty as defined in the regulatory code, and when the broker steps beyond the bounds of code-authorized conduct, he or she forfeits the commission. A contrasting case might be a corporate vendor listing its real property assets for sale, then transferring a controlling interest in the corporation to a prospect produced by the broker; in this situation, a commission would be due.

Example 6

V orally agrees to list her farm, Blackacre, with B, who then advertises the farm for sale and makes contact with several prospects. V then notifies B that she is trying to sell the farm herself and a week later executes a contract of sale with P1. B then produces a contract executed by P2 to buy the farm for a higher price. V and P1 close the first contract. B sues V for a commission. What result?

Explanation

Judgment for V. Absent a written listing or an express agreement to the contrary, most courts will construe a listing as open, which has two characteristics relevant here. First, the B-V agreement is an agency agreement but not an exclusive agency—it is not V's agreement to deal with only one broker. Second, in an open listing the vendor retains the right to sell the property herself without liability for a commission. This implied term of the listing is made express by V's notice to B. Finally, the listing agreement cannot be construed as just an agreement to sell for the highest price offered. A vendor can refuse a contract tendered by a broker for many reasons, price being just one of them.

Example 7a

V executes a brief but enforceable[2] listing agreement granting B, a broker, an "exclusive right to sell" V's farm, Blackacre. During the listing period, V executes a contract of sale for the property with P. B sues V for a broker's commission. What result?

Explanation

Judgment for V. The negation of the vendor's right to deal with the property, when expressly stated in the listing agreement, results in an exclusive right to sell. However, there is no magic in those four words, standing alone and without spelling out their implication for the vendor. Thus, unless B could show that P came to V through his efforts, V has no liability to B for a commission.

Example 7b

Would your answer change if the listing agreement provides that a commission would be due B if "the undersigned, or any other broker" procured a purchaser for the farm?

Explanation

Probably. The negation of V's right to deal with the property is express here, although even more explicit language is possible—and would show a litigation-avoiding prudence.

Example 7c

Before B procures a purchaser, V leases the farm for the listing period and beyond. Is B entitled to a commission?

---

2. Read this phrase "brief but enforceable"—which appears often in this book—as one meaning that you should assume that the contract is enforceable unless the context, the facts presented in the problem, indicate otherwise.

Explanation

Yes. The broker would be due the commission because V's action here has made the broker's procuring a suitable purchaser impossible. V must deal in good faith with B, and the execution of the lease is not good faith dealing.

Example 8

After listing and advertising V's house for sale in local newspapers for a month, what if there are no offers and B proposes to hold a public "open house"? Is an open house a good idea?

Explanation

Only if it sells the house. Will it? The answer is that it might, but seldom does. Most brokers would like to hold an open house, though. Why? Because (1) it shows broker activity for the listing owner, (2) it allows the broker to meet curious neighbors who might one day be clients, as well as purchasers who are in the market, but not for this house, and (3) it gives the novice salespersons employed by B a chance to get field experience. B probably knows that the open house seldom sells the property, so he or she will probably be doing something more important during it. V should ask what other ideas B has. One better idea would be to hold an open house for other brokers, because it is the broker's peers who will actually sell the house. Another would be a "virtual tour" video that can be posted on the broker's firm's website. It's possible that V has listed with a broker who collects listings—too many to give each personal attention—but relies on selling a certain percentage of the listed properties through other brokers. A short term for the listing agreement is the best antidote for this problem.

THE MULTIPLE LISTING SERVICE

The mechanics of the Multiple Listing Service (MLS) affect the types of listings discussed so far. Most MLSs are organized as a nonprofit corporation run by the local real estate brokers' trade group. Its regulations permit member brokers to list properties with the Service, to share their listings with other MLS members, and to sell any property so listed. Its records constitute an inventory of all properties available for sale at any one time. For purposes of effecting any one sale, the MLS divides its members into listing brokers and selling brokers; its regulations often also permit a broker to attempt to sell the property for which he has procured a listing himself for a short time (e.g., 72 hours) after the listing is obtained; thereafter, it must be submitted to the MLS.

Access to the MLS is limited to its members, and the MLS usually processes a listing only if it is based on an exclusive right-to-sell agreement. A description of the property is processed with the listing.

When a commission is due on a listed property, the listing broker and the selling broker (or their firms) split it. The split is sometimes a 50/50 one, but sometimes it is 40/60, respectively. Further, the commission will be split within the listing broker's firm between the listing salesperson and his broker; and the same split occurs in the selling firm.

In most areas with MLSs, over 90 percent of all residential vendors employing a broker have the listing submitted to it. Thus the MLS is a pervasive factor in residential sales. Without being a member, a broker would find it difficult to compete for this type of brokerage business.

EXAMPLES

Examples

Example 9

V executes a brief but enforceable listing agreement with B1, a broker. The agreement is entitled a "Nonexclusive Listing." It has a 90-day listing period. It also reserves a commission for B1 "if within a year after the primary listing period, V sells the listed property to any prospect B1 procures within the primary listing period." B1 procures customer P, but no contract results within the 90 days. On the 85th day of the listing's primary term, V cancels the listing, then lists the same property with B2, who receives an inquiry from P about the property. P purchases the property within a year after the execution of B1's listing. B1 sues V for a commission. What result? *See Galbraith v. Johnson*, 373 P.2d 587 (Ariz. 1962).

Explanation

Judgment for B1. The extension clause is meant to protect against vendor fraud. Such a clause may extend liability for the commission from 90 days to 1 year and 90 days. However long the extension period, it is always express. It is not intended to keep the broker working beyond the primary term of the listing agreement. As a result, the level of broker effort beyond the expiration can decline markedly; in *Galbraith*, the court only required that his effort be substantial during the primary term. In this sense, the extension clause becomes a separate agreement—or, an agreement within an agreement.

This result would not change if after V cancelled the listing she leased the property to P for two years with an option to buy effective at the end of the lease, and at the end of the first year of the lease, the tenant exercised the option. The vendor's fraud on the broker is then shown by the terms of the lease with the option, and the benefit that the lease confers on V is substantially the same as a sale. Thus both to discourage V's behavior and to prevent V's unjust enrichment, the judgment should still go to B1. An extension clause does not empower a broker who has produced several prospects but has no purchaser during the primary term to continue negotiations with any of his prospects during the extension period. The prospect's readiness, willingness, and ability to purchase is freeze-framed as of the expiration date of the listing's primary term. By the same token, the listing vendor's right to negotiate and sell the property herself is reestablished after the expiration of the primary term.

Example 10

A listing contract contains a provision stating that the commission is payable *inter alia* "when the listing owner, for any reason, withdraws the listing during the primary term of the agreement." Before the broker expends any significant amount of effort to sell the listed property, the owner withdraws and the broker seeks to enforce this provision. Can he?

Explanation

Yes. *See Blank v. Borden*, 524 P.2d 127 (Cal. 1974). Because the listing agreement is completely result-oriented—that is, the broker receives no compensation without a sale, with compensation measured by a percentage of the sale price and paid regardless of the amount of broker effort—the vendor's exercise of the "withdrawal from sale" is an anticipatory breach of the agreement, with the damage to the broker measured not by the amount of his effort but by his lost opportunity. The clause is also an indication that the prospective vendor has a choice. She can either accept the broker's services or withdraw from the agreement. *But see Wright v. Schutt Constr. Co.*, 500 P.2d 1045 (Or. 1972) (refusing to follow a California case similar to *Blank* involving a withdrawal from sale clause when the trial court found, as a matter of fact, that there was no reasonable probability of sale within the terms of the net listing). Alternatively, the withdrawal clause might be examined as a provision for liquidated damages, finding it either a reasonable calculation of damages or a penalty (in the latter instance, the clause would be avoided and the broker reduced to recovering actual out-of-pocket damages).

THE VENDOR'S LIABILITY FOR A COMMISSION

The vendor is liable for a brokerage commission when the broker procures a purchaser ready, willing, and able to purchase the listed property on the vendor's terms, unless the vendor and the broker agree otherwise. Procuring the purchaser is defined as being the proximate cause of the offer. The broker must set off a chain of events leading to negotiations and the offer. No sale is necessary; only an offer need be made.

As to the attributes of the purchaser, ready and willing means being in a state of mind (and *compos mentis*, at a minimum) to make the required offer. Able? That means financially able, not capable of buying for cash (unless the vendor required it in the listing) but appearing to be creditworthy. In most jurisdictions, it is largely for the vendor to decide when a purchaser is ready, willing, and able, up to the execution of a contract of sale. In many jurisdictions, when a vendor executes a contract of sale with a would-be purchaser, this act in itself indicates an acceptance of the fact that the purchaser is ready, willing, and able. The vendor's terms are stipulated in the listing agreement; the broker's duty is to procure an offer on terms substantially the same as, but not identical to, the vendor's. *De minimis* variations are permitted. The vendor may not add conditions after the listing is executed.

Examples

Example 11

O lists Blackacre with B. B introduces P to O during the term of an exclusive right-to-sell listing, but O and P do not execute a contract of sale until the primary term of the listing has ended and its extension period clause applies. Their contract's provisions are quite different from the terms with which the negotiations opened. Does O owe B a commission?

Explanation

A broker must "procure" a purchaser. The answer to the question posed is yes if this means that but for the broker, there would be no contract of sale, but no if the so-called procuring cause doctrine requires an unbroken chain of events leading to the contract. In some states, courts hold that an extension period clause is a waiver of the doctrine. The better view is that it applies all the time. If B had procured an option to purchase instead of a contract from P and the option was exercised during the extension period, O would still owe B a commission. This is a typical situation in which extension periods are useful for brokers, but it leads courts to the (mistaken) view that the doctrine of procuring cause does not apply during the extension period: Here B's efforts led to the sale, even though no further efforts were necessary during the extension period.

Example 12

When is a purchaser qualified as ready and willing? As able? Do these occur simultaneously or at different times?

Explanation

The times are different. A purchaser is ready and willing at the time the contract is executed, but is not yet financially able; her mortgage loan must be approved before she can be called able. Thus the latter term refers either to a finding that the purchaser is able at the time of the contract or to an allocation of the risk that the purchaser will be found "unable" later. In a majority of jurisdictions, the risk that the purchaser will prove unable to buy rests on the vendor.

Example 13

A contract of sale is executed by the vendor and the purchaser, but during the executory period the purchaser fails to qualify for a mortgage loan called for in the contract. Is the broker due his commission? What if the purchaser was qualified for the loan at the execution of the contract of sale but thereafter suffered financial reverses (through no fault of her own) that render her unqualified?

Explanation

As to the first question, the answer is yes in most jurisdictions. The risk that the purchaser will prove unable to buy is on the vendor when the issue is the vendor's liability for a commission. That is, the vendor must make a judgment when executing the contract that the purchaser is financially able to purchase the listed property. It is sometimes thought that the vendor's contract rights against the purchaser support this result.

As to the second question, the fact that the purchaser's financial reverses occurred during the executory period means that it is more difficult to allocate this risk to the vendor. Some authority supports the idea that the broker should not obtain a commission in this situation. This authority exists in jurisdictions that have adopted the (minority) rule governing the vendor's liability for a broker's commission: the rule of "no closing, no commission."

Example 14

V agrees in writing to permit B, a broker, to "handle the sale" of Blackacre. B produces a customer, C, with whom V executes a contract of sale for the property. C fails to close the transaction. B sues V for a commission. What result?

Explanation

As a matter of contract interpretation, the quoted phrase can be interpreted as providing that if there is no closing between the vendor and the procured purchaser, the vendor is not liable for the broker's commission. In short, "no closing, no commission" becomes the rule governing the broker's entitlement. As a matter of law, a minority of states beginning with New Jersey in 1967 have adopted such a rule as a matter of public policy and, later in Massachusetts, as a matter of contract law. Under either version of this rule judgment goes for V, although if the matter were to be decided under the majority "ready, willing, and able" rule, the word "sale" would be interpreted in accordance with prevailing law and found to mean "handle the procuring of a contract of sale"; judgment would then go for B. Language like the quoted phrase has provided the opportunity for a majority rule state to accommodate the purposes of the minority rule.

Example 15

The listing agreement states, without further elaboration, that the commission "is to be paid on the sale." If the broker procures a prospective purchaser who executes a binding contract of sale but later refuses to close, is the listing vendor liable for a commission?

Explanation

No, although the case presents (first) a question of fact—what did the parties mean by the word "sale"?—and (second) one of law. Because evidence on the fact question appears nonexistent, and the contract is construed against the drafter or its beneficiary, the broker, the second issue is a closer one than in Example 14 because the listing agreement might only be defining a time at which the commission is to be paid, not whether it is payable. A Massachusetts opinion held that the use of the word "sale" is to be given its common meaning and refers to a completed transaction—a closing is required before a commission is payable. *Tristram's Landing, Inc. v. Wait*, 327 N.E.2d 727 (Mass. 1975).

Ellsworth Dobbs, Inc. v. Johnson, 236 A.2d 843, 30 A.L.R.3d 1390 (N.J. 1967), is the leading case for the "no closing, no commission" rule. In this case, the facts indicate that the broker clearly brought the parties together, but the purchaser's inability to obtain financing several times postponed the closing until finally the vendor released the purchaser from further liability under the contract of sale. The broker sued the vendor. Holding for the vendor, the court said that the vendor, like most listing vendors, expected to pay the commission out of the proceeds of the closing, and further that the broker assumed the risk that the purchaser's inability to finance the sale would balk the closing. The broker was in the best position to assay the purchaser's financial worth. So when the purchaser expects to pay for property with the proceeds of a sale of stock, but the stock market drops so that the sale produces insufficient funds, the risk is the broker's. Thus the broker, under the rule of *Dobbs*, bears this risk as a result of his expertise. He also bears it because he is in the best position to, so if the property is destroyed by fire or is condemned, the risk is still on the broker. The court held:

> When a broker is engaged by an owner of property to find a purchaser for it, the broker earns his commission when (a) he produces a purchaser ready, willing, and able to buy on the terms fixed by the owner, (b) the purchaser enters into a binding contract with the owner to do so, and (c) the purchaser completes the transaction by closing the title in accordance with the provisions of the contract. If the contract is not consummated because of lack of financial ability of the buyer to perform or because of any other default of his, there is no right to commission against the seller. On the other hand, if the failure of completion of the contract results from the wrongful act or interference of the seller, the broker's claim is valid and must be paid.

236 A.2d at 855. The court held as it did as a matter of public policy, not as a matter of contract interpretation.

Example 16

What if the listing agreement says that the commission is payable "from the proceeds of the closing"? When is it due?

Explanation

There is a split in the cases here. Some cases (like Maine) hold that the phrase only defines the source of the commission payment, not when it need be made. For example, the "ready, willing, and able" rule is not trumped expressly by this language, nor should it be presumed to be. Others (like Arizona) hold that the phrase is more comprehensive, defining both the source and the timing of the payment.

Example 17

Using the two rules on vendor liability for a commission presented so far, consider the following: Vendor and Purchaser execute a brief but enforceable contract of sale, but the purchaser does not complete the purchase because she develops an acute phobia and refuses to leave her present residence. If the broker procuring the purchaser sues for a commission, what result?

Explanation

In a "ready, willing, and able" jurisdiction, the vendor's acceptance of the purchaser, evidenced by the execution of the contract with her, signifies the broker's procuring a purchaser and therefore an entitlement to a commission. *See Blackman de Stefano Real Estate, Inc. v. Smith*, 550 N.Y.S.2d 443 (N.Y. App.

Div. 1990) (holding that when the purchaser develops agoraphobia—an unreasonable fear of open places—the broker is nonetheless entitled to a commission under the "ready, willing, and able" rule).

Absent evidence that the broker should have known about the illness and its probable effect on the transaction, where the *Dobbs* rule is a matter of law, the vendor might still have expected to pay the commission out of the proceeds available to her at the closing, so the public policy basis of the *Dobbs* rule remains. Judgment for the vendor.

In a state in which the *Dobbs* rule is a matter of contract interpretation (such as Massachusetts), the answer may vary depending on the contract, for there the parties to the listing agreement may contract around the rule, and the question becomes whether they have done so. If an objective standard is used to interpret contracts, the broker will likely win a commission.

THE FIDUCIARY DUTIES OF REAL ESTATE BROKERS

Brokers owe certain duties to their principal (*i.e.*, their employer, usually the vendor but possibly the purchaser, so here we use the encompassing language of the law of agency). These duties are based on a preexisting relationship of trust and confidence, here normally shown by a previously executed employment agreement—the listing agreement. Fiduciary duties arise with that agreement and, as if attached to it, as implied terms.

A broker owes his principal three fiduciary duties: (1) loyalty, (2) dealing in good faith, and (3) the disclosure of facts material to the principal's acceptance of an offer. The duties of loyalty and good faith dealing are often lumped together. Taken together, these duties may occasionally give the broker a duty to investigate and disclose to a vendor facts material to a transaction, even if the vendor does not ask. They are clearly violated when the broker does not forward offers to his principal, reveals the latter's confidences, or engages in self-dealing—that is, buys the property himself or in some other way competes with the principal. Moreover, they do not end with the expiration of the listing agreement, in the sense that the broker cannot thereafter undercut the principal's position using information gained during the course of the listing.

The duty to disclose facts material to the principal is a mop-up duty breached when the broker does not reveal his violation of his first two duties or in some way misrepresents the purchaser's qualities—his readiness, willingness, or ability to contract. For example, while knowing that the purchaser's checks bounce, the broker fails to disclose this to his principal. Likewise, a failure to disclose a fact material to the vendor's view of the transaction violates this third, more encompassing fiduciary duty.

Examples

Example 18

A young couple has been driving around in Ben Broker's car for days viewing listed properties, and when getting out of the car, one says to the other, "Let's offer $250K, but we'll go as high as $300K, okay?" If Ben is listening, must he report this to the vendor?

Explanation

The answer is yes if Ben is a vendor's broker, but no if he is the couple's broker.

In many jurisdictions, the state's regulatory code for brokers will provide examples of the duties expected of brokers. Examples might be interpreting the sales contract or arranging for property inspectors and other settlement services. In some jurisdictions, these statutes (aka minimum service laws) list a range of services (uniform standards) that brokers must provide clients regardless of the commission rate. *See, e.g., Stone Creek Bus. Ctr. LLP v. Stone Creek-Colorado, LLC*, 2022 U.S. Dist. LEXIS 174197 (D. Colo., Sept. 22, 2022). Some of these statutes provide that clients may waive these extra services—many do not. Where no waiver is available, these statutes discourage lower flat fees for services and arguably inflate the cost of brokerage services. The services listed correlate with activities incident to the brokers' business, that is, services that brokers may perform under the jurisdiction's law of unauthorized practice. Such statutes have also been used to define the duty that brokers owe clients in nonregulatory or tort litigation against brokers. Notwithstanding these statutes, brokers have ample incentive to assist the parties in closing a transaction. Why? Because the easiest form of paying brokers is by a check cut by closing agents.

The default measure of damages for a breach of duty is the loss of a commission. *See Nichols v. Minnick*, 885 N.E.2d 1 (Indiana 2008). Consequential damages are also available for economic loss, particularly for cases of broker self-dealing. If the broker has already been paid a commission, its disgorgement is possible under a restitution theory; here the damages are measured by the broker's gain, even when the plaintiff has suffered no proven loss or damage. Some states, however, say that the commission amount is an upper limit or a cap on damages.

Examples

Example 19

B holds a valid listing of V's property for sale at $100,000. While showing it to P, who is hesitant to make an offer, B states that "the listing price is $100,000, but offer $85,000 and see what V says." V closes the sale at $85,000, but refuses to pay B his commission when she discovers the foregoing facts. B sues V. In this suit, what result? *See Haymes v. Rogers*, 219 P.2d 339, 17 A.L.R.2d 896, modified on reh'g, 222 P.2d 789 (Ariz. 1950).

Explanation

Judgment for B on the facts, not as a matter of law. The broker has come very close to breaching his fiduciary duty of loyalty to his principal; a slight variation in the broker's words or the lack of the prospect's hesitancy might mean a different result. For example, if the broker said that "V has an offer at $80,000, but offer $85,000 and see what she says," the fact that the broker has disclosed a prior offer might make a difference. Similarly, if the broker said, "the vendor hasn't budged off $100,000, but she desperately needs the listing price to pay for an operation for her mother," the broker might well lose. The facts and circumstances surrounding what is said also matter. B might say, "the listing price is $100,000 and that's it—that price is final" when in fact V is willing to bargain further. Such a statement, standing alone, well might be regarded by the courts as only a bluff and a negotiating posture.

If the broker knew and were to disclose the price at which V would likely consider an offer, the disclosure of such information in the face of a prospective purchaser's intransigence might not breach the duty of loyalty, on the theory that the broker may disclose confidential information when it is in the best interests of the principal to do so and here the broker was only encouraging negotiations.

Example 20

B holds a valid listing of V's property. P employs B to search for property suitable for her residence. P expresses an interest in V's property to B and offers to purchase it. B does not transmit P's offer to V, but instead buys the property himself and later sells it at a profit. On learning the foregoing facts, P sues B. What result?

Explanation

Judgment for P. A broker is required to transmit every offer received. While in the employ of P, B owes P his best efforts to find suitable property, and those efforts may not be diverted for the broker's personal gain. B has violated not only the duty of good faith and loyalty but capped his disloyalty with a failure to disclose self-dealing. Hiring a broker should mean just that—hiring a broker, not a competitor. The public expects brokers not to step out of their professional role, and violating those expectations by self-dealing is a breach of a broker's fiduciary duty.

What if there were no employment agreement between P and B? P's case would be more difficult to make out, but P's employment agreement might be implied in law—a quasi-contract—and, as such, have as its subject the transmittal of offers rather than the full services of a broker. Additionally, when dealing with breaches of a fiduciary duty, think in terms of the law of torts: B has denied P a business or investment opportunity by not transmitting the offer, and so interfered with a prospective advantage or the contract that P might have signed.

Perhaps the remedy (besides damages) is the most interesting part of this situation. P may impose a constructive trust on B's profits or, if B still owned the property, she might force its conveyance to her. *See* Funk v. Tifft, 515 F.2d 23 (9th Cir. 1975), noted at 1976 B.Y.U. L. Rev. 513 and 12 Idaho L. Rev. 217 (1976).

On the same facts, if V sued B, V would obtain judgment. He has a listing agreement on which to base a breach of fiduciary duties: the breach of the duty of loyalty—evidenced by the nondisclosed dual representation and the failure to forward the offer—and the self-dealing—B's buying the property for himself. V need not allege damages for breach of such a duty: The breach of the duty implies injury, at least to the relationship between broker and client, so no allegation of injury is required in the complaint; nominal or consequential damages will be awarded if shown at the trial, as well as recovery of the broker's profit from the self-dealing.[3]

Example 21

P hires B as her broker in a brief but enforceable agreement. B shows P property for sale by V for $100,000. B then learns that V, aware of P's interest, will not deal with P. V and B negotiate with a third party for a sale of the property at $100,000. While these negotiations are underway, P learns that the property is worth $110,000 and asks B to offer V $105,000. B does not transmit P's offer to V, who then sells to the third party for $100,000. P sues B for breach of the duty of loyalty. In B's action, what result?

---

3. Why do you think some states don't require any allegation or later proof of damages? It is because (1) the breach of duty nullifies the employment contract and the cause of action lies in restitution—it is one way to recover money falsely obtained or obtained under false pretenses when the commission is already paid out (and if no commission is paid out, the basis for the suit is the employment relationship in the listing agreement); (2) damages may be difficult to show [*see* Restatement (3d), Agency, §8.01, comment d(2) (2006)]; (3) disgorgement or loss of the commission removes the temptation to violate the duty in the hope that no loss or damages will result; and (4) it facilitates trust between broker and client—a trust on which the fiduciary relationship is based. Overall, this rule is more prophylactic than remedial.

Explanation

Judgment for P, but only for nominal damages. Although the refusal to transmit an offer is generally a breach of the duty of loyalty, the breach here caused the plaintiff P no injury because of V's refusal to deal. Disgorging or denying any commission or fee is P's only remedy. (Typically B will share a commission with V's broker if any—so don't think that B is out in the cold here.)

Example 22

V owns Blackacre. B, a broker, approaches V with the information that someone is interested in purchasing the property. V replies that she does not deal with brokers and does not pay them commissions. B replies that he will get his commission from the interested party, P. Although thereafter V thought that she was selling Blackacre to P, she in fact was selling it to B, who promptly turned around and sold it to P. Discuss V's rights against B.

Explanation

V has a cause of action in tort for the misrepresentation and for the interference with a prospective advantage. However, without an intent to deal with B, V has no listing or other employment contract on which to bottom a breach of fiduciary duty, so there is no cause of action against B on any express or implied contract claim.

Fiduciary duties are grounded in a preexisting relationship of trust and confidence. Typically, that relationship is shown by the listing agreement. Hence, fiduciary duties are a major source of *vendors'* rights against brokers. They may impose duties to speak and act on the vendor's behalf, even when the broker is a volunteer; for example.

BROKER DUTIES TO THE PURCHASER FOR MISREPRESENTATIONS

Fiduciary duties arise from the broker's employment agreement, but typically they are of no help to a party to a transaction (usually but not always the purchaser) not employing the offending broker. A broker, acting as the agent of a disclosed vendor, is not liable to third-party purchasers for actions and representations authorized and within the scope of his agency. (As the authorizing party, the broker's action may be attributed to the vendor.) Absent some special undertaking, a broker alone is liable when his representations are unauthorized and outside that scope; as a matter of law, the vendor does not authorize tortious misrepresentations. *See Kennett v. Marquis*,

798 A.2d 416, 418-419 (R.I. 2002). Nonetheless, for purchasers the law of torts provides default rules governing the broker's conduct. A representation of fact that the broker knows or should know is false, but which is material to a plaintiff's transaction, is made with the intention that the plaintiff will act in reasonable reliance on its truth, and causes the plaintiff injury, may be actionable in one of three forms: as an intentional (or fraudulent), negligent, or innocent misrepresentation.

The materiality of a fact is crucial to a cause of action for misrepresentation, but it is often black-lettered as the distinction between alleged patent and latent defects. A patent defect is subject to inspection, and the risk of its presence is allocated to the purchaser. The underlying premise is that if the purchaser could see it, then she adjusted the bargaining over and the price of the property to take account of it. A latent defect is by definition not subject to inspection, not bargained over, and actionable on that account. All states recognize an action for some type of misrepresentation. Not all states recognize an action for each type.

An intentional misrepresentation is the most widely accepted and is akin to fraud. Here the broker as a defendant has actual knowledge of the falsity of the representation. Another common type of liability here is for a fact of which the broker has actual knowledge, but about which the broker is silent even though aware that the fact is material to the purchaser. For example, often a broker introduces a purchaser to an area by taking the latter around to see the unsold inventory of listings. The broker knows the area, the purchaser doesn't. In this situation, brokers have been held liable to disclose that the property is affected by a nearby toxic landfill or rock quarry, on the theory that the broker's peripheral vision as to what is material to the purchaser's decision to buy is broader than the purchaser's. So while there might not be a duty to disclose (say) the lack of potable water in a property's well, there may be a duty to disclose features of the neighborhood that might adversely affect the value of the property, or a soil condition that, in a wet season, results in soil expansion that can crack a house's foundation.

A negligent misrepresentation may be based on a broker's affirmative statement that turns out to be false, even though the broker did not know that at the time the statement was made. If the broker speaks, the risk that the statement is false is quite commonly the broker's. A negligent misrepresentation can be made honestly and in good faith but still be negligent because it involves facts that the broker should have investigated beforehand. Many states have imposed such liability on brokers. When a vendor's broker shows the listed property to the purchaser, if the vendor and the broker permit the purchaser free access to the property to inspect it, if they make no affirmative misrepresentations, and if they do not conceal any defects in it, or if information about the defect is available from third-party sources known to the purchaser (say public records of some type[4]), then there is no breach of a duty to disclose. Although there is some split in the cases, silence alone is seldom actionable as fraud. When a broker believes that a house was designed by a famous architect, and says so to the purchaser when in fact it was not, and if a purchaser pays more on that account, the broker's statement isn't the sort of thing that can be checked on a public record or that can be characterized readily as a patent condition, so it may be actionable as a negligent misrepresentation.

Finally, an innocent misrepresentation is one that, although made honestly and in good faith, turns out to be false after a reasonable investigation of the facts. Only a few states impose liability on a broker for such a statement because liability in this instance is in effect strict or absolute liability: a decision to put the risk of a misrepresentation on the broker. Only actual, nonconsequential damages are given in this instance.

When a broker and a vendor inspect property together, signs of water seepage into the attic may indicate a leaky roof. If they do not conceal those indications, or don't replace light bulbs that would, if replaced, render the signs of the leaks visible, a purchaser will almost surely have no provable tort action for intentional misrepresentation. Active concealment is the legal equal of intentional misrepresentation. If the broker inspected and saw signs of a leak, but relied on the vendor's statement that it had been repaired when it had not, the vendor's liability will be for intentional misrepresentation, but the broker's will be for negligent misrepresentation. It is not fraudulent, but it's not innocent, either. The broker who neither extols the soundness of the roof nor downplays the purchaser's need to check it out for herself is probably free of liability in most states.

If a vendor discovers cracks in the foundation slab of her house, but recalls her broker's prior advice (given without knowing of the cracks) to install wall-to-wall carpet over the slab, the vendor is liable for intentional misrepresentation, but the broker is not. The broker is also not negligent in this instance. Presumably the vendor would mind the broker's ripping up the carpet to inspect the slab, so the broker's duties are at an end. If the situation were reversed, and the broker discovered the cracks, installed the

---

4. A zoning ordinance is an example. Thus property may even be described by a broker as multi-family on an MLS listing or data sheet, and there is no duty to investigate the zoning on which that description depends. *See* Craig v. ERA Mark Five Realtors, 509 N.E.2d 1144 (Ind. App. 1987). The purchaser best knows whether zoning is important to his future use of the property, and the ordinance is available to vendor, purchaser, and broker equally. The same "no duty" rule applies to (1) any recent rise in the tax assessment of the listed property, (2) the property's location over an underground mine, or (3) its location on a flood plain; tax records and public geologic survey maps are public records and available for a purchaser to check. The constructive notice imparted by a public record is another rationale for such a "no duty" rule: Such notice trumps the broker's duty to investigate. The equal availability of the record also supports the argument that only intentional misrepresentation should be actionable in such instances.

carpet, and did not tell the vendor of the cracks, the broker has concealed what would otherwise be a patent defect in the property and is liable for fraud, but so might the vendor be, on a theory that the broker's knowledge may be imputed to his principal. However, here the broker is the ultimate pocket from which a judgment will be paid.

One state, California, requires that a broker conduct a reasonably prudent visible inspection of normally accessible areas on a listed property and disclose the results to prospective purchasers. *See Easton v. Strassberger*, 199 Cal. Rptr. 90 (Cal. App. Ct. 1984), narrowed by Cal. Civ. Code §2079. Most state courts have not gone so far as to impose such a duty of investigation.

Alleged misrepresentations, besides giving rise to a suit in tort, may also violate state ethics and regulatory rules for brokers, state unfair trade practices acts, and tort duties to convey accurate information when a defendant's business regularly deals in such information.

In summary, an actionable misrepresentation requires (1) a statement of (2) a material fact, which (3) the defendant either (a) knows is false (an intentional misrepresentation) or (b) should know is or will prove false (a negligent misrepresentation) or (c) does not know to be true or false (an innocent misrepresentation) but which (4) meanwhile the defendant intends the plaintiff to act on, and on which (5) the plaintiff does rely, (6) without having a reasonable basis for doing otherwise, to (7) the latter's loss or injury. *See Bortz v. Noone*, 729 A.2d 555 (Pa. 1999) (containing a good summary of the law).

This discussion has proceeded on the premise that a broker's misrepresentation may also be attributed to the listing vendor. This attribution or imputation may seem counterintuitive, but it is based on the assumption that absent a showing otherwise, the broker is carrying out his principal's wishes and fulfilling his duties under the listing agreement, and more generally on the identity that is presumed to exist between principal and agent; a broker's actions are coextensive with the principal's capacity to act in person.

Examples

Example 23

B, a broker with a valid listing to show V's residence, shows it to P, but misrepresents its condition. V and P then execute a brief but enforceable contract of sale for it. The contract provides that the residence is sold by V "as is." P sues B on account of the misrepresentation. In P's suit, what result, and why?

Explanation

The result will depend on the type of misrepresentation alleged and whether the "as is" provision is a defense. The provision tends to show that no matter the misrepresentation, P did not rely on it when purchasing the residence. It was material to neither the transaction nor the proximate cause of the contract damages that P allegedly suffered. If P's suit is for negligent or innocent misrepresentation, this defense is a good one in some states. However, if it is for an intentional misrepresentation, the vast majority of states deny B the defense. The better view is that no matter the type of misrepresentation, the provision is no defense and does not bar the suit, but is admissible and relevant, though not necessarily conclusive evidence that P did not reasonably rely on the misrepresentation. Most states permit B to claim the benefits of the provision, however limited its effect. P's suit is based on a tort, not a contract. The more intentional the tort or active the concealment, the greater the need for the suit and the less scope the provision should have. Moreover, as the facts warrant, this provision is easily confined to patent defects that can appear "as is" on the listed property, is interpreted only as a negation of implied warranties, or is not intended to bar suits based on dangerous conditions on it.

Nor is there generally any duty on brokers to investigate or disclose stigmas that attach to a property—for example, that a former owner had AIDS or that the property was the site of a suicide, multiple murders, poltergeists, or ghost sightings. Not that such things have not produced litigation. They have. But when the litigation has resulted in broker or owner liability, a follow-up statute has often been enacted to reverse the result for the future. *See, e.g.*, Idaho Code §55-2701 (no action for failure to disclose property "psychologically impacted," meaning one near which a sex offender resided, that was the site of a suicide, or on which a prior occupant had a nontransmissible, widely feared, disease). A dozen or so states have also exempted brokers from having to disclose that a convicted pedophile, registered under a so-called Megan's Law, lives nearly. However, some state statutes leave such duties unaddressed. If the law's purpose is to increase public awareness of the offender's presence, then brokers might increase that awareness by disclosure. On the other hand, there is no statutorily prescribed duty to disclose, arguing for no disclosure. Moreover, the registry is in the public domain and available to a purchaser.

If the broker were to make a statement about the scope of Megan's Law, or who must register under the law, that turns out to be false, the statement may be considered legal advice, and just as a broker is not liable for statements regarding the adequacy of a survey or legal description for the property—that's a legal matter—the purchaser should know that a broker's legal advice is not only the unauthorized practice of law but useless as well. The broker is not an attorney and so is without a duty to investigate legal matters.

Brokerage boards are well counseled, and generally when a broker is found liable for a misrepresentation of any type, soon thereafter some disclaimer for the type of information involved is likely to appear in their standard form listing agreements presented to clients. Likewise the subject is likely to be covered by some statement required of a vendor under the disclosure statutes now nearly universal and discussed in the next section.

DISCLOSURE, BUYERS, AND TRANSACTION BROKERAGE STATUTES

In response to the many misrepresentation suits against brokers brought over the past two decades, brokerage trade associations have lobbied for and many state legislatures have enacted vendor property report and disclosure statutes. These cover a range of conditions, so that when the broker is accused of misrepresenting the condition of the property, its permitted uses, or its profitability, the broker can turn to the vendor and say, "She told me to say it." Most misrepresentations may thus be laid at the vendor's feet. This may not keep the broker from being sued, but it may lessen liability: An early disclosure by the vendor may not render the broker immune from suit, but it will provide the broker, once held liable for a misrepresentation, with a vehicle for seeking indemnity from the vendor.

Under such statutes, a property report and disclosure form is filled out by the vendor at the time of the listing. It provides the broker with a report on the physical condition of the property as well as inherent environmental hazards. Vendors disclose whether they have "actual knowledge of current or past conditions" regarding water, plumbing, sewer, septic, heating, air conditioning, and electrical systems; roof; basement and crawl spaces; structure (foundations, walls, and floors); insect infestations (termites, ants, and other wood and masonry borers); and drainage, soil, or erosion problems.

Many states—about two-thirds—now require (mandate) some similar form of disclosure and use brokers to procure it. In the remaining states, brokers use some sort of disclosure form as a matter of prudence. These disclosure forms are many pages long, and often, in addition to the items mentioned previously, cover a long list of appliances, as well as ask questions about the title to the property, earthquakes, wetlands, radon, asbestos, lead paint, and mold on the property. The lists tend to lengthen with each legislative session or brokers' board meeting. There is generally no duty imposed on brokers to see that vendors fill out these forms truthfully. *See McKiernan v. Green*, 2005 Conn. Super. 1527 (Conn. App., June 10, 2005).

Typically, a state statute enumerates the conditions subject to disclosure and (as is again typical) delegates to the state Real Estate Commission the drafting of the mandated property report and disclosure form, leaving it to the Commission to decide whether a vendor will be asked questions like "Are there defects in the walls?" or be presented with a statement like "The walls are defective," and asked to check yes or no in response.

Such statutes and practices encourage the use of property inspectors. They are often paid by vendors. In most states, having inspections done does not waive the statutory requirement for the mandated disclosures. But *see Alires v. McGehee*, 85 P.3d 1191 (Kan. 2004) (vendor's misrepresentations subject to inspection require an actual inspection as a precondition to suit), noted at 44 Washburn L. Rev. 475 (2005).

Examples

Example 24

How might such a disclosure statute change the preexisting common law of misrepresentation?

Explanation

Two changes are illustrative: (1) No longer is the vendor merely required, as at common law, to disclose only latent defects; by using such forms, the vendor may be required to disclose both patent and latent defects. (2) A defect might be defined as a physical defect, or one materially decreasing the value of the property, thereby limiting the reach of these statutes. In any event, the use of these forms will cause vendors to think twice about the listed property's condition and provide brokers with some assurance that the claims they make regarding the property are correct, as well as some defense against the allegation of intentional misrepresentation.

Example 25

A broker says that the property is "new and modern." When a condition subject to disclosure turns out to need replacement, is such talk actionable under the statute?

Explanation

Yes. *See Cruse v. Coldwell Banker, Inc.*, 667 So. 2d 714 (Ala. 1995) (holding that a broker's description of the property as "new" is not just a descriptive term or sales talk, but instead negates the doctrine of *caveat emptor* and making "new" mean "not needing replacement within a reasonable time").

Example 26

A broker presents a property disclosure report form to her client vendor and the vendor hands it back, asking the broker to hire a property inspector to fill it out. What would you advise the vendor who is concerned that some items on the report the inspector fills out may be false?

Explanation

Written instructions to the broker are advisable so that the broker may be held liable for negligence in hiring the inspector. *See Thomson v. McGinnis*, 465 S.E.2d 922 (W.Va. 1995) (recognizing a cause of action for negligent hiring of a property inspector).

Example 27

What if the vendor found a leak in the roof after executing the disclosure report and passed that information along to the broker to reform the report? May the vendor thereafter be liable for the inaccuracy on the form?

Explanation

Yes, although the vendor might also reasonably expect that the broker will update the form as needed and as new information comes to her attention, particularly when that information is supplied by the vendor. *But see Barta v. Kiondschuh*, 518 N.W.2d 98 (Neb. 1994) (holding that when a broker negligently failed to reform a disclosure statement with new information about a leaky roof, provided by the vendor to the broker, the vendor who signs the incorrect statement thereafter has no cause of action against the broker). *Barta* bucks the trend incorporated in a doctrine of reasonable expectations, permitting vendors to rely on their brokers' actions—here, a correction of the disclosure form—once the condition is known. The vendor's reliance on the broker's acting to correct the form is reasonably foreseeable in this case. The broker would have to ask the vendor to review the form anew for the result to be otherwise.

A second response by brokerage groups to purchasers' tort suits has been to represent purchasers rather than vendors. Some state statutes create a presumption that a broker working on the purchaser's behalf is a buyer's broker, unless that broker expressly agrees to a subagency with the vendor's agent(s). Inaccurate information about the property provided by the vendor or the vendor's broker cannot be attributed to such a broker. Fiduciary duties may simply be negated, as in Georgia, or they may be listed, as in Oregon, as loyalty, obedience, disclosure, confidentiality, reasonable care and diligence, and accounting. Or. Rev. Stat. §696.810(3)(a)-(g). At least seven other states—Connecticut, Maine, Michigan, Missouri, South Carolina, Virginia, and Washington—have similar statutes. They purport to limit a purchaser's rights and remedies to a suit against his own broker. In addition, a buyer's broker has whatever duties the purchaser himself would have to the vendor, so the vendor may hold the broker liable for nondisclosures and misrepresentations about the purchaser—about (say) the purchaser's financial ability to close the transaction. *See Lombardo v. Albu*, 14 P.3d 288 (Ariz. 2000).

A third industry response further limits a broker's role. Statutes expressly eliminate the broad prohibition on dual agencies for brokers and provide for a "transaction broker" working for neither the vendor nor the purchaser but facilitating the transaction for each. "A broker engaged as a transaction-broker is not an agent for either party." Absent an agreement otherwise, these statutes create a presumption that a broker acts as a transaction broker. A Colorado transaction broker statute defines and severely limits a transaction broker's duties to transmitting offers, advising the employment of legal counsel, providing full information to all parties, assisting parties to a contract of sale in complying with and closing it, and disclosing adverse facts of which the broker has actual knowledge pertaining to the title, the physical condition, and environmental hazards affecting the property. Such a broker is not liable for disclosing a willingness to accept less than the listing price, the motives of the parties, or stigmas affecting the property, and has no duty to conduct either an independent financial audit or inspection of the property, or to verify "the accuracy or completeness" of disclosure forms or inspection reports that the vendor presents. The disclosure duties of a "limited agent" are to disclose "adverse material facts actually known" by the agent. In the same spirit, an Alabama statute gives its transaction brokers duties of "honesty, reasonable skill and care, confidentiality, and accounting." Omitted here is any duty of disclosure—a way of distinguishing a transaction broker from the buyer's brokers discussed previously. Statutes similar to the ones just discussed have been enacted in Florida, Georgia, Texas, Minnesota, and several other states.

Example 28

B, a broker, explains to P, a prospective purchaser of an office building, the services that she provides as a transaction broker, claiming that they include a verification of financial audits. P employs B with an oral employment agreement incorporating the terms of the Colorado statute described previously. P purchases the building. What recourse has P against B if the financial audit turns out to be inaccurate?

Explanation

The statute is probably no defense to P's action for breach of B's fiduciary duty of loyalty and due diligence. Brokers should be aware that, when explaining this new type of agency to buyers, they should not overpromise—and thus possibly place themselves in a conflict of interest—before the statutory agency arises and protects them from a charge of breach of duty. There is no reason to construe the transaction broker statute to protect the broker from the traditional grounds for liability before the employment of the broker as a transaction broker.

Example 29

In a state requiring that listings be in writing, B, a licensed broker, orally agrees that B will assist P, a prospective office building purchaser, in finding a suitable property. B does so and the office building proves to be a financial success. B demands her fee from P, who resists payment of the transaction broker's fee, alleging that in this jurisdiction all employment contracts for brokers must be in writing. Is this defense valid?

Explanation

A regulatory requirement that listings be in writing applies to all vendor's brokers, but less often to buyer's brokers. Typically, these special-purpose statutes of frauds have requirements that a buyer's broker will find impossible to meet—for example, accurate description of the property, and the statement of the vendor's asking price. There is no reason to prohibit an oral employment contract here unless the authorizing statute for buyer's brokers explicitly does so. This same result may also apply to transaction brokers.

ADMINISTRATIVE REGULATION OF BROKERAGE ACTIVITIES

The complaint that fails against a broker in court may be sufficient in a regulatory forum. In each state, real estate brokers are licensed and governed by a statute setting out grounds for revocation of that license. This statute is implemented by an administrative body, often called a Real Estate Commission. A substantial misrepresentation or the suppression, concealment, or omission of material facts are grounds for an administrative invesstigation into a transaction conducted by a licensee. Scienter is usually a requirement of these statutes, but they can, at the same time, be very general. For instance, "untrustworthiness" is sometimes a ground for revocation of a license. Whether a private cause of action arises to enforce the standards imposed on brokers in these statutes is a question on which the courts addressing the issue have split. In addition, if a successful plaintiff is unable to collect a judgment obtained against a broker for fraud, misrepresentation, or financial crimes such as embezzlement, an administrative fund is available (in 34 states) to pay it. Such a fund is generally known as a real estate recovery or guaranty fund. It is funded by brokerage license fees and disciplinary fines paid by licensees.

CHAPTER 3

Contract Risk of Loss and Equitable Conversion

In a majority of American jurisdictions, the courts have adopted the rule that absent an express provision of the contract, the risk of loss of the property during the executory period of a contract of sale for real property is on the purchaser. *See Brush Grocery Kart, Inc. v. Sure Fine Market, Inc.*, 47 P.3d 680 (Colo. 2002). This rule applies to a fortuitous loss, not one for which a party to the contract is responsible. Once the contract is binding, it applies even if the purchaser is not in possession of the property during that period and, however much it diminishes the vendor's rights in the property, it does not change the rule that the vendor must be able to convey, and the purchaser must accept, a marketable title at the closing. The rationale for the majority rule is found in the equitable principle that regards the contract as performed once binding: "Equity regards as done what ought to be done."

At the same time, if the vendor has insured the property, he will often be found to hold the proceeds of the policy in trust for the purchaser. This is one way of ameliorating the unexpected effect of the majority rule on the purchaser, who often will not have anticipated the need for insurance on the property during the executory period. This trust theory takes account of the rule that an insurance contract is personal to the parties to it. Thus this theory is another attempt to ameliorate the effects of the majority rule.

The majority rule on this risk is made for the contract that has no provision about the risk of loss. None of the foregoing says that the drafters of a contract of sale should not change or modify it. It is a court-made rule. Even though the parties to a contract may be unaware of it and its consequences, a vendor staying in possession is more likely to protect and to have insured the property. Still, litigation may be required to establish its applicability to the particular situation—and to a particular contract. The same is true for the purchaser's rights in the vendor's insurance. Better to have the vendor endorse his policy for the benefit of the purchaser during the executory period or while the purchaser procures his own insurance. Better yet to have the purchaser named as an insured party in the vendor's policy.

THE DOCTRINE OF EQUITABLE CONVERSION

The majority rule depends on the doctrine of equitable conversion of the property. The doctrine is adopted in 32 jurisdictions in this country.[1] It is applied at the signing of a binding contract of sale. After that, under the doctrine, the vendor (1) holds the legal title to the property in trust for the purchaser and (2) also holds a lien for the amount of the purchase price.[2] This doctrine regards the purchaser as the owner of the property, able to enforce the contract in an action for specific performance, and as a debtor for its purchase price: It regards the vendor as a trustee of the title, held for the purchaser, and a secured creditor for the price. In short, the purchaser owns real property, the vendor personal property—the right to the payment of the purchase price. Nothing to the contrary being said in the contract, the doctrine enables the purchaser to mortgage the equity in the property or to assign his interest in it. The purchaser can also devise his interest by will, or it can descend to his heirs under the jurisdiction's canons of descent. It is chargeable with his debts and a judgment by his creditors can attach to it. It is, in other words, alienable, devisable, descendible, and attachable. *See O'Brien v. Paulson*, 186 N.W. 440 (Iowa 1922) and *Stiles v. Montana Seventeenth Judicial District*, 286 P.3d 247 (Mont. 2012). The doctrine applies no matter how short or long the executory period might be.

The doctrine is based on the equitable maxim that "treats as done what in good conscience should be done." It arose first in cases in which the vendor died during the executory period, and a court of equity,[3] using a

1. In one state, adoption of the doctrine occurs because "it is the uniform opinion of the bar . . . that the doctrine of equitable conversion was the law. . . ." *See Briz-Ler Corp. v. Weiner*, 171 A.2d 65, 67 (Del. 1961).

2. This statement on the status of the vendor's interest is the most in dispute. Courts split on the issue of whether a judgment lien against the vendor can attach when the vendor has already contracted to sell. *See* Roger A. Cunningham, William B. Stoebuck, & Dale A. Whitman, Law of Property, § 10.13, p. 738 (2d Ed., 1993) (reporting a slight majority favoring attachment).

3. The doctrine was in its origins, a work-around in equity of the rule that the promises or covenants in bilateral contracts were independent of one another so that a vendor could not refuse to convey land even though the purchase price was unpaid. Professor Samuel Willison, a critic of the majority rule, thought the doctrine unneeded once the doctrine of independent covenants was no longer the law. *See* Samuel Williston, 7 Law of Contracts, § 933 (3d ed., 1963).

decree of specific performance for the purchaser, found that the contract was performed by the vendor during his life; nothing more needing to be done except to convey the title, equity regarded the transaction as closed. Neither could (in a state in which a marital estate attaches at the time of death) the vendor's spouse claim dower or curtesy in the property when the vendor died during the executory period—the vendor did not have a sufficient interest in the property (he was not "seised" of the property, said the common law) when he died.

The doctrine works on a completed, enforceable contract of sale. It is a doctrine limited to real estate contracts. *See Devine v. Buki*, 767 S.E.2d 459 (Va. 2015). It does not work on an option to purchase real property—it is said that the option "works" no equitable conversion. If the purchaser improves the property during the executory period, the vendor cannot enjoin the removal of the improvement because the vendor's lien on the property for the purchase price is measured at the time the lien arose—that is, at the time of the execution of the contract—not thereafter. If the property contracted for is timberland, the vendor could enjoin the purchaser's removal of the timber during the executory period for the same reason. The value of the timber measures the value of the lien for which the vendor bargained, and if that value is impaired the vendor can get an injunction. (In some states, the impairment of value will have to be sufficient to put the remaining value of the property below the unpaid purchase price before the vendor can have an injunction.) Based on the doctrine, the purchaser during the executory period can also sue the vendor for waste, sue any trespasser on the property for damage to it, and sue any tenant of the vendor for breach of a lease covenant. Because of the doctrine, a purchaser taking possession during the executory period does not owe rent to the vendor.

However, the doctrine does not give the purchaser all the benefits of ownership right away. Absent a contract provision to the contrary, the purchaser is not entitled to the rents, profits, and other benefits of the use of the property. The vendor gets the rent up to the closing; that is, the right to rents is regarded as personalty until then. In the same vein, during the executory period the vendor is responsible for real property taxes up to the time that the purchaser takes possession.

The emphasis on the doctrine of equitable conversion thus permits the risk of loss (considered as the subject of a separate (implied) provision of the contract) to be shifted to the purchaser immediately on the execution of the contract. So the purchaser bears this risk but receives some benefits as well. What if the property is condemned or minerals are discovered on the property during the executory period and at the time of the destruction, the risk of loss is on the purchaser? The person bearing the risk of loss in fairness receives either the condemnation award or the benefits of the appreciation in value. Further, neither that award nor the appreciation in value, occurring during the executory period, is a bar to the purchaser's obtaining specific performance of the contract. This resulting benefit also modifies the harsh effect of the majority rule—at least in a rising market.

Examples

Example 1

V and P[4] execute a brief but enforceable contract for Blackacre. P pays V a portion of the purchase price. J's judgment lien is then docketed against V. Does the contract trump the lien?

Explanation

Yes, the doctrine of equitable conversion means that Blackacre is no longer considered V's property, so the lien does not attach to it. If it were otherwise, P would have to check the judgment docket before paying any part of the purchase price. When V and P close the sale, V will have the proceeds of the sale and, in a slight majority of the states, J will be able to enforce the lien against the proceeds. *See Grant v. Kahn*, 18 A.3d 91 (Md. Spec. App. Ct. 2008).

The enforceability of the contract defines the time at which the risk shifts to the purchaser. Here the equitable maxim shifts to say that a contract "is performed not necessarily when made, but when according to its terms, it should be performed." Only at that point does the doctrine apply to the contract. The modern contract, loaded with contingencies or "subject to" clauses, is in this regard seldom capable of specific performance much before the closing. So, in some jurisdictions, the doctrine might shift the risk of loss, but the contract might not. That is, early in the executory period, the contract might not be capable of specific performance. Only later, at the end of the period, will the contingencies, material to the closing and thus a precondition to it, be satisfied. So an alternative application of the doctrine and by extension the risk of loss rule is not to shift the risk of loss until all the material contract contingencies are satisfied. Only then is the contract capable of specific performance. That is, this equitable action will not lie until the purchaser obtains all that he expects the contract to provide. This better takes account of the harsh effects that the majority rule may have on purchasers.

Examples

Example 2a

In a majority rule jurisdiction, after the destruction of property the vendor may argue that even though the contract had unperformed contingencies,

4. Hereafter in the chapter, vendor and purchaser respectively.

they are immaterial to the contract. If there is some doubt as to the materiality of the contingency to the question of risk of loss, how can a purchaser in a majority rule state further protect himself?

Explanation

There are several methods. (1) By expressly negating the rule by contract. (2) By requiring the vendor to restore the premises by the time of the closing should they be destroyed during the executory period of the contract. (3) By the use of an escrow as a closing device. (4) By bargaining for a credit against the purchase price due at the closing in the amount of the value of any improvement destroyed. That value might be determined to be either (a) the replacement cost of the improvement, or (b) the proceeds of the insurance policy held by the vendor on the improvement. From the purchaser's perspective, the vendor's assignment of these proceeds may be insufficient: The purchaser does not know when or if the company will pay, what defenses the insurer has against its insured, and so forth.

Example 2b

In the course of negotiations over Blackacre, V and P discuss the subject of risk of loss. Blackacre is located in a majority rule jurisdiction. V and P propose to agree that P, the purchaser, will assume the risk and V will guarantee that if the property is destroyed by fire, flood, winds, or earthquake, V will restore it to its condition at the time of the contract's execution. P is your client and presents this proposal to you for your advice. What advice would you give?

Explanation

There may be other types of destruction possible—lightning strikes, for example. Should they be included? Is the property likely to be condemned? Vandalized? Those risks might be included as well. A guarantee is more than an agreement to indemnify. The distinction might be clearer than the language P used—for example, "V guarantees personally to restore to P's satisfaction. . . ." Moreover, how much "destruction" is contemplated? Just total destruction, or do the parties contemplate that a loss of (say) one-third of the purchase price or fair market value is sufficient? More definition rather than less typically will avoid future disputes and litigation. Unless V has ready cash to restore the property, V's restoration of the property will probably only be possible if V's property insurance is adequate. If V's policy underinsures Blackacre or is subject to large deductibles, then some further financial assurance to P by V may be necessary—perhaps a letter of credit or a surety bond. Finally, P will also want to inspect and oversee the restoration, so provision should be made for that oversight.

Example 2c

V and P's contract of sale provides that "the risk of loss or damage to the property by fire or otherwise, except ordinary wear and tear, is on the vendor until the closing."[5] The contract also represented that the "hot water heating system is in good working condition and shall be at closing," and "this representation shall not survive the closing of title." V and P and their closing agent meet to close the transaction at a time with the purchase price for the property had been wired to V's bank but had not yet cleared. To take account of this fact, V, P, and the agent prepare an escrow agreement stating: "all closing proceeds, the keys, and the deed to Blackacre are to be held in escrow until the funds clear." While the check for the purchase price is in transit, during some very cold weather, the water pipes on Blackacre burst, substantially damaging Blackacre. Which party to the transaction, V or P, bears the risk of loss for this damage?

Explanation

P does, absent evidence that V shut off the heat, causing the pipes to burst. V had done all that was required by turning over the keys and the deed to the agent, while P had not yet made the purchase price funds available to V. The language of their contract, referring to the "closing" of the transaction, customarily refers to the time designated for the passing of the title to real estate from the vendor to the purchaser and the ending or the "closing" of the transaction. Thus at the closing, the deed is constructively delivered to P when in escrow: The agent was V's agent handling the deed and P's agent for receipt of the funds—and the contract thus assigns the risk of loss to V. *See Bianchi v. Ladjen*, 2018 N.J. Super. Unpub LEXIS 943 (N.J. Super. Ct., Apr. 23, 2018).

Example 2d

V and P execute a contract of sale as before. P is a real estate developer who intends to develop Blackacre for a more profitable use but needs it rezoned to do so. P files a rezoning application but is denied standing to do this by the zoning officials. Does P have standing?

Explanation

Yes. The equitable title conferred by an equitable conversion gives P a sufficient interest in Blackacre to appear before the officials in a majority rule state.

---

5. This is the customary provision of the N.J. Ass'n of Realtors.

CRITICISMS OF THE MAJORITY RULE AND THE MINORITY RULE

Two criticisms have been aimed at the majority rule. First, equitable conversion is a legal fiction and it depends on the availability of specific performance, a remedy in which a court has so much discretion that its application is often uncertain. Second, the implied condition on risk of loss (however it allocates the loss) is itself based on a more fundamental (and also implied) point: The contract was executed on the assumption that the property is a fair consideration for the purchase price, so after the property is substantially destroyed, the exchange is no longer fair and should not be enforced in equity by specific performance. The practical result is that the contract should be viewed as a nullity and the parties should negotiate it again.

This second criticism of the majority rule is in fact the basis for the minority American rule—the so-called Massachusetts rule. This minority rule holds that absent a contract provision to the contrary, the risk of fortuitous loss of the property during the executory period is on the vendor. Under this rule, a contract of sale in effect provides that "the risk of loss or damage to the property by fire or other casualty occurring prior to the time the vendor delivers an executed deed to the purchase is expressly assumed by the vendor."

The minority rule rests on two rationales: first, that the destruction of the property results in a failure of consideration in the contract, and second, that the contract itself contains an implied condition that the contract would not be enforceable in the event of substantial destruction. *See Anderson v. Yaworski*, 181 A. 205 (Conn. 1935) (adopting the minority Massachusetts rule), noted in 49 Harv. L. Rev. 497 (1936).

In a minority rule state, is specific performance with an abatement in the purchase price available to the purchaser? The answer is no. The contract should become a nullity, leaving the parties free to renegotiate a new one. Anytime courts are asked to grant an abatement, they in effect are rewriting a crucial term in the contract—the price term. They should do that carefully, only when they have some basis to tell what the parties would do in this situation. So forcing the parties back to the negotiating table is better than having the court rewrite the old contract. If abatements are permitted, the open issues are: What is the amount of the abatement? Should the price be abated down by the amount of any insurance claim, the replacement cost of the property destroyed, or the contract price of the destroyed property? For a discussion of this issue, *see Burack v. Chase Manhattan Bank*, 194 N.Y.S.2d 987, 988 (N.Y. App. Div. 1959) (permitting abatement for the present value, not the replacement cost, of the property destroyed).

Despite criticisms of the majority rule, as well as the adoption of the minority rule in a substantial number of states, the majority rule has survived. Its survival is explained perhaps because a bright line is needed and the rule at least supplies that, as well as a basis on which the vendor and purchaser can plan their relationship during the executory period. The parties to a contract should ask which of them—vendor or purchaser—is the most efficient risk bearer or avoider? Often the answer will be the party in possession. Possession gives the possessor knowledge about the property, making that party the most efficient risk avoider.

Beware also of the halfway drafting solution. Consider the following.

Examples

Example 3a

The same problem that was presented in Example 2d: V and P execute a brief but enforceable contract of sale. P is a real estate developer who intends to develop Blackacre for a more profitable use but needs it rezoned to do so. P files a rezoning application but is denied standing to do this by the zoning officials. Does P have standing in a minority rule state?

Explanation

No. If the contract is a nullity for a failure of consideration and works no equitable conversion, P's interest is wiped out and is by no means sufficient to authorize P's appearance before the officials. Both V and P will have to appear together before the zoning officials to present P's plan of development. Some type of cooperation clause to this effect should be in the contract of sale.

Example 3b

V and P execute an otherwise binding contract of sale for Blackacre. A fire occurs, destroying the principal improvement on Blackacre and materially affecting its fair market value. The contract provides that "this property is sold 'as is.'" Does this language have an effect on the allocation of the risk of loss in a minority "risk on the vendor" jurisdiction?

Explanation

No. The weight of the case law is that it does not. An "as is" provision is generally interpreted to negate the existence of a warranty of habitability or fitness of the premises for a particular use, and even then, the cases are split on this effect. The intent of this language is that the purchaser must take the property at closing as it was when the contract was executed—but always assuming that the property is in the same condition as it was then, and assuming it is not thereafter destroyed. The risk is still on the vendor in a minority rule jurisdiction.

Example 3c

Same facts, but the contract provides that "P shall maintain a policy of fire insurance to protect herself for the duration of this contract." Does this language have an impact on the allocation of risk in a minority rule jurisdiction?

Explanation

No. This provision is a recognition of the rule that once a contract of sale for real property is executed, both the vendor and the purchaser have an insurable interest in the property. An insurable interest is an interest sufficient to compel an insurer to honor a claim. Viewed in this light, such a provision does not directly affect the allocation of the risk of loss: It only recognizes that both parties have an insurable interest. *Hans v. Lucas*, 703 N.W.2d 880 (Neb. 2005). However, this provision might *indirectly* affect that allocation: Its presence in the contract might encourage a court to rule that where the purchaser procures a policy during the executory period and the vendor lets his lapse, the proceeds of any purchaser's claim are held in trust for the vendor to compensate for the latter's loss. Thus the effect of such a provision has been held to create a constructive trust for the benefit of the noninsured party. Likewise, if a vendor were to undertake to maintain insurance during the executory period in a majority rule jurisdiction, such a result only mitigates the harsh, unexpected consequences of the majority rule.

Example 3d

Same facts, but the contract provides, in a majority rule jurisdiction, that "the vendor is responsible for the property until the deed to it has been delivered to the purchaser." What is the effect of this provision on the allocation of the risk of loss?

Explanation

This language is probably sufficient to place the risk of loss on the vendor, al-though it is less clear than the provision given in the preceding text. It might be the equivalent of saying that the vendor is responsible for the physical condition of the property until closing. In that case, extrinsic evidence—for example, testimony that the language was specially inserted in the contract and was intended to pertain only to vandalism and other noncasualty, intentional actions of the vendor and others—may limit its impact and leave the risk of casualty losses with the purchaser. When the language is preprinted on a standard form contract, such testimony (unless the witness was involved in the form's drafting) is of little weight. The vendor's "responsibility" for the property can reasonably include a casualty loss. *See Bryant v. Willison Real Estate Co.*, 350 S.E.2d 748 (W. Va. 1986).

Example 3e

If a contract of sale provided, in separate paragraphs, that "Blackacre is sold as is" and "purchaser to carry enough fire insurance to protect self" and "vendor is responsible for the property until delivery of deed at closing" and "sale includes all fixtures," would these four provisions, taken together, allocate the risk of loss to the vendor in a majority rule state?

Explanation

It wasn't sufficient in the *Bryant* case. One judicial approach (the one used in *Bryant*) is to try to narrowly construe each of the clauses in turn, rather than together, and, unless the negotiations provide evidence of a link between them, all of them are not likely to amount to more than the sum of their parts. *See also MidFirst Bank v. Graves*, 943 A.2d 923 (N.J. Super. Ct. 2007). Another approach is to attempt to construe the contract as a whole, harmonizing all the clauses.

Example 3f

V and P execute a contract of sale for Whiteacre, providing that "should the property be materially damaged by fire or other causes prior to closing, this contract shall be voidable at P's option." Is this language sufficient to invoke the minority rule?

Explanation

Giving P the right to void the agreement and shifting the risk to him meanwhile would be inconsistent, so this language is sufficient to avoid an equitable conversion, the majority rule, and to invoke the minority rule. *See Holscher v. James*, 860 P.2d 646 (Idaho 1993). When the purchaser takes out insurance and the vendor's insurance lapses during the executory period, a court might hold that the purchaser's interest (for purposes of giving him an insurable interest in Whiteacre) was subject to a condition subsequent, terminating it at his option when material damage by fire occurred, and the vendor should arrange to become a named insured or a third-party beneficiary of the purchaser's policy, thus gaining a legal, contractual right to its proceeds.

THE UNIFORM VENDOR PURCHASER RISK ACT

The most sensible rule on risk of loss is often said to be that of Professor Williston, long a critic of the majority rule and the drafter of the Uniform Vendor Purchaser Risk Act (UVPRA). This act has been adopted in 12 states, including New York and California. The act provides as follows:

> *Any contract* hereafter made in this State for the purchase and sale of realty shall be interpreted as including an agreement that the parties shall have the following rights and duties, unless the contract expressly provides otherwise:
>
> (a) If, when neither the legal title nor the possession of the subject matter of the contract has been *transferred*, all or a material part thereof is *destroyed* without fault of the purchaser or is *taken by eminent domain*, the vendor cannot enforce the contract and the purchaser is entitled to recover any portion of the price he has paid.
>
> (b) If, when either the legal title or the possession of the subject matter of the contract has been transferred, all or any part thereof is destroyed without fault of the vendor or is taken by eminent domain, the purchaser is not thereby relieved from a duty to pay the price, nor is he entitled to recover any portion that he has paid.

The rationale behind this statute is that the party in possession of the property is in the best position to safeguard it, minimize any damage, and know any loss or destruction. Its complementary rationale is that, once the purchaser takes legal title, he has had sufficient time to safeguard his interest by procuring insurance and arranging for repairs.

First, let's consider some of the terms that this act employs.

Any Contract? This means any document or documents functioning as a contract. It means any document lacking the essential requirements of a contract when those essentials can be supplied by the common law—for instance, a contract without a closing date can be presumed to give the parties a reasonable time to close, or a contract not prescribing the quality of title to be conveyed is presumed to require a marketable title. The law of contracts of the state enacting the act generally applies. *See Cohen v. Holder*, 167 N.Y.S.3d 973 (N.Y. App. Div. 2022) and *Armonk Snack Mart, Inc. v. Robert Porpora Realty Corp.*, 984 N.Y.S.2d 630 (N.Y. Sup. Ct., Westchester County, 2014).

Destroyed? What is "destruction"? The word includes a fire, a flood, an earthquake, and a landslide, but what about vandalism? *See Onondaga Sav. Bank v. Wagner*, 420 N.Y.S.2d 657 (N.Y. Sup. Ct. 1979) (holding that vandalism is included). Some courts have interpreted the word expansively. *See Sprouse v. North River Ins. Co.*, 344 S.E.2d 555 (N.C. App. Ct. 1986) (judicial sale also included). A judicial sale destroys the vendor's ability to sell but does not result in physical destruction. The destruction necessary for the act to apply must be more than a loss of the property's value during the executory period. That does not affect the vendor's ability to sell. *See Latipac Corp. v. DMH Realty LLC*, 938 N.Y.S.2d 30 (N.Y. App. Div. 2012).

In the same vein, what is a "material" destruction? It can either mean "material" to the contract or to the identity of the property. Because of the difficulties involved, New York courts have tended not to distinguish between nonmaterial and material destruction. Considering the intent of the act's drafters, the meaning of this word should probably be confined to the physical destruction of the property.

Transferred? What is a "transfer"? It either refers to a closing or to a right given under a contract that is subject to specific performance. The former is the likely plain meaning of the word in its context—"transfer of the legal title" (as opposed to the transfer of an equitable interest created in the purchaser by a contract of sale).

Taken by eminent domain? Following the lead of the previous definition, the phrase probably refers to a completed condemnation, rather than a pending one. *See Creative Living, Inc. v. Steinhauser*, 355 N.Y.S.2d 897 (N.Y. Sup. Ct. 1974), aff'd, 365 N.Y.S.2d 987 (N.Y. App. Div. 1975) (so holding). And it probably does not include a judgment in inverse condemnation.

That the terms of the act need further definition is only to suggest that the parties to contracts in the states adopting the act should supply them. But if they do, have they "agreed otherwise" and put themselves beyond the reach of the act? No, not if their intent was to flesh out the agreement the act assumes they meant to make.

The act applies to contracts of sale and to any document functioning like a contract of sale. The act's applicability should not depend on the title on the first page. Examples of documents with similar legal effects are an option to purchase contained in a lease, a freestanding option, or an installment land sales contract (or contract for deed, as it is called in some jurisdictions)—even the terms under which a foreclosure sale is conducted. *See U.S. Bank Natl. Assn. v. Cedano*, 880 N.Y.S.2d 876 (N.Y. Sup. Ct. 2009). An installment land sale contract functions like a contract of sale, but an option often does not: It is more like a contract to make a contract, and this may limit the remedies available to its holder—specific performance, for example. If specific performance is available, however, there is no reason why Professor Williston's statute should not apply.

When the act does not apply, the doctrine of equitable conversion does, unless the parties agree to the contrary. *See Latipac Corp. v. DMH Realty LLC*, 938 N.Y.S.2d 30 (N.Y. App. Div. 2012).

Are the act's provisions rules of law or presumptions about the intent of the parties? Unless the parties contract around the terms of the act, those terms are presumed to constitute their intent as to the matters covered by the act. The first paragraph of the act makes an assumption about the general or presumed intent of the parties to the contract. The act's provisions apply to contracts for both residential and commercial properties. They apply up to the transfer of title or possession of the subject matter of the contract, but not afterward: After the closing or the transfer of possession, the common applies. See *Burkins & Foley Trucking & Storage, Inc. v. County of Albany*, 11 N.Y.S.3d

351 (N.Y. App. Div. 2015).The parties to a contract might agree (say) to opt out of the act for condemnations, but not other types of destruction of the property subject to the contract. After all, physical destruction and condemnation present very different threats to the stability of the relationship created by the contract.

Examples

Example 4

V and P execute a contract of sale providing that the property will be delivered "as is" at the closing. Has this contract "expressly provided otherwise" under the UVPRA?

Explanation

No, that phrase is taken to negate a warranty of habitability, suitability, or fitness, but no more than that. *See Or Home Inc. v. Purrier*, 851 N.Y.S.2d 71 (N.Y. Sup. Ct. 2007).

Consider the following examples arising under the act. In each, assume that there has been a destruction of the property so substantial that the act applies.

Example 5

What if the vendor has rented the property to a third party during the executory period and either (1) the contract never mentioned which party was to receive the rents during that period or (2) the contract assigned the rents to the purchaser?

Explanation

The issue is whether the legal title and possession must actually be transferred. If not, the right to receive the rents is the right to receive the profits of title and possession, so in the former instance, §(a) applies, but in the latter, §(b) applies.

Example 6

What if the vendor and the purchaser agree that the purchaser is to have the right to possession during the executory period? The vendor moves out, but P never moves in, when a fire destroys the property. Who has the risk of loss?

Explanation

What is "possession"? Is it actual possession? Constructive possession? Possession given under the color of the contract? Or, as here, a contract right to possession, whether or not exercised? *See Rego Crescent Corp. v. City of New York*, 323 N.Y.S.2d 994 (N.Y. App. Div. 1971), aff'd mem., 300 N.E.2d 435 (N.Y. 1973) (holding that even though neither legal title nor possession was actually transferred, the entry of an order for the vendor granting him specific performance was sufficient to invoke the provisions of §(b) and defining possession more broadly than just actual possession). The contrary argument is that acquiring a mere right to possession may be insufficient to become a "transfer" of possession under §(b).

Example 7

Assuming that neither legal title nor possession (however defined) has been transferred at the time of a substantial destruction by fire, must the purchaser, to avail himself of the remedies in §(a), claim those remedies by the closing date when the contract makes the time for a closing "of the essence"?

Explanation

No, he has a reasonable time to claim the remedy. *See Stork v. Felper*, 270 N.W.2d 586 (Wis. App. Ct. 1978).

Example 8

Under what circumstances would a court give an abatement in the purchase price but award specific performance, even though the improvement has been totally destroyed by fire during the executory period?

Explanation

Among states adopting the UVPRA, there is a conflict in the case law on this point. *See, e.g., Skelly Oil Co. v. Ashmore*, 365 S.W.2d 582 (Mo. 1963), which presents this situation, and *Dixon v. Salvation Army*, 191 Cal. Rptr. 111 (Cal. App. 1983) (denying a purchaser specific performance with the abatement under §(a) of the UVPRA and contrasting this result with the New York cases). The issue is whether the act provides the exclusive remedies for the situations within its scope. Can the purchaser have an action for specific performance when §(a) applies and his only remedy express in the act is the recovery of installments paid under the contract? In New York he can, but in California he cannot. In New York, the courts note that the act does not repeal the purchaser's other remedies, and when specific performance with an abatement in the price is one such remedy, the purchaser should not be denied it by negative implication; in California, the purchaser is denied specific performance by negative implication.

Example 9

The act requires that the property be destroyed without fault of the party walking away from the contract. What if the purchaser has not made a good faith effort to satisfy the terms of a financing contingency clause at the time of the destruction? Who then has the risk of loss?

Explanation

The act's terms expressly consider fault only in the context of causing the destruction. Good or bad faith in carrying out the contract is not such fault as would affect the provisions of §(a), but the act does not prohibit and so does not preclude other remedies, such as the vendor's action for damages on the contract in this instance.

INSURING THE PROPERTY DURING THE EXECUTORY PERIOD

What's the practical answer to all of these problems? In a word, insurance. At the start of the executory period, and particularly when the property is insured, the vendor will usually carry it. His policy will typically be required by a lender-mortgagee. Keeping this policy in effect during the executory period is probably, in the small transaction, the simplest method of handling the risk of loss problem. Either the purchaser is named an "insured party" in the vendor's policy or the vendor can add an endorsement to the policy giving the purchaser the right to share in any proceeds.

What is the difference between these two methods? Naming the purchaser as an insured party gives the purchaser the right to participate in the settlement of the claim; not so if the policy is endorsed for his benefit. This latter method leaves the vendor with the sole right to settle the claim but gives the purchaser the right to share the proceeds of that settlement. From the purchaser's perspective, then, naming him as an insured party is preferable.

If neither method is used, then the party suffering the loss under the rules is left to the mercies of equity—in particular, to the operation of the equitable doctrines of subrogation and constructive trusts. Those doctrines, present in the case law of most jurisdictions and used in tandem with the doctrine of equitable conversion, result in a blurring of the distinction between majority and minority rules in this area of law. For example, although an insurance policy is a personal contract for the benefit of the named insured party—whether vendor or purchaser—this fact alone does not prevent equity from imposing a constructive trust on the proceeds of the policy, once received by the insured, for the benefit of the party found to have the risk of loss, while still holding that the claim is personal to the insured. Thus the vendor might hold the proceeds of a policy in trust for the purchaser if the latter has the risk of loss. (In 15 jurisdictions, the vendor is the purchaser's trustee when the latter bears the risk.) This theory also works in reverse—that is, that the purchaser might hold the proceeds in trust for the vendor, who in a minority rule state, or by agreement, might have the risk of loss. Of this, more later.

Often an escrow of the insurance policy is a useful device for implementing any such trust recognized under local law or by agreement of the parties.

Examples

EXAMPLES

Example 10

If in a majority rule state, the purchaser bears the risk but the vendor holds the policy, should the purchaser reimburse the vendor for premiums paid to the insurer during the executory period?

Explanation

No, not if no loss has yet occurred, because the trust arises only when the vendor receives the proceeds of the policy, not before. The policy remains the vendor's personal contract with the insurer. However, once a loss occurs and the vendor has the right to make a claim, the answer might change if the equitable nature of the constructive trust is followed to its logical conclusion. Sometime after a loss occurs, the purchaser has the benefit of the insurance and should reimburse the vendor for the premiums. The trustee is then entitled to reimbursement for the reasonable expenses of maintaining the *res* (the thing that is the subject of the trust—here the policy). Some courts might not maintain the distinction between the policy and the proceeds, and in such courts, the court might find that the trustee has the right to set off the premiums when, as things turn out, the purchaser receives the benefit of the policy in the form of proceeds. Vendor and purchaser might usefully execute an agreement on this point and not leave it to the operation of equity.

Example 11

In a majority rule state, what if the vendor has the policy but after an insured loss occurs will not negotiate the claim with the insurer: Can the purchaser, as the beneficiary of a constructive trust, compel the vendor to do so?

Explanation

Yes, the *res* of the trust can be broadly taken to be either the policy or the policy proceeds. Cf. *Dubin Paper Co. v. Insurance Co. of North America*, 63 A.2d 85 (Pa. 1949) (holding that when a vendor settled the claim but returned the proceeds, the purchaser could sue the insurer to compel the issuance of the proceeds again, but this time to him (the purchaser)).

Example 12

What if the purchaser has the insurance during the executory period, but the vendor is found to bear the risk of loss when a claim arises: Can the constructive trust theory work in reverse?

Explanation

Probably, but there may be a problem with the case law in some jurisdictions: Sometimes the doctrine of equitable conversion is premised on a rationale using the language of constructive trusts. When such case law is present, the vendor is a trustee of the title for the benefit of the purchaser during the executory period and, after the contract of sale, is subject to specific performance. This "title trust" should become the basis for the "proceeds trust" as well, but the result is not compelled. A problem remains: The vendor might hold the title in trust, but the fruits of the property, such as its rents, have been held not to be subject to the "title trust." On this authority, the proceeds of the policy benefit the vendor, but not because of the trust; instead, a principle of mutuality favors permitting the vendor to secure the purchaser's insurance proceeds. Finally, as a matter of the expectations of the parties, the vendor might expect to be named as the purchaser's trustee after agreeing to sell the property, but since the purchaser might not have the same expectation after agreeing to buy, this is a matter best handled in the contract of sale. Otherwise, the purchaser might expect to insure only his own interest in the property, knowing that both he and the vendor will have separate interests in it during the executory period.

Example 13

If the vendor has overinsured the destroyed property for an amount greater than the contract price would call for, does the vendor hold all the insurance proceeds in trust for the purchaser, or just that portion of the proceeds needed to satisfy the contract?

Explanation

The latter. The *res* of the trust is the amount that the vendor needs to perform his obligations under the contract. *See Estes v. Thurman*, 192 S.W.3d 429 (Ky. App. Ct. 2005).

A FINAL NOTE ON EQUITABLE CONVERSION

Considered by itself, outside of its utility in underpinning rules on the risk of loss, the doctrine of equitable conversion might be said to be effective when a contract of sale for real property is executed. Its effectiveness may be maintained even if the contract is a contingent one in the following sense: For example, when the contract has a provision making it binding on the purchaser only when she obtains third-party financing for the purchase price, this purchaser-friendly contingency need not prevent the contract's being specifically performed against the vendor. Why? Because, in order to bring an action for specific performance, the purchaser will have to show the court that the contract is fair and binding and that she is ready and willing to perform it. To do this she will have to either have the financing contingency satisfied (by having a loan commitment by the third party in hand) or waive it. Either way, once the purchaser shows that she is ready to perform the contract, the vendor becomes subject to an action for specific performance.

A moment's reflection on the example just presented should tell you that specific performance for purchasers requiring waiving the financing contingency puts the purchaser in a difficult position: She will have to come up with cash to pay the purchase price. A contract with no provision for financing is presumed to require the purchaser to pay all cash to close the transaction. Likewise, other contract contingencies will have to be satisfied or waived. They will present their own difficulties: What if the contract was contingent on the sale of a prior residence, or on the rezoning of the property? Each presents the same problem of showing that the purchaser is continuously ready to perform the contract during the pendency of the suit for specific performance.

CHAPTER 4

The Statute of Frauds in Real Property Transactions

INTRODUCTION

The Statute of Frauds provides that agreements (read the term broadly to include not just contracts of sale, but installment sale contracts, memorandum of understanding, and even, in some jurisdictions, options to purchase) for the sale of real property "shall not be enforced unless they are in writing and signed by the vendor." *See Hostetter v. Hoover*, 547 A.2d 1247, 1250 (Pa. Super. 1988). Thus, even if there is ample proof that the parties *intended* an agreement, it is not enforceable. All American jurisdictions have adopted the statute in some form. The primary purpose of the statute is to provide clear and easily enforced evidence of the agreement. It is meant "to intercept the frequency and success of actions based on nothing more than loose verbal statements." *See Yates v. Ball*, 181 So. 341, 344 (Fla. 1937). It also reinforces the prudent practice of formalizing an agreement and forces parties to distinguish clearly between preliminary negotiations and their final agreement. It thus protects (1) the evidence of an agreement, (2) a prudent business practice, and (3) a done deal. Under the "no enforcement" language of the Pennsylvania statute quoted above, when the purchaser is the defendant the statute's terms must be satisfied, but there is no need for the purchaser to sign it as a precondition to enforcing it.

The statute is applicable to contracts and agreements, but not to a deed or conveyance of an interest in real property—separate statutes in every jurisdiction govern those; thus, the agreement presented to satisfy the statute need not specify the type of deed nor the type of title to be transferred. Interests in realty created by operation of law are also not included.

Typically the statute requires that "the party to be charged," meaning the party conveying the interest and sued on it (the defendant, whether vendor or purchaser), must sign it. Mutuality of obligation is not required. Such statutes are closely patterned on the English Statute of Frauds. *See Smith v. Boyd*, 553 A.2d 131, 132 (R.I. 1989); and *see generally* E. A. Farnsworth, Contracts §6.1, at 363 (3d ed., 1999).

The English statute, enacted by Parliament in 1677, came in the wake of the 1666 Great Fire of London (in which many landowners lost their title deeds). At that time juries were able to act on testimony known to them personally; they were not required to act only on the evidence presented to them. This made them more likely to be misled by perjured testimony in cases to reestablish land ownership. The statute's purpose was to reduce that likelihood. Section 4 (of its 25 sections) of the English statute applied to real estate transactions. With the exception of section 4, Parliament repealed its statute in 1954. Section 4 was still necessary because of real estate transactions' reliance on documented agreements and their function in maintaining public land records. That rationale still justifies American statutes today. In this country, the statute's primary use lies in its policing of real estate transactions.

When the statute is cut from the English pattern, a defense based on it must be specifically pleaded; a failure to plead it waives the statute as a defense, and a general denial as to the existence of a contract is insufficient to raise the defense.

Examples

Example 1

O, the owner of Blackacre, writes to P, a prospective purchaser, "I, O, agree to sell P Blackacre for the price of $100,000." Has V "signed" the writing?

Explanation

Yes, the signature need not appear at the end, except in some of the states where the statute provided that it must be "subscribed" rather than "signed." If V accepts by telegram, fax, or email, that should, with proper proof, suffice as a "signature."[1] So may the signature being a party's printed name, initials, or cross mark be equally valid. The Statute of Frauds does not specify a particular form of signing. *See Waddle v. Elrod*, 367 S.W.3d 217 (Tenn. 2012).

1. "E-signatures" satisfy the statute too. *See* 15 U.S.C.A. §7001(a) (providing that an electronic signature or document has the same legal effect as a handwritten signature or printed document); *id.*, §7006(13)(B) (covering real estate transactions); and statutes in nearly all jurisdictions. *See* Waddle v. Elrod, 367 S.W.3d 217 (Tenn. 2012).

The effect of the statute is to render oral contracts or agreements unenforceable, but not invalid or *void ab initio*—that is, enforcement of oral agreements may be barred only when a party affirmatively pleads the statute and while specific performance is not possible, an action for restitution and damages may be. *See Waddle v. Ford*, 367 S.W.3d 217, 223 (Tenn. 2012). The measure of damages is the money paid, plus any expenses incurred on account of the contract. *Hostetter*, 547 A.2d at 1250-1251. Thus the statute precludes some actions, but not others—and usually not tort claims for misrepresentation either. *See Fericks v. Lucy Ann Soffe Tr.*, 100 P.3d 1200, 1204 (Utah 2004).

The original English statute, enacted in 1677, provided that all interests and estates in real property

> made or created by livery of seisin only, or by parol, and not put in writing, and signed by the parties so making or creating the same . . . shall have the force and effect of leases or estates at will only.

Statute of Frauds, 1677, 29 Car. 2, ch. 3, §4. Many states pattern their statute on the original one or use some portion of it. Often the statute appears in the following form:

> No action shall be brought . . . whereby to charge any person upon an agreement or promise upon the sale of any interest in real estate, unless the promise or agreement upon which such action shall be brought, or some memorandum thereof, shall be in writing, and signed by the party to be charged. . . .

R.I. Gen. L. §9-1-4.

Examples

Example 2

In a jurisdiction with a statute such as you just read, A orally promises to give Blackacre to B but later refuses to do so, arguing that the Statute of Frauds renders the gift unenforceable. Will A's argument succeed?

Explanation

Yes, it will succeed. Although it is possible to make a gift of real property, the evidentiary requirements for doing so will resemble recognized exceptions to the statute discussed later in this chapter. *See Everett v. Elliott*, 321 A.3d 944 (Pa. Super. Ct. 2024). An "agreement . . . upon the sale of any interest in real estate" as used in the statute, refers to the alienation of real property by one's own act or agreement, and not by descent. *See Bailey v. Henry*, 143 S.W. 1124, 1127-1128 (Tenn. 1912).

The required "writing" or "memorandum" may be more than one document so long as all the documents taken together include all required terms and are signed, or are incorporated into a document signed, by the party to be charged. Any type of writing, ranging from a formal contract of purchase and sale, an installment sales contract, a contract for deed, an option, or even a settlement agreement ending litigation, to an exchange of letters, emails, or texts, may satisfy the requirements of the statute.

Any material modification to a document seeking to satisfy the statute must also comply with the statute. In some states, an oral rescission is not subject to the statute, although one might ask why, when a modification is subject to it. (That rescission is not enforcement of the agreement might be one reason for the distinction.)

Whatever type of writing is required, it need not be either acknowledged or delivered to satisfy the statute. The delivery adds nothing to achieve the purposes of the statute. *See Rulon-Miller, III v. Carhart*, 544 A.2d 340, 342 (Me. 1988). The purposes of the statute are evidentiary, and the statute requires no more evidence than a writing. Indeed, a writing not having the essentials dictated by the statute may be used to show an intent *not* to contract, as when a person signs a letter of intent to make later purchase of real property. Moreover, the statute does not require the "writing" to include the whole of a document. Instead, the "writing" needed to satisfy the statute means one of two things:

1. a document with the following "essential" terms: the names of the parties, an identification of the property, the title to be conveyed, the price, and the signature of the party to be charged; or
2. a document, with the material terms of the transaction, and signed by the party to be charged.

Often the second version of the statute's requirements incorporates the first, but also includes other "material" terms.

Sometimes the price term is left unspecified, but an appraisal procedure is agreed on as a means of arriving at the purchase price. This is sufficient to satisfy the statute. Likewise, all prior oral agreements on matters that the statute requires, such as the price, must be expressly incorporated into a final agreement. Thus an oral agreement on the price, referenced in a writing "to buy your place as agreed," does not satisfy the statute. *See Thurlow v. Perry*, 77 A. 641 (Me. 1910).

Sometimes the identity of the purchaser is unknown. For example, a vendor might put property up for auction. After the vendor and the auctioneer prepare and execute a sales agreement for the signature of the winning bidder, may the latter refuse to sign it, invoking the statute's requirement that the parties be identified? Participation in the auction bidding authorizes the auctioneer, as the bidder's agent, to sign on his behalf, thus satisfying the statute. Further, the impartiality of the auctioneer is an adequate substitute for the protections otherwise provided by the statute. Auctions would routinely be undone if it were otherwise. *Schwinn v. Griffith*, 303 N.W.2d 258 (Minn. 1981).

When a vendor throws out an offer to deal with any person unconditionally meeting her terms, the resulting agreement lacks mutuality, and the vendor may change the terms before hearing of an acceptance. The statute is not satisfied beforehand. *See Irvmor Corp. v. Rodewald*, 171 N.E. 747, 748, 70 A.L.R. 192 (N.Y. 1930) (discussing this situation, Cardozo, J., states: "There is nothing more than an offer lanced into the void").

Sometimes the property is not identified. Some statutes provide that the writing must "provide a definite description of the property." In many states, a street address is insufficient, so a deed description (a boundaries or plat description) either must be used or must be referenced in the writing so that it can be proven by extrinsic evidence.

The second, "material terms" version of the statute is not a good idea. Why? Because if the law does not have a very bright-line idea of what satisfies and does not satisfy the statute, parties will be encouraged to think up material terms after the fact, and many will use the statute as a means of evading transactions to which they would otherwise be bound. The statute should provide a clear method for sorting enforceable from unenforceable contracts. For the basis of the second version of the statute in one state, *see* N.Y. Gen. Oblig. L. §5-703 (2025), *interpreted in Tamir v. Greenberg*, 501 N.Y.S.2d 103, 105 (N.Y. App. Div. 1986).

Nevertheless, in jurisdictions adopting the second version, the resulting rules are as follows: If the parties agree to a term of the contract and it is not incorporated into the memorandum, that document is insufficient and does not satisfy the statute. If the parties did not discuss a term, and the resulting memorandum is silent as to that term, a court can imply a reasonable or customary term on the same subject. This result is based on what the court finds that the parties would have done had they discussed the subject. Such an inference might be made even for the most basic of terms—for example, the price or title to be conveyed. If the parties discussed a term, but did not reach agreement on it, then what's a court to do? Now, of course, we are brought back to the evidentiary uncertainties and temptations raised as criticisms of this second version of the statute at the outset. To avoid these problems, it is better, therefore, to leave this second version to situations in which the parties agree that they either did, or did not, discuss the term.

Examples

Example 3

O agrees orally that P can purchase Blackacre from her for $100,000. Later, O denies that she agreed to sell and points to the lack of a written agreement with P as proof that she did not intend to sell. O consults you for advice. What do you say to her?

Explanation

Options to purchase real property should satisfy the Statute of Frauds. An option is an agreement to enter into a contract of sale. A contract of sale creates an interest in real property. An option is therefore an agreement to create an interest in real property in the future and should be written and satisfy the statute. *See Best v. Edwards*, 176 P.3d 695 (Ariz. Ct. App. 2008). Otherwise, an option will be little more than an invitation to a lawsuit. Measuring its terms against the requirements of the statute is itself a way of preventing fraud, promoting certainty in real property transactions, and encouraging parties to think out the terms of such transactions. Exceptions to the statute should be permitted only when a clear equivalent of a contract is present.

Example 4

V and P1 negotiate for the sale of Blackacre for several months, but before the negotiated terms are written down, V obtains a better offer from P2 and accepts it in writing. Does the statute entitle P1 to have her deal specifically performed?

Explanation

No. There was no meeting of the minds. There is no agreement to which the statute can attach. The statute isn't yet an issue.

Example 5

V and B enter into a brief but enforceable broker's listing agreement for Whiteacre. P signs an offer accepting the terms in the listing, and gives B a check with B as the payee, for a down payment. Is the Statute of Frauds satisfied by these documents?

Explanation

Probably not. The documents taken together will satisfy the statute only when they constitute an offer and acceptance. Here it is difficult to know to whom P makes the offer. An offer is a promise conditional on acceptance—but it must be made to someone. Without a memo line on the check mentioning the use of the funds and the vendor, the check is directed to the broker, who under the listing is without authority to enter into a contract. Moreover, at the time of the listing, there was no reason to imply the existence of any particular potential purchaser like P. These factors suggest that many courts will have difficulty integrating the three documents into a coherent substitute for one integrated writing necessary to satisfy the statute. Reference to one transaction is not the same as reference to a party to be charged. *See Banta v. Newbold*, 196 P. 433 (Kan. 1921) (holding that the documents satisfying the statute must not only identify the party to be charged but also the party in whose favor he is to be charged). Without the identification of both parties, there is no contract for purposes of the statute.

New means of communication have presented courts with new problems in applying the statute. As each came along, telegrams, faxes, voice recordings, emails, and text messages have all required new applications of the statute, presenting anew iterations of the same issues. The telegram, for example, resulted in two "writings"—one received by written instructions to the telegraphic operator, and one received by the recipient of the telegram. *See Howley v. Whipple*, 48 N.H. 487 (N.H. 1869) (holding that the words given to the telegraph operator, telegraphing as the agent of the sender, was evidence of a contract, and equating the telegram to a "writing" with a pen that may be "a thousand miles long," the electronic Morse Code impulses being the ink). If what was sent and what was received matched, they could be examined like any contract or agreement. When they did not, the first might trump the second. If the first was missing, the second might suffice as proof of an agreement. In any event, courts had a "writing" with which to ask whether it satisfied the statute. *See Yaggy v. B.V.D. Co.*, 173 S.E.2d 496 (N.C. Ct. App. 1970).

Likewise, faxes requiring two copies—one sent and one received—were consistently held to be a "writing" for purposes of the statute, even when the message was generated electronically on a computer. *See Bazak Int'l Corp v. Mast Indus., Inc.*, 535 N.E.2d 633 (N.Y. 1989).

A tape recording was definitely not a "writing" until the word was used broadly by courts as any means of communication that can be reduced to a tangible, written form in which the parties are clearly identified, the identification providing the "signature" on the "writing." Then, when both parties to the recording agreed to the taping, it might satisfy the statute's purpose of preventing perjuries. *See Ellis Canning Co. v. Bernstein*, 348 F. Supp. 1212 (D. Colo. 1972).

As to emails, when not copied and printed, they raised the issues of (1) whether electronic computerized storage data was a "writing" and (2) whether the typed name at the bottom of an email was a "signature." *See McClare v. Rocha*, 86 A.3d 22, 27 (Me. 2014) (holding that an email can constitute a "signed writing" based on the historically broad interpretation of the term). Multiple emails exchanged thus can satisfy the writing requirement of the statute. *See Millennium Funding, Inc. v. Priv. Internet Access, Inc.*, 2022 U.S. Dist. LEXIS 187487 (D. Colo., Oct. 13, 2022) (collecting cases).

Text messages again raised the same issues anew. *See Perl v. Grant*, 542 P.3d 396 (Mont. 2024).[2] When the text's sender typed his or her name at the

2. Because of an amendment to its statute of frauds, text messages did not satisfy the California statute. Cal. Civ. Code § 1624(d) ("electronic messages of an ephemeral nature that is not designed to be retained or to create a permanent record" does not satisfy the statute). California real estate brokers associations instigated this amendment because they did not want their members to have to retain all text messages relating to their business.

bottom of the message, it was taken as a "signature"—but for most courts, when the text was unsigned, the text message did not satisfy the statute. Here the issue was not whether the text message was a "writing" (most courts held that it was); rather, the issue was whether the writing had a "signature" indicating an intent to be bound. *See St. John's Holdings LLC v. Two Electronics LLC*, 24 LCR 654 (Mass. Land Ct. 2016).

With each of these iterations of issues arising under the statute, courts emphasize that, because the statute when applied narrowly and technically, might encourage as much as prevent frauds, the statute should with each new method of communication be applied flexibly and less technically. With each method, the majority of cases found there was a writing "signed" by the party to be charged, whether affixing a name is by signing, printing, lithography, or some other mode, so long as the act was done with the intention of signing. *See Schneider v. Norris*, 105 Eng. Rep. 388 (K.B. 1814). In part because federal and state statutes had validated electronic signatures for many purposes, the issue of whether a writing has a "signature" might easily be answered "yes."

Example 6

V and P exchange a series of texts about the purchase and sale of Blackacre. One exchange satisfies the statute requirement that the parties to the sale be identified, another describes the property in such a way that the statute be satisfied, and yet another sets the purchase price. In the last exchange over the price, V types his name at the bottom of the text and P ends his response with a "thumbs up" emoji. Does this exchange of texts satisfy the Statute of Frauds?

Explanation

No. No court has yet decided this issue. No previous means of communication has had to deal with the type of characters used in a writing. Though many languages use pictographs, the English language does not. The meaning of this emoji is unclear—a thumbs up might mean, "I agree," or it might mean, "I'm with you so far," inviting a further response. Even if a court were to find that the emoji was part of a "writing" reduced to a tangible form, it still might not be a series of letters or a word, and here there is no certainty about which series of letters or words it represents. While the evidentiary function of the statute is arguably satisfied, the exchange of texts does not provide the parties with the prudent business practice of taking an opportunity to review their agreement as a whole and to reflect on the legal implications of what they are doing—clarifying the whole series of exchanges and referring one exchange to the rest of them. This uncertainty of meaning suggests that this exchange of texts might not be a done deal.

LISTING AGREEMENTS AND THE STATUTE

In many states, statutes require that a real estate broker's listing agreements be in writing. The listing is technically a contract for the personal services of the broker and so arguably falls outside the purview of the usual Statute of Frauds. However, the listing is likely to lead to a transfer of real property and will control some of the terms of that transfer. So some jurisdictions have enacted special-purpose statutes that require a written listing. *See Mutual Dev. Corp. v. Ward Fisher & Co.*, 47 A.3d 319 (R.I. 2012). In other jurisdictions, a writing is required because of a regulation of the Real Estate Commission or other state agency regulating the licensing of brokers. As to the remaining jurisdictions, the listing agreement remains beyond the reach of the statute, even though this might be unwise as a matter of policy.

Such statutes do not, by the weight of the cases deciding the issue, prevent the enforcement of the listing by a broker who has fully performed. Brokers who do not satisfy these statutes are also generally denied causes of action for restitution and unjust enrichment.

EXCEPTIONS TO THE STATUTE

The statute is inapplicable to fully performed agreements. Such performance provides evidence of what the agreement would have been if written, and that evidence is an adequate substitute for the protections the statute would otherwise provide, rendering the statute irrelevant. So the statute may not be used to rescind such agreements.

What if an incomplete agreement is admitted as evidence in court? An admission of the essential terms of an agreement in pleadings, depositions, affidavits, or testimony in court is not a waiver of the statute's protections and any defense based on it. Although the safeguards surrounding judicial proceedings should be an adequate substitute for the statute's protections, most states refuse to create an evidentiary exception to the statute on this ground. Why? Because to do so would take as true what is only meant to be an intermediate step in the process of ascertaining the truth of the matter in litigation. On the other hand, once the admission is necessary for the court to support and enforce its judgment, the whole record of the litigation underlying the judgment becomes a writing sufficient to satisfy the statute. *See Smith v. Boyd*, 553 A.2d 131 (R.I. 1989).

The courts have fashioned two other exceptions to the statute. Both are designed to carry out its purposes and prevent the statute from itself encouraging fraud. Such is the strength of the policy behind the statute, that both must be shown by clear and convincing evidence. *See, e.g., Sullivan v. Porter*,

861 A.2d 625, 630 (Me. 2004). Both are affirmative defenses. They are typically asserted in an answer to a complaint and may give rise to a motion to dismiss. These two exceptions are the doctrines of (1) part performance and (2) equitable estoppel.

It should be noted that part performance (the most common exception recognized in this country) is really a black-letter version of the second and that it developed out of cases recognizing the second.

Equitable estoppel applies to promises that otherwise would be unenforceable. It is invoked to enforce such promises so as to avoid injustice. It requires that the purchaser reasonably and detrimentally rely on a transfer insufficient to meet the requirements of the statute. There must be some, albeit insufficient, writing, and the purchaser must pay some money or incur some liability (take out a purchase money mortgage loan, perhaps) in reliance on the document's validity. *See Baliles v. Cities Serv. Co.*, 578 S.W.2d 621 (Tenn. 1979), noted in 10 Memp. St. U. L. Rev. 107 (1979); and *see generally* Note, The Doctrine of Equitable Estoppel and the Statute of Frauds, 66 Mich. L. Rev. 170 (1967). Equitable estoppel also arises from the conduct of a party—through speech, silence, action, or inaction—by which a party secures some benefit. For example, an oral agreement for the sale of a residence might be equitably enforced against vendors after the purchasers sold their existing residence in reliance on the agreement. The evidence of reliance need not involve the property at issue directly—in the instance of purchasers selling their existing residence. Nor need it affect any improvement in the property, as when purchasers incur liability for a loan related to their purchase. *See Chapman v. Bowman*, 381 A.2d 1123 (Me. 1978). Likewise, no direct promise is required. (That would involve promissory estoppel.) In *Baliles, supra*, the defendant vendor would have had a windfall and been unjustly enriched by obtaining a lot improved with the proceeds of the plaintiff's loan; likewise, the plaintiff's benefit was clear: He obtained clear title to the lot as improved. Thus this doctrine scrutinizes the conduct of both parties, not just the purchaser's. Because of this, equitable estoppel may also serve as a basis for restitution.

Likewise, because the statute applies to express easements as well as purchase and sale agreements, an oral agreement between two neighbors to improve a common driveway may be enforced through the doctrine, resulting in a monetary judgment for the unpaid amount in favor of the non-breaching neighbor and the creation of a permanent easement for the joint use of the driveway. *See Key v. Renner*, 2017 Tenn. App. LEXIS 780 (Tenn. Ct. App., Nov. 30, 2017).

Part performance is only available as an exception to the statute in cases when specific performance is sought. This exception generally requires that (1) the purchaser take possession of the property (in some states exclusive possession is required), and (2) pay all or part of the purchase price, and/or (3) improve the property in some way. *See Kiernan v. Creech*, 268 P.3d 312 (Alaska 2012). The first element of this doctrine applies in all states recognizing the doctrine. As to the second and third elements, they are sometimes both required, but sometimes only one of them is required. You might notice that the doctrine distinguishes between facts undertaken in contemplation of eventual performance and those undertaken in part performance. So facts related to obtaining mortgage financing are not sufficient to constitute partial performance of a contract of sale.

Thus, the four elements of the part performance doctrine are

1. possession,
2. possession plus payment,
3. possession plus improvements, and
4. possession plus payment and/or improvements.

See 3 American Law of Property §11.7 (A. J. Casner ed., 1952). As you can see from its elements, it is a doctrine for the benefit of purchasers, not vendors. Because there are several versions of this doctrine, beware of generalizations about it. The courts are using it equitably, and that effort may produce results in any one jurisdiction that defy a concise black-letter restatement. Eighteen states have codified the doctrine.

This doctrine was first recognized only 23 years after the enactment of the statute. *See Lester v. Foxcroft*, 1 Eng. Rep. 205 (H.L. 1700). In this country, Judge Cardozo gave it voice in *Burns v. McCormick*, 135 N.E. 273 (N.Y. 1922), saying that it applies when the performance is "'unequivocally referable' to the agreement" and is that "which alone and without the aid of words of promise is unintelligible . . . without the incident of ownership." The doctrine makes the contract enforceable in equity, for specific performance, but not in a damage action. All but four states recognize the doctrine. Only Kentucky, Mississippi, North Carolina, and Tennessee do not. In those states, equitable estoppel is the principal exception to the statute.

The first element of the part performance doctrine is thought to provide the same evidence as would a writing, and the second and third are thought to incorporate or black-letter the reliance element of equitable estoppel.

Once the purchaser invokes either equitable estoppel or part performance and validates an oral agreement through either doctrine, the vendor may not resist specific performance of the agreement by offering to reimburse the purchaser for his out-of-pocket expenses incurring related liabilities and improving the property. *See Smith v. Smith*, 2005 Tenn. App. LEXIS 733 (Tenn. Ct. App., Nov. 22, 2005).

Examples

Example 7

Ask yourself why the statute renders oral contracts unenforceable but not invalid.

Explanation

One instance in which the distinction might apply is where the purchaser makes an improvement to the property that is readily compensable in money. Thus the alleged vendor can make restitution. Where it is not readily compensable, then the doctrine of part performance is applied. This makes the statement quoted the basis for a restricted statement of that doctrine. This distinction is generally recognized.

Example 8

P builds part of a house on land purchased from V pursuant to an oral installment land contract unenforceable under the Statute of Frauds. P wishes to recover the value of the partially completed house from V. Does P have a cause of action against V?

Explanation

Yes. P has a cause of action for unjust enrichment. V and P have made a mistake of law about the unenforceability of the contract. There is no complete improvement, so the equitable exceptions to the statute may not apply in most jurisdictions. However, the statute does not bar all equitable actions under these facts—a decree in specific performance would be barred, but an unjust enrichment action would not be. *Redland v. Redland*, 288 P.3d 1173 (Wyo. 2012).

Example 9

Is an oral judicially supervised agreement to settle litigation over a disputed purchase and sale, when made by an attorney with a general authority to settle, sufficient compliance with the statute?

Explanation

Yes. While any admission of the terms of the agreement would not be a waiver of a defense based on the statute, the completion of the settlement agreement is the equivalent of a court's using an admission made in the course of litigation to enforce its judgment. Moreover, because the attorney is the agent of the party authorizing the settlement, his fiduciary obligations are a sufficient substitute for the statute's protections, and, finally, as a policy matter, judicial economy is promoted by the settlement. *Waddle v. Elrod*, 367 S.W.3d 217 (Tenn. 2012); *Ogden v. Griffith*, 236 P.3d 1249 (Idaho 2010); *Halstead v. Murray*, 547 A.2d 202 (N.H. 1988).

Of the two exceptions, equitable estoppel is the one likely to apply to the greater number of factual situations. This is so because it applies not just to actions involved in taking actual possession, but also to any action constituting detrimental reliance, whether or not the expense improves the property itself. Architectural fees evince detrimental reliance, regardless of whether the architect's plans are ever used on the property. So does procuring a mortgage. Estoppel arises from the conduct of a person, whether or not the conduct occurs on the land. On the other hand, part performance is shown by what happens on the land.

Finally, the parties to an agreement, whose terms must comply with the statute, cannot modify the agreement without again complying with the statute. What is required to be in writing in the first instance cannot be altered by parol evidence—true in most, but not all, states. In some states, the modified agreement is judged according to whether, as modified, it is of a type that is subject to the statute. If not, then the modification need not be in writing.

Example 10

V and P orally agree that P will purchase two parcels. P proves that the oral agreement satisfies the part performance exception to the Statute of Frauds. V receives a better offer for one of the parcels and sells it to a third party. P sues V for specific performance of the oral agreement. The court grants specific performance of the agreement as to the parcel remaining in V's hands. Should the court also award P damages for V's failure to convey the parcel he sold?

Explanation

Yes, as to any money paid so far by P, P should receive a credit, up to the amount of the damage award toward P's remaining purchase price for the parcel subject to specific performance. Damages should be measured by the opportunity costs arising due to P's not owning both parcels. *See Thornton v. Marcum*, 2008 Tenn. App. LEXIS 194 (Tenn. Ct. App., Mar. 31, 2008).

A CONCLUDING NOTE

No discussion of the requirements of the Statute of Frauds should be confused with a discussion of the needs and requirements of your clients in a transaction. Generally, it is good practice to memorialize all the terms they wish in a written contract of sale, whether or not those terms are required by the statute. For example, absent an agreement otherwise, it is presumed that the purchase price in a contract of sale will be paid in cash—this is the "all cash" presumption—and the statute only requires that a price be stated; nonetheless, it is a standard practice to require that if not paid in cash, it be paid either with a certified or cashier's check. Getting all the terms of an agreement into a written document is preferable to leaving them to the vagaries of memory.

CHAPTER 5

Contract of Sale Conditions

The period of time between the completion and execution of a contract of sale for real property and the closing is known as the executory period. Often it is the broker who guides the parties in filling in the blanks on a standard form contract. But no matter who fills in the blanks, it commences when the parties sign or "execute" the contract. It is typically a time when the contract is not yet fully performed—that is, it is subject to contingencies (aka "subject to" clauses). The purchaser is most likely to apply for a mortgage loan, have the property inspected and appraised, and deal with attorneys searching the title and determining its marketability. All this cannot be done overnight. The usual executory period is 45 to 90 days long. As you read this chapter, consider this somewhat informal letter as an executory contract of sale.

September 1, 2026

Victoria Vendor
Blackacre Farm
Eden Heights, MD

Dear Vivi:

Thank you for walking the bounds of your farm with me over the weekend. I intend to purchase it and with this letter make the following offer to purchase. Your acceptance of my offer can be indicated by signing the line after my signature.

The price is $500,000, or $10,000 an acre. Enclosed is a check for $25,000, tendered as a down payment, to be credited toward the full price, which is payable as follows:

—$75,000 upon the offer of title proof,
—$400,000 payable as the proceeds of a first deed of trust.

I will make application to the Myerstown Federal Savings Bank for a $400,000 loan, to be secured by an appraised first mortgage lien upon the farm, at a satisfactory, conventional rate of interest, for a term of 20 years. Settlement shall occur by December 15, 2014, at a place mutually agreeable to both of us and subject to the following three conditions:

1. Title to Blackacre shall be insurable and marketable. Proof of title shall be in a form acceptable to my attorneys, Ketchum & Skinner.
2. A survey is done indicating that the boundaries of Blackacre are more or less as we saw them last weekend.
3. The sale of my house in town is completed, with the proceeds free and clear.

Very truly yours,

Peter Purchaser

This _______ day of September, 2026, I have read and accept the terms and conditions of this letter.

____

Victoria Vendor

As this contract clearly indicates, the modern contract of sale for real property is replete with "subject to" clauses—as in "the closing of the title involved in this transaction is subject to" or "only to be held when the following conditions are met." The contingencies become preconditions to a closing. A precondition is an event not certain to occur that, unless its occurrence is waived, excuses further performance of a contract.

"Contingencies" is a word of double meaning. A contract provision may state, "this contract is made subject to the ability of the purchaser to sell his existing residence, and if he is unable to do so, this contract shall be null and void." First, this language is more precisely defined as a condition—that is, it defines an event annulling the contract. Moreover, it is a condition subsequent—that is, it states that the purchaser has a contractual interest in the vendor's property until he fails to sell his residence, but that meanwhile that interest continues. Defining a contingency as a condition subsequent may have important consequences for the purchaser if (say) the improvements on the property burn to the ground while the interest continues. In a majority of states, by placing the risk of loss on the purchaser, the doctrine of equitable conversion operates even though the purchaser's interest is subject to a condition subsequent.

Other cases interpreting contract contingencies have assigned them a second meaning. A contract provision may state, "this contract is made subject to the rezoning of the property from residential to commercial use." Most courts would interpret this provision to mean that the purchaser, the party to benefit from the rezoning, is under an obligation to pursue the rezoning application. The basis for such an obligation is an implied covenant of good faith and fair dealing. Breach of such a covenant can be the subject of waiver (by the party benefited) or an action for breach of contract, while the occurrence of a condition subsequent is not. Its breach or performance is a precondition to the sales contract; upon its breach, there is no sales contract on which to base a suit. *See CAL, SD, LLC v. Interwest Leasing LLC*, 15 N.W.3d 433 (S. Dak. 2024). In some jurisdictions, unperformed contingencies of the second type delay the applicability of the doctrine of equitable conversion. However, the traditional rule is that a contract with unperformed contingencies that are nonetheless capable of performance does not prevent an equitable conversion.

"SUBJECT TO FINANCING" CLAUSE

The most litigated contingency clause is a "subject to financing" clause, in which the purchaser agrees to close only after he has applied for and received a lender's commitment for a type of mortgage financing outlined in the clause. This type of clause is generally of benefit to the purchaser; he can thereafter waive its benefit by, for example, agreeing to close with cash instead of the proceeds of a mortgage loan. But the clause may arguably benefit the vendor as well: It assures him of the purchaser's financial ability to close the transaction by requiring the latter to produce a firm commitment for financing within a reasonable time of executing the contract. Better yet, this clause should provide that a commitment be in hand within (say) 30 days. Thus the purchaser's waiver may not always remove the clause from the contract.

The usual material terms of this type of clause are (1) the amount of the mortgage loan to be obtained; (2) the term of that loan, stated as a minimum term acceptable to the purchaser; and (3) the maximum interest rate acceptable to the purchaser. These three terms are necessary to avoid a charge that the clause is void for vagueness, indefinite, or ambiguous in its provisions. Such a finding results in the parties being able to rescind the contract, and rescission will require the other party to tender back any benefits received under the contract, including the purchaser's deposit. *See Perkins v. Gosewehr*, 295 N.W.2d 789, 791-792 (Wisc. Ct. App. 1980).

However, less is sometimes made to serve. The third paragraph of the letter beginning this chapter has the first term, a vague reference to the second, and part of the third, so the acceptance letter back will have to provide more.

Other terms might include a minimum appraised value for the mortgaged property, a maximum amount payable in closing costs on the loan, a maximum amount necessary to satisfy the lender's requirements for a mortgage escrow account for real property taxes and property hazard insurance, and a maximum amount necessary each month to repay the loan. *See* Perkins, *op. cit.*, 295 N.W.2d at 792-793) (warning that "excessive detail may be counterproductive to enforcement of the contract by . . . narrowing the contingency clause to an extent that makes its fulfillment improbable.").

Why is this clause so important? Consider the following.

EXAMPLES

Examples

Example 1

P informs her broker that she cannot afford V's home if she's required to finance more than 80 percent of the purchase price, but executes a brief but enforceable contract of sale for it without a clause mentioning financing. If P does not qualify for the loan she needs, can V keep her deposit?

Explanation

Yes. The default rule is that the sale is "all cash at closing," whether the cash is provided by P or by a lender. P might consider a suit against the broker here, but that is no sure thing.

Executing a contract expressly calling for "all cash at closing" may seem like a good deal for the seller. However, such a clause should only be in a contract calling for a short executory period and obligating the purchaser to close even if the purchaser is unable to come up with the necessary cash through third-party financing. Because an "all-cash-at-closing" provision is presumed to be for the sole benefit of the purchaser, the contract should also provide that it is non-waivable by the purchaser. Such a provision imposes a condition on the contract rather than a contingency, annulling the contract and denying the buyer further remedies on it. *See Dygert v. Crouch*, 36 S.W.3d 1, 11-12 (Mo. Ct. App. 2001).

Executing a contract with an adequately detailed subject to financing clause, the purchaser undertakes the implied obligation to make a reasonable effort to obtain the outlined financing. *See Williams v. Ubaldo*, 670 A.2d 913, n.1 (Me. 1996). Often the purchaser will apply for a preapproval of a mortgage loan application before executing a contract; such an early application has been held to satisfy part of the effort required of the purchaser. Often it is held that the vendor may, but need not, search for the purchaser's financing, too, but the vendor may not force the purchaser to accept financing not called for in the clause. Much depends on the words of the clause. Some examples follow.

Examples

Example 2

Vivi (V) and Peter (P) execute a brief but enforceable contract of sale for Blackacre for $375,000. The contract provides in part "if P is unable to obtain this loan [described below] within 60 days from this date, P's deposit will be returned to him in full." The contract is further conditioned on P's ability "to borrow $300,000 at a conventional, fixed interest rate of 4 percent, for 20 years." The parties reduce the contract price in the contract to $350,000 but do not otherwise change the terms of the contract. P files one mortgage loan application. In response to this application, the lender appraises the property and offers a commitment for a mortgage loan whose principal amount is $260,000 and whose interest rate is 4.25 percent. Ninety days after the date of the contract's execution, P requests the return of his deposit. V refuses. P sues V for its return. What result?

Explanation

Judgment for V, who is entitled to keep the deposit. While V will have to concede that the benchmark for P's satisfaction of the clause is a commitment for a loan, V has at least three arguments to make. First, V will argue that the risk of not procuring the required loan in 60 days is P's. Second, on the amount of the required loan, V can argue (considering the declining contract prices that this transaction reflects) that the reduction in the purchase price implicitly amends the subject to financing clause, reducing the principal of the required loan to an amount bearing the same loan-to-price ratio as $375,000 is to $300,000—80 percent. V should argue that P has a duty to keep trying. *See Binford v. Shicker*, 553 N.E.2d 845 (Ind. App. Ct. 1990) (applications rejected by three lenders excusing the purchaser from the contract) and *Grayson v. LaBranche*, 225 A.2d 922 (N.H. 1967) (purchaser excused after filing two rejected applications). V might also offer to make up the difference with a second mortgage loan, so that P will have the financing he contracted to take. V can either offer a loan with an 80 percent loan-to-price ratio or offer a second mortgage that, when added to the lender's, provides total financing for 80 percent—$280,000—of the revised contract price. (P does not have to accept V's offer of a loan: P agreed to the vendor-purchaser relationship and may well be uninterested in being V's long-term debtor. However, such an offer will tend to show V's good faith.) Third, as to the interest rate, V can argue that P's application to only one lender cannot establish a conventional interest rate.

Courts have validated subject to financing clauses that provide for financing "ASAP 2025" or "at prevailing conventional rates and terms." Such language applies to all the terms of the financing, not just the interest rate, although in the instance of the latter phrase, financing must be obtained in 2025 or else the contract is null or void in 2026. *See Rogers v. Cardinal Realty*, 339 A.2d 23 (N.H. 1975). How are the missing rates and terms to be ascertained? In a majority of jurisdictions the answer comes through the good-faith, reasonably diligent efforts of the purchaser in seeking the loan. Such an effort becomes the subject of an implied covenant attached by many courts to this type of clause. *See Farnsworth/Samuel Ltd. v. Cerini*, 492 So. 2d 1245 (La. App. 1988). If the purchaser makes a good-faith effort to obtain financing and the transaction does not close due to the vendor's default, the purchaser will recover his deposit; on the other hand, when no good-faith effort is made, the vendor not otherwise in default may retain the deposit. *See Hunt v. Shamblin*, 371 S.E.2d 591 (W.Va. 1988). Only one of the parties—the non-defaulting one—will "win" the deposit when satisfying the good faith covenant is the issue. In contrast, if the clause were to be found indefinite and the contract null and void on that account, the deposit would be returned to the purchaser.

Moreover, when the purchaser makes a good faith effort and does not obtain financing, the contract is null and void. *See Rousset v. Smith*, 176 So. 3d 632 (La. App. 2015) (the "subject to financing" clause being a condition in the contract). Further, when the financing clause is initially satisfied, but no closing occurs through no fault of the purchaser, the burden of the failure should not fall on the innocent purchaser.

Another answer is that for purposes of fleshing out the contract as to this term, P becomes, upon the execution of the contract, V's agent for the purpose of establishing what a conventional interest rate is. Here the good faith covenant is an implied term of the agency. This agency argument may at first seem strange to you: Why should parties who are in an adversarial relationship when negotiating a contract suddenly become principal and agent for purposes of carrying it out? The answer lies in their mutual interest in implementing the contract and the narrowness of the scope of the agency. As an agent, P owes a fiduciary duty of acting in good faith for the principal. This duty is breached when only one financing application is filed. An application must be filed with a reasonable number of lenders, and until P does this, or else shows why one application is a reasonable number, he is in breach and not entitled to his deposit. *See Liuzza v. Panzer*, 333 So. 2d 689 (La. App. 1976). P might argue that the purpose of the clause was to provide a third-party appraisal of the property, but if that was the case, this purpose was not expressed clearly in the clause used in this example.

Example 3

Would the result change if the contract called (as did the letter, *op. cit.*) for P's filing one loan application with a named conventional mortgage lender?

Explanation

No, arguably because once the agency is created its duties can supersede the contract's words, which in any event can be taken to mean that the agent has a duty to apply not just to the one named lender, but also to lenders like the named one. This rule will depend on a showing of the parties' intentions. The support for such a view is not overwhelming (but the leading case is in many casebooks). *See Kovarik v.Vesely*, 89 N.W.2d 279 (Wis. 1958).

Example 4

If the contract did not contain all of the definitive material terms for the loan, what would be the legal effect of establishing the purchaser as an agent?

Explanation

Then the filing of a loan application has the effect of providing material terms for the contract. Without it, the time and manner of the payment of the purchase price—an essential term for the contract of sale—become uncertain. These terms are filed on behalf of both the vendor as a principal and the agent on his own behalf. The application, agreed to by both parties, can then be incorporated into the contract for two purposes: to satisfy the Statute of Frauds and to supply material terms for the contract.

Example 5

No matter what it provides, must this condition be unconditionally fulfilled?

Explanation

No, because it seldom can be when a "commitment" is the benchmark for performance. The commitment will have other terms and conditions: The lender will want the title searched, appraisals done, and so forth. The terms in the contract are unlikely to cover all the ground the commitment will.

Once a mortgage commitment is obtained, the purchaser-borrowers are under a duty not to hinder the closing on the mortgage loan. *See Bruyere v. Jade Realty Corp.*, 375 A.2d 600 (N.H. 1977) (holding that when the commitment was withdrawn because of the purchasers' divorce, the covenant was breached).

Example 6

V and P execute a brief but enforceable contract for the sale of Greenacre, containing a brief but enforceable subject to financing clause. P writes a letter to V, asking V to approve a modification of the clause. V construes the letter as an anticipatory repudiation of the contract, noting that the letter does not deal with any term already in the clause. Is V right?

Explanation

Yes. P should have written, "If you can't modify the clause, I will be forced to withdraw from the contract," indicating that he has not already done so.

Example 7

V and P execute a brief contract of sale for Blackacre. The contract conditioned the closing on "P's obtaining satisfactory financing." Is this contract unenforceable on account of this language? What other language might be substituted?

Explanation

Yes. Again, obtaining a commitment is the benchmark, but "available financing" would be better. From the vendor's perspective, words like "satisfactory" or "suitable" may be ambiguous, indicating either financing offered by the mortgage market or financing that the purchaser can afford. Any meaning encompassing the purchaser's financial ability gives the purchaser too easy an out. Availability, on the other hand, is a standard subject to verification in the marketplace and, further, need not depend on the personal ability or satisfaction of the purchaser with what's offered. *See Gildea v. Kapenis*, 402 N.W.2d 457 (Iowa 1987). "Conventional Financing" is another term achieving much the same result. *Stackhouse v. Gaver*, 801 N.W.2d 260 (Neb. Ct. App. 2011). An objective, rather than subjective, standard for fulfilling the contingency is more likely to pass judicial muster on issues such as indefiniteness and mutuality of obligation; moreover, the purchaser's good faith in satisfying the subjective standard is likely to become an issue. "Satisfactory" financing makes the contract resemble an option.

Example 8

V and P execute a brief contract of sale for Blackacre. The contract conditioned the closing on "P's applying for available financing from an institutional lender within 10 days of the execution of this contract." The next day P fills out an application, gives it to a mortgage broker to submit to a qualifying lender, and does nothing more. Ten days later, the broker submits the application to the lender, who 30 days later rejects the application. Has P failed to satisfy the clause?

Explanation

Yes. The application was submitted not to a lender but to a broker, so upon its rejection, P is bound to go through with the closing. A mortgage broker is not a lending institution. The language here implies that P will be dealing directly with the lender(s) — promoting speedy responses to lender inquiries, and so on — so P makes other arrangements at his peril. What the broker does, as P's agent, is imputed to P. *See Vafa v. Cramer*, 622 N.Y.S.2d 567 (N.Y. App. Div. 1995), discussed at 17 Cardozo L. Rev. 299 (1995). P has not satisfied the clause. It is no longer a precondition to a closing.

Example 9

V and P execute a brief contract of sale for Blackacre. The contract provides for a closing only after "P obtains a firm mortgage commitment." After searching for a mortgage loan, P obtains a commitment that requires that P have the proceeds of the sale of his present residence in hand, in an amount not less than $100,000. Can V compel P to go through with the transaction?

Explanation

No. The commitment is not "firm" and the precondition for the closing is not met. P cannot be compelled to proceed further. *See Farrell v. Janik*, 542 A.2d 59 (N.J. Super. 1988) (holding that under these facts, purchasers were free of further liability on the contract when it proved impossible to sell at the required price).

"SUBJECT TO SALE OF PRIOR RESIDENCE" CLAUSE

A contract condition making a closing "subject to the sale of the purchaser's existing residence" is not a statement that the purchaser will not close without being able to use the proceeds of that sale to reduce his mortgage loan amount used to finance a new residence. *See Agnew v. Stitch Assocs.*, 214 A.2d 134 (Conn. 1965). Neither does the statement in a contract that a further deposit will be paid at the time the purchaser's existing residence is sold make the prior sale a precondition of the closing on the contract for the purchaser's new residence. *See George v. Oswald*, 78 N.W.2d 763 (Wis. 1956). Without a clear expression of intent, then, the sale of a prior residence is not a material term of the subject to financing clause in a purchaser's contract of sale for a new residence.

In the letter at the beginning of this chapter, the clause requiring "the sale of my house in town," and the phrase "with the proceeds free and clear" will not be read together as a part of the subject to financing clause. Any such dependency between the various provisions will have to be clearer to create a contract "subject to financing after the sale of my prior residence."

"SUBJECT TO EXISTING MORTGAGES" CLAUSE

A related topic is presented by a provision that the closing is "subject to an existing mortgage." What does this mean? Is the price term in such a contract definite? It is not unless the parties have provided that the purchaser is to take the title assuming liability for repayment of those mortgage loans. "Assuming" such liability is the traditional way of saying two things: (1) the purchaser has taken title to the property subject to the existing mortgage lien, and (2) the purchaser has undertaken personal liability on the note for the existing loan. If the title is taken "subject to" an existing mortgage, that usually means that the purchaser accedes to the first proposition just explained but not to the second. *See Daugharthy v. Monritt Associates*, 444 A.2d 1030 (Md. 1981).

The distinction between a sale of property "subject to an existing mortgage" and a sale with "an assumption of existing mortgages" exists in all jurisdictions. The sale of property "subject to a mortgage" does not create a personal obligation on the purchaser's part to pay it. The sale of property with "the purchaser assuming payment of an existing mortgage" creates a duty (1) to satisfy the obligation when due, as well as (2) to protect the vendor against any demands made for payment of the debt that mortgage secures. As between the vendor and purchaser, the assumption is a matter of contract. That contract may be written or implied, made in the deed conveying the property or in a document separate from the deed of conveyance.

The interplay between the price term for a property and an implied assumption by a purchaser, arises when a purchaser elects to "deduct" the principal amount due on an existing mortgage from the purchase price. Here courts draw the inference that he must have "deducted" that amount to pay the mortgage. This inference gives rise to the rule that absent an express agreement to the contrary, a purchaser's assumption of the mortgage will be implied when the amount due on the mortgage equals the amount deducted from the purchase price. *Daugharthy, op. cit.*

No matter what the purchaser's liability, a severable issue is whether the vendor is released from his liability to the mortgage lender by the assumption. Unless there is a novation[1] of the mortgage, the answer is no: A mortgage lender is under no obligation to release a selling mortgagor upon a purchaser's assumption. Otherwise a unilateral change in the loan agreement would be forced on the lender, denying him his original bargain. So such a release is likely to occur only if the purchaser agrees to pay the mortgagee a higher rate of interest than the vendor has been paying; it amounts to a novation of the original mortgage agreement.

Examples

Example 10

Suppose a vendor is not personally liable on the existing mortgage, but instead of assuming the mortgage, took title subject to it and later convinces his own grantee purchaser to assume this liability. May the lender then sue the grantee?

Explanation

There is a split of authority on the issue of whether before a mortgagee can proceed directly against an assuming grantee, it must prove that the vendor was personally liable as well. There is a title view and a contract law view of this problem. Some courts take the view that if the vendor has no liability, he cannot pass any on to his own purchaser. That is the title view. However, other courts (most recently) take the view that if the vendor and the purchaser intended to benefit the mortgagee, the latter is the third-party beneficiary of their contract.

"SUBJECT TO REZONING" CLAUSE

If the purchaser needs to rezone the property, the contract should make the closing conditional on obtaining the needed change. Otherwise the law presumes that the parties have executed the contract recognizing the present zoning and the purchaser will bear the risk that an existing zoning regulation does not permit the future use that he wishes to make of the property. The contract should specify the type of zoning classification sought, the party who will seek it, the date by which it must be finally approved,

1. A novation is an agreement that replaces the existing mortgage obligation with a new one, signed by the purchaser with the mortgage lender. It replaces the vendor/mortgagor/debtor with the purchaser and voids the vendor's original obligation to pay the mortgage debt. In this respect it differs from an assignment, which does not release the vendor from an ultimate responsibility to pay the debt when the assignee does not pay.

and the use permissible after the rezoning is obtained. Because obtaining a rezoning is often a negotiation with zoning officials, many rezoning clauses should reflect the fact that many rezoning applications are not denied, but are granted with conditions attached. *See Steele v. Pack*, 674 S.E.2d 134 (Ga. App. 2009) (rezoning not "denied" as subject to rezoning clause required when a condition made its satisfaction impossible). If possible, a specific rezoning application should be incorporated by reference. A contract simply stating that it was "subject to rezoning" without more, will fail for being vague and indefinite. *See Hitt v. Lord*, 391 S.E.2d 681 (Ga. Ct. App. 1990).

If the zoning ordinance applicable to the property subject to a contract of sale is changed during the executory period, judicial opinions divide on whether the parties are excused from the performance of the contract or are presumed to have contracted with the knowledge that the zoning might change. The latter view rests on the doctrine of equitable conversion reviewed in Chapter 3. The former depends on contract theory: If the parties are deemed to have contracted in light of existing regulations without at the same time allocating the risk of a change in it, the continuance of that law becomes an implied condition of the contract. Both of these theories are well established. So there is an acute need for an express provision allocating the risk of an unforeseen change in zoning during the executory period.

A "subject to rezoning" clause is sometimes presumed to be to the benefit of both vendor and purchaser. The vendor benefits when the rezoning to a denser use makes the land more valuable; the purchaser benefits by using the rezoning to develop the property to that new use. The result of this presumption is that, absent an agreement to the contrary, the clause is not waivable by either party alone; both must consent to its removal from the contract. This view is particularly appropriate when the vendor takes back a mortgage on the rezoned property from the purchaser. *See Knight v. Princess Builders, Inc.*, 899 A.2d 157 (Md. 2008). Otherwise, when the purchaser does not obtain the required rezoning, the vendor's obligation to close the contract is at an end, regardless of the purchaser's willingness to waive the clause.

Other courts view the clause as for the sole benefit of the purchaser who will use the rezoned property and thus may waive its benefit. *See Brotman v. Roelofs*, 246 N.W.2d 368 (Mich. Ct. App. 1976) (also holding that once a rezoning denial is issued, the contract "lapses" and the purchaser may not specifically perform it) and *Litvak v. Smith*, 636 S.E.2d 327 (N.C. Ct. App. 2008).

Examples

Example 11

A city publishes a notice of a public hearing affecting the permitted uses of Blackacre. Several days later, V and P execute a brief but enforceable contract for Blackacre. At the hearing, the use of the land that P proposes for Blackacre is changed from a permitted to a prohibited use. The effectiveness of the use change relates back to the date of the notice of the hearing. The V-P contract is silent on the allocation of the risk of a rezoning. P sues V to rescind the contract. In this suit, what result?

Explanation

Judgment for V. The traditional rule applies even here: The risk of a rezoning during the executory period is on the purchaser. Some courts say that the risk shouldn't be on the vendor—after all, what control has he over the local legislature responsible for the ordinance? That the purchaser has no control either is the ready reply to that line of argument. But, say the courts adopting this traditional view, the purchaser is in the best position to know the use that he plans to make of the property and whether that use is permitted by the ordinance.

Example 12

Same facts as in the previous Example, but in addition, V knew that P wished to use the property in a way possible at the time of the execution of the contract but impermissible after the rezoning without a hearing to obtain the special exception.

Explanation

Judgment for P, on the grounds of a mutual mistake of fact. The facts underlying the traditional rule are distinguishable from this case. *Dover Pool & Racquet Club, Inc. v. Brooking*, 322 N.E.2d 168 (Mass. 1975); *see generally* Restatement (Second) of Contracts §§151-152 (1977).

"SUBJECT TO ATTORNEY REVIEW" CLAUSE

The organized bar has long argued that attorneys become involved in the typical residential purchase and sale transaction only when they can't be of much help to either party—the reason being that by the time they are involved, the rights and duties of the parties have been fixed by the terms of the contract. One remedy for this situation is the insertion in standard form contracts of an attorney review clause. Under the terms of such clauses, the parties are given the right to seek legal advice within a certain time of the execution of the contract, and the attorney whose advice is sought is given the right to disapprove the contract, rendering it null and void.

The terms of the clauses used in this fashion vary considerably. Sometimes the contract binds the parties if not disapproved within the time set; sometimes the attorney's approval must be express before the contract becomes binding. Most courts considering such clauses that are otherwise silent find them to be conditions subsequent, akin to a right of rescission. They do not, however, give the parties themselves the right to repudiate the contract unilaterally during the review period.

These clauses are routinely used in only a few jurisdictions. Why? Because the brokerage trade groups resist their use. Consider the situation in New Jersey. In the mid-1960s, the state bar and the state brokerage board engaged in litigation over the brokers' alleged unauthorized practice of law. The discovery stage of the case dragged on into the 1980s, when it was settled by consent. *See N.J. State Bar Assn. v. N.J. Assn. of Realtor Boards*, 461 A.2d 1112, modified, 467 A.2d 577 (N.J. 1983) (holding that a broker-prepared residential sales contract is not the unauthorized practice of law provided that the contract prescribes a three-day attorney review period). The consent decree required that the Board place in bold, ten-point type the following statement at the start of the board's standard form contract, which is in widespread use in the jurisdiction:

> **THIS IS A LEGAL DOCUMENT. IT CREATES RIGHTS AND DUTIES ABOUT WHICH YOU MAY NEED LEGAL ASSISTANCE. YOU HAVE THE RIGHT TO CONSULT AN ATTORNEY FOR THREE BUSINESS DAYS FROM THE EXECUTION OF THIS DOCUMENT. UPON THE ADVICE OF AN ATTORNEY, YOU HAVE THE RIGHT TO REVOKE THIS AGREEMENT WITHIN THAT TIME.**

Since the 1980s, this statement has been modified and elaborated from time to time. It need not be included in a sales contract resulting from an absolute auction of property so long as the parties are advised of the importance of an attorney review. *See Sullivan as Trustee of Sylvester L. Sullivan Grantor Tr. v. Max Spann Real Estate and Auction Co.*, 276 A.3d 92 (N.J. 2022). It is also inapplicable to a palimony agreement *See Moynihan v, Lynch*, 269 A.3d 435 (N.J. 2022). In effect, the statement creates a right of rescission. In whom is this right created? The "you" could refer to either the vendor or the purchaser, although the purchaser is the most obvious beneficiary: It gives him a three-day cooling-off period after the contract's execution. This period is also intended to provide professional review of the contract. The three days, then, does not include weekends and holidays. The parties could agree to extend the three-day period but not to shorten it. When the broker holds on to the contract after the vendor executes it, the period runs from the time the contract is actually delivered to the purchaser, and perhaps even from the time the purchaser executes it. Otherwise the broker would have the unilateral power to render the clause useless. *Peterson v. Pursell*, 771 A.2d 666 (N.J. Super. 2001).

The New Jersey clause does not say so, but it applies only to broker-prepared contracts of sale. Because the contract is prepared by a third party, the rescission period should run from the time it is delivered to both the vendor and the purchaser. There is but one rescission period, running for the benefit of both parties. The period starts to run when the contract comes into existence, and that event only occurs when both parties are bound by it. There cannot therefore be two independent rescission periods. *See Gordon Dev. Group, Inc. v. Bradley*, 827 A.2d 341 (N.J. Super. 2003).

Examples

Example 13

V and P executed a brief but enforceable contract. It contains an attorney review clause, but the purchaser does not submit the contract to her attorney. The time for review passes. May the purchaser walk away from the contract at this point?

Explanation

It depends. If the clause is viewed as a conditional acceptance or a condition precedent to the contract, then the answer is yes. However if, as most courts think, the clause is seen as a condition subsequent, then the purchaser may not walk away, because the contract is binding unless disapproved. Under either view, the duty to perform does not arise until approval or disapproval by the attorney. The majority view avoids the contractual problem of having an agreement that the parties to it expect to be binding, but which is not. So the clause terminates an otherwise valid, existing contract. *See Hubble v. O'Connor*, 684 N.E.2d 816 (Ill. App. 1997). As a matter of contract law, this approach separates the time the contract becomes valid from the time at which specific performance is available. This separation suggests that the attorney must review the document as a whole and clearly and unequivocally accept or reject it as whole. A purchaser attorney's "disapproval as is, but approving if modified" will be construed as disapproval so that the vendor can resell the property. *See Gaglia v. Kirchner*, 721 A.2d 1028 (N.J. Super. 1999). Disapproval with modifications is not a counteroffer. *See Asonia Props., LLC v. Vasili*, 2015 Il App (1st) 133846-U (Ill. Ct. App. 2015). In New Jersey, the disapproval must be sent to the broker. *See Conley v. Guerrero*, 157 A.3d 416 (N.J. 2017) (holding that the disapproval must be by certified mail, telegram, or personal service and that this provision must be strictly enforced). Weighing the pros and cons of approval or disapproval is likely to take the attorney some time, and the short three days in the New Jersey forms and many others is likely to mean that in doubtful cases, the attorney will recommend disapproval. This suggests that parties may wish to bargain for a more extended review period.

Example 14

Two days after V and P together execute a contract, P's attorney advises him to revoke it. V inquires as to the reason for the revocation. In response, P's attorney gives no reason. May P still revoke?

Explanation

Yes. P's attorney is entitled to remain mute and ground her muteness on the attorney-client privilege. In some of the cases involving such facts, the attorney is assigned a duty to the parties to provide advice in good faith, but the burden of showing the attorney's bad faith is on the complaining party. Cf. *Indoe v. Dwyer*, 424 A.2d 456, 15 A.L.R.4th 760 (N.J. Super. 1980) and *Ulrich v. Daly*, 650 N.Y.S.2d 496 (N.Y. App. Div. 1996). This suggests that the clause should clearly specify whether extrinsic facts (facts beyond the four corners of the contract) may be used as grounds for an attorney's disapproval, but a purchaser's request for such grounds may be met with a request to be more specific. The purchaser might then suggest that such matters as extrinsic evidence of (say) prevailing mortgage rates, or execution of a favorable listing for his existing residence, be sufficient grounds. Rather than bargain back and forth, however, the parties might settle on a clause that permits rescission "for any reason whatever." They might reason that if they are to enter an executory period together, each wants the other to be comfortable with the transaction—such comfort is a good indicator that the closing will be problem-free. *See Stevens v. Manchester*, 714 N.E.2d 956 (Ohio App. 1998).

Example 15

Two days after V and P execute a contract, V is advised to rescind and thereafter resells the property for a higher price. Can P get specific performance of the contract?

Explanation

No. *See Trenta v. Gay*, 468 A.2d 737 (N.J. Super. 1983). However, V himself would be well advised to follow carefully the contract mechanism for giving notice of the disapproval to the other side. *See Denesevich v. Moran*, 512 A.2d 505 (N.J. Super. 1986) (holding that notice to broker is insufficient when contract requires the purchaser to give notice to both the broker and the opposite party).

Example 16

Two weeks after V and P execute a contract together, P delivers a signed waiver of the contract's subject to financing clause. The waiver was prepared by the broker. Does the attorney review provision apply to the waiver document?

Explanation

Yes. If the clause applies to broker-prepared contracts, it should also apply to broker-prepared modifications of those contracts—but only then permitting rescission of the modification, rather than the original contract. *See Freedman v. Clonmel Constr. Corp.*, 587 A.2d 1291 (N.J. Super. 1991). In effect, when contract modifications of a broker-prepared contract fly back and forth, the broker can start the recession period running only by delivering to both parties a final contract that each has signed. *See Morton v. 4 Orchard Land Trust*, 849 A.2d 164 (N.J. 2004).

MARKETABLE TITLE CLAUSES—EXPRESS AND IMPLIED

Implied in every contract of sale is a covenant (a promise) that at the closing of the transaction the vendor will produce evidence that his title is a fee simple absolute that is merchantable or marketable. This implied condition refers only to the title to property; it does not refer to a property's physical condition: So the presence of toxic or hazardous materials on a property does not prevent its title from being marketable. In this sense, a marketable title may refer to property that is valueless. For instance, landlocked property may be of little value, but it is marketable in some (though not all) jurisdictions. A decision about the marketability of a title is a question of law, not fact.

The production of a marketable title is a condition precedent of the closing. A marketable title is one that a reasonable and prudent purchaser would accept, that is both free from reasonable doubt and reasonably free of the possibility of litigation. "A marketable title is one that may be freely made the subject of resale." *See Trimboli v. Kinkel*, 123 N.E. 205 (Cardozo, J., N.Y. 1919). Whether a title is marketable is a question of law.

This implied condition is the product of the state's interest in cleansing real property title from encumbrances at the time of each and every closing within its jurisdiction. For this purpose, an encumbrance may be a lease, mortgage, marital right, mineral right, easement, party wall agreement, contract, and options such as a right of first refusal and of first offer. The doctrine of marketability frees up the fee and enhances the purchaser's freedom to deal with the property during his tenure. Unlike some other legal doctrines that are based on strong public policies, this doctrine can be modified and even waived by the purchaser by some agreement to the contrary. The marketable title standard is a default standard. (Some encumbrances may be of no concern to particular purchasers and the benefits to them of certain encumbrances, such as utility easements, must be considered as well.) The doctrine also prevents the purchaser and his attorney from flyspecking the title—objecting to minor encumbrances that in fact do not cloud the title—as a way of avoiding the closing. The vendor has the burden of proving the title marketable, although in many regions of the country the purchaser may actually pay for the title search and examination.

Often, almost as soon as a purchaser receives a marketable title at a closing, the purchaser will want to mortgage it. Thus the title need not actually be subjected to an adverse claim when received. To render a title unmarketable, it is enough that the encumbrance exist, even though it is not asserted.

A higher title standard is a title "marketable of record," meaning that each link in the chain of title leading to the vendor is evidenced by a deed or other public document or recorded instrument.

Examples

Example 17

V and P execute a brief but enforceable contract "subject to P's attorney's approval of the title." Is this title call more or less than a marketable title?

Explanation

More, because the attorney's disapproval, if exercised in good faith, may be based on considerations other than whether the title is marketable. The disapproval is in effect a rescission of the contract. Normally V would have the right to make the title marketable during the executory period and up to the closing, but here the attorney may short circuit that right.

In some regions of the country, the mechanics of showing a title to be marketable work like this: First, the vendor produces his evidence of title; second, the purchaser examines the evidence. Elsewhere, the purchaser assembles the title evidence from the public records and then examines it. No matter how the evidence is produced, it is the purchaser's obligation to object to any defects in the title and to have the vendor cure them by the time of the closing. If a defect is not objected to and cured by then, it is deemed to be waived by the purchaser.

Examples

Example 18a

V and P execute a brief but enforceable contract of sale calling for V to deliver to P a marketable title to Blackacre at the closing in exchange for $100,000. Thereafter, during the executory period the abstract of title presented to P's attorney contains a break in the chain of deeds coming down to V. The break is a probate court decree. Is V's title marketable?

Explanation

Yes, it is marketable. It is also "marketable of record," because the decree is a public record, regarded then as admissible and self-proving in court. A marketable title can consist not just of a chain of deeds (A to B, B to C, C to D, etc.), but also of many other types of documents that are "public records," meaning that they are self-proving in court.

Example 18b

The evidence of V's title relies on a sworn affidavit showing adverse possession in V's predecessor. Is V's title marketable?

Explanation

No, not on the basis of an unproven affidavit. A judicial decree would establish a public record link in the chain of title rendering it marketable. However, a title depending on adverse possession, and proven to be such, is generally considered marketable. *See Conklin v. Davi*, 388 A.2d 598, 601 (N.J. 1978). It is not, however, marketable of record. A contrary rule that a title subject to proof by adverse possession is unmarketable casts the burden of litigation proving the title on the vendor. *See Tri-State Hotel Co. v. Sphinx Investment Co.*, 510 P.2d 1223 (Kan. 1973).

Example 18c

The abstract shows that the title is subject to an unsatisfied mortgage with a 15-year term and a $20,000 principal amount. The mortgage was executed a decade ago, but the holder of the mortgage note and lien cannot be located. Is V's title marketable?

Explanation

No. The mortgage lien could be foreclosed anytime within its term, plus whatever time the applicable statute of limitations for mortgages provides. When the term of the mortgage is 15 years, the mortgage is still enforceable, and the title is thus not reasonably free of the possibility of litigation, the mortgagee having ample time to show up, demand the payments due, and bring an action to foreclose the lien. The very existence of the inchoate mortgage lien is sufficient to render the title unmarketable. However, with the vendor and purchaser's agreement at closing, any encumbrance that can readily be monetized—here, if the unpaid amount of the mortgage principle and the mortgagee can be ascertained—might be the subject of a post-closing escrow for the amount due, held back from the purchase price and paid to the mortgagee.

Example 18d

If in the prior example the mortgage were executed 60 years ago, would your answer change?

Explanation

Yes. The probabilities are that the mortgage is now unenforceable by an action in foreclosure. The mortgagee has probably abandoned or waived enforcement of the lien and the statute of limitations has run on its enforcement. A finding of marketability requires no more than a reasonable degree of freedom from foreclosure litigation; it is not a guarantee to the purchaser that no litigation will occur or that no encumbrance exists.

Example 18e

The abstract shows a power line easement running along one boundary of Blackacre. Is V's title marketable?

Explanation

Yes. An easement located on the property renders it unmarketable unless it is at the same time beneficial to the property. Although the title is technically unmarketable, this is likely not to be objected to. The same rule is sometimes applied to easements that are visible, common in the jurisdiction, or otherwise implicitly accepted by the purchaser. What if the easement ran through the property? Now the title is unmarketable because it is not likely to be beneficial. What if the easement reduced its fair market value to $90,000? (Same answer.)

Example 18f

The abstract shows that a mechanic's lien for $5,000 has been filed on Blackacre. Is V's title marketable? If not, what is P's remedy?

Explanation

No. The title is unmarketable, but the remedy is again a simple escrow established at the closing in an amount sufficient to pay off the lien and prevent it from being foreclosed.

Example 18g

Would your answers to any of the foregoing questions change if the contract called for "an insurable title"?

Explanation

No. This title standard is generally taken to mean "marketable and insurable"—marketable, as that basic title call is incorporated by implication into every contract of sale, as well as insurable with a title insurance policy customarily used in the jurisdiction. *See Conklin v. Davi, supra,* 388 A.2d at 602.

Example 18h

How about if the contract called for "a marketable and insurable title"?

Explanation

No. The second adjective adds nothing. It does imply, however, that the title insurance policy called for will contain the usual coverage and the usual exclusions and exceptions, and be issued at regular premium rates. *Conklin v. Davi, supra.* Thus the word "insurable" in the letter at the beginning of this chapter adds nothing to the purchaser's legal protections. The title insurer will provide coverage for unmarketability in many jurisdictions, and if the title is unmarketable, it will not provide title insurance.

Example 18i

What if the contract called for "a title insured by the XYZ Title Insurance Corporation"?

Explanation

There is nothing wrong with this title call as a matter of law. Indeed, in many regions standardized contracts of sale are printed by title insurers. Decades ago, the name of a title insurer might be printed as a part of the standard language in the contract, but today a blank is likely so that the name can be inserted. (Business tie-ins between brokers and title insurers are regulated by federal and often state statutes.) It is advisable for a party to test any preprinted insurer's name to make sure that another, equally reputable title insurer would be acceptable as well. If another is not, then the possibility of a business tie-in with the named insurer should be considered—and avoided—by the party to whom the suggestion is made. Indeed, instead of a contract provision calling merely for an insurable title, it is prudent for a purchaser to name in the contract not just the title insurer but also the policy wanted, and the coverage, exclusions, and exceptions acceptable to the purchaser in that policy.

Example 18j

Would your answers change if the contract called for V to deliver a quitclaim deed at the closing?

Explanation

No. A provision in a contract of sale calling for the use of a quitclaim deed at the closing is not a waiver of an implied condition that the vendor produce a marketable title at the closing. A purchaser should not be held to have waived such an important protection unless he does so clearly. By definition, a quitclaim eliminates the vendor's warranties but need not affect the standard of marketability of the title that the vendor must produce.

Example 19

V and P execute a brief but enforceable contract of sale for Blackacre. The contract calls for V to deliver a fee simple absolute to P "subject to easements of record." During the executory period the adverse user of an undocumented easement over Blackacre ripens into adverse possession. Is V's title marketable?

Explanation

No. P as the purchaser of the servient estate should not be forced to buy a lawsuit. Marketability is shown at the closing and here the title will then be burdened with the easement. Title is unmarketable and purchaser need not accept it, absent his agreement to the contrary. Whether the "subject to easements of record" language is an agreement to the contrary is a matter of contract interpretation. The language means "subject to easements existing on the record as of the closing date." An easement arising by adverse possession is not one evidenced on the public records; rather, it arises through the actions of the adverse possessor. The purchaser has not agreed to accept it. Finally, suppose that the adverse user reduced the easement to judgment by the closing date. Would the judgment be "of record"? Yes, then the "subject to" language applies to encumber P's title. An examination of V's title to determine its marketability is no substitute for P's inspection of Blackacre for signs of adverse use.

Example 20

V leases a portion of Greenacre to L. V and P then execute a brief but enforceable contract of sale. What if the contract calls for a fee "subject to leases" and "marketable of record" and during the executory period V's lease to L expires and V executes a new lease with L? Is V's title marketable?

Explanation

No. In the prior Example, the vendor was sleeping on his rights during the executory period, but here V is actively creating an encumbrance on the title. The "subject to leases" language means "subject to existing leases when the contract is executed." Thus V's executing the new lease renders the title unmarketable. P is entitled to have Greenacre vacant at closing. Marketable title requires a fee simple absolute with *seisin*—possession with all its rights. In addition, when a title is unmarketable, it is also unmarketable "of record."

When presented with an unmarketable title at closing, a purchaser has several remedies: (1) rescission and restitution of payments made, with a discharge of the contract; (2) specific performance of the contract, with the abatement of the purchase price for the title defect, lien, or encumbrance; (3) a cause of action for damages, including nominal damages or out-of-pocket costs, and here in Example 20, substantial, benefit-of-the-bargain damages because of V's creation of the encumbrance when executing the lease. Executing the new lease is also a slander[1] of the purchaser's equitable interest in the title. Vendor's title is unmarketable because the purchaser need not accept a title subject to the lawsuit he would have to bring, for slander of title, against the vendor. The contract at a minimum should permit a purchaser to review leases entered into during the executory period.

Example 21

V and P execute a brief but enforceable contract of sale calling for V to transfer title to "Lot 1, Blackacre Subdivision, Smith County, Nevada, as shown on Plat 73-123 held by the Recorder of Deeds of said County." (This lot description is a recorded, public record in county land records: A plat reference is everywhere by statute a valid method of describing property.) P's mortgage company reports that its employee cannot locate one of the four boundaries of the lot on the ground, and the mortgage company then reports that V's title is unmarketable. Is this correct?

Explanation

No. The description references a plat or map of the subdivision that contains the dimensions of the lot and locates it within the subdivision. The mortgage company may want more as a business matter before loaning P mortgage money to buy the property, but its business practices do not affect the marketability of V's title. The fact that the boundaries are not located on the ground by stakes or survey markers might affect the land bought and sold, but not the title. The title is marketable.

---

1. Slander of title is a tort action requiring the plaintiff to prove that the defendant "uttered a false statement" about the plaintiff's title to real property, which statement resulted in actual loss by the plaintiff. Likewise, anyone recording a contract of sale with the knowledge that it is unenforceable for any reason is liable in an action for slander of title. Recording the contract is the utterance, and when the recording is made with knowledge that the recording party does not have an enforceable interest in the property, malice is sometimes presumed by the fact of the recording itself, although in some jurisdictions, actual malice must also be shown. *See Rogers Carl Corp. v. Moran*, 246 A.2d 750 (N.J. Super. 1968).

On the other hand, an actual conflict between the legal descriptions used in two land surveys does render the title unmarketable. P may not be forced to bring a quiet title action to settle the conflict. If P decides to use one of the surveys as the basis for the legal description in his deed, he should obtain, from the surveyor, a certification that the survey is correct.

Example 22

V and P execute a brief but enforceable contract of sale for an unimproved parcel of land. The contract calls for the land to be sold "as is." P then discovers that the land contains a heretofore undiscovered archaeological site, giving the state archaeologist a right of entry for exploration of the site. Exploration will require two years. Is P's title unmarketable due to this discovery?

Explanation

No, because the assertion of public rights, even though resulting in an easement for public officials to enter the land, is not an encumbrance on the title. Eminent domain, for example, results in a physical invasion of land, but its assertion is not an encumbrance. Even if the contract called for a title marketable of record, this highest type of title standard would not be affected. In addition, the "as is" provision in the contract is typically only a reference to the physical and use characteristics of the land, for example, improvements on it, and not to its title; neither will this provision be read as a call for a quitclaim deed to be used at closing. The law's strong implication that a marketable title will then be presented survives all these claims. Likewise, attempts to modify the doctrine of marketable title must be clear and unambiguous. "This contract is conditional only on purchaser's acceptance of the title report." "Vendor will convey an indisputable title." Neither language will vary the purchaser's right to a marketable title.

Example 23

Same facts as in the last example, but in addition the parcel is located on the coast where P intended to moor his yacht. No mooring is possible (1) due to currents rendering riparian wharf-out rights attaching to Blackacre useless and (2) the assertion of an aboriginal trail by Native Americans along the coast, preventing P's construction of a wharf. Does either of these additional problems render the title unmarketable?

Explanation

No, the riparian right is a natural use right, inherent in the land, not the title, so the denial of the right to wharf-out does not affect the marketability of the title. Neither does the assertion of native rights: They are based on custom, not title.

Example 24

V and P execute a brief but enforceable contract of sale for Blackacre, calling for a purchase price of $100,000 and for V to present P with "a marketable title, subject to covenants, conditions, and restrictions of record at the time of the closing." As provided in the contract, P pays V 10 percent down. During the executory period, V executes a restrictive covenant with his neighbor, promising that each owner will use their property "for residential uses only." The covenant is recorded. P contends that the covenant is invalid as to him because he is a bona fide purchaser (BFP) for value and that the doctrine of equitable conversion has not left V with an interest in the property sufficient to create this covenant. Are P's contentions correct, and what advice would you give him?

Explanation

P's contentions are substantial, but not always successful. A BFP is a common law, as well as a recording act term. In some states, the execution of a contract is an insufficient basis for asserting BFP status and the contract language here lends some support for using this rule. However, a majority of states say that P is a BFP to the extent of any payment made under the contract. *Fong v. Hashimoto*, 951 P.2d 487 (Haw. 1998). In most jurisdictions, then, the title is also unmarketable. If P wishes, he may elect to receive Blackacre free of the covenant. If the quoted contract language was intended to give V authority to create covenants during the executory period, it is ambiguous and should be construed in P's favor, leaving the doctrine of marketable title untouched. *See Daniels v. Anderson*, 642 N.E.2d 128 (Ill. 1994).

MARKETABLE TITLE AND ENVIRONMENTAL LIENS

For purposes of the doctrine of marketable title, an encumbrance rendering a title unmarketable is a broad concept, including any estate or interest in real property that might render the title subject to a reasonable doubt or prospect of litigation. When a toxic or hazardous substance is discovered on property, however, the traditional rule is that the marketability of the title is not affected: Even if the vendor has dumped the substance on the land under contract, there is as yet no defect, lien, or encumbrance on the title and, though the land's physical attributes may affect its use, the title remains unaffected. In this instance, absent a contract provision to the contrary, a purchaser may be forced to accept the vendor's title.

Under federal and many state statutes, disclosure to the government and the purchaser of the toxic substance is required, and its cleanup can be ordered by the government's environmental regulators. When a cleanup is not accomplished in this manner, the government itself may clean up the property, and its cleanup costs can be recovered from the property's "owner or operator." To enforce this recovery, the government has a lien on the property. 42 U.S.C.A. §9607(1) (2002). Strict liability is imposed on "owners or operators" of property for the amount of the lien. This lien is sometimes called a superlien because it takes its priority not on a first in time, first in right basis but is superior to preexisting liens. If the contract does not take account of this risk, purchasers take title subject to it.

However, once any environmental lien for cleanup costs, superlien or not, is filed on the public records and not discharged, the marketability of the title is obviously affected, for the marketability doctrine is concerned about the possibility of litigation over the title (in this instance, the foreclosure of the lien): The purchaser of real property is not, under the doctrine, to be compelled to buy a lawsuit. Moreover, the doctrine is concerned not with the outcome or results of litigation, but with its prospect. *See Myerberg, Sawyer & Rue, P.A. v. Agee*, 446 A.2d 69, 72 (Md. App. Ct. 1982).

The marketability doctrine thus has two concerns: (1) with the existence of an encumbrance affecting the title as well as the reasonable possibility of litigation, and (2) with distinguishing between land use and land title matters. Just as the presence of hazardous or toxic substances on property subject to an executory contract does not affect marketability, neither can a purchaser invoke an express warranty or contingency in the sales contract to the effect that the land comply with applicable land use controls. Nor can a title insurer be subjected to liability under the provisions of a title insurance policy. *See South Shore Bank v. Stewart Title Guaranty Co.*, 688 F. Supp. 803, 805-806 (D. Mass.), aff'd in memo. op., 867 F.2d 607 (1st Cir. 1988).

Given these considerations, purchasers rely on negotiating specific contract provisions that assign the risk of the property being subjected to an environmental lien to one party or another. Several types of contract provisions are currently in use, for example, a provision that (1) the vendor will hold the purchaser harmless by indemnifying the purchaser if toxic substances are discovered by an environmental audit ordered for the property; (2) the vendor will purchase property insurance whose coverage extends to the presence of toxic substances; or (3) the vendor warrants that there are no toxic substances on the property. All three leave open the possibility that the purchaser must accept title to the property, subject to the vendor's performance. Singly or in combination, however, they are not as good as a walk-away provision for the purchaser, voiding the contract if toxic substances are discovered.

In commercial transactions, the presence of environmental problems is often made a deal-breaker in the contract.

"TIME IS OF THE ESSENCE" CLAUSE

Traditionally, time was of the essence in a contract of sale involved in a cause of action at law. So, in an action for damages for breach of contract, a call for a closing on a certain date is sufficient to make damages available from the party not ready to close on that date when the party seeking damages tenders whatever performance is due at the closing, unless that performance is excused, for example, by the nonperforming party's anticipatory repudiation. *See Cohen v. Kranz*, 189 N.E.2d 473 (N.Y. 1963). That is the effect of the words in the letter at the beginning of this chapter: "Settlement shall occur by [a date certain]." Likewise, a provision calling for a closing "ASAP 2025" means that, even though no date is given, the closing must occur on or before December 31, 2025. Further, the use of the phrase "time is of the essence in this contract" extends this rule and means that each action required in the contract's provisions shall be performed promptly at the time or date specified. Performance of a provision—for example, for a provision requiring a down payment or a "subject to financing" clause—may also be made "of the essence" separately from the call for a closing. *See Strohm v. Morgan*, 876 S.E.2d 913 (N.C. Ct. App. 2022). A failure to perform then is taken as a waiver of the other party's performance. *See Marioni v. 94 Broadway, Inc.*, 866 A.2d 208, 220 (N.J. Super. Ct.), cert. denied, 874 A.2d 1109 (N.J. 2005).

However, in equity, time was not of the essence unless expressly made so in the contract or implied from circumstances available to interpret the contract. Time not being essential in equity, a standard of reasonable diligence is substituted. Thus, specific performance is available to a purchaser, even after the date fixed for performance of some action or the closing in the contract. Such an equitable action is available for a reasonable time after the closing date.

Today, in both legal and equitable actions, time is not of the essence unless the contract (1) expressly stipulates this, (2) necessarily implies it, or (3) the parties' actions imply it. Fixing a specific date for closing in a contract does not, standing alone, make time of the essence. *See Kalalik v. Bernardo*, 439 A.2d 1016, 1019 (Conn. 1981). Thus, a failure to perform or close on a stipulated date is not, *per se*, a breach of the contract actionable by the nonbreaching party. Delays are frequent in real property transactions, and a later performance might well be found to be substantial performance. Equity does not infer that time is essential unless clearly indicated. When clearly indicated, the clause becomes a condition subsequent to the contract and when enforced, voids the contract. *See Owen v. Kessler*, 778 N.E.2d 953 (Mass. Ct. App. 2002).

If no time is set for a closing, a reasonable amount of time is implied. *See Estate of Osborn v. Kemp*, 991 A.2d 1153 (Del. 2010) (finding a 90-day delay reasonable as a matter of law). But a contract lacking a "time is of the essence" clause does not excuse a party's not closing on the day and at the time named in the contract. The reason for the nonperformance is for the judge sitting in equity; he must review its reasonableness. *See Mouat v. Wolfe*, 556 A.2d 99, 101 (Vt. 1989) ("Where time is *not* of the essence, the buyer who tenders payment late *may* bring a suit in equity, depending on the reasonableness of the delay, to compel delivery"). What is a reasonable time depends on the subject matter of the contract, the situation of the parties to it, and the circumstances surrounding performance. *See The Winterton LLC v. Winterton Investors LLC*, 900 N.E.2d 754 (Ind. App. 2009).

In a contract of sale silent as to time, the rule of reasonable diligence applies in two situations. First, the contract may set a date for closing, but when that date is past, either of the parties can make time of the essence, in both law and equity, by a clear notice setting a future closing date, reasonably distant from the time of the notice. Thus, even when the parties to a contract postpone a closing twice but thereafter agree to make time "of the essence" for a third closing, the mere use of those words allows a court to refuse to examine extrinsic evidence of the parties' intent to determine whether both parties knew the words' impact.

Second, when the contract is silent on a closing date, either party during the executory period may call for a closing within a reasonable time.

When a contract expressly provides that "time is of the essence" and sets a closing date, performance must occur at the time specified in order to entitle the performing party to specific performance. An equitable action for specific performance requires, as a precondition, a tender of performance by the plaintiff. Courts in some states like Florida, New York, and Tennessee strictly enforce such a requirement. In Illinois, for example, if the provision is found material to the contract, a delay of a day voids it. *See Arnhold v. Ocean Atlantic Woodland Corp.*, 284 F.3d 693 (7th Cir. 2001) (citing these four states and D.C. cases). Substantial, though late, performance is insufficient. *See* Samuel Williston, 15 Contracts §44:53, at 225 (2000). Such a provision may be waived. This provision coupled with a forfeiture can easily make a contract into an option, as in "time is of the essence of this contract: If the purchaser does not make full settlement within 90 days, the deposit is forfeit as the vendor's sole remedy and purchaser relieved of all further liability hereunder." *See Dixon v. Haft*, 253 A.2d 715 (Md. 1969), discussed in *Green Manor Corp. v. Tomares*, 295 A.2d 212 (1972).

Examples

Example 25

A contract of sale calls for "a closing of this contract by March 1st." Is this statement sufficient to make time of the essence?

Explanation

No. The designation of a date for the closing does not by itself make time of the essence.

Example 25a

What if a contract of sale contains a strict forfeiture clause providing that "this contract is null and void and the purchaser's equity in the property is forfeited if the closing is not held within 60 days"? Is time of the essence in this contract?

Explanation

Yes. From the strictness of the forfeiture, a court may infer that time is of the essence.

Example 25b

In a land market in which prices are falling, a farmer agrees to sell his farm to a developer. The contract of sale calls for a closing "within three months." After three months and one week, the developer has not closed the deal. Is time of the essence in this contract?

Explanation

Yes. Here the essentiality of the time of the closing can be implied from the market circumstances surrounding the contracts. Time may be of the essence if by holding it so, a court could prevent the developer from waiting to make a better deal with the farmer. *See Kasten Constr. Co. v. Maple Ridge Constr. Co.*, 226 A.2d 341 (Md. 1967); *Doering v. Fields*, 50 A.2d 553 (Md. 1947).

Example 26

A contract of sale calls for "a closing of this contract by March 1st." On that date, neither party appears at the date, time, and place scheduled for the closing. What then is the status of the contract?

Explanation

The contract is still subject to performance within a reasonable time unless and until either party sets a reasonable date for the closing. If time had been of the essence (this contract "shall close by March 1st, time being of the essence"), cases split: A court would either discharge the contract or automatically extend it, using the rule of reasonable diligence.

Example 27

A contract provision states that a failure to make any one of two executory period deposits on the date named "is essential to the performance of this contract" and, when P fails to make any one of these, the sums so far on deposit are forfeited to V. P makes the first but not the second deposit. Thereafter P brings an action for specific performance of the contract. May P have a decree in specific performance?

Explanation

Yes, but only if P is willing to put all of the purchase price into escrow with the court, to fulfill his contract obligations. The chancellor will also require that P pay the full purchase price, without any credit for the first deposit. That deposit is forfeited under the terms of the contract. As to the closing date, that has not been set; therefore, the equitable rule of reasonable diligence controls, and the decree of specific performance can set a closing date. Decree for P, without any abatement of the purchase price for the first deposit.

Example 28

V and P execute a contract of sale that provides in part as follows: "Settlement within thirty days or as soon thereafter as a title report is delivered to the purchaser and reviewed. If the purchaser fails to close, the deposit herein *may* ["may" was deleted and "shall" inserted in its place] be forfeit *at the vendor's option* [the four italicized words were deleted], in which case purchaser is relieved of further obligation under this contract." After the title report is delivered, reporting a fee simple absolute in the vendor, purchaser refuses to close. V sues P for damages. What result?

Explanation

Judgment for P. The changes in the form contract indicate that the parties intended that the agreement become an option to purchase, by which V agrees to take the property off the market for a certain time in consideration of the deposit paid by the potential purchaser. In an option, no equitable conversion is worked at the execution of the document; P acquires no equitable interest in the property and no right to have the option specifically performed. Although legal rights may be inferred from its provisions—that is, a party in breach may be liable for damages—P, as the optionee, bought the right to walk away from the transaction without further liability. This is consistent with an option.

At law, in an action for damages, time is of the essence. This supports the inference that V gained the right to be free of P's claims after the time during which V agrees to hold the property off the market. Moreover, in an option, time is of the essence because it is what is bargained for. The optionee must exercise his rights within the option period, and P did not do so here. *Schlee v. Bryant*, 234 A.2d 457 (Md. 1967).

Once exercised, the optionee's rights become those of a contract purchaser. He holds an equitable interest and, in equity, time is no longer of the essence. The purchaser has a reasonable time to close the transaction, regardless of the call for a closing within a reasonable time after the title report's issuance.

ACREAGE AND PRICE TERMS

When the purchase price in a contract of sale for real property is stated as a whole or "in gross," the risk of a deficiency in the acreage contained within the legal description or described in the contract is on the purchaser. The statement of the price in gross indicates that the purchaser regards the acreage as immaterial to the closing. *See Turner v. Ferrin*, 757 P.2d 335, 337 (Mont. 1988). Stating a specific number of acres in a description of land does not prevent a sale from being considered in gross. Even if the statement is substantially in error, that error does not create an automatic right to rescind the contract. *See Perfect v. McAndrew*, 798 N.E.2d 470 (Ind. App. 2003). Including the term "more or less" or "+/−" after the stated number of acres in the legal description indicates that the parties to the contract did not intend the acreage given to be precise. This inclusion is a bad idea from the purchaser's perspective; its inclusion throws the risk of an insubstantial deficiency onto the purchaser. *See Marcus v. Bathon*, 531 A.2d 690, 694 (Md. App. 1987), cert. denied, 547 A.2d 189 (Md. 1988). When the sale is in gross, the purchaser is not entitled to an abatement in the purchase price to take account of the deficiency before closing.

On the other hand, if the price is stated on a *per acre* basis, the risk is on the vendor; the statement of the price per acre indicates that the purchaser regards the acreage as a material term of the contract. If the acreage deficiency is substantial and a price *per acre* is stipulated, the purchaser can decide to reduce the price proportionately and sue for specific performance at the abated price. He might also sue for reliance damages or rescind the contract and avoid the closing altogether, although these alternative remedies are suggested in the probable order of difficulty in obtaining them. *See Hinson v. Jefferson*, 215 S.E.2d 102 (N.C. 1974). Why? Because here rescission must be based on a mutual mistake of fact. Turner, *supra*, at 153 ("Equity will provide a remedy when by mutual mistake the land contains materially more or less acreage than the parties believe. A slight disparity will justify equitable relief if the sale is by the acre, but, if the sale is in gross a great disparity must exist to authorize relief."). If the vendor has already received more money than the acreage warrants, the purchaser's cause of action lies in contract for damages.

If the price is stated in gross but the parties agreed to compute it on an acreage or area basis, parol evidence is admissible to show the true nature of the transaction. The contract, after all, is not inconsistent with the area computation, and parol evidence can explain how the parties arrived at the price. Use of parol here is particularly useful when urban commercial space is involved and the price is computed on a *per square foot* basis. Similarly, the sale of land in a residential subdivision may be on the basis of the number of buildable lots or parcels involved.

Any representation of the vendor as to the acreage will often change the results of these rules. The same is true as to vendor's representations about boundaries.

Examples

Example 29

V and P execute a brief but enforceable contract for lakefront property. The purchase price is "$500 a front foot, or $250,000." When surveyed, the property is found to have only 400 front feet on the lake. Should this price statement be treated as an in gross price, or not?

Explanation

If this property is undeveloped land, the arguments for treating the price as if it were stated on a *pro tanto* basis, not in gross, are substantial. This would force V to reduce the price to $200,000. On the other hand, if the property has a residence on it or has picturesque geographic features, treating the price as if it were stated in gross is preferable. Which will be used is a matter of ascertaining the intent of the parties as a matter of fact, and because the contract is ambiguous on this point, extrinsic evidence will be admissible to show this.

Example 30

In the letter at the beginning of this chapter, the price is stated in both acreage and gross terms. It is implied that dividing the latter by the former will compute the acreage contemplated by the purchaser. Will such an implication in an offer give rise to a warranty by the vendor that the farm contains 50 acres?

Explanation

Not likely. The purchaser must clearly indicate reliance on either one price or the other in the offer or contract. Here this warranty is unlikely because the purchaser inserted a contingency in the offer relating to a survey. The results of the survey will have to be reviewed by the purchaser before closing, and if the legal description produced by the surveyor fails to enclose 50 acres, the purchaser closes this transaction at his peril.

Example 31

V and P execute a brief but enforceable contract of sale for Blackacre. The purchase price is $100,000 and the contract describes the property as "containing 1,000 acres, more or less." In fact Blackacre contains 900 acres and therefore is worth only $90,000. Can V obtain specific performance of the contract? Can P?

Explanation

It depends. If the purchase price was negotiated on a per acre basis, the acreage is a material term of the contract. So V cannot get specific performance or, at best, can get specific performance subject to an abatement in the price. If P shows acreage material to the contract, he can get specific performance with an abatement, unless the vendor can show that it was an "all or nothing" transaction. The latter situation is unlikely here because of the "more or less" language in the contract. That language also indicates that acreage was not material to the whole deal, which means that either V or P can have specific performance, but without any abatement in the price.

PRICE ESCALATOR CLAUSE

Dealing in a vendor's market, a contract purchaser may wish to set a price in the contract (say, for example, $500,000) but also provide that the offering price can increase, in a set number of increments (of say, $5,000), to meet competing offers. It is prudent to provide for a cap on such escalations in the price (say, not above $550,000).

ANTI-ASSIGNMENT CLAUSE

During the negotiations for a contract, vendor and purchaser have had an opportunity to size each other up. Vendor has decided to sell to purchaser—and in some cases, may have dealt with several prospective purchasers before making this decision—and should realize that the general rule is that unless the assignment of the contract is expressly restricted, the purchaser will, immediately upon executing it, have the right to assign it. As with other types of contracts, free assignability is the rule. This may lead the vendor to conclude that if other prospects are waiting in the wings to buy, this assignability should be restricted. Or the vendor may wish to propose some restriction in order to see if the purchaser is the agent of an undisclosed principal. (There is nothing fraudulent about being such an agent if no misrepresentations are made.)

When the purchaser resists a blanket prohibition on an assignment, one alternative might be: "This contract shall not be assigned unless the vendor consents in writing, such consent not to be unreasonably withheld." This gives the vendor an opportunity to determine if the proposed assignee is just as (say) creditworthy as the purchaser. Another alternative is for the vendor to permit assignability more freely but insist on the right to capture some or all of the profit the purchaser makes "flipping" the contract.

Like the contract itself, its assignment is subject to the Statute of Frauds and must be in writing. The purchaser/assignor does not warrant the marketability of the vendor's title or the contract's performance; he only warrants its existence. If the title is unmarketable, this is not a failure of consideration for the assignment: The assignee may not thereafter recover the money paid for it. (This means that the assignee will likely insist that the money he paid be put into an escrow pending the closing.) Likewise, the assignee takes subject to any defenses based on the contract and available to the vendor. An assignment in violation of any anti-assignment clause is nonetheless a valid contract between the assignor and the assignee for purposes of the latter's suit for damages.

WARRANTIES OF GOOD WORKMANSHIP

A warranty of good workmanship is implied by law or imposed at a duty sounding in tort in every contract of sale for the construction, repair, and first-time purchase of residential real property from a professional builder-vendor. It provides that the property is built in a workmanlike, skillful manner, free of substantial defects in its major latent structural components and features and fit for its intended purpose. *See Blue Water Construction, Inc. v. Hill*, 2022 V.I. LEXIS 15 (V.I. Super. Ct., Feb. 11, 2022) (collecting the cases). It has been applied not only to the construction of a new home, but also to other ancillary buildings, the installation of a new roof, plumbing, heating or septic system, or the drilling of a well. It is often distinguished from an implied warranty of habitability imposed or implied in residential leases and providing that a dwelling is fit for occupancy. When this warranty is imposed as a matter of public policy or as a duty in tort, it is neither waivable for the purchaser nor exculpable by the vendor. *See Jones v. Centex Homes*, 967 N.E.2d 1199 (Ohio 2012). When imposed as a matter of implied contract, it generally can be both waived and disclaimed, although the waiver or disclaimer is subject to close judicial scrutiny. This warranty is not merged into the deed delivered at the closing, being considered a provision collateral to the deed's intrinsic function of transferring title. It is the product of judicial decisions in most jurisdictions, but provided by statute in some.

Patent defects are not covered; thus, the drywall, because it is subject to inspection, is not covered by the warranty. If in replacing the drywall, however, the purchaser discovers that the framing is defective, that (being a latent defect) is covered. When the warranty is based on an implied contract, the purchaser may have a duty (to mitigate) by bracing the framing uncovered in replacing the drywall—and in any event, a purchaser has the duty not to hinder a vendor's efforts to repair. In some jurisdictions, the warranty is extended to the soil conditions and drainage on the lot, as when the soil contains radon or is unsuitable for a septic system.

A builder-vendor otherwise subject to the warranty does not escape liability under it by residing in a structure. Sometimes nonbuilder vendors have been subject to the warranty, as where a vendor builds and sells houses one at a time, even if the time taken is spare time.

The measure of damages for the warranty's breach is contractual. Some courts use the difference in the fair market value of the property as warranted and as delivered, while others use the replacement cost for the materials needed to remedy the breach—plus the expenses of dealing with the breach and the loss of the expected use of the property. Sometimes economic losses are recoverable as well. In rare cases, a house tainted by ghosts, or the scene of a grisly crime or multiple murders, gives rise to damages based on emotional distress.

Jurisdictions disagree as to whether the tort, contracts, or property statutes of limitations apply to the warranty. Many but not all jurisdictions apply a discovery rule when deciding when the statute of limitations starts to run. In about a dozen jurisdictions, the warranty is extended to subsequent purchasers suing professional builder-vendors. Likewise, occasionally lenders who unduly involve themselves in the business of a builder-vendor to whom they lend, and so control the business, have been held to be liable for the warranty's breach. A few jurisdictions have extended the warranty to developers of commercial properties.

Some courts considering the issue have held that the warranty may be waived (by a purchaser of a new residence) or disclaimed (by its vendor). *See O'Mara v. Dykema*, 942 S.W.2d 854 (Ark. 1997). Any disclaimer of the warranty must be specific, conspicuous, and agreed to by the purchaser. Integration or "entire agreement" provisions, representations that the purchaser has inspected the property, and "as is" clauses are insufficient.

Examples

Example 32

Purchaser discovers mold growing on the joists of her new residence. She asks you whether this is covered by the implied warranty of habitability.

Explanation

Mold (mildew or fungus) is a naturally occurring organism, but needs moisture and air to grow. The joists would need to retain water and be subject to air currents carrying fungal spores to grow, damage the joists, and perhaps become a health risk. The spore's growth thus results from a design flaw permitting their growth. That, strictly speaking, is not a defect in the residence's physical structure and components breaching the warranty, but the warranty is also a warranty of workmanlike construction, and encompasses construction that supplies mold with a food source. So mold should be covered by the warranty.

HOUSING INSPECTIONS

Often a purchaser will make the contract contingent on the inspection of the property by a private housing inspector. *See Hanscom v. Gregorie*, 562 A.2d 1232 (Me. 1989). The inspector will examine the condition of the property's improvements, particularly the heating, air conditioning, plumbing, and electrical systems, as well as the roof, foundation, walls, and basement, and the inspector's finding that the property is unsatisfactory in some respect may give rise to a mutual right to rescind the contract, a right to abate the purchase price by some measure, or a right to sue for damages.

Such inspections are useful to vendors as well, particularly in jurisdictions giving broad reach to vendor disclosure statutes, implied warranties of habitability, and liability for misrepresentations as to the condition of the premises. However, the purchaser's use of an inspector will not generally render the vendor immune from a duty to disclose. *See Caple v. Green*, 545 So. 2d 1222 (La. App. 1989).

These inspections result in the issuance of certificates by the inspector. These documents "warrant the statements in the report about the condition of the inspected items are substantially accurate and acknowledge responsibility for substantial inaccuracies." The latter are usually subject to some deductible amount that the purchaser, then usually owner, must spend on repairs before contacting the inspector and invoking the claims procedure set out in the certificate, and only inaccuracies reported within one to two years of the closing give rise to a claim. Also excluded from any claim are normal maintenance costs, personal injury damages, consequential damages, or the cost of repairing code violations. If an inspection report describes a code violation, the cost of bringing the property up to code standards is not covered, but if the inspected system fails during the claims period, the fact that the failure was due to a code violation is no bar to a claim. Limitations of the inspector's liability for defects subject to inspection, when permitting only minimal recovery, have been found unconscionable. *See Pitts v. Watkins*, 905 So. 2d 553 (Miss. 2005) (citing *Lucier v. Williams*, 841 A.2d 907, 909-910 (N.J. Super. 2004) (limitation of the lesser of $500 or one-half the inspector's fee unconscionable), noted at 33 Real Est. L.J. 70, 74-76 (2004)).

"Subject to inspection" clause A contract clause may make the closing "subject to an inspection of the property by the ABC Home Inspection Company." *See Estey v. MacKenzie Engineering Inc.*, 927 P.2d 86 (Or. 1996). This clause will help the purchaser find and foresee repair and maintenance costs, but the consequences of a finding that major repairs are advisable should be spelled out.

Such clauses are encouraged by the enactment of statutes mandating residential vendor disclosure reports, as discussed in the next section of this chapter. Such disclosures, which are made on state-prescribed standard forms, often leave the purchaser receiving them wanting further information. For example, a question about whether the property has a septic system, answered yes on the form, leaves the purchaser wondering whether the system is in working order and whether the vendor guarantees it is working. An inspector is useful at this point, but, as previously discussed, the usefulness of their certificates is often limited. *See Herner v. Housemaster of America, Inc.*, 2002 N.J. Super. LEXIS 139 (N.J. Super., Mar. 11, 2002) and *Thomson v. McGinnis*, 465 S.E.2d 922 (W. Va. 1995) (recognizing a cause of action for a broker's negligent hiring of an inspector). Here again, clauses limiting damages or exculpating inspectors are subject to strict judicial scrutiny. *See Sanislo v. Give Kids the World, Inc.*, 157 So. 3d 256 (Fla. 2015) (collecting cases).

Examples

Example 33

P executes a contract with V in which P "agrees that he has inspected the property and agrees to accept it in its present condition, except as is otherwise provided" and "has the further right to walk through and inspect the property 48 hours prior to closing." What is the extent of P's right to a later "walk-through" inspection? Can P refuse to close the transaction if the property is not, at the time of the later inspection, in a condition satisfactory to him?

Explanation

The right to a walk-through inspection is not an independent, freestanding condition. Unless the contract clearly provides otherwise—that is, spells out the necessary condition of the property at the time of the inspection—the contract will be interpreted to require only that the vendor keep the property in the condition it was in when the contract was executed. This is in accord with the general rule that a contract is interpreted in light of the circumstances surrounding its execution, unless the parties provide otherwise. A rational and plausible view of the purpose of the inspection is to check whether the property's condition is the same as it was when the purchaser agreed to buy it. *See Brooks v. Bankson*, 445 S.E.2d 473, 476 (Va. 1994).

DISCLOSURE REPORT STATUTES

Required in two-thirds of the states by statute and regulation, but prudent in all states, is a residential property report and disclosure form. This is typically filled out by the vendor when listing the property and provides the broker and the purchaser with a report on the physical condition of the property as well as environmental hazards inherent in it. The vendor is asked about his actual knowledge of current or past conditions regarding water; plumbing; sewer; septic; heating; air conditioning; electrical systems; the roof, basement, and crawl spaces; structure (foundations, walls, and floors); insect infestations (termites, ants, and other wood and masonry borers); and drainage, soil, or erosion problems. The vendor is required to disclose both patent as well as latent defects.

The questions the vendor is asked may be phrased in any one of several ways. *See Lindberg v. Roseth*, 46 P.3d 518, 526 (Idaho 2002). The format might require checking statements such as "the walls are defective" as correct, incorrect, or not applicable. (As in Wisconsin, where purchasers might wonder, "what defects?") Or the vendor can be asked to answer yes or no to questions such as "are there defects in the walls?" (South Dakota) Or the vendor can be asked, "has the soil been subjected to a percolation test?" (Arizona, leaving one to wonder "when?" and "recently enough to be useful?" and "with what results?")

Disclosure forms will cause the vendor to think twice about the listed property's condition, but the extent to which a vendor must investigate a condition before filling out the form is often unclear. *See Barta v. Kiondschuh*, 518 N.W.2d 98 (Neb. 1994). California requires that the broker perform a visual inspection of the property. Such forms aid brokers in seeking indemnification from vendors, as well as in protecting brokers from claims made by vendors found liable for a misrepresentation.

A WORD ON OPTIONS

When would you expect to use an option agreement instead of a contract of sale? (1) An option is advisable when a purchaser has reservations about the transaction that cannot be resolved by objective standards incorporated into a contingency clause in a contract. (2) Similarly, perhaps the vendor has agreed to sell the purchaser some of his land, but which portion will be conveyed is unclear; because the conveyed portion cannot be described yet, an option might be used. (3) Or the purchaser may be a land developer. She might use an option to assemble large tracts of land, not wanting to be bound by contracts until all parcels in the tract are available to her; in this situation, an option ties up the parcels available early in the assembly process and gives her a time during which to work on the more difficult acquisitions. Further, a purchaser having difficulty obtaining financing has time to work out those difficulties if she holds options.

An option is generally an offer to sell, irrevocable for a certain time. (It can be an offer to buy as well, but that is rarer.) Thus the vendor is bound to sell, but the purchaser is not obligated to buy; in this sense, it is a unilateral contract binding the offeror to enter into a contract of sale. Often the contract, unexecuted, is attached and incorporated by reference to flesh out the terms of the offer. Some jurisdictions apply the writing requirement of the Statute of Frauds to an option, although it does not create an interest in real property. Rather, it is only an offer to enter into a contract of sale. Traditionally time is of the essence in option contracts. *See Scotti v. Mimiaga*, 323 A.3d 900 (R.I. 2024). Traditional contract remedies apply. When exercised, the option will "ripen" into a contract.

Examples

Example 34

LO executes a valid option with D. Before D exercises the option, but within its term, LO executes a contract of sale with T. What remedies has D?

Explanation

In general, D as the optionee will have an action for specific performance of the option. However, T may be a bona fide purchaser, without notice of D's right to purchase, and if so, T will prevail over D. However, if the problem arises during the LO-T executory period, equity will enjoin the closing. If the closing has occurred, equity may undo the LO-T transaction. Casting the option in a recordable form is the best method of avoiding this problem; under many recording acts, an option is a recordable document.

A lease option A property that does not sell after some time on the market gives the vendor an opportunity to rent and combine a traditional lease with the option to purchase. *See Stubbs v. Ramsey*, 2025 Miss. App. LEXIS 217 (Miss. Ct. App., June 10, 2025) (traditionally in such a contract, time is not of the essence unless made expressly so). The rental covenant in the lease typically provides in part that all or some of the rent is credited toward the purchase price when and if the lessee/purchaser exercises the option. The option must have its own, separate consideration, all or some of which is nonrefundable upon the option's exercise and not credited to the purchase price. The purchaser, as a lessee, in effect saves up for part of the purchase price, but meanwhile gets possession in exchange for a lower investment in it, is permitted to improve it, and locks in the purchase price. Vendors keep the title, obtain tenants with the interest in maintaining the property, rent at a higher rate, and after a while perhaps qualify their property for a tax-deferred exchange. Similarly, a lease might be combined with a contract of sale, effective at the end of the lease term.

Examples

EXAMPLES

Example 35

Would you recommend to a vendor client using a lease option that separate lease and option documents be used, or is it advisable to combine the documents?

Explanation

Separate documents are best in case the lessee has to be evicted. The vendor wants to be able to use summary procedures available to a landlord and does not want the lease to be subject to recharacterization as a contract of sale.

Example 36

What advice would you provide a vendor client using a lease option and wanting to make the rent credit as small as possible?

Explanation

That the credit has to be large enough to encourage the lessee to exercise the option, so a smaller credit may be self-defeating. However, if the credit is too large, the vendor's profits may be lost. If the vendor's maintenance costs are high or expected to rise, a smaller credit is warranted. Purchasers need to feel that their "forced savings account" is building them equity in the property, so it should be a healthy percentage of the rent—say, one-third over a one- to two-year lease, perhaps less if the term is longer.

BACKUP CONTRACTS OF SALE

Backup contracts of sale are common in "hot" markets for real property or for popular properties within any market. They are effective when a prior contract is terminated by its parties. Thus they are used when more than one purchaser wishes to execute a contract of sale. When the primary contract is terminated within a short period of time after the execution of the backup contract, the backup then becomes the primary contract. However, a backup purchaser may wish to set a date certain for termination of his own contract; if this proves unacceptable, then the purchaser should have the right to terminate at any time before receipt of the vendor's acceptance of his contract as the primary one.

Disputes are likely to develop over whether the purchaser should pay a deposit. Perhaps the check for the deposit should be in escrow, uncashed until the backup becomes the primary contract. If the backup contract contains contingency and conditional clauses, the time for fulfilling the conditions may run either from the date of its execution or the date on which it becomes the primary contract. So the parties to the backup contract should specify which date controls.

Examples

Example 37

V executes a brief but enforceable contract of sale with P1 and a backup contract with P2. The primary contract is contingent on the sale of P1's existing residence. The sale of the existing residence falls through. V agrees to waive this condition, but P2 insists that he now has the right to buy V's property. Does he?

Explanation

The issue is whether V and P1 can renegotiate their primary contract. Good drafting should settle this issue expressly, but failing that, the issue is whether the parties to the primary contract intend to create a new one. That they cannot do. That would be its "novation—the legal equivalent of termination. Whether the parties to the primary contract intended to create a new contract is a matter of intent. Here the removal of a condition is not a novation. Adding a condition might be. Absent some provisions controlling the permitted scope of any renegotiation of the primary contract, the parties to it should negotiate carefully.

CHAPTER 6

Remedies for Breach of Contract

The following remedies are available to both vendors and purchasers for a breach of contract of sale of real property:

1. damages,
2. specific performance of the contract,
3. rescission, and
4. foreclosure of a vendor's or vendee's lien.

DAMAGES

The traditional rule is that upon a vendor's breach of contract, a purchaser of real property is entitled to only nominal damages. Such damages usually are measured by the out-of-pocket expenses incurred in the purchase up to the point at which the vendor breaches the contract. This limited measure of damages is explained historically by the vendor's limited responsibility for the review of the title. She was not expected to know the state of the title—she needed an attorney to review it—so why hold her to pay more than nominal damages when it proved unmarketable and the purchaser refused it? This traditional rule—also known as the English rule in some jurisdictions or as the *Flureau* rule, after its leading English case—applies only when the vendor is in breach, or when the breach is neither intentional nor willful, or involves a non-curable title defect. *See Flureau v. Thornhill*, 96 Eng. Rep. 635 (K.B. 1776). Conversely, the *Flureau* rule does not apply when the vendor's breach is willful or in bad faith—and this means that the exceptions to *Flureau* severely limit the situations to which it is applied. This rule of nominal damages is also explained by the early judicial preference for specific performance of the contract of sale and that preference in turn is explained by the limited measure of damages available. These two preferences are, in other words, mutually reinforcing—and of historical interest today. Indeed, with the question put another way, why limit even a good faith vendor's liability to nominal damages? When a title search is cheap and readily available, the *Flureau* rule has little to commend it today.

The alternative to the traditional rule of nominal damages is "benefit of the bargain" damages. This latter measure of damages requires that the fair market value of the property be computed. That computation was difficult when real property sales were not as common as they are today. Thus a further explanation for the grip of the traditional rule may lie in the erratic and small markets that once existed for real property.

Whatever the historic preference of the courts, about one-half of the states in this country have gone beyond the traditional and limited measure of damages and award benefit of the bargain damages, plus consequential damages. The benefit of the bargain is the difference between the fair market value of the property and the price reserved in the contract—aka difference money measure of damages.

Upon a purchaser's breach of contract, vendors are likewise restricted to nominal damages in many states. Where benefit of the bargain damages are also permitted, as in California under its Civil Code §3307, remember that no such damages exist for the vendor unless the property's fair market value, on the date of the breach of contract, is less than the contract price, for only then will the difference be greater than zero. As a practical matter, the market value will have to fall substantially before a lawsuit to recover the difference money is worthwhile.

States permitting a vendor more than nominal damages often permit a vendor to recover consequential damages too. Consequential damages are those whose proximate cause is, and which flow naturally from, the purchaser's breach. They must be computed as those incurred by the vendor, upon a resale of the property within a reasonable time after the breach. The most common type of consequential damages is the expense of reselling the property. Determining what these expenses are requires a close examination by the purchaser's attorney. Some will have been the vendor's responsibility during the first sale and should not be included. Some will duplicate expenses incurred by the vendor during the first sale but incurred again on the resale and should be included—for example, the vendor might be responsible for two brokerage commissions.

Deposits and Down Payments

After an involuntary breach of contract by the purchaser, most preprinted contracts will permit the vendor to elect to retain the purchaser's deposit, usually construing the retention as the vendor's acceptance of liquidated damages. Some courts reach this result without much analysis of the effect of a provision for liquidated damages in a contract, citing the inherent uncertainties about prices in real estate markets. Here the retention of the deposit shows the vendor's election to take no further legal action based on the contract.

At the same time, there is general agreement that a purchaser can bring an equitable, specific performance action even though the contract contains a liquidated damage provision. *See K.G.M. Custom Homes, Inc. v. Prosky*, 10 N.E.3d 117 (Mass. 2014). As to an action for damages, when the contract contains a liquidated damage provision, the situation is more complicated: Some courts permit a vendor to retain the deposit even when the vendor has sustained no damages, as when the vendor resells the property at a higher price. *See Karimi v. 401 N. Wabash Venture*, 952 N.E.2d 1278, 1288 (Ill. App. 2011). This result is based on the rule that the provision's reasonableness is evaluated once, when the contract is formed, not thereafter; this is the so-called "single look" approach. A slightly greater number of courts have rejected this result, adopting a "second look" approach evaluating the reasonableness of the provision at the time of the breach. *See Wasserman's Inc. v. Middletown*, 645 A.2d 100 (N.J. 1994) and *Kelly v. Marx*, 694 N.E.2d 869 (Mass. App. Ct. 1998) (discussed *infra*, this chapter).

When a purchaser agrees to accept a refund of all or part of any deposits that she has made "as full settlement upon the vendor's default," the clause is evidence that the parties to the contract intended to bar the purchaser from obtaining additional damages. Nonetheless, the cases are split on the issue of whether to give the quoted provision this effect. Compare *Tanglewood Land Co. v. Wood*, 252 S.E.2d 546 (N.C. App. 1979) (provision prohibited additional damages), with *Melcer v. Zuck*, 245 A.2d 61 (N.J. Super.), cert. denied, 246 A.2d 456 (N.J. 1968) (purchaser enabled to collect benefit of the bargain damages in addition to recovering the deposit).

In summary, when the purchaser is in breach, no matter what measure of damages is permitted, in a majority of states the vendor is entitled to retain the deposit as liquidated damages, so long as its amount is no more than the customary. *See Leeber v. Deltona Corp.*, 546 A.2d 452, 456 (Me. 1988) (finding 15 percent of the purchase price customary). Retaining substantially more than is customary is unconscionable. *See Olmo v. Matos*, 653 A.2d 1, 3 (Pa. Super. 1994).

For residential transactions, California by statute adopts the single look approach and prescribes the maximum amount that a vendor may retain as liquidated damages as 3 percent of the purchase price; this effectively sets an upper limit on deposits. Likewise, Louisiana adopts a single look approach by statute. Oklahoma by statute creates a presumption of reasonableness for a liquidated damages provision of no more than 5 percent of the purchase price.

Evidence of arm's-length bargaining is usually sufficient to sustain a liquidated damages provision. *See Proulx v. 1400 Pennsylvania Ave.*, S.E., LLC, 199 A.3d 667, 674 (D.C. 2019). However, absent an agreement otherwise, the burden of litigation falls on the purchaser to sue for its return. The vendor is free, upon the purchaser's breach, to declare the deposit forfeited, and in most states is then still free to sue for damages, so long as she applies the deposit against those damages. Likewise, absent a contrary contract provision, a defaulting purchaser is not barred from recovering the deposit, to the extent that its amount exceeds the vendor's actual damages and (some states add) so long as the purchaser's default was involuntary and in good faith. *See Kutzin v. Pirnie*, 591 A.2d 932 (N.J. 1991).

Keeping in mind the foregoing splits in the authorities, examine the following problems. They are arranged according to who is in breach—vendor or purchaser—and according to the type of remedy sought—damages or specific performance. First, consider some problems concerning whether that ever-present out-of-pocket expense, the purchaser's deposit, is recoverable after the deal goes sour. These problems assume that the contract is silent on the subject of the vendor's right of retention. The facts in Examples 1b through 1e are variations on Example 1a.

EXAMPLES

Examples

Example 1a

V and P execute a brief but enforceable contract for the sale of V's residence. The purchase price is $100,000. P makes a $10,000 down payment but then locates another property that she likes better and refuses to close the V-P contract. V quickly finds another purchaser, B, to buy the residence. B pays $100,000 for it. P asks you to recover the deposit. Will you take P's case?

Explanation

Probably not to court. Nominal damages may be recovered, but V's sale to a third party at the same price means that she has suffered no loss of bargain damages, so a forfeiture of the deposit by P might arguably make V more than whole. Does P's willful default defeat her recovery? Some courts would say so. They describe the deposit as "earnest money"—its deposit with the vendor is the purchaser's guarantee of performance of the contract and of making a good faith effort to close the deal, in which case neither nominal nor loss of bargain damages could be recovered.

The difficulty with such a description is that whatever creates a fear of forfeiture can also be described as a penalty for nonperformance. Thus a guarantee of performance is easily construed as a penalty for nonperformance. A contract's statement that the deposit is partial payment of the purchase price will override a clause permitting the vendor to retain it as liquidated damages. However, without the credit toward the purchase price, penalties will not often be found in contractual silences. They require intent. Permitting V to retain the deposit is a rough way to measure damages, with something leftover to pay V for her expenses on the V-P contract. A brokerage fee, for example, could be 5-7 percent of the purchase price, so V surely has some damages. A close case, but obtaining a judgment for P would cost more than the deposit itself. *See Edwards v. Inman*, 566 S.W.2d 809 (Ky. App. 1978) (in a purchaser's suit for the return of a deposit, the court ordered its return subject to a deduction for the defendant vendor's incidental damages, in the amount of a real estate commission, survey costs, and attorneys' fees).

Example 1b

You ascertain that a 10 percent deposit is usual and customary in the area. What difference does this make to P's attempt to recover the deposit? Would your answer be different if P had paid $30,000 down?

Explanation

Following the custom and usage in the area lends an air of reasonableness to the amount of the deposit here. Compliance with the local custom may provide V with a way of satisfying the burden of proof on the question of whether the amount was a penalty. However, a complete inquiry into whether the forfeiture of a deposit constitutes a penalty requires (1) a reasonable preestimate of damages, (2) bargaining in which something is exchanged for the forfeiture, and (3) a fair result. The custom need not be a code word for a reasonable preestimate of damages; indeed, the local custom shows it likely that no actual preestimate was made. So the presence of such a custom is not conclusive but strengthens V's position. She still has an argument that the contract is fair in its result, even if no bargaining over the forfeiture took place, so long as the 10 percent deposit level is not exceeded. Exceeding the 10 percent is then evidence of a penalty and weakens V's right to retain the deposit.

Example 1c

The fair market value of the residence soars after P's breach. P's deposit is the usual and customary one, but P wants it back. Will you take her case?

Explanation

No. P is not looking at the relevant time frame. The measure of damages is taken on the day of the breach, not thereafter, and not even when the vendor benefits in the long run from P's default, as here. Damages are measured by comparing the contract price with the value of the property on the date of the breach. *See White v. Farrell*, 987 N.E.2d 467 (N.Y. 2013); *Vines v. Orchard Hills*, 435 A.2d 1022 (Conn. 1980). This is the rule in a majority of states. Courts following this rule justify it as follows: (1) it is in harmony with general rules of contract damages; (2) it puts the vendor in as good a position as if the purchaser had performed, meeting the vendor's expectations for the transaction; (3) it is consistent with the contract rule on mitigation of damages: Because the vendor has the risk of further declines in the property's value, he will be quick to resell, thereby mitigating the purchaser's damages; and (4) if the vendor does not have an adequate remedy at law because of this measure, he can bring an action for specific performance (unless, as a practical matter, the defaulting purchaser is financially unable to purchase the property).

In a few states, the date for measuring damages is the date of the resale. In this minority of states, all using the benefit of the bargain damages, the date is the date on which the vendor resells the property, so long as the vendor has diligently pursued the resale. This rule measures damages by comparing the contract price with the resale price. Courts following this "time of resale" rule justify it as follows: (1) it puts the risk of lost value during a falling market on the defaulting purchaser and gives purchasers an incentive to close; (2) it gives the vendor the benefit of a completed sale—what she bargained for in the first place; (3) it reflects the realities of the real estate market—real estate is not fungible, and real estate transactions take time, are undertaken in a cyclical market, and involve many time-consuming services; (4) it uses the date that in most cases offers the strongest proof of a property's fair market value.

Example 1d

V decides not to sell but instead sues P for damages. What must V prove in this action for loss of bargain, substantial damages?

Explanation

An action for damages will require proof of the fair market value of the property. The measure of damages is the difference between the fair market value of the property and the contract price, both measured on the date of the breach. This is a "difference money" measure of damages. In applying this measure of damages, one party's opinion about the money lost in an incomplete transaction, an unaccepted offer to purchase, or the exchange value of real property is not evidence of its fair market value. Offers and exchanges may be motivated by many factors unrelated to market values; an accepted purchase price, paid in a voluntary purchase and sale of the same property or comparable properties, is the best evidence available and, while subject to examination in litigation, is most likely to withstand opposing scrutiny.

Example 1e

The fair market value of the property remains stable. V quickly finds another purchaser, T, willing to pay $130,000. Now will you sue V to recover P's deposit?

Explanation

Yes. Even if P's was a willful default, V's net gain on the resale appears to outweigh any damage arising from P's default. California cases analyze the problem this way. *See Smith v. Mady*, 194 Cal. Rptr. 42 (Cal. App. 1983) (holding that a quick, profitable resale not only precludes benefit of the bargain damages for the vendor but also may offset any consequential damages incurred by her). They presume that the property was worth the higher price on the day of P's breach. In some states (e.g., New York), courts would still hold that P should not gain a cause of action by reason of his own default; forfeiture of the deposit incentivizes performance. *See Maxton Builders, Inc. v. Lo Galbo*, 502 N.E.2d 184 (N.Y. 1986) (holding that a purchaser may not recover the deposit when defaulting without a lawful excuse), noted in 38 Syracuse L. Rev. 471, 479-481 (1987). So there is variation among jurisdictions.

In summary, when the vendor has suffered no damages, the purchaser can in a majority of states recover the deposit. In some states, however, the willful default of the purchaser is sufficient grounds for refusing to return the deposit. If the purchaser refuses to close, the vendor may retain a deposit, reasonable in amount, regardless of what happens after the breach.

Example 2

V agrees to sell her farm to P, a real estate developer. V and P execute a contract of sale providing in part that upon V's default, P may recover her down payment or seek specific performance of the contract, but that V "shall not be liable for money damages for any default." V's title proves unmarketable because V had previously conveyed part of the farm to her children. Meanwhile, P's financing commitment has run out and P sues V for damages. In P's suit, what result, and why?

Explanation

Unless there is some violation of public policy, fraud, misrepresentation, or overreaching, the limitation on the damages remedy is valid and not unconscionable. *See Leet v. Totah*, 620 A.2d 1372, 1379-1380 (Md. 1993).

SPECIFIC PERFORMANCE

From an early date, our courts granted purchasers of real property specific performance when the plaintiff could show (1) a contract of sale, binding and enforceable between the parties to it; (2) that the plaintiff was not in breach at the time of the defendant's breach and was capable of tendering performance[1] (e.g., tendering the purchase price); (3) that the contract is fair and there is no reason equity should not enforce it (e.g., the price and other provisions in it are fair and it involves mutual rights and duties); and (4) that the plaintiff does not have an adequate remedy at law (often this involves a showing that damages would be difficult to measure). *See Keystone Props. & Dev. LLC v. Campo*, 989 A.2d 961 (R.I. 2010). These elements are typically present, and so in some jurisdictions a presumption for specific performance as a preferred remedy arose. *Johnson v. Sellers*, 798 N.W.2d 690 (S.D. 2011). This presumption typically arose out of the fourth element with a showing that the property was unique, without comparable properties on the market when the contract was made, so that duplication of the contract was impossible. *See Estate of Younge v. Huysmans*, 506 A.2d 282, 285 (N.H. 1985) ("Specific performance is ordinarily granted to enforce a contract of sale of real property, unless circumstances make it inequitable or impossible to do so"); and compare *Humphries v. Ables*, 789 N.E.2d 1025 (Ind. App. 2003) (granting specific performance without proof of the fourth element) with *Kesler v. Marshall*, 792 N.E.2d 893 (Ind. App. 2003) (denying specific performance without such proof), both cases discussed at 37 Ind. L. Rev. 1307 (2004).

A decree in specific performance may be accompanied by an abatement in the purchase price. An abatement is granted when the vendor's title is defective and so the vendor cannot convey the title that the purchaser bargained for. *See Merritz v. Circelli*, 64 A.2d 796, 7 A.L.R.2d 1325 (Pa. 1949). The purchaser still has the right to whatever title the vendor can convey, with the abatement measured by the cost of curing the defect but not by the attorney's fees payable in the action for specific performance. If the defect were to be measured in terms of its effect on the fair market value, purchasers

1. "He who seeks equity must do equity," said the chancellors. This is often known as the "perfect tender rule."

would obtain in equity a kind of benefit of the bargain denied in an action for damages.

Being an equitable remedy, specific performance is granted only as a matter of judicial discretion. *See Davis v. Harmony Dev., LLC*, 460 P.3d 230 (Wyo. 2020). That is, it is not granted when doing so would itself work an injustice. For example, it is not granted when the subject matter of the contract is destroyed or the contract is rendered impossible to perform—for instance, when the improvements on the property are a large part of its value and are destroyed by fire. *Merritz v. Circelli*, *supra*.

Specific performance is more readily decreed for purchasers than for vendors. After all, the purchaser wants the property, whereas the vendor has agreed to take money for it. Thus as to the purchaser, the transaction is unique. When the property is a condominium or a house in a cookie-cutter subdivision, the contract is arguably not unique, even for the purchaser. Then the purchaser might allege that it was particularly beneficial—for example, giving her the property at a low price. However, the purchaser runs a risk in asserting that the contract is unique because of its low price, because the contract must be reviewed to the court and only a contract fair to the parties gets specific performance. When it appears that the purchaser overreached, specific performance is less likely to be given. This is the purchaser's "fair price" dilemma.

In helping a purchaser evaluate whether to bring a specific performance action, an attorney needs to make a purchaser appreciate what it will take—for example, keeping the cash requirements of the contract available and keeping the loan commitment alive during the pendency of the action. This is the purchaser's "tender dilemma." *See Francassa v. Doris*, 876 A.2d 506, 508 (R.I. 2005).

The vendor, in contrast, only has to be counseled to keep the title marketable and be ready to tender a satisfactory deed to the property. Some states routinely deny a vendor specific performance, forcing the vendor to resell and then sue for damages. Other states regard the vendor as having an action for specific performance just because the purchaser does, on a principal of mutuality of remedies. Looking beyond this justification, the vendor may be land-poor, her assets illiquid, or a resale at the contract price difficult, and in these instances, the transaction for the vendor may be unique.

In further support of the vendor's right to specific performance, difficulties of gathering information about market prices and conditions might justify, in some real estate markets, extending the remedy to vendors. This is to say that damages may be too expensive or difficult to calculate or, once calculated, unreliable. On the other hand, in a mass market specific performance would not lie for vendors, market information being more easily obtained.

A plaintiff's position has the advantage of being able to plead in the alternative and to elect either specific performance or damages. For the purchaser, if the market drops, then damages, measured at the date of the breach, are preferable; if the market rises, then specific performance, in effect measuring the value at the date of the decree, is preferable. For the vendor, the situation is reversed, but for both, this election puts either party in a win-win position and may leave either overcompensated.

Examples

Example 3

V and P execute a brief but enforceable contract of sale for Blackacre for $100,000. V discovers that the western boundary overlaps that of a neighbor and undertakes to buy the additional acreage required to settle the dispute and provide P with the acreage described in the contract. The boundary dispute drags on. P sues V for specific performance, escrowing the remainder of the purchase price with the court and demanding also that V settle the dispute with the neighbor. V raises the defense that P has imposed a new condition on performance and is not entitled to specific performance. Is V's defense valid?

Explanation

No. P is requiring of V no more than the initial contract did—that is, the conveyance of a marketable title, one free of reasonable doubt (as to the boundary) and litigation (here, the threat that the boundary dispute will become the subject of litigation). P's tender is complete. *Kelley v. Leucadia Financial Corp.*, 846 P.2d 1238 (Utah 1992).

Example 4

On June 1, B executed a brief but enforceable contract with O to purchase Ranchacre, O's ten-acre tract of land improved with a ranch house. Ranchacre is one of 2,000 tracts located on O's 20,000-acre land holdings and similar to most of the other 1,999 tracts there. B's purchase price was $1,000,000, payable in full at the closing on September 1. Pursuant to the contract, B paid O $50,000 on July 1, this payment to be held in escrow and applied as liquidated damages if either O or B defaulted. On July 10, B agreed in writing to sell Ranchacre to K for $1,250,000.[2] Ten days later, K received an appraisal putting Ranchacre's market value at $1,400,000. B, O, and K never met, all doing all the foregoing through the mail. On July 21, O told B that O would not convey Ranchacre to B and offered to pay B $20,000 either to cancel the contract or to convey another tract O owned,

2. B's new contract is known in real estate jargon as a "flip contract"—B is parlaying a short-term interest for a relatively large profit.

a tract adjacent to Ranchacre and similar in most respects to it. What are B's remedies, if any, against O?

Explanation

B may obtain specific performance of his contract. Although the tract is not unique land, B's flip contract with K gives it a unique value to him, and assuming the contract to be fair on its face and K does nothing further, specific performance lies against O. That the liquidated damages clause gives B $50,000 while perhaps incurring a much larger liability to K means that B's damage remedy is "under-liquidated" and so inadequate, and also raises the inference that B's liquidated damages were not intended to be B's exclusive remedy. Neither will O's unilateral offer of alternative performance limit equity's discretion to award B specific performance.

How much then might B recover from O in damages? If the liquidated damage remedy is limited to a good faith default, B's damage remedy will yield bad faith, benefit of the bargain damages ($1,250,000 − 1,000,000 = $250,000, B's profit flipping his contract to K), of which B may owe K $150,000 (because the tract's fair market value was $1,400,000), netting B $100,000 in damages.

Example 5

In the foregoing Example, what are K's remedies against B?

Explanation

Were K to elect $150,000 in damages from B, the rationale previously discussed for awarding B specific performance would collapse. This is because it is B's contract with K that makes a damages remedy inadequate—and further indicating that if B is thrown back on a damages remedy, B may be compensated with damages either measured by B's liability to K (as discussed, $150,000) or by his lost opportunity (a $250,000 profit flipping his contract).

If K elects specific performance, his action is dependent on B's, but K cannot force B to pursue this remedy. This is so because B's flipping his contract for a 20 percent profit in a short time makes B seem to be overreaching or acting unfairly: A contract fair in its terms between the parties is a precondition to specific performance. So a court could conclude that specific performance would not promote fairness between O and B. The unstable market for O's tracts indicated by the $1,400,000 appraisal is a further indication that specific performance is an inappropriate remedy between any of these parties. This would limit K to damages.

K's damages are $150,000 ($1,400,000 − $1,250,000) because (1) B's breach is in bad faith (he agreed to convey a title he did not possess), so benefit of the bargain, not just nominal damages, should be awarded, and

(2) the $1,400,000 appraisal is evidence of the tract's fair market value closest to the date of B's breach of K's $1,250,000 contract.

Example 6

On June 1, V and P execute a brief but enforceable contract for the sale of Blackacre, P thinking that it "is the perfect place for my mother-in-law to live." The contract price is $100,000. The contract calls for closing the transaction on September 1. Just before closing, V decides not to sell and offers to pay P $20,000, the difference between the contract price and the fair market value of Blackacre—then $120,000. P refuses V's offer and instead sues V for specific performance. Will P win?

Explanation

Yes. V's offer of difference money, substantial measure of damages, does not compensate P either for P's nominal damages, incurred for transaction and closing costs during the executory period, June 1 to September 1, or for any consequential damages he might have, so P's damage remedy is not adequate. Any consequential damages, even P's idea that Blackacre is the ideal place for his relative, makes Blackacre a unique property from his perspective. P's consequential damages may be non-monetary, but so what? The court will not inquire into them. P's risk is that the fair market value of Blackacre may fall. But again, so what? The future market for the property is irrelevant to equity's jurisdiction. Further, the court's discretion to grant or deny specific performance would only be used to deny the remedy when it works a hardship on V, but no hardship is shown when V is only forced to do what V previously agreed to do. Otherwise, absent fraud or oppression, the cause of action for specific performance is a matter of right for P. It may not do perfect justice between the parties, but it is a shortcut to an efficient remedy. Equity will enforce P's contract as written.

The Vendor's Right to Specific Performance

It is common for many courts to award a vendor specific performance without inquiring into the adequacy of his legal remedies: To make V whole, V must have the benefit of his bargain; in jurisdictions where only nominal or out-of-pocket damages are available in an action for damages, a specific performance is the only way to achieve that. In other jurisdictions, where substantial damages are available, they may be difficult to calculate. Indeed, when P is in breach, V's suing in contract for the purchase price is the equivalent of asking for a decree in specific performance. Specific performance is thus a very efficient remedy making the vendor whole. *See Maisano v. Avery*, 204 A.3d 515, 522 (Pa. Super. Ct. 2019). Finally, if the purchaser can have such a remedy so should a vendor, on a principal of mutuality. *See Ash Park, LLC v. Alexander & Bishop, Ltd.*, 783 N.W.2d 294 (Wis. 2010). When inquiry is made, V's chances of obtaining specific performance increase, for example, when V has the benefit of a very high contract price (particularly when only nominal damages are available) in excess of the fair market price and has not overreached to get it. Likewise, proof that V is land-poor (lacking in other assets) or needs the proceeds of the sale for some purpose disclosed to P will also increase V's chances. *See Finley v. Aiken*, 1 Grant, Cas. 83 (Pa. 1855).

If in the following two Examples P may have specific performance, may V have the same remedy?

Examples

Example 7

If V was a farmer and P a real estate developer, may V, when bringing an action for specific performance, make a tender of her obligations after P's loan commitment has run out during the pendency of the specific performance action?

Explanation

Yes. V's decree in specific performance might be adjusted so that P is given a reasonable time to procure an alternative commitment from a mortgage lender and thus make a perfect tender. Maintaining a long-term, outstanding loan commitment is time-consuming and expensive. A perfect tender is traditionally required when the suit is filed, but equitable discretion should allow the court to adjust the decree to the realities of financing.

Example 8

What if V's contract calls for a series of deposits payable by the purchaser during the executory period but, upon the nonpayment of any of these, provides that "the deposits shall be forfeited and this contract of no further effect." Can V, upon the purchaser's nonperformance, retain the deposits thus far paid but still sue for specific performance?

Explanation

Maybe. The forfeiture clause will not *per se* preclude the action, but the clause, with its no-effect corollary, is some evidence, but is not dispositive, of the intention of the parties intended to preclude specific performance. *See Martin v. Dillon*, 642 P.2d 1209, 1211 (Or. 1982).

THE DAMAGE REMEDY FOR A VENDOR'S BREACH

Nominal Damages

The willful-nonwillful breach distinction, mentioned earlier, grew out of cases in which the vendor's title proved unmarketable, with the result that the transaction could not be closed because of the *vendor's* default in delivering the title promised in the contract. In these situations, the purchaser could only recover nominal damages—the expenses she was "out of pocket." This nominal measure of damages assumes that absent some fraud or misrepresentation on the vendor's part, she is not responsible for knowing the state of her title; that is a matter for an attorney to investigate. Moreover, the vendor could not make the title good, so why hold her to a futile act? *See Flureau v. Thornhill*, 96 Eng. Rep. 635 (1776) (involving a sale of a leasehold), discussed in *Basiliko v. Pargo Corp.*, 532 A.2d 1346 (D.C. App. 1987).

When the vendor is unable to deliver a marketable title and the transaction fails to close on that account, the purchaser may claim that she obtained the cash to put up the down payment and/or the purchase price from the sale of securities that since the breach have risen in value. After the default, the purchaser is left with depreciated cash and no property. She claims that it is not fair to permit her only nominal damages. These facts are the very facts in *Flureau*.

The nominal damages rule made sense in an era of stable property values and short executory periods, but fluctuating values and long executory periods characterize real property markets in this country, so why apply this English rule? One answer often given is that when title fails and neither vendor nor purchaser is responsible, the rule carries out the contract principles of mutual mistake and impossibility of performance.

Examples

Example 9

V and P enter into a brief but enforceable contract of sale for V's residence. The purchase price is $100,000. The title search discloses that V has granted an interest in the property that interferes with P's plans for the property. What if that interest is an easement over the backyard? Or a "residential use only" covenant that prevents P from having a home office? Should P sue V for damages or specific performance?

Explanation

In both situations, it is V who has granted the interest making the title unmarketable. Because under the *Flureau* rule, V is responsible for the decrease in value, V's breach is willful, and P should recover, in an action for damages, the benefit of her bargain, or difference money: in this case, the difference between the fair market value of the property with and without the easement, both measured on the day of the breach (which here is the day the contract was executed, the title already being unmarketable). Establishing this difference money probably will require expert opinions by appraisers, and the trial is likely to wind up as an expensive "battle of the experts" in front of a jury or the trier of fact. In contrast, specific performance may be the least costly remedy. As to the second question, in a jurisdiction in which easements are conveyances of an interest in real property and covenants are executory contracts or promises, they may have different effects on the marketability of the title. The easement definitively affects marketability; the covenant may not. Whatever these substantive differences are, the remedial consequences of the conveyance/contract distinction are unimportant today.

Example 10

Suppose that in the previous Example V does not have title to the residence when the contract is executed, but in fact has only an option to purchase it. What if (a) the optionor breaches or (b) V defaults on the option? What measure of damages can P thereafter recover from V?

Explanation

In both cases, absent an appropriate disclosure to P, V has misrepresented (indicating that he had title when he did not) the state of the title by executing this contract. In every contract of sale, the vendor makes a representation, implied by law if not express, that she will convey a marketable title at the closing. *See Luette v. Bank of Italy Natl. Trust & Sav. Assn.*, 42 F.2d 9 (9th Cir.), cert. denied, 282 U.S. 884 (1930).

That V's breach of the contract was not willful when the optionor defaulted, but was when V herself defaulted on the option, makes no difference. In the first set of circumstances V has a cause of action for damages against the optionor, and because of this "action over" P obtains difference money damages. In the second situation, V brought this trouble on herself and doesn't deserve much sympathy. In both cases, V assumes the risk that she cannot fulfill her obligation to have a title by the closing. Moreover, when she only has an option, V could not yet know whether she will have a marketable title. Judgment for P for substantial damages. *See Kooloian v. Suburban Land Co.*, 873 A.2d 95, 100 (R.I. 2005).

Example 11

What if V loses part of her backyard to an adverse possessor during the executory period of her contract with P?

Explanation

Flureau does not apply. The vendor's sleeping on her rights caused the loss of title, and P should get more than nominal damages for V's omissions, as well as for fraud and misrepresentations; the effect of all three is the same as far as P is concerned. *See Smith v. Warr*, 564 P.2d 771 (Utah 1977).

Example 12a

Same facts as in Example 9, but in addition B offers V $130,000 for the residence. What if P finds out about B's offer before V and B both execute a contract of sale? What can P do at this point?

Explanation

P can enjoin V's proceeding further with B and obtain a decree in specific performance. This is a classic case for specific performance. The offer may not be evidence of fair market value but is evidence that P's damage remedy is inadequate.

Example 12b

Same facts as in Example 9. V decides not to sell. What can P do at this point?

Explanation

P can get specific performance or bring an action for damages. The election is P's. Because the change of mind on V's part indicates a willful breach, more than nominal damages—that is, difference money damages—are available.

Example 12c

Same facts as in Example 9. P finds out about B's offer after V and B execute a contract of sale. What now?

Explanation

Specific performance is still available to P. P's prior contract takes precedence over B's. Also available is a temporary restraining order or injunction against V and B closing the second contract. A *lis pendens*,[3] filed with P's specific performance action, is available as well. The court would grant the order or

3. A *lis pendens* is Latin for "pending suit." It refers to a recorded notice that the title is the subject of litigation; it provides constructive notice of the suit to all who thereafter deal with the title; any later acquired interest is not void, but is taken subject to the judgment or decree in the litigation. For more, *see infra*, this chapter.

issue the *lis pendens* to protect its own ability to enforce its decree should P prevail.

Example 12d

Same facts as in Example 9. What if P doesn't find out about the V-B contract of sale until after V closes this contract with B?

Explanation

Now specific performance is unavailable if B is a bona fide purchaser; an action for damages is then P's only remedy. Now the sale to B is good evidence of the residence's fair market value, but more evidence of comparable transactions will be needed to establish that value for the trier of fact. P will get her deposit back, as well as the expenses that she is out of pocket, subject to a caveat to the effect that those expenses are reasonable in amount. If B is not a bona fide purchaser, then P can elect between the action for damages and specific performance. The decree in specific performance will declare B's title subject to the equities of P's contract, void that title, and transfer it to P.

DEFINING SUBSTANTIAL DAMAGES

Consider what type of damages are available in states that reject the rule of *Flureau* as a limitation on further damages and instead permit both out-of-pocket expenses *and* difference money or benefit of the bargain damages. *See Basiliko v. Pargo Corp.*, 532 A.2d 1346 (D.C. App. 1987). Approximately, half of the states use this expanded measure of damages.

Examples

Example 13

V and P execute a brief but enforceable contract for the sale of V's residence. P secures a mortgage commitment with an 8 percent rate of interest. V breaches the contract and does not close the transaction. The commitment expires, and P's later commitment, secured for a postponed closing, contains an interest rate of 11 percent. P wants V to pay for the difference in the costs of the resulting mortgage and asks you to represent her in this matter. Will you?

Explanation

Yes. Such additional *purchaser's* damages are reasonably foreseeable, either arising naturally from the breach or contemplated by the parties at the time the contract was executed, placing the injured party in the position achieved had the contract been completed. *See Hadley v. Baxendale*, 156 Eng. Rep. 145 (Ct. Ex. 1854). Such damages must be proven by a preponderance of the evidence. P can recover the difference in her monthly mortgage payments extended over the likely term (not necessarily the contract term) during which the loan will remain unpaid. Proof of the likely term is a question of fact. P will bear the burden of showing its length—probably around a decade. *See Donovan v. Bachstadt*, 91 453 A.2d 160 (N.J. 1982). How will the damage award be paid? A lump sum is preferable, but periodic payments on a monthly or annual basis eliminate the possibility of overpayments to P, who may, after all, decide to prepay a loan for many reasons. In the alternative, V could purchase an annuity yielding the annual difference in mortgage costs and retain the right to the principal amount. Often V will have an amount sufficient for this purpose taken from the closing proceeds, although it may be tied up in V's new residence. Garnishment of the proceeds needed might be in order. (If you see this remedy as complex, then you have found yet another rationale for limiting damages to out-of-pocket damages.) It is unclear whether any such award represents general or consequential damages. If the latter, P will have to show the foreseeability of the damages, which might be shown by the widespread press coverage given mortgage interest rate changes.

What other consequential damages might available? What if P has valuable rose bushes in her present garden and loses the opportunity to transplant them to V's garden? Foreseeability here would be more difficult to show unless V has knowledge of P's plans. P's loss of a profitable sale of her existing home would make an easier case.

Example 14

Same facts, but the damages concern rising construction costs for a residence to be built on V's unimproved land. Same result?

Explanation

Yes. Substantial damages have long been awarded purchasers in this situation, and they are measured by the difference between the construction contract available on the day of the breach and that obtained at the time of the balked closing. If P were to buy another ready-built residence instead, the difference between the cost of financing the house she was to build and the house she bought would measure her damages.

Example 15

Same facts, but the commitment to lend was made initially by V. Same result?

Explanation

Yes. However, the remedial possibilities in V-P litigation are now broader. A court might give specific performance of V's promise to lend the money or give specific performance of the original transaction, but with an abatement in the purchase price equal to the damages. The latter is the crisper remedy.

Example 16

Same facts, but this time V resells to G at a profit. When closing her transaction, G was aware of P's situation. Will you as P's attorney seek to join G as a third-party defendant in the V-P litigation?

Explanation

Yes, if V is judgment proof, but otherwise, but the court will probably prefer restitution of V's profit from her, using the resale as the measure of the damages. If you can still add a tort claim to your complaint, however, then a suit against G may have some additional advantage. This claim against G is for her interference with a prospective economic advantage—interference with the closing of the V-P contract.

No matter whether the rule of the jurisdiction permits the recovery of nominal or substantial damages, a purchaser can recover for any improvements made during the executory period. Some jurisdictions limit such recoveries to the amount by which such improvements increase the property's fair market value, so not all purchasers will recover these costs. Were recovery denied, a defaulting vendor will be unjustly enriched; the recovery is, in effect, the foreclosure of a lien for the amount of the improvement.

Example 17

V and P contract for the purchase and sale of Blackacre in a jurisdiction permitting substantial damages. V willfully defaults. P then incurs costs preparing Blackacre for her move to the property. Later, upon V's petition, V is adjudicated bankrupt and her assets, including Blackacre, are subjected to the jurisdiction of the bankruptcy court. The court-appointed trustee in bankruptcy lawfully repudiates the V-P contract. This leaves P with a damages action in the bankruptcy proceedings. When P attempts to recover the move-in costs incurred after the default, V resists, saying that the contract damages are measured at the date of the breach, not thereafter. What does P reply?

Explanation

P's reply is that the date on which the contract was repudiated in the bankruptcy court is a further breach and damages up to that point are recoverable. That P continued to incur expenses shows that she wished to proceed with the contract, and V's actions prevented this by denying P an action for specific performance. That denial is a further default on the contract, and damages should be measured as of the time P lost this remedy. *See Beard v. S/E Joint Venture*, 581 A.2d 1275 (Md. 1990). More generally, a purchaser may offer proof that an item of damages is related to the particular action alleged to be a breach, or that the vendor has the burden of showing that the purchaser acted unreasonably after the vendor's first breach.

THE DAMAGE REMEDY: DEFINING THE DATE OF THE BREACH

As the last Example indicates, the majority of jurisdictions measure damages for the breach of a contract of sale for real property as of the date of the breach. So substantial damages are measured by the difference between the contract price and the fair market value of the property on the date of the breach. E. Allen Farnsworth, Contracts, §12.12, n. 31 (3d ed. 2004). This is consistent with the general rule in contract law—for all types of contracts. When the date of the breach is otherwise unproven, the breach is taken to occur as of the date of the closing—when nonperformance of the contract is a sure result. This traditional rule for when to measure damages is consistent with the parties' expectations and with a vendor's duty to mitigate damages, putting the risk of further declines in market prices on the vendor: She cannot sit back, not attempt to resell, and thus run up the damages on the purchaser. When the purchaser is suing for damages, the rule puts the purchaser in as good a position as she would have been had the vendor not been in breach and had performed.

However, when the vendor sues a purchaser for damages, some courts have measured damages as the difference between the contract price and the vendor's resale price, so long as the resale takes place within a reasonably short period of time. The allowable time period might reasonably be 8-12 months after the breach, but this period might be longer or shorter according to the circumstances of the case and the market for the resale. Some have labeled this "time of resale" measure as a minority rule when really it is a court's short-circuiting the evidentiary search for the value of the property on the date of the breach with a number that's readily available; it puts the risk of a falling market for the property on the defaulting purchaser; and it recognizes that sales of real property are difficult and time-consuming.

THE DAMAGE REMEDY FOR A PURCHASER'S BREACH

Upon a purchaser's breach, the vendor is often confined to recovering nominal damages. In about half the states, she is also entitled to the amount of the difference between the contract price and the fair market value of the property, measured in most jurisdictions on the day of the breach. *See White v. Farrell*, 987 N.E.2d 244 (N.Y. 2013) and *Royer v. Carter*, 233 P.2d 539 (Cal. 1951). The vendor will have no damages unless prices for his property are falling and the property's fair market value is less than the contract price, except for her nominal, out-of-pocket expenses. In a rising market, resale of the property may recoup the vendor's nominal damages and then some, making the vendor's damages not worth the costs of litigation, considering that in many states the vendor can retain the purchaser's deposit.

When suing, a vendor may recover the expenses that are (1) incurred in any resale, (2) duplicative of the expenses of the original sale, and (3) reasonable in amount. The expenses for maintenance and upkeep of the property from the date of breach to the date of the resale are not recoverable. Were it otherwise, there would be insufficient incentive for the vendor to resell, thus mitigating damages. A vendor's damages should equal the value of the purchaser's unperformed promise, less the savings the vendor has at any resale.

The resale price is evidence of the fair market value. *See Webster v. Di Trapano*, 494 N.Y.S.2d 550 (N.Y. App. Div. 1985). It may be *prima facie* evidence of that value in some jurisdictions. However, that value is a question of fact, subject to proof. In a falling market, for example, a purchaser may not want the fair market value established by this resale price alone. In a steady market, there will be no benefit of the bargain damages for the vendor, or at least they will be slight compared to the difficulties and costs of proof, which is why vendors often want to retain the deposits paid by purchasers. Neither will a vendor in a rising market pursue damages in litigation: He can just resell the property for more money and forgo what damages he might otherwise prove.

The vendor is only going to use the damage remedy in a sharply falling market, and here purchasers may well be hard to come by. After all, a falling market is often accompanied by hard times generally. Maybe we should admit that fair market values in a falling market are very difficult to measure, and measure the vendor's damages as of the date of the resale, assuming that the purchaser cannot show that an unreasonably long time has passed between the date of the contract and the resale and taking account of the fact that a reasonable amount of time will be much longer in a falling market than in a rising one. *See Kuhn v. Spatial Design, Inc.*, 585 A.2d 967 (N.J. Super. 1991).

Although a vendor's nominal damages are often restricted to the expenses of resale, some states also permit vendors to recover *special* foreseeable damages. For example, in a residential setting, after a purchaser's breach the vendor may wind up owning two residences, and his duplicative expenses in this situation are recoverable. Special damages are available alone, even in a rising market, when the vendor's resale price is higher than the breaching purchaser's. *See Jones v. Lee*, 971 P.2d 858 (N.M. 1998). Special damages must be reasonably foreseeable by the parties at the time of the contract. *See Hadley v. Baxendale*, 156 Eng. Rep. 145 (Ct. Ex. 1854). So if the vendor intended to shut down a home office on the property, loss of income from using it after the date of the purchaser's breach is not recoverable. *See Turner v. Benson*, 672 S.W.2d 752 (Tenn. 1984). Consider two problems involving a vendor's damages.

Examples

Example 18

V and P agree to buy and sell Whiteacre for a purchase price of $500,000. P makes a down payment, but breaches this contract four months later when she is unable to obtain financing for the purchase and Whiteacre is worth $450,000. V resells Whiteacre for $400,000 four months after P's breach (when Whiteacre's value was $50,000 less than it was on the date of P's breach). V sues P for damages. The jurisdiction uses a substantial, difference money benefit of the bargain measure of damages. What will be the amount of V's recovery?

Explanation

Again, the date for measuring a vendor's damages will either be the date the purchaser breaches the contract (in a majority of states) or the date the vendor resells the property. So the amount recovered by V will be $50,000 in a majority rule state and $100,000 under the minority rule. *See Williams v. Ubaldo*, 670 A.2d 913 (Me. 1996). In both instances, however, a setoff for the amount of the down payment will be given, reducing the amount of the judgment. The amount of the down payment will, then, affect the decision about whether to bring suit. In addition, in a minority rule state, the burden of proving that the resale was not made within a reasonable time or with due diligence is on the purchaser, so that there, if the record is devoid of facts tending to show that the resale did not occur reasonably promptly, the vendor will recover the difference money, measured on the date of the resale.

Example 19

Same facts, except that V, during the period before a reasonably prompt resale takes place, pays an additional installment of real property taxes when due. May V recover this payment?

Explanation

No. The vendor retains ownership during the period between the default and the resale, has the use and benefit of the property for that period, and so, by a principle of symmetry, should also have the burden of taxation. There is no authority for the idea that avoiding tax liability is part of the benefit of the bargain. Would this answer change if the state adopted the minority rule, date of resale, for determining when to measure damages? Probably not. It is the benefit of the bargain that is given in damages, not a reallocation of real property tax liability. *See Rowan Constr. Co. v. Hassane*, 549 A.2d 1085, 1090 (Conn. App. 1988), aff'd, 567 A.2d 1210 (Conn. 1990).

Example 20

V and P contract for the purchase and sale of V's residence. After a willful default by P, V resells the property and with the proceeds makes a down payment for a new residence. V finances her new residence at a time when the mortgage interest rate has risen by 2 percent. V then, in an action for damages, attempts to recover additional financing costs that she incurs in financing the purchase of a new residence after the resale of the property originally contracted for by P. Will she be successful?

Explanation

The vendor's damages must be reasonably foreseeable. *See Hadley v. Baxendale*, 156 Eng. Rep. 145 (Ct. Ex. 1854). Foreseeability, however, is a question of fact, so there is no clear answer here. For a case denying V recovery, *see Gryb v. Benson*, 406 N.E.2d 124 (Ill. App. 1980) (vendor's additional finance costs are not recoverable). However, vendors have, as defendants, been made responsible for the costs of increasing mortgage interest rates, so shouldn't they have the same as a plaintiff? *See* Example 13, *supra*.

LIQUIDATED DAMAGES

Liquidated damages clauses in a contract of sale are commonplace; they save vendors and purchasers the time and expense of proving damages, and courts the trouble of supervising such proof. In real property transactions, their validity is often questioned when a purchaser seeks to recover a down payment even though the contract provides that the vendor "may retain the deposit as liquidated damages." Deposits and down payments will take effect as liquidated damages only with proof the parties intend them to be that. In cases litigated in rising markets, the vendor's retaining it often overcompensates him: He can keep the deposit and still resell at a higher price, so the vendor's real damages are zero. Nonetheless, a clause specifying, in good faith and in advance, an amount that is (1) intended as damages (and not a penalty), (2) then difficult or impossible to anticipate, and (3) a reasonable estimate of whatever damages the parties might anticipate at the time of the negotiation, will be upheld. *See Kelly v. Marx*, 694 N.E.2d 869 (Mass. App. 1998), 705 N.E.2d 1114, 1117 (Mass. 1999), noted at 28 Real Est. L.J. 232 (2000). Let's enforce the contract as written, say many courts.

Courts refusing to enforce these clauses, while viewing them as a substitute for compensatory damages, are sometimes willing to take a second look at the reasonableness of the estimate, based on evidence gathered at the time of the breach, often involving the resale price. *See Grossinger Motorcorp, Inc. v. Am. Natl. Bk. & Tr.*, 607 N.E.2d 1337, 1347 (Ill. App. 1992). The black letter does not usually find such evidence admissible, but many courts find it hard to resist. *Kelly, supra*, at 694 N.E.2d at 873-874 (reporting that 20 states permit a retrospective "second look" while 22 do not, looking only to the prospective reasonableness of the estimated damages at the time the contract is formed). Such a second look is likely to encourage litigation and ignores the facts that liquidated damages are not just an estimate of compensatory damages; they are also the price that vendors extract from purchasers against the risk of undercompensation, assuming that this risk not only involves the loss of a resale, but also attempts to estimate the price of taking the property off the market. Enforcement gives the parties their due and defers to their initial intention of avoiding later cost and litigation. Wash. Rev. Code §64.04.005 (providing a vendor's not incurring actual damages is no bar to enforcing a liquidated damages clause when deposit does not exceed 5 percent of the purchase price and providing mandatory language for the clause). Even when the contract gives the non-breaching party the option of choosing liquidated or compensatory damages, this option is no bar to courts enforcing a liquidated damages clause as written. *See Ravenstar, LLC v. One Ski Hill Place, LLC*, 401 P.3d 552 (Colo. 2017). Likewise, courts do not pay heed to the seriousness of the breach when enforcing these clauses. Perhaps this is because courts tend to think of these clauses as a partial settlement of an otherwise litigated dispute. *See XCO Int'l, Inc. v. Pac. Sci. Co.*, 369 F.3d 998 (7th Cir. 2004).

RESCISSION

Rescission is the unmaking of a contract. It is a cause of action for the cancellation of a contract of sale by one of the parties to it. In many jurisdictions, it is unclear whether this is a legal or an equitable remedy. The grounds for cancellation are mutual consent to the cancellation, execution of the contract under a mutual mistake of material fact, fraud, undue influence, duress, a failure of consideration, illegality, or, occasionally, some statutory ground (such as under a consumer protection statute that permits a cooling-off period during which a party can cancel the contract). *See Hilton Hotels Corp. v. Piper Co.*, 519 A.2d 368, 372 (N.J. Super. 1986) (finding it a remedy granted when the contract was invalid at its formation); *Moonves v. Hill*, 360 A.2d 59, 60-61 (Vt. 1976) (involving mutual mistake of fact about the acreage sold in gross).

One ground for rescission—a failure of consideration—need not apply to both parties as, for example, when a substantial portion of the property is destroyed. The destruction is only of the vendor's consideration. The purchaser's consideration is the price, and that's still extant. So this ground only works for the vendor. For this remedy to work for the purchaser, then, a contract should provide that destruction permits rescission, when the risk of loss would otherwise fall on the purchaser. Likewise, in some jurisdictions, courts restrict purchasers to rescission when there is a substantial deficiency in acreage.

Early election between rescission and damages is not, under modern rules of pleading, necessary, but the facts required to prove damages are likely to be antithetical to those that show rescission. Filing for damages affirms the contract and is itself an election not to pursue rescission. To avoid this effect, the trial must proceed in stages—rescission first, and then, if no rescission is found, a trial on the damage cause of action follows. This emphasizes also that rescission is effective when decreed by the court, not when the facts on which it might be based occurred.

A precondition to bringing an action for rescission is an offer to restore the opposite party to the condition in which he was prior to the contract. Rescission and restitution go hand in hand. This follows (1) from the maxim that he who seeks equity must do equity and also (2) from the sequence of complaints and petitions just mentioned available to undo a transaction. So an action for restitution, or foreclosure of a vendor's or vendee's lien, should be followed by a decree or judgment for rescission.

The maxim about seeking and doing equity means the purchaser's giving any rents from the premises back to the vendor. The rents actually received, not just the fair rental value of the property, must be tendered. *See*

Metcalfe v. Talarski, 567 A.2d 1148, 1151-1152 (Conn. 1989). For the vendor as plaintiff, this means giving back the portion of the purchase price already paid. A contract provision allowing retention of a deposit is all the more important in this regard because it indicates that the parties just intended to walk away from the agreement and forgo its further performance—in effect a mutual rescission. Otherwise, from the vendor's perspective, good pleading can make it clear that the offer to tender back is effective when the decree or judgment is rendered, not when the cause of action is brought. When the parties "cannot be returned to the ground on which they stood," rescission is refused. *Hilton Hotels*, *supra*, 519 A.2d at 372-373.

Rescission based on a contractual right is assignable, but if it is based on fraud, it is often not. A cause of action for rescission is consistent with one based on the torts of fraud or misrepresentation, so no election between the two is necessary. Thus, when the value of the tort action is higher than that involving damages or recovery of property in specific performance, rescission becomes the preferred remedy. As a matter of prudence, then, rescission should be by written agreement, if only expressly to preclude one party or another from later bringing a suit in tort. *See Evergreen Land Co. v. Gatti*, 554 S.W.2d 862 (Ky. App. 1977).

A unilateral rescission is often possible, but seldom prudent: There should be a property drafted agreement to rescind, recordable where contracts are recordable.

Examples

Example 21

A vendor, V, contracts to sell Blackacre to P on Monday morning, neither party knowing that the property was totally consumed by a fire the previous Sunday evening.

Explanation

Since both V and P assumed that Blackacre was in existence when the contract was formed, their mistake was a mutual one. Both parties hold beliefs that are not in accord with existing facts. Thus, when (say) the house destroyed on the property was most of the property's value, the mistake was material and both V and P will be relieved of all their contractual rights and obligations.

Example 22

Same facts as in Example 21, but there has been no fire. The contract was for a price of $100,00, but in fact it was worth $80.000. May either V or P rescind their contract?

Explanation

No. This mistake goes only to the value of Blackacre, not to its existence. It does not justify rescission.

Example 23

A vendor, V, sues to rescind a contract of sale because neither he nor the purchaser, P, knew whether the property contained valuable minerals. V asks for a jury trial. Will he get it?

Explanation

No. If the suit is to prevent the unjust enrichment of the defendant, P, the action looks equitable in nature. In equity the judge sits as the trier of fact. No jury trial. A complaint asking for a jury trial would make the remedy sought a legal one; the complaint asking for the judge to try the case makes the remedy sought an equitable one. The distinction between law and equity in mistake cases still matters here—but will matter in few other cases.

This Example blurs the existence/value distinction used to solve Examples 21 and 22. If both V and P might know that valuable minerals have been discovered on neighboring properties, their betting on their being found—or not—on Blackacre is insufficient reason to rescind their contract. When both are conscious of their own ignorance in the matter, their mistake cannot be said to be mutual. To justify rescission by either party, theirs must be a "mistake of fact," not one of ignorance. P cannot get rescission if Blackacre is found to have no minerals, and V cannot rescind if minerals are later discovered there. This Example tracks the leading case of *Sherwood v. Walker*, 33 N.W. 919 (Mich. 1887) (the "pregnant cow" case).

Example 24

Purchaser sues to rescind his purchase contract but has had possession during the executory period and wants payment for improvements made to the property during his possession. Will the issue of the value of the improvements reach a jury?

Explanation

Yes, because this compensation (really a part of the duty of restoration and restitution) makes the action look like an action for damages—a legal cause of action—for which a jury is available.

Example 25

Vendor sues to rescind his purchase contract of Blackacre for mutual mistake, but while in possession P has timbered a portion of its land. May V still have rescission of the contract?

Explanation

Yes. The traditional rule is that the tender back must put the parties in *status quo ante*, as they were at contract formation "on the ground on which they stood." Another way of saying this is that rescission and tender back must be total. Here that is not possible. Blackacre cannot be tendered back to P *in specie*—specific restitution is impossible. However, when Blackacre is tendered back and an amount of money representing the value of the timber harvested on Blackacre is also given to P, "value rescission" with restitution is possible—and that's what should be done here.

Example 26

V executes a brief but enforceable contract with P for Blackacre for $100,000. P gives V a $10,000 deposit and takes possession of Blackacre. P then refuses to go through with the contract. In a falling market, P sues V for rescission. What result?

Explanation

Subject to proof of facts about the purpose of the deposit, P's refusal to perform is an abandonment of the contract, and if V acquiesces, the rescission is completed by mutual consent. The duty to restore possession applies when P obtains a decree against V. In a falling market, V cannot be restored to his *status quo ante* without retention of some of the deposit—how much depends on the fair market value on the day of the breach. And P must give V the fair rental value of the property for the time P was in possession. In this case, where one party is in breach, the duty to restore might be applied to put the parties as they were on the day of the plaintiff's breach.

Example 27

V executes a brief but enforceable contract of sale for Whiteacre to P for a purchase price of $100,000. P goes into possession and, at the same time, makes a deposit of $10,000. P then makes installment payments totaling $50,000 when V says that he will not close the transaction because a better offer has come along at a higher price—$120,000. What is the measure of P's recovery if she sues in rescission?

Explanation

Whatever P has paid thus far—$50,000—plus the costs of carrying the property for the time during which he was in possession. Carrying costs might include repair-maintenance costs, insurance premiums, taxes, and the capital value of any improvements made to the property. Carrying costs are recoverable in part because P will only have to surrender the property on the date of the decree. In some jurisdictions, P is also entitled to $20,000 for benefit of the bargain damages—damages for the lost opportunity to sell Whiteacre herself at the increased fair market value, shown in part by the higher offer—certainly some evidence of the fair market value of the property on the day of the breach. But an offer is not the best evidence, and more will have to be proffered.

The presence of this last element of damages indicates that it is going to be difficult to restore the parties to their *status quo ante*. However, you could think of these damages instead as flowing from a tort, a business tort of interference with a prospective advantage. This requires delicate pleading because it is a tort bottomed on a contractual duty.

VENDOR'S AND VENDEE'S LIENS

Upon the execution of an unconditional contract of sale, or at the time during the executory period when all conditions have been satisfied, there arise two types of equitable liens for the benefit of the vendor and the vendee respectively. They are implied; provision for them need not be express. They are inchoate; they need to be exercised or perfected to attach to the property. They are perfected through an action to foreclose them. Such an action is everywhere regarded as an equitable one.

Vendee's Lien

This is an equitable lien for the benefit of the purchaser for any payments made under the contract. It attaches to the real property subject to the contract. For the purchaser, it arises during the executory period when the vendor refuses, without excuse, to close the contract. It is generally assignable, insurable, and survives the titleholder's bankruptcy because it attaches to the property and does not create a personal liability in the party subject to it. (Even when the trustee in bankruptcy rejects the contract of sale, the lien survives as one attaching to the bankrupt's property. Bankr. Code §365(j).) The lien must be exercised or perfected before the vendor conveys the title to a bona fide purchaser, a person who pays value and accepts the title in good faith, without actual or constructive notice of the lien, or without any fraud, collusion, or participation in the foregoing transaction. Such a purchaser cuts off the lien.

Examples

Example 28

If the contract of sale provides that the purchaser will pay insurance premiums and taxes during the executory period, may he foreclose a lien for these carrying charges?

Explanation

Yes. The contract controls the scope of the lien. Its subject can be either payments of money or other services if the contract obligates the purchaser to make these payments or render services benefiting the property. The purchaser does not even have to be in possession when making the payments in this scenario. She needs no special equities to assert the lien. The only precondition to recovering is the contract status of the claim. It allows the purchaser to add up all expenditures made under the contract—the deposit or down payment, payments applied to the purchase price, as well as expenditures for insurance and taxes required by the contract. Traditionally no recovery for title search, abstracting, and insurance expenses is permitted; such expenses look beyond the closing to protecting the purchaser once in possession. (In some jurisdictions, however, these expenses will be recoverable because standard form contracts expressly provide for their recovery.)

Example 29

If the purchaser makes payments, takes possession, and makes improvements to the property, may the cost of the improvements be recovered in the foreclosure of the lien?

Explanation

Only if the contract is the basis for the purchaser's possession and, in some other cases, only if the improvements themselves are called for in the contract. The same rules apply to any repairs made to the property.

Example 30

Must the contract satisfy the Statute of Frauds to be the basis of this lien?

Explanation

No. The lien is equitable, so legal requirements for the contract are not a precondition to its assertion. Likewise, the purchaser does not have to show that his legal remedies for damages are inadequate; the rationale is that a purchaser performs the contract *pro tanto* with each payment and is asserting, through the lien, an equitable interest *pro tanto* in the vendor's title. If the vendor is a concurrent holder of the title, the lien is assertable only against the vendor's interest in it. This lien rests on a theory of proportionate equitable conversion. Its assertion is inconsistent with rescission.

Example 31

Is the assertion of the lien also inconsistent with a suit for damages for substantial or benefit of the bargain damages?

Explanation

No. Foreclosing the lien does not provide this type of damages. No incidental, consequential, or benefit of the bargain damages is recoverable. Reimbursement for money spent made because of the contract is the object of the foreclosure.

Example 32

P has a vendee's lien against V's title to Blackacre but does not foreclose it until V conveys the title to P1, a bona fide purchaser who has no notice of the lien. Can P now foreclose the lien against P1's title?

Explanation

No. P1 is a bona fide purchaser and cuts off the lien. However, if the proceeds of V's sale can be identified, the lien attaches to those proceeds.

Example 33

What if a vendor takes out a mortgage loan in exchange for a note and mortgage in favor of the Greenville Savings and Trust Bank while the vendee has an unperfected vendee's lien? Which of these liens — the mortgage lien of the bank or that of the vendee — has priority?

Explanation

The purchaser prevails, unless the bank is a bona fide purchaser. If the bank is a bona fide purchaser, its lien has priority.

Example 34

What if in the previous problem, the bank took the mortgage lien to secure a prior, unsecured debt. Would that change your answer?

Explanation

Yes. In most real property matters, an antecedent debt is not "value" for purposes of defining a bona fide purchaser: Such a purchaser is one who takes in good faith and gives value for his interest.

Vendor's Lien

This lien secures all or any portion of the purchase price for the benefit of the vendor. It can be enforced through foreclosure. In theory it arises with the execution of the contract of sale, but since the vendor still has title, in the typical purchase and sale it is meaningless until the closing. It typically gains value at the closing or conveyance by the vendor. Nonetheless, its arising before the closing has importance when it attaches to the purchaser's equitable interest under a long-term installment land sale contract, or in jurisdictions where contracts of sale are recordable and the vendor might bring foreclosure to eliminate the contract interest of the purchaser as a cloud on the vendor's title. To arise before the closing, it has to attach to a contract interest of the vendee capable of performance — in other words, a contract with all contingencies and conditions satisfied — and subject to the doctrine of equitable conversion. A majority of jurisdictions recognize a vendor's liens.

It is usually an implied lien, although it has been the subject of a statute in some jurisdictions (such as Texas). When the vendor sells both real and personal property using one contract for both types of property that names a price that does not attribute a portion of the purchase to the realty, a court may refuse to foreclose it because of the difficulties of attribution and a fear of rewriting the contract's price term. Likewise, when the vendor has taken a mortgage lien from the purchaser, the equitable lien is generally held to have been waived by the vendor's acceptance of the express lien in the mortgage documents. Refusing to imply the lien is also justified when the vendor, who at a closing has had the opportunity to insist on a mortgage lien, does not do so and takes only a note instead; its waiver might here be inferred. In this situation, if the vendor wants the protection of a lien, he can ask for it. There is no reason to distinguish between such an inattentive vendor and the purchaser's other, unsecured creditors, and if the vendor wants to sue on the note and, if successful, levy on the property, he can in this manner later attach a lien to it.

Like a vendee's lien, a vendor's lien is assignable, insurable, and survives the vendee's bankruptcy. A bona fide purchaser cuts it off.

Remember that both vendor's and vendee's liens are creatures of equity and thus are subject to discretion in their imposition. They are no substitute for good, preventive legal planning and drafting. They exist to provide remedies when no other remedies are available.

Examples

Example 35

V executes a valid contract of sale for Blackacre with P for a purchase price of $100,000. P gives V a $10,000 deposit and a note for $10,000 as a down payment, both credited in the contract toward the purchase price. The contract also provides that P will secure a mortgage loan for $80,000 from the Greenville Savings Bank. P informs V that the bank has agreed to make the loan secured by a note and mortgage. Both the title and the loan transaction are closed. P defaults on both V's note and the Greenville loan. V brings a foreclosure action to enforce a vendor's lien, and the bank brings a similar action to enforce the mortgage lien. These actions are joined. Which lien has priority?

Explanation

A close case. Some authority holds that the mortgagee bank has priority. V knew of the mortgage lien and his not insisting on priority over it at the closing might be construed as a waiver of priority. More generally, his acceptance of only the note and thus an unsecured creditor's status after the closing might mean waiver of the right to assert a vendor's lien, no matter what its priority. On the other hand, the existence of the note is not inconsistent with the existence of a vendor's lien. The latter merely adds a remedy for enforcing the former. V might have been counting on the lien all the more when he accepted the note alone. In addition, the bank knows of V's existence and, in a jurisdiction recognizing a vendor's lien, should check to see that the down payment is paid in full before funding the rest of the purchase price and closing the loan transaction; not checking might deny it bona fide purchaser status as to V. V's lien here functions as would an equitable mortgage.

As a matter of prudence, liens on title should in this situation be in writing; the danger otherwise is that vendors will conceal from unsuspecting purchasers their right to such a lien. Undocumented interests in real property are not favored.

LIS PENDENS

At common law, the filing of a lawsuit was constructive notice of its pendency. Today, in all states, anyone filing a cause of action and wanting that action, while pending, to have the benefit of such constructive notice must file a separate notice as required by statute. This is a *lis pendens*, a notice that an action is currently pending that may affect the title to specifically described real property. A person filing a *lis pendens* warns everyone that the specified property is the subject matter of litigation and that any interests acquired or filed during the pendency of the action are subject to its outcome and final judgment. A *lis pendens* is a prejudgment remedy. The person filing this notice does not have to show that he or she will prevail in the underlying lawsuit, only that he has a good faith belief that the facts underlying the suit will sustain the claim. This notice is indexed in the public records maintained by the clerk of the court or the recorder of deeds in the county in which the action is pending. This makes the title to the affected property unmarketable; by definition, a *lis pendens* is intended to create a cloud on the title. Some statutes limit the effectiveness of the notice to a definite period of time—say, three years. The more common rule is that a *lis pendens*' effectiveness ends with the final judgment—or settlement—of the underlying suit.

The statute requiring this notice also defines the causes of action for which a notice may be filed. Typically those filing any "action affecting the title to real property" are entitled to a *lis pendens*. Sometimes the scope of the statute encompasses any "action affecting the title *or possession* of real property." (Inclusion of the two extra words would permit persons filing an ejectment action to also file a *lis pendens*.) Occasionally the words "directly or indirectly" are added at the end. (These words would extend the reach of the statute to lawsuits for damages against a corporation or partnership whose primary assets are real property.)

These definitions are exclusive—actions not included do not have the benefit of a *lis pendens*—and improperly filed *lis pendens* notices give rise to an action for slander of title. Plaintiffs asserting adverse possession qualify for *lis pendens*. So do plaintiffs claiming a less-than-fee interest in a title—such as an easement, or the benefit of a real covenant. *Lis pendens* notices are intended to protect a court's remedial powers by making the property available to satisfy its judgment or decree and to prevent defendants from avoiding payment of a judgment by conveying, during the pendency of the action, to any potential good faith purchasers. *See* 5303 *Realty Corp. v. O & Y Equity Corp.*, 476 N.E.2d 276 (N.Y. 1984).

Owners suing to set aside a fraudulent transfer of real property may obtain a *lis pendens*. Purchasers suing for specific performance of a contract are entitled to file a *lis pendens*. So are secured mortgage lenders suing to foreclose a mortgage or deed of trust. Unsecured lenders—say, of money lent to purchase real property—have no such entitlement. Neither do purchasers filing for contract damages, although after realty is attached to satisfy a damages judgment, a *lis pendens* is then available. A landlord suing for back rent is suing for damages and is not entitled to a *lis pendens*. Purchasers suing to rescind a contract are not entitled to a *lis pendens*: The court is not, in this action, asked to convey title to the plaintiff, and the tender back required of those seeking rescission may be satisfied with restitutionary payments of money. Neither are plaintiffs suing in nuisance entitled to a *lis pendens*, because that action involves the unreasonable use of property and is not a title matter. When the applicable statute protects possession of real property, however, courts split on whether a *lis pendens* is available. A rough test for the reach of a *lis pendens* statute is whether the interest at issue is recordable in the land records or whether a title insurance policy could be obtained for a transaction.

To the extent that there are due process problems with *lis pendens* statutes, legislatures generally handle them with expungement and bonding procedures. The case law on expungement procedures is extensive. The reason may be that a motion to expunge a *lis pendens* from the land records precedes the discovery process in the underlying lawsuit and so may be used to reveal a weakness in a plaintiff's case in that lawsuit.

SLANDER OF TITLE

One response to the unjustified filing of a *lis pendens* might be a suit to expunge the *lis pendens* notice from the records and a claim for slander of title. The latter claim involves the intentional disparagement of a person's title, and is a tort—aka the tort of injurious falsehood. It is the uttering, making, or publication of an unjustified and false statement about the title, depriving the titleholder of a beneficial relationship with another, the benefit of which would otherwise have accrued. *Wharton v. Tri-State Drilling & Boring*, 824 A.2d 531, 536-537 (Vt. 2003). Its elements must usually be shown by a preponderance of the evidence. An escrow agent does not "publish" a statement about title when carrying out escrow instructions, even when the statement is false. However, a broker who records a contract of sale has published a disparaging statement because he has no right to do so, as has a title abstractor who files a mechanic's lien for title work.

In many jurisdictions, actual malice is an essential element of this tort. Its presence is a question of fact. *See Arnold Road Realty Assocs. v. The Tioge Fire Dist.*, 873 A.2d 119 (R.I. 2005); *Saddlewood Downs, L.L.C. v. Holland Corp.*, 99 P.3d 640, 649 (Kan. App. 2004); Ala. Code §6-5-211. The statement must have been made with the intent to injure the titleholder. *See Colquhoun v. Webber*, 684 A.2d 405, 409 (Me. 1996). In other jurisdictions, malice may be implied from the recordings previously mentioned. In fact, the recording of a false or nonexistent interest is "published," and it is difficult thereafter for the person doing the recording to deny that the publication was intentional.

Resulting damages must be financial (as opposed to reputational) and might include impairment of one's property values or expenses incurred in counteracting the statement, such as litigation costs in a quiet title or declaratory judgment action. Two further examples are an abstractor's false title report causing denial of a mortgage loan application and a nonexistent interest reported by a title insurer causing a vendor to lose a sale.

Often the transaction interfered with involves a contract of sale, but the measure of damages that a plaintiff would obtain in a contract action is only part of what might be obtained in a slander of title action. Consequential and foreseeable damages are available as well. So are expenses unforeseen before the tort was committed. *See Rite Aid Corp. v. Lake Shore Investors*, 471 A.2d 735, 44 A.L.R.4th 1063 (Md. 1984). In some cases, damages for mental suffering and punitive damages may also be available. Restatement (Second) of Torts, §774A (1979).

Examples

Example 36

If the false document is recorded, does the statute of limitations run from the date of recordation, or is the action available continuously thereafter, running from the date of recordation so long as the document remains on the public records?

Explanation

The cases are split on this issue. *Compare Hosey v. Central Bank of Birmingham*, 528 So. 2d 843 (Ala. 1988) (holding that the statute runs from the date of filing, but not continuously), *with Green v. Chamberlain*, 60 So. 2d 120 (La. App. 1952) (holding the action a continuous one so long as the document is of record). Reframing the issue slightly may give way to better analysis of it. This is a tort: The action lasts so long as the defendant falsely claims or disparages the title. The time during which the document is on the record is one way of measuring its duration, absent further proof, but as of the time the defendant does not claim an interest in the title, the action is tolled and the statute runs from the date of the last claim.

Example 37

A defendant's actions cause a third party to breach a contract of sale. The breach is clearly unjustified under the contract. As a result, a plaintiff has a cause of action for breach of contract against the third party, as well as a slander of title action against the defendant. Can the plaintiff sue the third party in contract, and then the defendant for slander of title?

Explanation

Yes. The defendant is liable for the damages, even though the third party is also liable. However, the plaintiff may not actually recover the same damages twice. If the third party is successfully sued for breach of contract and in fact pays contract damages, the plaintiff may not recover them from the defendant as well; in this situation, the defendant should not pay damages over and above the contract measure already recovered. Restatement (Second) of Torts §774A(2) (1979).

CHAPTER 7

Deeds

DEEDS AND CONVEYANCES

The end of the executory period is known as the closing or the settlement. At the closing the vendor will deliver a deed to the property bought and sold to the purchaser. The delivery of a deed is known as a conveyance. The ceremonial aspects of a modern conveyance are an outgrowth of the enfeoffment with livery of *seisin*—the ceremonial handing of a twig or bit of soil from vendor to purchaser—providing evidence of the transaction and delivering the deed as well. Today the delivery of a deed replaces the ceremony of livery of *seisin*. In the nineteenth century in some jurisdictions, the person handling the closing and the delivery of a deed was a layman. Today, particularly in complex commercial transactions, he or she is more likely to be an attorney. A deed creates additional rights and obligations when included in them are specified "covenants" or promises. Deeds are "successor contracts": They to some extent displace and discharge the contract of sale that called for the closing.

When a transaction is closed, the crucial document for the purchaser is the deed to the property. A deed is a translation of the Latin word *factum*, meaning a thing that is done—in the instance of a deed, that it is effective on delivery. Thus a deed is a writing, with (1) an identifiable grantor and grantee, (2) words operating to effect a transfer of legal title to interests in real property not less than a fee simple, (3) identification of the property being conveyed, and (4) the grantor's signature. Its recitations and component parts should therefore become familiar to you. Familiarity is in fact essential.[1] Why? Because a writing in the form of a deed is presumed to be a deed.

THE COMPONENTS OF A DEED

A deed contains four parts: (1) the premises, which includes the granting clause; (2) the habendum, including the warranties; (3) the execution, including the attestation clause; and (4) the acknowledgment. The first and third parts of the deed are necessary for the document to be a legally effective conveyance between the parties to it. You should be able to break down each deed into those four parts and, in the course of doing that, examine each component.

The deed's *premises* include its date, the names of the grantor and grantee, the operative words of conveyance, and a legal description of the property, together with all the appurtenant rights of the grantor in the identified property. It may also include as *recitals*,[2] a reference to a past conveyance of the same property—for example, "being the same property conveyed to the grantor . . ."—and any exception to the property granted, for example, a garage on the boundary of neighboring property. In short, the *premises* is anything appearing before the *habendum*. Deeds can be either short or long form deeds. Short form deeds are statutory creatures, and as such they contain words of art that the statute authorizing them defines—that is, the statute provides in part that the word "grant" used in the short form means that certain warranties to title are given by the vendor, whether or not the deed actually contains such warranties. Thus short form deeds (1) omit the habendum to the extent that it is a repetition of the granting clause and

1. In preparation for a closing, an attorney is likely to prepare a deed to present to the purchaser. Its preparation is undertaken, however, for the attorney's client, (say) the vendor. May an attorney for the vendor be liable to the purchaser when one of its provisions is defective? *See Collins v. Binkley*, 750 S.W.2d 737 (Tenn. 1988), held yes. There a defective acknowledgment failed to contain words necessary to make the deed recordable. The deed was in fact recorded, but the vendor then filed for bankruptcy and there was able to void the deed. The purchaser then sued the attorney and the attorney was held liable for the purchaser's damages, notwithstanding the lack of an attorney-client relationship: The purchaser's recording the deed was foreseeable; the attorney has a professional responsibility to make it recordable; and the lack of privity between the vendor's attorney and purchaser was no bar to the purchaser's suit. *Collins* and other cases are discussed in *Robinson v. Omer*, 952 S.W.2d 423, 427-428 (Tenn. 1997).

2. A recital is a statement in a deed not necessary for its legal effectiveness. It contains information about the purpose of the deed, the background of the grantor and grantee, etc. Many facts often included in a deed actually are recitals, such as the date, the marital status of the parties, their addresses, and the consideration given for the deed. For example, the consideration is only necessary to the deed's effectiveness when covenants including a promise by the grantee, perhaps pertaining to the use of the property, are included.

(2) incorporate many of its warranties into the granting verbs. 3 American Law of Property §12.47 (A. J. Casner ed. 1952).

Unaided by statute and left to themselves, conveyancers are prolix and have a tendency to copycat forms. They use many words when one would do, particularly if the purchaser is their client and they want to make sure that he gets the full fee simple absolute. So, although the word "grant" may suffice as a legal matter, the conveyancer may say that "the grantor . . . *gives, enfeoffs, grants, bargains and sells,* as well as *leases and releases, surrenders, remises, yields up, alienates, confirms, assigns, covenants to stand seised of, quitclaims,* and *conveys* . . . to the grantee."

Only one of these words—*conveys*—actually refers to a transfer of title by use of a deed. Most of the others refer to other, older forms of conveyancing.

Gives? That verb refers to the operative word in a charter of enfeoffment.

Enfeoffs? This is the handing over of the fee simple absolute in the ceremony known as livery of *seisin*, in which the transferor picks up the proverbial twig, clod of earth, or peppercorn and hands it to the transferee.

Grants? If an interest was incapable of livery, as with an interest that is nonpossessory (e.g., an easement), then it was granted the transferee.

Bargains and sells? This is what the gentry in the privacy and remoteness of their London townhouses did to transfer real property, without going on the land, and without standing before the witnesses to the livery. These verbs, in this sequence, refer to the making of a contract of sale or transfer that a court of equity will enforce and execute under the Statute of Uses.

Leases and releases? A popular form of transfer just after the Statute of Uses. The transferor leases a term for years to the transferee and thereafter releases his reversion to the same person. After the release, the transferor has handed over her simple absolute in two steps instead of one. Its virtue lay in that it also did not require livery because it was recognized in equity without that ceremony.

Surrenders? The giving up of a less-than-fee interest—usually for life or for years—so that it merges into the following future interest, either a remainder or a reversion. A surrender was usually by deed but could also be by operation of law.

Remise? This includes both a surrender and a release of rights in the real property.

Yields up? In the feudal system, one yielded up service to the lord of the manor. Examples were knight service and money tributes; or a duty to work the lord's fields, on the roadways of the parish, or on the parish church. The words came to refer to the transfer of the obligations of the transferor. Often in leases the lessee "yields and pays" the reserved rent.

Alienates? A recognition of the transferor's giving up her power to dispose or deal with the real property. It "disposes" of the transferor's title to one heretofore "alien" to it.

Confirms? It recognizes that if the transferor has created voidable rights by the transfer, such creations are made absolute by the use of this word.

Assigns? The use of this word in a deed references the assignment of any causes of action necessary to protect the property of the transferee.

Covenants to stand seised? This means "promises to defend the *seisin* of the transferee." It is another form of transfer possible after the Statute of Uses and is used often in intrafamilial transactions in which the consideration was love and affection, rather than money.

Quitclaims? An American invention, the quitclaim conveyance grew out of the release and came to mean that the transfer is an "as is" transaction in which the transferor says in effect, "I'm not sure what I have, but whatever it is, I give it to the transferee." The quitclaim is much used in the United States in the absence of attorneys, as well as by attorneys when less than a full fee simple absolute is conveyed or when title defects have arisen and are to be cured with the conveyance of the present deed.

A quitclaim deed should be used cautiously. Traditionally, it does not transfer after-acquired property—that is, when its grantor does not own the property the deed purports to transfer at the time of its execution but later acquires it, a quitclaim does not later transfer it to the grantee. Further, in a minority of jurisdictions, its grantee may not become a *bona fide* purchaser of the property it purports to transfer. Further still, and by definition, it contains no deed warranties; thus, the grantee's only remedies lie in tort—for example, for fraud or misrepresentation as to the property by its grantor. Because of these limitations, some title insurers will not issue a title insurance policy to its grantee.

Conveys? This is a reference to the use of a deed. The description of the land or property conveyed completes its premises. Some Eastern and Southeastern state statutes (and good drafting practice) require that the source of the title conveyed in the deed be indicated by book number and page on the public land records. This information is inserted just after the legal description, with the words "Being the same interest, title, and estate that John Doe conveyed to the" vendor at Book #________, page ________.

The other three parts of the deed use their own distinctive language as well. The second part, the *habendum* clause usually begins with the words, "To have and to hold, . . . together with (all improvements, later acquired improvements, mineral rights, and so forth)." It follows immediately after the premises. It defines and for estates less than freehold, limits the estate or interest granted in the premises. For a fee simple the words used are, "to have and to hold for the grantee, his heirs and assigns forever," or more simply, "to the grantee and his heirs." Most states have, either by statute or case law, abolished the requirement that the word "heirs," or more generally, words of inheritance, are necessary to create a fee simple in the grantee. Nonetheless, deed forms in most jurisdictions continue the use of the words "and his heirs." Why? Because the use of those traditional words makes the intent behind the deed clearer. The *habendum* may also include a *reddendum* reserving (e.g.) a right-of-way easement across the property and a *condition* specifying the consequences of a change in land use of the property. In addition to the reservation of an easement, a *reddendum* may be used when the parties agree that the grantor retains a ground rent, a reversion, or a profit *a prendre* that did not exist prior to execution of a deed. The habendum usually includes warranties or covenants of title. More on these later. It may also include an express release of any dower, curtesy, or marital rights of the grantor. Thus when the marital status of the grantor is recited in the granting clause, the well-informed person reading the deed should look for a release of any marital rights available in the jurisdiction. The *attestation* or *testimonium* clause typically begins with the language "In Witness Whereof I (we) have set our hands and seals." Signatures follow this phrase, often in old deeds with the initials "L.S." under the signature line. L.S. stands for *legilis sigli*—Latin for legal seal. A seal is unnecessary in most all states today, eliminated by statute. Except in a few states, deeds don't need to be witnessed. The attestation of any witnesses to the execution of the deed as may be required by state law must be done in the presence of the grantor when he executes it.

The fourth part of a deed is another recital; it is not necessary for the validity of the deed as between the parties. This is the vendor's acknowledgment of the deed as her free, voluntary act. Completion and notarization of this part is necessary for recording the document.

This description of the four parts of a deed is the work product of a well-informed drafter. However, the model form of a deed is not infrequently muddled. The premises may include words defining the estate or interest granted—likewise, the *reddendum* may appear in the premises, or the title covenant may refer to an estate not appearing in either the premises or the habendum.

Following is a deed. Identify each of its parts.

DEED

This *indenture,*[3] made on (month) (day), (year), between [name(s)], Grantor(s), of (name of city or town), (name of county), (name of state), and [name(s)], Grantee(s), of (name of city or town), (name of county), (name of state), witnesses that, in consideration of (here name the purchase price or other *consideration*[4]), paid on the *delivery*[5] of this deed, by which delivery receipt is acknowledged, *have granted*[6] (*etc.*[7]), and with this deed, do now grant (etc.) to the Grantee(s) and (his/her/their) heir(s), all the land described as[8] follows:

[Here insert legal description of the land granted.]

Shown on [insert reference to any plat or survey of the land, with any notations necessary to locate it in the public records], and *being [part of] the same land* conveyed [insert reference to that last previous deed to the land to the grantor(s)[9]], and *together with* all the improvements, ways, waters,

---

3. Indenture? It was a deed written in duplicate, one on the top half of sheepskin or parchment, the other on the bottom, with the Latin word "chirographum" written between the halves in capital letters. A chirograph is just a two-part document. Both parties signed it, and then the whole was indented, or cut in half along a ragged or serrated edge, the Latin capitals being cut in two. The parties then had a record of the transaction and could put the two together along the edge to prove the authenticity of each. Trusting, huh? Of course that was the point: trust, but keep the evidence. An indenture is the next best thing to the transaction itself. The other type of deed begins, "Know all persons by these presents that . . ." This is the signal for a deed poll, one "polled" or shaved along its edges, signed only by the vendor, and customarily used in all but a few states. It was regarded as merely evidence of a past transaction. Today there is little difference in form between the two types, except in the organization of the premises. With both these types of deeds, the underlying premise is that grantors don't guarantee the title they present, they only give whatever (and presumably it's the best) evidence they have of it.

4. Is a consideration necessary? Not in a conveyance, as opposed to a contract: A deed is evidence of a transfer of title and delivery of the possession of the property. However, after the Statute of Uses, deeds recited a consideration to make them valid in equity as well as in the law courts, and this as a matter of prudence, is still customary.

5. Delivery may refer to the assent of the grantor alone, so that it's prudent, depending on the law of a state, to add the words "and acceptance" at this point, to refer to the grantee's assent to the transfer as well. If the word means more—i.e., refers to actual, physical delivery—recall that the law presumes that a deed has been delivered if it is found in the possession of the grantee, that an unrecorded deed is presumed not delivered if found in the grantor's possession, and (in some states) a recorded deed is presumed to have been delivered.

6. In the last two words that you've read, notice the tense of the verb to grant, and contrast it with the present tense used five words on. This deed is both evidence of a past transaction and the transaction itself. In modern deeds, the evidence and the thing itself are inseparable.

7. Add here any of the variations of this verb, as needed by the law of the jurisdiction in which the deed is used and which is the location of the transferred property.

8. Instead of "described as" the phrase "known as" may be used when a number or other identifier has been assigned to the land, e.g., "known as Lot 3, Burke's Subdivision, Smithville, in the State of" (state).

9. This reference to past deeds is required by statute in some states and even where it is not, it's a good idea, because it might (say) provide an opportunity to further explain that the

watercourses, and minerals, with all the easements, covenants, rights, royalties, rents, and profits issuing therefrom, whether held in present or future interests by way of reversion, executory interest, or remainder, and being all of the estate, right, title, and property of the Grantor(s) in law and equity in and to the same and each and every part thereof.[10]

To have and to hold all the same previously mentioned, in the Grantor(s) and their heirs for their use and *benefit*[11] forever.

The Grantor(s) do(es) hereby specially (or generally) covenant and *warrant*[12] that (he/she/they) have *seisin and the right to convey*[13] the described property, that it is free of encumbrances, and that they *will further defend*[14] the quiet enjoyment and provide such further assurances as may be demanded by the Grantee(s).

In witness whereof the said parties have set their hands and seals[15] on the date and year written above.

____
Grantor(s)[16]

---

grantor Liz Jones is in fact the same person as the Elizabeth Jones named in the prior deed as the grantee. Some states also require that its preparer so indicate by signing it.

10. Is all this necessary? On the one hand, a grantor is presumed to transfer all that he has, and any ambiguities on this point are construed against the grantor and in favor of giving the grantee the larger estate or interest. On the other hand, recitals are presumptive proof the facts recited and a deed should be construed as a whole, so it is arguable that this language adds something.

11. The traditional word for benefit in this context is "behoof." It is part of the reference to a deed of bargain and sale. Such a deed is supported by consideration, is thus enforceable in equity, and operates through the Statute of Uses in the law courts as well. A deed for "the use—as the word is used in the Statute—and behoof" of the grantee and his heirs, is one intended to execute any equitable interest for the grantee's benefit.

12. Often all deed warranties are, as here or by custom, all given either specially or generally. It need not be this way—any one of the following five covenants may be as needed, given in a form that is either present and general, future and general, present and special, or future and special. *See infra*, next section.

13. Perhaps because of the syntax used here, the warranty of *seisin* and the right to convey are taken to be the same.

14. At this point a covenant of warranty might be incorporated. Some states regard this covenant as the equivalent of the covenant of quiet enjoyment. In other states, a "warranty deed" is a deed with a covenant of either special or general warranty, perhaps containing other covenants as well. A covenant of warranty might more readily be thought of as an indemnity agreement: the covenant of *seisin* protects against the risk that someone will have a valid claim, while the covenant of warranty additionally protects against the actual assertion of such a claim.

15. Any mark may be a seal if so proven. It is a question of fact whether the grantor used it. So L.S., "seal," or an "X" in a circle suffices in states still requiring it. When a document is not a deed because it lacks a seal, it still may be enforced as a contract.

16. This is a conveyance, so only the grantor(s) need to sign it, but the grantors want the grantee(s) to sign as well when there are (say) restrictive covenants in the deed, usually inserted in the *habendum*, or when the grantees make some contractual agreement with the grantors, in which instance the deed should also recite a consideration to make the contract binding.

The undersigned appeared before me and acknowledged that the execution of the foregoing document was his free and voluntary act.[17]

____

Notary Public.

CANONS OF CONSTRUCTION FOR DEEDS

Canons of Construction are guidelines and rules for interpreting documents of various types—some are general rules, some more specific. They can be used for ascertaining the meaning of a contract, insurance policy, or statute. The case law of a state may include some but not others, but all the canons detailed in this section are available in some states. All travel well across jurisdictional lines and when used, present questions of law for a court.

Here some of the most used canons have been adapted for interpreting deeds, as follows:

(1) A deed should be construed as a whole; its provisions should be construed as in harmony with one another; and every word and phrase should be given effect, to determine the intent of the parties to it.

Sometimes this is called the "four corners" canon, meaning that the deed is to be interpreted within the four corners of the paper on which it is printed. It assumes that the parties to a deed intended every word and phrase to have meaning and did not use superfluous words nor intend words to contradict themselves. The reference to the "intent of the parties" is not meant to authorize a free-wheeling investigation of the parties' intent: In a more limited sense, courts determine that intent as incorporated into and using only the plain words of the deed.

(2) The words of a deed are to be given their "plain meaning," or their "ordinary and natural meaning," unless this reading leads to absurd or mischievous results or thwarts the manifest intent of the parties.

17. What does an acknowledgment add to a deed? In an earlier time, when illiteracy was widespread and seals required, deeds were often proven in court, and the acknowledgment made the deed self-proving. It serves the same function today in that, if the deed is unambiguous on its face, the parol evidence rule bars its signatory from introducing evidence that he didn't sign it.

(3) Extrinsic evidence is inadmissible to alter, add to, or contradict the plain meaning of words of a deed, but is admissible to clarify an ambiguous word or phrase. When there is no plain meaning, ambiguities in the deed should be construed according to the intent of the parties to it, with extrinsic evidence of the circumstances surrounding its execution admissible. (a) The ambiguous words of a deed are construed against the grantor and in favor of the grantee, unless the grantee is the drafter: Then the words of a deed are construed against that drafter, or as appropriate, against the beneficiary of the word or phrase at issue. (b) Extrinsic evidence is admissible to show fraud, mistake, or duress in the execution of a deed.

Construing a deed against its grantor is often known as the canon *contra proferentem*. It assumes that the grantor is the deed's drafter and can look out for himself, while the grantee may not be as familiar with its terms as is the grantor. Its purpose is to encourage clear language and punish unclear language. It also provides a clear, efficient method for ascertaining a deed's meaning. Sometimes it is based on the idea that the grantor has easier access to information underlying the transaction giving rise to the deed. A clear exception to this canon is found in a deed of gift—as with any gift, it is the donor's or here the grantor's intent that controls.

Extrinsic evidence is in many courts used sparingly to give certain meaning to a deed. This is reflected in courts requiring "clear evidence" that its use will with "reasonable certainty" give meaning to the deed. Such evidence may be taken from trial testimony or documents related to the underlying transaction and the negotiations for the deed. It may also involve the physical condition of the land, the prior use of the land, the use of adjacent lands, customary practices in the neighborhood, and the subsequent conduct and activities of the parties. Its probative value may be reduced by the passage of time or its source, as when the evidence comes from third persons not a party to the deed. The less probative the evidence, the more weight a court is likely to give the four corners canon.

Fraud is typically subject to a high standard of proof—clear and convincing evidence is needed. A mistake of fact leading to the execution of the deed may lead to its reformation, duress to its rescission.

(5) The same word or phrase used repeatedly is presumed to have the same meaning, unless disregarding this presumption is necessary for consistency. (a) A word or phrase that has previously been construed judicially is to be understood as construed, unless a different meaning is clearly required. (b) A word or phrase is construed according to the grammatical effect of its arrangement, unless strict adherence to the rules of grammar defeat the intent

> of the parties. (c) An adjective or limiting word or phrase refers to the prior preceding antecedent, unless its plain meaning requires otherwise. (d) A reference to a document in a deed is incorporated by reference, meaning that it is given the same effect as if it had been set forth at length.

A deed may be incorporated into a later deed for the purpose of proving the grantor's source or chain of title. The words "Being the land previously owned or titled to . . ." make clear that the incorporation is intended to prove the grantor's title, but for no other purpose. A subdivision map or plat may be incorporated by reference to show the legal description, boundaries, or acreage of the land. Care should be taken not to incorporate a plat too broadly, however, because methods and technology used in surveying land have changed over time. A plat may most safely be used to incorporate a legal description than to incorporate a recital of boundaries or acreage.

Some canons of construction are more specific and have been black-lettered, as follows:

(6) When two clauses in a deed conflict and cannot be reconciled, the first should be given priority.

This canon is a black-letter version of the doctrine of repugnancy, followed in a few states—for example, California and Texas—and providing that a deed provision may be rejected when repugnant to the rest of the deed or when inadvertently inserted in it. Often but not always, this canon results in the later provision being severed altogether from the deed. It is also based on the assumption that the most important provisions of a deed appear up front, in the earliest of its provisions, so . . .

(7) The granting clause of a deed controls other clauses repugnant to it. When the granting clause and the habendum or recital in a deed are in conflict, the granting clause controls.

(8) Recitals in a deed are presumed correct, but subject to rebuttal by extrinsic evidence.

(9) Specific words control general words.

This canon is based on the assumption that specific words and phrases are more likely than not to have been thought out by the parties or negotiated by them. It has also given rise to the following, even more specific canon.

(10) More specifically still: When there is a conflict, handwritten words control typed words, and typed words control printed words; without a conflict, they are all given equal weight.

Some canons intended to protect the grantor's right of alienation, as follows:

(11) A deed is construed to grant all the grantor's estate, absent an expression of a contrary intent.
(12) Conversely, a deed should be construed to transfer the greatest estate possible to the grantee.
(13) A deed should be construed to render it legally effective and valid as a conveyance.

These three canons are based on that doctrine that a grantor is estopped, by the omnipresent and often implied covenant of general warranty, from asserting that he did not convey all that he owned. They also are a generalized version of the canon that construes the words of the deed in favor of and for the benefit of the grantee. *See generally* Robert G. Natelson, Modern Law of Deeds to Real Property 92-103 (Little, Brown & Co., 1992); 3 Am. L. Property 376-396, §§ 12.89-12.97 (A. James Casner, ed., 1952); Karl N. Llewellyn, Remarks on the Theory of Appellate Decision and the Rules or Canons about How Statutes are to be Construed, 3 Vand. L. Rev. 395, 401-406 (1950).

DEED WARRANTIES

Warranties are classified in two ways. First, they can be either special or general warranties. A special warranty is a statement by the vendor that the estate transferred is not otherwise than as stated in the granting clause and the premises because he himself has not encumbered that estate. A general warranty carries the same message except that the vendor warrants that neither he nor any predecessors in title have encumbered it.

Second, warranties can be either present or future warranties. Present warranties are the vendor's representations about the title at the time of the closing. There are three of them. They are the warranty

of seisin—a warranty that the vendor owns the estate conveyed; it is breached when the grantor promises a fee simple, but only holds (say) a fee simple determinable fee, a life estate, a future interest, an executory interest, right of entry, or a right of reverter. It also assures the grantee as to the extent of the land conveyed—so when the mineral estate has been severed from the surface, or when the acreage is not substantially as represented, the warranty is breached. Typically, this warranty is given with the words that the grantor is "seized of a indefeasible estate in fee simple—that is, a mere "cloud" on title does not breach this covenant. It is also not breached when the fee is encumbered by a lien or an easement—likewise, encumbrances do not breach this warranty. Identifying the indefeasibility of the necessary estate avoids the possibility that only common law *seisin* is required of the grantor.

of the right to convey—a warranty that the vendor has the right or authority to sell or convey the estate. It is breached if the grantor is a limited partner or a trustee without authority to convey a fee simple absolute. Like the warranty of *seisin*, it is not breached by an encumbrance or a cloud on title. In a minority of jurisdictions, it is held to be implied in a warranty of *seisin*—after all, a right of alienation is implied in every common law estate. It is not the same thing as a warranty of *seisin*: Trustees and persons holding a power of appointment have no *seisin*, but when given express authority, may have right to convey. Thus, persons with a power of appointment or trustees will not normally give a warranty of *seisin* when exercising their authority. A breach of the warranty of *seisin* will usually—but not always—trigger a breach of the warranty of the right to convey.

No particular words or combination of words—no words of art—is necessary to create either the warranty of *seisin* or the right to convey. For this reason, a warranty that the grantor has made no prior conveyances to third parties impairing the title or right to possession presented the grantee, that the grantor has the same right to convey as did his predecessors in interest, and that the grantor (if an agent) has the same right to convey as does his principal, has the same effect as either of these two present warranties.

against encumbrances—a warranty that no interest held by a third party limits or qualifies the estate being conveyed. *See Ochse v. Henry*, 33 A.3d 480, 486 (Md. Ct. Spec. App. 2011) (a good discussion of the covenant against encumbrances). Examples of encumbrances are easements, running covenants, profits, divesting conditions, concurrent tenancy rights, marital interests, profits, leases, mortgages, or other liens. The warranty against encumbrances may be special or general—warranting that neither the grantor nor in the case of a general warranty any prior grantor in the chain of title respectively, has created any legal interest that diminishes the value of the title or limits the use that may be made of the land. Hazardous substances, wetlands, and assessment not yet liens are all not encumbrances. In some jurisdictions, a building code violation may be an encumbrance. *See Holmes Dev. Co. v. Cook*, 48 P.3d 895 (Utah 2002) (containing a good discussion of warranties). But the violation of a zoning or land use ordinance is not an encumbrance. *See Hoffer v. Callister*, 47 P.3d 1261, 1264-1265 (Idaho 2002).

Examples

EXAMPLES

Example 1

In V's deed to P, V warrants that he owns a fee simple absolute when in fact he owns no interest at all. Is the covenant of *seisin* breached?

Explanation

Strangely, no. Why not? Because if V's deed is void, he has no estate to convey. Only valid common law estates can breach this warranty. Thus when P proves that V has no such estate, there is no breach. This is strange because it seemingly makes the warranty useless when most needed. The rationale for this perhaps lies in the remedy for this warranty. The usual remedy is in damages: the difference between the estate as represented and the estate actually conveyed, with the upper limit on damages being the consideration given for the deed. When the consideration is recited in the deed, it is not necessary to make the deed effective as a conveyance; it is a recital of a contractual aspect of the deed. Returning the consideration is thus not a matter of property law, it is a contractual matter.

Example 2

In V's deed to P, V has obtained a fee simple absolute title by adverse possession. Has V breached any of the three present warranties?

Explanation

Once the statute of limitations has run or tolled, there is no breach of either the warranty of *seisin* or of the right to convey: The grantor has obtained both *seisin* and the right to convey from the dis-seissed owner and can convey both to P. If V has not confirmed his title either by a judicial decree or assembled the proof that the statute has run out, the warranty against encumbrances may be violated. However, the right to sue is a cloud on title, not a legal interest in it—on that score the warranty against encumbrances is not breached. However, in many jurisdictions, the warranty is often regarded as a right of indemnity. Thus, the potential assertion by the dis-seissed owner of the right to eject V will certainly diminish the value of the title to the extent that P cannot sell it or obtain title insurance on it. If the statute of limitations was still running, the right of the third-party owner to sue V may be an encumbrance, giving P damages for the diminished value of his title or, in some jurisdictions, giving P the right to the cost of curing the title by bringing the action V has to assert it.

Example 3

In V's deed to P, given at the closing of the purchase and sale of V's property Blackacre, the premises' words of grant are "to P and his heirs."[18] In the

18. Recall that in attorney-speak the words and his heirs are words of limitation—that is, the heirs of the grantor take nothing because of their use. Instead, the words indicate that the grantee has an unlimited right to dispose of the estate granted to successor grantees, unless of course the grantee dies intestate.

deed's habendum, P is to "have and hold Blackacre during his natural life." What estate is P given in this deed?

Explanation

The premises and the habendum are here using mutually exclusive language. Because the traditional purpose of the habendum is to limit P's estate, one would argue that the habendum controls the premise's granting clause. However, most courts hold that the granting clause language controls, either as a rule of law or a canon of construction. Courts view this result as one required by the doctrine of repugnancy: That is, reading the deed as a whole, from first to last, the earlier version of the estate granted controls the later version. In the alternative, if the earlier estate were "to P," and the later version were "to P for life," the result might be different. The later version is an example of the canon of construction holding that specific language controls more general language. That is, when the granting clause does not indicate that the intent of the deed is not to create a fee simple, the more specific words in the habendum are to be preferred, even though in most states the words "to P" would create a fee simple.

Example 4

V owns Blackacre Farm in fee simple. By deed, V transfers title to the farm "to the City of Goodhope." The habendum to V's deed states that the City will retain title to the farm "so long as the farm is used as a public park" for City residents." What estate does the City receive?

Explanation

The City receives a fee simple determinable. The specific words of limitation in the habendum control the more general wording of the granting clause. The state in which transaction occurs most likely has the rule that no words of inheritance are used to create a fee simple; thus, "to the City" indicates a fee simple. However, the City not being a natural person, it cannot have heirs. Words of limitation are unnecessary and so here their omission does not bear on V's intent, allowing the words of limitation in the habendum to control. Restatement (Property), § 35 (1936).

Example 5

V transfers a deed to Blackacre "to P." V continues after the transfer to reside on Blackacre. The habendum clause states that P is "to have and to hold Blackacre for P and his heirs, successors and assigns" In the covenants and warranties of title, V states that V warrants that P has "full title to Blackacre." V then sues P to reform the deed to include what was mistakenly left out—the reservation of a life estate for P. Will P succeed?

Explanation

This is a question of what evidence P has of her intent to reserve such an estate. The evidentiary bar is a high one: She must prove by clear and convincing evidence among other things, P's continued residence, her paying no rent, paying the taxes on the property, and P's delaying the recordation of the deed P received up to the time of V's lawsuit. Showing these things, the court might find V reserved a life estate even though the deed was absolute on its face. V's case will be strengthened if V and P are members of the same family, and V is of an older generation than P. The language in the warranty of title might be taken by the court to be a recital, but the language in the habendum must be overridden by the evidence indicated previously.

Example 6

New York's Real Prop. L. §253.6 provides that a deed warranty that the vendor has not encumbered the conveyed property shall mean that she "has not made, done, committed, executed or suffered any acts . . . whereof . . . the premises may be . . . charged or encumbered." V conveys New York land to P using a short form deed stating that it contains all "statutory covenants." Later a previously undisclosed easement across the land is discovered in V's chain of title. The easement is an encumbrance under §253.6, but V had no actual or constructive knowledge of the easement before the closing. P argues that the deed and §253.6 should be construed broadly to include all encumbrances, even those of which a vendor has no actual knowledge. Is P's argument valid?

Explanation

The whole of the statute—and most of its verbs—say that P's argument will fail and that §253.6 is intended only to provide purchasers with a special warranty. The New York statute is discussed in Natelson, Modern Law of Deeds to Real Property 334-335 (1992) (an excellent treatment of deed warranties, *id.*, at 309-346). Why would a vendor give a general warranty? Acting as the vendor's attorney, you wouldn't routinely permit him to.

Example 7

V, a minor, owns Blackacre and conveys it to P by a deed containing the three present, special warranties. Which of them is breached by this conveyance?

Explanation

The warranty of V's right to convey. V, being a minor, lacks the legal capacity to alienate the land, and so has breached this warranty.

A title defect can be waived at the closing and excepted in the deed. A defect presented to the purchaser but not objected to may be deemed waived at the closing. If not waived, the defect covered by a present warranty is said to be broken, if at all, at the closing. It must be asserted during the period of limitations running from that date. In this sense a present warranty is personal to the purchaser; it doesn't run to future purchasers. Its limited life magnifies the importance of the closing and forces the purchaser to investigate the status of the title beforehand. As a rationale for present warranties, however, it ignores the effect of statutes of limitations, which start to run at the closing but continue a purchaser's ability to claim a breach of warranty on account of the defect for the limitations period thereafter.

Taken together, the three present warranties of title are the equivalent of the covenant of marketable title implied in every contract of purchase and sale for real property.

Future warranties are not merely warranties, but also covenants or promises to indemnify the purchaser if there is an assertion of an adverse claim, to cleanse the title, or to pay damages. They are three in number. They are a covenant . . .

of warranty. It promises to indemnify the grantee against the actual assertion of an adverse claim against the grantee's title. No particular words of art are necessary to create it. A promise to "defend" the title suffices; so does "shall and will warrant and defend," or "defend forever." It is the covenant most widespread in its use in this country. In contrast to the warranty of *seisin*, which protects the grantee against the risk that someone might assert a claim, the covenant of warranty only protects against the actual assertion of a claim. It is breached only when an actual claim is asserted. In many states, a grantee may be constructively evicted: as when, for example, the grantee yields possession to a claimant while invoking the covenant. *See* Annot., 172 A.L.R. 18 (1948) (on such constructive evictions).

This assertion is called an "eviction." The statute of limitations on this covenant begins to run from the time of the assertion or eviction—really from the time the grantee has notice of the defect. An eviction is defined as the assertion of a title defect invoking any of the three present covenants. This covenant is particularly useful when at closing, the parties are aware of a defect that is remote and unlikely to be asserted, so that the grantee does not want to hold the grantor liable as of the closing; instead, he wants an indemnity should the defect ever be asserted later.

Once the grantee is on notice, the grantee must notify the grantor and demand that the grantor defend the title. If the grantor refuses, the grantee may proceed to defend the title, and if unsuccessful, demand indemnification against both the loss of title and litigation expenses. If successful, the grantee may still recover litigation expenses.

The covenant of warranty may be either special or general, covenanting respectively against defects created by the grantor or by any of his predecessors in title. In some states, by statute, a covenant of warranty is implied by the use of the word "grant" as an operative word of conveyance. See *Chicago Title Ins. Co. v. Cochran Invs., Inc.*, 602 S.W.3d 895 (Tex. 2020) (asking whether when the implied covenant of special warranty incorporates present warranties, the scope of those warranties is narrowed).

The measure of damages under this covenant is difference money damages when the grantee loses a part of or all his possessory estate—that is, the measure is the same as with the warranty of *seisin*. When the asserted defect is a lien, the grantee may cure or remove it when the payment required is less than the grantee's purchase price—that is, the measure is the same as for a breach of the warranty against encumbrances. In both instances, reasonable attorney's fees are also recoverable.

Unlike present warranties, this future warranty runs with the land, meaning that future grantees are also indemnified, even though their deed does not contain a covenant of warranty.

of quiet enjoyment. This promises that the grantee will have possession of the property free of the threat of ouster or "eviction" by a person with a title superior to the grantor's. This gives the grantee the right to enter and remain on the property free of ouster by the grantor or any person claiming through her, bona fide purchasers excepted. Like the covenant of warranty, it runs with the land, is breached only upon the assertion of paramount title—the assertion of an adverse encumbrance will not do—but does not require the grantor to put the grantee into actual possession: The grantee must sue in trespass for that. It appears in leases as well as deeds. Only in some jurisdictions does it convey an after-acquired title, but where it does, courts sometimes assert that it is identical to the covenant of warranty.

for further assurances. This is the promise of the grantor to do such things as are necessary to put the grantee in possession of the title warranted at closing. Often this means executing documents to complete an imperfect conveyance, cure clouds on title owned by third parties, and transfer a grantor's after-acquired title or interests retained by the grantor. It does not require the grantor to do anything illegal or impractical. It may be enforced by an action for specific performance. This last warranty is often known as the English warranty and not often used in the United States (except in jurisdictions where it is customary, as in Virginia).

Minor differences in these definitions exist from state to state. The two classifications just outlined also encounter certain difficulties. For example, what of a mortgage only discovered after the closing? The present warranty against encumbrances provided initial protection against such an interest. But if a later discovered interest is not asserted, the statute of limitations could have run on a present covenant, and the nonassertion of the interest by its holder means there is no breach of the quiet enjoyment warranty— and therefore no remedy under any type of warranty for the purchaser. *See Brown v. Lober*, 389 N.E.2d 1188 (Ill. 1979). Present warranties are properly thought of as representations of the status of the title, and future warranties as covenants or promises to defend, indemnify, and cure the title or pay damages if the cure is not successful.

Some states have enacted statutes for all forms of deeds that incorporate certain covenants or warranties into the verbs used to grant or convey the title. A reference in a Virginia deed to "English covenants of title" incorporates a warranty of the right to convey, of quiet enjoyment, and for further assurances. Va. Code. Ann §§55-70 to 55-74.

The burden of proof with regard to a present warranty varies according to its type. The grantee must allege a breach of the warranty of *seisin* and the right to convey, but thereafter the grantor has the burden of proof. For the warranty against encumbrances, the rule is sometimes different because the grantor may not have created the alleged encumbrance and the grantee then has the burden of proof to show its breach.

The measure of damages for a breach of a present warranty, in the case of the covenant of *seisin* and right to convey, is a fraction of the purchase price, representing the percentage of the price for which title failed. This is a restitutionary or rescission measure of damages; that is, the warrantor must give back a fraction of the price she received, in proportion to the failure of the title. The consideration paid the warrantor is the upper limit on any recovery. For the warranty against encumbrances, it is the cost of removing the defect if that is possible with the payment of money, and when it is not possible, it is the fair market value of the title with and without the encumbrance, fixed at the time of the covenant's breach.

For a future warranty, the measure of damages is the difference between the fair market value of the title as the deed purported to convey it and as received, and its fair market value as measured at the time of the ouster. In each instance, the recited purchase price received by the warranting vendor provides an upper limit on damages. Attorneys' fees are more likely recovered in a successful action based on a breach of a future warranty. Reasonable costs and attorneys' fees are usually recovered as well when the warrantor fails to defend or cure the warranted title against the assertion of an adverse claim.

Example 8

Are the present covenants implicitly assigned with each successive transfer of the same property?

Explanation

No, in most states; yes, in others. The American majority rule is that present covenants are unassignable. This rule stems from the fact that a cause of action was not assignable at common law; any assignment was "champerty." While this explains the genesis of the rule, one might ask: What justifies it today? Today each grantor is presumed to have made her own bargain over covenants and should not be held to have liabilities granted in the course of negotiations conducted by other, unknown, and perhaps deceased parties. So each covenantee-grantee can sue her immediate grantor-covenantor but not grantors "remote" to her — that is, those further up the chain of title.

In a minority of states (the leading cases are from Iowa), the cause of action on the warranties is deemed assigned with each successive transfer of the title. Here the warranty "runs with the title," not the land. No grantee has to take possession to gain the benefit of this implied transfer; taking title is sufficient. This assignment means that the last assignee-grantee, though remote from the grantor giving the covenant, is the one with the right to sue the breaching grantor, even if remote to him. This has the advantage of judicial economy: It prevents a line of lawsuits back up the chain of title. Only the present holder of the cause of action, the latest grantee, can sue the breaching covenantor; interim ones cannot sue. It often has the disadvantage of lengthening the time of that warrantor's exposure to liability.

Example 9

Assume that the Statute of Limitations for real property matters is six years. In a jurisdiction permitting the assignment of present warranties, when does the statute run when the first warrantee's prior link in the chain is three years long?

Explanation

The assignment is really of the right to sue the warrantor, and it runs to a remote grantee for the last three-year period of the six years originally allowed for bringing suit.

Example 10

In a jurisdiction permitting the assignment of present warranties, can a *mesne* or interim holder of the title sue her vendor if a true owner ousts her purchaser from possession?

Explanation

No. If the covenant has been assigned by its beneficiary to her purchaser, that purchaser has the right to sue and the interim titleholder (the original beneficiary) no longer has it. That purchaser must now sue the remote vendor liable on the covenant. Its original beneficiary cannot.

Example 11

If a chain of title is subject to a latent defect, such as a forgery, do the warranties run down the chain in a minority rule state if the deeds in the chain are void?

Explanation

Yes. The latent defect destroys the estate of each grantee in turn, but if it were to destroy the warranties as well, they would not be available when most needed and just when the parties probably intend them to be used. Courts regard them as corollary agreements, not dependent on the validity of the deed in which they appear. To enforce them, privity of estate between their holders is not required. However, if any grantee knew of the presence of the true owner, estoppel may be invoked against her enforcement of the covenant.

Example 12

What if the deed with the breached warranty recites a purchase price of \$100,000, but in fact the vendor received nothing for the deed?

Explanation

The immediate grantee is estopped from asserting any damages for a breach of the warranty or from claiming more than the price actually paid. A remote grantee might be similarly estopped in a minority rule state on the theory that when the implied assignment of warranties is made, it is subject to any defenses the vendor might have. When a remote grantee relies on the record, this seems unfair, unless there is a release of liability from the immediate grantee on the record as well. (The recorded release puts the remote grantee to the duty of inquiring into whether the purchase price might have been rebated in exchange for the removal of the grantee's warranty protection.)

THE DELIVERY OF DEEDS

A deed must be delivered to be effective. A delivery requires an intent to deliver the deed, as well as the actual, physical delivery, or manumission, of the deed. Its proof is a matter of gathering evidence extrinsic to the document itself. A delivery requires evidence of (1) the physical presentation of the deed from vendor to purchaser with (2) the vendor's intent to create a present interest in the purchaser at the time of the document's execution and presentation to the purchaser. It has three functions: (1) it makes the grantor aware of the serious consequences of the transfer of title, thus functioning as a protection for the unwary grantor; (2) it provides evidence of the transfer to the grantee and often to third parties; and (3) its ceremonial aspects mark the beginning and end of rights in the property, as did the ceremony of livery of *seisin* at common law.

Only an irrevocable delivery is effective. The grantor must put the control of the deed beyond her power and control. A grantor's placing the deed in her safety deposit box will not be an effective delivery. Putting it in a box, giving the box to the grantee, but retaining the key to it is equally ineffective. A physical handing over is required in most cases. Giving the key to the box is probably not a substitute for delivery of the deed, until the grantee actually uses the key and removes the deed from the box. (If the box were big and heavy, the result might be different, as then the delivery of the key is all the more equivalent, from the grantor's point of view, to delivery of the deed.) After obtaining the deed, a grantee who returns the deed to the grantor for safekeeping may not intend to alter her right to the deed but subjects herself to the hazards of proof about the grantor's intent.

Neither can the grantor give the deed to her agent, with instructions to deliver it to the grantee, and expect the delivery to be complete at the time the instructions are given; the agency itself implies the right to direct the agent. For example, giving the deed to the grantor's attorney is ineffective as a delivery. This result might change when the agent is a dual one or when, on the way to deliver the deed, the agent recorded it. In all other instances, only when the deed is actually delivered by the agent has it been delivered.

Acceptance of the deed by the grantee who benefits from the delivery is presumed and so rarely is the subject of litigation.

In a majority of jurisdictions, a condition on delivery to the grantee, not written into the deed actually delivered to the grantee, is ineffective—the conditions are ignored once the delivery is complete. To maintain such a condition in force, delivery must be to a third party, such as an escrow agent. Only a condition that is written into the deed itself (and not in some other document) survives its delivery to the grantee.

When a deed with blank spaces on it is physically delivered to a grantee, the grantee can complete them when doing so accords with the grantor's intent. Here there is a physical delivery, but an intent to deliver must be established.

Courts have established four presumptions to deal with problems of delivery. All of them are rebuttable. First, the deed in the possession of the vendor is *prima facie* not delivered. Second, the deed in the possession of the purchaser is *prima facie* delivered. Third, recording the deed creates a presumption of delivery; it is usually *prima facie* evidence of the vendor's delivery, although in some states the presumption is irrebuttable. Fourth, acceptance by the purchaser is presumed; its nonacceptance must be clearly evidenced by the grantee.

Examples

Example 13

V prepares a deed of Blackacre to P. The deed is valid on its face. V gives the deed to P on condition that P pay V $100,000. P does not pay as required. What can V do?

Explanation

This deed has been delivered and the condition voided by the delivery. V can assert a vendor's lien for the purchase price on Blackacre, but the deed has transferred Blackacre's title to P.

Example 14

V prepares a valid deed to Blackacre, leaving the space for the grantee blank but intending later to convey the property to P. V gives the deed to P, telling P to have her attorney review it. After further negotiations for the sale of the property fall through, P inserts her name and refuses to return the deed. Can V force its return?

Explanation

Yes. V did not intend to deliver the deed, so the delivery is ineffective. In a declaratory judgment action, V is entitled to have the delivery held void. In an action for slander of title, V is also entitled to judgment for whatever damages P has caused.

Example 15

V prepares a deed of Blackacre, valid on its face, to P. V gives the deed to P's attorney for review. The attorney records it and sues V for ejectment. What can V do?

Explanation

V is entitled to have the deed declared void. Two deliveries are required—one to the attorney and another to P—and only one has occurred. The deed has not been effectively delivered.

THE DOCTRINE OF MERGER

The undertakings in the terms and conditions in a contract of sale last only so long as the contract remains executory. When a deed is accepted as called for in the contract, the contract terms calling for the transfer of title are satisfied and those aspects of the contract are extinguished and merged into the deed. *See Towsley v. Stanzak*, 519 P.3d 817, 824 (Mont. 2022). This doctrine implies an integration clause into every deed, saying, in effect, "this deed is the full agreement between its parties on the title" to the transferred property. The underlying rationale for this doctrine is that contractual obligations dealing with the title are normally expected by the parties to be performed by the closing or else become part of the deed; thereafter, the deed is the best and final evidence of the contract and substitutes for it. The contract calls for a vendor to convey a marketable title, but when the purchaser accepts a deed for less at the closing, the contract provision on the title is merged into the deed. The deed's acceptance by a purchaser is in effect the vendor's substituted performance of the title call in the contract. When the risk of loss is on the vendor during the executory period, acceptance of the deed allocates the risk to the purchaser. So, at the closing and with the acceptance of a deed, the risk of loss, and the risk of the later discovery of an encumbrance, falls on the purchaser.

Traditionally this doctrine has been regarded as a rule of law. In some jurisdictions, however, it creates a presumption that once the deed is accepted, provisions in the contract of sale preceding delivery of the deed are merged into that deed. This in effect turns the doctrine into a canon of construction, so that evidence that the parties to the deed did not intend merger to occur will override the doctrine. No matter its status in your jurisdiction, it is easy to override it with a survival provision in a contract of sale.

The doctrine of merger is usually a protection for the vendor and discharges him from further liability on the contract, but when the deed provides greater protection than the contract did during the executory period, the doctrine protects the purchaser as well. *See Reed v. Hassell*, 340 A.2d 157 (Del. Super. Ct. 1975).

Only the contract is merged into the deed; however, if the parties have an "ancillary" agreement, it is not merged, even if it is a provision in the contract. A contract provision allocating responsibility for a brokerage commission is ancillary and not merged into the deed. A contract provision giving a third party (such as the vendor's neighbor) a right of first refusal to buy the property concerns the title to be given the purchaser at closing; on that account it is merged into the deed and after the closing the neighbor loses the right.

Suppose the legal description of the property in the contract conveys less land than the deed's description. Is the purchaser's right to sue for the discrepancy merged into the deed? The answer is no if the discrepancy was the result of error, but yes if the suit is filed after an unreasonable amount of time has passed following the closing.

Often such ancillary agreements concern aspects of the physical condition of the property. An agreement concerning them would not fit into the components of the deed presented earlier in this chapter; such an agreement becomes an ancillary one. For example, a contractual agreement that "the air conditioning is in good repair" would not be included in a deed; such an agreement is ancillary and is not merged. Neither is it necessary for the deed to be effective. When the deed's effectiveness is the touchstone of the doctrine, the purchaser's post-closing recovery for an acreage deficiency would be barred by the doctrine: The legal description is an essential component of the deed. If the purchaser's claim is for the potability of the water on the property, however, the agreement is an ancillary one and recovery is not barred. A restrictive covenant is another example of an ancillary agreement within the deed: It too is not necessary for the passage of title; it concerns the use of the property, not its title. In addition, implied warranties of habitability in the contract are usually not merged into the deed. Neither are promises to clean up toxic substances on the land, or to pay a brokerage commission. None of these things are necessary to the passage of the title. Besides an exception for ancillary agreements, additional exceptions to the merger doctrine exist for contract provisions produced by fraud, mutual mistake, or inadvertence. *See Cooper Realty Invs., Inc. v. City of Bentonville*, 643 S.W.3d 816, 819 (Ark. Ct. App. 2022).

CHAPTER 8

Deed Descriptions

There are three methods of description land in common use in the United States. In the states and jurisdictions that were originally colonies or were carved out of their territory (Maine, Vermont, parts of Ohio, West Virginia, Kentucky, and Tennessee), conveyances are described by **metes and bounds**, using distances and directions starting from an identifiable point. In the rest of the country (Texas and parts of California excepted), the legal description of real property begins on the macro level, with the Jeffersonian **governmental or rectangular survey**. Along with both of these methods, one is likely to find a recorded **subdivision plat**, with lots numbered for identification—this is used particularly in urban areas. This last method is perhaps the easiest to describe, so let's deal with it first.

SUBDIVISION MAPS IN DEED DESCRIPTIONS

Whenever a tract of land is broken up—or subdivided—into smaller parcels, a plat map is recorded showing where each of the parcels or lots in the subdivision is located. The dimensions of each lot are shown on the plat and each lot is identified by number, hence "lot 10, Burke's subdivision, recorded in Book 230, at page 57, in Winsor County, State of Grace ..." Plat maps are typically first prepared by a land developer (or his agent or employee—a surveyor or civil engineer) and presented to municipal planning officials for approval and then to the appropriate governmental body for a final approval. After approval, the land is staked showing the bounds of each lot. Only then can the developer sell the lots to builders or consumers to erect improvements on them. If the subdivision is in a jurisdiction using the rectangular survey, somewhere on the plat map will be a description of the outside perimeter of the plat, described by Township and Range, east or west of a principal meridian.

THE RECTANGULAR SURVEY

Surveyors began this survey (long ago) by establishing a *principal meridian*—a north-south line—established by compass (magnetic compass before 1881 and solar compass after that). The first meridian used was the western boundary of Pennsylvania. There are 35 principal meridians in the United States, six with numbers, the rest named. The locations of most are arbitrary. *See* Figure 8-1. Each meridian intersects with a *base line*, running east and

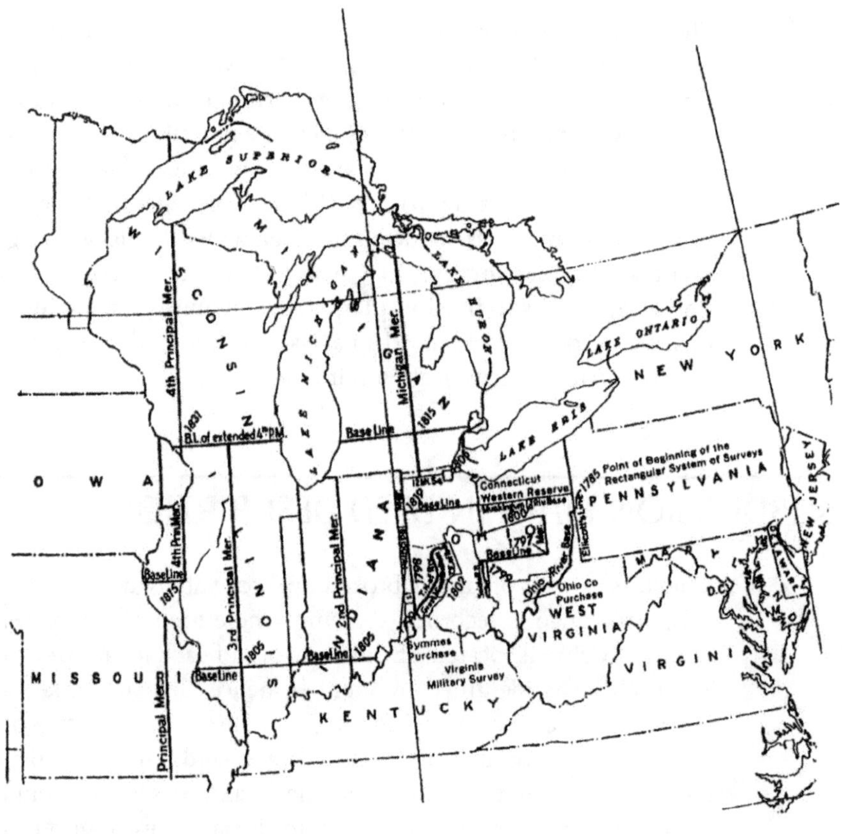

Figure 8-1. Section of U.S. Principal Meridian Map

west. Think of these two lines as the x and y axes familiar to you from high school geometry.

Parallel to the principal meridian, running north and south, are *range lines*. Six miles apart, the range lines form six-mile strips called *ranges*. Parallel to the base line, and also six miles apart, are *township lines*. The six-mile strips bounded by the township lines are called *townships*, as are the six-mile squares formed by the intersection of range and township lines. *See* Figure 8-2.

Each township is located between two parallel lines, known as *standard parallels*, extending out from a principal meridian in an east-west direction. With reference to the x-y axes of the standard parallels and ranges, particular townships are found by combining "Township 1, or 2, North or South" and

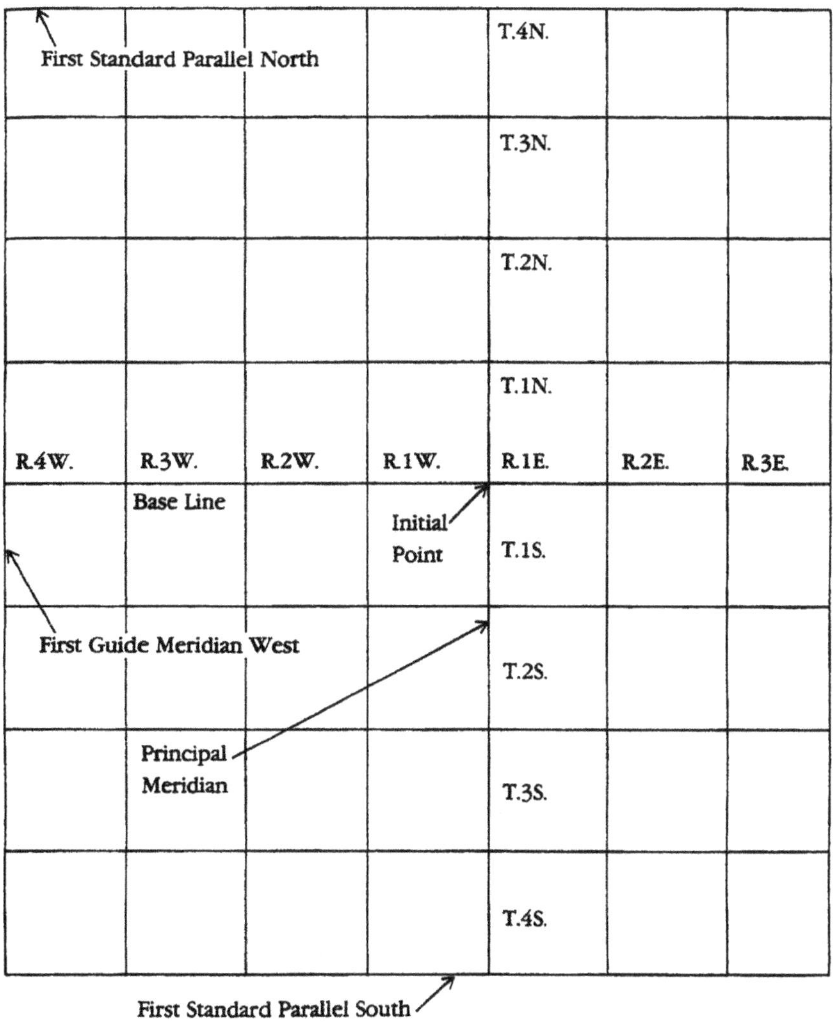

Figure 8-2. Principal Meridian and Base Line, Showing Townships and Ranges

6	5	4	3	2	1
7	8	9	10	11	12
18	17	16	15	14	13
19	20	21	22	23	24
30	29	28	27	26	25
31	32	33	34	35	36

Range Line

Township Line

Figure 8-3. A Standard Township, with Sections Numbered in the Typical Order

"Range 1, or 2, East or West" of a principal meridian. Thus, Township 30 North, Range 5 East, is 30 townships north of the base line, and five ranges east of the principal meridian in question. Only one such township exists.

From this larger grid (Figure 8-2), the land is divided into sections of one square mile each. Thirty-six sections form one six-square-mile township. The sections are numbered from 1 in the northeast corner, running across the top, to 6 in the northwest corner, with 7 just below, 8 to the right, and so on to 12 on the eastern boundary, dropping down to 13 just below it, running back to the western boundary, and so on, until reaching 36 in the southeast corner of the township. *See* Figure 8-3.

To describe land under this survey, the smallest unit of land goes first and builds to a reference to the principal meridian used in the region. Thus Section 12, Township 5 South, Range 2 West, Salt Lake Meridian—or Sec. 12, T5S, R2W, Salt Lake M.—describes land in northern Utah.

Township sections can be further divided into quarters. When only a part of a section is conveyed and that part is rectilinear in shape, the description reads: "the NW 1/4 of the SW 1/4, of Section 12." *See* Figure 8-4. If

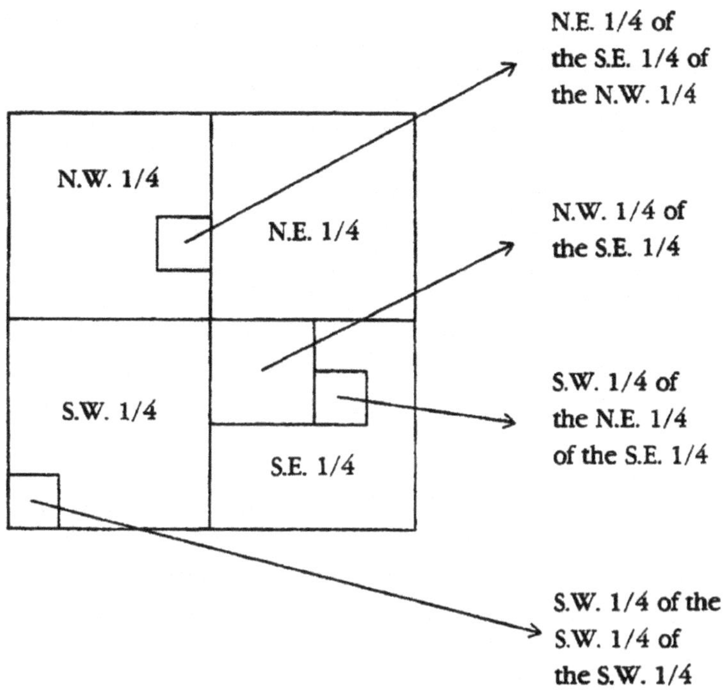

Figure 8-4. Quarter Sections of Sec. 12, T5S, R2W, Salt Lake M.

a smaller parcel is conveyed, or if it is not rectilinear, a metes and bounds measure must be used in addition to the rectangular survey description, usually preceding that description in the deed; or a smaller parcel might be referred to as a numbered parcel in a platted subdivision. None of these, however, is a substitute for incorporating a statement of the city, town, or village and the state into a description. Otherwise, a mistake in the rectangular survey description can land you in an adjoining state (or, if on the coast, in the ocean!).

PREFERENCES AMONG CONFLICTING ELEMENTS OF A METES AND BOUNDS DESCRIPTION

As discussed previously, the first two sections of a deed are in the premises, followed by the *habendum* clause. Between these two sections generally appears the legal description of the transferred property. The deed description must identify that property with reasonable certainty.

When metes and bounds—or distances (aka "courses") and compass-point directions are used to describe property, the description proceeds in much the same way you might direct a friend to trace the boundaries around a land parcel: You would tell him or her where to start, where to go from there, point to point, and at each point or "call," where to turn and in what direction, to get back to the where he or she began. Each of your "calls" would give both a distance and a direction. This dictates a trip from monument to monument—"monument" being either a natural object like a rock or tree, or an artificial object like an iron stake or rod. Thus, the description begins from some visible starting point ("Starting at the middle of the intersection of Oak and First Street . . ."), and continues the description "thence 1,000 feet north, 500 east, 1,000 feet south, thence to the point of beginning." If the components of a description are internally consistent, the description will "close" or end at its point of beginning. The description in this paragraph is of a lot or parcel on the northeast corner of Oak and First Street in a named municipality, county, and state of this country.

When the elements of a description are internally inconsistent, boundary descriptions are controlled by a well-established order of priorities: Monuments, courses, distances, and quantity prevail in that order, unless it produces absurd results. A monument is generally a stake in the ground with metal button atop it, left by the last surveyor to work out the description. The physical disappearance of a monument does not defeat its priority if it can be reestablished by the surveyor's field notes or other evidence. If the surveyor makes a mistake and the monument is wrongly located, the monument as located on the ground is preferred to its true location, particularly if relied on to improve the property. A monument established before the date of the deed, and referred to in it, is preferred to a monument later established. A natural monument controls an artificial one. An artificial monument is one that either calls for a change in courses with reference to adjoining property later established by survey, or is a natural monument set in the ground after the deed is given (one that uses the description and so relies on it). If there are two conflicting surveys of adjoining property, the one in existence at the time of the deed controls. *Stransky v. Monmouth Council of Girl Scouts*, 925 A.2d 45 (N.J. Super. Ct. 2007).

"Courses control distances." This is true in most, but not all, states. This means that a boundary line need not stop at a certain distance when the direction it is given would take it further, to a monument further on. Moreover, "to" used in this sense is a word of exclusion. "To the old oak tree" means "to this side of the old oak tree," not to its center or far side. Both courses and distances yield to monuments. "First courses control last courses." If the error cannot otherwise be isolated, the last course described often absorbs the error.

Natural monuments have the highest priority, but they might not be used everywhere they are available. In urban areas, they can easily disappear during the process of urbanization. Trees can die and disappear, rocks be moved when improvements require it, and so forth. Moreover, distances originally marked out in surveyors' chains (80 to a mile) might be converted to feet, rods to yards, and so on, as surveying methods change and adapt to GPS locations and advanced mapping techniques. The most reliable legal description might be one that has worked in the past, not the product of the most modern surveying method.

The rule of reasonable certainty is judge-made law. In most states, the rule is the same for both contracts of sale and deeds for real property, so it is best to incorporate the fullest available description into a contract. However, the state of Washington requires that a legal description be used in the contract. Its state courts formulated this rule as an interpretation of the state's Statute of Frauds. In this case, however, the statute may work a greater fraud than it would otherwise.

The rule of reasonable certainty is usually not a problem in states using a rectangular or other governmental survey, but in the former colonies (and Texas) it presents a somewhat greater problem. A person who is about to sell real property should have her tax assessment reference number, lot and block number, or title insurance policy handy so that she can incorporate the description by reference into any contract executed during nonbusiness hours. If these are unavailable, the plat number or the book and page number in the public records where the last recorded description appears can be used, but only as a backup.

Examples

Example 1

O conveys to A "Lot 1" with a reference to a subdivision map, lot and block number, "per the recorded plat thereof." Unknown to A, amendments to the plat were also recorded, changing the boundaries of Lot 1. Does the reference to the lot revise the boundaries?

Explanation

Yes, it does. *Goad v. Urich*, 13 S.W.3d 738 (Mo. App. 2007).

The rule of reasonable certainty requires that there be a point of beginning to the survey. It further requires that the description close. When abstracting a title, the title searcher will generally omit the premises of a deed when a fee simple absolute is conveyed, naming only the parties to it. However, he will generally copy the description meticulously, compare it with past descriptions, and note any discrepancies. He probably hopes that the same description is used all the way down the chain of title. If not, a resurvey of the property may be indicated. If he finds that a description contained less than a grantor owned, he is generally put to an extra search; for example, he might search the land records past the next transfer date until he is sure that successive grantees held for the period of adverse possession.

Examples

Example 2

What if a deed description is "such land as the grantor (a living person) owns upon her death"?

Explanation

This description is void for uncertainty. The description must be certain at the time the deed is effective, and this description is not. It has a testamentary aspect to it, but as a will, it would fail, not being in the proper form. However, if it read "all the lands unsold to other parties on January 1," this is a definite description because the public records will ascertain the land retained by the grantor as of that date. The extrinsic evidence giving certainty to the description is in the public domain and is customarily gathered by abstractors.

Example 3

What if the description is "the house that Bill now occupies"?

Explanation

This may be a valid description. If the property is the only one Bill owns, then the description can be given certainty by extrinsic evidence. However, if that evidence creates ambiguity because, for example, Bill owns two houses in the area, the description fails.

Example 4

What if the description is of the "Joe Brown Farm"?

Explanation

This description is one that can be fleshed out by extrinsic evidence. If extrinsic evidence is successfully used, the description is reasonably certain. The use of this evidence creates some corollaries to the general rule. For example, the mention of the city or county in which the property lies may be omitted when the grantor owns only one parcel in that jurisdiction. Likewise, omission of the state in which the property lies is not fatal because the law will infer that the place of contracting or closing is the state in which the property lies. Such omissions are curable, even if not prudent.

Example 5

What if a legal description in a deed reads "all the land that I now possess"?

Explanation

The holdings can be established by extrinsic evidence as of the date of the deed, and so the description is definite. Further, there is no ambiguity patent on the face of the deed to render a description uncertain. Remember, latent defects are cured by extrinsic evidence, patent ones are not.

Example 6

What if the description is "part of lot 2"? Which part? What shape?

Explanation

This description is indefinite and patently ambiguous. A description that reads "one and a half acres in the northwest corner of lot 2" is similarly ambiguous. There would have to be some customary shape for the subdivision lots in the region for this description to be valid. The Jeffersonian survey (if used in the region) not only will provide the meta-descriptors for the property, but also might provide a customary shape, but otherwise this description fails. (In some states, if the property conveyed is smaller than (say) one-sixteenth of a section, a plat must be filed for it and then it is the plat that determines the shape.)

Example 7

How about a description reading "the north side of lot 2"?

Explanation

Courts have held this to mean that the northern one-half of the lot is conveyed. This is a rule of law, not a matter of the intent of the parties. Most of the questions that arise regarding deed descriptions are questions of fact and for the trier of fact.

Example 8

What if the deed says "to A and her heirs, that certain parcel, being one-half of my estate Blackacre"?

Explanation

Here the "one-half" does not describe a certain acreage, so the description is patently ambiguous and fails. If the vendor and purchaser are tenants in common with regard to Blackacre, another problem arises because this description on its face does not describe an undivided one-half in the whole of Blackacre.

Example 9

What if the description is of the "western 50 feet" of a lot?

Explanation

There may be no problem if extrinsic evidence shows that the lot is either a square or rectangle. If the lot is irregularly shaped, however, a problem arises. Similarly, a reference in a description to 50 feet of frontage on a street will imply a rear line of the same length, but unless the property is (again) a square or a rectangle, courts cannot make that implication. How are these problems resolved? They are generally resolved by a presumption that the grantor intended to convey away the larger of the two possible acreages. This is a matter of construing the deed against the grantor. Armed with this rule of construction, there is a latent ambiguity in the deed, and the trial court should admit extrinsic evidence to explain it. If that evidence is conflicting, however, the court will be unable to establish the intent of the parties to the transaction. In many deed description cases, that intent will have receded so far into the past that it will be impossible to establish. In this situation, the courts are likely to reject the extrinsic evidence because of the improbability of its being credible and instead rely on the paper record, on which present-day grantors and grantees most often have to rely.

Example 10

O mistakenly believes that she owns a parcel 500′ by 100′—in fact, it measures 450′ by 100′. O subdivides it into five equal-sized parcels. O sells each lot to A, B, C, D, and E, in that sequence. How big is each lot?

Explanation

Each gets a parcel 90′ by 100′. All share equally in the shortfall. The sequence of the conveyances is irrelevant because the rule is that the lots in the subdivision are created at the same time, and simultaneous purchasers share the pain equally since all their rights are derived at the same time, the time of subdivision—that is, in most states, to the time the subdivision plat was recorded in the land records.

Example 11

O, under the same mistaken belief as in the previous example, conveys part of his 500′ by 100′ parcel without subdividing it, conveying to A a 300′ by 100′ portion of it by metes and bounds. Then O conveys the rest of the parcel to B, describing the rest as a 200′ by 100′ lot. What does B get?

Explanation

B's lot absorbs the entire shortfall and so B obtains a 150′ by 100′ lot.

MONUMENTATION AND SURVEYING

What if a surveyor running a metes and bounds description makes an error and his plat plan or field notes conflict with the marker he leaves on the ground? Which controls? If the marker is in its original position, it controls because judicial emphasis in this area is on what the surveyor did, not what he meant to do. This encourages reliance on the facts of possession (which after all creates rights superior to the record) and prevents overlaps or deficiencies on the ground. So when the original monument can be established, it prevails over a plat. But if the plat conflicts with the field notes of the surveyor and no monument can be found, the field notes control because they show what the surveyor did; the plat is then regarded only as a copy of the notes. If there is a conflict between the original monument and the notes but the plat has been recorded in a state that conveys according to a plat reference, the plat controls and inconsistent evidence is inadmissible unless the monument is misplaced, in which case, the monuments on the ground control.

If a monument is lost, it may be reestablished by witnesses, fences, sworn affidavits, and so forth. A lost but remembered monument may be established by extrinsic evidence. Once established, it must be put back where it was, even if it had been misplaced on the ground by surveyor error. If a monument is lost and no extrinsic evidence is available to reestablish it, the courts then go to the nearest two existing monuments and measure the distance between them, dividing the line proportionately to fix the point lost. This rule has the effect of containing errors within the smallest possible land area. In some situations, however, a deficiency in the legal description may be prorated, as where there are more than two lots and a deficiency in the frontage measurements between two monuments encompassing all of the lots is in dispute.

The American Land Title Association (ALTA), the American Congress on Surveying and Mapping (ACSM), and the National Society of Professional Surveyors (NSPS), all trade groups, jointly issue what is titled "Minimum Standard Detail Requirements for ALTA/ACSM Land Title Surveys." This document is available at www.acsm.net. A new version was issued in 2026. Although state standards may require more detail (some do and some require less), these standard requirements have become the norm for surveyors and attorneys reviewing their work. One consequence of this is that many of the standard recitations in a surveyor's certificate can be incorporated by a reference to the survey's compliance with ALTA/ACSM survey standards in the document just cited. For example, the Minimum Standard Requirements provide that the surveyor give professional licensing information on the plat or map—so there is no need for a recitation that in fact the surveyor is licensed.

The survey certificate needs to provide that the surveyor has prepared the survey, plat, or map known by whatever job number the surveyor assigns it with its date of preparation given. A description of the property surveyed and the title insurance policy (or more likely, the title report or commitment) will also be recited as having been used for surveying the property.

Generally speaking, ALTA and ACSM require that the following be shown in a survey: boundaries; differences between the measured and the recorded boundaries; distances to the nearest public street; recording act data; all monuments; the character of all evidence of possession; the location of all buildings, and particularly those buildings and other improvements located within five feet of a boundary; all easements; all alleys and driveways crossing the property; and the location of cemeteries, burial grounds, and waterways.

ALTA, ACSM, and NSPS have also provided additional documents adopting both survey measurements and standards of accuracy, so a certificate should also provide that a survey, plat, or map is based on measurements in "Minimum Angle, Distance, and Closure Requirements for Survey Measurements Which Control Land Boundaries . . ." and the Accuracy Standards in effect as of the date of the certificate.

Examples

EXAMPLES

Example 12

What provisions would you expect to see in even a brief survey?

Explanation

One such provision might pertain to the assignability of the certificate, entitling, for example, a vendor's purchaser, mortgagor, mortgagee or lender, its assignees (including, for example, any servicer or successor trustee), and the title insurer issuing the title report used to prepare the survey to rely on it. Defining who may rely on the certificate may prevent costly litigation.

The Standard Detail Requirements document has a blank space for other, negotiable items that a surveyor might provide. Other inclusions might be the provision of new monuments, a vicinity map, flood zone designations, acreage or square footage of the surveyed property, its elevation and contours, zoning regulations, exterior dimensions and footprints of buildings and other improvements, parking areas, access to public roads and ways, the location of utilities, or compliance with governmental survey requirements. This is a long list of items, but each can generally be incorporated in the certificate by reference to its number in an ALTA/ACSM document.

Example 13

As counsel for a purchaser of surveyed land, what further steps, beyond a review of the survey, should you undertake?

Explanation

You might notify your client that the survey is available for her inspection and, at closing, ask her to sign an affidavit to the effect that she has inspected and examined it, noting all encroachments, easements, and rights of way; building locations; driveways, fences, and other improvements, and found them acceptable.

TAGALONG WORDS IN DEED DESCRIPTIONS

Many deed descriptions contain the words "more or less" at their end. These words either mean that some deviation from the legal description is to be permitted (and the parties should then agree on how much) or they are an allocation and assumption of risk or a deficiency. The risk will generally be assumed by the person taking the deed—that is, the grantee or purchaser. In some states, these words are not part of the description; rather, they control it. Whether they indicate an allocation of risk of a shortage in the description or a rule of substantial deviation is a matter for local law to be determined from the whole contract or the intent of the parties; for example, unless the sale is on a per acre basis, the purchaser has likely assumed the risk of any deficiency.

When added to the deed description at the end, an accurate statement of the amount of acreage can supply missing boundaries and close the descriptions that don't otherwise close. So if you have an accurate idea of how much acreage is involved in a sale, it is a good thing to include an acreage statement at the end of the description.

The words "to or along" a named street mean that the grantee takes to the middle of the street. This is a matter of construing the deed in favor of the grantee and assumes that the grantee receives ownership of the street from her vendor. If the boundary were a stream, the result is the same. At common law, the grantee takes to the thread or middle of the stream. If a lake or pond were involved, however, a different result obtains: A purchaser takes to the low-water line of the lake.

To litigate a boundary dispute in most jurisdictions, a plaintiff does not have to prove title to the land bounded by the line in dispute. After all, it's the boundary that is in dispute, not the title. Possession is sufficient here. This rule originates in the notion that a boundary dispute is really a trespass action. In some jurisdictions, like Texas, the cause of action is appropriately entitled trespass to try title, but the same result would be reached today in states in which a quiet title action or an ejectment action is used.

CHAPTER 9

Recording Acts

Every state or jurisdiction has enacted a statute establishing the office—usually a part of a municipal or county government—for the receipt and maintenance of documents relating to the transfer and ownership of titles to real property. The public official in charge of this office is generally known as the recorder or register of deeds. The documents presented to this official are thus "recorded" and thereby become "public records"—that is, they are maintained for and accessible to the public at large.

The legislative objective in enacting recording acts is to encourage purchasers to put their deeds and other ownership documents on the public record. *See Board of Selectmen of Hanson v. Lindsay*, 829 N.E.2d 1105, 1109-1110 (Mass. 2005). One consequence for a purchaser is that, once on the record, the recorded copy provides notice to others that the purchaser holds the title or interest referred to. The notice effect of the recording is the same whether or not the third party actually knows of the recording—that is, the third party has "constructive notice" of the recorded document. The flip side of this effect is that persons can rely on the record and safely ignore the threat of unrecorded matters of which they have no other, actual notice. Another consequence of recording is that, again by statute, the document is self-proving—that is, it becomes admissible in court without further proof (although it is still subject to challenge there). Thus the recording acts provide grist for determining which of two or more conflicting titleholders have priority, as when the same interest or property is sold more than once.

The protection of subsequent purchasers is the main purpose of the acts. They, however, must qualify for the protection by meeting the acts' requirements. Their principal protection is derived not only from what the recording act states, but also by searching the public records and saving themselves from unwise investments in real property that is subject to prior interests which would defeat their plans for it. The acts also preserve the history and state of a title by giving everyone an incentive to record and protect their interests in turn by giving purchasers subsequent to them notice of it. So the notice provided by the acts is prospective, and when the protection of the act is given, it is not taken away by another conflicting claimant thereafter recording a prior conveyance.

This conflict is a zero-sum game: Someone wins the title, and the loser (or losers) is relegated to a suit for damages. To the extent that conflicting titles and interests are not prioritized by the acts, the common law rule concerning them controls—just as with any statute, so too here: When a statute does not expressly change the law, it is presumed to leave the common law intact.

THE COMMON LAW RULE: "FIRST IN TIME, FIRST IN RIGHT"

The common law for determining the priority of title between two persons sold the same property interest was first in time, first in right. Thus if O conveys to A and then conveys the same real property to B, A's title prevails over B's. In this way, we say that A has priority of title over B. A better statement of the rule might be prior in time, prior in right. How does that rule apply to the following situation?

Examples

Example 1a

O contracts to sell Blackacre to A, who does not record. O then conveys Blackacre to B, who pays a deposit but also does not record. So what happens when neither of two conflicting purchasers records in a state (like every state) with a recording act?

Explanation

Under the common law rule, B has priority and thus his title prevails over A. The common rule applies as between legal interests, but in this case only the conveyance (the very word says to the legal mind that a deed was used) to B was a legal one; the contract to A creates an equitable interest in A as a transferee of the property. So B now has priority, but that can change. Here A and B might race to otherwise complete and record their transactions, and the first to do so prevails. For example, if B closes his transaction, takes a deed from O, and records it, B then cuts off A's interest if, when B records, A hasn't yet paid O the purchase price. (In any case, the inferior interest holder is left to his rights and remedies against O, if any.)

Based on the answer that common law judges gave to the preceding problem, it is not strictly true that the rule was based on the idea that if O transferred the property once, he could not thereafter transfer the same interest again—often it was said that O had nothing to give after giving it away once. That is only true if interests of the same type (legal and legal, or equitable and equitable) are transferred to different persons.

Example 1b

If B receives a contract, not a deed, who would prevail?

Explanation

A would. If both of the conflicting interests are equitable, the first in time prevails. If both A and B have executory contracts for Blackacre, they will be involved in a race to close their transactions, and the first to do so prevails. Thus A prevails, for now. But the priority as of now could change if B continues with the transaction and beats A to the closing table.

The common law rule applies in all states, absent the applicability of the state's recording act. That is a big proviso. It often swallows the rule. But the rule is worth remembering nonetheless.

THE RECORDING ACTS: "FIRST TO (VALIDLY) RECORD, FIRST IN RIGHT"

There are three types of recording acts: race, notice, and race-notice acts. In a race jurisdiction, the first to record is first in right. This result obtains even when the purchaser who first records takes with notice (meaning actual knowledge of a properly executed document) of the prior transfer. Thus the knowledge of the winning transferee is irrelevant. The objective of such acts is to promote the use of the public records and give them certainty. The following statutory language is typical of a race statute:

> No conveyance of real property is valid as against a purchaser, but from the time of its recordation.

Few jurisdictions today have race statutes. Louisiana and North Carolina have one generally applicable to conveyances; Pennsylvania and Arkansas have one applicable only to mortgages.

A notice recording act protects the subsequent purchaser who is a bona fide purchaser (BFP). A BFP is one who takes his interest without either actual or constructive notice of the prior transfer and pays value for the interest. The value paid must be real, as opposed to a legal consideration or an executory promise; it must be new or present value, as opposed to past consideration; and it must be adequate, meaning a substantial amount of the fair market value of the interest taken. In a notice state, a subsequent BFP prevails over a prior unrecorded transferee, regardless of whether he records first. If the prior transfer is recorded, the subsequent purchaser cannot become a BFP. Why? Because the prior recording gives, by law, constructive notice of the interest whose instrument is recorded. Twenty-one jurisdictions have this type of recording act today. They typically read as follows:

> No conveyance of real property shall be valid against subsequent purchasers without notice, unless that conveyance is recorded.

Historically, a notice act replaced the race statute of some jurisdictions; their legislatures recognized the fact that the winners of the race to the courthouse were arriving at the recorder's offices with a malicious gleam in their eyes. The trouble with their reform was that the change in the law protected the lazy—later purchasers protected by the notice act had little incentive to record. They had only to remain subsequent purchasers. This did not promote use of the records, and their certainty was diminished to that extent.

With the defects in notice statutes in mind, 25 states and the District of Columbia amended their acts still further. They enacted race-notice acts. In these jurisdictions, the protected class of subsequent purchasers is narrowed. To come within it, a subsequent purchaser must not only be a bona fide purchaser, as in a notice act state, but must also be the first to record, as in a race act state. *See Friendship Manor, Inc. v. Greiman*, 581 A.2d 893 (N.J. Super. 1990). What follows is typical race-notice statutory language:

> Every conveyance of real property which is not recorded is void as against any subsequent purchaser, in good faith, of the same real property, whose conveyance is first recorded.

When litigation occurs between prior and subsequent transferees of the same property, the only issue is priority of title: The effectiveness of the deed or other conveyance, as between the parties to it, is not the issue. The recording acts do not render conveyances ineffective as between the parties.

No one disputes that the titleholder who conveys the same property twice is a bad actor and perhaps liable for fraud or misrepresentation. If O conveys property to A who does not record, and then conveys the same property to B who records, who as between O and A is at fault? On the one hand, A did not record and so set up the situation bringing the loss of title on himself. On the other hand, if O had not conveyed to B, A would have suffered no loss. O's and A's equities being equal, the doctrine of unclean hands cannot resolve this matter. If the A, the prior transferee, loses the recording act litigation, O's misrepresentation in his use of the second deed involves a breach of an implied promise to A not to sell the same property again, not to empower a subsequent purchaser to defeat the prior purchaser's interest. O thus tortuously interfered with A's title and incurs liability on that account. *See Jones v. Garden Park Homes Corp.*, 393 S.W.2d 501 (Mo. 1965). Were B the subsequent purchaser somehow to lose, the misrepresentation involves the status of O's title. *See Patterson v. Bryant*, 5 S.E.2d 848 (N.C. 1939) (involving two deeds to the same timberland). In either event, O's is liable in either tort or quasi-contract.

Recording acts (of any type) put state legislatures in the unenviable position of choosing which of two parties is going to lose the title that both thought was conveyed and that both expected to receive. Usually both parties are innocent. Hard choices are involved, but clear rules are needed if the conveyancing system is to work smoothly.

Examples

Example 2a

O conveys to A, who does not record. Then O conveys to B, a BFP who does not record. Who has priority of title and prevails, A or B? The applicable recording act is a notice statute.

Explanation

B. She is a subsequent purchaser in good faith because she is without notice of A's claim. When A does not record, A effectively gives O the power to defeat the O to A conveyance.

Example 2b

O conveys to A, who does not record. Then O conveys to B, a BFP who does not record. O then conveys to C, also a BFP. The applicable act is a notice statute. Who prevails?

Explanation

This is a horror story for subsequent purchasers in notice jurisdictions. B would be a subsequent purchaser protected by the act except that O conveyed to a person subsequent to him. If that latter person is a BFP, then he becomes the protected party. If O was a bad actor to start with, the fraud he perpetrated once likely won't stand in his way (unless B threatens him with mayhem). Thus in a notice state, it is not strictly speaking true that B has no incentive to record.

Example 2c

What if A paid $10,000, B paid $5,000, and C's deed recited that its consideration was "love and affection, and $1 paid in hand"? Now who prevails?

Explanation

C prevails if he can show that he is not a donee and is a BFP. Donees do not prevail even though they promptly record, except in Colorado. If C is a donee, then B prevails. B prevails (if he does) regardless of the fact that the fair market value of the property is $10,000 (what A paid). A donee is not a BFP. A BFP must pay something more than nominal damages. "Love and affection" does not qualify C as a BFP. Neither does $1, particularly when the value-to-payment ratio is apparently 10,000 or 5,000 to 1. Although C may be able to show that love and affection involved the provision of something more tangible of value, B will prevail if C cannot make that showing.

Example 3

O conveys to A, a donee, who does record. O then conveys to B. Who prevails?

Explanation

A prevails not as a donee, but because his recording is constructive notice to B, who cannot thereafter become a BFP exactly because he has constructive notice of A's conveyance. B will be treated as if he had searched the title, found A's deed, and thus gained notice of it. Otherwise, B's actions are not the sort that the recording acts wish to encourage. Why, after all, encourage people to be willfully ignorant? The recording acts do not prohibit transfers to donees. (They might not protect them much, as in the prior problem, but that's another matter.) Imagine where intrafamily conveyancing would be if it were so! Finally, it makes no difference whether the first transferee is a BFP or not—it is the subsequent purchaser who, under notice and race-notice acts, must qualify as a BFP.

"FOR VALUE"

Some recording acts provide that the subsequent purchaser "for valuable consideration" is protected by the act (if he meets the act's other requirements). When this proviso is not express in the act, the provision is implied by the courts. The subsequent purchaser's reliance on his grantor's clear title causes him no injury until he pays value. Taking the title as a donee causes the subsequent purchaser no injury; it is only when that purchaser subsequently pays the purchase price that he suffers injury. To qualify as a subsequent purchaser "for value," one must pay more than nominal consideration. How much more? Enough to support a deed with a covenant given for consideration? Judges are probably hesitant to make the lines too bright. More than earnest money or a contract down payment should probably be given; otherwise, a court can use the contract itself as a guide in putting the subsequent purchaser back in his place, *status quo ante*. Reasonably adequate consideration is required of the subsequent purchaser. *Alexander v. Andrews*, 64 S.E.2d 487 (W. Va. 1951) (finding that payment of $1,000 for property valued at about $4,000 is inadequate, but that $1,000 plus an agreement to care for and bury the grantor was adequate), discussed in detail by John W. Fisher, The Scope of Title Examination in West Virginia: Can Reasonable Minds Differ?, 98 W. Va. L. Rev. 449, 464-469 (1996).

Examples

Example 4a

O conveys to A, who does not record and pays less than full market value. O then conveys to B, a donee, who records. Who prevails between A and B?

Explanation

Under all types of recording acts, judgment will go for A (again, except in Colorado). *See Eastwood v. Shedd*, 442 P.2d 423 (Colo. 1968). Subsequent donees don't win, even when they record promptly to protect their interests. They are not financially harmed and defeating their interests restores the status quo ante of the whole messy situation.

Example 4b

Same facts, except that A paid full value and B, no longer a donee, paid enough to believe that he was getting a good deal but not so little as to become suspicious that O had previously conveyed.

Explanation

Judgment for B. Courts do not inquire too closely into the consideration for a conveyance once past the threshold at which B passes for a BFP. Only if B has actual knowledge of the prior transfer would the result change.

Example 4c

Same facts, except that B takes title as a donee and then goes into possession and improves the property.

Explanation

Most courts require that B pay the purchase price or contract with a third party to pay it (e.g., take out a mortgage loan from a bank), to satisfy the requirement that the class of purchasers protected by the statute take title "for value." The detriment that B suffers by expenditure of time, effort, or money for the improvement can be compensated with a lien on the title, measured by the addition of fair market value or the cost of labor and materials. See *Lown v. Nichols Plumbing & Heating, Inc.*, 634 P.2d 554 (Alaska 1981).

Example 4d

Same facts, except that B takes title, records his deed, and also applies for a mortgage loan, but mortgage financing problems prevent closing of the title and the loan at the same time, so that B holds the title not having any debt to repay yet. Between the title and the mortgage closing, A records. B's deed recites a substantial consideration, but the deed is held in escrow pending delivery when financing is arranged.

Explanation

The cases are split. Giving B judgment is supported by a policy of penalizing A for not promptly recording. On the other hand, A can argue that B has not yet qualified himself for statutory protection: B should search the record again before closing the loan, and his search should stop only on the date the loan is closed and statutory protection achieved. A's argument rests on the premise that B's lack of notice is insufficient when he has suffered no injury as a result. B's response is that it is A who should be charged with notice of documents on record at the time of his recordation and that he should not be charged with two checks on the record.

Judgment for B.[1] A's recording affords no notice to someone who has already recorded, and meanwhile B has contracted to pay the consideration through mortgage financing and the escrow. Compare *Lown*, *supra*, with *Lowden v. Wilson*, 84 N.E. 245, 249 (Ill. 1908). More to the point, "value" should be measured at the point of taking one's estate or interest in the property, not thereafter. Once taking the title, B is entitled to arrange for a loan or make a contract to pay O—just as he would be entitled to turn around and transfer

1. For a contrary but well-articulated view, *see* Taylor Mattis, Recording Acts: Anachronistic Reliance, 25 Real Prop., Prob. & Tr. J. 17, 56-62 (1990).

the title for value. The court should protect his right to alienate and can do so only if it protects his right to use his title as security for a loan too.

SUBSEQUENT PURCHASERS

A subsequent purchaser is generally broadly construed and includes any person taking a deed to real property, mortgagees, assignees of a mortgage lien, and sometimes lessees. Often leases with a term of three years or more are expressly made recordable, but leases for a lesser term are not recordable. The term "subsequent purchaser" also, and often expressly, includes a person paying a portion of the agreed purchase price under an installment or executory contract of sale for real property.

Examples

Example 5

In a jurisdiction in which contracts of sale are recordable, O conveys to A, who does not record, and then contracts to sell to B, a BFP who pays a down payment and records. Who has priority of title?

Explanation

Judgment for B, but the court should condition the granting of title upon B's payment of the outstanding portion of the purchase price to A. O is estopped to protest this condition, and A is assigned O's rights in the contract, unperformed at the time B learns of A. *See Mitchell v. Dawson*, 23 W. Va. 86, 88 (1883).

Example 6

In a state with a notice act, O conveys to A, who does not record. A conveys to B, who records. O conveys to C, who records. Who has priority of title?

Explanation

Judgment for C, as he is the subsequent purchaser entitled to the act's protection. If the facts were revised so that A's recorded conveyance to B occurs after O's conveyance to C, however, would B then be the subsequent purchaser entitled to protection? His receipt of the title is certainly the last one, and for many courts that is sufficient to give B judgment in this revised situation. But is this correct? (This discussion will be continued in later examples, asking whether "subsequent purchaser" might mean "a purchaser on a subsequent chain of title." But you need some more information about the statute to engage in it.)

JUDGMENT HOLDERS AS PROTECTED PARTIES

Some (about one-half) of the recording statutes expressly provide that subsequent judgment lien creditors are protected. Subsequent creditors, as such, are not protected; it is only when a creditor reduces a debt to judgment that the issue arises of how to treat the judgment lien created when the judgment is docketed or entered on the court records.[2] *See generally* Dan S. Schechter, Judicial Lien Creditors Versus Prior Unrecorded Transferees of Real Property: Rethinking the Goals of the Recording System and Their Consequences, 62 S. Cal. L. Rev. 105 (1988).

Examples

Example 7

Suppose O conveys to A, who does not record and who pays value, but who is without actual notice of any difficulties with O's title. B then obtains a judgment lien, which is docketed before A records his conveyance. Who prevails?

Explanation

In some jurisdictions it is held that a judgment lienor does not fall within the class protected by the recording act because he has not paid value in reliance upon O's title to his real property. Unless provided by statute, a judgment lien is subordinate to prior conveyances, even when these are unrecorded. *See Hunnicutt Construction, Inc. v. Stewart Title and Trust of Tucson*, 928 P.2d 727 (Ariz. App. 1996) (collecting the cases and authorities). Judgment for A on that account; even though A was not the first to record, he was the first to record "for value," meaning value given on account of the real property. The arguments for B would involve interpreting the phrase "subsequent

---

2. The law governing judgment lien creditors is state statutory law. Many statutes provide that a state court's granting a judgment itself creates a general lien on all of the debtor's real property (as defined by state law) in the county in which the judgment is rendered. Other statutes provide that docketing of the judgment in the county in which the debtor has real property creates the lien. In the former category of jurisdictions, the creditor need do no more than secure the judgment; in the latter, the creditor has to do more—that is, he must have the judgment docketed in the appropriate book of judgments, under the name of the debtor named in the judgment. In Alabama, Georgia, and Mississippi, a judgment lien reaches both real and personal property; in California, business personal property is reached. Federal court judgments are subjected to the rule of the state in which the federal district court sits, except that federal court judgments cannot be treated more stringently than a state court's. *See* 28 U.S.C. §1962. Out-of-state judgment creditors must generally bring an action to enforce the judgment of another jurisdiction's courts.

purchaser" to include B—quite a stretch! (Al-though there are cases that do just that.) Check local law and the wording of the statute on this.

Example 8

In a jurisdiction in which subsequent purchasers include judgment lienors, does B, a person who records a mortgage taken to secure or in exchange for a preexisting debt, prevail over A's prior unrecorded mortgage or deed?

Explanation

The weight of authority says that a lien creditor like B has not relied on the records in extending the initial loan or credit that created the debt and so is not a creditor protected by the act (of any type). B must show himself to be one who in the initial credit transaction customarily searches and relies on the public records. In addition, the execution of the mortgage in exchange for the preexisting debt requires some additional consideration if the mortgage transaction is to avoid the charge that the lien creditor did not take his interest in the property "for value." A preexisting debt is not "value" as required for an effective recording. There must be some additional consideration given at the time of taking the mortgage. *See Osin v. Johnson*, 100 U.S. App. D.C. 230, 243 F.2d 653 (D.C. Cir. 1957); *Gabel v. Drewry's, Ltd.*, USA, Inc., 68 So. 2d 372, 39 A.L.R.2d 1083 (Fla. 1953). Judgment for A then. Even when an attaching creditor has searched the record, he is often less interested in the priority of his lien than he is in financial planning and learning how many other creditors have recorded. *See Amoskeag Bank v. Chagnon*, 572 A.2d 1153 (N.H. 1990). While a contrary result might be justified as a means of punishing A, the prior grantee who does not record promptly, the lack of reliance by the subsequent mortgagee B represents a better rationale.

BRINGING THE RECORDING WITHIN THE CHAIN OF TITLE

Incorporated into the recording act (of any type) are the practices of the local abstractors or searchers of titles. They search the public records by first chaining the title and then searching for conveyances from the owners forming the chain. *See Bank of New York v. Nally*, 820 N.E.2d 644 (Ind. 2005). Chaining the title involves a search backward in time. A prospective purchaser knows the name of his vendor. He searches for that name in the index of grantees (or purchasers), and when he finds it, he looks across the page for the cross-reference to the name of the vendor involved in the last completed purchase and sale transaction—in which his vendor was the purchaser. The chaining search then continues by repeating this process, looking for the name of the last-found vendor in the index of grantees. When this process has been repeated enough to find out who held the title for the search period (60 years at common law, but often back to the date the property came out of the public domain), the chain is complete.

After the chaining search is complete, the searcher shifts to the grantor indexes, looking for conveyances out of the owners in the chain. This involves a search that goes forward in time, back to the present. The result of this part of the title search is a series of references, by book and page number, to a series of deeds, mortgages, and other documents. The searcher then goes to the books referenced and obtains copies of the documents conveying the title, or encumbering it, down to the present.

In the following problems, there is case authority for the results indicated, but there is also often a split in the cases. Purging the title of out-of-the-chain documents has a title cleansing effect, provides abstractors of title with clear rules for guiding their work in the record room, and encourages all transferees to record their documents promptly. In this light, consider the following problems.

Examples

Example 9a

O conveys to A, who does not record. A conveys to B, who records. O then conveys to C, a BFP who does not record. Who, B or C, prevails in a race state?

Explanation

No one wins under a race recording act. A's recording is not within the chain of title that C will search. C will be looking for conveyances out of O and will not, using the records arranged by the names of grantors and grantees, find A's conveyance. A might have priority of title, but not because of the recording act. Rather, B wins because the common law rule prefers his chain of title; it is first in time.

There is authority for the foregoing result, but the cases are not uniform. First to record, under a race statute, is thus interpreted to mean first to effectively give notice by recording. The tension here is that the recording statute in grantor-grantee index states nowhere mentions the need to record within the chain of title.

B should have recorded A's conveyance, and only after that recording put his own conveyance on the record. Then there would be a chain of title leading subsequent purchasers like C to the record of his interest. Bringing one's recording within the protection of the act means recording not just one's own interest but also any interests leading to it.

Example 9b

Same facts, except that the recording act is a notice type.

Explanation

C wins under a notice recording act because it requires only that C be a subsequent BFP. He is and prevails on that account.

Example 9c

Same facts, except that C is no longer a BFP but does record, and the recording act is a race one.

Explanation

C wins. He has become the first to record in such a way that his chain of title can be searched; he is the first to validly record. If C still had his bona fides, he would also win in a race-notice state because he would then have done both of the things required by that type of recording act: been the first to record validly and been a BFP.

Sometimes the person protected by a recording act has not fulfilled all of the requirements of the act himself. He then relies on the actions performed by his predecessors in his chain of title. Consider the following examples.

Example 10

O conveys to A, who does not record. B has notice of the O-A conveyance. O then conveys to B, who records. B then conveys to BFP C. Who prevails?

Explanation

C prevails in all jurisdictions. Under a race recording act, B is the first to record and his knowledge is irrelevant to his protection. B conveys his priority of title over A in his conveyance to C. Conversely, it is said that C shelters under the right of B to alienate a title superior to A. This rationale is often described as the "shelter rule." The rule is also a recognition that in this instance, B is permitted to convey a better title than he has. Under a notice act, C is a subsequent BFP and that qualifies him for protection under the act. Under a race-notice act, C wins again. If he won under the first two types of acts, he automatically wins in the race-notice act because this third type of act combines the elements required for protection in the other two. He satisfies the BFP requirement of notice states himself and takes his recording priority over A from the actions of his grantor, B, regardless of B's knowledge. C takes free of the taint of that knowledge. (C is often said to be "freed of the equities" that might attach to B in this situation.) *See Morse v. Curtis*, 2 N.E. 929 (Mass. 1885); *contra Woods v. Garnett*, 16 So. 390 (Miss. 1894).

The previous problem is an example of the working of the recording acts through the concept of a chain of title. The mechanics of abstracting a title in a grantor-grantee index is important to the functioning and interpretation of the recording acts, although nowhere mentioned in the acts themselves. Consider the following example in this regard.

Example 11a

O conveys to A, who does not record. O then conveys to B, who does not record. A then conveys to C, who does record. Who prevails?

Explanation

Under a race recording act, C's recording is ineffective. B or B's abstractor cannot find it. Either one will be searching the record for conveyances by O, and because they can't find A on the public records, they also can't find C. A race act, then, requires an *effective* recording. In this situation, effectiveness means enabling an abstractor to reach the recorded documents—which can't be done here! Under a race act, the first to record between A and B will establish priority of title. Neither has done that, and the common law rule still applies as between A and B. The further question is, should A's common law priority be given to C? The better view is, probably not. This for the reason that, if it is, C will have no incentive to record A's deed, and then his own, to complete the chain of title down to himself. If the recording acts are seen as an incentive to keep the public records in the best shape possible, reflecting the true state of a title, then C should be given every incentive to get his grantor's deed on the record.

Under a notice act, B wins if he is a BFP. In a race-notice state, no one is yet protected by the statute.

So when a purchaser seeks the protection of a recording act, she must make sure that unrecorded documents in her chain of title are recorded in an order that will enable an abstractor to reach her once the chain of title is established.

Example 11b

Using the same facts, if A recorded after C, that recording would be ineffective in all states. Do you see why?

Explanation

A's failure to record before C puts A's later recording outside the chain of title. A must record first, followed by C, to establish an effective chain.

Example 12

O conveys to A, who does not record. O conveys to B, who does not record. A records. B conveys to C, a BFP who records. What arguments can you make for A and C?

Explanation

A argues that C should extend the period of search out of O to the date on which C takes. If he does so, he or his abstractor will discover A's recorded conveyance. C argues that A's failure to record promptly permitted O to convey again and that the title search should be conducted in the usual manner. Title searches would be too expensive otherwise. (If the facts were changed slightly—and if B had recorded, but not promptly—this efficiency argument is diminished. How would a prudent abstractor search C's title?)

Example 13

Would your answers to these problems change if the abstractor used a tract index instead of a grantor-grantee index?

Explanation

Yes, if by statute the tract index has the notice-giving, self-proving legal consequences attributed to the grantor-grantee index. Then a subsequent purchaser could not ignore out-of-chain documents; rather, he would have to make a reasonable inquiry into the transaction that the documents purport to reflect, and be on constructive notice of what that inquiry would yield. However, if the statutes are not clear on the legal effect of the tract index, the answers probably would not change. Even if the title searcher consults a tract index and there finds a document recorded outside the chain of title, the legal effect of seeing the document may be nil. This is so because the legal record often remains the grantor-grantee index, not the tract index. What is recorded there provides the notice with which subsequent purchasers are charged. "Recording outside of the grantor-grantee index, as in the tract index, is recording merely for convenience." *See Skidmore, Owings & Merrill v. Pathway Fin.*, 527 N.E.2d 1033, 1035 (Ill. App. 1988). What purpose is left for a tract index? Well, remember that it is just that—an index—and, as such, is a useful corrective for the recorder's mistakes in indexing by name. So assuming that the "recording" is within the chain of title, the tract index serves as a check on the name index.

Finally, no matter what type of index is used, what if the formalities required by the recording acts are not met? The acknowledgment may not be valid. *See Messersmith v. Smith*, 60 N.W.2d 276 (N.D. 1953) (held that no constructive notice is imparted by a defectively acknowledged deed). This result has been much criticized. *See Amoskeag Bank v. Chagnon*, 572 A.2d 1153

(N.H. 1990). If the defect in an acknowledgment is not apparent on its face, the majority of cases hold that the defect does not deny the document its function in providing constructive notice through the record, so a title searcher may rely on it. Only patent defects render a recorded document ineffective to provide such notice. *See in re* Sandy Ridge Oil Co., Inc., 510 N.E.2d 667 (Ind. 1987), noted at 22 Ind. L. Rev. 369, 394-397 (1989). Finally, some jurisdictions will have a statute curing defect such as this when the document has been on the record and unchallenged for one to three years. Of such curative statutes, further discussion is in Chapter 10.

CIRCUITY OF INTERESTS

O conveys to A, who does not record. O then conveys to B, who records first but takes with notice of A's interest. O then conveys to C, who takes without notice of A but with notice of B, and records.

This scenario results not only from a series of voluntary transfers, such as contracts, deeds, and mortgages, but also from a series of involuntary ones (arising out of judgment liens). Under nonrace acts, A, B, and C are each superior and at the same time inferior to each other: A has priority over B, B has priority over C, and C has priority over A. Circuitous priority results: There are more than two liens, and each is inferior to another.

One solution to this problem is to say that here we have a situation that the recording acts are incapable of handling and that therefore the common law controls: First in time, first in right, then, is the governing principle. This solution might be appealing when A's failure to record is due not to his own efforts, but to the misindexing of his interest by the recorder of deeds.

What should be done? In reaching the preferred solution, assume that the fair market value of the property is $100,000 but that a judicial sale brings only $80,000. That amount ($80,000) is what is available to satisfy all claims. Further assume that A's claim on the $80,000 is $40,000, B's is $20,000, and C's is $40,000, but not all of these amounts can be paid in full.

First, take the $80,000 and subtract the amount of the claim about which C had notice. This latter amount is the amount of B's claim, or $20,000. So $80,000 − $20,000 = $60,000. Sixty thousand is the amount available to satisfy C's claim. C's $40,000 claim falls within this latter $60,000, so C will be paid in full. Hold $40,000 for C.

Second, with the same amount available ($80,000), subtract the amount about which B knew: $80,000 − $40,000 (A's claim) = $40,000. This is more than B's claim of $20,000, so B will be paid in full too. Hold $20,000 for B.

Third, take the remainder and pay A with it. Because $60,000 is now held for payments to C and B ($40,000 and $20,000, respectively), only $80,000 – $60,000, or $20,000, is left to pay A. Thus, A will *not* be paid in full; A gets $20,000 or half of his claim.

There is a general principle at work here: Everyone competing for the available fund is paid from that fund, minus the amounts of which each had notice, and the last transferee, as the subsequent purchaser protected in some form by the recording act, is first paid. For a recent use of this method in a personal property case, *see ITT Diversified Credit Corp. v. First City Capital Corp.*, 737 S.W.2d 803, 804 (Tex. 1987), noted at 19 Tex. Tech. L. Rev. 1511, 1518-1522 (1988) (providing a good summary of the various solutions) and discussed in George Nation, Circuity of Liens Arising from Subordination Agreements: Comforting Uniformity No Longer, 83 B.U. L. Rev. 591 (2003).

This problem of circuity arises in several contexts. The first we have seen. The second is a land development problem in which A is a farmer, holding land that O, a developer, would like to develop. Being thinly capitalized, O agrees with A that A will take back a purchase money mortgage for some portion of the price of the land. O also agrees with A that A in the future will subordinate the priority of his lien to a later construction loan and mortgage lien. This subordination agreement is not recorded. A sells the land to O and takes back this mortgage lien. O then mortgages the land again to B, who knows of A's lien. What B doesn't know, however, is that C, appropriately here a construction lender, makes a construction mortgage to O, takes back a lien, and claims the benefit of the off-record, subordination agreement giving C priority over A. A, B, and C all record their liens promptly.[3] *See In re Petition of Price Waterhouse*, 46 P.3d 408 (Ariz. 2002).

In some cases, B is paid first, then C, and then lastly A. Sometimes this solution is known as the New Jersey rule. B knew nothing of the A-C subordination agreement and should not suffer for it. C is next preferred because this preference gives him the benefit of his agreement with A, who is left with the residue of the available funds.

Is this fair? To the extent that B is preferred first even though he never should expect to take priority over A, it is not. Also, C has his expectation defeated when he expected to step into A's shoes.

Is there a better solution? Again, yes. Assume that A's claim is $40,000, B's $10,000, and C's $40,000, and that a judicial sale brings $50,000. Then, out of the $50,000, set aside the amount of A's claim, or $40,000; then pay out the $40,000 first to C, up to the amount of his claim, then to the extent there is a balance remaining, pay out the remainder to A. (So far, C will be paid $40,000 and A nothing.) Pay the remainder of the available fund to

---

3. Second lien mortgage financing has made this type of contractual circuity the subject of intense scrutiny in the economic hard times of 2007-2010.

B, so B gets the remaining $10,000. There is nothing left to pay A any of his claim.

Paying C and A out of A's claim, first set aside, prevents B from getting a windfall from a priority that he never expected to have. However, the subordination agreement is enforced only to the extent that it can be satisfied out of A's claim, of which B knew. Then B is paid, out of the fund available, minus A's claim of which he had notice. This gives B the benefit of the priority that he did expect, irrespectively of the subordination agreement. Then, if proceeds are still available, the subordination agreement is enforced again to the extent of any funds not yet paid out: first to C, as the agreement anticipated, and then to A.

A third context in which circuity is a problem involves mortgages and federal and state income tax liens. *In re* Holly Knitwear Inc., 356 A.2d 405 (N.J. Super. App. Div. 1976). Thus if A is a mortgagee, B holds a state lien, and C holds a federal lien, the federal lien is superior to a state lien but must be recorded to be effective against mortgage liens previously recorded. Moreover, state liens are superior to all recorded mortgages, and A and B record promptly; thus, circuity results again (with the same solution).

INDEXING

The majority of jurisdictions hold that the index is not a part of the official record. The consequence of this holding is that a purchaser, recording and thus relying on the records to give notice to subsequent takers, is not responsible for checking the index to find out if the document is properly indexed. *See First Citizens Bank v. Sherwood*, 879 A.2d 178 (Pa. 2005); *Haner v. Bruce*, 499 A.2d 792 (Vt. 1985), noted in 12 Vt. L. Rev. 283 (1987); *see generally* Annot., Failure to properly index conveyance or mortgage of realty as effective constructive notice, 63 A.L.R. 1057, 1058, n.12 (1929). Thus in only a few states—Iowa, Maryland, New Jersey, New York, North Carolina, Washington, and Wisconsin—is indexing regarded as the final step in recording and the purchaser given the responsibility of checking the record for mistakes in the index. *See Greenpoint v. Schossberg*, 888 A.2d 297 (Md. 2005); *Compiano v. Jones*, 269 N.W.2d 459 (Iowa 1978). How sensible is the majority rule on indexing? Doesn't a holding that the recorded but misindexed document imparts constructive notice set off a search for a needle in a documentary haystack?

In a jurisdiction in which the index is not part of the record, an attorney may nonetheless be liable for malpractice in not checking the record for proper indexing of a client's deed. *See Antonis v. Liberati*, 821 A.2d 666, noted at 49 Vill. L. Rev. 233 (2004).

E-RECORDING

Statutes permitting recorders of deeds to accept electronic recordings are common. *See, e.g.*, Va. Code Ann. §17-83.1:1-3 (enacted 1997). They are often accompanied by statutes authorizing e-signatures (*id.*, §17-83.1:4), but the latter type of statute does not usually authorize the former. Electronic notarial act statutes, authorizing and prescribing formats for such acts, are often another precondition for successful e-recordings. The Uniform Electronic Transactions Act encompasses all three types of statutes and is perhaps the safest safe harbor for electronic recordings. It has been the pattern for congressional legislation preempting aspects of state law not conforming to the Uniform Act. This act was followed by the adoption of the more specific Uniform Real Property Electronic Recording Act in 2004. It has been adopted in several states. *See, e.g.*, Ariz. Rev. Stat. §§11-487.01-.06 (2005). These Uniform Acts hold the greatest promise for uniformity among the states in this area.

Evaluating an e-recording statute thus requires that it be checked for all of the components of a traditional recording. How will it authorize and handle the use of scanned and digital images, signatures, and acknowledgments, and how will it handle some matters not discussed here but that are crucial to the operation of a recorder's office: security/encoding systems, payment systems, and receipts? E-recording must be hacker-free, and it will require escrow funds to pay for recordings established by frequent users of the recorder's office, like law firms, abstractors, and title insurance companies.

RIGHTS OF PARTIES IN POSSESSION

A final point: A right to real property manifest by the possession of its holder (or his agent) takes precedence over any right arising under the recording acts. Indeed, remember that the recording acts do not create any rights that would not exist independently of the documents recorded; they only establish a priority of rights. Another way of saying this is that establishing priority of title under the acts is no substitute for a thorough inspection of the property itself. *Sanborn v. McLean*, 206 N.W.2d 496 (Mich. 1926) (finding reciprocal negative easements through inquiry notice). Not only is an inspection valuable to a purchaser interested in the physical condition of the property, but it also will reveal any rights in possession—for example, a tenant who can tell the purchaser of the possessory rights of his landlord, a visible easement across the property, an adverse claimant in possession, or a neighbor adversely possessing land along the boundaries to the property.

The problems that can arise from this inspection can be tough ones. For example, a tenant in possession consistent with a lease does not provide the prospective purchaser with notice of an unrecorded option to purchase the property, which is not a part of the lease itself. And a tenant in common, when in possession, has the right to possession of the whole property, but that is not inconsistent with the rights of other cotenants who all own undivided fractional shares of the property. An unrecorded prior conveyance by an out-of-possession cotenant may be effective against the subsequent purchaser who does not track down all the cotenants and have them execute deeds of their interests to him. What if the spouse of the record owner is in possession? Today one can't assume that this possession is consistent with the record without some further inquiry.

Examples

Example 14

In a jurisdiction whose recording act protects judgment creditors, V (holding record title to Blackacre) is constructing a house there. V and P sign a brief but enforceable contract to sell Blackacre, with its half-built house, to P. P does not record the contract. P continues construction using subcontractors, erecting a "P's Construction Co." sign advertising Blackacre for sale and displaying P's phone number. J acquires and dockets a judgment against V for nonpayment of construction supplies. Does J or P have priority of title?

Explanation

J has. J was entitled to rely on the public records, so unless he has either actual, constructive, or inquiry notice of P's contract interest, he has priority. No actual notice is indicated, and because P did not record, no constructive notice is present either. Are these facts sufficient to put J on inquiry notice? P is not in possession, and his subcontractors' presence is consistent with the activity that gave rise to J's judgment in the first—the construction process. A similar consistency is displayed by the sign. Thus J's judgment has priority because, finally, the facts are insufficient to put J on inquiry notice either. *See Nussbaumer v. Fetrow*, 556 N.W.2d 595 (Minn. App. 1996).

CHAPTER 10

Title Searches, Abstracts, Title Insurance, Reforms, and Torrens Laws

The executory period is the time when the vendor presents the purchaser with what evidence he has that he owns the property. The procedures followed to present this evidence to the purchaser—or to the purchaser's attorney—involve a search of the title as evidenced by the documents relevant to the title and recorded in the public records. This title search is performed by one of three types of persons: (1) an attorney, (2) a title abstractor (a professional title searcher), or (3) a title insurance company.

Thereafter the "abstract" (or précis and summary of the results of this search—for a fuller discussion of the term, *see infra*, this chapter) is reviewed by an attorney, working for either the vendor or the purchaser, or as an attorney/employee of the insurer. The review provides the point at which the legal consequences of the documents are determined. It results in one of two types of documents presented at the closing: either (1) an attorney's opinion letter or certificate concluding that, based on the records searched, the title is a marketable one, or (2) a title insurance policy showing a marketable title or otherwise satisfying the provisions of the contract of sale. When a title insurer employs in-house abstractors, it compiles a preliminary report on title, showing the interests that it will list in its policy as exceptions to coverage. This report functions in some regions of the country as (1) an abstract, giving the parties notice of less-than-fee interests to be cured or dealt with in other ways before closing, as well as (2) a commitment to issue a title insurance policy effective at closing.

THE TITLE SEARCH

A title search is important first because all jurisdictions, often counties, by statute maintain real property title records. Again by statute, such records impart constructive notice to purchasers, whether or not they actually search those records and find the documents that pertain to the title that they wish to purchase. On the other hand, if they search those records and these records do not disclose any defects in the title that might be reflected there, then they may, absent actual knowledge of a defect, be a good faith purchaser for value entitled to rely on the title as shown in the records.

A second reason for a title search is that, under our common law system, no vendor is able to convey to a purchaser more than he or she has; in law Latin, *nemo dat qui non habet*, "he who hath not cannot give." Hence each purchaser of real property has to find out what it is that his or her vendor has to sell. There are no guarantees that the vendor owns what he is purporting to sell.

A title search has two major steps. The first is finding the names of all the past owners and holders of interests in the title under scrutiny for a sufficient period of time that the examiner may be reasonably sure that no other interests exist. This is called "chaining the title," each owner being one link in the chain. At common law, this search period was 50 to 60 years. In states with so-called marketable title acts, the period is shortened to between 30 to 50 years. In some complex or very costly transactions the period may be longer, and may go back to the time when the patent to the land came out of government hands or when the recorded instruments refer to boundaries marked by monuments long removed or disappeared.

At a minimum, a title search is a search of those public records that, by statute, provide constructive notice of their contents. (Tort actions for professional incompetence in conducting the search are available against title searchers/abstractors.) As related to real property, the public records are found in the office of the registrar or recorder of deeds. Also searched will be the records of the state and federal courts in the jurisdiction, the local tax assessor's records, and other specialized dockets and records. In one jurisdiction, the "lunacy docket" is searched; it shows the names of those persons declared mentally incompetent. Other records, even more specialized, are searched as well.

To find the names of prior owners for the chain of title, the abstractor or title examiner starts with what he probably already knows—that is, with the name of the present owner. In jurisdictions in which the indexes to the land records are arranged according to the names of the grantors and grantees of the titles, the examiner searches for the present owner's name in the grantee index until finding it beside either a document reference (a book and page number at which the record of the deed under which the present owner took title can be found) or the name of the owner's vendor. In either case, it is the latter name that interests the examiner at this stage, for with it he can find, again using the grantee index, a cross-reference to the name of the next prior owner, and proceeding in this manner he can develop a list of all prior owners and (again from the referenced deeds) the dates of their ownership.

Although many jurisdictions (particularly in states outside the eastern United States) index the records by tract number, most maintain and index their records according to the names of the owners. Where numbers are used, tracts are assigned a reference number unique in that jurisdiction, usually starting with a township, range, and section number that allows the parcel to be located under the federal public lands survey. Some jurisdictions require the recorder to maintain both a tract index and a grantor-grantee index. In such jurisdictions, the examiner may use both indexes by using one and checking its accuracy with the other. Typically, however, the name indices are the official ones.

Once the examiner has chained the title, he is in a position to embark on the second major step in a title search: to use the tract or grantor index to check for any conveyances made by each owner during the period of his or her ownership. The abstractor uses the names of the grantors, previously found cross-listed in the grantee index, in order to search the grantor indexes forward in time, for the time period involved in each link of the chain. What did each grantor, while the holder of the title, do with it? Mortgaging it, suffering a judgment lien, and/or conveying a less-than-fee interest are all possibilities, and any such transaction may destroy the marketability of the title being tendered.

The result of this search for conveyances by present prior titleholders or owners, conducted in the grantor indexes, reveals some basic information about each document located in this manner. This information is then compiled into an "abstract of title." Once both the grantee and grantor indexes have been used, the full texts of all the documents found in the indexes are located for later review.

An abstract of title can be composed of many types of documents, not just deeds and other documents of voluntary transfer. For example, the title to the property in question might have been subject to probate, and a transfer of title effected by the order of the probate court. The court order or the decree would then become a link in the chain of title. Likewise, when the property has been through the hands of a judicial or tax sale, the deed from the public official in charge will become a link in the chain. State statutes sometimes provide a general definition of an abstract.

REVIEW OF THE TITLE

So far in the process, the title search has been a mechanical, even routine process. Title examiners or abstractors are not usually attorneys. Their work can be conducted in the public records office and in whatever other records office might be involved—for example, if a title insurer maintains a private system of records in the insurer's office. Next comes a more complicated task: The abstract is reviewed, usually by an attorney, either working for one of the parties, typically the purchaser, or for a title insurer. His or her task is to make the legal judgments to determine the marketability of the title just searched. This requires, in part, determining the strength of the chain of title, the validity of the legal descriptions, the scope of any encumbrances or less-than-fee interests disclosed by the search, and the rights of any parties in possession. For example, if the chain involves a person named Elizabeth who, as a grantee, took title to the property in the past, the reviewer will want to know whether the Betsy, Liz, or Beth who granted the property to establish the next link in the chain is the same person. See the discussion of the doctrine of *idem sonans* a little later in this chapter. Likewise, the legal description must be the same in each deed in the chain of title; it must also close and encompass the acreage the purchaser expects to obtain, and moreover there must be no restrictive covenant prohibiting the use the purchaser proposes for the property.

An attorney working for a purchaser then advises the client on marketability and issues a certificate of marketability to the client, typically the purchaser. An attorney working for an insurer then prepares a title insurance binder, which is both a preliminary report on title and a commitment to issue a title insurance policy reflecting the status of the title revealed by the search. The commitment is sometimes, depending on the complexity of the issues involved, submitted to the title insurance company for approval, but often the attorney, acting as an agent for the company, has authority to issue the policy. Once the title has been searched and reviewed, the attorney often drafts the documents necessary to conduct the closing of the transaction—for example, the deed.

Some Title Search Rules

The abstractor or title searcher has several rules to limit the length and cost of a title search.

Chain of title A title search starts with a name search in the grantee index. The search is for the name of the person now proposing to sell the title to a property, listed alphabetically as a grantee, and cross-listing the name of his or her grantor. That grantor's name is located in the grantee indexes, along with the cross-listed name of the party from which he or she purchased. With these three names located, you have established one link in the chain of title. Each link runs from closing date to closing date, except in jurisdictions where contracts of sale are recordable: There a link runs from contract date to closing date. The process is then repeated to establish the earlier links in the chain, searching as appropriate in the various indexes (probate for wills, etc.) when the link is not established by the recording of a deed. Still using the grantee indexes, the abstractor proceeds, searching for the names of the parties involved in the various transactions involving the title, backward in time for 60 years or so, to a "root of title," meaning the first transaction prior in time to the period of search.

This back-in-time use of the grantee indexes establishes the chain of title. Documents not later located within this chain, even if found by an abstractor through inadvertence, do not provide constructive or any other type of notice under the recording acts. They are said to be "wild" deeds or documents. The effectiveness of the chain in this way occurs even if the jurisdiction in which the search is conducted maintains tract indexes along with the grantor/grantee indexes. Only documents within the chain of title can affect the marketability of a title.

Rule of specific reference A document in a chain of title may describe some of the property conveyed or some ancillary right or interest, such as an easement or restrictive covenant, in general language. "General" for this purpose means without identifying the record book (by volume or year), as well as the page within that book, where the legal description or interest referred to appears on the public records. A specific reference is to the book and page where the property or interest appears on the records.

General language, while valid to give rights or assign duties as between the parties to the document in which the general description appears, is not binding on a good faith purchaser for value, unless that purchaser has actual knowledge of the interest. Specific language is binding on good faith purchasers.

The rationale for such a rule is to save the purchaser, and all other later purchasers, the time and expense of searching the records. A search for a general reference, lacking a book and page number to which to turn, is like looking for a needle in a haystack. This may be unfair to the holder of the interest who cannot enforce it against the bona fide purchaser, but it is even more unfair to put the purchaser to a daunting search when the holder of the interest can see to its recording, whether in a deed or in an affidavit, giving a specific reference.

This rule requires a specific reference when the legal rights and duties involved in one recorded document are sought to be incorporated into another. It might be called a rule of specific incorporation by reference.

***Doctrine of* idem sonans** When a party's name is misspelled on a deed or other title document, the identity of the party is presumed from the similarity of sounds between the correctly spelled pronunciation and the pronunciation of the name as written. Similarly, names can be either fully spelled out or appear as nicknames: A presumption arises that William is the "Will" referred to on the record. In the context of a dispute about the marketability of the title, this doctrine prevents a purchaser from objecting when all of the names in the chain of title are not identical, as between a person's name first appearing as the purchaser and later as the vendor of the same property. Similar names used in both appearances in the records are sufficient to establish the marketability of the title. When the same doctrine is used by a purchaser later searching the records after closing, the function of the doctrine is different: Now the doctrine is likely to be narrowly construed or rejected, because the consequence of using it may be to subject a purchaser who appears otherwise to be a good faith purchaser to an interest unanticipated when he or she made his bargain for the property.

ABSTRACTS OF TITLE

An abstract of title is the result of the title search. It is the title searcher's written memorandum and work product. As such, it is a summary of the documents comprising the chain of title, as well as any liens or encumbrances on that title, all arranged in chronological order. Each document noted in the abstract is called a link in the chain of title, and the links, taken together, constitute the chain going back in time for the period of the search. In many jurisdictions, an abstractor works in the public records office (or offices) to compile the documentary material that goes into the abstract. When a title insurance company compiles an abstract, it often uses documentary materials in its own possession, together with its own indexes; thus, it does not rely wholly on the public records. Some larger title companies, singly or in combination with other companies, retrieve and copy or "take off" the public records customarily searched in the jurisdiction, and the "take-offs" become the company's "title plant."

Examples

Example 1

What if in the course of reviewing a title you discover that in one document in the chain of title, nine months elapsed between the date of the deed and the date of recording?

Explanation

The delay in recording is suggestive of a conditional delivery and inquiry of the parties about the condition is in order.

Example 2

What if you discover that the grantee in one deed in the chain is Billy Joe Barton, but later, as a grantor, the name on the deed is William Barton?

Explanation

The doctrine of *idem sonans* states that like-sounding name variations between the name of a person taking title as a grantee and a name used as the next grantor in the chain of title do not render the title unmarketable. The cure is an affidavit to the effect that the different names were used by one and the same person. *See J. I. Case Credit v. Barton*, 621 F. Supp. 610 (D. Ark. 1985). Such an affidavit need not be made under oath, but it will have the effect of estopping the person(s) making it from denying the facts recited as well as preserving them against death. Taken in advance of any later litigation, they also may permit invocation of the "ancient document" exception to the hearing rule.

ABSTRACTORS' LIABILITY

Williams v. Polgar, 204 N.W.2d 57 (Mich. App. 1972), aff'd, 215 N.W.2d 149 (Mich. 1974), held that an abstractor employed by a vendor could foresee that the abstract would be given to a purchaser, and so the abstractor could be liable to the latter for negligent misrepresentation. The Michigan Supreme Court also held that the statute of limitations on this cause of action ran from the time of the discovery of the omission in the abstract, rather than from the time the abstract was issued.[1] Not just an abstractor, but also, today, an attorney performing abstracting work is generally liable not only to the party for whom the abstract or legal work is prepared, but also to those who did in fact or who would foreseeably rely on it. *McCarnish v. E.E. Appling Interests*, 991 S.W.2d 787 (Tex. 1999). There is no danger of unmanageable liability for the work resulting from its holdings: The limited number of parties to any real property transaction precluded such a possibility. Nor will a client lose control over the attorney-client relationship. Many jurisdictions have grounded this liability to third parties in the Restatement (Second), Torts, §552.

Consider the following short abstract, based originally on Flick, 1 Abstract and Title Practice 22-40 (2d ed. 1958). What problems do you see in constructing a chain of title, and what types of defects or encumbrances

1. Only a minority of cases on the subject today are contrary. *Anderson v. Boone County Abstract Co.*, 418 S.W.2d 123 (Mo. 1967).

should you be concerned with before advising a purchaser to close on the title offered by the last purchasers (the Symes) who appear in it?

TITLE ABSTRACT

Caption

Located in Burke's Addition Division, lot number five, in the Township of West Comfort, in the County of Myers, State of Ohio, and being in the Southwest quarter of the Northeast quarter, Section 16, Township one North, Range five SouthWest; and containing one-quarter acre of land, more or less.

John Burke to Samuel Bond	Date: July 29, 1926 Recorded: August 5, 1926 Recorded at: Vol. 15, p. 278, of Recorder of Deeds, Myers County, Ohio Consideration: $8,500.00 Estate Conveyed: Fee, with Minerals Reserved Defect in Deed: None
Samuel and Mary Bond to Samuel Bond, Jr.	Date: April 21, 1955 Recorded: November 4, 1957 Recorded at: Vol. 45, p. 10 of Recorder of Deeds, Myers County, Ohio Consideration: $4,000 Estate Conveyed: Fee Defect in Deed: None
In re Estate of Samuel Bond, Deceased	Application to Probate Will Date of Death: February 19, 1956 Widow: Mary Bond Heirs named in Will: Phillip Bond Elizabeth Marie Bond Sanford Issac Bond Petitioner: Samuel Bond, Jr. Certificate to Record: None
Sam and Marie Bond to Myers Savings and Loan Bldg. Assn.	Date: November 24, 1967 Recorded: December 1, 1967 Recorded at: Vol. 53, p. 145 of Recorder of Deeds, Myers County, Ohio Consideration: $3,500 Estate Conveyed: Mortgage Lien Defects: *No Acknowledgment*

Samuel and Marie Bond to John and Issac Clark	Date: September 15, 1977 Recorded: October 2, 1977 Recorded at: Vol. 102, p. 374 of Recorder of Deeds, Myers County, Ohio Consideration: $21,000.00 Estate Conveyed: Fee Defects: Residential Use Only Covenant
John and Issac Clark to First Federal Savings Assn.	Date: September 16, 1977 Recorded: Vol. M184, p. 262 of Recorder of Deeds, Myers County, Ohio Consideration: $17,000 Estate Conveyed: Deed of Trust Trustee: Robert Willing, V.P. Defects: None
John and Issac Clark to Ohio First Bank	Date: September 18, 1982 Recorded: September 20, 1982 Recorded at: Vol. 143, p. 752 of Recorder of Deeds, Myers County, Ohio Consideration: $4,000 and release of liability Defects: None
Ohio First Bank to James and Jane Symes	Date: May 12, 1983 Recorded: September 22, 1983 Recorded at: Vol. 151, p. 34 of Recorder of Deeds, Myers County, Ohio Consideration: $35,000 Defects: None

Some Comments on the Abstract

1. As to the legal caption and its legal description: Is a range for a township described as *SouthWest?* No, a township is either east or west of the baseline. So the caption should probably read "West" here. This township is located on the baseline and has as its eastern boundary the First Guide Meridian.

2. Is a title search back to 1926 sufficient, or should the search go back to the patent, or title issued by the state? Compare *Palamarg Realty Co. v. Rehac*, 404 A.2d 21, 28-29 (N.J. 1979) (noting that "it is the custom of title searchers and conveyancers in New Jersey to search a title only for sixty years and until a warranty deed is found in the chain of title," but remanding for expert testimony to determine the custom), with *Midway Assoc. v. Shoneck*, 1992 Conn. Super. LEXIS 1799 (1992) (finding that a marketable title act reduces

the necessary time period of searches). Ohio has a marketable title act. Its 40-plus-year search period affects the answer, but in 1994 the root of title under the act is still the 1926 transaction.

3. Notice that the deed to Samuel Bond, Jr., was executed two years before it was recorded. What might have intervened during such a lapse of time? What document intervenes in this chain of title? The probate application. That might make you want to inquire whether the deed whose recording was delayed was the subject of a death escrow or is a will substitute.

4. *Mary* Bond might not be the same person as *Marie* Bond. What if they are the same? What if they are different people? See the discussion of the doctrine of *idem sonans*. Is Elizabeth Marie, mentioned as one of Samuel's heirs, the same person as one of the grantors in the 1977 deed, where the name given is Marie Bond? What are the current rights of Phillip and Issac Bond? *Colonial Bank & Tr. Co. v. Sheehan*, 258 N.E.2d 306, 307 (Mass. 1970) (involving a name change upon marriage and quoting the rule that when recorded deeds and other documents are then given or received by persons or entities known by different names, the records may fail to furnish exact information on the parties making up the chain of title, but nonetheless reflect genuine transactions, executed in good faith, and sufficient to furnish constructive notice of the transaction); *Grygorewicz v. Domestic and Foreign Discount Corp.*, 40 N.Y.S. 2d 676 (1943) (holding that judgment entered against the name of "Mary A. Pender" was not a lien on the real property of "Alice Mary Pender" and therefore did not provide notice to a good faith purchaser of real property from her).

5. The lack of *acknowledgment* of the mortgage to Myers Savings may affect its validity. *But see Sweatman v. F.D.I.C.*, 418 So. 2d 893, 894 (Ala. 1982) ("Mortgage is not invalid from lack of, or because of, an improper acknowledgment"). There is some earlier authority to the contrary.

6. There should be deeds of release for the mortgage lien and the deed of trust, and you should be concerned if neither is recorded. If the 1967 mortgage lien was not released in 1977, when the property was conveyed to the Clarks, the mortgage they took out to First Federal was in reality a second or junior lien on the property. A title is unmarketable without release deeds or other evidence that the mortgage or trust deed liens are in fact unenforceable, satisfied, or otherwise released. *Alling v. Vander Stocken*, 194 S.W. 443 (Tex. App. Ct. 1917) (holding against vendors promising a marketable title, but failing to produce a release for mortgages).

7. What should be done (if anything) about the reservation of minerals in the 1926 deed? *Heifner v. Bradford*, 446 N.E.2d 440 (Ohio 1983) (mineral reservation not extinguished when recorded subsequent to the date of the root of title); *see generally* Lewis Simes & Clarence Taylor, Model Title Standards 32 (1960) ("The recording of an instrument of conveyance subsequent to the effective date of the root of title has the same effect in preserving any interest conveyed"). The purchasers could not develop this property without some resolution of the reserved mineral estate issue raised in the first entry.

8. The conveyance to and from Ohio First Bank is some indication that the property was the subject of a foreclosure action against the Clarks based on a further or third mortgage or deed of trust. That would make the Clark's 1982 deed (for which no estate is given) a deed given in lieu of foreclosure. Making sure this deed is not subject to challenge in equity may be a problem, but the statute of limitations has probably run on such a challenge after ten years.

TITLE INSURANCE

The Policy

Title insurance policies[2] insure "against loss or damages, not exceeding the amount of insurance stated in Schedule A, plus costs, attorneys' fees, . . . sustained or incurred by the insured," by reason of (1) the title to the estate or interest described in Schedule A "being vested otherwise than as stated"; (2) a "defect . . . on such title"; (3) "lack of a right of access to and from the land"; and (4) the unmarketability of the title. For the policy, the holder pays one premium, for which she obtains coverage for as long as she holds the insured title, and even beyond, in the situation in which she is asked to make good on the deed warranties she gives later as a vendor of the insured title. It also "continues in force" for insured vendors who later finance the purchaser of the insured title with a take-back or purchase money mortgage, insuring the lien of that mortgage. This said, no title insurance policy is assignable.

Schedule A is the first of three component parts to a title policy. It defines the estate or interest that the policy insures. It is a statement of coverage. What Schedule A gives, however, the second component, Schedule B, limits, for it is a statement of the results of the title search. Thus, if the search uncovers defects on the title, they are recited as exceptions to coverage in Schedule B. With these recitations, the insurer can do a great deal to limit its risk of having ever to pay a claim. Schedule B provides information that might otherwise be disclosed on an application for insurance used in other types of insurance. The information it contains is used to assess the risk of issuing a policy. Often this schedule contains preprinted, standardized exclusions from coverage as well.

A third component of the policy is its "Conditions and Stipulations," covering such topics as the insurer's duty to defend the insured title, the procedures for making a claim and defining a loss, the measure of damages, and other subjects.

---

2. The phrases quoted in this and subsequent paragraphs are found in the owners and loan policies issued by the American Land Title Association (ALTA), the major title insurers' trade group.

In all, title insurance has three aspects. It is an indemnity agreement (not a guarantee of the status of the title); it is litigation insurance; and, perhaps above all, it involves the hiring of experts in title matters.

As to the first (indemnity) aspect of the policy, the policy should be seen as looking both backward and forward in time. Its two faces pivot around the date of the policy. One face looks back, to determine the facts and the interests that the policy both insures and excepts. The other face looks forward into the future, after the date of the policy, to await the assertion of a claim adverse to the insured title. This aspect of the policy has an impact on the measure of damages as well. Only losses that are "actual" and "sustained or incurred" are insured.

The second, litigation aspect is triggered by the insurer's duty to defend the insured title. This duty is sometimes analogized to the title covenants in a deed. The duty to defend is broader than the duty to pay a claim. Because the duty must be performed before the duty to pay becomes clear, the insurer will often have to defend in instances in which it ultimately will not have to pay, as for example when its defense is successful.

The third aspect of the policy is a matter of the expectations of the insured. Nowhere in the policy does the insurer undertake to make a search of the title, but why else would many insureds be interested in a policy? This insurance covers both "on-record" and some "off-record" title defects. The former are defects reflected on the public records, the latter those unreflected on the records, such as a lack of delivery of a deed in the chain of title, or a deed subject to revocation because it was executed under duress or was fraudulently obtained. So even for a client who has either been given or inherited the title, or obtained an attorney's title certificate, title insurance may be advisable because it covers off-record defects that the certificate does not.

The following short-form policy is typical. The *italicized* words are the subject of further commentary following this policy.

OWNER'S POLICY OF TITLE INSURANCE

Subject to the exclusions, exceptions, and conditions later appearing, The Blank Title Insurance Company *insures as of the date of the policy, against loss or damage* not exceeding the amount of insurance shown herein, and costs, attorneys' fees and expenses which the Company may become obligated to pay, *sustained or incurred* by the insured by reason of:

1. *title to* the estate or interest described in Schedule A being *vested otherwise* than as stated therein; or
2. any defect in or lien or encumbrance on such title; or
3. lack of a right of access to and from the land; or
4. the unmarketability of such title.

SCHEDULE A

Policy No.: ____________________
Date of Policy: ____________________
Amount of Insurance: ____________________
Name of Insured: ____________________
Estate or Interest Insured: ____________________
Description of Land: ____________________

EXCLUSIONS FROM COVERAGE

1. Any law, ordinance, or *governmental regulation* (including but not limited to housing or building codes and zoning or subdivision regulations).

2. Rights of eminent domain or governmental rights of police power unless notice of the exercise of such rights appears in the public records at the date of this policy.

3. *Defects,* liens, encumbrances, adverse claims, or other matters (a) *created, suffered, assumed, or agreed to* by the insured; (b) *not known to the Company and not shown on the public records, but known to the insured* at the date of the policy or at the time the insured took the estate or interest insured; (c) resulting in no loss or damage to the insured; (d) attaching or created subsequent to the date of this policy.

SCHEDULE B

The Company does not insure

1. rights or claims of parties in possession;
2. what an accurate survey would disclose;
3. easements not shown on the public record;
4. mechanic's liens;
5. taxes not yet liens on the date of this policy;

and [here are noted the results of the title search].

CONDITIONS

The coverage of this policy continues so long as the insured retains an estate or interest in the land or has liability by reason of covenants of warranty, provided that coverage shall not continue in favor of any purchaser from the insured of such estate or interest.

The Company, at its own cost and without undue delay, shall *provide for the defense* of the insured in all litigation consisting of actions or proceedings against the insured to the extent that the litigation is founded upon an alleged defect, lien, encumbrance, or other matter insured against by this policy, provided the insured notifies the Company promptly in writing of such litigation and cooperates with the Company during it. The Company has the *right* to prosecute any action or proceeding to *establish* the title as insured, whether or not liable hereunder. Whenever the Company interposes any defense or brings any action or proceeding to establish the title as insured, the Company may pursue any such litigation to final determination and reserves the right to conduct all appeals from any adverse judgment or order. The insured shall cooperate with the Company in any such litigation and appeal.

The Company shall have the option to pay or settle any litigation, action, or proceeding for or in the name of the insured or terminate all liability to the insured by payment of the amount of the insurance shown herein, together with the payment of all costs, attorneys' fees, and expenses incurred up to the date of payment.

The Company's liability under this policy shall in no case exceed the least of (a) the actual loss of the insured, or (b) the amount of insurance stated in Schedule A, payable within 30 days after the amount of loss or damage is definitely fixed.

No claim under this policy is maintainable (a) if the Company removes the defect, lien, or encumbrance or establishes the title as insured, or (b) until there is a final determination and disposition of all appeals adverse to the title, or (c) for liability voluntarily assumed by an insured in settling any claim or suit without the prior written consent of the Company.

All payments under this policy or another policy insuring any mortgagee of the insured title reduces the amount of insurance pro tanto. Whenever the Company settles any claim under this policy, all right of subrogation shall vest in the Company, which shall thereafter be entitled to all rights and remedies which the insured would have had with respect to the insured title. This policy is the *entire contract* between the insured and the Company and any claim for loss or damage, whether or not based on negligence, shall be restricted to the provisions, conditions, and stipulations of this policy. Notice of loss or claim required by the policy shall be sent in writing to the principal place of business of the Company, __________.

Policy Highlights

Title insurers give some of the phrases of the policy particular meanings or a particular emphasis. Consider the phrases italicized in the short policy you just read.

Insures as of the date of the policy This phrase emphasizes the risk elimination aspect of title insurance. The insurer does not insure future events or nonevents. This type of insurance is unlike health, accident, or life insurance. It looks into the past, not the future: It reflects the state of the title as of the date of the policy. The "description" of the insured title in Schedule A (referred to in the first statement of coverage) reinforces this notion, and exclusion 3(d) provides the mirror image of this phrasing. The date of the policy is not necessarily its date of issuance. In many regions of the country, it is issued after the closing and after the insurer has had a chance to perform a last-minute search for documents both affecting the insured title and recorded up to the time the deed is filed for record. This can be many days after the closing, but the policy might still be dated either as of the closing or the date on which the bring-down search is completed. When the later date is used, the insured's attorney should ask for "gap" insurance—for the period between the closing and recording.

Against loss or damage . . . sustained or incurred These phrases, particularly the verbs "sustained or incurred," serve to emphasize the indemnity aspect of the policy. Title insurance is a reimbursement or indemnity agreement, not a guarantee or warranty of a title. The policy is not breached simply because the title is defective when issued. It is only breached on the assertion of the defect that the insurer, upon notice, fails to cure, remove, or pay for within a reasonable time. If the insured title is encumbered by an interest covered (and not excepted or excluded) by the policy, the encumbrance must result in an actual loss to the insured. Often this means that the encumbrance must be asserted, rather than merely discovered, to exist. Exclusion 3(c) mirrors this phrasing.

Title to Notice that in the statements of coverage the references are to the title to an estate or interest, any defect or lien on the title, or a right of access. The insurer is taking pains to emphasize that the land, or possession of the land, is not insured—only title to an interest in the land is covered. The first three standard exceptions, shown here in Schedule B, reinforce this point: The "rights or claims of parties in possession," "what an accurate survey would disclose," and "easements not shown on the public record" are not insured.

Vested otherwise This phrase, found in the first statement of coverage in the policy, has two meanings. Primarily it is a reiteration of the requirement of a loss or damage. That the insured title is not as described is insufficient for a claim; the title must also be "vested otherwise," meaning that it must exist in someone other than the insured—a someone who is presumably capable of asserting it as well. Secondarily, the phrase is also taken as a negation of the requirement of an insurable interest in the insured. Insurers sometimes attempt to argue that if the title or interest insured never was in the insured, then there never was any coverage. Title insurance is a policy issued against the possibility that the insured may be found to lack the insurable interest that she was thought to hold.

Exclusions for . . . governmental regulations This, as well as rights of eminent domain and the police power, all contained in the first two exclusions, makes the fundamental point that only private interests are insured. Assertions against the insured title based on public rights are excluded. Notice, however, that some public rights are excluded categorically; those related to building and housing codes, zoning, and subdivision regulations are examples. Others, such as those based on eminent domain and the police power, are excluded, unless exercised and appearing of record—in which instance, they can be searched for and discovered in the course of a title search.

Defects . . . created, suffered, assumed, or agreed to This is the broadest, most litigated of the exclusions. It is typically known as Exclusion 3(a). It is in part a reiteration of the principle stated in the Conditions, to the effect that "liability voluntarily assumed" by the insured in settling a claim without prior consent of the insurer creates no coverage. Its objective is to prevent the insured from creating a defect on the insured title and then basing a policy claim on it. An actual intent is necessary on the insured's part. If the defect is the unintended legal consequence of the insured's act, it does not apply. However, the cases often treat this string of verbs as if they have different—and increasingly broad—meanings. With this in mind, the phrase "defects . . . and other matters" may also be given generous meanings, and the doctrine of *ejusdem generis* may not apply. Remember that exclusions in any policy of insurance, not just title insurance, are to be narrowly construed, particularly so when they defeat the expectations of the insured. This exclusion, known as Exclusion 3(a), prevents the insured from recovering on a defect arising because of faulty closing procedures at the insured's own closing.

Defects . . . not known to the Company and not shown on the public records, but known to the insured This is the second most often invoked exclusion—Exclusion 3(b). Here insurers eliminate from coverage those defects for which no search of the public records can be conducted but of which the insured knows when the policy is issued. This exclusion is reinforced by a Condition in the policy—typically "A Duty to Cooperate" with an insurer when asserting a claim on a policy.

Conditions The Conditions generally commence with a series of definitions. They make plain that the insured's coverage continues indefinitely. This is not term insurance. However, under Condition 1, the coverage cannot be assigned, except as expressly permitted by the policy, to any purchaser of the insured. Under Condition 2, once the insured sells the insured title, the policy is converted into coverage for any further liability that the insured may have for warranties given in the deed or other document by which the sale is accomplished. Only this warranty coverage survives the sale of the insured title by the insured.

The Conditions contain a *duty to defend* (as in *provide for the defense of*) the insured title, as well as the *right to establish* it. The words are litigation-oriented, but they extend to an administrative proceeding as well. If there is a right to establish the insured title, there may also be a duty to establish the title. A principle of mutuality supports such a duty. However, this duty, once undertaken, can be pursued through all appeals. A condition in the policy, 7(b), reiterates this principle. Condition 8 states that an insurer will pay the "least" measure of the value of a claim on the policy. Condition 10 states that "a voluntary satisfaction of the insured lien shall terminate all liability" of the insurer. A good faith duty to settle the claim (not express in the policy) may in many cases result in speedier settlements of the dispute for the insured. Once undertaken, any litigation is in the insurer's hands. Successful litigation is, in these conditions, clearly an alternative to payment of the claim. The insured cannot have both payment of the claim and the title as insured—that would be a windfall to her. Payment of the claim gives the insurer a subrogation right to any entitlement previously held by the insured.

The policy attempts, through an "*entire contract* or agreement" clause, to restrict any claim based on negligent abstracting or title search. This attempt has often been unsuccessful. Tort claims for defective searches are often (not always) allowed.

In the following examples involving either an owner's or a lender's title insurance policy, assume that O purchases an ALTA policy that has a policy date the same as the date on which O closed the purchase of the interest. Assume that the interest insured in the policy is a fee simple absolute unless otherwise noted.

Examples

Example 3a

O purchases a subdivision lot on a dirt road. The lot is in a subdivision for which a plat map was filed and accepted by the municipality as part of its land records. The surrounding municipality refuses to issue a building permit to construct a house on it because it is on a dirt road. Does O have a claim under her policy?

Explanation

No. A title to the lot can be a "marketable title" in the legal sense, but without fair market value in the economic sense. Thus, an insured can have a perfect legal title, worth nothing—and no claim under the title policy. *See Hocking v. Title Ins. & Trust Co.*, 234 P.2d 625 (Cal. 1951) (a leading case). Title insurance does not insure the physical condition of the lot: If it contained toxic substances and was unbuildable, the result would be the same.

Example 3b

The lot turns out to be surrounded by a trackless swamp and is accessible only by four-wheel drive vehicles. Does O have a claim for the lack of access to the lot?

Explanation

No. The policy insures that there is a *right* of access to the lot, not that a low-slung car can reach it without damage. So long as there is a legal right of access, there is no claim. An access easement, even a revokable license, suffices if in existence at the time the policy is issued. Title insurance is not property insurance. *See Title & Trust Co. of Florida v. Barrows*, 381 So. 2d 1088 (Fla. App. Ct. 1979).

Example 4

O purchases a house and lot along with a title policy. Five years after moving in, O discovers that one of the deeds in her record chain of title was executed by a man adjudicated incompetent three years before the date of execution. Does O have a claim against the insurer?

Explanation

Yes. *See Citicorp Sav. Bank of Illinois v. Stewart Title Ins. Corp.*, 840 F.2d 526, 531 (7th Cir. 1987).

Example 4a

Same facts, but the adjudication of incompetency takes place after the date of the policy. The finding of incompetency, nonetheless, is based on facts occurring before that date. Does O have a claim against her insurer?

Explanation

Yes, O still has a claim.

Example 4b

Same facts, but O has notice of the incompetency proceedings and does not disclose what she knows to the insurer. Does she have a claim against the insurer?

Explanation

Yes. This hypothetical presents an Exclusion 3(b) question. O still has a claim because the proceedings are a public record of which the insurer also knows.

Example 5

O purchases and insures a 99-year leasehold on a condominium unit in a large resort. O agrees not to occupy the unit for more than one week per year and to permit a development company to manage the unit, along with all other units, and share pro rata in the profits from the rentals of all units. Ten years later, the creditors of the resort force it into bankruptcy. The trustee in bankruptcy seeks to evict O for nonpayment of maintenance fees. Does O have a claim against her insurer?

Explanation

No. The policy does not insure against the risk of bankruptcy as such but may insure against a bankruptcy court finding that the insured title or interest is invalid. *See First National Bank & Trust Co. of Port Chester v. New York Title Ins. Co.*, 12 N.Y.S.2d 703 (Sup. Ct., Westchester County, 1939). Bankruptcy is a business, not a title risk. Maintenance fees in a condominium are given priority over the interest insured as a leasehold.

Example 5a

Same facts, except that the trustee argues that the leasehold interest insured was really an equity contract, subject to the securities laws, and O is not the holder of an interest in real property, but an investor in the resort. Does O now have a claim against her insurer?

Explanation

Yes. The question of whether the policy insures against the risk of bankruptcy is unchanged; it does not. However, the resort-wide management of the units for the owners is a violation of the securities laws, and the trustee has authority to recharacterize the leaseholds as "equity" interests in the resort—the securities law equivalent of shares. Thus, when the policy was issued, the interests insured were not leaseholds—indeed, were not property interests insurable with a title policy—and were unmarketable as such. Titles to the leaseholds were not as represented in Schedule A of the policy: they were "vested otherwise" in the development company. O does have a claim. *See Allison v. Ticor Title Ins. Co.*, 907 F.2d 645 (7th Cir. 1990).

Title insurance policies are issued in two forms: One standard policy is issued to owners and another to mortgage lenders insuring the priority of their lien. As between the two policies, there are differences in coverage. Think about whether an insured lender must foreclose before making a claim. How feasible is that in the context of the national secondary market for mortgages? Defining the "actual loss" a title insurer must indemnify is different for an insured owner and an insured lender. An insured owner receives the full value of the interest or estate insured when a title defect appears. An insured lender's "actual loss" cannot be determined until the note is not repaid and the security for the mortgage lien proves inadequate. *See Centerpoint Mech. Lien Claims, LLC v. Commonwealth Land Title Ins. Co.*, 569 P.3d 796, 2025 Ariz. LEXIS 187, **17-18 (Ariz. 2025). Thus, an insured mortgage lender must typically assert the lien, foreclose on it, and find the proceeds of the foreclosure sale inadequate.

Example 6

O wishes to refinance her residential mortgage. ME1 holds a mortgage lien on the premises. O approaches ME2 about a new lower-rate loan and mortgage. ME2 agrees to extend the new loan to O. An escrow account is established by ME2 with a subsidiary of a title insurer to pay off ME1's old loan, release ME1's lien, transfer a new lien to ME2, and insure ME2's lien priority. ME2 pays the proceeds of its loan into escrow, and ME1 receives the escrow agent's check payable to it to release its lien; ME2's title policy is released from escrow and delivered to ME2; the check payable to ME1 is returned for insufficient funds. The escrow agent absconds with the funds intended to pay off ME1. Does ME2 have a claim under its lender's title policy against the insurer?

Explanation

No. The risk of loss for insufficient funds is ME2's, who established the escrow. Why? Because at the time the check was returned uncashed, the agent held the funds for ME2, not ME1. *See Jones v. Lally*, 511 So. 2d 1014 (Fla. App. 1987). However, the resolution of the risk of loss issue does not answer the question of whether this risk is covered by its title policy. It is not. Title insurance does not cover losses incurred in the closing of a transaction leading to insurance. The risk of insolvency of the agent relates to a separate function—escrowing the title, not insuring it—and should be separately treated unless the insurer agrees to hold harmless those of its agents using its escrow services. Title insurers sometimes do this for approved attorneys closing a transaction with a "closing protection letter." This is an agreement (not part of a lender's title policy) by an insurer to indemnify a mortgage lender whose lien is about to be insured, from the misconduct, negligence, fraud, or embezzlement of its agent at closing.

Example 7

Big Bank loaned money to Mortgage Bank to finance a large subdivision project. The project was secured by a mortgage lien, and its developer purchased a lender's title insurance policy. The market for subdivision lots slowed, and the costs of construction exceeded the revenue to pay off the loan. As a result, mechanics' liens were filed against the subdivision developer. After litigation over the priority of various mechanics liens conducted by the title insurer, the insurer reached a settlement with the mechanics to release their liens. Big Bank then bought Mortgage Bank, the insured under the title policy, for a sum that repaid the initial mortgage loan. Does Mortgage Bank have a claim under its policy?

Explanation

No. Even though Mortgage Bank might *de facto* still exist as an insured entity, the repayment of the loan means no coverage under the policy, for, if the lender owes nothing on the loan, the lien insured is of no value. The adage is, "the mortgage lien lives and dies with the note." The satisfaction or release of the insured mortgage lien terminates the insurer's liability under the policy: A lender's policy limits coverage to damages "sustained or incurred" because of the subordination of the insured mortgage lien to other liens or encumbrances—here the mechanics liens—and then only to the extent that the mortgage loan remains unpaid. Since the loan here was fully repaid—not in a formal sense, but by the buyout of Mortgage Bank—nothing was owed on the loan: When the loan disappears, so does the insured lien securing it, and a decline in value of the lien is *pro tanto* a decline in coverage—here down to zero. *See Centerpoint Mech. Lien Claims, LLC v. Commonwealth Land Title Ins. Co.*, 569 P.3d 796 (Ariz. 2025). Had the insurer not defended its insured, it would have been liable for the costs of the defense; here, however, the insurer fulfilled its duty to defend.

Example 8

Brown Title Ins. Co. and Burke Title Ins. Co. each insure a mortgage on Blackacre. Brown's mortgage closing was in the morning and Burke's in the afternoon of the same day. The next morning, both mortgages are recorded and because local custom permitted title companies access to the recorder's office before the office opens to the public, both mortgages were stamped as received by the recorder at exactly 9 a.m. on the day following the closings. The applicable Recording Act is of the race-notice type. Does each mortgage have equal priority?

Explanation

No. Although as a legal matter and for purposes of assigning priority, each was recorded simultaneously, neither is a "subsequent purchaser" as required by the recording Act. So, when the Act is inapplicable, the common law rule of "first-in-time, first-in-right" controls. Thus, the mortgage lien insured by Brown has priority. Regarding both mortgage liens as having "simultaneous" priority is impractical because both would then have to be foreclosed at the same time, in the same foreclosure, denying both mortgagees the remedy they bargained for. *See First Bank v. East West Bank*, 132 Cal Rptr.

3d 287 (Cal App. Ct. 2011). The two mortgages might be assigned priority as of the time each was indexed; however, most jurisdictions do not regard the index as part of the official record, so this solution too is impractical.

Example 9

V and P sign a brief but enforceable contract of sale for Blackacre. The transaction goes smoothly until the final preparations for closing. P then insists that V deliver a general warranty deed to him, citing remote but still enforceable title defects in V's chain of title. P's title insurer states that, as is local custom, every link in the chain involves a special warranty deed. As P's attorney, what advice would you give P on this matter?

Explanation

Your advice should have three parts. After first explaining the difference between a general and a special warranty deed, you might point out that the former provides greater protection for P against V upon the assertion of the remote title defect. Second, explain that insurers are often said to prefer the use of special warranty deeds: A special warranty deed, when insured, enables the insurer to narrow its policy obligation after P sells the insured title and his Warranty coverage kicks in. However, you should also explain that P's closing by choosing and accepting a general warranty deed, gives rise to an argument under Exclusion 3(a), that P "suffered" or "assumed" the defects created by a remote grantor in the chain of title, thus excluding a claim on that defect from coverage. Third, explain to P the widely recognized difference between coverage issues under the policy and the insurer's duty to defend its insured against the assertion of a past title defect. The duty to defend is broader than the duty to cover a claim; it does not depend on whether there is coverage. If the insurer does not fulfill its obligation to defend, it cannot later contest issues of coverage. It is for this reason that many people buy title insurance—it's really litigation insurance. A general warranty of title does not require V to remove or cure the defect until it is asserted; thus, it is useful when the defect is remote and unlikely to be asserted. When an insurer is likely to argue—this will not be everywhere—that accepting a general warranty deed gives rise to an Exclusion 3(a) defense, a fourth piece of advice for P might be that he should ask for an Endorsement on the policy providing that the insurer will not use the Exclusion 3(a) defense against P. As a general matter, when an attorney is dealing with a title insurer, it is prudent, as problems arise, to have the insurer's Endorsement Guide handy. Each insurer will issue its own set of standard endorsements—some for an extra fee and some *gratis*. Further, endorsements can be tailored to particular transactions and problems raised before closing. With proper endorsements, we can deliver a general warranty deed to P.

MEASURING THE DAMAGES OF THE POLICYHOLDER

As discussed generally in the prior section of this chapter, in situations involving a partial failure of an owner's title, an insured is entitled to either (1) the actual loss caused by the defect or (2) the difference between the fair market value of the title with and without that defect, whichever is less. In instances of a total failure of title, the insured is entitled to the fair market value of the title that she thought she had. The amount of the policy serves as an upper limit on the insurer's liability under the policy and is subject to the requirement that the insured show the loss or damage. The traditional date for measuring damages is the date of the closing on the insured title, but reliance damages have also been awarded when the insurer knows that the property, title to which is insured, is to undergo development of some type; thus, damages have also been measured on the date on which the title defect limiting development is discovered.

Examples

Example 10

O starts to develop land but discovers an easement across it. The insurer admits that its title searcher missed this interest when conducting the search but argues that the value of the easement is measured as of the date of the policy, not the date of the easement's disclosure. On this argument, what result?

Explanation

Compare *Overholtzer v. Northern Counties Title Ins. Corp.*, 253 P.2d 116 (Cal. App. 1953); *Hartman v. Shambaugh*, 630 P.2d 758, 761-763 (N.M. 1981) (preferring the date of discovery of the defect), with *Glyn v. Title Guaranty & Trust Co. of New York*, 117 N.Y.S. 424 (1909). The modern view is that the date on which the defect is discovered is the date for measuring the "actual damages."

Example 11

O purchases and insures the title for land that she plans to develop. O procures development and construction mortgage loan financing, and closes on the mortgage loan. The market for the development collapses. O's development is stymied by the assertion of an easement across the land. O files a claim with the insurer, and the insurer argues that the measure of damages on the claim should be measured as of the date the easement is discovered. Is the insurer correct?

Explanation

No. In a falling market that, as here, hits bottom at a value close to zero, the modern view may result in a claim with a very low monetary value. However, cases like *Hartman*, declaring that the date of discovery is the one on which damages are measured, are an example of a rule seeking indemnity for the insured who has started to develop the property and relied on the title permitting that development. When the insured has committed herself to a mortgage, she in effect has used the title as would any developer, as a source of funds. She remains liable to repay that mortgage loan, and the title insurer, if otherwise liable, should pay as of the time of the closing on that loan.

Another way to handle this is for O to argue that damages should include economic or opportunity cost damages—here, the lost resale of the development. *See Native Sun Inv. Group v. Ticor Title Ins. Co.*, 235 Cal. Rptr. 34, 37-38 (Cal. App. 1987). Damages caused by the defect in the title are compensable, no matter the date on which the defect is measured.

CONVEYANCING REFORM BY STATUTE

Perhaps the most effective statutes for quieting titles and removing defects and encumbrances on them are statutes of limitation, along with the law of adverse possession, viewed, as it should be, as a gloss on these statutes. Statutes of limitation fix a time beyond which ancient claims, defects, and encumbrances may no longer be the subject of judicial action and determination; they withdraw the privilege of litigating and deny the aid of the courts to the claimant who waits too long. They thus reinforce the title of any possessor of land. At the same time, however, they are ineffective against the holders of future, nonpossessory interests, against persons under a disability (such as incompetents), against the government at its various levels, and against cotenants or mineral estates. These defects in the title-curing features of statutes of limitations have led to the enactment of other, more specialized types of statutes.

MARKETABLE TITLE ACTS

These acts have been adopted in almost 20 states. They are modeled on a statute promulgated by the Commissioners on Uniform State Laws. The Model Marketable Title Act is a legislative attempt to shorten the chain of title required for a title search. Searches are confined to a period of 30 to

40 years, plus the number of years it takes to search back to the next title transaction in the chain. These acts do not confine the title search to a prescribed number of years but rather set a search period for each title based on the legislative period, plus the number of years required to get back to the next prior transaction. The next prior transaction becomes what is called in these acts the "root of title," and the title searcher begins in the grantor index from that transaction, searching forward in time from it to the present. *See Blanton v. City of Pinellas Park*, 887 So. 2d 1224, 1228 (Fla. 2004).

When a vendor can present a purchaser with a "marketable record title" of the length required by the act, all previous claims, defects, and encumbrances on the title (but based on documents preceding the root of title) are extinguished, whether or not the interest has ever been a possessory one. ("Marketable" in the sense used in such an act is not to be confused with the doctrine of marketable title; that doctrine is unchanged by any of these acts.) Not only do these acts limit the period of search, but they also extinguish the majority of interests that would be discoverable in any title search extended beyond the period of marketable record title. *See State of Minnesota v. Hess*, 684 N.W.2d 414, 422-423, 426-427 (Minn. 2004).

In order to preserve a claim, the claimant must file (or refile) it in the public land records within the 30- to 40-year statutory period. This filing requirement becomes particularly important for mortgagees, holders of deeds of trust, and other security interests in real property. However, once extinguished, a claim or interest is not thereafter revived by refiling or rerecording; however, a claim arising subsequent to the root of title, recorded but not within the chain of marketable record title, may not be extinguished by the act. *Heifner v. Bradford*, 446 N.E. 2d 440 (Ohio 1983). So these acts are no substitute for being able to check the results of a grantor/grantee search with a tract index. The constitutionality of such statutes has been upheld in numerous state courts against arguments based on the due process clause, the takings clause, and the contracts clause of various state constitutions.

Exceptions A marketable record title is subject to certain exceptions, also enumerated in acts of this type; a landlord's reversion, for example, is often excepted, and so are public utility easements and governmental interests—particularly the interests of the federal government, which may not be affected by state law without consent under the supremacy clause of the U.S. Constitution. Rights of persons in possession are routinely excepted, as are the workings of the doctrine of adverse possession. A person with a marketable record title cannot defeat the interests of a party in possession for the period of marketable title. In oil and gas and mineral-rich states, certain mineral estates are likely to be excepted as well. As to the last exception, another type of legislation—known as a dormant minerals act—is increasingly likely to have been enacted to deal with mineral-related defects in a title. A dormant minerals act requires that an unused mineral estate lapse after a statutory period tolled without refiling the interest or estate in the public land records. *Texaco, Inc. v. Short*, 454 U.S. 516 (1982) (upholding a dormant minerals act). *Short* is taken to uphold, as a matter of federal constitutional law, the constitutionality of marketable title acts as well.

A shortened version of the text of the model act follows.

MODEL MARKETABLE TITLE ACT

Section 1. Any person having an unbroken chain of title of record to any interest in land for 40 years or more shall be deemed to have a marketable record title to such interest, as defined in Section 8 and subject to the matters stated in Section 2.

Section 2. Such marketable record title shall be subject to:

(a) All interests and defects which are inherent in the muniments of which such chain of record title is formed; provided, however, that a general reference in such muniments to easements, use restrictions, or other interests created prior to the root of title shall not be sufficient to preserve them, unless specific identification be made therein of a recorded title transaction which creates the interest preserved.

(b) All interests preserved by the filing of proper notice or by possession by the same owner continuously for a period of 40 years or more.

(c) The rights of any person arising from a period of adverse possession, which was in whole or part subsequent to the effective date of the root of title.

(d) Any interest arising out of a title transaction which has been recorded subsequent to the effective date of the root of title from which the unbroken chain of title of record is started; provided that no interest extinguished by Section 3 shall be revived.

(e) The exceptions stated in Section 6.

Section 3. Subject to the matters stated in Section 2, such marketable record title shall be held by its owner and shall be taken by any person dealing with the land free and clear of all interests whatsoever, the existence of which depends on any act, transaction, event, or omission that occurred prior to the effective date of the root of title. All such interests, however denominated, whether legal or equitable, present or future, whether such interests are asserted by a person who is sui juris or under a disability, within or without the state, natural or corporate, private or governmental, are hereby declared to be null and void.

Section 4. Any person claiming an interest in land may preserve it by filing for record during the 40-year period immediately following the effective date of the root of title of the person whose record title would otherwise be marketable, a notice in writing, setting forth the nature of the claim. No disability or lack of knowledge of any kind on anyone's part shall suspend the running of this 40-year period. A continuous 40-year period of possession, during which no title transaction appears of record in this chain of title, shall be deemed the equivalent of a filing under this section.

Section 5. The notice shall contain an accurate description of the land affected, which is at least as full as the description in any recorded instrument on which the claim is founded. It shall be filed in the records of the county in which the land is situated, entered in the records in the same manner as other recordable transactions, and indexed both by the name of the claimant in the grantee index and by legal description.

Section 6. This act shall not be applied to bar any lessor or his successor as a reversioner of his right to possession on the expiration of any lease; or to bar or extinguish any easement clearly observable by physical evidence of its use; or to bar any right, title, or interest of the United States, by reason of failure to file notice as required by Section 4.

Section 7. This act shall not change or modify any applicable statute of limitations.

Section 8. Definitions.

(a) "Marketable record title" means a title of record, as indicated in Section 1, which operates to extinguish such interests existing prior to the effective date of the root of title, as are stated in Section 3.

(b-c) "Records" includes probate and other official public records, as well as records in the registry of deeds. Recording, when applied to court records, includes filing.

(d) "Person dealing with the land" includes a purchaser of any estate or interest therein, a mortgagee, a levying or attaching creditor, a land contract vendee, or any other person seeking to acquire an estate or interest therein, or impose a lien thereon.

(e) "Root of title" means that conveyance or other title transaction in the chain of title of a person, purporting to create the interest claimed by such person, upon which he relies as a basis for the marketability of his title, and which was the most recent to be recorded as of a day 40 years prior to the time when marketability is being determined. The effective date of the "root of title" is the date on which it is recorded.

(f) "Title transaction" means any transaction affecting title to any interest in land, including title by will or descent, title by tax deed, or by trustee's, referee's, guardian's, executor's, administrator's, master's, or sheriff's deed, or decree of any court, warranty deed, or mortgage.

A marketable record title protected by this act can consist of a chain with a single link. If O conveys to A who records in 1949, A will in 1990 have the protection of the act. The 1949 conveyance is the root of title and the single link in the chain of marketable record title. On the other hand, if the O-A 1949 conveyance is not recorded until 1959, A will not gain the protection of the act until the year 2000 because the recording is what establishes the root of title, and that has been moved forward ten years by the failure to record for that time.

A marketable record title is likely to have more than one link. If O conveyed to A who records in 1949, A to B who records in 1950, and B to C in 1960, but C does not record and conveys to D in 1970, the break in the chain of recording denies D a marketable *record* title until such time as the chain of title is one completely of record—even if the unrecorded transaction can be proven by extrinsic (meaning here, outside the public records) evidence. A person seeking the protection of the act must have unbroken record title back to, but also including, the root of title.

Section 2 defines some interests to which a marketable record title is subject. Thus, if the root of title states that the title transferred is "subject to all easements and covenants of record," the title searcher has no duty to go back, past the root of title, to ascertain what these interests might be. The lack of a specific reference, in a book number and page, is fatal; only a specific reference preserves them. However, a reference in the root of title to a preexisting easement conveyed by deed recorded in book number 65, page 670, would preserve the easement. *See* §2(a).

Likewise, interests conflicting with a marketable record title, predating the root of title and recorded during the period of marketability commencing with the date of the root of title, are preserved. So if O conveys to A in 1950 and that conveyance becomes the root, but in 1948 O had conveyed an interest to X in conflict with A's deed, and X conveyed the interest to Y in 1960, Y's interest is preserved. However, if X had waited until 1991 to convey to Y, the interest would not be preserved because it was not the subject of a conveyance within the 40-year period of marketability running from the date of the root of title. *See* §2(d).

Marketable record title is also subject to persons establishing adverse possession or prescriptive rights (*see* §2(c)), rights held in possession for 40 years, or rights preserved by a notice (§2(b)).

Examples

Example 12

O and S (a married couple) move to Blackacre in 1949, purchasing the property together from V. O and S record V's deed to them; they raise their family on Blackacre, but by the 1990s their children are grown and have moved away and O and S are ready to move to a smaller property. In 1995, O and S sell Blackacre to P. With the Model Marketable Title Act in effect, what should the title abstractor/searcher do to prove their title to P?

Explanation

The title searcher first must determine how far back to search. This is not a matter of ascertaining a particular date or year, but of finding what the act calls the "root of title" as defined in §8(e). In this case, the root is the 1949 purchase of Blackacre. The absence of a transfer of title for 40 years, between 1949 and 1989, does not prevent O and S from obtaining a "marketable record title"; it can consist of a chain with a single link (although most marketable record titles are likely to have more than one link). Thus the title abstractor need only search back to the 1949 deed, thereafter searching forward for conveyances out of O and/or S. O and S are also protected by §4 of the act, which provides that they need not file a claim to preserve their title;

consistent with the common law, the act provides that possession trumps written interests.

Example 13

A took a deed to Blackacre in 1925, but the deed had no witnesses, as required then by statute. A conveyed Blackacre to B in 1935, but the description was ambiguous, not following precisely that of earlier deeds. B conveyed to C in 1945. C died in 1970, and H was her heir. H is given a deed by the executor of C's estate. All of the forgoing deeds were promptly recorded. H wishes to sell Blackacre to P in 1996. Does H have a marketable record title?

Explanation

Yes. Here the act eliminates any objection to H's title based on the unwitnessed, 1925 deed and the ambiguous description in the 1935 deed. All this is accomplished because the "root of title" is the 1945 deed, on the basis of which H acquires a marketable record title in 1985.

Example 14

What if the 1945 deed was a forgery?

Explanation

H no longer has marketable record title, because the "root of title" is subject to a defect "inherent in the muniments of title of which record title is formed." *See* §2(a). Thus a further inquiry is now necessary to determine if B engaged in any "title transaction" protected under §2(d) and occurring within the period of marketable title before an attorney can say that H has a marketable record title.

Example 15

What if the 1945 deed granted not a fee simple absolute, but instead a fee simple determinable?

Explanation

Same result. B here reserved a possibility of reverter. This estate is not extinguished by the lapse of the period of marketable record title. *See* §6. So C does not have a fee simple absolute, and neither do his transferees. Some other type of statute is necessary to deal with this problem. (In some jurisdictions, such statutes have been enacted, providing for a limited life or duration of a right of reentry and a possibility of reverter, terminating them 30 to 40 years after their creation.) By the same token, remainders and reversions are not extinguished by (say) the possession of a life tenant for a number of years in excess of the period. However, were the life tenant to mortgage the property, then default on the mortgage and, in the mortgagee's foreclosure action, a purchaser at the foreclosure sale took title in fee simple absolute, and then possessed the property for the period, the future interest holder's rights would be extinguished.

Example 16

Does the act extinguish an unrecorded party wall agreement made over 40 years ago for a duplex residential structure?

Explanation

Section 2(d) would seem to require two things that this agreement does not have: first, that the agreement be linked to a title transaction making up the marketable record title, and, second, that its recordation be within the period of marketable title. However, the two other sections (§§4 and 6) suggest that if this agreement can be treated as one involving a visible, possessory interest, then it will be preserved and marketable record title is held subject to it.

Example 17

Does the act require recordation of a boundary agreement between neighbors established by mutual acquiescence?

Explanation

No. Unwritten agreements need not be recorded.

Example 18

Is a reciprocal negative easement, established by judicial decision as in *Sanborn v. McLean*, 206 N.W. 496 (Mich. 1925), valid for no longer than 40-plus years in a state adopting the act?

Explanation

To the extent that such an easement arises from the inquiry notice given by the construction of improvements implementing the larger scheme of restrictive easements and covenants in the neighborhood, it might be regarded as a possessory interest covered by §§4 and 6. But to the extent that it is a mistake or gap in the written scheme, it must be filed every 40 years, and if not filed is extinguished by the act.

Example 19

Your client, John Smith, wants to sell Blackacre to P. Having established the root of title in Smith's chain of title to Blackacre, you find that, in the deed that is the root of title and other deeds leading the deed to Smith, Blackacre is conveyed by the following language: "Lot 10 in Block 2 of Sunshine Acres, according to the Plat Plan thereof, as recorded in Plat Book 16 at page 234 of the Public Land Records" of your county and state. The plat plan was filed before the root of title. It shows a restrictive covenant that would prevent further development on Blackacre by P. Can Smith transfer a marketable record title to P?

Explanation

No. Two arguments should be considered. First, the restriction is preserved as being "inherent in the muniments" language of §2(a). What are "muniments"? They might be narrowly defined as documents of title or more broadly defined as evidence of title. When the latter definition is used, this argument carries the day. Second, the deed's incorporation by reference of the plat may also be a "specific identification" of a "title transaction" rather than a general reservation of rights under §2(a). However, a "title transaction" is arguably too narrowly defined to include a plat plan. *See* §8(f). So this second argument is a weak one. *See Sunshine Vista Homeowners Assn. v. Carana*, 623 So. 2d 490 (Fla. 1993) [where the statute was clear, made so by a reference to "plats" in the Florida version of §2(a)]. In related cases, the reference to a plat in a deed's legal description incorporates the plat's terms into the description, but a reference to a plat in a title insurance policy does not give rise to a policy claim based on the plat's terms; presumably such a policy is not evidence of a title transaction, but a plat may be.

Example 20

O executes an installment land sale contract for Blackacre with A. O conveys Blackacre to B, who records his deed. How does the act treat this type of contract?

Explanation

From the definition of a "title transaction" in Section 8(f), it does not appear that an installment contract falls within the definition. Notice also that a "person dealing with the land" (so protected by the act) under §3 is B, not the contract vendee.

Example 21

O conveys to A 42 years ago; A records and remains in continuous possession of Blackacre to the present. Forty-one years ago, B conveys Blackacre to C. B had no prior interest in the property. C records and, one month later, conveys to D. Today D wants to sell to your client. What advice would you give this client? If A had been out of possession for 20 of the last 42 years, would your advice change?

Explanation

Here there are two "roots of title" leading to two chains of marketable record title. This is arguably a situation that the act was not intended to handle, so one might argue that the act is inapplicable. *See Exchange Natl. Bank v. Lawndale Natl. Bank*, 243 N.E.2d 193 (Ill. 1968) (holding that a wild deed cannot serve as a root of title). The better answer is that this client will have to yield to A's rights under §4 of the act, which take precedence over an out-of-possession, but otherwise marketable, record title. If A were out of possession for 20 of the last 40 years and does not qualify for §4 rights, then your advice would change and your client's filing a Section 4 notice is in order, but the timing of that notice is unclear. *See Marshall v. Hollywood*, 224 So. 2d 743 (Fla. App. 1969), aff'd, 236 So. 2d 114 (Fla. 1970) (holding that a wild deed can serve as a root of title and, as such, extinguish the true title), noted, 29 U. Fla. L. Rev. 916, 927-931 (1977).

In this connection, notice that a "root of title" is given the legal effect that it "purports" to have. *See* §8(e). Thus a valid root might even be a sheriff's tax deed subject to some defect not evident on its face, perhaps arising from the sheriff's failure to comply with the tax sale statute. If, however, the reference to a possibly adverse instrument is clearly indicated in the deed so that the title searcher can locate it in the records or with a reasonable investigation, the deed containing such a reference will not serve as a valid root of title to extinguish that adverse interest. So don't let the number of situations acceptable as a root of title get out of hand. A quitclaim deed, for example, is not a valid root of title, because the root must be a "title transaction" and that last term requires a "warranty deed" in §8(f).

Example 22

Forty-five years ago, O mortgages Blackacre to M. O makes regular payments under the mortgage, but the principal is not fully repaid today. Thirty-nine years ago, O conveys Blackacre to A. When should M file a §4 notice? What if the act were amended to provide, at the beginning of §1, "No action shall be brought affecting the possession or title to real property, except by . . ." (thereafter continuing as in the model act); would this amendment affect your answer?

Explanation

Probably the notice filing, if it occurs today, comes too late to preserve the effectiveness of the mortgage. The §4 notice must be filed within 40 years of the root of title, and the facts indicate that the root is removed by more than 45 years from the present day. Thus, to preserve M's interest, he would have to file a notice in the public records at least once every 40 years. An act set up like a statute of limitations would more clearly yield the same answer.

Example 23

O has a recorded title in 1945. X, having no title, receives a deed from Y in 1948. O dies in 1994, devising his real estate to H. O's will is duly probated and the decree putting the title in H is recorded the same year. Can X claim to have a marketable record title at the end of 1998?

Explanation

No, because the intervening O/H probate decree operated just like notice under the recording statute and protects H's title. Section 2(d) operates to prevent X's title from becoming a marketable record one. Because there has been a recorded "title transaction," defined in §8(f) to include an executor's deed or court decree, within the period of marketable record title, this record is just as effective as a filed notice under §4.

Example 24

If O had lived until 1999, would the result be the same?

Explanation

Yes, it would, but in this situation, the provision equating a 40-year possession with a statement of claim (in §4) would protect H. The act reinforces adverse possession law in §2(c) and reinforces the law of possessory rights. *See* §2(b).

CURATIVE STATUTES

A curative statute is retrospective legislation reaching into the past to operate on past transactions in order to render valid those transactions that would otherwise be ineffective to do what the parties to the transaction intended. It provides that after the lapse of a specified number of years, a document's failure to comply with a certain formal requirement of the law not only is immaterial to the effectiveness of that document to provide constructive notice through the public records, but also ceases to affect its admissibility as evidence. (An alternative, less frequent type of curative statute cures all documents on the record with defects of a certain type as of the date of the statute's enactment.) Such statutes exert their effect on the record at a time removed from a document's recordation, but not at a time so close to its drafting as to encourage carelessness in drafting.

Curative statutes correct frequently recurring conveyancers' errors. They reach back and, for example, cure a defectively executed or missing acknowledgment on a deed once it has been recorded a certain length of time; thereafter, the title searcher or reviewer may disregard the error or defect. Such statutes generally cure the formalities of conveyancing by assuming that, once the defective document has been long recorded—say, three to five years—the parties to the document intended it to be effective, and that the defect should not thereafter defeat that intention. Thereafter, the statute regards the defective document as having been fully effective from and after the date of its initial recordation and as cutting off intervening interests and estates. Curative statutes create more than a presumption about the parties' intent. Once cured, forever cured, regardless of the real intent of the parties; these statutes are aimed to give repose and reliability to the public records.

In addition to defective acknowledgments, other subjects for curative statutes have included the absence of a seal on a document, a defective power of attorney, defectively executed deeds from corporations (e.g., one executed by a corporate officer without authority) or partnerships (e.g., a conveyance in partnership name where the names of the partners are required), and defective judicial sale records.

Dealing as many such statutes do with the formalities of conveyancing, these statutes affect legislatively created requirements. What the legislature requires, it can also waive—and the statutes are also regarded a legislative waiver of the requirement in enumerated instances.

Difficulties with these statutes arise when during the period in which the defective instrument was on the record, an intervening and competing interest is created. Does the lapse of the period specified in the statute cure the defect in the sense that the formerly defective document relates back to the date of its first recording? If so, the curing of the defect will create a document trumping the intervening interest.

Massachusetts and Wisconsin have the greatest variety of these statutes. *See, e.g.*, Mass. Gen. L., ch. 184, §24. The following is a paraphrase of the statute just cited:

> When any written instrument, in any manner affecting or purporting to affect the title to real estate, has been recorded for a period of ten years and such instrument, but because of any defect, irregularity, or omission, fails to comply in any respect with any statutory requirement relating to the execution,

attestation, acknowledgment, or recording, such instrument and the record thereof shall be fully valid, binding, and effective to the same extent as if the instrument had in the first instance been in compliance with any such statutory requirement.

Examples

Example 25

In a state in which a curative statute like the one just cited is enacted and has been in effect for 20 years, assume that 10 years ago last month, O conveyed Blackacre, in an unacknowledged deed, to a joint tenancy with a right of survivorship, composed of O, A, and B. This deed is otherwise valid to create a joint tenancy and is promptly recorded. O died one year ago, leaving her widower as her sole heir. Who owns Blackacre today?

Explanation

It depends on whether the defective deed, when "cured" of the defect by the statute, is given the priority it would have had had it not been defective when first recorded, or is given the priority it has as of the time it is cured of its defective feature. There is generally little hesitancy in holding today that the reach of the statute is retroactive and that the deed takes the priority it had ten years ago. If so, the widower loses any interest in Blackacre because his spouse's death activates the right of survivorship, and A and B thus succeed to O's interest in the property. *See Dennen v. Searle*, 176 A.2d 561 (Conn. 1961), noted in 36 Conn. B.J. 642 (1962). As to this type of defect, moreover, the requirement (of an acknowledgment) is one that is created by statute. What the legislature can create, it can modify—or abolish. On that ground, the retroactive effect of the curative statute cannot be beyond the power of the legislature.

Finally, if the purpose of the curative statute is to do what the parties intended to do in the beginning, why not give the statute the power to correct the defect in what they did, as of the time they intended that the transaction be effective. The intervening interest of the widower is defeated on that basis as well. *See Watson v. Mercer*, 33 U.S. 88 (1834) (Story, J.); *Weeks v. Rombaugh*, 12 N.W.2d 636 (Neb. 1944).

PRESUMPTION STATUTES

Most jurisdictions have statutes that create a legal presumption (rebuttable by clear and convincing evidence to the contrary) that in a deed or other instrument of transfer, grantors, or transferors intended to transfer their whole and entire interest or estate in real property. Such statutes apply to a fee simple absolute as well as interests less than a fee simple absolute and make necessary a title search of the property to determine what the largest estate or interest was that might have passed to a transferor. Having determined that, the statutory presumption can be applied. In addition, many jurisdictions also have statutes in their probate codes that provide that a will or valid testamentary instrument shall convey all real property belonging to the testator, unless a contrary intent is clear. Thus, absent contrary evidence, a grantor or testator's transfer is presumed to grant or devise their whole interest or estate.

TITLE STANDARDS

Title standards are a fourth type of conveyancing reform often available today. These standards are promulgated by state bar associations and are intended to prevent attorneys from raising minor objections to a title's marketability when mechanisms, statutory and otherwise, are available for cleaning up that title. A little less than half our jurisdictions have such standards. They do not have the force of law; they are guidelines. However, in one state, Nebraska, the legislature periodically enacts them as statutes. They often appear as appendices in state codes. One such provides that "inconsistencies in recitals or indications of dates, as between dates of execution, attestation, acknowledgment, or recordations, do not, in themselves, impair marketability." Okla. Bar Ass'n Title Std. 6.2. Another typical standard relates to mortgages on the records that might be presumed stale: Mortgages with a stated maturity date can be presumed satisfied (say) 10 years after that date or, if lacking a maturity date, 40 years after filing. These standards extend the reach of a curative statute. Finally, they also insulate the conveyancing bar from charges of malpractice when following the practices recommended in a standard.

THE TORRENS SYSTEM

We have been discussing the recording acts and their uses by abstractors and attorneys—but in the eyes of many there is a better way. Instead of just presenting the documents needed to examine the current state of a title, what if references to all the interests encumbering a title were assembled in one place and the title guaranteed to be otherwise unencumbered by the governmental officer in charge of the records? Such a system would be a tract index, an abstract of title, and a guarantee of the title—all reduced to one document. The public records would then present not just evidence of title, but the thing itself. A present-day analogy would be the registration certificate to your automobile.

Such a system would, furthermore, eliminate the need to present a chain of title. The title on the document would present the results of an evaluation of a chain of title, and rather than chaining the title each time the title was transferred, one final title search that resulted in a certificate of title would be guaranteed as the state of the title. That title would then be "registered."[3]

In fact, such a system is used in most nations outside the formerly communist bloc, except for the United States. Even Great Britain, the country from which we inherited our system, uses it. So do most of the countries formerly part of the British Empire, although the system is more widespread than that. This system is called the Torrens system, named for a British civil servant and state premier in Australia, Sir Robert Richard Torrens. As a customs collector in Australia, he noticed the way the titles to ships were transferred. S. R. Simpson, Land Law and Registration 68 (1976); V. DiCastri, Thom's Canadian Torrens System (2d ed. 1962).

The Torrens system works on three basic ideas: the *mirror* principle, the *curtain* principle, and the *fund* principle. Simpson, *supra*, at 22. The *mirror* is the idea that the certificate of title reflects the state of the title at the time of issuance; all interests unnoted on the certificate do not exist. Thus the mirror may not reveal the whole history of the title; nevertheless, all unnoted interests—easements, mortgages, deeds of trust, leases, and other liens—are extinguished.

The *curtain* principle holds that the issuance of the certificate brings down the curtain on all unnoted interests. All adverse possessors, holders of secret liens, equities, and future interests or estates are bound by the certificate's description of the title.

Thereafter, they must look, under the *fund* principle, to a guaranty fund for compensation for the loss of any valid, but unnoted interest—even if that interest was in possession at the time at which the certificate was issued. No action for possession (e.g., foreclosure, perfection of a mechanic's lien, or ejectment) is thereafter held by the interest holder; thereafter, money from the fund, rather than possession, must suffice. *Canadian Pacific Ry. Ltd. v. Turta*, [1954] 3 D.L.R. 1. Compensation by the fund is given on an indemnity basis. Overall, the biggest advantage of the Torrens system is that it makes the public records subject to automation and computerization.

This system still uses contracts of sale and deeds, not as a means of conveyance but usually as evidence that the grantors wish to have a new

3. "Registered" is used here to distinguish the process from recording, although in some jurisdictions the recorder is called the registrar of titles. For the present, forget this fact; registration is a reference to a guaranteed title, recordation to the present system of laying title evidence on the public record.

certificate of title, naming the purchasers as the titleholders, issued by the registrar. Only the issuance of a replacement certificate acts as a conveyance. Transactions must be registered against the title enrolled in the state-operated land title office to be valid and are not valid until registered. When less than the full fee simple is transferred, the holder of the interest files to have a "caveat" enrolled in the certificate; unless so enrolled, the interest is not valid. Two certificates are in existence: One remains with the registrar, and another is held by the current owner. If the current owner resists having her certificate "charged" through enrollment of a less-than-fee interest, then the interested parties resort to an administrative hearing or judicial review of the dispute, or both.

At one time, 22 states in this country had a Torrens system. However, the number of user jurisdictions has dwindled to just a few: to the island of Oahu, Hawaii; to Cook County, Illinois, where it is now being phased out; to the Suffolk and South Shore counties in Massachusetts; to Hennepin, Ramsey, and Saint Louis counties in Minnesota, the Twin Cities, and the Duluth area. *See Doyle v. Commonwealth*, 830 N.E.2d 1074, 1078-1079 (Mass. 2005); *Aames Funding Corp. v. Mores*, 110 P.3d 1042, 1047-1048 (Haw. 2005) (both reviewing the history and purpose of their state's systems). Puerto Rico and Guam also use it.

There are several variations in the way the Torrens systems work in the United States. Two states, Massachusetts and Minnesota, provide the clearest contrasts. In Massachusetts, the system is administered by the courts; the Land Court, a limited-jurisdiction court, supervises all registrations in an action that resembles a quiet title action. Mass. Gen. L. Ann. ch. 185. Thus, parcels with title problems are good candidates to be "torrenized." Also good candidates for using the system are parcels whose acreage is uncertain. The Land Court has high surveying standards. In addition, the system was given a healthy boost with a strong judicial opinion in its favor, an opinion written by no less than Justice Holmes while sitting on the Supreme Judicial Court of Massachusetts. *Tyler v. Judges of the Court of Registration*, 55 N.E.2d 812 (Mass.), app. dismissed, 179 U.S. 405 (1900).

In Minnesota, the system is administrative in nature; attorneys are appointed by system administrators to perform a title search before the issuance of a certificate. Here the system was established before title insurers were on the scene to provide competition, was backed by strong advocates, and was located in a jurisdiction with a tradition of good municipal government, and was, as in Massachusetts, the subject of a strong, favorable judicial opinion.

But the system did not last. First, it had fierce competition from title insurance companies. Second, the guaranty funds have provided inadequate compensation: Large claims made during the 1930s depleted them and made the system unreliable and unattractive to mortgage lenders. In

California, for example, the system had been widely used in the four counties around Los Angeles, but one claim wiped out the entire fund. Third, unsympathetic courts rendered decisions making the certificates of title inconclusive. Behind this judicial sympathy for ousted interest holders often lay administrative sloppiness or an unprofessional title search. Fourth, many special-purpose title searches were still necessary in some jurisdictions; for example, searches were often needed to locate encumbrances such as tax liens or to determine the acreage of a parcel. Often such limited searches were made necessary by judicial decisions or by statutory exceptions to the conclusiveness of the registered title. Finally, a pre–New Deal tradition that limited delegations of authority made to administrators—bolstered by the ideas that land titles were a matter for attorneys and the judiciary, and that due process problems with statutory procedures often flawed the system—worried the system during its decline. Thus the causes of the system's decline were many. Nonetheless, the system has its present-day defenders. McCormack, Torrens and Recording: Land Title Assurance in the Computer Age, 18 Wm. Mitchell L. Rev. 61 (1992). Most propose a gradual, noncompulsory introduction of the system by administrative officials with the help of the bar.

Examples

Example 26

Dan Developer torrenizes the title to Whiteacre, a tract of land that he is subdividing. The land registration and then the subdivision process is completed according to the provisions of state law. Dan incorporates the Whiteacre Property Owners Association to provide services to the subdivision, including the maintenance of its roads, a beach, and other community facilities. All Whiteacre's lots have certificates of title, on most of which appear a notation of a covenant that the holder will pay for the association's services. Some certificates, however, do not contain such a covenant. The holders of Whiteacre lots without the notation refuse to pay for these services. The association sues them to compel payment. What result?

Explanation

Judgment for the defendants. A person dealing with registered property need look no further than the certificate, unless the statute provides otherwise. *See Popponesset Beach Ass'n, Inc. v. Marchillo*, 658 N.E.2d 983 (Mass. App. Ct. 1995) ("Title to registered land is free of encumbrances that are not noted on the certificate of title, either by express grant or reservation or by express reference to a registered document that contains the grant or reservation"). No notation on the certificate, no covenant.

Example 27

The same facts as in the previous example, but in addition the association recorded an affidavit containing the covenant before the first purchaser of the defendants' lots took their certificates to their parcels. Same result?

Explanation

Yes. Registering property abrogates the doctrine of constructive notice contained in the recording act as to registered land. The holder of a covenant omitted from the certificate, and preexisting it, is reduced to a money claim, and its holder recording later is performing a futile act (in most Torrens jurisdictions).

Example 28

V is about to sell part of Blackacre to P. They dispute the scope of an easement over P's portion, but both agree that the easement exists, although it is not noted on the certificate tendered by V and accepted by P. Is the certificate thereafter subject to reformation for mutual mistake between parties transferring the registered title?

Explanation

Yes. To the extent that the Torrens law does not repeal the common law, it is not repealed.

CHAPTER 11

Closings

CLOSINGS

The end of the executory period is known as the closing or the settlement. It is the time when the last steps in the transfer of the title are completed: A cashier's or certified check for the purchase price is exchanged for the deed to the property. In many areas of the country, it is a ceremony that both the vendor and the purchaser attend. It is also the time when final documents accompanying the delivery of the deed are reviewed by the parties and their attorneys or other representatives. Often the broker attends too, because he is holding the down payment to be credited toward the purchase price and he expects to take away a check for the commission, paid out of the sale proceeds received by the vendor at this time.

In some jurisdictions, the parties meet and the closing takes place in an attorney's office—this is often the case in New England—or at a title insurance or escrow company. Sometimes, as in Massachusetts, it takes place at the public records office so that the deed can be recorded immediately by the purchaser.

In states in the Pacific West and in the Southwest, the parties do not meet face-to-face. There, the final steps—indeed, all the steps necessary to satisfy each and every condition in the contract of sale—are overseen by an escrow company that, when the final steps are taken, clears the check for the purchase price, delivers the deed to the purchaser, and distributes the proceeds of the sale to the vendor and others.

Examples

Example 1

A client of yours is careful about your billing fees. You tell her that it will take you several hours to prepare to close on a property he is purchasing. He asks, "why bother with a closing anyway?" Reply to his concern.

Explanation

Preparing for a closing is an opportunity to see that all of the contingencies and conditions in the contract of sale are satisfied altogether by the time of the closing. You might delegate some of the work to a paralegal, but if you are to attend the closing, delegation is an opportunity lost for you to think through the closing process. Yes, you say, we might record the contract of sale and take a quitclaim deed, but many title insurers are wary of insuring a quitclaim deed, and if something were to go wrong at the closing, the contract would be a cloud on the vendor's title and have to be removed with a quiet action and a bill to remove a cloud. In that action, your client would be the defendant!

PREPARATION FOR A CLOSING

Closing a real estate transaction is not a legal process. It provides a method for seeing that all of the contingencies and terms in the contract of sale are satisfied. An attorney approaches a closing with a checklist of items that the client needs. That checklist may be assembled not only from the terms of the contract of sale, but also from documents and services generated by the parties during the executory period.

One of the staples on such checklists is a statement of taxes and other monies due at closing from the vendor and purchasers. Taxes and assessment payments will have to be prorated as of the closing date. Vendor and purchaser are responsible for real estate taxes accruing during their tenure. Likewise, the federal income tax deduction for property taxes is apportioned in a similar manner. When the purchaser is assuming the vendor's existing mortgage, mortgage payments will also be apportioned around the closing date. Less common, but possible, is the apportionment of insurance premiums when the purchaser continues the vendor's existing property and casualty insurance policies with a change in beneficiary.

Examples

Example 2

Your client, the purchaser, asked for your advice on procuring property and casualty insurance policies for the property. What advice should you give?

Explanation

None, unless you are an expert. Policies are changing all the time, and your advice should be to consult an insurance broker up on the changes in coverage. The broker, however, should assure you that the policy procured covers all insurable perils, with a replacement cost endorsement and with the lender named as a beneficiary and additional insured and loss payee, and the insurer rated excellent by a reputable rating company.

The abstractor or title insurer searching the title may have discovered and disclosed less-than-fee interests encumbering the title. These interests will first come to the attorneys' attention in a title commitment (aka a preliminary report on title—the term used in most Western jurisdictions of the country). The commitment thus is a list of items that will appear as exceptions from coverage in Schedule B of the title policy when it is issued, unless the insurer agrees to insure over it. The commitment is sometimes referred to a title binder, referring to the promise of the insurer to issue a policy reflecting what the state of the title as reported.

Other steps taken during the executory period may indicate a need for endorsements to the title policy. An endorsement is a change in coverage, usually an increase in coverage. It sometimes begins with a statement by the insurer that it will not invoke certain named provisions of the policy as a defense to a claim on it. A zoning endorsement may thus constitute a promise not to invoke a policy exclusion for zoning as well as a statement of the uses of the property that are currently in compliance with existing zoning.

Likewise, when the property has been surveyed anew during the executory period, a purchaser might seek endorsements that the surveyor produced an accurate survey or that the property is located where the survey indicates it is. An accurate survey endorsement and a location endorsement thus assure the purchaser that legal description used in the deed to be delivered as closing gives him the property he thought he was buying.

Before issuing an endorsement, the title insurer may demand a back-up assurance. In the case of a zoning endorsement, an opinion from a land use attorney that the zoning is as stated in the endorsement—and, in the cases of an accurate survey endorsement, a certificate from the surveyor that the survey work was accurately performed. Thus if the endorsement becomes that basis of a claim on the policy, the insurer, once paying the claim, can assert its subrogation rights in the policy and turn around and sue the attorney or the surveyor

Examples

Example 3

Your client is about to close on a luxury home last renovated several decades ago. The renovation the client proposed will take about six months, but will increase the value of the property substantially. What advice would you give this client about his title policy?

Explanation

The client needs the policy endorsed to increase its face amount. Such an endorsement gives the policy holder the right for a limited time after the policy is issued to increase the face amount by a set percentage of the original amount. (In some regions of the country, this is known as a "Sears endorsement.") This eliminates the risk that the insurer will refuse to reinsure after renovation or construction increases the fair market value of the property. Title insurers typically issue policies for either the purchase price or, when presented with a post-closing appraisal of the property, its fair market value. A further endorsement might insure against mechanics liens filed by workers performing the renovation.

Example 4

Your client is a mortgage lender and you are preparing for a loan closing on a substantial property. You find out that the state license of the title insurance agent issuing the Loan Policy for this transaction has lapsed. What action should you take?

Explanation

You should check the closing protection letter issued by the title insurer for this transaction. Such a letter insures a lender against actions by the agent not in compliance with the lender's instructions for the disbursement of funds and other matters. If the agent is unlicensed, the insurer may disavow the letter, so you now need to see that the agent has renewed the license and that the lender reissues the letter.

Other items in the title commitment may indicate the need to expand the attorney's closing checklist to include a particular type of survey. Reading the deeds in the chain of title might reveal that the legal description does not close, an inspection of the property might fail to find the monuments referred to in the legal description, or the legal descriptions of abutting properties leave a gap or are inconsistent with the description in the deed being offered your client—in all three of these situations, a new survey is warranted. In turn, ordering a survey will require an attorney to tell the surveyor the level of accuracy wanted. The level may depend on whether the property is an urban, suburban, or rural one.

Likewise, the loan commitment may require an "ALTA/ACSM survey." It is expensive, but adds value to the property. It will provide information on the following: the precise location of the property, the precise location of any improvements on the property, the footprint of those improvements in square feet, the dimensions of those improvements, any utility lines and other easements running over it, the location of improvements on it, and any encroachments on it. Many mortgage lenders will also specify other matters that are to appear on the survey—so-called "Table A" matters: Examples might include the location of parking spaces, their dimensions and the total number of them, as well as those reserved for handicapped persons, the location of the means of access, including (for commercial properties) curb cuts, and physical evidence of underground utilities such as manholes and storm drains. In order to perform such a survey, the surveyor will need copies of the deed, abutting owners' deeds, and all the relevant easements.

Examples

Example 5

What besides a survey meeting its guidelines might a lender or a title insurer require?

Explanation

A surveyor's certificate. It should be given by the surveyor performing the survey, stating that he or she is licensed and bonded in the jurisdiction in which the property is located, bearing his or her stamp, seal, and registration number, certifying that the survey was performed according to required standards, and dated (typically for a date not less than 60 days preceding the closing). When title defects are later discovered, the certificate provides a basis for an insurer's recovery through subrogation of any claim made by an owner or lender.

Example 6

The title search performed for your client produces only a few exceptions in the title commitment. What might still prompt you to advise obtaining a survey?

Explanation

Even in this situation, a survey may still be useful to disclose flood plains, building setback lines, or steep slopes. These are not title matters, but may be important to a prospective purchaser who is looking to improve the property further.

Preparing for a closing is like a sentence game: One word is followed by another, one thing leads to another. Land surveys, for example, should be ordered early in the executory period since it may lead an attorney to investigate aspects of the property not heretofore known to present a problem.

The need for documents well in advance of the closing has led to the practice, in commercial property closings, of dividing the period after the execution of a contract of sale into two parts—a so-called due diligence or study period, followed by what in residential transactions would normally be the executory period. During the due diligence period, the prospective purchaser may be given access to the financial records of the vendor for the purpose of working up a financial analysis or pro forma for the property. Land surveys, environmental reports, soil analyses, energy efficiency reports, use and occupancy permits, hazardous materials surveys, and zoning compliance reports, among others, may also be provided during the due diligence period.

Examples

Example 7

Your client is preparing to accept a deed from her vendor. The vendor is a legal entity such as a Limited Liability Company or Partnership. What steps should you take in this situation?

Explanation

Not only will you need a chain of title leading to the LLC or Partnership, but you will also need a paper chain of authority leading to the person(s) who will sign the deed delivered to your client at closing. This in hand, you should then check the applicable state LLC or Partnership Act to determine whether the entity can do business as an entity or only as the aggregate of its members or partners. Such Acts will typically be some modified version of the Uniform LLC Act, the Uniform Limited Partnership Act, or the Uniform General Partnership Act. Each is annotated by the Commissioners on Uniform State Laws. Finally, you should insist that the closing be in person and not through a power of attorney; a natural person can give such a power, but a legal entity may not be able to do so.

Example 8

Checking the formation documents for an entity purporting to have authority to transfer property to your client, you discover that the entity was formed a week after it accepted the delivery of a deed from its vendor. What is the effect of this?

Explanation

This will require an extra check of the land records to assure your client that the names in the chain of title indicate the title's marketability of record and in fact. Also required is a check of the vendor's closing documents to find out whether any brokerage commissions on the sale were paid, or whether there might be a broker awaiting a commission.

Example 9

You receive a pay-out letter from an existing holder of a mortgage on the property your client is buying. It shows the amount of outstanding mortgage debt. You find that the letter is undated. What should you do?

Explanation

Ask for a new letter, dated as of the closing date. The amount needed to repay the debt is a moving target when interest on the mortgage loan accrues on a daily basis.

Example 10

Your client is considering taking title to a substantial property in the name of a two-member LLC, the second member being his spouse. What advice would you give on this matter?

Explanation

Many mortgage lenders and title insurers are leery on insuring properties titled to new LLCs. They question the LLC members' motives when using such an entity. Lenders in particular may reduce the loan-to-value ratio for loans given to LLCs. Lenders know that LLC Acts are frequently amended, particularly in Delaware (where some lenders want the LLC established), and amendments may require periodic changes in loan documents. In addition, LLCs incur set-up fees, legal expenses in drafting an operating agreement, and accounting and tax preparation expenses. For a client with a large income and net worth, the use of an LLC might be advisable, but for a client with less to insulate from lawsuits and liens, it's of much less value.

Moreover, comprehensive liability and casualty insurance policies provide an alternative to the limited liability aspects of an LLC. Still, for an individual whose living expenses consume much of his income and savings, the use of an LLC is worth considering.

Example 11

While preparing for a closing in which your client has decided to purchase property using an LLC, you discover that the client has yet to form the entity. What concerns might you have about this matter?

Explanation

Several concerns. If the purchasing entity did not execute the brokerage listing or the contract of sale, those agreements might be subject to attack and nullified. Both should be amended. This may further require an adjustment of the timelines established in the agreements. *See R&J Enterprises v. Ware Creek Real Estate Corp.*, 2018 Va. Unpub. LEXIS 30 (Va. Oct. 4, 2018).

Example 12

The vendor asks your client, the purchaser, for permission to remain on the property for a week after the closing. How should you respond?

Explanation

You should obtain the right to reinspect the property in a week and prorate insurance premiums, taxes, assessments, and maintenance costs anew, all the while making sure that the continued possession is under a license, not a lease, for the week. A license is easily revoked, and the licensee is not given the many rights tenants have today.

CLOSINGS AND THE REAL ESTATE SETTLEMENT PROCEDURE ACT

The federal Real Estate Settlement Procedure Act (RESPA), enacted in 1974, requires that a federally related mortgage lender provide the borrower, at the time he or she applies for a mortgage loan, an estimate made in good faith of the settlement costs to be paid by the borrower. The Act also provides authority for the federal regulator overseeing the Act's enforcement—originally the federal Department of Housing and Urban Development, now the Consumer Financial Protection Bureau—to issue a booklet, which the lender may adapt for its own use, describing those costs and fees. Further authority has been given the regulator to issue a uniform closing statement (HUD-1, as amended) reconciling the financial terms of a transaction. Current regulations require the person preparing the HUD-1 to reference each good faith estimate fee on the HUD-1, so that the borrower can see how the estimated fee compares to what is charged at closing.

The most litigated section of the Act is its §8(b). It provides:

> No person shall give and no person shall accept any portion, split, or percentage of any charge made or received for the rendering of a real estate settlement service in connection with a transaction involving a federally related mortgage loan other than for services actually rendered. 12 U.S.C. §2607(b).

Both lenders and loans may be federally related when they are federally insured, regulated, or (as to loans) sold into the secondary market, The Act's reach is broad indeed. Likewise, a settlement service includes any person or firm providing services necessary for a loan closing—brokers, appraisers, surveyors, title companies and insurers, or escrow firms—any and all third-party servicers are included. Violations of this section may result in substantial penalties and may also result in criminal liability, including imprisonment.

The intent of the Act is to control so-called reverse competition—that is, the competition of settlement service providers for business through solicitation of other providers, as a title company might solicit business from real estate brokers, or appraisers might solicit the business from mortgage lenders.

Examples

Example 13

A mortgage lender hires an appraiser during its underwriting process for a federally related loan. The appraiser charges the lender $200 for its services. The lender charges the borrower $250 for the service when noted on the HUD-1. Has the lender violated RESPA §8(b)?

Explanation

No. There is no "person giving" and no "person receiving" the markup. This Act is not intended to control prices charged for real estate settlement services. It does not prohibit unreasonably high fees. It is only intended to prohibit kickbacks. There is no giver or receiver of a kickback in this situation. Markups are not a violation of RESPA.

A kickback, however, need not be money given or received. It can be anything of value—for example, tickets to a football game, or the provision of business equipment. However, a broker's being taken out to dinner to thank her for a past referral is not a violation of the Act. Neither is a title insurer prevented from holding a conference for all lenders to educate them about the provisions of its insurance policies, regardless of whether or not the insurer does business with the conferees.

Example 14

A mortgage loan borrower finds that the appraiser whose fee is listed on her HUD-1 is not licensed in the jurisdiction where the property appraised is located. Has the appraiser "actually performed" the appraisal under §8(b)?

Explanation

Yes. He has. This section of the Act is not intended to enforce the requirements of state law—such as a licensure requirement here.

Example 15

An attorney refers title search and insurance business to a firm in which the attorney is a major stockholder and from which she receives payments based on a percentage of the amount of the title insurance premium charged purchasers and borrowers. Is §8(b) violated by this arrangement?

Explanation

Yes. The referrals result in a giver (the firm) and receiver (the attorney) required by this section. That the payment is based on a percentage amount of the premium makes it unrelated to the services actually performed by the attorney.

ESCROW PRACTICE

A deed delivered to a person other than the grantee, with instructions to that person to deliver it to the grantee upon the performance or happening of some condition, has been placed "in escrow." Thus, a traditional escrow is a mechanism for the delivery of a deed in two steps: first, to the escrow agent,[17] and second, to the grantee. The concept of an escrow originated with real estate closings. 2 Wm. Blackstone, Commentaries 307.

17. Escrow "agent" is an imprecise term because the law of agency does not explain all of this person's rights and duties. Nonetheless, the term is widely used to indicate a person who has agreed to carry out the parties' contract of sale according to their previously agreed-on instructions.

The elements of an escrow are: (1) the deposit of property (e.g., money or a deed), upon the agreement of parties, (2) with a third party with fiduciary duties to both for purposes of the escrowed property, (3) who will hold the property beyond the depositor's control, and (4) who will deliver the property to the opposite party when a condition is performed.

In many jurisdictions in the western United States, the use of escrows is commonplace in all types of real property transactions. They are used for both residential and commercial transactions and replace the formal ceremony known as a closing in the East and Midwest. In the West, "going into escrow" refers not just to the delivery of a deed. It also refers to a vendor's and purchaser's setting up a procedure by which the agent oversees the completion of the many steps required to exchange both a deed for the purchase price and a mortgage lien for the purchase money loan proceeds. In the West, it is a mechanism to close both the title and the mortgage transaction simultaneously. An escrow agent's employment agreement is commonly known as the escrow instructions.

These instructions authorize the agent to accept for deposit in the title transaction: the documents showing compliance with the various contingencies and "subject to" clauses in the contract of sale, the deed executed by the vendor, and the payment of the purchase price by the purchaser. In the mortgage transaction, an escrow agent is authorized to accept: a note and mortgage lien from the purchaser for the lender, documents outlined as necessary preconditions of a mortgage loan, and, finally, the mortgage loan proceeds from the lender. All of the documents, checks, and payments required for a closing pass through the hands of the escrow agent. She discharges all liens affecting the marketability of the title, pays for the services rendered in the course of the transaction, and finally disburses the proceeds.

Escrow instructions usually contain both general provisions and those tailored to the particular transaction. The former often state the agent's accounting practices and responsibility for funds. Generally, the instructions are not subject to the jurisdiction's Statute of Frauds. They are agreements for personal services, not transfer of title documents. Customarily, however, they are in writing nonetheless.

Everywhere, there are many reasons why the parties to a transaction might consider using an escrow agent instead of closing the transaction themselves. The agent is often an expert at handling such transactions. Using the escrow avoids a face-to-face closing, and this might be expedient when the vendor is moving some distance away or the purchaser is moving into an area from a distance. When there are questions about the state of the title, an escrow agent can be instructed to have an updated search performed just before recording the deed, or to record it only after all liens and encumbrances are paid off.

If routinely handled, an escrow is a two-step delivery of title. First, the deed is handed to the escrow agent, and second, the agent delivers the title deed to the purchaser when all the conditions in the contract and the instructions are performed. The second delivery is deemed effective as of the date the deed is deposited in the escrow agent's account. This is the doctrine of "relation back": The effectiveness of the deed is measured by the date of the first delivery. This legal fiction cuts off intervening interests. The death, incompetency, or insolvency of the vendor does not destroy the validity of the second delivery.

A valid escrow requires two preconditions: (1) a valid and binding contract of sale and (2) escrow instructions in which the vendor does not reserve the power to recall the deed in the escrow account, absent a breach of the contract or the instructions by the purchaser. As to the first requirement, today a line of authority holds that the instructions, if complete in themselves or as augmented by other documents, can suffice for a contract of sale. The second requirement is that of irrevocability, which should not be confused with contract conditions and contingencies. A conditional deed may be put irrevocably into an escrow, and the completion of the escrow awaits the fulfillment of the contingencies.

The escrow agent should act independently of the vendor and purchaser, but must act as agent for both; if the agent were the vendor's agent alone, the delivery of the deed into escrow would not put the deed beyond the vendor's control. If, on the other hand, the agent were the purchaser's agent, the rule that conditional delivery to a grantee vests title in the grantee unconditionally would mean that the conditions in the contract of sale could not be enforced. Once the contract of sale is binding and the escrow created by instruction of the parties, the vendor's placing the deed in escrow puts his ability to deal with the title further on hold. If he marries thereafter, no marital rights will attach to the title. Likewise, the vendor's creditors will not be able to enforce a judgment against the escrow—a result that is of benefit to purchasers if the vendor is debt-ridden. Neither will a vendor be able to make a will devising the title conveyed in the deed. And, if the vendor dies, the deed already in a valid escrow will be beyond the reach of his estate—the same result that the doctrine of equitable conversion accomplishes for a conveyance without an escrow. *See* Chapter 3.

With the escrow established, an escrow agent is a fiduciary of both parties to the escrow, bound to carry out the escrow instructions and to comply strictly with them. The fiduciary duties of the agent are generally limited and defined by the duties assumed in and sometimes arising out of those instructions. In many regions of the country, a title insurance company may assume the duties of an escrow agent, but limited to the closing of a transaction. An attorney may also assume the duties of an escrow agent so long as the Rules of Professional Conduct permit and informed consent of the parties is obtained. Whether an attorney's assuming this role is wise or prudent is another matter—one the attorney should scrutinize carefully. Assuming such a role does not diminish the attorney's duties to a client.

Consider the following bare-bones escrow agreement between the parties to the contract at the beginning of Chapter 5.

ESCROW INSTRUCTIONS

This agreement is made between *Vivi Vendor* and __________ escrow agent, on this __________ day of __________, 20 __________.

Vendor has agreed to convey, and *Peter Purchaser* has agreed to purchase, Blackacre Farm, Myerstown, Maryland by contract dated September 5, 2026, and described as follows:

[legal description inserted here]

being 50 acres, for a price in gross of $500,000 and free of encumbrances except as are set out in the preliminary title report of Title Guaranty Insurance Co., Mooers City, delivered to the escrow agent at the start of the escrow.

Vendor and Purchaser agree to deliver irrevocably all forms and instruments necessary to close this escrow by December 5, 2014.

Vendor shall deliver a special warranty deed to the property upon request of agent, and Purchaser shall deliver all monies necessary to complete the purchase, including all prorated adjustments and closing costs appearing on Form HUD-1, last revised _________, 20 _________.

Vendor and Purchaser agree to release agent from all claims arising under this agreement, except for claims based on the fraud and gross negligence of the agent. Agent shall have a lien on all funds on deposit to secure payment of its fee.

Agent's fee shall be _________ % of all monies on account.

Executed at _________ on _________

____

Vivi Vendor

____

Peter Purchaser

Compare this set of instructions with the contract of sale beginning Chapter 5. If the provisions of the contract are inconsistent in any way with the instructions, the instructions prevail. They are generally written later in time than the contract is and, being the latest evidence of the parties' agreement, prevail. Regardless of when they are written, however, they prevail for an additional reason: They often are more detailed than the contract and therefore fill in the contract's gaps and silences without necessarily being inconsistent with it. Their specific provisions control the more general ones of the contract. If the two documents can be read in harmony, courts will do so. So when clear inconsistencies appear, the terms of the instructions control those in the contract, and if the instructions merely flesh out the contract, the two documents will be read harmoniously.

In the last paragraph of the instructions, the agency exculpates itself from all liability regarding claims based on the agreement, except for fraud and gross negligence. This is common and such exculpations are not unconscionable. As to their substance, they are commercially reasonable, considering the relationship of the agency's fee to its possible liabilities; and as to their procedures, they are not exacted under duress. Inequality of bargaining power alone is not enough to show procedural unconscionability as a matter of law. *See Hurst v. Enterprise Title Agency, Inc.*, 809 N.E.2d 689 (Ohio App. 2004).

Which of the terms of the escrow instructions provided in this chapter conflict with those of the contract (Chapter 5)? Consider the items in the following examples.

Examples

Example 16

Is the instruction regarding the preliminary title report a modification of the contract's provision for a marketable title?

Explanation

The instruction's reference to the preliminary title report has the effect of accepting all encumbrances mentioned in the report, whether or not they affect the marketability of the title. In a preliminary report, the title searcher for the insurer will list all encumbrances, whatever their effect on the title to be insured. Further negotiations are required to make sure that the encumbrances rendering the title unmarketable are not accepted by the purchaser executing these instructions.

Example 17

When will the closing be held? The contract calls for a date certain, but is time made "of the essence" in this contract? Is that aspect of the contract modified by the instructions?

Explanation

Yes, so the client should consent to this. The instructions advance the date of the closing by ten days, from the 15th of December in the contract to the 5th in the instructions. Since the instructions are the last agreement of the parties on this matter, the former controls. When considered with the next paragraph of the instructions, its terms can be said to make time of the essence with this change—and the date for the closing will become December 5th unless the parties change the terms of the instructions.

Example 18

What other problems do you foresee if these instructions are not modified?

Explanation

Perhaps the most important matters not yet included in the instructions would (1) incorporate the contract of sale into the terms of the instructions, and (2) give the agent express authority to oversee the performance of the terms and conditions of the contract. Another matter concerns the relationship of the acreage and the price. Here the acreage is stated, as it was not in the contract (there two prices were named, one in gross and the other on an acreage basis). So the ambiguity in the contract persists here; taken together, the addition of the instructions as they stand show that the acreage is a concern of the purchaser. Moreover, a statement of the price in gross is not inconsistent with this concern. Thus the vendor should inquire about the impacts of an acreage deficiency on the transaction, a survey should be ordered, and the procedure for the agent's handling of the survey should be added to the instructions.

Example 19

When is the escrow effective? In other words, when does the escrow agent have authority to act for the parties? When does that authority end?

Explanation

The receipt of the preliminary title report is the start of this escrow, and that may be too late. Unless the parties mean to see and review the state of the title before going into escrow, this provision should be modified so that the agent can act for the parties as soon as the agreement is executed. Probably the termination of the escrow should not be a date certain but an event certain, such as the satisfaction of the last performed contingency in the contract of sale. The contract called for a survey (previously discussed in the prior Example) and the sale of a prior residence as conditions or contingencies on the closing—and the specific escrow instructions should tell the agent how to handle these matters.

Example 20

Escrows must be irrevocable. Is this one?

Explanation

Arguably not, at least not without a start date. The start of the escrow may now be the delivery of the preliminary title report, and the parties should clarify this matter with an express provision.

Example 21

Who bears the risk if the escrow agent embezzles the funds on deposit with her?

Explanation

Until the title is ready in escrow for delivery to the purchaser, the risk of the agent absconding with the funds on deposit lies with the purchaser. Up to that time, the purchase money in escrow was awaiting title and so was still subject to the purchaser's direction and control. After the title is proven and the deed is put in escrow, the risk lies on the shoulders of the vendor. (The first sentence of this explanation is consistent with risk of loss rules in a majority of states. The last sentence is, however, inconsistent. The difference is explained by the fact that the rationale for these rules lies in the ownership of the funds, not ownership interests in the property.) Several jurisdictions, however, have harmonized this inconsistency by adopting the rule that the person owning the property at the time of the embezzlement bears the loss. *See Johnson v. Schultz*, 691 S.E.2d 701 (N.C. 2010); *Stuart v. Clark*, 619 A.2d 1199 (D.C. App. 1993). *See generally Boozer v. Fischer*, 674 S.W.3d 314, 323-330 (Tex. 2023). This rule is often known as the "entitlement rule": If money or a deed is in escrow and is lost or embezzled, "the loss falls on the one who owns the property as the time of the loss or embezzlement." *Id.*, 674 S.W.3d at 330. In other words, when the conditions of the escrow are satisfied, the loss is the vendor's because he is entitled to the deed; when the title is unproven and the conditions unperformed, the loss is on the purchaser for the same reason—he is entitled to get the escrowed purchase money back. The purchaser 'owns" the money until the escrow closes.

Example 22

The escrow agent has duties to both parties. If the agent notices that the purchaser's check for the earnest money deposit bounces, must she inform the vendor?

Explanation

Yes. However, while fiduciary duties are sometimes imposed on agents, don't count on such duties in every situation. Escrow agents are often said to be authorized by the instructions to perform "merely ministerial acts" in implementing the escrow. So the agent has no duty to notify a party that the amount of the lien was more than the loan proceeds. *See Lee v. Title Ins. & Trust Co.*, 70 Cal. Rptr. 378 (Cal. App. 1968). And if the purchaser proves to be without the financial ability to complete the sale, the agent has no duty to disclose this. Were it otherwise, when would this disclosure be made? When the first mortgage loan application is denied? The second? Third? But if a signature on an amendment to the instructions does not match the signature on the original instructions, the agent has a duty to inform the opposite party. *See Lee v. Escrow Consultants, Inc.*, 259 Cal. Rptr. 117, 123 (Cal. App. 1989) (an agent must verify signatures). More generally, in some jurisdictions, an act amounting to fraud gives the agent a duty to disclose what she knows. *See Mark Properties, Inc. v. Nat'l Tit. Co.*, 34 P.3d 587 (Nev. 2001) (involving a double escrow concealing an assignment of contract rights). *But see Berry v. McLeod*, 604 P.2d 610 (Ariz. 1979) (finding no such duty).

Example 23

If and when Vivi and Peter mutually agree to cancel this escrow agreement, is their contract of sale also rescinded?

Explanation

No, unless that intent to do so is clear. Escrow instructions are the implementation of the terms of the contract. They do not supersede it. The underlying contract remains in force. The parties need to be counseled that their contract must be expressly rescinded as well.

Example 24

V and P (vendor and purchaser) execute a brief but enforceable contract of sale for Blackacre. The contract provides that the vendor will present a standard title insurance policy showing a marketable title. The parties then enter into a brief but valid escrow agreement establishing an escrow account with E as their escrow agent. V deposits a deed, and P deposits a substantial down payment, into the account. V remains in possession. Fire destroys the residence on Blackacre, and E absconds with P's down payment. Advise P about the legal consequences of these facts.

Explanation

In a majority of jurisdictions, absent fault by either party or a contract or escrow provision to the contrary, P bears the risk of loss by fire during the executory period; she also has the risk of E's absconding with the down payment. The allocation of the loss of the residence is based on the doctrine of equitable conversion, holding that P is the equitable owner of the real property and so subject to specific performance. The allocation of the loss of the down payment is based on agency theory—that, before the satisfaction of the condition(s) of the escrow (here the delivery of the title policy to E) E holds the money as P's agent, not V's, and so the risk of its loss falls on E's principal P. Because P bears both of these two risks she must now purchase Blackacre, also coming up with money to replace his lost down payment while doing so. Generally, the rules for allocating these two risks are inconsistent with each other. They overlap: P is regarded both as owning the property and the money at the same time, premised on theories of ownership and agency.

MISDELIVERY FROM ESCROW

When a deed is delivered to a purchaser before the latter has performed a condition of the escrow instructions or the contract, the prevailing view is that the deed is void. Similarly, when a forgery of the vendor's signature is involved or fraud is involved in the execution, the deed delivered is void. Thus when the purchaser obtains a deed out of escrow without proper delivery by the agent, the deed is void and the vendor may cancel it.

In some situations, however, the misdelivered deed is voidable, not void. As in other situations, the voidable deed becomes good in the hands of a bona fide purchaser, whereas a void deed is no good no matter into whose hands it falls. A breach of fiduciary duty by the agent in misdelivering the deed results in a voidable deed; so does a mistake of fact, duress, or undue influence on the vendor involved in the establishment of the escrow. Here the vendor established the escrow, delivered the deed into it, and so suffers the consequences when the alternative is to visit a loss of the title on a bona fide purchaser. For example, a vendor might let his deed clear escrow in return for a check for the purchase price that later bounces, or give the purchaser a purchase money mortgage based on the latter's misrepresentation of his creditworthiness: The deed in the hands of the purchaser is voidable. In these instances, the vendor meant to deal with the purchaser, but dealt too readily, without escrow instructions that let the check clear or required a check of the purchaser's credit. Negligence on the vendor's and the escrow agent's part does not prevent a misdelivered deed from becoming voidable.

The rationale for finding a deed voidable often sounds like a characterization of facts estopping the vendor from denying the bona fide purchaser's title, rather than an examination of the purchaser's bona fides—and in truth, estoppel and an innocent purchaser are the best arguments for characterizing the deed as voidable. Thus, on the one hand, when the deed is stolen from escrow, it is void, but when there is an inadvertent misdelivery of a deed by the agent out of escrow, the deed is voidable.

CONTRACT OR POST-CLOSING ESCROWS

In jurisdictions that do not routinely use escrows to close a transaction, special-purpose escrows may still be used. For example, what if the heating system breaks down during the executory period? No one's at fault, the vendor expected that it would be working at the closing, and vendor and purchaser still want to close, but the purchaser realizes that once closing occurs, she will be in a poor position to bargain for the vendor's fixing it. The purchaser may still have rights—the implied warranty of habitability applies, but it may require litigation to enforce, and the law may find it waived by the purchaser closing the transaction; or the doctrine of merger might fold an express warranty about the heating system into the deed; or the contract may make time of the essence, and postponing the closing might create a breach. There are any number of reasons why the closing should be held but part of the purchase price withheld from the vendor until the system is fixed. The partial postponement of the closing—withholding the price, and requiring the repair—is the subject of a contract escrow. *See Van Vorgue v. Rankin*, 41 So. 3d 849 (Fla. 2010). The same might be used when the contract contains a minor, unfulfilled, condition at the time of the closing—sometimes this can be as simple as a typo in the deed or other document required at the closing.

The contract escrow agreement should be written, but may be in letter form, addressed to the escrow agent and signed by the vendor and purchaser. It should identify (1) the problem or the unfulfilled condition, (2) a timetable for fixing it, (3) any maximum amount that the vendor is willing to spend to fix the problem, (4) objective proof that the problem is fixed (i.e., an invoice, a bill of sale, a warranty certificate for new equipment, a governmental certificate, all as appropriate—the point is to give as little discretion as possible to the agent), (5) the vendor's right to inspect after the repair (particularly if the vendor has such a right pre-closing), (6) how, when, and to whom the escrowed funds are to be released, (7) procedures for resolving problems interpreting the agreement, and (8) any exculpatory limitations on the agent's duties. To avoid multiple responsibility problems, attorneys involved in a closing should not become the agent for a contract escrow.

Examples

Example 25

What if funds are held back from closing to cure title defects, but then embezzled by the agent?

Explanation

This arrangement is a post-closing escrow. Since the vendor has the obligation to use the funds to cure them, then the loss is the vendor's, and the vendor will have to deposit more money after the loss to cure the defects outstanding.

CHAPTER 12

Mortgage Lenders and Markets

Up to the 1930s, mortgage capital was distributed in short-term loans, usually payable in interest-only installments until the end of the term, when the total amount of principal outstanding was then due in what is known as a "balloon payment." Terms were not likely to be more than ten years in length, and the balloon payment at the end of the term often meant that the loan was refinanced rather than repaid.

During the Great Depression of the 1930s, amid its bank failures, the federal government stepped up its regulatory interest in the banking system—particularly for the mutual banks and savings and loan associations, which were then the major providers of residential mortgage capital. The source of this capital was the money in these banks' saving accounts. The interest rate payable on these accounts was protected by statute; that is, the rate payable was higher than rates on comparable accounts held with commercial banks. With these higher rates, the associations were sheltered from competition and able to attract deposits that could then become the basis for loans secured by mortgages. The associations were restricted in their geographic lending area and most of their capital had to be put into residential mortgage loans. In effect, the federal government underwrote the primary lenders of mortgage loans by helping to making capital easy to attract.

These savings banks held either state or, after the 1930s, federal charters, or were mutual banks owned by shareholders with saving accounts. Many had their accounts insured by the federal government; they did not have to hold a federal charter to obtain federal deposit insurance. Another by-product of this federal intervention was a wave of standardized mortgage terms: amortized monthly payments, containing a little repayment of principal as well as the payment of interest; level monthly payments; longer terms for repayment; and no balloon payments at the end of the term.

This type of federal support—sheltered interest rates and deposit insurance—worked well until the mid-1960s. Then the system started to fail to attract sufficient capital to meet the nation's housing and building needs. The reason was the availability of alternative investments for those who, up to this time, would otherwise invest their savings with savings banks.

Up to this time, only a small secondary market for mortgage loans had existed. A secondary market is defined as any market in which participants buy and sell things that have their first sale elsewhere. Thus, the assignment of a mortgage is a secondary market transaction. Such assignments were well known to the common law starting in the 13th century. Once in the secondary market, a mortgage (but not necessarily the note as a negotiable instrument subject to the Uniform Commercial Code's Article 3) is subject to the same federal and state regulation controlling its initial creation—if a mortgage loan was usurious when made, it is usurious in the secondary market.

Prior to the 1970s, some savings associations, mutual banks, and other private mortgage lenders, when strapped for cash or new loan funds, sold portions of their portfolio of loans to larger banks. Usually, the purchasers in such markets were large commercial banks.

In the late 1960s, however, the federal government created several new types of purchasers in the secondary market. With federal funds it capitalized several quasi-public corporations, with charters authorizing them to buy mortgage loans, pool them in amounts totaling millions of dollars, and then use the proceeds of these pools to pay the holders of securities backed by the pools in which the mortgages are retained. Investors in the securities would then provide funds for creating new pools, into which mortgages could again be put. On and on, in an endless cycle of floating securities, creating pools, and eventually getting new money into the hands of mortgage lenders.

Most likely borrower-mortgagors never know that their loan documents have been assigned to a purchaser in the secondary market because the original lender would become the "servicer" of the loan. The monthly mortgage payment is still sent to the same place but is passed on by the servicer. Many mortgage lenders came to depend on the fees received for servicing the loans they had originated. With time, some lenders became servicing specialists.

These quasi-public corporations established to support what quickly became a huge secondary market for mortgages are the Government National Mortgage Association, the Federal National Mortgage Association, the Federal Home Loan Mortgage Corporation, and the Federal Agricultural Mortgage Corporation. They are known as Ginnie Mae, Fannie Mae, Freddie Mac, and Farmer Mac, respectively. Fannie Mae and Freddie Mac underwrite the conventional mortgage market. In 2005, these two corporations owned or guaranteed about 45 percent of the country's total residential debt. Combined, all have been major players in the market for mortgage capital since the 1970s; as we will see, they have also been major forces tending to standardize mortgage note and mortgage lien and deed of trust documents, standardization that has meant fairer, more evenhanded treatment of mortgagors. And since 2010, they have been major factors in the (slow) recovery of the housing market after the financial crisis of 2007-2008.

Fannie Mae came to be among the 25 largest corporations in the country, which was why, in the years 2007 to 2014, its work (in its accounting, underwriting, and risk departments) came to be such a force in the mortgage capital crisis of those years. The underwriting available from these secondary market purchasers has enabled new types of mortgage lenders (some eventually seen as predatory lenders) to gain a strong position as originators of residential mortgage loans. Often they are corporate subsidiaries of commercial banks and savings banks, but just as often they are stand-alone mortgage lenders—all capable of rapidly closing mortgage transactions and servicing mortgage payments, passing on the long-term risk to secondary market investors in mortgage securities.

MORTGAGES

What is commonly referred to as a mortgage is, in reality, two documents. The first is a promissory note, in which the debtor-borrower promises to pay back the loan of the creditor-lender. The second is the document in which the debtor *qua* mortgagor conveys a lien to the creditor *qua* mortgagee. In various regions of the country this second document is called a mortgage or a deed of trust. "Although a deed of trust is technically distinct from a common law mortgage, it is common both colloquially and in legal parlance to use the term 'mortgage' as a shorthand for financing that involves a deed of trust." *See Nationstar Mortgage LLC v. Kemp*, 258 A.3d 298, 300 (Md. 2020). (There are differences between a mortgage and a deed of trust, but in those situations in which the differences have no practical effect on the problems being discussed, the word mortgage will be used.) Properly speaking, then, a mortgage is a document conveying a lien. This lien typically attaches to property improved or purchased with the loan proceeds.

THE TITLE THEORY OF MORTGAGES

At common law, as the colonies received that law from England, a mortgage was a conveyance of the legal title to the mortgagee (the lender). He was vested with the legal title to the property securing the loan, subject, however, to the condition that the lien could not be foreclosed after the loan was repaid. The mortgagee had a defeasible or conditional fee simple absolute: "to the mortgagee so long as the loan is unpaid"—defeasible fee language—or "to the mortgagee, but if the loan is repaid, to the mortgagor"—a fee simple, subject to a condition subsequent. The mortgagee holds the legal estate, and the mortgagor the equitable one. *See Key Bank Nat'l Ass'n v. Keniston*, 298 A.3d 800, 805 (Me. 2023) and *New Milford Savings Bank v. Jajer*, 708 A.2d 1378, 1382 and n.11 (Conn. 1998) (describing mortgagee's title as a fee simple determinable subject to an equitable right of redemption). In other words, the common law mortgage was a conditional conveyance. This is the title theory of mortgages. Today it has some lingering effects on the law of mortgages.

THE LIEN THEORY OF MORTGAGES

A second theory of mortgages is the lien theory of mortgages. Under it, the debt is the principal obligation and the mortgage a collateral agreement to secure the debt. The mortgage becomes a lien on the secured property, not a common law estate in it. It was regarded as personal property of the mortgagee, should he die, for purposes of administering his estate, and the mortgagor is given an equitable estate, called the equity of redemption. This equity has all the attributes of ownership, except that it can be terminated by a proceeding to enforce the mortgage lien. This proceeding is an equitable one and is called foreclosure.

Most states and jurisdictions have adopted the English equitable or lien theory of mortgages, and the title theory is used in only a few states today. However, the two theories are just that—*theories*—and when applied to particular documents, the distinctions between them become blurry.

Examples

Example 1

MR (mortgagor) executes an enforceable[1] mortgage in favor of ME (mortgagee). C, a creditor of ME, asks you whether he can enforce a judgment against ME by levying against MR's property. What do you say? If C were a creditor of MR, would your answer change? *See* Wesley Sturges & Charles

1. The use of "enforceable" in this chapter means to indicate that unless the content of an Example expressly indicates to the contrary, the mortgage is enforceable and not subject to hidden defects, such as a failure of delivery or other legal problems not indicated on the face of the document.

Clark, Legal Theory and Real Property Mortgages, 27 Yale L.J. 691 (1928) (the leading article on the lingering distinctions between the two theories of mortgages, written by two of the founders of the legal realist movement).

Explanation

No and yes, respectively, in both lien and title jurisdictions. A summary of these results and further examples of the lack of difference between lien and title theories are found in the commonly accepted answers to the following questions.

Issue	Lien	Title
Can ME's creditors reach land?	No	No
Can MR's creditors reach land?	Yes	Yes
Will a judgment against ME be levied against the land?	No	No
Will a judgment against MR be levied against the land?	Yes	Yes
Does the existence of a mortgage determine whether MR's spouse has a marital estate in the land?	No	No

These results should confirm your expectations about the relative rights of lenders and borrowers. *See Case v. St. Mary's Bank*, 63 A.3d 1209 (N.H. 2013) (mortgagee in a title theory state is not the owner liable on a covenant of quiet enjoyment given the mortgagor's tenant). Now for some examples in which the theory of the mortgage makes a difference.

Example 2

MR executes an enforceable mortgage in favor of ME. MR defaults, and ME begins foreclosure. Can ME go into possession of the land before the foreclosure decree is issued?

Explanation

This is one of the few areas of mortgage law in which it matters whether a lien or a title theory is used. In title jurisdictions, absent agreement otherwise, the mortgagee can gain possession of the land immediately after the mortgagor's default. Think about the analogy to a fee simple determinable followed by a possibility of reverter in this regard. *See Trannon v. Towles*, 75 So. 458 (Ala. 1917) (dismissing a mortgagor's trespass action brought against a mortgagee who took possession of the secured property under authority of a title mortgage).

In lien jurisdictions, the right to possession does not arise immediately after default, but later. How much later varies from jurisdiction to jurisdiction. Some lien theory jurisdictions speak of a hybrid or intermediate theory of mortgages. The date on which the mortgagee is entitled to possession can be the date the mortgagee files for foreclosure, the date of the decree in foreclosure, or the date on which the decree becomes final. *See Glover v. Marine Bank of Beaver Dam*, 345 N.W.2d 449, 453 (Wis. 1984) (holding that a mortgagor under a lien mortgage retains the title and the right to possession until the date of the foreclosure decree). In this regard, think about the analogy to a fee simple subject to a condition subsequent: The right of reentry is not automatic—as it is with a possibility of reverter following a determinable fee—but instead it must be exercised by the mortgagee. Its exercise is not one of self-help, but commences with the filing of a foreclosure suit.

Example 3

MR executes an enforceable mortgage in favor of ME. The mortgage covenants contain a use restriction on the land. MR conveys the property to X, who does not assume the mortgage. Can ME enjoin X from violating the use restriction?

Explanation

Again, the theory matters. If a lien theory applies, then ME and X are not in privity of estate and, because they are also not in privity of contract (the nonassumption makes that certain), there is no link between the interests of ME and X to provide the basis for enforcing the restriction against X. If a title theory underlies the MR-X mortgage, there is still no privity of contract, but there is privity of estate, and the use restriction can be enforced by ME against X. The latter succeeds to MR's title diminished by the conveyance of the benefit of the use restriction, and so X takes title subject to it. If the restriction was important enough to ME that he negotiated for it in the first instance, it is no less important to him after the MR-X conveyance because the property still secures the mortgage debt.

Example 4

MR executes an enforceable mortgage in favor of ME. The land subject to the mortgage gains acreage through the accretion of land near a water boundary of the property. MR defaults and ME brings a foreclosure action against MR, including the accreted land as part of the property subject to the mortgage. MR moves to strike the accreted land from ME's complaint. Will MR be successful?

Explanation

Yes. in a lien jurisdiction, but no, in a title jurisdiction. If in a title jurisdiction ME may be regarded as the titleholder during the term of the mortgage, ME has the right to the accreted land as it accretes. In a lien jurisdiction, this isn't so; MR will be successful unless the mortgage document gives ME an express right to property acquired after the mortgage's execution (a so-called after-acquired property covenant).

These four examples represent contemporary differences between the two theories, but don't generalize from them. They are confined to very specific areas of the law.

THE ACCUMULATION OF MORTGAGE REMEDIES

The history of mortgages is a series of remedies provided to the lenders, to which the borrowers react, so that the law swings first in the lenders', then in the borrowers' favor. This history is one in which remedies are piled on top of another so that the most recent ones do not alter or abolish older ones.

Thus, the title theory of mortgages provided for a "law day" or final payment date. This was a date on which either all payments—and usually it was just one lump sum payment—were due or the conditional title of the lender became absolute. If the mortgagor "doth not pay, then the land which he puts in pledge . . . is gone from him for ever, and so dead." Littleton's Tenures §332 (E. Wambaugh ed. 1903). What if the borrower did not pay on the day the debt was due but had a good reason for not doing so (e.g., he was robbed on his way to the lender's)? Or what if the lender hid from the borrower? What if the time and place of payment were unclear? The borrower then went to an equity court and asked that he be granted an *equity of redemption*—the right to pay the loan off after payment day. It came to be the practice of the courts to grant a six-month period, running from the date of the decree and during which the mortgagor must pay the debt or else lose the title. *See* Anonymous Case, 27 Eng. Rep. 621 (1740). Once the courts got used to granting one extension, they sometimes granted several in a row. *See Nanny v. Edwards*, 38 Eng. Rep. 752 (1827) (noting that three extensions were usual). Such an equity of redemption could not, at the execution of the mortgage, be bargained away.

Once this became a matter of routine for borrowers, lenders felt insecure in dealing with the secured real property, even after payment day, because the borrower might ask for an equity of redemption. *See Novosielski v. Wakefield*, 34 Eng. Rep. 161, 162 (1811). To foreclose this possibility, lenders started asking for a decree to confirm their absolute title to the secured property; in return they agreed not to pursue the other assets of the borrower further (i.e., they agreed not to sue on the note for a deficiency judgment). *See Toro Credit Co. v. Zeytoonjian*, 267 A.3d 71, 77 (Conn. 2021). This confirmatory decree was a decree of *strict foreclosure*. *See Perine v. Dunn*, Johnson's

Ch. Rep. 140 (N.Y. 1819). To "foreclose" means to shut out or bar; what is being barred here is the equity of redemption. When we speak today of foreclosing a mortgage, the reference is really not so much to enforcing the lender's rights, but to barring the rights of the borrower in the property.

What survives the uniform use of strict foreclosure today is the equity of redemption. It gives rise to the perception that the law of mortgages has a pro-mortgagor bias, and the perception is strengthened by a further rule—a prohibition on "clogs" on the mortgagor's right to access the courts to exercise the equity of redemption. Finding that a provision in a mortgage is a clog renders it void; so a clog is any agreement contemporaneous with the mortgage that cuts off or modifies the equity of redemption. This prohibitory rule is aimed at preventing the mortgagee's overreaching at a time when the mortgagor is most vulnerable to such activity. For example, an option to purchase mortgaged property at a fixed price cannot be given to a mortgagee at the same time the mortgage is executed. That option is a clog because the option price is likely to be too low. However, what if a lessee improves leased premises and also negotiates an option to buy them? And what if that option provides that if the lessor cannot give a marketable title when the option is exercised, the option becomes a mortgage for the value of the improvements? No clog is present here. The mortgage is part of the option, not the other way around.

Once strict foreclosure was well established, borrowers asked some state legislatures for a *statutory right of redemption*. This referred to the borrower's right to redeem or pay off the debt during a statutory period after the foreclosure decree and receive back a clear title to the real property. The period of statutory redemption is piggybacked onto the process of obtaining the decree. This right is statutory, is strictly construed and not implied, and not available in all states.

Lenders responded to this change, which they regarded as too borrower-oriented, by inserting into the mortgage document a *private power of sale*. This power enabled them to bypass the judicial process altogether. This power involved the appointment of a trustee, with the power to sell the foreclosed property, usually at a public auction.

Borrowers responded to this private power with a further petition to the legislature, asking that foreclosure be made a mandatory remedy. As a result, *judicial foreclosure codes* were enacted in every state. The statutes comprising these codes supplemented, but did not supplant the common law and the equitable right of redemption; they implemented important public policies relating to foreclosure—providing procedural safeguards on the use of the private power of sale, such as notice and timelines for conducting such sales. *See Keybank, N.A. v. Yazar*, 297 A.3d 968, 977 (Conn. 2023). Thus, notwithstanding these codes, a foreclosure action is commonly described as equitable in nature, a reference to the continuing use of the equity of redemption and the use of judicial discretion in the conduct of the action.

Lenders responded to such codes by elaborating on their private powers of sale and transferring such powers to a trustee who, during the term of the loan, would hold the title and, upon notice of default from the lender, would sell it. If the codes barred the mortgage lender from using the power, they did not bar the trustee, who after all was the mortgagor's agent as well as the mortgagee's. The document creating this trust is known as a *deed of trust.* For a lender, the deed of trust has some procedural advantages: With a mortgage, the lender initiates a suit in foreclosure, but with a deed of trust, the lender tells the trustee to foreclose and the borrower must object, bringing an action to enjoin the foreclosure.

Some states responded to the deed of trust with several statutes requiring a *judicial confirmation* of the trustee's private sale.

The pendulum of remedies thus looks like this:

Advantage to Lenders	Advantage to Borrowers
the title mortgage	equity of redemption
strict foreclosure	statutory right of redemption
private power of sale	judicial foreclosure codes
deeds of trust	confirmation of sale

Two caveats about this table are needed. First, this is a historical pendulum; it is not meant as a graphic picture of any state foreclosure code. For instance, in some states today, a power to cure the default is provided before the decree is final. Second, recall again that these remedies are cumulative; that is, the availability of one does not mean that other earlier remedies are denied. Later ones don't repeal early ones.

These remedies all have modern applications. For example, the equity of redemption cannot be waived by a mortgage covenant in the same documents as are executed at the time of the original mortgage transaction. Neither can a mortgagor agree, at the time of the original mortgage closing, to convey the property to the mortgagee after a default in lieu of the mortgagee's bringing a foreclosure action. Both of these covenants would be a clog on the equity of redemption, available to mortgagors even in the midst of foreclosure. This prohibition against clogging the equity of redemption is today seen as protecting (1) a method of keeping negotiations in advance of a foreclosure evenhanded and (2) the integrity of the judicial process involved in a foreclosure, as well as a type of consumer protection device. For example, any expansion of the mortgagee's common law right to a receiver to manage the secured property and to collect its rents and profits may be seen as a clog on the equity of redemption; granting of the right to a receiver, in advance of the need for the remedy, will likewise provoke strict judicial scrutiny of the provision when it appears in a mortgage document.

Examples

Example 5

Planetary Real Estate Trust (PRET) owns $50 billion worth of office buildings all over the United States and borrows $50 million from Mammoth National Bank (MNB) to acquire another property for its portfolio. PRET's loan is secured by a note and a mortgage, one covenant of which provides that on default, the property will be turned over to MNB. Two years later, PRET defaults and, in order to prevent PRET from repaying its outstanding loan amount, MNB seeks to enforce its contractual rights. May MNB do so?

Explanation

No, not without dealing first with the equity of redemption. The equity is an implied, unwaivable aspect of every mortgage, regardless of the parties' wealth, status, or contract rights. It distinguishes mortgage finance from all other types of secured transactions. Contractual rights in the mortgage covenant applicable after default and before foreclosure, as here, cannot defeat the equity or prevent PRET's payment of the outstanding loan and release of the mortgage lien. It creates a right for the mortgagor just by the latter's being a mortgagor—a status right that trumps contract rights. Once a mortgage, always a mortgage. It is not preempted by any other statutory borrower protections or any other type of foreclosure proceedings. After default, it provides leverage for the mortgagor in refinancing negotiations.

Example 6

Suppose that a developer D needs construction financing, but the capital market for such financing is tight. A mortgage lender L is willing to make a loan in an amount representing 80 percent of the fair market value of the land plus the improvements that D proposes to construct, evidenced by a note and secured by a mortgage lien. In addition, L proposes that D convey to L an option to acquire a 20 percent interest in the land and the improvements at the completion of construction. D agrees to the conveyance in writing. The loan agreement is executed, the note and mortgage executed, and L disburses the loan principal. But when L exercises his option, D refuses to convey the 20 percent interest. L sues D for specific performance of D's agreement to convey the interest. Will L obtain specific performance of this agreement?

Explanation

80% +20% = 100%. This being so, L is asking that D convey away his equity in the property—the amount of the market value in excess of the loan amount—at the time of the execution of the loan documents before foreclosure. So D's equity of redemption is involved. (Statutory redemption, in contrast, arises only at the time of the foreclosure sale—and then only in states with a statute establishing this right. No foreclosure yet, so statutory redemption is not involved.) Further, the equity of redemption is only valuable if there is a portion of the market value over the amount of the loan available to the borrower like D at the time of the loan. Otherwise, strict foreclosure is possible for L because D's remaining interest has no monetary value.

L is thus asking that the amount representing the equity of redemption be conveyed away at the time of the loan so that D will have no equity in the property. The issue then is whether the equity of redemption can be conveyed at the same time as the lien. The common law answer was clearly in the negative: Common law lawyers said that the equity of redemption could not be "clogged" or waived in advance of foreclosure. Specific performance of L's option on the 20 percent is in effect a clog and so is unenforceable when executed as part of the original mortgage transaction. The common law requires later execution of such an option and independent consideration for it in order to validate it; otherwise, D's entire interest in the project is extinguished. If the equity of redemption is to provide D with an interest in the secured property, then L has clogged it with his option. Thus no specific performance, and judgment for D.

Consider the other point of view: If consumer protection statutes, usury laws and cases, and doctrines of good faith, unconscionability, and equitable mortgages are in place in the jurisdiction, when there is no collateral advantage taken by L in securing the option—all legal devices aimed as accomplishing some of the results achieved by the equity of redemption—why should D and L not be permitted to make a deal that suits their circumstances, notwithstanding the doctrine of clogging? If L's interest rate is a conventional one, the usury ceiling is not exceeded, and the option is not an equitable mortgage, there is no clog.

Thus, although two answers are possible, this scenario is likely to be seen as a clog on the equity of redemption. The presence of other consumer protections for D should not be seen as an abrogation or implied repeal of his common law rights to avoid foreclosure by exercising his equity of redemption. The common law–property law point of view will probably prevail over one resting on the parties' freedom of contract.

NOTE AND MORTGAGE TERMS

The note is an IOU: the personal promise of the debtor to repay the loan and is evidence of the debt. If the debt is paid, released, or invalid, the mortgage underlying the debt is also terminated. The note's essential terms are a promise to pay a definite sum, the terms of the payment, and the signature of the borrower(s). *See Devlin v. Wiener*, 656 A.2d 664 (Conn. 1995). It also defines a right to prepay the loan (if the lender wants to extend that right) and prepayment charges. In many jurisdictions, there is no right to prepay unless the note extends it, and then only to the extent defined in the note. Any charges levied on late payments, often imposed after a grace period has passed, are also set out. Often a procedure for giving the debtor notice of a late payment is set out as well, along with a waiver of some common law debtor's rights (e.g., presentment, or notice of dishonor) and a statement of joint and several liability for the debt on the part of every debtor executing and delivering the note.

Following is a shortened version of a standard-form Fannie Mae/Freddie Mac note.

NOTE

________, ________		________, ________	
date	year	city	state

____

property address

In return for a loan, I promise to *pay* U.S. $_____ (the principal), plus interest, *to the order of the lender*, that is, to _____. *Interest will be charged at a yearly rate of* _____%. Payments of principal and interest will be due every month, on the _____ day of the month, at _____. My monthly *payments* will be _____ and will be *applied to interest before principal.* I can *make principal payments* anytime *before they are due*, in whole or part.

If the loan is found *usurious*, the excess over the permitted limit will be severed from the amounts due and refunded to me.

If a monthly payment is unpaid _____ calendar days after it is due, I will pay the lender *a late charge* of _____% of the overdue payment; if a payment is overdue, I am in default and the lender may notify me that, 30 days after receipt of the notice, I will be *required to pay the full principal amount not paid* and all interest due on that amount, plus the lender's costs and expenses. This notice is effective when sent to me at the property address above.

Every person signing this Note, and every *guarantor*, surety, or endorser, is obligated to keep all the promises contained in it, and all such persons waive any right to *presentment and notice of dishonor*. In addition to the protections given to the Note holder herein, a Mortgage or Deed of Trust, dated the same date as this Note, also protects the holder and describes how, when, and under what conditions immediate payment in full of all amounts owing under this Note, might be required by its holder. Such conditions include the sale or transfer of the property without the consent of the holder of this Note.

WITNESS THE HAND(S) AND SEAL(S) OF THE UNDERSIGNED:

______________________________ *(LS)*
Borrower

______________________________ *(LS)*
Borrower

The note is (once again) the *personal* promise of the borrower to repay the loan. "Personal" means that it can be enforced by a judgment against the personal assets of the borrower, and in this context a "personal asset" means any asset besides the real property securing the loan. The loan is, in other words, a "recourse" loan: The lender has recourse, through all appropriate legal remedies, to any and all of the borrower's other assets; that is, all the borrower's wealth stands behind this loan. In contrast, a nonrecourse loan is one in which only the property stands as security for the mortgage.[2]

Typically a lawsuit to recover the outstanding amount of the debt after the borrower's default will be brought in two stages. The first will be brought on the basis of the mortgage lien ("to foreclose" or perfect it); in this action for foreclosure, the secured property will be sold to satisfy the debt in whole or part. After the foreclosure action, a second suit may be brought on the note; its purpose will be to recover any difference between the amount of the debt and the amount realized by the lender from the proceeds of the foreclosure sale. This second suit is known as an action for a deficiency judgment[3]—the deficiency being that difference just referred to. To satisfy the deficiency judgment, the court can order a levy and sale on the debtor's personal assets.

Let's consider some of the key phrases italicized in this note.

In return for a loan? First thing, the note establishes that the borrower has received the proceeds of a loan—a fact that he or she cannot thereafter deny. After all, the note has been signed. Thus, the maximum amount of the borrower's liability is also established. Because as later provisions in the note indicate, the loan will be repaid in installments, usually made monthly, the amount of the loan does not establish the amount of the debt due at foreclosure. Here, the provisions of the judicial foreclosure code intervene: The lender, usually the plaintiff, has the burden of proof to establish the amount of the debt due and outstanding. The assignment of this burden is in line with civil actions generally. Asserting possession of the note and submitting an affidavit of intervening payments by the borrower up to the time of his or her default in payments, is typically sufficient to meet this burden, Thereafter, unless the borrower raises a sufficient defense, the burden of

---

2. A nonrecourse note contains a covenant limiting the mortgagee/lender to a remedy, known as foreclosure, in which the property is sold to satisfy the loan and, after payment of the expenses associated with the sale, its proceeds, up to the amount needed to pay the outstanding debt, are given to the lender, with any excess going first to other, junior lenders whose loans are secured by the same property and made a party to the foreclosure action, and then to the borrower.

3. Certain types of mortgages—e.g., purchase money mortgages and vendor-financed mortgages—sometimes require either a first suit on the mortgage in foreclosure, or an election by the lender of either a suit on the note or on the mortgage; these limitations on deficiencies are generally imposed by state statute.

proof remains with the lender, but further proof typically involves live testimony of the lender's employees, the discovery of the borrower's loan file; disputes over the trustworthiness of that file depending upon evidentiary rules involving the hearsay rule, business records exception to that rule, and so forth. When the note has been the subject to a lender's merger or acquisition of another lender—usually a larger bank—or sold into the secondary market and the right to service the loan has been separately sold, further complications of proof arise. Enough said here!

Pay . . . the lender? These words make the lender's possession of the note at the time of its enforcement of the mortgage in foreclosure a precondition to bringing the action on the mortgage. The note is the principal instrument, and the accompanying mortgage is an accessory. *See MB Fin. Bk. v. Rao*, 239 A.3d 181, 186 (Pa. Super. Ct. 2020). Although lost note affidavits are available, they are not self-proving. *See Jones v. Ward*, 270 A.3d 1024, 1031-1032 (Md. App. 2022) (detailing the elements of a lost note affidavit). When a borrower defaults, moreover, the lender has a choice of suing on the note, which creates liability *in personam*, subjecting all the borrower's assets to repay the debt evidenced by the note, or suing *in rem* on the accompanying mortgage securing the note and subjecting the mortgaged property to its payment. *See Archie v. U.S. Bank*, NA, 258 A.3d 1005, 1012 (D.C. 2023). The relationship between the note and its accompanying mortgage has been stated in many ways, but always to the same effect:

> "If the note is void, the accompanying mortgage is a nullity and void as well."
> "The mortgage follows the note."
> "The mortgage lives and dies with the note, and satisfaction destroys it."[1]

Archie, op. cit., 258 A.3d at 1015.[2]

Pay . . . to the order of the lender? These are important words: On a bank check, where they routinely appear, they permit endorsement of the check by its payee. The same rule applies here. The borrower should sign only one of these, and not sign copies—to sign more than one would mean that as many copies as were signed are subject to endorsement and assignment. These words make the note negotiable. This means that it can be assigned

---

1. *See Moore v. Burnet*, 11 Ohio 334, 341 (Ohio 1842).
2. However, the note and mortgage are not considered one instrument for purposes of tolling a Statute of Limitations: The note may be time-barred while the mortgage is still enforceable under a longer Statute. *See Bank of Wildwood v. Kerl*, 189 So. 866, 868 (Fla. 1939). Thus, in this situation, the right to a personal judgment may be lost, while the right to enforce the mortgage still exists in foreclosure. In the same vein, a person not signing the note may still be liable on the accompanying signed mortgage.

or transferred by its payee (the lender) to another and that the assignee, if a bona fide purchaser for value, takes it free of any defects in the interest of the transferor or defenses that the transferor may be subject to when such defenses are raised by the debtor (the borrower). A note purchaser protected in this manner is known as a holder in due course. The language here is the equivalent of making it payable to its bearer, or "to bearer." Most notes are negotiable. A nonnegotiable note would not be payable "to order" or "to bearer," but would instead be payable to a named and specific person. A nonnegotiable mortgage instrument is, after assignment, still subject to defenses arising in the original mortgage transaction such as illegality, fraud, or unconscionability. More will be said about negotiable notes in Chapter 13, on transfers of the mortgage.

Interest will be charged at a yearly rate of _____%? This is a fixed-rate note; its interest rate does not vary over the term of the loan. That term is typically 15 to 30 years. In contrast, many borrowers use an adjustable-rate mortgage, in which the provisions of the note are changed so that the lender may (but need not) vary the rate of interest during the term. Changes in the interest rate must be adjusted in accordance with the provisions of the note. An adjustable-rate note typically provides for (1) advance notice of the change to the borrower, (2) an adjustment made according to the movement of a predetermined index (the index may be the T-bill rate or some other widely available financial benchmark), and (3) an upper limit on an increase in the interest rate (e.g., no more than one increase in any 12 months, or no increase of more than 1 percent per year).

Payments . . . applied to interest before principal? Each monthly repayment of the note is applied to the whole debt according to this order of application, so if, for some reason, interest on the loan is overdue, the next monthly payment will be applied to interest due first, and only if and when there is money left over, to the repayment of principal. In the accompanying mortgage, this order of application is repeated and elaborated in a covenant. The mortgage has more detail on the order of application; this detail reflects the need of the lender to recover its costs in enforcing the mortgage's covenants as soon as possible.

Make principal payments . . . before they are due? In a majority of jurisdictions, absent statutory authority or express contrary language in the note, there is no right to prepay the loan given to the borrower; so a prepayment right must be expressly stated—and here it is. There is, however, a split in the cases considering this matter. *Compare* Ex Parte Brannon, 683 So. 2d 994 (Ala. 1996) (the majority rule), *with Mahoney v. Furches*, 468 A.2d 458 (Pa. 1983) (the minority rule: a right to prepay is implied).

Two rationales are commonly advanced for the majority rule. First, the lender has made an investment in the loan and is entitled to the bargain that was initially struck; a prepayment would deprive it of its bargain. This is known as the rule of perfect tender in time. Some courts have justified the perfect tender rule by looking at the hardship on the lender—finding that, were the rule otherwise, the lender would suffer economic hardship: the loss of the expected rate of interest, the need to reinvest the principal, and so on. Under the majority rule, the prepayment was thus regarded as a default or breach of the terms of the mortgage. Another rationale for the rule is a principle of reciprocity: Because the borrower cannot be compelled to make early payments, the lender should not be compelled to accept the prepayment. Mortgagees should not, if they wish to invoke the majority perfect tender rule, avoid provisions that make all repayment due "on or before," "no sooner than" a date certain, or "within" a period of time. Such phrases are an invitation to litigation.

The minority rule is that absent statutory authority or express, contrary language in the note, there is a presumption that the borrower has the right of prepayment. A policy promoting the alienability of real property underlies this rule.

Fixed prepayment fees (e.g., 3-2-1 percent; declining over the term) were once the condition of a mortgagee's permitting prepayment. For commercial mortgage loans, litigation ensued over whether these were a liquidated damages covenant in disguise. If they were, these provisions had to anticipate and bear a reasonable relationship to the mortgagee's economic loss, or else they were an unreasonable penalty. This possibility, and mortgage securitization, prompted lenders to adopt so-called yield maintenance and defeasance provisions instead.

Yield maintenance refers to the interest or yield lost on a total prepayment when interest rates decline. It is measured by the spread between the contract rate and the rate current when the prepayment is made. It assumes that the prepayment can be invested and that annuities substituted to cover the spread will leave the lender whole. A defeasance provision is also a substitution of collateral. Usually a portfolio of U.S. Treasury bonds is substituted for the property, these bonds yielding amounts comparable to the payments that the lender loses after prepayment. After substitution, the mortgage is released, but the note remains outstanding. Once purchased, the bonds are held in escrow until maturity and then delivered back to the borrower.

Defeasance requires the borrower's setting aside a portfolio of bonds, to cover the outstanding mortgage debt. Lenders prefer defeasance to yield maintenance: It maintains yields, does not interrupt the lender's income stream (important for a securitized loan), moves the collateral up-market (bonds being safer than mortgages as investments), sells bonds, is most securely insulated from the charge of being liquidated damages, and locks in the original bargain of the parties—thus permitting the lender to have the financial advantage of the perfect tender rule even in minority rule states.

Usurious? Usury is (1) a loan of money (or forbearance on the recovery of a loan) (2) made on terms that make it repayable absolutely and (3) with an intent to charge a rate of interest on it that is (4) higher than that permitted by law. *See Britz v. Kinsvater*, 351 P. 986 (Ariz. 1960). When raised as a defense by the borrower to a suit for repayment of a loan, usury is typically viewed as an affirmative defense.

A "usury savings clause" such as the one that this note has is generally enforceable and effective to prevent a finding of usury. It overrides a stated rate of interest that is usurious on its face. *See in re* Dominguez, 995 F.2d 883 (9th Cir. 1993). Such a clause is useful because the impact of applicable usury laws is not always clear. It preserves enforceability as to any part of the loan remaining legal after the usury statute (if applicable) is applied to it. The effect of this clause is to sever the illegal from the legal portion of the interest charged—and save the latter.

Usury is the subject of state statutes and case law. A usurious intent is generally inferred from the loan documents; proof of an actual, subjective intent to violate the law is not necessary, and a mistake in interpreting the usury law is no defense. So a loan agreement for interest greater than permitted is sufficient evidence of a usurious intent and is presumed usurious, whether or not the lender is aware of the violation. Neither is a disclaimer or waiver of the usury law permitted: When a borrower makes a usurious payment, the lender acquires no claim of waiver or estoppel.

On the other hand, when repayment of a loan is subject to a bona fide contingency or the risk of loss of the principal, as with the investment of equity capital so that the loan is not absolutely repayable, the usury law does not apply.

Statutes prescribe "the legal rate of interest" above which a loan is considered usurious, but they are typically subject to numerous exceptions for certain types of lenders and loans. Lenders generally investigate what type of charges and fees will be considered "interest" for purposes of an applicable usury statute. In general, if the lender passes along a fee to a person providing a legitimate service to the lender, the fee is not "interest." Appraisal fees, brokerage commissions, title and casualty insurance premiums, housing inspection fees, and escrow fees are not interest on this account. On the other hand, origination fees, unrelated to the administrative costs of placing the loan, may be interest; and points and discounts deducted from the principal amount will likely be found to be interest. A lender's counsel will study these matters and tailor the terms of the loan accordingly. He might provide that the excess over the legal rule be refunded or applied to the outstanding amount of the debt. But the results of litigation being uncertain, a usury savings clause is necessary.

Usury penalties can be severe. Forgoing the usurious component of an interest charge, forgoing all interest, and invalidation of the loan are common. Generally these penalties and statutes have been considered to impede the interstate movement of mortgage capital and the use of non-fixed rate mortgages. In 1983, Congress responded to these two concerns and preempted state usury statutes for many "federally related" first-lien residential notes and mortgages. 12 U.S.C. §1735f-7a. Federally related mortgage loans include those eligible for purchase by Fannie Mae, Ginnie Mae, or Freddie Mac, or loans made by a lender who regularly makes loans totaling over $1 million a year. 12 C.F.R. pt. 590.2(b)(6). State legislatures were given an opportunity to opt out of the preemption, and only about ten states did so.

Transactions structured to avoid the impact of the usury laws sometimes might involve, for example, an installment land sale contract, a sale and repurchase of property, or the incorporation of the borrower (to take advantage of a statutory exemption).

A late charge? This note computes a late charge as a percentage of the amount overdue. This presents a problem: As the unpaid monthly payments mount, does a percentage actually reflect the administrative costs of overseeing the delinquency? Maybe not, and if not, then this charge will result in a windfall for the lenders. A set amount might be fairer. Moreover, a court might find it to be a liquidated damages clause that lacks a reasonable foundation in that it has not been bargained for, nor has it been based on a reasonable estimation of the lender's actual damages. As such, it becomes invalid as a contractual penalty.

Required to pay the full principal amount not paid? The judicial foreclosure code typically will establish the period after which the borrower is required to pay the full principal and all interest due on the loan. This is known as the acceleration clause of the note, typically found there, and sometimes cross-referenced in the accompanying mortgage. Acceleration of the loan advances a note's maturity date so that the payment of the entire debt is due immediately. Its purpose is to prevent the lender from having, after the borrower's default, to sue separately for each and every payment on the note as it falls due, thus preventing a multiplicity of suits and fostering judicial economy of the foreclosing court's resources.

Examples

Example 7

A late charge in a borrower's mortgage is computed as a percentage of the amount overdue. When the lender levies this charge on the borrower, the latter objects that the charge is effectively "interest" subject to the state's usury statute. Is this objection valid?

Explanation

No. This charge is not part of the lender's bargain when that bargain is made: It is not a return on the investment made by the lender. It is a charge made instead after a default. So usury restrictions do not apply to a late charge or a penalty payable on a default in repayment of the note—even when the charge is computed as a percentage of the interest due. Even if interest were charged on the delinquent amount at a higher rate than in the note, the determination of the effective rate of interest for usury purposes would not include any charge or penalty. *See First American Title Ins. & Tr. Co. v. Cook*, 90 Cal. Rptr. 645 (Cal. 1970).

Following are a few more explanations of phrases in the note.

Guarantor? This is a third party that promises to pay the debt when the debtor defaults and does not pay. Such a person is liable for the debt in the same way that an assignee of the borrower might be. A guaranty is a credit-enhancing contract and can take several forms. It typically has a maximum dollar amount, reduced with the "first dollars" or "last dollars" repaid, the latter being the most common form. It can be either total or partial. (Most are partial guarantees.) For example, a "carry guarantee" is an agreement, on default, to pay not the principal of the loan, but the interest, taxes, and insurance required to carry the loan out of default. A "springing guarantee" is effective only on some specified event, often the bankruptcy, fraud, or waste of the property by the borrower. A *surety* does not guarantee repayment, but will instead indemnify the lender when the lender sustains an unrecoverable loss after a default and after the lender pursues any remedies (such as foreclosure) available to it. All persons assuming the duties of a guarantor, surety, or endorser are also liable to the same extent as the original party—and have no extra defenses against the lender because of their third-party status.

Presentment and notice of dishonor? Presentment is the right of the borrower to require that the holder of the note demand payment of the amount overdue. Notice of dishonor is the right to require the holder of the note to give notice to other persons that the overdue amounts have not been paid; thus, when the borrower pays an insolvent lender when an assignee of the lender is actually due the payment, the borrower may have to make the same payment twice. Servicing contracts (defined *infra*), sometimes sold and sometimes held by the originating lender, obviate this problem, but the language remains useful if a foreclosure action is brought.

The statement of a definite sum that the debtor must repay is an essential term of the note. The computation of this sum is possible using four of the note's provisions: (1) the loan amount or principal, (2) the interest rate, (3) the term or duration of the repayment period, and (4) the monthly payment. They are all set out in the note. Once any three of these are set, the fourth can be determined.

LS? The words *leglis signi*, law Latin for a seal, are not much used today, but still they indicate the borrower's intent to make the promises in the note.

A trio of crucial terms—the principal, the interest rate, and the term of the loan—are necessary to compute a monthly payment of interest in an interest-only loan. Up to the 1930s, payments made on most mortgage loans consisted of interest only; the principal was due at the end of the term, on "law day," payable in a lump-sum balloon payment that in the Depression of the 1930s, fewer barrowers could make; this meant refinancing the loan on law day, but in the 1930s, much less capital was available to do that even if the borrower qualified, the balloon payment being more than the property was worth. Thus, in the 1930s, through the influence on mortgage lenders of the Federal Housing Administration and its standardized residential notes and mortgage covenants, monthly payments were made constant and amortized. Amortization means that each payment contained some repayment of principal and payment of interest, paid on a declining balance as the principal is repaid. In this manner, at the end of the last payment, the loan was completely repaid. Payment of interest on a declining balance requires that the early payments be mostly interest, which suits the borrower just fine, considering that the interest portion of the payment is deductible from income taxed by the Internal Revenue Code. In addition, in the 1930s the terms of such residential loans were lengthened from 5- to 10-year to 20- to 30-year terms.

The **mortgage** (or deed of trust) contains a conveyance of the lien; it is like a deed of the lien in this regard, containing the usual components of a deed. Both the note and the mortgage are sometimes written in "plain language"; that is, without legalese and words of art. State statutes that require plain language exist in about a dozen states. The sellers of mortgage-backed securities—Fannie Mae and Freddie Mac—have redrafted some of their notes and mortgages for use even in states where plain language is not required by statute.

MORTGAGE

This mortgage is made this _____ day of ___, ___ (year), between the Mortgagor, _________, (herein Borrower) and the Mortgagee, _________, a corporation organized and existing under the laws of _________ and of the United States, whose address is _________ (herein Lender). Borrower is indebted to Lender in the principal sum of _________ dollars, as evidenced by Borrower's Note dated _________, _________ (year), and providing for monthly payments of principal and interest, with the balance of the debt, if not paid sooner, due on _____.

To secure to Lender (a) repayment of the debt evidenced by the Note, with all interest, and payment of all other sums, with interest, advanced to protect the security of this Mortgage, and all covenants and agreements made herein, and (b) *repayment of all future advances*, with interest, made hereunder, Borrower grants and conveys a mortgage to Lender on the following described property in the County of ________, State of ________, described as follows:

[THE LEGAL DESCRIPTION OF THE SECURED PROPERTY IS INSERTED HERE.]

whose address is __________ __________.
Property Address

Together with all present and future improvements, all easements, rights, appurtenances, rents, royalties, mineral, oil and gas rights and profits, water and water rights, stock, and fixtures now or in the future attached to the property, including all replacements and additions thereto, all referred to as the "Property."

Borrower covenants that Borrower (a) is seised of the estate conveyed and (b) has the right to mortgage, grant, and convey the Property, that (c) the Property is unencumbered, and that (d) Borrower will defend title to the Property against all claims and demands, subject to restrictions listed on a schedule of exceptions to coverage in any title insurance policy insuring Lender's interest in the Property.

The mortgage secures *repayment of all future advances*. What are they? When the principal amount of the loan is not completely disbursed at the execution or closing of the mortgage, then further disbursements are known as future advances and the provision for them is known as a dragnet clause. *See Central Natl. Bank v. Bd. of Comm'nrs*, 270 P.3d 1229 (Kan. App. 2012). Because a competing lien or encumbrance on the title intervenes between an initial and any future advance, the lender is concerned that the priority of its mortgage be fixed as of the time of the initial disbursement. For example, suppose the borrower needs more money and executes a second mortgage on the same property; the lender does not want any later future advance to be junior to that other mortgagee. That would mean that the advance would be paid off, from the proceeds of a foreclosure sale, only after the other lien is satisfied; thus, the advance would have the status of a third mortgage. To avoid this, the mortgagee here will record this mortgage and so put the junior mortgagee on constructive notice of future advances so that their priority relates to the date of the execution and recordation of this mortgage.

Thus far, the mortgage looks like a deed to the secured property: There is a *premises* (naming and identifying the parties to the mortgage, referencing the note and its debt, a granting clause, and describing the property and its attendant rights); a *habendum* clause, including present and future deed covenants; and, upcoming, a *testimonium* clause (with signatures) and an acknowledgment by the borrower. In the covenants, there is a reference to the requirement of most lenders that a title insurance policy list no exceptions to the priority assigned the mortgage lien, as it might be assigned into the secondary market. That policy is another document that ensures the smooth operation of such markets.

However, the difference between the conveyance of a mortgage lien and of a fee simple absolute, though barely noticeable up to this point in the document, is great: Now come the various covenants that describe and control the ongoing relationship between mortgagor and mortgagee—not just about the debt and the lien, but about the property securing that lien as well.

The mortgage covenants are twofold. In the mortgage forms drafted by Fannie Mae and Freddie Mac, there are uniform covenants, applicable in all states and used in the forms intended for each and every state; and there are nonuniform covenants, applicable in only one state and tailored to the law there, and varying according to the form used (e.g., the mortgage form intended for use in Alabama).

Interspersed between the deed-like aspects of the mortgage are (in the residential mortgage forms used by Fannie Mae and Freddie Mac) a series of covenants, used uniformly in each state in which a lender does business. These uniform covenants are promises by the mortgagor. They (1) promise prompt payment of the debt; (2) establish a mortgage escrow account for property taxes, insurance premiums, and ground lease payments; (3) settle on how payments will be applied (to late fees, prepayment fees, interest, and principal due, generally in that order); and (4) promise further (5) payment of prior liens, (6) maintenance of hazard and mortgage insurance policies, and (7) not to commit waste. They also give the lender (8) the right to inspect the property and a share in (9) insurance and (10) condemnation proceeds to satisfy the debt. Further covenants give the mortgagee (11) the right to satisfy prior liens, and (12) exercise any and all rights in the covenants without being estopped or waiving any other right or remedy, as well as (13) set out a notice procedure for defaults in the covenants, (14) determine which law controls the interpretation of the mortgage, and (15) set out the severability of each covenant.

Uniform covenants are, more generally, intended to accomplish four things for the lender. First, they are meant to prevent interests superior to the lender's lien from arising, and to prevent events from occurring that render the lender and the loan insecure. For example, a uniform covenant establishes a mortgage escrow account into which the borrower pays monthly amounts for the eventual payment, by the lender, of real property taxes. The lender is concerned that these taxes be paid because, if they are not, a lien for payment arises that will have by statute a superior position to the lender's. In a tax lien foreclosure, then, the lender would be paid only after the taxing authority is paid out of the proceeds. Similarly, the lender is concerned that improvements on the property be insured against loss by fire; many times, such a loss would make the lender's lien worth less than would be needed to repay the loan.

Second, the uniform covenants are meant to provide further security for the loan. For example, the mortgage escrow funds "are pledged as additional security for all sums secured by this Security Instrument." In addition, a covenant provides for an "order of application." That is, any funds received from the borrower are applied first to pay any prepayment charge due under the note, then to amounts due (if any) to the escrow account, then to loan interest, then to principal, and finally to pay late charges due under the note.[4] This order of application permits the lender to spend money to protect its lien priority and the value of the property as collateral and recover those costs from monthly payments before accepting further repayment of the debt.

Third, uniform covenants protect the lender in actions and proceedings that may affect the title of the borrower in the future. When the borrower does not appear and defend the property, the lender may appear and charge the costs of doing so to the borrower.

Fourth, and finally, they are meant to foresee situations in which the security for the loan is converted into cash, and to assure the lender a share of that money. The two primary examples of such covenants provide (1) for the use of awards made in condemnation proceedings concerning the property to pay off the loan, and (2) for the use of money paid on insurance claims on hazard and fire policies when all or part of the improvements on the property have been destroyed. Lender has a right to share in the condemnation award or insurance money to satisfy repayment of the loan before it is reinvested in new property or the destroyed property is rebuilt.

Mortgage escrow accounts put on deposit with the lender, every month and with each mortgage payment, contain funds to pay real property taxes and property hazard insurance premiums as they are due. The account accumulates these funds until they need to be paid out to taxing authorities or insurers. Distinguish this use of an "escrow" from the escrow previously discussed as an alternative to the direct delivery of documents and the face-to-face closing of the transaction. The mortgage escrow has

---

4. This covenant states: "Unless applicable law provides otherwise, all payments received by Lender under [the covenant to repay the loan and to pay escrow amounts] shall be applied: first, to any prepayment charges due under the Note; second, to amounts payable [into the escrow account]; third, to interest due; fourth, to principal due; and last, to any late charges due under the Note."

a much narrower purpose. Its maintenance is controlled by the terms of Uniform Covenant 2 of the FNMA/FHLMC mortgage and reads in its opening sentences as follows.

> Subject to applicable law or to a written waiver by Lender, Borrower shall pay to Lender on the day monthly payments are due under the note, until the Note is paid in full, a sum ("Funds") equal to one-twelfth of (a) yearly taxes and assessments which may attain priority over this Security Instrument, (b) yearly leaseholds payments or ground rents on the Property, if any, (c) yearly hazard insurance premiums, and (d) yearly mortgage insurance premiums, if any. These items are called "escrow items." Lender may estimate the Funds due on the basis of current data and reasonable estimates of future escrow items.

Thus far, the covenant first explains the types of monies to be escrowed, either in order to preserve the status and priority of the lender's lien or to protect its security. However, when the jurisdiction's statutes require that the mortgagor be given a choice as to whether to maintain an escrow with the mortgagee, that statutory requirement controls: Often when the mortgagor pays down more than the usual percentage of the purchase price (and so is not financing the purchase *pro tanto*), the mortgagor will be given the option of paying the escrow items himself. This covenant places a maximum on the amount that can be collected with any one monthly payment. The total amount estimated by the lender to be necessary for each item is part of the borrower's monthly payment—and each item can be estimated separately rather than as a group. No matter how the estimating is done, the mortgagee is subject to a good faith and fair dealing requirement of the common law. This covenant continues.

> The Funds shall be held [in a federally or state-insured institution]. Lender shall apply the Funds to pay the escrow items. Lender may not charge for holding and applying the funds, analyzing the account or verifying the escrow items, unless Lender pays Borrower interest on the Funds and applicable law permits the Lender to make such a charge. Borrower and Lender may agree in writing that interest shall be paid on the Funds. Unless an agreement is made or applicable law requires interest to be paid, Lender shall not be required to pay Borrower any interest or earnings on the Funds. Lender shall give to Borrower, without charge, an annual accounting of the Funds. . . .
>
> If the amount of Funds held by Lender, together with the future monthly payments of Funds payable prior to the due dates of the escrow items, shall exceed the amount required to pay the escrow items when due, the excess shall be, at Borrower's option, either promptly repaid to Borrower or credited to Borrower on monthly payments of Funds. If the amount of the Funds held by Lender is not sufficient to pay the escrow items when due, the Borrower shall pay to Lender any amount necessary to make up the deficiency. . . .

Thereafter, this covenant imposes on the mortgagee the duty to make a prompt refund of all funds on account at the time of the release of the mortgage lien or, when the property is sold, application of all funds on account to satisfy that lien. The account is required unless waived by the lender or requiring it is in violation of *applicable*[5] law. 12 U.S.C. §2609 (1974) (a federal statute, part of the 1974 Real Estate Settlement Procedures Act, authorizing escrows for "federally related" or most residential mortgages).

Examples

Example 8

MR's mortgage documents require that the borrower (MR) pay into an escrow account maintained by the lender (ME) the amounts necessary to pay the premiums on a fire insurance policy for the secured property. MR makes the payments, but ME does not pay the premiums when due. A fire occurs after the policy has lapsed. MR sues ME for breach of the contract and consequential damages. In this suit, what result, and why?

Explanation

In this situation, some borrowers have recovered against the lender, sometimes for not notifying the borrower that the policy was about to lapse, and sometimes for a breach of contract to pay the premiums. The difficulty with the latter result is that the covenant says nothing about a promise to pay the premiums. Some courts have, however, implied such a promise. *See Cromartie v. Carteret Savings & Loan Assn.*, 649 A.2d 76 (N.J. Super. 1994). Based on the language that the lender "shall hold . . . [and] apply to pay" funds on account, some other suits have been based on an alleged fiduciary duty owed borrowers by lenders, on a trust or pledge theory. Most courts have dismissed suits seeking to imply a trust and impose fiduciary duties on lenders as the basis for these accounts. Implied contract has been more successful. The measure of damages here is the amount that would have been due a claimant under the policy, had it been purchased. *See Brooks v.Valley National Bank*, 539 P.2d 958 (Ariz. 1976).

Following are some of the other important covenants included in most residential mortgages today, with some explanation following each.

5. "Applicable" law is a term used repeatedly in Fannie Mae/Freddie Mac mortgage forms and refers either to federal and/or state, case and/or statutory law. Over the last several decades, the federal courts have been fashioning a federal common law of mortgages, preempting state laws when they impede the uniformity needed for implementation of federal housing programs.

> **Charges and Liens.** Borrowers shall pay all taxes and levies on the Property which may attain priority over this Mortgage. Borrower shall pay these obligations into escrow as before provided, or if not so paid, Borrower shall pay them on time directly to the person owed payment. Borrower shall promptly notify Lender of amounts to be paid under this paragraph. If Borrower makes these payments directly, Borrower shall promptly furnish to Lender receipts evidencing payments.
>
> Borrower shall promptly discharge any lien which has priority over this Mortgage unless Borrower: (a) agrees *in writing to the payment of the obligations secured by the lien in a manner acceptable to Lender;* (b) *contests in good faith* the lien by, or defends against enforcement of the lien in, legal proceedings which prevent the enforcement of the lien; or (c) secures from the holder of the lien an agreement satisfactory to Lender subordinating the lien to this Mortgage. If Lender determines that any part of the Property is subject to a lien which may attain priority over this Mortgage, Lender may give Borrower a notice identifying the lien. *Borrower shall satisfy the lien or take one or more of the actions set forth above* within 10 days of the giving of notice.

Under this covenant's second paragraph, the borrower is given a procedure to use when improvements on the property are subject to (say) a mechanic's lien, filed by a person the borrower believes performed work on the premises in a shoddy or unsatisfactory manner. But the paragraph is ambiguous, in that the lender might require the borrower to agree to the lien's payment *in writing . . . acceptable to the lender* at the same time that borrower *contests* [the lien] *in good faith.* The issue is whether the lender may use any of the methods of subparagraphs (a) through (c) all at once, or whether the introduction of the last subparagraph [(c)] by a disjunctive "or" indicates that each is independent of the others, and the borrower need agree with the lender on only one of them. The last sentence in this paragraph of the covenant indicates that the lender can insist on an agreement to satisfy a superior lien for the lender's benefit during the "contest" with the mechanic: It states that the *Borrower shall satisfy the lien or take one or more of the actions set forth above.*

> **Hazard or Property Insurance.** Borrower shall keep the improvements now existing or hereafter erected on the Property insured against loss by fire and any other hazards, including floods, *for which Lender requires insurance* and in amounts and for periods which Lender requires. The insurance carrier providing the insurance shall be chosen by Borrower subject to Lender's approval which shall not be unreasonably withheld. All insurance policies and renewals shall include *a standard mortgage clause.* Lender shall have the right to hold all policies and renewals and they shall name lender a *loss payee.*

There was no duty to insure secured property imposed on borrowers at common law. The rationale for this rule developed in an agricultural era, when the value of the land was sufficient to secure the debt. Thus, even today, when the land value is sufficient security, the borrower has no duty to insure absent an express covenant on the subject. Hence this covenant.

For which Lender requires insurance? Any lender has legitimate concerns that the secured property be insured. The lender also has an insurable interest in the property. What the lender wants is to be able to step into the shoes of the insured for purposes of filing and negotiating a claim, so most lenders will require that the policy name the lender as an insured, not just a beneficiary of the policy, in an endorsement.

A standard mortgage clause? The lender wishes to protect his insurable interest in the property, regardless of any defenses that the insurer might have against the insured. This clause provides that the lender takes insured interest in the policy free of any such defenses, including the intentional destruction of the property by the insured borrower. So in the instance of a fire policy, the borrower's arson will not defeat the lender's policy claim.

The right to hold all policies? Before the standard mortgage clause was in common use, a so-called open mortgage clause was used. Here the mortgagee was deemed to be the mortgagor's appointee for dealing with the insurer, and was subject to defenses available against the mortgagor, but was not subject to defenses based on misrepresentation made in the application. But what if the mortgagor repaired the damage to the secured property after a casualty loss: Could the mortgagee recover on a claim? Not if the mortgagee has no damages. *See Savarese v. Ohio Farmers Ins. Co.*, 182 N.E.2d 665 (N.Y. 1932). However, courts have found that because the mortgagor and the mortgagee have separate insurable interests and the mortgagee's claim is a contract matter requiring no showing of insecurity, the mortgagee has the right to elect to repair or file a claim, and the mortgagor's repair should not diminish that right, the repair being a third-party modification of the mortgagee's contract with the insurer.

This right to hold policies is not, however, a right to hold the proceeds of a claim, although express rights to hold such proceeds have been upheld, even when the mortgage is not in default. *See Kasden, Simonds v. World Savings & Loan Assn.*, 317 F.3d 1064 (9th Cir. 2003). A full credit bid (one for the outstanding amount due on the loan) at foreclosure ends the mortgagee's right to hold the policies. *See Norwest Mortgage Inc. v. State Farm Fire & Casualty Co.*, 188 Cal. Rptr. 2d 367 (Cal. App. Ct. 2002).

Loss payee? This is the person—here the lender—to whom insurance claim proceeds are to be paid, to the extent of that person's insurable interest, so the phrase gives the lender the right to receive the proceeds and saves the insurer from having to bring an interpleader action to determine who is entitled to them.

> **Occupancy and Waste of the Property.** Borrower shall *occupy and use the Property* as Borrower's principal residence within sixty days after the execution of this Mortgage and shall continue to occupy the Property as Borrower's principal residence for at least one year after the date of occupancy, unless Lender otherwise agrees in writing (*which consent shall not unreasonably be withheld*) or unless circumstances beyond Borrower's control exist. Borrower shall not *destroy, damage or impair* the Property, *allow the Property to deteriorate*, or *commit waste* on the Property. Borrower shall be in default if any proceeding, whether civil or criminal, is begun that could result in forfeiture of the Property or materially impair the lien created by this Mortgage.

Why must the borrower *occupy . . . the property?* Because common wisdom among lenders is that unoccupied property is neglected property, deteriorates in value, is more likely to be vandalized, and so affects the security of the lender's lien.

Which consent shall not unreasonably be withheld? This language has been implied by many courts, so in that sense it is superfluous. The lender may have a good reason for refusing consent to the borrower's not occupying the property, but the borrower will have to provide some alternative use of the property satisfactory to the lender.

In every state, a lender has a cause of action for any *waste* committed by the borrower. Waste might be narrowly defined as a prohibition on a borrower's changing the use or physical identity of the property as it existed on the execution date of the mortgage; the lender expects that this identity will be maintained over the term of the loan, but is not, a court might hold, entitled to more than that. Such a narrow construction of the term "waste" leaves the borrower free to do anything not inconsistent with that identity, such as expand the existing use or neglect improving the property so long as it remains physically the same. Not satisfied with that construction, the drafters of this document have expanded the lender's protection: Borrower covenants not to *destroy, damage, or impair* the property, *allow the property to deteriorate*, or *commit waste*. The lender may police practically any change in the use of the property. There is also some case authority holding that a mortgagor's failure to insure the secured property is waste under these covenants.

Waste, when coupled with the insolvency of the borrower, is grounds for the appointment of a receiver to manage mortgaged commercial property. Otherwise, the routine remedy for waste is damages, measured either by the loan balance as a ceiling on damages, the amount of the waste (measured in turn either by the loss of the secured's property's value or the cost of repair), or the impairment of the lender's security (often the amount required to restore the lender's bargained-for loan to value ratio). Often damages are, in addition, set by state statute as two or three times the actual damages to the property.

So a suit for waste is a particularly powerful remedy for lenders pre-foreclosure. Post-foreclosure, when the lender has entered a full credit bid, the lender may have waived or extinguished this remedy—the bid is in effect an admission that it cannot be damaged further. Such a bid also takes on added importance when, as will be later explained in Chapter 15, the note is nonrecourse.

> **Protection of Lender's Rights in the Property.** If Borrower fails to perform the covenants and agreements herein, or there is a legal proceeding that *may significantly affect Lender's rights* in the Property (such as a bankruptcy, probate, condemnation, or forfeiture action, or an action to enforce laws or regulations), then Lender, *at its option*, may do and pay for whatever actions are necessary to protect the value of and Lender's rights in the Property. Lender may, among other actions, pay any sums secured by a lien which has priority over this Mortgage, appear in court, paying reasonable attorneys' fees, and enter the Property to make repairs. Any amounts disbursed by Lender hereunder shall become additional debt secured by this Mortgage. Unless Borrower and Lender agree to other terms of payment, these amounts shall bear interest from the date of disbursement at the Note rate and shall be payable with interest upon demand.

May significantly affect Lender's rights? A proceeding might be significant, but still not impair the lender's security. Here the lender can appear in court when the borrower fails to appear. This language is intended to give the lender the option of appearing and determining whether the effect is significant enough to warrant that appearance, regardless of whether any impairment of the lender's security would result.

At its option? The lender has no obligation to do anything under this covenant. If its actions are optional, the lender has no correlative duties under it. For example, if the property deteriorated to the point that it was in violation of the building code applicable to the property, the lender cannot be made to repair it to comply with the code.

Any sums expended under this paragraph are added to the principal amount of the debt and bear interest at the note's specified rate of interest. They are payable upon notice and demand by the lender. This covenant in effect secures a type of future advance.

> **Borrower Not Released and Forbearance by Lender Not a Waiver.** Extension of the time for payment or modification of amortization of the sums secured herein to any successor in interest of Borrower shall not operate to release the liability of the original Borrower or Borrower's successor in interest. Lender shall not be required to commence proceedings against any successor and may refuse to extend time for payment or otherwise modify amortization of the sums secured by this Mortgage by reason of any demand made by

> the original Borrower or Borrower's successors in interest. Any forbearance by Lender in exercising any right or remedy shall not be a waiver of any other right or remedy.

Under this covenant, the mortgagor/borrower becomes the surety of any successor in interest. This leaves unclear whether the borrower as a surety is entitled to the benefit of any extension of time or re-amortization of the loan negotiated by the successor, or whether the borrower is held to the original bargain. If the lender asks the borrower for consent to the modifying agreement, the new terms control. If not, and that agreement is more onerous in its terms, the borrower does not lose the benefit of the original covenants through the unilateral actions of the lender. In the second sentence, it becomes clear that the lender need not do anything prior to making a demand on the borrower as a surety.

> **Successors Bound Jointly and Severally; Co-signers.** *The covenants and agreements of this Mortgage shall bind and benefit the successors and assigns of Lender and Borrower. . . .* Borrower's covenants and agreements shall be joint and several. Any Borrower who co-signs this Mortgage but does not execute the Note: (a) is co-signing this Mortgage only to mortgage, grant, and convey that Borrower's interest in the Property under the terms of this Mortgage; (b) is not personally obligated to pay the sums secured by this Mortgage; and (c) agrees that Lender and any other Borrower may agree to extend, modify, forbear or make any accommodations with regard to the terms of this Mortgage or the Note without that Borrower's consent.

Here a borrower may "co-sign" or execute the mortgage, but not the note. Who might do this? A spouse not wishing to be obligated for the personal debt of the other spouse might do this. So might a co-tenant of the borrower, or his business partner. Such persons may take the property or an interest in it subject to the mortgage, but not assume a personal obligation to pay the debt that accompanies it, subject to the right of the lender to execute an extension agreement with the borrower(s) obligated under the note.

Except for this acceptance by the lender of a nonassuming borrower, all other successors or assigns of the borrower(s) to the latter's interest in the property are assuming the debt in the note. This is the impact of the first sentence and the general rule of this covenant: *The covenants and agreements of this Mortgage shall bind and benefit the successors and assigns of Lender and Borrower. . . .* This liability is joint and several; the lender has an election to make. The lender can choose either to sue any successor for the whole outstanding debt, or to sue the borrower.

> **Transfer of the Property or a Beneficial Interest in Borrower.** If *all or any part of the Property* or *any interest* in it *is sold or transferred* (or if a beneficial interest in Borrower is sold or transferred and Borrower is not a natural person) *without Lender's prior written consent*, Lender may, at its option, require immediate payment in full of all sums secured by this Mortgage. This option shall not be exercised by Lender if exercise is *prohibited by federal law* as of the date of this Mortgage.
>
> If Lender exercises this option, Lender shall give Borrower notice of acceleration. The notice shall provide a period of not less than 30 days within which Borrower must pay all sums secured by this Security Instrument. If Borrower fails to pay these sums within this period, Lender may invoke any remedies permitted by this Security Interest without further notice or demand on Borrower.

Is sold or transferred? This is a so-called due-on-sale covenant. It is a version of the acceleration clause found in the note, accelerating the maturity date of the loan and requiring immediate payment of the whole debt all at once. Here i is in a form dictated by federal statute, hence the reference to *federal law* in the last sentence of the first paragraph. 12 U.S.C. §1701j-3 (1982) (known as the Garn–St. Germain Act). A regulation similar to this statute was held to have preempted state law on the subject. *Fidelity Fed. Savings & Loan Assn. v. De La Cuesta*, 458 U.S. 141 (1982). So the federal statute is commonly assumed to do the same thing.

All or any part of the property? If even a portion of the property is sold, a portion so small that the lender is not rendered insecure, the borrower has violated this covenant and the debt is accelerated. The lender does not have to prove that it is insecure before invoking it. This issue is settled in the act, which states that the covenant shall be enforced according to its terms (not according to the facts and circumstances surrounding its use by a lender). When violated, the lender may exercise rights under the covenant for reasons not relating to the particular mortgage transaction and so may invoke the covenant for market reasons, for example, to help increase the interest rate yield on its portfolio of loans.

Any interest? The clause here applies to the sale or transfer of any interest in the property—even a less-than-fee estate. It might apply to the creation of a junior mortgage or a conveyance of the property into a trust. It might also apply to a contract of sale, although a lender would probably be unwise to invoke it so soon. (Many contracts don't close.) It might also apply to a lease, particularly one with a long term or one containing an option to buy the property. It also applies when the borrower executes an installment land sale contract. (Not all these transfers are violations of the regulations issued under the Garn–St. Germain Act, but the covenant is arguably violated in each instance.)

This covenant applies only at the lender's option—that is, to optional clauses of this type, not mandatory ones. The covenant mimics the act in this instance. Congress intended to encourage negotiations between lenders and borrowers by making its use optional on the lender's part. The next italicized phrase plays into this rationale as well.

Without lender's prior written consent? A sale or transfer not consented to by the lender accelerates the due date of the whole outstanding debt: It is then due immediately. But such consent may not be unreasonably withheld: A lender cannot refuse to consent without having good cause for doing so and must use this covenant in good faith: A good faith refusal would occur if the proposed borrower and purchaser of the property are found uncreditworthy (or at a minimum lacking the same credit rating of the original borrower); if intervening changes in the mortgage markets have rendered the loan unmarketable, the mortgagee's seeking a higher interest rate does not show a lack of good faith.

The purpose of this clause is thus threefold: (1) it enables the lender to renegotiate the interest rate with the transferee as a condition of giving its consent; (2) it gives the lender an opportunity to check the credit rating of the transferee; and (3) it gives the lender an opportunity to reappraise the property and adjust the loan agreement accordingly.

Prohibited by federal law? This refers to the Garn–St. Germain Act, but also makes the point that the covenant is governed by and is the subject of federal common law.

> **Borrower's Right to Reinstate.** Subject to conditions stated in this paragraph, Borrower shall have the right to have *enforcement of this Mortgage* discontinued at any time prior to the earlier of: (a) 5 days (or such other period as applicable law may specify) before sale of the Property pursuant to any *power of sale contained in this Mortgage*; or (b) entry of a judgment enforcing this Mortgage. Those conditions are that Borrower: (a) pays Lender all sums which then would be due under this Mortgage and Note as if no acceleration had occurred; (b) cures any default of any other covenants or agreements; (c) pays all expenses incurred in enforcing this Mortgage, including, but not limited to, reasonable attorneys' fees; and (d) takes such action as Lender may reasonably require to assure that the lien of this Mortgage, Lender's rights in the Property and Borrower's obligation to pay the sums secured by this Mortgage shall be reinstated and continue unchanged. Upon reinstatement, the obligations secured by this Mortgage shall remain fully effective as if no acceleration had occurred.

Enforcement of this Mortgage? This is a reference to an action to foreclose the lien of the mortgage. Such an action may be a judicial one, involving first a finding that there is a default, then a decree ordering the sale of the secured property. This sale is conducted by court-sanctioned auction. The foreclosure decree provided that the court will convey the title to the property to the successful bidder at the sale. At this auction, the lender is a "certified" bidder; the lender automatically has the right to bid in the amount of the outstanding debt and does not have to present a certified check for this amount to the auctioneer. Other bidders have to certify their bids.

Power of sale contained in this Mortgage? This refers to an alternative to the judicial foreclosure just described. Under a power of sale covenant, a private sale is held and then, in some states, confirmed by a court. The sale is conducted not by a public official such as the county sheriff, but by a private person, acting as a trustee for both lender and borrower. Typically, the sale is conducted at a public auction, held not at the courthouse as with a judicial foreclosure, but at the office of the trustee.

The right to pay off the mortgage in the last sentence gives the borrower the right to be shucked of the lender before the latter exercises any other of its remedies.

> **Sale of Note and Change of Loan Servicer.** The Note or a partial interest in the Note (together with this Mortgage) may be sold one or more times without prior notice to Borrower. A sale may result in (1) a change in the entity (known as the "Loan Servicer") that collects monthly payments due under the Note and Mortgage and (2) one or more changes of the Loan Servicer unrelated to a sale of the Note. If there is a change of the Loan Servicer, Borrower will be given written notice of the change in accordance with applicable law. The notice will state the name and address of the new Loan Servicer, the address to which payments should be made, and any other information required by applicable law.

The advent of the secondary market has given rise to another method of lender's revenue: The originating lender often remains, after the loan is sold, as the servicer of the loan. As its servicer, this lender receives the monthly payments and forwards them to the loan purchaser. This service is performed for a fee—and such fees have kept many a lender solvent in the past two decades. This paragraph recognizes that servicing rights may be transferred separately from the loan. Servicers that are not originating lenders, doing nothing but service loans, have sprung up as separate businesses.

APPLYING FOR A MORTGAGE

In the residential mortgage situation, many cases state that the application is an offer and the commitment letter an acceptance. A corollary to this rule is that the verification by the lender of the matters contained in the application completes the application and the offer. That would mean that a contract is established at the time of the commitment to lend. A properly drafted loan application will identify the borrower (usually as the purchaser identified in a contract of sale) and the property securing the loan applied for (also identified in a contract of sale). A lender often requires the purchaser/borrower to present the contract to the lender. If nothing else, the lender may want to determine the timelines established in the contract for the closing, which will be the date that the title deed is delivered and the date of the loan closing.

When the application is filed, the residential lender is required to present the potential borrower with an estimate of the fees and settlement charges that the borrower will be charged at closing. This is a requirement of the federal Real Estate Settlement Procedures Act for loans extended by a lender who is federally insured or regulated in some manner. 12 U.S.C. §2601, et seq.

The receipt of the application is accompanied by the payment of an application fee, usually for the credit report and property appraisal. The acceptance of the application establishes a contract to process it. *See Jacques v. First Natl. Bank of Maryland*, 515 A.2d 756 (Md. 1986) (finding such a contract, to which a standard of due care and reasonable consideration of the application within a reasonable period of time attaches). The applicant pays some fees at the filing of the application, seeks the advantage of obtaining and accepting a commitment to loan, and forgoes other applications (this forbearance might be detrimental consideration for the processing contract). The lender gains the benefit of reviewing the application. The Jacques won their case for negligent processing of the loan application. Damages included the difference between the costs of financing that they would have obtained but for the negligent processing and the higher-cost financing they were obliged to accept. *See Larson v. United Fed. Sav. & Loan Assn.*, 300 N.W.2d 281, 21 A.L.R.4th 855 (Iowa 1981) (negligent appraisal of property).

Appraisals are a key tool that lenders use to review a mortgage loan application. In the residential mortgage market, appraisers must use data generated by recent sales of comparable properties to determine the property's fair market. Other appraisal methods may be used in the review of a commercial mortgage application. Secondary market purchasers require that their appraisal forms be used for loans they purchase; this requirement has done a great deal to standardize appraisal practices and lenders' review. In addition, federal legislation enacted in 1989 created new, stricter standards for appraisers working in large "federally related transactions." Mortgagees increasingly give the management of appraisers to outside firms, bidding for the work on a least-cost basis, and thereafter hiring the cheapest, but not necessarily the best, appraisers.

Starting with a credit report, qualifying for a residential mortgage generally requires that the borrower's (or borrowers') monthly mortgage payment be no more than 28-35 percent of his or her (or their) monthly income.

No other segment of the real estate industry has been affected more by e-commerce than the mortgage application process. Applications and documents can often be reviewed online in the borrower's home—and later, before a closing, so can notes and mortgages. In addition, Fannie Mae is capable of purchasing e-mortgages in the secondary market.

Examples

Example 9

H and W, husband and wife, file an application for a residential mortgage. It is accepted by letter, but when the day of the loan closing arrives, they find that the lender is only willing to lend at a rate of interest 1 percent higher than requested in the application. Can they obtain specific performance of the application and acceptance letter as a contract?

Explanation

As a general rule, commitments to lend money through residential mortgages are not subject to specific performance. H and W would, however, have a cause of action for damages against the mortgage company. If they wish to bring this cause of action, they should not close the loan. The leading and classic case is *Rogers v. Challis*, 27 Beav. 175, 54 Eng. Rep. 68 (1859), discussed in Roger Groot, Specific Performance of Contracts to Provide Permanent Financing, 60 Corn. L. Rev. 718 (1975). There are some cases contra, but they involve commercial mortgages. Practically speaking, they might close and then rely on statutory rescission rights, shopping around for a better rate in the interim.

Example 10

MR's broker advises her to set a closing date late in the month. Is this good advice?

Explanation

Yes, because most lenders require a borrower to pay at the closing all the mortgage interest from the date of closing until the next monthly mortgage payment is due, typically the first of the month—so the borrower who closes early in the month will have to come up with more cash at closing.

MORE ON POST-CLOSING MORTGAGE ESCROW ACCOUNTS

In the course of applying for a mortgage, mortgagors often agree to put on deposit, every month and with each mortgage payment, money to pay real property taxes and property hazard insurance premiums as they are due.

The account maintained by the mortgagee for the purpose of accumulating these monies until they need to be paid out is called a reserve account, or a mortgage escrow account. The maintenance of this account is controlled by the terms of the mortgage or deed of trust. Uniform Covenant 2 of the FNMA-FHLMC mortgage, discussed *supra*, this chapter, explains the types of monies that may be escrowed and imposes on the mortgagee the duty to make a prompt refund of all funds on account at the time of the release of the mortgage lien or, when the property is sold, application of all funds on account to satisfy that lien.

The issue that has worried many courts since the 1970s was whether the language of this covenant creates a trust, of which the mortgagor is the beneficiary and the mortgagee the trustee. Most courts held that no trust was created. *See La Throp v. Bell Fed. Sav. & Loan Assn.*, 370 N.E.2d 188 (Ill. 1977) (mere mention of the word "trust" in an escrow account covenant is insufficient to establish a trust relationship), cert. denied, 436 U.S. 925 (1978), noted in 7 Real Est. L.J. 163 (1978). The presence of a late payment penalty, for example, tended to show that the account was for the mortgagee's benefit, not the mortgagor's.

Covenant language such as "the Lender shall hold the funds" and "the Lender shall apply the funds" likewise failed to indicate a trust relationship. Such language does, however, indicate that the mortgagee undertakes some duty in relation to the funds, so a contract duty may still be found. Thus some courts held that the mortgagor had contractual rights against the lender. *See Brooks v. Valley Natl. Bank*, 539 P.2d 958 (Ariz. 1976). In the 1990s, there was renewed interest in litigating some mortgagees' practices regarding these accounts. *See Cusack v. Bank United of Texas*, 159 F.3d 1040 (7th Cir. 1998) (reporting over 100 class actions on the subject). These suits have been based, in part, on the 1974 Real Estate Settlement Procedures Act (RESPA) requirements. RESPA sets maximum permissible balances in escrow accounts maintained for federally related mortgages. *See* RESPA, §2609(a) (RESPA, §10). Section 10 prohibits escrow payments greater than (1) required to meet estimated disbursements plus (2) a cushion calculated to be no more than one-sixth of the estimated disbursements over any one year, unless the mortgage documents provide for a lower amount.

However, §10 does not expressly permit its enforcement in private causes of action. There is today a split in the opinions of federal circuit courts as to whether §10 nonetheless authorizes such an action by implication. *See McAnaney v. Astoria Financial Corp.*, 357 F. Supp. 2d 578, 590-591 (E.D.N.Y. 2005) (collecting the cases). The Fourth, Fifth, and Seventh Circuits say no. They find that the silence of the statute is deliberate, that amendments subsequent to some of their holdings providing only administrative remedies for other RESPA sections reinforce their conclusion, and that some other RESPA sections do provide for treble damages and attorneys' fees. The Sixth

Circuit disagrees. However, most federal district courts have followed the lead of the Seventh Circuit.

Examples

Example 11

What if a mortgagee's employee absconded with the escrowed funds or is negligent in making the payments for escrow items when payments are due the tax collector or insurer? Does the mortgagee or mortgagor undertake this risk?

Explanation

The mortgagee, as a matter of contract. Inadequate supervision of an employee may give rise to an action for a negligent implementation of a contract duty. Likewise, the mortgagee is an agent of the mortgagor for paying over funds on account and a failure to pay is a breach of the agency.

Example 12

In an action by mortgagors for an accounting of funds on deposit, may the plaintiffs include an unjust enrichment count in their complaint?

Explanation

No. A person may not recover under a theory of unjust enrichment when the claim arises out of conduct already covered by a contract. Here the express covenant establishing the account gives rise to the claim. However, until the court finds that a contract duty exists, it is prudent pleading to include an unjust enrichment count, just in case the court does not find a contract governing the issue being litigated. So dismissal of such a count at the pleading stage may also be premature.

Example 13

May any servicer of the mortgagee's accounts also be sued for an accounting?

Explanation

Yes. The servicer may be sued alone or together with the mortgagee. There are advantages to suing the servicer as opposed to the mortgagee. The servicer has conducted the communications with the mortgagor and has knowledge of what was said. Discovery will likely be more productive on this account. It may also be easier to bring a federal mail fraud or state deceptive trade practice action with the servicer as a defendant.

Example 14

Mortgagors using escrow accounts subsequently sue the mortgagee for improper accounting and escrow practices, resulting in the mortgagee agreeing to change its practices. What further remedy should the mortgagor seek?

Explanation

A refund for excess deposits and a credit against future estimated amounts due the account, valid for a certain number of years. *Cusack*, *op. cit.* (approving such a remedy).

Example 15

Title insurers often issue "closing letters" to their insured mortgagee, guaranteeing that the mortgagee's closing agent, typically the insurance agent issuing its policy, will not negligently or improperly handle the closing. When a title insurer pays a mortgagee a claim based on the agent's conduct, may the title insurer then sue the servicer to enforce statutory account requirements?

Explanation

Yes, as the subrogee of its insured mortgagor. *See Lawyers Title Ins. Corp. v. United American Bank of Memphis*, 21 F. Supp. 2d 785 (W.D. Tenn. 1998).

CHAPTER 13

Variations on Conventional Mortgages

ALTERNATIVE MORTGAGE INSTRUMENTS

Alternative mortgage instruments (AMIs)—alternative, that is, to fixed interest rate instruments—come in many forms, but they have a common genesis in (1) the credit problems experienced by mortgage lenders themselves during the 1970s and early 1980s, (2) the lenders' desire to maintain demand for their portfolios in the secondary market, and (3) the impact of inflation on those portfolios. So the first type of AMI was the adjustable-rate mortgage (ARM), which satisfied lenders on all three counts.

AMIs are created by redrafting the covenants of a note, rather than changing the provisions of the mortgage; in most cases, these changes form a contract on the borrower's part to pay a higher interest rate upon the happening of some event or contingency. In an ARM, for example, the interest rate floats, up and down, according to some predetermined index spelled out in the note's covenants. State legislatures, and Congress, responded to the idea of a free-floating rate with limitations on any one change—for example, limitations on the amount the monthly payment can change, or a ceiling on the interest rate changes that may be imposed. So limited by federal regulation and the legislatures of several states, the interest rate of an ARM loan is typically stable for the first two or three years of the term, and then may be adjusted at (say) annual intervals. For the borrower, then, the total amount of future monthly payments is not known at the closing.

Some AMIs were designed particularly for certain demographic groups. The reverse annuity mortgage (RAM), for example, is designed to advance the loan proceeds in installments to the elderly who are "land-rich, cash-poor"— who own their homes outright, having paid off their mortgages, but who are short on income after retirement. It provides them an annuity, resulting in a lien growing in amount, up to a preset amount, which can be recouped out of the mortgagor's decedent's estate. It is, in effect, a mandatory, future-advance mortgage.

Another AMI, the graduated payment mortgage (GPM), is intended to be a mortgage without a level series of amortized repayments; rather, the GPM is paid off in a series of payments that rise over the term of the loan—low at first, so low perhaps that no principal is amortized, but increasing as the income of the mortgagor rises. This mortgage is intended for youthful, first-house purchasers or low-income but upwardly mobile persons. A mortgage loan that defers interest, principal, or both in some prearranged way is a variant of a GPM. GPMs are relatively high-risk loans and not much used because they do not appeal to secondary market investors.

To solve the problem of fluctuating interest rates, without using the short periods of readjustment used in an ARM, another AMI, the rollover mortgage (ROM) refinances ("rolls over") the outstanding loan principal at three- to five-year intervals. The ROM has a long-term payment schedule but an interest rate that is renegotiated at intervals. Sometimes the refinancing is obligatory, sometimes optional, with the mortgagee. ROMs are like a rolling, balloon payment mortgage.

Shared appreciation mortgage Lenders often wish to share in the appreciation in the fair market value of the secured real property. In exchange for a reduced interest rate, borrowers are sometimes willing to let them do so. Three types of "equity mortgages" will be discussed here: the shared appreciation mortgage (SAM), the participating mortgage, and the convertible mortgage. For the mortgagee, each type has the advantages of a higher overall return and a hedge against inflation. For the mortgagor, the advantages are a larger loan principal, lower initial interest payments, and perhaps a lower initial cash investment in the property.

Typically, a SAM is an inflation hedge. It permits the mortgagee in the note to charge deferred interest based on a percentage of the net appreciation of the fair market value of the secured property. Such a charge is contingent on the property appreciating in value. The appreciation is usually computed when the property is sold or otherwise transferred at some (fixed) date in the future. In addition, the mortgagee also charges interest at a fixed rate, a rate below the prevailing rate for conventional mortgages. In this manner, a SAM enables a mortgagor who would not otherwise qualify for a conventional mortgage to do so. Sometimes a SAM is used as part of a workout for a conventional loan in default.

SAMs have been challenged as an unreasonable restraint on alienation, but most courts have found them to be a reasonable restraint. To avoid the charge of its being an unreasonable restraint, a provision in the note adds the appreciated value, on an annual basis, to the principal amount of the loan, instead of charging it to the mortgagor's interest account. Other drafting problems arise (1) when property subject to a SAM agreement is to be improved in some way, the parties have to choose one of two methods to measure that appreciation: by either (a) the cost of improvements to the property or (b) the value of those improvements. Some improvements may cost a lot but only add a little in value, or vice versa. For example, a swimming pool typically adds little value relative to its cost, while the cost of a new kitchen is likely to add greatly—at least dollar for dollar—to value. (2) Another drafting issue is how to distinguish a repair from an improvement. Replacing a roof can be costly, but every building needs one. (3) Buyout provisions also need drafting attention: Will the mortgagee be permitted to buy out the mortgagor's interest to prevent having to do business with a stranger? Will the right to a buyout be mutual? Will the mortgagee have a right to possession of the property upon the mortgagor's default? If the mortgagor and mortgagee are deemed to be tenants in common, will ejectment be available to the mortgagee?

This last question, put another way, is whether the SAM transaction is the beginning of a partnership, a joint venture, or a concurrent interest between the putative mortgagor and mortgagee and is subject to an action for reformation and recharacterization. When the note contains an unconditional obligation to repay the initial principal of the loan, a fixed interest rate, and security for the obligation to repay in the mortgage lien and covenants, the SAM transaction is given the three essential features of a true loan between the parties. Further, when the mortgagee contributes no services, an essential feature of a general partnership or joint venture is lacking. The contingent interest feature tends to show a joint venture, but it is arguably outweighed by the other loan attributes of a SAM that would point to a debtor-creditor relationship. The *tax consequences* of this classification are several: (1) if the contingent interest is paid to a creditor, the debtor mortgagor can deduct it on federal income tax returns; if a joint venture results, this deduction is lost; (2) the treatment of the contingent payment as interest means that it is ordinary income to the creditor mortgagee; if it is not so treated, then the payment will be treated as the distributive share from the sale, transfer, or exchange of the property.

All of these subjects are interesting and present drafting challenges, but they also show why SAMs are infrequently used in residential mortgage transactions.

Participating mortgage This is a mortgage with a fixed interest rate, with a contingent interest feature measured by (1) a percentage of the mortgagor's gross receipts or income, (2) a percentage of the cash flow from the property, (3) a percentage of the resale value, or some combination of the three. Typically the contingent interest feature of such a mortgage is known as a "sweetener" or "equity kicker" for the mortgagee's rate of return. Some of the same legal uncertainties associated with a SAM recur in the context of a participating mortgage. Further, the participating feature might render the mortgagee liable on warranties of habitability and suitability when these are extended by the mortgagor. Finally, for purposes of federal and state environmental statutes, the mortgagee may be deemed to be an "owner or operator" of the property and thereby responsible for any cleanup of toxic substances later discovered on it.

Convertible mortgage This is a fixed or adjustable-rate mortgage in which the mortgagee also has an option to purchase all or some portion of the secured property at some time in the future. The option is exercisable either at a date certain, or on several dates during the term of the loan, or during some predetermined period of time. The mortgage is convertible, in the sense that the mortgagee can convert his debt obligation into an equity interest in the property, typically in exchange for releasing the mortgagor from the obligation to pay all or part of the debt. This type of mortgage is often used as a long-term, permanent mortgage taking out a construction loan. From the mortgagor's perspective, the mortgagor combines financing with the possibility of a future sale, with the result that the property can be sold with lower closing costs. Frequently, the mortgagor continues in the capacity of property manager after the complete sale of the property to the mortgagee, thus generating management fees. The advantage of this mortgage for the mortgagee is that it gets to test the market for the property and then buy a stake in or all of an up-and-running, seasoned property, with all the bugs worked out of its operation. The option to purchase is usually assignable; if so, the mortgage and the option are typically in separate documents.

Two other features of this mortgage include (1) an option price set in advance, or by a predetermined formula or appraisal method, and (2) a statement that the right to purchase is at the mortgagee's discretion (a call), or a right of the mortgagor to force the mortgagee to purchase (a put). An option price set in advance acts as a hedge against inflation. Some convertible mortgages also contain a right to repurchase the property or interest of the mortgagee. This right may be included in order to cap the mortgagee's gain, or to cancel the option at a preset price.

To avoid having the convertible feature of the mortgage transaction characterized as a common law clog, five drafting devices can be used: (1) the mortgage documents and the option should be in separate documents, (2) they should be separately recorded, (3) the option should not be exercisable upon a default in the note and mortgage covenants, and (4) it should be exercisable at the then-fair market value of the property or interest purchased. When a nonlender entity is operated by the mortgagee, (5) the option should be put in that entity's hands. In response to cases finding the convertibility to be a clog, convertible mortgages are sometimes expressly authorized by state statutes. Besides providing immunity from the charge that they are clogs, these statutes typically give the option a title priority as of the time it is recorded.

Should the option, when separate from the mortgage, be recorded before or after the mortgage? If recorded before, it may well chill the bidding at a later foreclosure sale, making that remedy less valuable. If recorded after, any later foreclosure will extinguish the option, rendering it worthless thereafter. Further, is the optionee a bona fide purchaser protected by the applicable recording act? Arguments can be made either way.

For all of these "equity" mortgages — SAMs, and participating and convertible mortgages — three common problems must be borne in mind: First, the mortgagee may become unsecured (as to the equity feature or portion of the loan) in a later bankruptcy of the mortgagor, where the option may be treated as an executory contract and avoidable under §365 of the Bankruptcy Code by the bankruptcy trustee. This is particularly likely with a convertible mortgage. Second, the mortgagee may have to take a junior position (as to the equity feature) in any later foreclosure. A junior claim on the proceeds of a foreclosure sale is subjected to the risk of insufficient proceeds. With a participating mortgage, for example, the mortgagee might be wise to insist on a floor or baseline percentage of the gross income or cash flow in order to protect its position in foreclosure. Third and finally, the equity feature may render the interest rate usurious under state law, particularly when the equity feature is a substantial portion of the consideration for the loan.

FUTURE ADVANCE MORTGAGES

In mortgages and deeds of trust, after providing that the instrument secures the principal amount of the debt disbursed at the loan closing, the following provision often appears:

> Also secured by this mortgage are all future advances and indebtedness of the borrower up to the maximum amount of $100,000. Such sums as are advanced in the future are to be used by the borrower for the improvement, renovation, and rehabilitation of the property described in this instrument. Such advances will be made upon the presentation of executed job orders for the improvement, rehabilitation, and renovation of the subject property.

With this clause a mortgagee is attempting to gain priority for any future advances made to the borrower over intervening lienors — that is, lienors who file (say) mechanic's liens after the date of recording of the initial mortgage but before the date on which the advance is to be made. If the clause binds the lender to advance the money, and a lawsuit might result if the advance were withheld, the lender has obligated himself through this clause to make the advance. Obligatory advances generally gain a priority over intervening lienors, and such liens are subordinated to the obligation stated in the initial mortgage plus the amount of the advance.

In a majority of states deciding the question, the mortgagee is protected for all future advances up to the time at which he has actual notice of intervening liens later recorded. No constructive notice is charged to the mortgagee through the recording acts. And in most jurisdictions, no payment schedule for the advances is necessary to enable the mortgagee to assert that the advances are obligatory. In such jurisdictions, if the advance is made under progress payment schedules, it is obligatory by definition: When a future advance mortgagee is committed under a recorded mortgage to lend a specific sum, or up to a specific sum, and once several advances are made, with more to follow to complete the lender's agreement, the majority of courts treat the transaction as a continuous one, and neither actual nor constructive notice of intervening liens will defeat the lender's priority. The mortgagee has no duty to recheck the public land records with each advance for the existence of intervening liens. Thus, neither actual nor constructive notice defeats the intent of the parties to treat the loan transaction as a continuous one.

In a minority of jurisdictions, the mortgagee is required to check the records before making each future advance. In such jurisdictions, no advance is deemed obligatory unless the lender first checks the records.

When a future advance is optional on the mortgagee's part, however, actual notice of an intervening lien will subordinate its advance to the amount of an intervening lien. In a majority of jurisdictions, a mortgagee's constructive notice of an intervening lien does not defeat the priority of an optional advance.

Thus two rules govern future advance mortgage clauses. (1) Obligatory future advances have priority over intervening liens. (2) When the advances are optional, they are subordinated to the intervening lien if the mortgagee has actual knowledge of the intervening lien (the majority rule) or constructive notice of it (the minority rule).

The distinction between obligatory and optional advances is a matter of judicial interpretation in most jurisdictions. Optional advances are generally found where (1) the mortgagor abandons the property, (2) the procedure for disbursement of the advance has not been followed by the lender, (3) the advances were made before they were due to be paid under the payment schedule (in this case they can later become obligatory at the due date), and (4) the mortgagee represents that intervening lienors will get the advance.

The mortgagee may most readily defend his priority when advancing the money, even though state law might find that the advance was optional, by showing that the money was spent to perform duties under the mortgage covenants or was an assertion of a right to preserve the encumbered property from waste or deterioration, as when money is spent for tax payments, restoration of the property, or janitorial service. What is required of the mortgagee under the mortgage's covenants is determined in these cases by what objectively is necessary to keep the mortgagee's lien position. What matters is not what the mortgagee may elect to do personally, but what keeps the value of the security intact.

On the other hand, advances are found obligatory under state law if definite sums to be advanced have been stated on the face of the loan agreement, or if the loan application by the borrower and the mortgagee's loan commitment constitute offer and acceptance so that the lender would be liable in damages if he did not make the advances.

A future advance clause for a construction loan might be interpreted as the mortgagee's offer to advance the money, but it may not yet constitute an obligation to do so. In the typical case, the process of constructing or improving a property is itself the subject of the loan agreement: Here the mortgagee will typically require proof of (1) the work performed and (2) some inspection of that work by a qualified individual such as an architect. Only upon presentation of this third party's certification that the work has been performed according to prearranged plans and specifications is an advance actually disbursed; in such situations the mortgagee might be construed to have contracted for an optional advance and thus should check the public land records for intervening liens before each advance is made.

Many legislatures have been dissatisfied with judicial distinctions between obligatory and optional advances, particularly as the distinction might apply to construction loans. Their statutes take one of four approaches. (1) Some jurisdictions declare future advances invalid unless they are expressly referred to in a mortgage and a maximum amount is set for them there. Some other jurisdictions, either by statute or judicial decision, have set the same requirements, not for the advance's validity, but in order to maintain its priority. About 15 jurisdictions require both an express reference and a maximum amount for one or the other purpose. (2) Some other state codes provide that the mortgagor may give the mortgagee a notice stating that the future advance covenant of the mortgage is no longer valid. Again, about 15 jurisdictions fall into this category. (3) Some jurisdictions have codified an actual notice rule: Only the mortgagee with actual notice of an intervening lien need search before advancing a disbursement. (4) Finally, some jurisdictions give the mortgagee a priority for future advances for a fixed period of time (say, 18 to 24 months) after the mortgage's execution, and following such a grace period apply the common law. All four approaches leave ample room for the workings of the common law, and in many states it remains the primary source of law. *See* Restatement (Third) of Property (Mortgages) §2.1 (1997), at 53, 55 and table ff. at 56.

As previously noted, many standard form mortgage covenants authorize the mortgagee to make advances to pay taxes, insurance premiums, and maintenance costs that prevent the secured property's "waste or deterioration." Many jurisdictions have statutes complementing these covenants and giving the mortgagee's future advances priority when made for the protection of the security. Such protective advances include those for property tax payments (liens for which might otherwise trump the mortgage lien), insurance premiums, and maintenance expenses. *Id.* at 54. The priority for insurance and maintenance is presumably also based on the mortgagee's right to prevent waste of the secured property.

In the Federal National Mortgage Association form Uniform Covenant 3, there is a reference to future advances in the schedule for applying the payments of the borrower. If the loan was given many years ago, this reference may be unnecessary because, although there is no reference of future advances in the mortgage agreement, all advances extended to the borrower within the principal amount stated on the face of the mortgage are likely to be secured. So if the mortgage was given for $500,000 and had declined to $450,000, the mortgagee could make a $50,000 advance to the borrower after the initial loan closing and feel secure that the loan would receive priority over intervening liens.

Examples

Example 1a

MR executes a brief but enforceable residential mortgage in favor of ME. The mortgage advances MR the purchase money for the secured land and contains the clause "also secured by this mortgage are all future advances and indebtedness of the borrower up to a maximum amount of $50,000" and also provides that ME will advance MR the full $50,000, in increments of $10,000, as MR builds a house on the land. MR promises to use the whole $50,000 to improve the land. ME also later agrees to disburse the first $10,000 when the foundation is finished. ME later refuses. May MR then compel the $10,000 disbursement?

Explanation

Yes, because it is an obligatory advance under the loan agreement. A right to inspect the progress of the construction, when used to verify that the loan is being properly applied, does not turn an obligatory advance into an optional one. To do so would defeat the purpose of the loan. The inspection is intended to prevent the MR from diverting the loan proceeds to other uses. *See Southern Trust Mortgage Co. v. K & B Door Co.*, 763 P.2d 353, 355, n.2 (Nev. 1988). Neither is the answer to this question likely to change when the agreement to disburse was executed separately and later than the loan agreement.

Example 1b

What if C had filed a mechanic's lien before ME's disbursal?

Explanation

ME would have priority over the mechanic's lien, on the same rationale. In addition, consider that C, the mechanic, wouldn't be working and paid—on this job site, anyway—unless the proceeds of the loan are disbursed; those proceeds make his work possible, so C shouldn't complain about ME's priority. ME should prevail.

Example 1c

Same facts as subparts (a) and (b). The MR-ME agreement calls for the second $10,000 disbursement when the first floor is in place. ME now knows that MR has diverted some funds from the first disbursement to improve another lot that MR owns. MR is therefore in default on the loan agreement. C, a mechanic working on MR's improvement, files a mechanic's lien before ME makes the second disbursement. Who has priority as to this second disbursement, C or ME?

Explanation

ME, who has made the disbursement as required by the terms of the agreement. MR's default should not—and usually does not—make this disbursement optional. A disbursement made subject to a commitment to disburse is obligatory, not optional.

Example 1d

Same facts, but in addition C disputes with ME a payment made by MR to C. Next week, ME makes another advance to MR. State the priority of the mortgage and mechanic's liens.

Explanation

Now ME has actual notice of the claim of C. In many jurisdictions, that would turn the obligatory advance into an optional one. ME ought not to have to search for mechanic's liens before making each advance, but here he has more than the constructive notice that the recording acts would provide. Whether C files a lien is irrelevant.

In summary, a mortgage may secure a future advance (making it obligatory) by expressly providing that the repayment of future advances is secured, stating a monetary amount not to be exceeded by these advances, and recording the mortgage with this provision—and then by the mortgagee's not in fact exceeding the stated amount. Restatement (Third) of Property: Mortgages, §2.1 (1997).

DRAGNET CLAUSES

This type of clause provides that the mortgage secures all present and future debts of the mortgagor, whether or not contemplated at the time of the execution of the mortgage in which the clause appears. Thus it is like a future advance clause but is broader and open-ended—that is, unlimited in amount. Courts often take a cue from this similarity and construe the clause to apply only to future loans originated (as opposed to acquired by assignment) by the same lender. This clause permits the mortgagee to consolidate multiple suits against the mortgagor.

Examples

Example 2

MR executes a brief but enforceable residential mortgage in favor of ME. The mortgage stated that it "secures all debt now due or hereafter due that ME holds against MR as maker, surety, guarantor, partner or otherwise, whether contracted directly or purchased by ME." MR executes this mortgage on his farm for a loan to finance his farming operations. Later he ceases those operations and secures a mortgage on a residence in town from the same mortgagee, but the farm mortgage is not in default, not paid off, and not released. What type of transaction will this clause reach? Who has the burden of showing its intended effect?

Explanation

Most courts strictly construe a dragnet clause. The differing purposes of the two loans is sufficient to find that the clause in the first mortgage does not mean that the title to the farm stands as security for the loan on the residence in town or vice versa. *See Decorah State Bank v. Zidlicky*, 426 N.W.2d 388 (Iowa 1988); *First Security Bank of Utah v. Shiew*, 609 P.2d 952 (Utah 1980) (contains a good recitation of the black-letter law on these clauses). Their strict construction is necessary because otherwise the clause provides no notice of the extent of its reach. Title searchers and abstractors cannot define the reach of the clause without the strictest construction, particularly as to a search for other transactions between the same parties. *Amos v. Lance*, 355 So. 2d 84 (Miss. 1978), noted in 50 Miss. L.J. 124 (1979). Some courts even require that the later mortgage refer back expressly to the mortgage with the dragnet clause; they presume that if a separate mortgage without a reference back is used, the waiver of the clause is intended. Parol evidence is generally admissible to show how the parties intended the clause to function. *See Canal Natl. Bank v. Becker*, 431 A.2d 71 (Me. 1981).

Example 3

If the earlier mortgage with the dragnet clause requires a specific type of foreclosure, is an expressly referenced later mortgage between the same mortgagor and mortgagee for a similar purpose limited to the same remedy?

Explanation

Yes. A dragnet clause usually benefits the mortgagee, but it need not be so. The benefit of the clause can run to the mortgagor, too, as when a statutory protection is given the mortgagor of the first mortgage. Thus the protection given in a specific type of foreclosure then runs to the mortgagor in later secured loans, too.

Example 4

MR executes a brief but enforceable 20-year mortgage on Blackacre, securing $100,000 in debt "and all other debts owed" ME. MR receives the $100,000 from ME, who records the mortgage. Five years later, ME has expended $5,000 to maintain the property in the condition it was at the time of the mortgage's execution and has made future advances of $30,000. Later, when the outstanding amount of MR's initial debt to ME is $75,000, MR takes out another $50,000 mortgage on Blackacre, extended by Consumer's Bank. MR defaults on both loans and a resulting foreclosure sale of MR's interest in Blackacre then fetches $150,000. What portion of these proceeds will ME receive?

Explanation

ME holds outstanding debts of $75,000, $5,000, and $30,000, or $110,000 in all. Unless the quoted "other debts" phrase is construed broadly, however, Consumer's Bank has notice of only a $100,000 debt. There is no sound reason to construe the phrase as a future advance covenant for anything more than the $100,000 amount of debt appearing on the face of the mortgage. Consumer's Bank might reasonably assume that MR's "other debts" are those incurred when ME's future advances increase the paid-down outstanding debt, but such increases, if consistent with the notice provided Consumer's, cannot be more than $25,000. So the ceiling on ME's future advances under this phrase is the amount that brings the outstanding debt (here $75,000) back up to its original $100,000 face amount. ME obtains $100,000 of the $150,000 foreclosure sale proceeds.

CHAPTER 14

Equitable Mortgages

An equitable mortgage is one that the parties intended to have function as a mortgage, but that does not. Equity will impose an equitable mortgage when the facts surrounding a transaction evidence that the parties intended that a specific piece of property secures a debt. A document may be treated as an equitable mortgage because either the form of transfer does not create a lien—rather, it creates less (as, for example, where a contract of sale is executed) or creates more (as, for example, where a deed, absolute on its face, is used)—or because the alleged mortgagor has himself only an equitable interest in the secured property. *See Moon v. Moon*, 776 N.Y.S.2d 324, 325 (N.Y. Sup. Ct. 2005) ("[A]n equitable mortgage has been described as a transaction that has the intent but not the form of a mortgage and that a court will enforce in equity to the same extent as a mortgage"). Thus an equitable mortgage is the triumph of substance of a transaction over its form: An equitable mortgage may be recognized when there is a deficiency or uncertainty in a document that purports to create a mortgage, or by implication under principles of equity. The question: When will a document that is not styled as a mortgage be treated as if it were a mortgage because, in the context of the transaction in which it is used, a court will find that the parties intended that it function as a mortgage?

In a majority of jurisdictions a deed in fee simple absolute, valid as such on its face, can be shown, using parol evidence presented by the mortgagor, to have been intended as a mortgage by the parties. This is so even without the presence of fraud or mistake. It is a mortgage disguised as another type of transaction. When a lender holds a promissory note and the borrower conveys property to the lender as security for repayment, but the conveyance is in the form of a deed absolute, with no indication on its face that it was given as security for the preexisting duty to repay, a court will cut the effect of the deed back and recharacterize the deed as a mortgage, rather than a true conveyance of title. This will give the grantor all the protections that a mortgagor has in any attempt by the grantee to collect the debt. These protections will permit the grantor to repay the debt, leaving the title to the property as it was before the deed was given.

Likewise, in another example, when a person promises to care for another (perhaps a sick or aged relative) and the relative conveys property in anticipation of and in exchange for that care, when the care is not given, a court will recharacterize that deed as a mortgage for which there is no preexisting debt and so cancel the deed. The grantee's performance being executory, the terms of the deed may not be specifically performed.

Likewise too, when a person purchases property using a contract with an extended executory period, during which the purchaser pays the purchase price in installments, much as an owner would pay off a mortgage, that contract takes on the attributes of a mortgage. Moreover, when the installment sale contract contains a draconian forfeiture clause, permitting the vendor to repossess the property upon any default in payments, the purchaser losing all the payments made thus far, a court will recharacterize the contract as a purchase money mortgage. This forces the vendor to foreclose the contract much as a mortgage would be.

Another common situation, perhaps the most common situation, giving rise to an equitable mortgage is a defective legal mortgage. *See e.g. Flexter v. Woomer*, 197 N.E.2d 161 (Ill. Ct. App. 1965) (a mortgage that omits its maturity date and the amount of the debt gives no constructive notice when recorded but is still valid and subject to reform as between its parties). In such situations, courts confer on the borrower or grantor the equitable right to redeem the debt. This is called the equity of redemption. It is not subject to waiver. As we shall see when discussing mortgages in upcoming chapters, it confers a cause of action on the debtor, grantor, or assignee to repay the debt and cancel or reform the document in accordance with the original intention of the parties to it.

That a document was knowingly cast in its absolute form is no defense to this cause of action; that the document was not the subject of fraud, duress, or undue influence is not a defense either; and neither is the fact that possession of the property was given to the grantee. Parol evidence is still admissible to establish the parties' true intent to execute a mortgage.

The relevant cause of action is either one for unjust enrichment or to quiet title. However, the burden of proof for such a showing is sometimes a preponderance of the evidence, but often it is higher—clear and convincing evidence of (1) unjust enrichment and (2) an intent to create a mortgage. Both are needed. The most satisfactory evidence is, of course, another document showing the parties' agreement; next best would be a completed transaction supporting the idea that the deed was intended to function as a mortgage. The completed transaction is treated as part performance of the intended mortgage transaction. Once deemed an equitable mortgage, the exercise of some form of the foreclosure remedy is typically mandatory because the state statutes governing it have many built-in protections for the mortgagor (as we will see).

If the parties to a transaction intend to create an equitable mortgage, that intent must be shown by a totality of the circumstances surrounding the transaction. Restatement (Third) of Property, Mortgages, §3.2, comment e (1997). The existence of a debt is essential, and other relevant factors might be prior unsuccessful attempts to obtain a mortgage loan, the sophistication of the parties, the adequacy of consideration, an agreement to repurchase, and the continued possession of the property by the alleged mortgagor. Aside from the debt, no one factor is determinative or more important than the others.

Would-be *mortgagees* have also used the doctrine. They have a more difficult task. On the one hand, a party seeking to become a mortgagor must show that a deed, absolute on its face, is really a mortgage attempting to cut back the reach of the document, and so parol evidence to support his showing is not necessarily inconsistent with the facial contents of the document. On the other hand, one seeking to become a mortgagee is attempting to show that a document purporting to do less than create a mortgage actually does more; and parol evidence inconsistent with the agreement is inadmissible, so there must be some ambiguity in the document rendering parol evidence admissible before clear and convincing evidence of its true function can be presented.

Why does the evidence of an equitable mortgage usually have to be clear and convincing? Why so high an evidentiary standard? Suppose that A agrees to sell Blackacre to B and immediately lease it back on terms somewhat like mortgage terms. If either A or B believes that the courts would find the transaction a mortgage, is that sufficient to make it one? No. The parties are entitled to cast the transaction in the form they wish. The intention of the parties (plural, not singular) controls. Otherwise, every transaction could be upset by a party dissatisfied with the financial terms of a transaction—when there is a disparity between the fair market value of the property and the sale price, or when the rent in the leaseback is below the fair rental value.

Examples

Example 1

Ben and Dan are brothers with a remainder interest in their multimillion-dollar family summer home. Dan is a hedge fund who manages substantial assets. Ben is just graduating from college where he was on the golf team. Ben wants to become a professional golfer, but to go on tour, he will need money. Dan loans Ben money to get Ben started on tour and in exchange, Ben assigns his remainder in the summer house to Dan. After touring unsuccessfully for a year. Ben takes a regular job. The next summer, after the death of their mother, the life tenant of the summer house, Ben, arrives for his vacation and is told by Dan, "if you want to take a shower here, you'll now need my permission." Ben asks you if he can take back the assignment he signed. What is your advice?

Explanation

Ben may bring a quiet title action to cancel the assignment so long as he redeems the debt, repaying his brother Dan for the loan. *See Seaman v. Seaman*, 477 A.2d 734 (Me. 1984). The controlling issue is the brothers' intention in making the loan. On this issue, Ben bears the burden of proof, established by a preponderance of the evidence. (In some jurisdictions, proof must be clear and convincing.) The true intent may be gleaned from the surrounding circumstances of the loan. Here the adverse financial condition of one brother compared to the other and the fact that the loan was for seed money to get Ben started on tour, a small sum compared to the value of the home, is sufficient to establish that the assignment absolute on its fact, was a mortgage. *See Koenig v. Van Reken*, 279 N.W.2d 590 (Mich. Ct. App. 1979). It is no defense to Ben's action to redeem that the remainder has vested in possession in his brother.

Example 2

Owen purchases a home using a bank loan and an installment sale contract with a harsh forfeiture clause. Later Owen finds out that the contract terms for repayment are similar to the terms extended by the same bank to friends whose creditworthiness is equal to Owen's but who were given a mortgage. Owen seeks to have his contract cancelled and a mortgage given to him. Would you take Owen's case?

Explanation

Yes. Owen's contract interest functions here like a mortgage, albeit with harsher terms than a mortgagor would have. The differing remedies extended to Owen when compared to those given his friends and the similarity in contract and mortgage terms permit a court in equity to replace his contract with a mortgage on terms similar to those of the friends: When Owen defaults on the contract, the bank can be forced to foreclose it instead of enforcing the contract's forfeiture clause.

Example 3

Olive purchases Blackacre executing a promissory note for the purchase price and a mortgage conveying a lien on Blackacre as security for repayment of the note. The mortgage misstates the amount of the debt, having dropped two zeros from the true principal amount stated on the face of the note. The holder of the notes and the mortgage is Big Bank. Olive later defaults on the obligation to repay. The Statute of Limitations for contracts is four years. The Statute of Limitations for property interests is eight years. Five years after Olive's default, having done nothing in the interim to make Olive repay, Big Bank sues for repayment of the note. Olive defends the suit, alleging that the Statute of Limitations has run out. Counsel for Big Bank then argues that the mortgage is still enforceable as an equitable mortgage. Is it?

Explanation

Yes, it is. As an equitable mortgage, the defect in the statement of the principal can be corrected and the mortgage foreclosed. The note may not be directly enforced due to the tolling of the Statute of Limitations, but within the longer time period given for a suit based on a property interest such as a mortgage lien, it can still serve as evidence of the outstanding mortgage debt. Thus the mortgage, reformed in equity, can be foreclosed. The mortgage lien, defective at law, may be enforced as an equitable mortgage. Once again, the bank has the burden of proof to show that the principal amount of the debt stated in the note is the true amount of the debt as the parties originally intended it to be. Reformation of the mortgage will require proof of a scrivener's error and a mutual intent to have the note's statement of the debt repaid. *See Etheridge v. TierOne Bank*, 226 S.W.3d 127 (Mo. 2007).

Example 4

O conveys Blackacre by a short-form warranty deed to X. X records. X agrees in writing to reconvey the property after three years, but the agreement is unrecorded. After four years in possession, X refuses to reconvey. Is the agreement to reconvey capable of specific performance? Would your answer change (a) if the agreement to reconvey is oral, or (b) if the deed and the agreement do not cross-reference one another? And (c) if the two documents taken together are construed as a mortgage, what type of mortgage is it—lien or title?

Explanation

Yes, no, no, and it depends. A deed taken together with a contemporaneous promise to reconvey may be construed as a mortgage. *See White v. Schader*, 198 P. 19, 21 A.L.R. 499 (Cal. 1921). (a) The Statute of Frauds creates legal defenses, but no equitable ones—it need not apply in an equitable action like specific performance or unjust enrichment. (b) No specific cross-reference is necessary between documents that, taken together, might be said to constitute a mortgage. (c) There is no prohibition on the resulting mortgage being construed as a title mortgage in any state, and the intent of the parties may show it to be a title mortgage—after all, the parties did use a deed. However, in every state foreclosure statutes are said to provide a mandatory remedy, indicating that the mortgagee's interest in the property is not regarded as vested until the remedy is used and only then results in a title that the mortgagee may retain or sell. Putting off the mortgagee's title in this way is a good indication of a public policy to prefer a lien theory mortgage, absent a clear agreement otherwise.

Example 5

P agrees to sell his house and pay the proceeds to his brother in exchange for a mortgage on the brother's house. P sells his house and pays the proceeds to the brother, who dies before executing the mortgage. P's sister-in-law, the brother's widow, refuses to execute a mortgage. Can she be compelled to do so?

Explanation

Yes. The sale of the house is a completed transaction and is part performance of the mortgage transaction. The so-called mortgagee relied to his detriment, and the brother received the benefit of the sales transaction. The sister-in-law's denial of the mortgage results in a type of fraud that equity will not countenance. *See Cauco v. Galante*, 77 A.2d 793 (N.J. 1951), discussed in *Poultrymen's Serv. Corp. v. Baer*, 164 A.2d 195, 197-198 (N.J. Super. Ct., Law Div., 1960) (reviewing N.Y. and N.J. cases).

Example 6

If the brother had agreed to use the proceeds of P's house sale to buy a house, would your answer change?

Explanation

No. Tracing the proceeds of the sale of the house in this way provides an example of the common law doctrine of a purchase money mortgage. P in effect said to his brother, "Here, take the proceeds and buy a house." The brother wouldn't be buying the house without P's urging and aid; P motivated the purchase and prevails over later lienholders, even if they had no notice of his interest. So such a mortgage prevails over any later third-party mortgage. This doctrine of a purchase money mortgage provides one example of the doctrine of part performance. *See Stewart v. Smith*, 30 N.W. 430 (Minn. 1886). (We will see the term "purchase money mortgage" used in other contexts, with different meanings, so be clear on the context when you use this term.)

Example 7

M furnishes materials used in the construction of O's house. M files no mechanic's lien, but after the statutory time for filing the lien has passed, M sues to foreclose an equitable mortgage on O's property. In M's suit, what result?

Explanation

The cases are split on this one. The court may regard the mechanic's lien statute as a mandatory, exclusive remedy. However, the statute also shows a legislative policy of benefiting mechanics; the mechanic added value to O's house, O received the benefit of his materials, and might in equity be compelled to satisfy an equitable mortgage. So O is unjustly enriched; the closer question is the intent element of the action. If in addition O sat back and watched while M furnished his materials, estoppel provides another gap-filling theory to support proof of intent and the imposition of an equitable mortgage on O's property.

Example 8

Mort is negotiating for a bank loan for real estate development. The bank agrees to loan him $10 million; in consideration for this Mort gives the bank a promissory note for that amount. The bank also requires him to execute a statement that provides "Borrower will not permit or create any lien or encumbrance other than those presently existing on [another piece of property he owns] without prior written consent of Bank." Mort defaults on his loan, and the bank seeks to foreclose the interest created by the statement as if it were a mortgage. In the bank's suit, what result?

Explanation

This statement is a so-called negative pledge. Such a pledge is a contractual promise not to further encumber Mort's title. The bank, not the mortgagor, argues that the pledge is an equitable mortgage. Its strongest argument is that upon breach of the pledge, the measure of damages is the amount of the debt in the note, which, when reduced to judgment and levied on, produces a judicial sale of the property—just as would a mortgage foreclosure. The bank, however, hid this legal consequence of the pledge from Mort and so shouldn't benefit from its nondisclosure. If it had wanted a mortgage, it easily could have requested one and didn't do so. *See Tahoe Natl. Banks v. Phillips*, 480 P.2d 320 (Cal. 1971). Typically, however, a negative pledge has not been found to be an equitable mortgage.

Example 9

Grammy, an 80-year-old woman, gives Sonny a deed to her farm in exchange for Sonny's agreement to pay the taxes and insurance on the farm and to provide Grammy with "food, shelter, and clothing so long as Grammy lives and the necessities of life to the extent that Grammy cannot provide these necessities for herself." Grammy brings suit to cancel the deed, alleging a breach of the conditions in the deed and Sonny's shattering of her emotional well-being. In her suit, what result, and why?

Explanation

Judgment for Grammy. *See Thompson v. Glidden*, 445 A.2d 676 (Me. 1982) (upholding generally the validity of this type of equitable "support" mortgage and finding that money as well as emotional support for the elderly are valid types of consideration for it). *See also Ripple v. Wold*, 549 N.W.2d 673 (S.D. 1995). If Sonny had recorded his deed as soon as he received it, it would not be a deed granted "for value" as the recording acts require. Consideration for the elderly may require judicial scrutiny of overreaching relatives—even if this violates the usual rules of construction. To be the subject of a mortgage, though, a promise must be readily translated into money. So Sonny had better keep good records; otherwise, Grammy wins.

CHAPTER 15

Junior Liens and Mezzanine Finance

When a titleholder mortgages property twice, the lien given and recorded first is called the senior lien, and that given second a junior lien. Each of the mortgagees holding a lien is entitled to the security in the property for which she bargained at the time of the transfer and recording of their respective liens. Thus, a senior lien is entitled to a foreclosure conducted as if the junior lien did not exist, and its foreclosure has the effect of wiping out any liens junior to the lien foreclosed. This effect means that a title sold at any foreclosure sale will be in the same state as it was when the senior mortgagee bargained for her security. In this way, she gets what she bargained for.

Foreclosure procedures typically involve a title search at some early point in the proceedings. Junior mortgagees discovered in the search are made parties to the foreclosure and receive some of the proceeds of the sale, if any remain after the satisfaction of all liens senior to them. Junior mortgagees and any holder of a junior interest in the property, such as a lease, are necessary parties to a senior foreclosure. In contrast, a senior mortgagee or other interest holder is a proper, but not a necessary, party to a junior foreclosure.

The holder of a senior mortgage lien has reason to worry about the presence of a junior lien. When a junior lien secures a commercial property, the existence of the junior loan represents an additional call on the cash flow generated by the property. For any type of mortgage, not only may the presence of a junior loan indicate a worrisome need for cash on the part of the mortgagor, it also reduces the mortgagor's equity in the secured property. This reduction in turn increases the likelihood of the mortgagor's defaulting on both loans. And if that default requires modification of the senior mortgage, the modification may require the junior's consent, lest the senior lose its lien priority. Moreover, when a default on the mortgagor's part renders him insolvent, the junior lienor may put the mortgagor into bankruptcy, eliminating the senior lienholder's ability to foreclose—and conversely, a junior lienor's bankruptcy will automatically stay any senior foreclosure. A final reason to worry arises upon the refinancing of property secured by a senior lien because then any junior's loan will have to be repaid: If it is not, the senior lien may lose its former priority.[1]

In a foreclosure of a senior lien, a junior mortgagee has the same right as a mortgagor to redeem the senior mortgage by paying the outstanding debt due on it. She can also sue the mortgagor for a deficiency judgment if the proceeds of the senior foreclosure sale are inadequate to satisfy the full amount of the debt owed to her at the time her lien is extinguished. Finally, she can purchase the property at the foreclosure sale.

Even after the foreclosure of a senior lien, a junior lienholder can exercise, in some jurisdictions and with others whose interests were extinguished as a result of a senior lien's foreclosure, a statutory right to purchase the (formerly) secured property at the foreclosure sale price. By this and other methods previously mentioned, mortgage law favors junior liens. The purpose of this favoritism isn't hard to understand: When most owners need a mortgage to purchase their property, the alienability of their equity also needs protection.

The doctrine of marshaling may further protect the junior lienholder when the mortgagor owns two properties, both of which are subject to the senior lien and one of which is subject to the junior. Under this doctrine, the senior can be compelled to satisfy her debt from the property exclusively available to her. The senior is still entitled to have her debt satisfied first, but she must foreclose first on property available only to her, and if part of her debt has not been paid in that foreclosure, she may then foreclose on the property, securing both mortgages. In a few states, this doctrine is codified. The senior and junior interests need not be of the same type for the junior to seek the protection of the doctrine (e.g., judgment creditors can use the doctrine against mortgagees, and vice versa). Marshaling is an equitable doctrine, subject to judicial discretion, and so is not everywhere seen as a right, although if a junior asserts it in a timely manner and shows

1. While the emphasis in this chapter is on the priority of liens and foreclosure, there are other situations in which senior and junior lienholders' interests may conflict. For example, a junior might pay real property taxes owed by a mortgagor and thus, to the extent of that payment, gain priority over a senior lien. Likewise as to property or fire insurance premiums: The senior and the junior lienholders might dispute the use of insurance claim proceeds once a claim on the policy is paid.

that, first, no prejudice to senior lienholders results, and, second, its use would not defeat any statutory rights, then it will be used.

The junior no less than the senior lienholder is entitled to the security for which she too bargained. The senior mortgagee cannot extend the time for payment, raise the interest rate on the note accompanying the senior lien, or raise the monthly payments without the approval of the junior. The reason for requiring the approval is that otherwise, the junior would be less secure than she bargained to be. If the junior becomes less secure, her lien will, in part, become senior (in any later foreclosure) to that portion of the payment of the senior note obligation that diminishes the security of the junior.

What the junior mortgagee cannot do is force the senior mortgagee to foreclose her lien, even if the titleholder is in default on the note or on a covenant in the senior mortgage. The principle is the same. The senior bargained for a remedy and is entitled to choose when and where to use it. She invested money for a certain period of time and is entitled to choose the time to recall that investment.

The junior mortgagee, however, can foreclose her mortgage lien separately from the senior lien. If she does this, she forecloses on the title as it was when she executed her mortgage. That is, the title sold at the foreclosure sale will be subject to any senior lien, and of course the obligation to pay the senior note still exists. The purchaser at the sale gets to step into the mortgagor's shoes on the secured property but also gets the title subject to the senior mortgage. She has no personal obligation to pay the senior debt, but if it is not paid, the senior mortgagee can foreclose and the junior mortgagee in possession, or the purchaser at the junior foreclosure, will lose the right to possession. In effect, the junior mortgagee forecloses on the title existing at the time she bargained for her security, and her foreclosure sale transfers that title along with the rights that the mortgagor has to participate in any future foreclosure of a senior lien.

In any foreclosure, questions of priority of title are resolved only to the extent necessary. There is no proceeding that will adjudicate the priority of all liens and other encumbrances attaching to the title. Foreclosure is not a proceeding *in rem*. To the extent that the proceeds of the sale must be distributed, that distribution will be in accord with the priorities found *inter se*. When junior liens are wiped out in a senior foreclosure, they are turned into a right to share in the proceeds; those junior liens are lined up in priority to receive whatever proceeds are available. If the junior is partially satisfied from the proceeds, the unpaid junior may sue for a deficiency. However, if no proceeds are available for distribution, no priorities will be determined. The junior lienholders left in the cold must enforce their notes against the personal assets of the debtor, no longer a mortgagor as to the wiped-out junior.

Thus the priority of a junior lien will be determined in a senior foreclosure in which the junior is joined as a party, but the priority of a senior lien will not be determined in a foreclosure of a lien junior to it unless the senior mortgagee joins in the action. These principles are in accord with the relativity of title underlying the common law.

EXAMPLES

Examples

Example 1

In a title state for mortgages, O executes a mortgage on Blackacre in favor of M1, and then later executes a mortgage on Blackacre in favor of M2. What interest does M2 take in Blackacre?

Explanation

The O-M1 mortgage is the conveyance of a defeasible fee to M1, who holds the title so long as the mortgage loan is unpaid but agrees that, upon repayment, she will reconvey the title to O. If M2's mortgage is executed while M1's is still outstanding, O has conveyed her possibility of reverter, including her equity of redemption, to M2, that being the right held by O after the execution of the first mortgage. *See J. M. Seward v. N.Y. Life Ins. Co.*, 152 S.E. 346 (Va. 1930) (discussing the theory of junior mortgages).

Example 2

If O's mortgages in the preceding explanation were executed in a lien state, what would your answer be?

Explanation

Both M1 and M2 hold liens on Blackacre. M1 holds the first lien, superior to M2's. M2 holds a second or junior lien—junior, that is, to M1's.

Example 3

If M2 forecloses in a lien state and purchases at the judicial sale, what is the state of her title?

Explanation

M2 takes over O's rights as of the time O and M2 executed their mortgage transaction. That is, M2 gets the title in the condition in which it was at that time. That's what M2 expected to have as security for her loan, and that's what she gets. So M2 gets possession of Blackacre, with its title encumbered with M1's mortgage lien—again, this encumbrance was attached to the title when M2 made her deal. M2 gets possession, together with the right to pay off M1's loan on the terms for which M1 had bargained. M2 takes title subject to the senior lien but absent some agreement to the contrary, without assuming the personal obligation to pay it. M1 remains liable on the note he signed.

Example 4

Can M2 force M1 to foreclose? Would your answer change if M1's mortgage were in default?

Explanation

No, M2 cannot force the holder of a lien senior to her own to foreclose. M1 bargained for the right to foreclose at a time and place of her own choosing; she cannot be forced to use what she bargained for as an elective remedy. Even if the senior lien is in default, the senior lienor cannot be forced to foreclose. In a few states, when and only when the whole senior mortgage debt is due, can M1 be compelled by M2 to foreclose her lien.

Example 5

A first mortgagee, M1, brings an action to foreclose her mortgage lien. A junior mortgagee, M2, with security in the same property is properly joined in M1's action. The mortgagor has a defense to the action that, if properly and timely asserted, would result in the action's dismissal. The mortgagor does not assert this defense but, over M2's objections, consents to a foreclosure decree binding M2, in exchange for M1's waiver of her right to a deficiency judgment. In a timely manner, M2 attempts to assert the mortgagor's defense. Should M2 be permitted to assert this defense?

Explanation

No. The defense is one relating to the first lien mortgage transaction, to which M2 was not a party. M2 is a poor source of evidence relating to this defense; M2 took her junior lien in the expectation that the senior lien was enforceable, and would otherwise be unjustly enriched (by having the first lien foreclosure dismissed).

Example 6

O executes brief but enforceable mortgages to M1 and M2 in that order. Before a large payment on M1's mortgage comes due, O asks X to make the payment and to pay the outstanding balance of M1's mortgage. M1 agrees to deal with X, and X pays off M1's mortgage. Can X assume M1's lien status over M2's protest?

Explanation

Yes. M2 never expected to have, as security for her loan, a title unencumbered by M1's lien. X assumes M1's lien position by virtue of subrogation: X steps into M1's shoes and takes over her rights and duties. Any other result would be a windfall for M2. It is said that X has an "equity of subrogation." When X assumes M1's lien status and forecloses, M2's lien would be wiped out in X's foreclosure because that is what M1 bargained for and what was transferred to X by M1. M1 bargained for security in a title in foreclosure unencumbered by M2's lien and, M1's remedy being transferred to X, X is entitled to the same remedy.

Example 7

What were M2's alternatives to taking a junior lien in the preceding examples?

Explanation

Some alternatives are M2's leasing the property and taking possession (when the rents and profits from doing so can satisfy the debt), buying the property and leasing it back to O (a sale-leaseback), taking a vendee's interest in a contract of sale (giving O an option to repurchase it), an installment land sale contract, or providing O with wraparound financing (to be discussed in Chapter 19, on construction financing). In addition, the junior mortgagee can take a participating note—that is, one payable in interest and a portion of the rents and profits from the property—or an equity interest in the property as partial repayment of the debt. *See*, in Chapter 13, the discussion on participating mortgages.

Example 8

M2 is owed $100,000 on its mortgage on MR's Blackacre, subject to M1's outstanding senior mortgage debt of $1,000,000. M2's mortgage goes into default and during its foreclosure, a title search for Blackacre shows that M3 has another, third, junior outstanding mortgage. M3 is promptly made a party to the foreclosure. Blackacre's fair market value is $1,250,000. What amount should M2 bid at the foreclosure sale?

Explanation

M2 has a creditor or certified bid of $100,000. Should M2 bid more? No. Should M2 bid less? Probably. Why? Because any excess over $100,000 (or over an amount necessary to satisfy M2's outstanding debt) will go to M3, whose debt will be extinguished by the foreclosure, and any excess over that will go to MR. None of this excess, in other words, will go toward paying down M1's mortgage (to which M2's rights will be subject). Think of this answer in terms of what a third-party purchaser at the foreclosure sale will bid: that is, no more than the property will be worth free and clear of all liens, less the amount of outstanding senior liens. M2's problem here also indicates why a junior mortgagee or lienholder is a necessary party to any workout or loan extension agreement between M1 and MR.

MEZZANINE FINANCING

In the 1990s, after the real estate recession of 1990-1991, stricter underwriting guidelines for commercial mortgages and lower loan-to-value ratios encouraged commercial mortgagors to look for junior or second mortgages. Lenders responded with prohibitions on junior mortgages, often framed as "due on encumbrance" covenants, justified by recently encountered problems posed by junior mortgages in bankruptcy proceedings. Thus throughout the 1990s, the use of junior mortgages sharply decreased, and commercial mortgagors searched for alternatives.

One alternative was mezzanine[2] financing. Typically mezzanine financing is a loan made in addition to a first mortgage loan and subordinated to it, but by agreement made senior in priority to both the mortgagor's equity in the secured property and the mortgagor's priority in the cash flow generated by the property. Mezzanine financing is in the sandwich position, between the senior mortgagee and the mortgagor/borrower/owner. In the traditional sense, it creates unsecured debt, "secured" by the cash flow from the realty, not the property itself. More accurately described then, it is personalty, not realty; it is only indirectly secured by real property owned by an intermediate entity owned in turn by the borrower. It takes the form of either an assignment, a pledge of cash flow, or an entity membership interest. If the borrower is a corporation, it may be an assignment of corporate shares, the dividends of which are sufficient to repay the loan. If the borrower is a partner or a member of a limited liability company, it may be a pledge of the borrower's partnership share or company membership—or an entity interest in a preferred position to receive the cash flow. In any event, the lender will typically require the personal guarantee of the debt by the borrower and be able to seize the shares or other ownership interests more quickly than if foreclosure (of any type) was required. Meanwhile, although a second mortgage would have to be carried as a liability on the balance sheet of the corporation, partnership, or limited liability company,

2. "Mezzanine" is a Wall Street term, referring to financing that is not investment-grade (as highly regulated institutions would require because their regulators require it) but not junk.

the mezzanine loan is carried not on those entities' books, but on the books of the borrower. Mezzanine financing is off–balance sheet financing.

Just as with junior mortgages, mezzanine financing is often used for (1) renovating commercial properties, (2) upgrading and repositioning a property in its market, (3) capturing the value of built-up equity in a property without the income tax liabilities of selling it, or (4) obtaining seed money for the owner's next project. As experience was gained with it, however, it was used more widely just to let the developer achieve greater leverage—that is, a higher loan-to-value ratio for all his development loans. For lenders, mezzanine financing offers a higher rate of interest than do second mortgage loans. Lenders engaging in such financing are usually seasoned real estate investors capable of evaluating the equity value that the owner/borrower has in a property. Mezzanine lending is unlikely if the owner's equity is not 20 percent or more of appraised value.

The typical mezzanine transaction has two to three components: (1) a promissory note, perhaps with a mortgage, unrecorded; (2) a pledge of entity interests; (3) an intercreditor agreement between the senior mortgagee, consenting to the mezzanine loan, and the mezzanine lender. This agreement also provides (a) for notice of defaults and an opportunity to cure defaults in the senior mortgage and (b) for defining the relationship and priorities of the two parties in foreclosure, sometimes permitting the mezzanine lender to step into ownership.

The mezzanine borrowers will likely be a special-purpose entity (SPE) that will own only the secured property, will conduct its business independently, and is bankruptcy-remote (often by promising not to file for bankruptcy or with the existence of a lender-controlled director, partner, or member who is not an obligor under the financing agreement and who will vote against the filing).

Repayment may also be guaranteed by the SPE's parent company or entity. This financing might also include a participating interest (at a slightly higher than first lien interest rate, plus a contingent return based on cash flow) or a shared appreciation feature based on an equity event (such as sale, condemnation, refinancing, or revaluation, etc.). These inclusions are drafted to avoid recharacterization as a clog, which usually results from lender control based on lender participation in management decisions after a default, pledge and participation rights, conversion options and equity kickers, and may also result in anti-clogging affidavits being required from the borrower, and sometimes an anti-clogging endorsement from a title insurer, with the insurer that issued the endorsement in turn requiring an indemnity agreement from the borrower.

Typical intercreditor agreement provisions are drafted to avoid the financial pressure points found in the senior note and mortgage. That is, any balloon payment or refinancing dates in the senior mortgage will not occasion similar obligations for the mezzanine borrower, lest the double pressure of the two loans tip the borrower into insolvency. In a similar vein, the mezzanine financing will have a term longer than the senior note and mortgage, tending to make mezzanine lenders look long and hard at the long-term prospects of the property. The mezzanine lender will have a right to cure defaults in the senior mortgage. The mezzanine lender and the senior mortgagee will agree on how to handle disputes that arise on leasing the property. One such dispute might arise, for example, when a mezzanine lender would willingly accept higher rents and a lower credit rating in tenants, while the mortgagee might want lower rents and a higher rating. When the mortgage has been used as collateral for a secondary market bond or other instrument, this type of dispute means that the senior mortgagee will require that the mezzanine lender obtain written confirmation from a rating agency that enforcement of any of the mezzanine lender's proposed remedies will not adversely affect the credit rating given to the instrument sold to investors in the secondary market.

The disadvantages of mezzanine lending are that (1) a 10-15 percent decrease in fair market value will erode the borrower's equity and put the lender at risk; and (2) the costs of underwriting and due diligence are high compared to the amount of the loan. So investigation of the market is crucial and risky, and this increases negotiation costs.

A mezzanine borrower responding to a senior mortgage lender who, when discovering mezzanine financing has been used, feels insecure and threatens to declare a default of the senior mortgage, might (1) offer a "lockbox" agreement, which would require tenants on the property to pay rents and profits constituting the cash flow from the property directly into an account controlled by the senior mortgagee, who would then pay the mezzanine lender out of cash flow in excess of amounts needed to make payments due on the senior mortgage, (2) also offer to put the management of the property in the hands of an agreed upon property manager, and (3) further offer the senior mortgagee a "carry guarantee" for that mortgage, or to purchase the senior note and mortgage upon default.

When mezzanine financing is being considered, title insurers should be consulted as additional issues with the borrower's title policy arise. Consider three that might arise. (1) Recall that claims on a title policy require a showing of damages "sustained or incurred"—that is, actual damages. The mezzanine lender, however, will want to get at the proceeds of a claim sooner, even though its loss will be contingent and may never arise by the time the claim is payable or paid. So an endorsement for this will be necessary. (2) Exclusion 3(b), giving the insurer a defense to a claim based on knowledge of the insured, may be a problem. Thus, affidavits from all the participants in the due diligence underwriting for the loan will be required, to the effect that they know of no matters, rights, claims, or interests affecting the property that are not represented in the application for insurance. (3) A Condition 1 or continuation of coverage problem may arise when the memberships in the borrowing entity change: This, too, will have to be the subject of an endorsement.

Examples

Example 9

A commercial mortgage lender, envious of the higher rates of interest given mezzanine lenders, offers a mortgagor a reduction of the principal amount of the loan secured by an outstanding mortgage in exchange for becoming a mezzanine lender in the amount of the reduction. What problems do you foresee with this offer?

Explanation

Those associated with a convertible mortgage, because that's what is being offered. *See Wonderland Shopping Center Venture Ltd. Partnership v. CDC Mortgage Capital, Inc.*, 274 F.3d 1085 (6th Cir. 2001). *See* Chapter 13, *supra* (discussing this type of AMI).

Example 10

What types of federal income tax problems might arise for mezzanine lenders?

Explanation

The purpose of the loan is to replace part of the owner's equity ownership in the property with the mezzanine lender's right to repayment. Equity ownership is the subject of the loan, and the lender then generally wants to be treated as an owner for tax purposes—that is, to be taxed at capital gain, not ordinary income rates. (1) To gain this treatment, the Internal Revenue Code's crucial factors are the purpose of the investment, the frequency of sales, and the management of the property. IRC §1221. So the more rights the mezzanine lender has to take over and manage the property, the more he will look like a real estate developer in the ordinary course of business and be denied capital gains treatment. Thus the lender's right to hire a management company, rather than manage directly, is useful on default by the borrower. (2) Another route to capital gains treatment is to characterize the loan as equity (and so a capital asset), not debt. IRC §385. The right to designate members or directors of the SPE, the avoidance of a fixed maturity or repayment date, and the lack of a sinking fund or an obligation to repay make the case for equity classification stronger and avoid the appearance of debt.

Additional protection of mezzanine lenders is provided by the Uniform Commercial Code. Under its revised Article 9, the mezzanine borrower's pledge is either an "investment property" or a "general intangible." UCC §9-102(42) and (49) for definitions. The former may be perfected by control (evidenced by possession or the right to possess in an assignment), by filing a financing statement, or (when certificated with a security under UCC Art. §8-301) by possession. The latter may be perfected by filing. UCC §§9-308, 9-310. Among interests perfectible by filing, the earliest to file has priority. Title insurers often offer either an endorsement for their loan policies or a UCC policy, insuring the Article 9 status of the lender's interest, but sometimes an attorney's opinion accomplishes the same result.

The UCC's protections are premised on the ability of the foreclosing lender to sell the property—but standard procedures for either such a sale have not developed. Why? Because potential purchasers cannot easily know what they are bidding on. Often it is a pledge or assignment of an interest in a single asset entity that owns the realty involved, and so the lender is one or two levels removed from the source of the cash flow upon which his loan was predicated. If the real estate is in trouble, the entity is in trouble and his cash flow is in double trouble.

Example 11

The senior mortgagee begins foreclosure. If the mortgagee succeeds, what is the mezzanine lender left holding?

Explanation

An equity interest in an entity with no assets, other than the surplus realized at the foreclosure sale over and above the outstanding amount of the senior note. The lender is subordinated to every secured creditor of the borrower so that any surplus is unlikely to reach him—and in a severe market downturn, it is unlikely that there will be any surplus. If the note for the mezzanine debt was accompanied by a mortgage, so far unrecorded, now is the time to record it. The mezzanine lender will in the meantime be under extreme pressure to realize some portion of the debt through assertion of his UCC rights.

Example 12

The mezzanine lender avoids the senior's foreclosure by assuming the senior note and mortgage. What did the lender purchase?

Explanation

The senior mortgagor's rights, subject to the covenants in that mortgage. Those covenants might include (among others) a due-on-sale clause, specifically tailored for this situation and restricting further sale of the secured property. This tailoring is likely if the property was to collateralize a bond sold to investors in the secondary market; rating agencies have insisted on this covenant as a means of stabilizing the investments made in the bond.

In the context of a senior mortgagee's foreclosure action, the mezzanine lender will realize that he lacks the protections afforded by the common law to mortgagees, even junior mortgagees: the right to record, the right to a receiver, a cause of action in waste, protections on the equity of redemption that the junior would receive, and the fact that the rights of the mortgage holder run with the land, binding subsequent purchasers. Indeed, his transaction was structured specifically to avoid these protections, and the law does not have equivalent protections for him. He is left with an action in debt on the contract to lend against the borrower.

In the past decade, the situation of the mezzanine lender worsened in other ways, too. Any slight downturn in real estate market values causes many mezzanine loans to become delinquent. The downturn that occurred in 2007-2010 was not slight. When commercial real estate in many markets lost more than 25 percent of its fair market value in those years, mezzanine lenders were caught in a larger capital markets crisis in 2007-2008.

CHAPTER 16

Payments, Prepayments, and Transfers of the Mortgage

PAYMENTS AND PREPAYMENTS OF MORTGAGE DEBT

Repayment of a mortgage debt is typically made so much per month for residential mortgages. Each repayment includes amounts allocated to principal and to interest, amortized so that at maturity the whole debt is paid off. However, payments can also be interest only, or amortized over a shorter or longer period than would be required to repay the entire debt. Indeed, the repayment schedule can be arranged so that the financing terms are more important than the purchase price of a property, conforming the repayments to the monthly budget or the pro forma financial analysis, thus making the property affordable for the mortgagor.

At common law, the mortgagor had no right to prepay the debt. It was thought that the mortgagee bargained for and expected a stream of payments up to and including the maturity date of the loan on which date the last payment was due. This "perfect tender in time" fulfilled the mortgagee's investment expectations. *See* Pittman v. Hamann, 24 N.W.3d 775 (Iowa Ct. App. 2025). By the same token, this common law "no right to prepay" rule turned the mortgagor's early prepayment of principal into a privilege to which the mortgagee did not have to consent, but for which the mortgagee when consenting might demand consideration. This consideration is the origin of prepayment fees.

Typically, today residential mortgagors have a right to prepay. Restatement (Third), Mortgages, § 6.1 (1996) (recognizing a right to prepay unless the mortgage eliminates the right). This right is either authorized by federal and state statutes or provided by a covenant in their mortgages. These covenants are prescribed for mortgages to be sold into the secondary market. Since such a sale is possible for any mortgage, virtually every residential mortgage contains such a covenant.

Not so for mortgages secured by commercial property. The legal landscape for these mortgages is much more complicated, varying by type of mortgagee, the extent of federal regulation, and state statutes.

Having a right to prepay does not mean that a prepayment is free of a prepayment fee. Quite the contrary is true, no matter whether the mortgage is secured by residential or commercial property.

Prepayment fees have taken several forms over the last several decades. For residential mortgages, six months' interest on the prepaid principal is common, with a mortgagor given the right to prepay up to (say) 20 percent of the outstanding balance in any one year of a mortgage's term. Commercial mortgages might use such a formula, but increase the amount of the fee by a percent or two as the mortgage debt is repaid on its original schedule.

These formulas do not account for the mortgagee's loss when the mortgage debt is repaid at a time when interest rates on mortgages are lower than they were on the execution date of a mortgage, nor for the mortgagee's gain when interest rates rise. This failure to account for fluctuations in interest rates motivated mortgagees to search for alternatives for fixed formulas. By the mid-1990s, two alternatives emerged for commercial mortgages.

Yield maintenance. This is a one-time prepayment fee. Its purpose is to make the mortgagee indifferent to whether the debt is paid early and to compensate the mortgagee for the interest payments lost when the debt is prepaid. However, it is more accurately called an acceleration fee rather than a prepayment fee since after the debt is partially or totally accelerated, the maturity date on the amount paid is past. When interest rates rise, yield maintenance covenants cost the prepaying borrower nothing more than a minimal fee (usually 1 percent of the prepaid amount), as the mortgagee can reinvest the prepaid amounts more profitably. When rates fall, however, the mortgagee cannot do this and is entitled to an amount of money that equals the difference between the mortgage's original rate of interest and the current rate. Often this amount is discounted to its present value. It is common to provide that the current rate is measured by the rate of U.S. Treasury bonds, typically a lower rate than the mortgage's original rate. In this way, yield maintenance covenants overcompensate the mortgagee. Using this formula makes it difficult for a mortgagor to argue that the fee is a penalty because it gives the mortgagee what the mortgagor originally found to be a reasonable return on the mortgagee's investment.

Defeasance. This is the process of replacing the collateral for a mortgage debt. It is not a prepayment of debt. The secured property is replaced with a portfolio of U.S. Treasury bonds yielding the same return as the mortgage would have yielded over the remaining term of the mortgage. After the replacement, the mortgage lien is released and in its place the bonds are substituted. The mortgage note remains, so there is no acceleration of the debt. The payment dates and income levels on the bonds must exactly match the dates and income expected by the mortgagee on the original debt. In addition, the bonds must not be callable; they must produce the income stream originally expected by the mortgagee. The defeasance process can be costly and time consuming, but for the mortgagor it can be worthwhile when he can refinance with a loan in excess of the original loan's principal—that is, sufficiently large and in excess to absorb the cost of the process. For the lender, it provides an alternative contract within the mortgage covenants, free from challenge as unreasonable liquidated damages or a penalty and replacing the mortgaged property with the securest type of collateral—U.S. Treasury bonds. For the remaining term of the loan, the bonds are typically held in escrow for return to the mortgagor when the maturity date is reached. Mortgagees typically prefer defeasance to yield maintenance because it has no relationship to market declines and interest rate fluctuations. It also keeps steady the loan's investment value in the secondary market.

In a general sense, maintaining the yield of the original loan is the purpose of both of these methods for handling early payments. In addition, however, mortgagees justify both of them by pointing out that their having mortgage capital on hand is not cost free; they too have their investors, whether shareholders, insurance policy beneficiaries, or other lending institutions. Their income stream must at least match their obligations for their investors.

Examples

Example 1

Mortgagor (M) executes a mortgage with a principal of one hundred thousand dollars ($100,000), an interest rate of 7 percent, and a term of ten years; his repayments under this mortgage are to be interest only. After the fifth year of the term, M wants to refinance when the current mortgage interest rate is 5 percent. The mortgage has a yield maintenance prepayment covenant. What is the yield maintenance amount M will owe his lender when he refinances?

Explanation

M's prepayment amount will equal the difference between the contract rate and the current rate: 7 percent and 5 percent, or 2 percent, discounted to its present value. His interest-only annual payments would be $7,000 a year for five years—the remaining term of the mortgage loan. When the mortgagee would earn $5,000 a year reinvesting at the current rate of interest in a U.S.

Treasury bond, the yield maintenance amount M will pay his mortgagee is \$2,000 times five, or \$10,000. (The same formula is used for an amortized mortgage loan, but is much simpler to compute with an interest-only loan.)

Example 2

A mortgagee client of yours is considering the insertion of either a yield maintenance or a defeasance covenant into a mortgage. Which would you advise him to choose?

Explanation

A defeasance covenant. While each prepayment method is based on U.S. Treasury yields, a defeasance might be preferred because: (1) it maintains your client's yield if the mortgage is sold into the secondary market; (2) it is less subject to challenge as a penalty: it is not interest rate sensitive, whereas yield maintenance is because the amount is computed by the spread between the contract rate and the current rate of interest; and (3) it has no relation to interest rate market declines; it merely locks in the mortgagor and mortgagee's original bargain.

ASSUMING DEBT VERSUS TAKING TITLE "SUBJECT TO"

When a mortgagor transfers his title to property securing a mortgage, the transferee will usually finance the purchase with the proceeds of a new mortgage loan. The new mortgagee will usually require that its lien be a first lien, thereby requiring that the mortgagor pay off the outstanding debt, usually from the proceeds of the sale. When this is not done, the grantee-transferee may take the title of the mortgagor-vendor subject to the outstanding lien of the preexisting mortgage (known as taking title "subject to," a subject we previously discussed in the context of contracts of sale). Taking title subject to does not oblige the purchaser to pay the debt evidenced in the note, but the property he receives may nonetheless be called on to secure repayment of that debt through a foreclosure sale, which will extinguish the purchaser's rights in the property. Such a purchaser is then the holder of an interest junior to that of the preexisting mortgagee. The purchaser takes title subject to the right to foreclose held by the preexisting mortgagee.

An assuming grantee or transferee is personally liable for the debt; he undertakes to repay the outstanding amount due on the preexisting note. Thus not only does the property remain the primary security for repayment, but the grantee, along with the mortgagor, is also personally liable for repayment. Restatement (Third) of Property, Mortgages, §5.1(a) (1997). As the result of an assumption, the assuming purchaser is primarily liable for the debt and the original debtor/vendor becomes a secondary obligee for its repayment. In a chain of assumptions, the grantees are primarily liable in the inverse order of assumptions. *See Swanson v. Krenik*, 868 P.2d 297 (Alaska 1994). When the transferring vendor was also personally liable for the debt and the mortgagee agrees to the assumption, that vendor becomes a surety, a secondary obligor for the payment of the debt. Restatement (Third) of Property, Mortgages, §5.1(d) (1997). Under the law of suretyship, the surety once asked to perform the duties of the primary obligee may seek reimbursement from that obligee and take over any suits and claims that the obligee would have under the mortgage.

Examples

Example 3

Your client is P, who is about to purchase Blackacre from V. Blackacre's title is encumbered by a mortgage from L, and since the interest rate on the note is lower than the present market rate, P wishes to assume the obligation on the note. L sends you an undated statement of the amount of the outstanding loan secured by the mortgage. Why would you object to the use of the statement in the upcoming closing?

Explanation

The amount to be paid off is a moving target: It likely accrues interest on a daily basis and the payoff must be precisely determined as of the closing date. In any event, it may be prudent to ask the title insurer issuing P's owner's policy to insure over the payoff of the preexisting mortgage. The payoff statement is not irrelevant to P's taking title subject to, but is crucial to an assumption.

Example 4

O sells Blackacre to MR, and takes back a brief but enforceable mortgage. MR later sells Blackacre to Beyer, who takes Blackacre's title in a deed providing that the title is "assumed subject to O's mortgage." Has Beyer incurred a personal liability for the mortgage debt? Would it matter if the deed referred to the "mortgage debt" or "O's note"?

Explanation

No and no. Using the canon of construction that permits the deed to be construed in favor of its grantee and (as is possible in many states) a presumption statute that states the greatest estate is conveyed to the grantee, the ambiguous language would be construed so that Beyer's deed was taken "subject to" the mortgage and that no assumption was included. *See McVeigh v. Marabito*, 556 So. 2d 1226 (Fla. App. Ct. 1990) (containing a good statement of the law). A more specific reference, such as those used in the phrases in the second question, would not change this result. Construing such words involves only presumptions about the parties' intent. The canon is an aid in determining the parties' intent, not a rule of law, so extrinsic evidence is still admissible to determine that intent, and, should an assumption agreement be found, a reference to the mortgage alone without any accompanying reference to the note will not affect that finding or cut back Beyer's liability. An assumption agreement is a contract incorporating not only the legal requirements of a contract, such as consideration, but also the same rules of construction that courts normally apply to a contract. Only when Beyer promises to pay MR's obligation to the mortgagee will an agreement to assume be inferred.

TRANSFERS BY THE MORTGAGOR

Let's now make further use of the distinction between taking title to real property subject to an existing mortgage and taking title while assuming an existing mortgage. Suppose that, in the context of a subdivision development, a developer-mortgagor finances the construction of houses with a blanket mortgage loan (in which the lien of the mortgage attaches to all lots in the subdivision), and the purchasers of each house and lot take title subject to the blanket mortgage. If the developer's mortgage is foreclosed, only so many of the purchasers who purchased last should be foreclosed on when not all lots are needed to satisfy the debt. The other purchasers (if foreclosure was brought against their lots) could assert the doctrine of marshaling as a defense. An inverse order of alienation will be used, foreclosing on only so many purchasers as are necessary to satisfy the debt and release the lien: so the last purchasers to take subject to would be the first foreclosed. Viewed from the perspective of the first purchasers in the subdivision, their purchase took place at a time when there was relatively more property to satisfy the blanket mortgage, but the last purchasers had no such cushion.

If each purchaser assumed the developer's loan, then the chronological order of alienation would control the sequence of foreclosure. Here the first purchaser was facing a potentially larger risk of foreclosure and liability, but subsequent purchasers take in reliance on the prior assumptions.

If some purchasers took subject to, but others assumed, the order of foreclosure and liability might go down the chronological order of assumptions, then back up the inverse order of "subject to" purchasers, on the theory that the assuming purchasers undertook the greater risk (of personal as well as grantee, subject to, liability).

Assuming that each of the lot purchasers financed their purchases with loans secured by junior mortgages on their individual lots, and then the blanket senior mortgage was foreclosed, how will the proceeds (assuming there are any) of the foreclosure sale be distributed to them? These junior mortgagees would either receive such proceeds in the order they recorded their liens or they would share those proceeds ratably, receiving only those proceeds derived from the sale of the lot securing their loan. *Metcalfe & Sons, Inc. v. Canyon Defined Benefit Trust*, 569 A.2d 669 (Md. 1990) (deciding that the latter, lot specific, distribution is best). The latter reinforces the need for good underwriting of each loan by each junior mortgagee.

Examples

Example 5

MR executes a brief but enforceable note and mortgage in favor of ME. MR conveys to A1, agreeing with A1 that A1 will assume MR's debt and take subject to the mortgage lien. Does this agreement have to be in writing?

Explanation

Most assumption agreements are contained in a deed covenant and so are in writing. Taking subject to does not require a writing. When the assumption agreement and the deed are independent of one another, a majority of courts addressing the question have held that the Statute of Frauds does not require a writing. *See White v. Schnader*, 198 P. 19, 21 A.L.R. 499 (Cal. 1921). For purposes of the statute, the assumption agreement does not create a new lien; it is only a delegation of contract rights and duties. Nor is it an agreement to pay the debt of another. Moreover, the original mortgagor, MR, is still liable to ME; if he were not, the note and mortgage terms would have been changed unilaterally by the MR-A1 agreement and, because ME was no party to this agreement, he is not bound by it. ME is, however, a third-party beneficiary of the agreement, so even when not a party, ME is able to hold A1 personally liable for breach of the agreement.

Example 6

Assume the facts in the preceding example. If A1 later contends that the agreement was really an agreement to take Blackacre subject to ME's mortgage lien, will A1 be able to show this? If MR wanted to show that A1 really meant to assume, but that they used the words "subject to" instead, would he be able to show that?

Explanation

The parol evidence rule does not prevent MR's proving that a "subject to" agreement is really intended, but it would prevent a showing that a subject to agreement was really intended to function as an assignment. It does not prevent cutting back the effect of the agreement, but it cannot be used to expand its legal effect.

Example 7

MR executes a brief but enforceable note and mortgage in favor of ME. MR conveys to P. MR's deed to P not only described MR's debt to ME, but also contained a reduced consideration, reduced by an amount reflecting MR's outstanding debt, and after the MR/P closing, P makes mortgage payments to ME when due. Would these facts establish an assumption agreement?

Explanation

Not in a majority of states. *See McVeigh v. Marabito*, 556 So. 2d 1226 (Fla. App. Ct. 1990). Absent an agreement, the reduction in price is just as consistent with MR's continuing duty to make mortgage payments as with imposing any implied duty on P to do so. Nothing has changed MR's contractual duty to do so; MR's sale of the property certainly does not affect ME's right to have the benefits of his bargain, which MR cannot unilaterally change. Restatement (Third) of Property, Mortgages, §5.2(b) (1997). The price reduction, while an admissible piece of evidence, will not provide the clear and convincing evidence that most states require to prove an assumption. In a few states, such as Oklahoma and Pennsylvania, an implied assumption agreement would be found when the purchase price is reduced by the amount of the outstanding debt. *See Heaney v. Riddle*, 23 A.2d 456 (Pa. 1942) (the leading case for this minority rule). Then the purchaser P will indemnify the vendor MR later forced to satisfy the debt. Under the majority rule, P's making payments after the closing will be construed as P's merely protecting her own interests, rather than as proof of an assumption agreement. Restatement (Third) of Property, Mortgages, §5.1, and Reporter's Note at 342 (1997).

Example 8

O sells Whiteacre to M(R) and takes back a brief but enforceable mortgage. M(R) later sells Whiteacre to Beyer, who takes Whiteacre's title in a deed stating that O's mortgage "is assumed and Beyer expressly agrees to repay O the debt secured by this mortgage." Beyer makes several mortgage payments to O and then defaults on several more. O sues Beyer for the amount of the defaults. Beyer defends the suit, saying that because O was not a party to the assumption agreement, O cannot enforce it. Will this defense succeed?

Explanation

No, even though not a party to the assumption agreement, O is a named, third-party beneficiary of it and so, by the weight of authority, has a direct cause of action against an assuming purchaser such as Beyer. Restatement (Third) of Property, Mortgages, §5.1(b)(3)(i) (1997). If Beyer had conveyed to another assuming purchaser, O would have the same right against that person, and so on: O has a direct cause of action against all assuming purchasers, each of whom, when holding title, is the principal obligor for the debt, the prior purchasers being his surety liable in inverse order (last first, etc.) of holding Whiteacre's title. If just the word "assumes" were used, the answer would be no different, because "assumes" is generally taken to mean "assumes and agrees to pay" the debt.

Example 9

MR executes a brief but enforceable note and mortgage in favor of ME and then conveys to A1, who conveys in turn to A2, who in her turn conveys to A3—all grantees assuming the original debt to ME. If on a default in payment ME can proceed either against MR or directly against A3, what theories permit that last cause of action?

Explanation

There are two theories. (1) The derived right theory means that the mortgagee ME derives his right by stepping into the shoes of the mortgagor MR, who has the right to go against the assuming grantees for the repayment of the outstanding balance of the loan. The theory is one of subrogation: ME is subrogated to MR's right to seek repayment from the assignee. *See Somers v. Avant*, 254 S.E.2d 722 (Ga. App. Ct.), rev'd, 261 S.E.2d 334 (Ga. 1979). (2) The third-party beneficiary theory. *See Hafford v. Smith*, 369 S.W.2d 290 (Mo. App. Ct. 1963). Under this theory, the mortgagee is the third-party beneficiary of the series of assignments between the MR and the first assuming grantee or between subsequent assuming grantees.

Which theory is used makes a difference in three instances. Let's add some more facts to the basic problem.

a. When ME has not foreclosed. The derived right theory depends on the enforcement of the mortgagee's rights, so A1, A2, and A3 are not liable for breach of the assumption agreement before MR incurs liability for ME's losses. In most states that won't happen before ME forecloses against A3's land, fails to satisfy the rest of the debt suing A3 for it, and instead obtains judgment for the unsatisfied amount against MR, who then uses his subrogation rights and sues the assuming grantees in inverse order. This theory defines ME's loss not at the time of a default in the mortgage, but only after ME exercises his rights. However, when ME is recognized as a third-party beneficiary of the assumptions, he achieves that status in contract when the assumption agreement is effective and foreclosure is not a prerequisite for ME's enforcement of the assumptions; ME's rights "vest" earlier than under the other theory. The third-party beneficiary theory gives mortgagees options besides foreclosure and is used in a few derived right jurisdictions to make sure that the breaches of the assumption agreement can be fully compensated.

b. When A2 does not assume, but instead takes subject to. A2 is now liable to lose the land in foreclosure, but is not personally liable on the debt. So there is a break in the chain of assumptions, and the question arises why A2 would make A3 assume. A2 might act out of an excess of caution, or because the law of the jurisdiction was unclear, or because he was about to default and executed an extension agreement (extending the time for payment) with ME. All are possible explanations. Some courts decide that ME can reach all assuming grantees, giving free rein to the third-party beneficiary theory. Other courts ask why A3 would assume a debt for which his grantor A2 has no liability. The break prevents after-assuming or remote grantees from deriving rights and incurring liability from those before (i.e., A3 is not in privity of estate with earlier assuming grantees, and any agreement to the contrary had to have been made in ignorance of the law). Frederic Storke & Don Sears, Transfer of Mortgaged Property, 38 Cornell L.Q. 185, 198-199 (1952).

c. When MR modifies or releases A3 from her assumption. In derived right states, ME's rights in the assumption agreement are extinguished unless the mortgagee has relied on it by beginning foreclosure or in an action on the debt. MR is denying ME the option of going against A3 but is also increasing his own potential liability by narrowing ME's potential pool of defendants. In third-party states, the assumption agreement may not be altered without the mortgagee's consent, because an alteration in the agreement denies the mortgagee rights already vested. In other third-party states, a later vesting is required; that is, ME must also show reliance on the assumption agreement.

In *Zastrow v. Knight*, 229 N.W. 925 (S.D. 1929), an extension agreement was executed between the mortgagee ME and an after-assuming or remote grantee. Does MR have to join in or consent to the agreement? The answer is yes in derived right states. The enforcement mechanism for this is the discharge rule. This rule states that the mortgagor who does not consent to a ME-A3 extension agreement is discharged. At common law the discharge was a total one. The mortgagor could not be held liable for any amount of the debt in an action to enforce a deficiency judgment. The majority of cases today hold that he is only discharged in part—that is, to the extent of his prejudice, measured by the amount the secured real property fell in value during the extension period. The answer is no in third-party states: MR, standing as the surety for the remote assuming grantee, receives a benefit from the extension agreement. The benefit is time. The march of litigation, back up the chain of title through interim grantees, is stalled by the agreement, and MR is given more time to make good on his suretyship obligation. The extension agreement is a change in the surety relations between MR and A1, A2, and A3, so MR must consent to the change.

Although one jurisdiction may adopt one or both of the theories, it is best to see the two theories as equitable adjustments to the circumstances of the case. Here it might be well to summarize the law as does the Restatement (Third) of Property, Mortgages, §5.1(c) (1997): ME's right to enforce remote and later assumptions exists whether or not the MR has partially or completely released the defendant, whether or not the defendant is a remote assuming grantee, and whether or not the mortgagee has first foreclosed. This may oversimplify the case law, but simplification gives certainty to the law and benefits everyone.

Example 10

FNMA-FHLMC Uniform Mortgage covenants make any of MR's grantees personally liable for the debt. They take advantage of both derived right and third-party beneficiary theory. The former theory will make everyone in the mortgagor's chain of title liable up to the nonassuming grantee, while the latter will make everyone liable below that point. What about the nonassuming grantee himself?

Explanation

He is typically made liable by being put on constructive notice under the recording acts and because the mortgage covenants aim at abolishing the rules of suretyship that would protect him at common law. *See First Fed. Sav. & Loan Assn. of Gary v. Arena*, 406 N.E.2d 1279 (Ind. App. Ct. 1980), noted at 15 Ind. L. Rev. 365-366 (1982).

Example 11

Can an assuming grantee of the mortgagor use any defenses that the mortgagor would have used against the mortgagee?

Explanation

If the defenses are raised in the mortgagee's foreclosure action, the answer is yes in derived right states, but no in third-party beneficiary states. In suits on the note, the answer is no when the note is negotiable and the defense is personal to the mortgagor—that is, intent-based, such as the mortgagor's lack of capacity, mistake of fact, or lack of consideration; but if the defense is policy-based, it is preserved for use by assuming grantees. *See Dunning v. Leavitt*, 85 N.Y. 30 (1881).

Example 12

O and P execute a brief but enforceable contract of sale for Greenacre. The contract states in part that P promises to assume O's mortgage of Greenacre to Big Bank as mortgagee and perform all the covenants of this mortgage. At the closing of this contract, O delivers a deed that makes no mention of the contract's assumption provision. Is the assumption agreement enforceable thereafter?

Explanation

Yes. Although an assumption agreement is typically part of the deed by which an assuming purchaser takes title, it may also appear in a contract of sale or an installment sale contract, or be a separate agreement altogether. Wherever it appears, the assumption agreement does not pertain to the title to Greenacre and is a collateral agreement to which the doctrine of merger (of the contract into the deed) does not apply. So it survives the closing. Restatement (Third) of Property, Mortgages, §5.1, illustration 3, at 330 (1997).

TRANSFERS BY THE MORTGAGOR: DUE-ON-SALE CLAUSES

"If all or any part of the property or any interest in it is sold or transferred . . . Lender may, at its option, require immediate payment in full of all sums secured."

In the late 1960s and early 1970s, institutional mortgagees found themselves having to borrow in capital markets with volatile, rising interest rates. Their loan portfolios had low-yield loans, insufficient to generate new mortgage capital, so they had to "borrow short and lend long"—borrow with short-term notes and pay off these short-term notes with the income from their (long-term) mortgage portfolio. The difference between the banks' receiving low rates of interest on their portfolio loans and paying high rates of interest as borrowers eventually meant a capital shortage for residential and other types of mortgagors. Mortgagees needed to turn over the loans in their portfolio more quickly so that the long-term mortgage rate could keep pace with the short-term capital markets the mortgage lenders found themselves in.

The partial answer to their economic problem was the just-quoted due-on-sale clause; another answer was the adjustable-rate mortgage note, discussed in Chapter 11. In tandem, then, the lenders hoped to become profitable again. In the meanwhile, they often lived off closing and servicing fees.

The due-on-sale clause was routinely used by the early 1970s. Most courts upheld the clauses against arguments that the mortgagee was (1) no less secure with an assuming grantee paying the loan than it was with the original mortgagor and (2) that its use was unconscionable, a penalty, and/or a restraint on alienation; most further held that the mortgagee could have automatic enforcement of the clause and thus acceleration of the debt. *See Lake v. Equitable Sav. & Loan Assn.*, 674 P.2d 419 (Idaho 1983) (containing a string citation to many cases). An influential few held that enforcement was not automatic and that the mortgagee had to make a showing of insecurity as a precondition to enforcement and acceleration. *See Wellenkamp v. Bank of America*, 582 P.2d 970 (Cal. 1978).

In the mid-1970s, federal banking regulators proposed regulations validating this clause and preempting state statutes and cases to the contrary for owners of one- to four-unit dwellings that are owner-occupied. The Supreme Court upheld the regulations and gave them preemptive effect. *See Fidelity Fed. Sav. & Loan Assn. v. De La Cuesta*, 458 U.S. 141, 147 (1982). The same year the Congress enacted legislation validating the clause. 12 U.S.C. §1701j-3 (1987) (the 1982 Garn–St. Germain Depository Institutions Act). Only four jurisdictions opted out of the Act's provisions for lenders they chartered. The result of this decade-long activity was the clause at the beginning of this section.

Any *sale or transfer* triggers the clause, but Garn–St. Germain established some exceptions—some situations in which the lender was not permitted to accelerate the debt. These were taken from clauses permissible under the regulations and often reflected the situations in which the early versions of the covenant had been successfully challenged in court. For example, the creation of a junior lien was not a sale or transfer, because the priority of the senior lien was undisturbed. This exception provides for "the creation of a lien or other encumbrance subordinate to the lender's security instrument which does not relate to a transfer of occupancy in the property." This exception allowing for junior liens was the product of heavy lobbying by the mortgage lending industry.

Examples

Example 13

A homeowner receives a home equity loan secured by her home. When learning of this loan, may a mortgagee holding a senior mortgage exercise the due-on-sale covenant in that mortgage and accelerate the loan?

Explanation

No. The exception for junior liens applies. If the senior mortgage was secured by commercial property, say an apartment house with more than five dwelling units, the exception would not apply.

Similar exceptions in the Garn–St. Germain Act were enacted for a purchase money security agreement for household appliances, for various intrafamily transfers including transfers made as part of a divorce proceedings, for decedent estate transfers after the death of the mortgagor to members of his family, for leases of the property for three years or less, and for transfers into *inter vivos* trusts. 12 U.S.C. §1701j-3(d)(1)-(8).

The Garn–St. Germain Act has some interesting provisions. Following are the crucial ones.

> Notwithstanding any provision of the constitution or laws (including the judicial decisions) of any State to the contrary, a lender may . . . enter into or enforce a contract containing a due-on-sale clause with respect to a real property loan.

12 U.S.C. §1701j-3(b)(1). This is the section that provides the mortgagee's basic authority to enforce the clause. The well-advised mortgagee, using the statutory authority here, will standardize its language.

> Except as otherwise provided in [the exceptions discussed previously], the exercise by the lender of its option pursuant to such a clause shall be exclusively governed by the terms of a loan contract, and all rights and remedies of the lender and the borrower shall be fixed and governed by the contract.

12 U.S.C. §1701j-3(b)(2). This federal statute applies in states that found such clauses an unreasonable restraint on alienation, as well as states whose courts upheld the clauses' automatic acceleration provisions—and to the extent that some states used their contract law to invalidate the clause, Congress intended to override such invalidation. However, all contract rules, canons of construction, and defenses not related to invalidation continue to apply: Examples are rules relating to the unconscionability of contracts or to contracts of adhesion. Most importantly, to the extent that the clause's enforceability is "governed exclusively" by its terms, the lender need not show itself insecure after the transfer; and, assuming that insecurity is relevant at all after the Act's passage (a big question in itself), the mortgagor has, in most jurisdictions deciding the issue, the burden of proving that the lender is no less secure after a transfer. *See Weiman v. McHaffie*, 470 So. 2d 682 (Fla. 1985).

Is the mortgagee's authority a matter of federal common law or of federal courts applying state law? Is the statute in the spirit of *Erie v. Tompkins* or

Swift v. Tyson? The *De La Cuesta* opinion suggests that federal courts must apply state law. Even if federal courts are authorized in this statute to develop federal common law rules, it should not control the equity powers of those courts. For example, a federal court may hold that enforcement of a due-on-sale clause along with enforcement of a prepayment penalty is a penalty and that the lender cannot enforce both together. If the mortgagee accelerates the debt at his option and then deducts the prepayment penalty from the amount to be credited toward repayment of the debt, it obtains a double benefit from its own unilateral action. *See in re* LHD Realty Corp., 726 F.2d 327 (7th Cir. 1984) (once accelerated, a debt by definition cannot be prepaid because it has matured).

The acceleration feature of a due-on-sale clause is defined in this act as "a contract provision which authorizes a lender, at its option, to declare due and payable sums secured by the lender's security instrument if all or any part of the property, or an interest therein, securing the real property loan is sold or transferred with the lender's prior written consent." 12 U.S.C. §1701j-3(a)(1). But what if the clause drafted by the mortgagee were mandatory and automatic? According to the literal reading of the definition, such a clause is not authorized by the statute: The only authorized clause is an optional one, working an acceleration only at the option of the mortgagee. Its optionality implies that the acceleration is not self-executing but is a right that should be elected by the mortgagee, with an appropriate notice to the mortgagor. This notice, not express in the statute, has been implied from it. Moreover, the acceleration operates when "all or any part of the property, or an interest therein . . . is sold or transferred." When is that? Although equitable title is transferred when an executory contract of sale is signed, that "sale or transfer" will remain unknown to the mortgagee unless it traced every one of its borrowers executing a contract of sale. As a practical matter, mortgagees will not enforce the clause at the time a mortgagor executes an executory sales contract. Too many such contracts are never closed. As a result, enforcement is not worthwhile. Notice to the mortgagee of a "sale or transfer" by deed will come through the public records for real property. (A deed is always recordable; often contracts of sale are not.)

When accelerating a loan under a due-on-sale clause, "a lender is encouraged to permit an assumption of a real property loan at the existing contract rate or at a rate which is at or below the average between the contract and market rate. . . ." 12 U.S.C. §1701j-3(b)(3). Thus a mortgagee might condition approval of an assumption on changing a fixed-rate mortgage to the current market rate of interest, or to changing a fixed-rate mortgage into an adjustable-rate mortgage. Otherwise this provision, read literally, is merely precatory.

EXAMPLES

Examples

Example 14

What if a mortgagor with a due-on-sale clause in his mortgage sells a portion of a large parcel but retains the rest? The clause, as authorized in the act, provides that it operates on a sale of all or part of the secured property, so it literally applies. But if the mortgagor claims that the retained portion of the property is sufficient collateral for the outstanding debt, may the mortgagee still invoke the clause? Does the mortgagee have the burden of proving that it has been harmed by the sale?

Explanation

Courts are divided about the result here. The Garn–St. Germain Act provides that "the exercise [of the lenders' rights under the clause] shall be exclusively governed by the terms of the loan contract." Its terms permit enforcement. *See Frets v. Capital Fed. Sav. & Loan Ass'n*, 712 P.2d 1270 (Kan. 1986) ("It is acceptable for a savings and loan association to enforce the due-on-sale clause for the purpose of improving its position in the money market"). A lender's decision to exercise its due-on-sale rights may thus be portfolio-based as well as transaction-based. However, if state contract law controls, some courts conclude that the law of adhesion contracts, unconscionable conduct, and the duty of good faith require that the mortgagee may be enjoined from exercising its rights in this instance. Some courts further hold that Congress could not have intended the act to restrict judicial power, particularly equity powers—if it did, it acted beyond its authority and, as a matter of separation of powers, acted *ultra vires*.

Example 15

Is an installment land sale contract a "sale or transfer"?

Explanation

Courts have divided on this issue, too. Regulations issued under the Act applied to installment land sale contracts, but the title under such an arrangement stays with the vendor. So there is no sale or transfer *of the title*. On the other hand, the purchaser acquires an equity in the title and the act covers the sale or transfer of "any interest" in the secured property. This equitable interest has the priority of a junior lien. This means that one of the exceptions in the act might apply and prevent enforcement.

Example 16

A mortgagor with a standard due-on-sale clause in a first mortgage executes a second mortgage. The second mortgage is foreclosed. The first mortgagee accelerates the amount due on the first. May he do so?

Explanation

Yes. The exception for junior liens is not applicable, because the foreclosure itself is a sale or transfer, albeit involuntary, of the secured property. *See Unifirst Fed. Sav. & Loan Ass'n v. Tower Loan of Mississippi*, 524 So. 2d 290 (Miss. 1986).

Example 17

When the due-on-sale clause provides that the mortgagee may accelerate upon any sale or transfer but shall not "unreasonably withhold consent" to the sale or transfer, is the mortgagee entitled to raise the interest rate as a precondition to giving consent?

Explanation

The quoted language is intended to allow the mortgagee to evaluate the creditworthiness of the borrower in the proposed assumption agreement in order to determine whether the transferee is of equal or better creditworthiness. If the transferee's creditworthiness is just as good, then the mortgagee has the equivalent of the initial bargain and is not entitled to more. The quoted language is a partial waiver of the mortgagee's rights. The benefit of this clause can be waived by the mortgagee. *See Cooper v. Deseret Fed. Sav. & Loan Assn.*, 757 P.2d 483 (Utah App. Ct. 1988).

Example 18

May an accelerating mortgagee also enforce a prepayment charge when the mortgagor pays the debt?

Explanation

No. *See Rodgers v. Rainier Natl. Bank*, 757 P.2d 976 (Wash. 1988). It is unfair to have the mortgagee benefit from his own unilateral decision to accelerate. The regulations of secondary market purchasers like Fannie Mae and Freddie Mac reach the same conclusion. Thus a mortgagee, particularly in a residential loan setting, will have to elect between enforcing any prepayment charge and accelerating the debt. Used in tandem, these two clauses can result in unfairness to the mortgagor.

The Garn–St. Germain Act does not say that it applies to commercial mortgage loans. But it doesn't say it doesn't, so it does—not impeccable logic in all situations, but good enough here. *McCausland v. Bankers Life Ins. Co. of Nebraska*, 757 P.2d 941, 81 A.L.R.4th 411 (Wash. 1988).

Some other exceptions to the reach of a due-on-sale clause otherwise made effective by the Act have been judicially created. For example, when a property is transferred to a trust of which the mortgagor is a beneficiary, there may be transfer, but the transfer is the mortgagor's creation of a personal property interest in the property. It is not a transfer of title to one beyond the mortgagor's direction and control; hence, arguably the due-on-sale clause is not breached. A second example might be a conveyance to a partnership in which the mortgagor has an interest: Arguably the mortgagor is both transferor and transferee here; the mortgagee is no less secure after such a conveyance, and so there is no transfer that breaches the clause. A third example might involve a sale and leaseback transaction in which the mortgagor conveys title to a transferee, who then leases the property back to the mortgagor, who in turn has an option to repurchase it. There is a transfer of title here, although this transaction might be the functional equivalent of a mortgage.

TRANSFERS BY THE MORTGAGEE

The transfer of a mortgage (meaning the mortgage lien) alone is a nullity. This is so because the express purpose of the lien is to serve as security for the accompanying note. The note is never transferred separately. When it is transferred, the mortgage follows it, willy-nilly, even in the absence of an express assignment. As the common law lawyers used to say, the note and the mortgage live and die together.

However, although no express assignment of the mortgage is necessary for it to follow the note when assigned, mortgage assignments are usually in writing. This practice is a matter of prudence on the part of the assignee, who seeks the writing to record it so as to achieve protection against subsequent bona fide assignees. In most states, the assignment of a mortgage is a recordable document, and, on the assignee's part, the practice is to record it. Recording is expensive, however, so assignments may not be recorded until after several assignments, when the mortgage and note come to rest in the secondary mortgage market. Without an assignment in the hands of a foreclosing party, there is no right to foreclose. *See Fleet Natl. Bank v. Nazareth*, 818 A.2d 69 (Conn. App. Ct. 2003). Since the mid-1990s, a book entry system of data retrieval (the Mortgage Electronic Recording System—MERS) has been used by major participants in the secondary market. Users can change the book entry with each assignment, while the publicly recorded record remains the same: MERS is typically named in the mortgage as "mortgagee solely as nominee of lender."

After an assignment, the mortgagor will want to assure himself that he is making payments on the note to the right party. If the note is nonnegotiable, he can pay the mortgagee any time prior to the time he has actual notice of the assignment. The assignee's recording does not affect the mortgagor; he need not check the record before each payment. In old cases, he does have a duty to make the mortgagee show him the note when making payment and a duty of inquiry if the note was not produced. Such a duty worked well for the one-payment, common law mortgage but is ill adapted to the many, level payments due in the modern amortized mortgage transaction. This duty persists until the final payment is made.

Examples

Example 19

A mortgage is transferred and registered in MERS. The mortgagor defaults and the transferee seeks foreclosure, presenting an affidavit that it is the holder of the mortgage note. The mortgagor objects. Will his objection succeed?

Explanation

Courts split on this issue. The mortgagee commencing foreclosure must produce the note, as only the note's holder is entitled to foreclosure. The creation of MERS does not change this requirement, but naming MERS as the lender's nominee might make MERS the initial mortgagee's agent so that MERS and the foreclosing transferee might then have the burden of proving that the transferee plaintiff holds a valid assignment.

THE TRANSFER, NEGOTIATION, AND ASSIGNMENT OF NOTES

The law that applies to transfers of notes involves two bodies of law separately governing their assignability and negotiability. Notes are either negotiable or nonnegotiable. Negotiability is governed by the Uniform Commercial Code (UCC), §3-104(a). Almost all the cases concerning Fannie Mae and Freddie Mac uniform residential notes have found those notes negotiable. If the note is negotiable, the mortgagor's duty is to demand production of the note before making any payment, and the mortgagor who does not runs the risk of having to pay twice—once to the mortgagee and again to any valid transferee of the note. If the wrong person is paid, the mortgagor will find himself paying PETER—the "party entitled to the economic return" on the note, including the amortized payments, any fees, prepayments, and the proceeds of a foreclosure. The mortgagor is presumed to know the legal effect of what he signed and, when he executes a negotiable note, is presumed to know that the mortgagee will use the authority to transfer or "assign" given in the note. Because of the practice of transferring residential mortgages into the secondary market, the elements of a valid assignment are crucial to the market participants and investors claiming to be PETER as well as to parties later asserting their right to foreclose. The prior example illustrates this point. In foreclosure, such an "assignment" requires a negotiable note's physical delivery (a requirement taken from the UCC's Article 9) into the possession of the party entitled to enforce it, aka PETE—the party entitled to enforce. The mortgagor as a defendant in foreclosure is presumed to know that PETE is bringing suit, and PETE, if challenged, must be prepared to show that he is in physical possession of the note.

Let's not forget about PETER, though. To receive the ongoing economic return on the note, it must have been either delivered or assigned to him. For purposes of foreclosure, however, it is PETE that counts: He is only party who can release or discharge the note—and because he alone can make a final settlement of the debt, he can also modify the note, accept a short sale or a deed in lieu of the note's payment, or otherwise settle the debt. So he is the *only* party entitled to bring foreclosure (PETE).

So why distinguish between PETER and PETE? PETER has ownership rights flowing from the note. Proving PETER status is an issue between initial mortgagees, secondary market investors, and loan servicers. PETER can either prove that the note was delivered to him or that he holds a valid assignment of it. Settling such issues is important to the smooth operation of the secondary market, and so is easier, as an evidentiary matter, with written assignments and properly endorsed notes. Here a separate, recordable, document or written assignment is useful. However, once a decree in foreclosure is final, any intervening transfer or assignment of the note is of no consequence. Why? Because if the mortgage instrument lives and dies with the note, the defendant in foreclosure need only be concerned with determining whether it is PETE bringing suit. To this defendant, PETER status is then irrelevant: PETE need not have an endorsed note, or a written assignment, or prove that a chain of written assignments leads to him; PETE's possession of the note is a sufficient basis for bringing suit.[1]

Notes used in commercial transactions are more often found nonnegotiable; they thus require close analysis to determine the issue of negotiability.

After any transfer or assignment, the mortgagor may want to assert the same defenses that he has against the mortgagee against the assignee as well. Whether he can depends on two issues: first, whether the note is negotiable, and second, whether the assignee is a "holder in due course." To take free of a mortgagor's defenses, the assignee must win on both issues. He must both (1) hold a negotiable note and (2) be a holder in due course. *See First Maryland*

1. An exception to the delivery requirement is typically made for destroyed or lost notes: There an affidavit is substituted for possession, although when used, the person filing the affidavit may have to give some form of indemnity to compensate the person asked to pay twice.

Fin. Servs. Corp. v. District-Realty Title Ins. Corp., 548 A.2d 787 (D.C. App. 1988). Let's now address each issue.

The negotiable note Negotiability is the authority to transfer a note for value by delivery, with or without endorsement. Thus negotiability is a type of transferability expressed in a note. A note payable "to ME or to his order" renders the note negotiable. Any check in your checkbook will have similar language just in front of the payee's name. That language makes the check negotiable, meaning it can be endorsed over to another. A note providing that "this note may be assigned or transferred to any person" is also negotiable (this language is often used in plain language notes); it is the equivalent of the "or order" phrase in common use. Similarly, a note with covenants in it requiring the mortgagor/debtor to maintain the premises, not commit waste, or insure the premises, remains negotiable. "The negotiability of an instrument is not affected by . . . a promise or power to maintain or protect collateral." UCC §3-112(1)(c). Such covenants do not affect the debtor's unconditional promise to pay the debt. Neither would a provision that "this note is secured by a mortgage executed contemporaneously with it." UCC §3-105(1)(e) ("A promise or order otherwise unconditional is not made conditional by the fact that the instrument . . . states that it is secured, whether by mortgage, reservation of title, or otherwise.") On the other hand, language in the note like "the debtor hereby grants a security interest in the property" would destroy negotiability. UCC §3-112(1). So the many covenants that a note might contain may affect the collateral so long as they do not refer to the actual transfer of a mortgage lien.

Examples

Example 20

A note provides that it is enforceable only through the mortgage executed contemporaneously with it. What is the effect of this language?

Explanation

This is so-called nonrecourse language. The mortgagee is to have no recourse against the assets (other than the secured real property) of the debtor. It does not destroy the note's negotiability. A reference to assets of the debtor does not affect an otherwise unconditional promise to pay nor is it the transfer of a lien.

Example 21

The language in the note referred to in the previous example is followed by the sentence: "The terms of said mortgage are by this reference made a part hereof." What is the effect of this addition?

Explanation

It is fatal to negotiability. *Holly Hill Acres, Ltd. v. Charter Bank of Gainesville*, 314 So. 2d 209 (Fla. App. Ct. 1975). "A promise or order is not unconditional if the instrument . . . states that it is subject to or governed by any other agreement." UCC §3-105(2).

Example 22

A note provides for a confession of judgment against the debtor anytime the noteholder selects an attorney for the debtor and directs that attorney to confess judgment. What is the effect of this provision?

Explanation

UCC §3-112(1)(c) authorizes a confession of judgment and that authorization encompasses selecting an attorney, a crucial step in the confession itself. Yet this note provision goes further, permitting a confession of judgment at "any time," even before the maturity of the debt, giving rise to the possibility that the note might be in circulation after its enforcement. This is fatal to negotiability: How would its assignee know? A confession of judgment waives the same defenses that a holder in due course takes free of and is distinguishable from a fatal waiver of all defenses: A waiver that is too broad destroys negotiability because the holder is left pondering what defenses were involved. *See Geiger Fin. Co. v. Graham*, 182 S.E.2d 521 (Ga. App. Ct. 1971). An early opinion found nonnegotiable a note containing both a confession of judgment and a waiver of the *maker's* right to have property appraised before it could be sold to satisfy the note. *See Overton v. Tyler*, 3 Pa. 346, 347 (1846) (Gibson, C.J., stating that "a negotiable bill or note is a courier without luggage").

Example 23

A note provision permits the acceleration of the debt or its prepayment upon any default in its terms of repayment. Does such a provision affect negotiability?

Explanation

No, it would not affect negotiability. UCC §3-105(1)(c). Provisions that affect the maturity date of the debt do not *per se* destroy the unconditionality of the promise to pay but merely change the payment day.

By now you will have noticed that the code glorifies negotiability. As Grant Gilmore so nicely said, it is "negotiability *in excelsis*." Formalism and the Law of Negotiable Instruments, 13 Creighton L. Rev. 441, 461 (1979).

Example 24

MR executes in favor of ME a brief but enforceable mortgage accompanied by a series of six notes, one of which is endorsed and assigned in writing to A, another to B, a third to C, and all of which are secured by the mortgage and are payable "to ME or order." A default occurs in all three notes, and the security of the mortgage is insufficient to cover the debts in the three notes. How should A, B, and C share the proceeds of any foreclosure? If the notes were endorsed "to the bearer," would your analysis of the sharing arrangement change?

Explanation

The courts would either use a first-in-time rule, satisfying them in the order of assignment, or else permit all the holders—ME, A, B, and C—to share equally in the proceeds of the sale of the security. The latter is the preferred view. Thus, if the notes are silent on the issue of priority, the priority of each note is equal. However, even where such equality is the general rule, the endorsement of each note is itself a guarantee of payment by the original ME, so the endorsement provides a partial solution to the priority question—that is, the endorsing original mortgagee goes last. If ME retains any of the notes, they are repaid after the ones endorsed and assigned. In addition, when the notes are assigned "to bearer," their satisfaction is premised on an implied warranty of repayment: ME is then estopped to deny repayment and cannot compete with the assignees; they must be paid first for this reason as well. If A, B, and C all execute an agreement in which each agrees to share the loan proceeds and each is assigned a certain percentage of those proceeds, that agreement will control the common law rule in the applicable jurisdiction. Absent the agreement, the four would share pro rata and equally. Because the agreement is an opportunity to negotiate over and sort out the status of ME as opposed to the assignees. No public policy forbids such tailoring of the common law.

Holder in due course (HDC) The second issue involved in determining whether the assignee can take free of the mortgagor's defenses is the status of the assignee. The assignee must show himself to be a holder in due course—one who takes the note for value, in good faith, and without notice that the note has been dishonored or is subject to a claim or defense to it by any person. A holder in due course is the term for the person whom you have met in other contexts as a bona fide purchaser.

If the note is negotiable and if its holder is a holder in due course, then the assignee takes free of personal defenses that the mortgagor has against the mortgagee. Examples are a failure of consideration, breach of a covenant, unconscionable conduct, or fraud. However, even a holder in due course takes the note subject to real defenses, such as a lack of capacity to contract due to infancy or mental incompetency, an illegal purpose in the contract, or an execution of the contract under duress. Real defenses are listed in UCC §3-305(2). The law develops the same sort of list when distinguishing between void and voidable deeds. Personal defenses relate to the terms of the original transaction between the mortgagor and mortgagee, but real defenses relate to the status of the parties to it.

Real defenses are subjected to a further scrutiny and classified in one of two ways—as either patent or latent. A patent defense is asserted by the mortgagor. A latent defense is asserted by a third party, as when, for example, the marriage of the mortgagor gives rise to a marital right that the spouse can assert. An assignee (whether or not he is a holder in due course) takes free of such a right.

An assignee will not be a holder in due course when he is too closely connected to the mortgagee. The close connection may be shown by the common use of forms by the mortgagee and the assignee, a corporate parent-subsidiary relationship, or a pattern of assignments by the mortgagee. An additional basis for denying an assignee rights as a holder in due course occurs when a statute limits this status. In jurisdictions adopting the Uniform Consumer Credit Code, for example, home improvement notes and mortgages cannot be a basis for holding in due course and taking free of defenses about the adequacy of the work. Likewise, the Federal Trade Commission by regulation has declared that it is an unfair trade practice for a home improver or service contractor to agree to provide and finance home improvements or services without including a covenant in the contract to the effect that its holder is subject to all defenses that the debtor would otherwise have; this effectively abolishes the HDC doctrine for these contracts. *See* 16 C.F.R. §433.2 (promulgated in 1986). However, this regulation does not apply to arm's-length, third-party financing for such improvements or services. In addition, for certain high-cost and predatory mortgage notes, the doctrine is abolished by other federal and state statutes. 15 U.S.C. §1641(d) (enacted in 1994) (abolishing the doctrine when an assignee can determine that the predatory lending statute applies from reading the face of the note or mortgage). Finally, the Truth in Lending Act (TILA) abolishes the doctrine for violations of its own provisions apparent on the TILA disclosure statement. 15 U.S.C. §1641(a).

Examples

EXAMPLES

Example 25

MR executes a brief but enforceable note and mortgage on Blackacre in favor of ME, who records and assigns to AE in writing. AE records. MR then conveys Blackacre to GE for value. State the title as between AE and GE. This explanation can be diagrammed as follows:

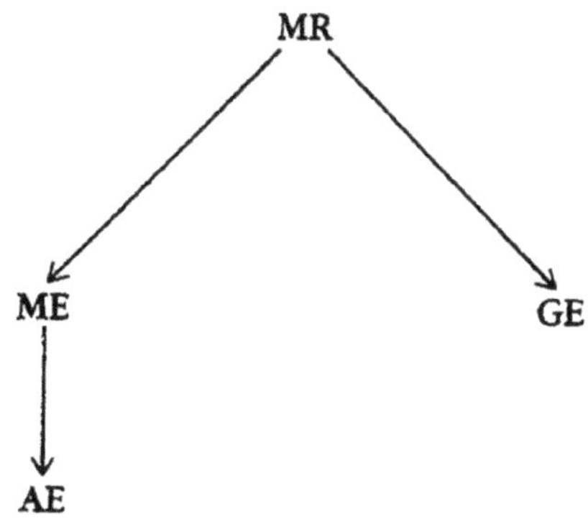

Explanation

As to the state of the title: If the note is negotiable and the AE is a holder in due course, AE's rights attach to GE's title. The recordings are irrelevant, and the rules of negotiability control. If the note is negotiable but the assignee is not a holder in due course, judgment still goes for the assignee because of the constructive notice given by the recording act.

Example 26

Assume the facts of the previous problem. What if MR tenders payment of the note, but ME and AE refuse it? Is the lien of the mortgage discharged?

Explanation

Yes. The mere tender of payment, when refused by the mortgagee, discharges the mortgage lien but not the underlying debt. *See Kortright v. Cady*, 21 N.Y. 343, 345 (1860).

Example 27

Assume the facts diagrammed in Example 25, except that the mortgagee ME assigns twice: once, as before, to AE, who records, and then later to AEE. What is the state and title between the two assignees, AE and AEE?

Explanation

If the note is nonnegotiable, then the recording act priorities control. In this event, AE, having recorded, provides constructive notice to any later assignee like AEE. If the note is negotiable, the law of negotiable instruments controls, and the holder in due course prevails.

Today the most common assignment of the residential mortgage is made by the original mortgagee who assigns or sells the loan with its documentation to an assignee-purchaser in the national secondary mortgage market.

The mortgagee here remains the servicer of the loan and, more important, the agent of the assignee-purchaser. The presence of this agency makes the possibility that the mortgagor will face a double payment less likely.

Example 28

Curtis conveys Blackacre to Armstrong, who records. Armstrong mortgages his interest back to Curtis, who records the mortgage. Curtis assigned his mortgage to the plaintiff, who does not record the assignment. Armstrong then conveys Blackacre to Curtis, who records, and then Curtis conveys to the defendant, who records. Plaintiff seeks to impose his lien on the defendant's title. Can he? The defendant cannot claim the protection of any type of recording act. What arguments are left to the defendant in a dispute with the plaintiff over priority of title to Blackacre?

Explanation

Defendant can argue that when Armstrong conveyed by deed to Curtis, the same person held both the mortgage and the deed (so far as the defendant can tell) and that the mortgagee's interest merged with that in the deed, giving Curtis the full, unencumbered fee simple absolute. Thus the mortgage is extinguished under the merger doctrine. In addition, some courts would permit the defendant to assume, when examining his abstract of title, that the deed was given in lieu of foreclosure and work a merger on that basis, giving broad effect to the record.

However, many courts would reject a merger argument and insist that the defendant in *Curtis* has a further duty of inquiry of his grantor. But why wouldn't a grantor like Curtis not say that the mortgage and note are destroyed or lost? Could the defendant-grantee trust the results of his inquiry? On that account, perhaps no duty of inquiry should be imposed. *See Curtis v. Moore*, 46 N.E. 168 (N.Y. 1897) (giving judgment for the plaintiff, ruling that the innocent payment by a mortgagor of a negotiable note, to an assignor of the note, is ineffective after the assignment is made, even though the assignment is recordable—as in most states it is—but not recorded by the assignee). The *Curtis* rule is a traditional one, so the mortgagor should demand to see the note when paying, even if he pays each month, and particularly when making the last payment and demanding a release of the lien. However, should not the defendant purchaser be able to rely on the state of the record? Rules governing negotiability are here getting in the way of the goal of certainty in the law.

Example 29

Mortgagor executes a mortgage note and lien in exchange for a loan extended to him in a transaction in which the loan originator is borrowing the capital for the loan with short-term financing. Traditional underwriting rules for the loan are not observed, the mortgagor does not have income sufficient to afford the repayment schedule established, and the originator assigns the mortgage promptly after closing the loan transaction. The loan is eventually "sold" to a trustee that holds it along with similar loans, in trust for investors in secondary mortgage market bonds. When the mortgage goes into default, the trustee sues in foreclosure. The mortgagor objects to the foreclosure, asserting defenses to the note's enforcement both real and personal. Will these defenses succeed?

Explanation

Probably not to the extent of halting the foreclosure. The fraud, misrepresentations, and conduct of the originator give rise only to personal defenses. This example is a typical secondary market transaction prevalent during the first decade of the twenty-first century. Unprofessionally underwritten in anticipation of mortgage brokerage fees and likely to default, they are nonetheless protected by the highly complicated tenets of the HDC doctrine when asserted by the trustee and the investors. It may be that the investors did not do enough diligence to become HDCs when the originator routinely and on a mass market basis passed along this and similar mortgages. It may be that there were warranties and representations made about the quality of the loans. Expensive litigation will be required to sort out these issues.

A legislative solution to the myriad, unresolved (as of this writing) issues of this example would be to amend Article 3 to exempt mortgage notes from its reach and provide that they are not negotiable.

FINAL PAYMENT RULE

Even if the note is pledged or assigned, and regardless of whether the mortgagee is an individual, a corporation, or some other legal entity, and whether the note and mortgage are for a residential or a commercial transaction, only one copy of the note should be executed by the borrower/mortgagor, in blue ink only, to make copying difficult when the print on the note is black. Why? Because the borrower wants to prevent double assignments and wants the note back when the final payment on the loan is made.

Once the note is delivered to an assignee, as previously discussed, the traditional common law rule was that the borrower who makes payment to any person other than the note's possessor does so at her own risk. What's the risk? The borrower may be paying someone other than the person then owning the note. Any payment made to the nonpossessor is not binding on the possessor/assignee. The rationale for this payment rule is that (1) it is the mortgagor's (imputed) negligence not to ask to see the note when the payment is made, and (2) under the holder in due course doctrine, the assignee takes free of personal defenses that the borrower would have against the mortgagee, in this instance the defense that the payment has already been made.

State and federal statutes qualify the effect of these rules for monthly payments—stipulating that the borrower is to receive notice of the assignment and so forth—but leave the traditional common law rule in effect for the final payment: Then the rule is that the final payment should not be made to someone who cannot deliver the note back to the lender. In a transaction in which the mortgagee is a large bank, this is a cumbersome rule—the note may be held in a distant vault or archive, and it may take weeks to recover. Nonetheless, the final payment rule is still the default rule, so the borrower should act in light of it.

Some state legislatures have reacted to this situation by enacting statutes extinguishing all mortgage-secured debts a certain number of years after their final payment date. *Pro-Max Corp. v. Feenstra*, 16 P.3d 1074 (Nev. 2000) (upholding a ten-year-from-due-date statute).

Once the note is paid, the well-nigh universal rule is, absent any statute on the subject, the mortgage is *functus officio*; it is a nullity, cannot be made to stand for any new debt, and cannot be reissued, recirculated, or otherwise used by the mortgagee. The payment of the debt divests the mortgagee of the lien or title transferred to it with the creation of the mortgage. The mortgage lives and dies with the note and the debt, and survives no longer than they do.

CHAPTER 17

Pre-Foreclosure Remedies

AN ASSIGNMENT OF RENTS

When a mortgage secures a commercial building and the mortgagor depends on its rents to repay the debt, when foreclosure is a slow and cumbersome remedy, when the mortgagor filed for bankruptcy to delay foreclosure, or when judicial foreclosure is mandatory, then an assignment of rents in the mortgage (essentially a mortgage on the rents often contained in a covenant in the mortgage—but sometimes in a separate document) is important to a mortgagee. From the mortgagee's perspective, the need for the assignment arises from the common law rule that the right to rents follows the right to possession. *See Town Ctr. Flats, LLC v. ECP Commer. II LLC*, 855 F.3d 721, 724 (6th Cir. 2017). With such an assignment, the mortgagee, without going into possession, may with notice to the tenants collect the rents and apply them to the outstanding debt. It is intended to prevent a mortgagor short on cash from stiffing the mortgagee, paying late, or milking the property. Its use has been widespread since the 1990s, when mezzanine lending replaced junior liens and senior mortgagees looked for further assurances of repayment.

The assignment needs to be effective "before the ink is dry" on the mortgage. An assignment of rents is a document delivering (1) the right to possess the rents—a "present, absolute, irrevocable, and unconditional" transfer of the rents, with (2) the mortgagor retaining a license to collect rents until a default. *See Freedman's Sav. & Tr. Co. v. Shepherd*, 127 U.S. 494, 502-503 (1888) (Harlan, J., approving an absolute assignment). The rationale for the license is in part to make clear to tenants that the mortgagee is not in possession and has not taken over the mortgagor's reversion and has not ousted him for all purposes.[1] To do so would give the junior interests the right to either attorn or vacate, and because most leases will be junior to the mortgagee's lien, the prospect of tenants vacating a property is not a happy one. Further, in many senior mortgage documents, the senior mortgagee often insists that a future, junior mortgagee become, by subordination or otherwise, junior to all lessees. This is a way of assuring itself that a junior mortgagee, either foreclosing or in possession, will not give lessees an opportunity to vacate their premises. The mortgagor's license to collect the rents (3) is conditioned on the mortgagor not being in default under the mortgage's covenants. The license (as distinct from the assignment itself) is thus revocable upon a condition subsequent (the default). The condition subsequent typically is (4) automatically triggered upon default, regardless of the mortgagee's taking possession, petitioning for the appointment of a receiver, or obtaining a judicial order sequestering the rents. Overall, the assignment of rents is not additional security for the mortgage. Even when the assignment states that it is granted by the mortgagor "as security" or is "contingent upon default," those words do not foreclose a transfer of absolute ownership of the rents or the transfer of a "contingent present interest" in them effective upon execution of the assignment. An assignment is routinely recorded in the land records. It is also typically effective upon delivery by the assignee to a tenant of a notice of mortgagor's default and a copy of the assignment.

A substantial majority of states enforce an assignment of rents according to its terms when it is executed contemporaneously with or is contained in the mortgage. Depending on whether they are lien or title mortgage jurisdictions, jurisdictions differ on when the assignment is effective between the parties and "perfected" against third parties (such as the tenants). Contemporaneous or early effectiveness is possible in title states, while effectiveness is postponed in lien states. For bankruptcy purposes, effectiveness and perfection are achieved when the assignment is filed for record. 11 U.S.C. §552(b). Earlier cases held that it was unperfected in lien states until rents were actually collected, foreclosure started, or possession taken—but in many jurisdictions those cases have given way to a rule of absolute assignment, meaning that it is in effect a sale of the rents, or the creation of a security lien in them, giving rise to the rule that it is in effect a title theory mortgage of them. In some states, the assignment is rendered absolute by statute or effective upon recording by the adoption of a provision from the Uniform Assignments of Rents Act, which also makes later

1. If it fails as an assignment for any reason, then it is sometimes treated as a pledge (an offer of property as security for a debt) or a bailment of rents, with (for both) delivery of possession necessary to complete it, but then giving possession for a limited purpose and not involving a transfer of the mortgagor's title or interest.

activation or enforcement possible by a notice to either the mortgagor or the tenants. As a practical matter, the assignment is effective when the mortgagee takes some affirmative action to collect the rents, even if it is only a notice to the mortgagor and tenants that it intends to do so. A demand for the rents, even when refused, will typically suffice.

A mortgage often, after the granting clause, will include language such as "together with all . . . rights, appurtenances, and rents." This is insufficient to assign the right to collect rents, particularly in a lien state where local law does not permit the mortgagee to have possession or rents before a default in repayment on affirmative attempt at collections.

Examples

Example 1

ME holds a mortgage containing an assignment of rents covenant and secured by MR's racetrack. Are the gate proceeds subject to the assignment?

Explanation

No. There are many cases holding that the proceeds are not rent, as they do not give the payor the right to occupy any predefined space within the track enclosure or in the stands: Instead, they provide a license related to the activities offered at the track akin to what tickets to the theater or golf course fees provide—a type of entertainment. The Restatement of Property (Third), Mortgages, §4.2 (1997), however, goes further and includes the proceeds of licenses as rents, reasoning that an all-inclusive definition will provide the law with needed certainty. The traditional rule remains that "rents" for purposes of an assignment, refers to lease proceeds that are paid primarily for the right to possess, occupy, and use real property.

Example 2

If an assignment is activated or otherwise enforced, MR refuses to turn the post-default rents over to the mortgagee. ME sues MR for waste. In this suit, what result, and why?

Explanation

Judgment for ME. After activation or other enforcement, it is a waste for a mortgagor to withhold or refuse to turn over the rents to the mortgagee. The measure of damages is the rents that would otherwise have been collected but not applied to the mortgage debt. This is not a suit for waste involving the property itself, so the ME need not show that it is insecure in order to bring the action.

Example 3

Why might a mortgagee prefer that an assignment of rents be in a separate document instead of in a mortgage covenant?

Explanation

A separate document might highlight it for the mortgagor and later persuade a court to enforce it more readily by encouraging the court to construe it as a stand-alone document not collateral to the mortgage. It can set out notice procedures for the mortgagor and tenants, procedures for paying rent, and even require that the mortgagor execute letters to tenants rerouting the rents to the mortgagee. Finally, it permits separate recording to provide notice to third parties. Following is such a document, given the form of a deed—a form that should provide you with a way to think about what should be included.

Sometimes but not typically, commercial mortgage covenants contain "lockbox provisions," drafted to work in tandem with an assignment of rents. A lockbox is a mortgagee-controlled bank account, into which rents are deposited by tenants. A "springing" lockbox is established for use when a mortgagor defaults by not repaying the loan as scheduled. That is, it is effective—or "springs" into existence upon default in repayment or another triggering event, such as the debt service coverage ratio falling or a signature lease on the property expiring.

Lockboxes may also be required of mortgagors routinely, regardless of whether the mortgage is in default. A "soft" box is a bank account into which rents are routinely deposited by tenants and subsequently released or "swept" to the mortgagor, or remain in the account until its balance equals the debt service due, after which the excess funds are swept to the mortgagor. Another version of a lockbox is a "hard" lockbox. Here the funds on account are disbursed to the mortgagor submitting vouchers to the mortgagee requesting the release of funds.

Example 4

Do you see why mortgagors resist the creation of lockboxes and settle for an assignment of rents?

Explanation

First, setup and maintenance fees for the lockbox account are paid by the mortgagor. Second, no matter the type of lockbox, it might create cash flow problems for mortgagors. If the mortgage payment is due on the sixth of each month, the rents will have to be received on the first in order to permit the bank to clear the funds for release. Moreover, the timing of rental receipts and debt service payments will have to be coordinated with the mortgagor's need for cash for maintenance and repairs to the secured property. Thus, from the mortgagor's perspective, a springing lockbox is the least objectionable.

ASSIGNMENT OF RENTS AND REVENUES

As consideration for the debt evidenced by the Note executed along with this assignment, ________ (Borrower) absolutely and unconditionally assigns and transfers to ________ (Lender), all rents and revenues of the Property securing that Note, including those rents and revenues now due or to become due by virtue of any lease or other agreement for the occupancy or use of all or any part of the Property, regardless of to whom they are payable. It is the intention of Borrower and Lender that this assignment be absolute, not an assignment for lien security only. This assignment binds its parties and their successors and assigns and is made for the Property secured by a Mortgage, executed simultaneously with it and the Note and describing the property as follows: ________.

This assignment is made together with the following: Borrower hereby authorizes Lender to collect said rents and revenues and directs each tenant of the Property to pay such rents to Lender, provided that prior to Lender's written notice to Borrower of the latter's breach of any covenant in the Mortgage, Borrower shall collect and receive all rents and revenues of the Property as trustee for Lender and Borrower, applying them to the sums secured by the Mortgage in the order described therein, with the balance, until such breach occurs, to the account of Borrower.

Upon a breach of any covenant in the Mortgage, Lender shall give written notice thereof to Borrower and then, without Lender's having to enter and take possession of the Property in person, by agent or by a court-appointed receiver, Lender shall be entitled to possession of such rents and revenues. This notice shall reference Lender's exercise of its rights under this assignment and its termination of authorization of Borrower's right to collect rents and revenues. Upon delivery of such notice, Lender shall make written demand that each tenant of the Property make such rents and revenues payable to and pay same to Lender.

Borrower warrants and covenants that (1) Borrower has not executed any prior rents and revenues assignment and has not made or done any agreement or act which would prevent Lender from exercising its rights under this assignment, (2) there is no anticipation or prepayment of any rents or revenues for more than one month prior to their due dates and Borrower will not hereafter collect or accept payment of any such rents or revenues more than one month prior to their due dates. Borrower also warrants that all leases pertaining to the Property are in a form previously submitted to the Lender for approval.

Executed this day _________ of _________, 20_________,

____

Borrower

[Borrower's Acknowledgment attached.]

____

Lender

Example 5

Would it be prudent to include the following in this document? "Borrower further covenants that Borrower will execute and deliver to Lender such further assignments of rents and revenues of the Property as Lender may from time to time request."

Explanation

Maybe not, because, depending on applicable state law, this might indicate that the assignment is conditional, not absolute, and so might be treated as an executory contract for Bankruptcy Code purposes.

Example 6

What other procedures might reinforce a lender's concern to have the assignment construed independently of the mortgage?

Explanation

A provision for tenants' paying their rents into a "lockbox," with distributions from the box to the mortgagee/lender for mortgage payments and to the mortgagor/borrower for the residue.

Example 7

ME holds a mortgage securing a commercial office building. The mortgage contains an assignment of rents covenant. The signature tenant in the building is behind in its rent payments. After revoking the mortgagor's license to collect rents, may ME recover this tenant's back rent?

Explanation

No. The right to the rents is just that: It is transfer of title to the rents, not the right to modify, extend, terminate, or enforce the lease. Moreover, the mortgagee doesn't want management control over the property. That control might bring liabilities in its wake—the liabilities of a mortgagee in possession.

In order to collect accrued but unpaid rents, the mortgagee needs an assignment of leases for the secured property. Like an assignment of rents, an assignment of leases is set up as would be an assignment of rents, as an "absolute, present, and unconditional" transfer of the rents. It is distinct from the assignment of rents.

MORTGAGEE IN POSSESSION

Today, when a mortgage document is silent about the mortgagee's right to possession, the mortgagee still has the right to bring a cause of action in waste to prevent the physical deterioration of the secured property. The typical mortgage covenant states that the mortgage "will not permit the property to deteriorate or commit waste" thereon. The mortgagee may, as a result of a judgment in this action, gain the right to take possession of the property to the extent necessary to prevent waste.

A mortgagee in title states is entitled in theory to possession to secure the debt after the mortgage is executed; in other states, this right arises upon default. *See 140 Reservoir Ave. v. Sepe Investments*, 941 A.2d 805, 811 (R.I. 2007). However, in lien states, it arises only after foreclosure. Because most states today regard themselves as lien jurisdictions, mortgage covenants typically provide the mortgagee with an express right to have a receiver appointed or to take possession upon default. *See Taylor v. Brennan*, 621 S.W.2d 592 (Tex. 1981), discussed at 60 S.M.U. L. Rev. 579, 590 (2007). The Restatement of Property (Third), Mortgages, §4.1 (1997) embraces the lien theory of mortgages on this issue.

A mortgagee might obtain possession by using the applicable summary procedure statute: It typically is available when the plaintiff in the action is one "entitled to possession" as might a mortgagee be after a default on the mortgage.[1] The mortgagee's interest in its right to possession may be keenest in the earlier years of the typical mortgage when the debt to equity ratio is highest. No matter when this right arises, however, few mortgagees wish to go into possession. If the property is subject to leases, they have little desire to collect rents or manage the premises. On the other hand, if the business conducted on the premises is one in which the mortgagee has experience, they may be less reluctant on that account. In any event, the mortgagee in possession must exercise reasonable care, being responsible not only for the rents and profits actually collected, but also in some jurisdictions for those that a prudent owner would collect. This prudent owner standard of reasonable care also applies to the expenditure of funds for operation and maintenance of the property. It arises in many jurisdictions out of the duty of a mortgagee in possession to account to the mortgagor; accounting is an

1. In some states, a mortgage cannot take possession of secured property even if the mortgage contains a provision entitling him to do so. "Kansas precedent is clear that the mortgage instrument alone is unable to provide the express consent necessary for a lender to take possession of real estate prior to a valid court action." *See Fairfax Portfolio LLC v. Carojoto LLC*, 472 P.3d 53, 57 (Kan. 2020).

equitable action, and as such discretion is accorded a court to which it is brought. A mortgagee in possession may have to guard against vandalism on the property but at the same time may have to take care that expenses incurred in guarding it are prudent. For purposes of environmental statutes on hazardous wastes, the mortgagee in possession may also incur liability for cleanup costs.

When the property is subject to leases, a mortgagee in possession has no right to disturb senior leases (those executed before his mortgage). Why? Because only the reversion of the landlord was bargained for and mortgaged to the mortgagee as security. So long as a senior tenant pays rent due under the lease and keeps its covenants, that tenant is secure in the possession of its term. That tenant could even prepay the rent under the covenants and would be secure from a claim for a second payment by the mortgagee in possession. Absent a special consent provision in the mortgage, the mortgagee in possession would have to evict the mortgagor-landlord and take over the reversion before being able to reach a senior tenant's rent payments.

A junior lessee, on the other hand, will be forced to recognize the mortgagee in possession and must "attorn" in the language of the common law. Thus a mortgagee will be able to take possession of a junior's leased premises unless the lessee attorns, and to relet because, as to junior lessees, the mortgagee bargained for the security of letting the premises in the future. (Unless taking possession of the junior lessee's premises, the mortgagee cannot reach the rent.) Thus the mortgagee can agree on a new lease with an existing junior lessee. The easiest agreement on this score will be to relet at the existing rent to the junior lessee, but in a rising rental market, the mortgagee may (and probably will) ask for more. Such rents are part of the security for which the mortgagee bargained when executing the mortgage.

The mortgagee's rights when taking possession are analogous to those of a foreclosing mortgagee. Thus a junior mortgagee in possession has the right to oust nonattorning junior lessees, but no such right with regard to senior lessees. Against the latter, the most that a mortgage gives is the right to collect the rent due.

In summary, a mortgagee in possession is a mortgagee who takes control and possession of the mortgaged property by agreement (usually expressed in a mortgage covenant) upon a mortgagor's default; a mortgagee cannot take possession without the consent of the mortgagor or otherwise enter, even when doing so peacefully and lawfully. Taking possession means acquiring the benefits of possession, including the value of the rents, profits, and use of the mortgaged property as well as taking on the duties and obligations flowing from possession. *See 6901 LLC v. Caputo*, 241 N.Y.S.3d 99 (N.Y. Sup. Ct., App. Div., 2025).

Examples

Example 8

Mortgagor (MR) vacates property on which mortgagee (ME) holds a mortgage. ME declares the MR is in default under the mortgage covenant requiring MR to occupy the property. MR sends ME the keys to the vacated property. When ME receives the keys, is ME a mortgagee in possession?

Explanation

No. Actual possession is required for ME to become a mortgagee in possession. Here possession is only constructive.

Example 9

Under applicable law, a commercial landowner is liable for clearing snow from the sidewalk. A residential landowner is not. Is a mortgagee in possession of its mortgagor's residence subject to this duty?

Explanation

Held, no in *Briglia v. Mondrian Mortgage Corp.*, 698 A.2d 28 (N.J. Super. Ct., App. Div.), cert. denied, 702 A.2d 352 (N.J. 1997). A mortgagee in possession does not benefit from the sidewalk to the degree its owner would, is not conducting a business on the secured property, and could not sell it until a foreclosure decree gave it title. Likewise, vacant property not put to commercial use is not subject to sidewalk liability. On the other hand, the mortgagee in possession has the ability to insure the premises and its decision to go into possession is related to its lending business and its profit-seeking activities; once in possession, it has the duty to make the property earn a reasonable return by leasing or using it. Courts have generally shown a reluctance to impute incidents of ownership to mortgagees in possession before they purchase at a foreclosure sale. *See Case v. St. Mary's Bank*, 63 A.3d 1209 (N.H. 2013). No mortgagee becomes the owner of the secured property by taking possession: Foreclosure is still necessary. Likewise, a mortgagee who changes the locks or winterizes property is preserving its *status quo*, not acting as its present owner or a mortgagee in possession. Before foreclosure, courts are quick to imply an agreement permitting the mortgagor to remain on the secured property, sometimes attempting to categorize the mortgagor as a tenant.

Example 10

For leased property, will the mortgagee in possession be affected by preexisting landlord tenant law?

Explanation

Yes *See New York & Suburban Fed. Sav. & Loan Assn. v. Sanderman*, 392 A.2d 635 (N.J. Super. Ct., Ch. Div., 1978) (as to providing security for tenants).

Example 11

ME takes possession of a condominium unit, the purchase of which it financed with the proceeds of a mortgage loan now in default. Does ME owe condo fees levied by the HOA, fees that have been levied but are unpaid?

Explanation

Yes, it does. It has the duties of a reasonably prudent owner in possession. If the condo owner would lose the property when the fees are unpaid, then the mortgagee must pay to avoid that result. *See Woodview Condominium Assn. v. Shanahan*, 917 A.2d 790 (N.J. Super. Ct. 2007).

Example 12

Mortgagee ME erroneously declares a default in mortgagor MR's mortgage on Blackacre, a residence, and ME orders MR to vacate the property. MR then sends the keys to Blackacre to ME and vacates. Is ME now a mortgagee in possession?

Explanation

No, so long as ME's activities are limited to paying utilities, taxes, and insurance premiums, it might be said to be in constructive rather than actual possession. *See in re* Dupell, 235 Bankr. 783 (Bankr. E.D. Pa. 1999). This sort of legal fiction is particularly likely in a lien state for mortgages where the mortgagee's right to possession is deferred. ME might take MR's sending the keys as authority to list the property for sale and as an agreement to cooperate with the listing and selling brokers, but further communication with MR will be necessary in order to close the sale, so ME does not yet have the rights and duties of a possessor. *See Kubczak v. Chemical Bank & Tr. Co.*, 575 N.W.2d 745 (Mich. 1998).

Example 13

Mortgagee ME brings a judicial foreclosure action against the mortgagor MR, but the court reviewing the foreclosure sale, voids it for procedural irregularities. Is ME a mortgagee in possession, or does MR resume possession and ownership?

Explanation

The latter—ME becomes a mortgagee in possession for the purpose of permitting MR to exercise his now reestablished equity of redemption. The court is in effect unwinding the foreclosure. While the mortgagee is in possession, however, mortgage interest continues to accrue, and the court will likely order an accounting in order to determine the current amount of MR's outstanding debt so that MR can in turn exercise the equity of redemption. *See SE Property Holdings, LLC v. Bama Bayou*, LLC, 329 So. 3d 1250 (Ala. 2020).

Example 14

ME is a mortgagee in possession. ME commits waste on the property. The waste reduces its fair market value by 40%. What is MR's (the mortgagor's) remedy?

Explanation

In MR's cause of action for waste, MR is entitled, among other remedies, to have his mortgage debt to ME reduced by the amount of the waste. When ME's tortious conduct reduces the value of the secured property, the debtor is discharged to the extent of the reduction. *See Riverview Apts. v. City Nat'l Bank*, 150 N.E.3d 164 (Mass. Ct. App. 2020). Should the reduction be 40% of the outstanding debt, or the cost of repairing the damage to the property—in other words, 40% of the property's reduction in value? ME has the duty to act as a reasonably prudent owner. MR's remedy should therefore reflect the damage done to him by the waste as an owner, not the waste's value to him as a debtor. If the cost of repair is more than the outstanding debt, the debt should be reduced to zero and MR is entitled to recover the difference. If the debt is more than the value of the property, MR might wish to give possession to ME and if ME accepts, MR should keep the money. Otherwise, ME would receive a reward for his tortious conduct

RECEIVERSHIPS

A receiver is a court-appointed officer or representative, appointed to preserve, control, and manage property that is the subject of prior agreement or litigation. A court may appoint a receiver to protect and conserve mortgaged property when a foreclosure action is pending. Generally, a receiver is appointed to protect any asset that is subject to litigation. It permits the receiver to control expenses and protect income. Although the appointment is often the subject of a state statute, courts also regard it as an extraordinary and equitable remedy, used cautiously and not automatic even when permitted under a mortgage. Its appointment is not restricted to instances where the mortgagor has committed fraud. *See Fannie Mae v. 204 Ellery St., LLC*, 2024 U.S. Dist. LEXIS 74046 (E.D. N.Y., April 23, 2024).

Thus, if a mortgagee does not wish to go into possession, he has an alternative—the appointment of a receiver. In a market in which real estate values have turned downward (where the mortgagor is, in common parlance, "under water"—that is, owes on a mortgage for an amount higher than the fair market value of the secured property), a receiver is particularly likely. *See New Haven Sav. Bk. v. General Finance and Mortgage Co.*, 386 A.2d 230, 231 (Conn. 1978). For any mortgagee, however, a receiver has several more advantages. First, the receiver can act as a stakeholder when the amounts due are in dispute. Second, a mortgagee in possession has a duty to account, which a receiver does not. Third, the mortgagee in possession is subjected to tort liability from which a receiver can provide a shield. Fourth, the appointment of a receiver does not terminate existing leases on the mortgaged property, because the receiver has duties to both mortgagor and mortgagee and is the agent of both; the distinction between junior and senior leases can be obviated on that account.

Thus the receiver, being a court-appointed person, is typically regarded as a mutual agent, not as (more important) the agent of the mortgagee. Where the income flow from leases is important to the mortgagee, the possibility that a mortgagee's taking possession will be construed as an ouster of the junior lessees is sufficient to make the mortgagee consider a receivership more desirable than taking possession. And, by the same token, many mortgagees will also consider an assignment of rents clause in the mortgage more valuable than a right to a receivership, and for the same reason: that assigning the rents provides one more step before the mortgagee need take possession. Thus a junior lessee does not have the right to vacate when the receiver takes over. In most courts that have considered the issue, the receiver is permitted to hold junior lessees to their lease obligations.

Receiverships are equitable in nature. This means, among other things, that a court, in considering a petition for the appointment of a receiver, is not bound by the covenants of the mortgage. Standards for the appointment of a receiver vary from state to state, but a petition for appointment will be heard only after a default.

A mortgagee seeking a receiver must establish (1) waste, (2) a default, and (3) insecurity. Insecurity can mean several things. First, that the fair market value of the property is insufficient to cover the outstanding debt—in parlance common when real estate values turn down, the mortgage is "under water." Second, that the remedies otherwise provided are inadequate—that is, that the mortgagor is insolvent so that the legal remedies on the note are inadequate, that the property securing the debt is threatened with loss or destruction, or that waste is being committed on the property. *See Union Guardian Trust Co. v. Rau*, 238 N.W. 166 (Mich. 1931) (holding that nonpayment of taxes constitutes waste and justifies receiver's appointment). Waste is perhaps the most commonly required element of proof necessary to justify a receivership. Besides fraud as previously mentioned, other factors used by a court considering the appointment of a receiver reflect its equitable nature and include whether the harm to the plaintiff caused by denying the appointment is greater than the injury to the mortgagor opposing it, and the mortgagee's likelihood of success in the underlying foreclosure action.

The grounds for a receiver are little different in title and lien jurisdictions, although perhaps the remedy traditionally has been granted more readily in lien theory jurisdictions (which means just about everywhere).

The rights of a mortgagee to have a receiver and take possession of the secured property depend on the distinction between title and lien mortgages. With a title mortgage, the mortgagee has the right to the possession, rents, and profits of the secured property. With a lien mortgage, that right arises only after a default—at the earliest. Some lien jurisdictions put the mortgagee off until after foreclosure.

A junior mortgagee is entitled to a receiver when the senior mortgagee has not yet petitioned for one's appointment, even when the senior mortgage contains a covenant currently entitling the senior to a receiver. That senior covenant is viewed as executory until the senior affirmatively acts upon it. Before the senior does so, the junior can have a receiver collect the rents and, once collected, cannot be forced to disgorge them if the senior later has a receiver appointed, although the senior's receiver will then have a superior claim to receive the rents and in effect trump the junior receiver's right.

Receivers are often appointed *ex parte*—on the sworn affidavit of the mortgagee. Such procedures have been challenged on due process grounds, but were upheld as constitutional in *Friedman v. Gerax*, 420 N.Y.S.2d 247 (N.Y. App. Div. 1979), so long as it is judicially supervised with an opportunity for a prompt hearing on the grounds for appointment. The professional qualifications of a person proposed to act as a receiver are independently reviewed by the appointing court.

Examples

Example 15a

MR executes a brief but enforceable mortgage in favor of ME. The security for the mortgage is Officeacres, a large office building. MR also executes a junior mortgage on the same property in favor of MEE. In a title jurisdiction, is ME entitled to the rents if MR is not in default on the repayment of the mortgage loan?

Explanation

Yes. ME is entitled to a receiver or to possession upon a showing of good cause (either waste, default, or lender insecurity) upon the execution of the mortgage, and of course he is entitled to file a petition later, at the time of a default in repayment.

Example 15b

Would your answer be the same in a lien jurisdiction? If so, how should ME react to the difference?

Explanation

The answer would be different. No to Example 13a in a lien jurisdiction, where the date on which ME is entitled to go into possession or to petition for the appointment of a receiver is either (1) the date of default, (2) the date of filing for foreclosure, (3) the date of the decree, or (4) the date on which the decree is confirmed. In a lien state, the mortgagee derives the right to the rents from the right to enforce the lien upon default. At the time of default, he is subrogated to the mortgagor's right to collect the rents — stepping into the mortgagor's shoes to do so. In reacting to the difference, ME should insist on an express covenant assigning the rents to him on default. Such a clause does not give the mortgagee a right to possession, and an entry to collect the rents may not be made unless a demand for them is first made of the landlord-mortgagor. Such a clause is one of the covenants distinguishing a commercial mortgage from a residential one. In a lien state, the courts sometimes treat such a covenant as an executory contract, executed upon default. Its subject is a lien on the rents, postponed until default and foreclosure is commenced.

Example 15c

Even if ME is entitled to go into possession, would ME want to? What if the leases for the offices in the building were made prior to the execution of ME's mortgage? Would that affect your answer?

Explanation

No. ME may not want to run the risks associated with being a mortgagee in possession, particularly if going into possession would constitute an ouster of existing lessees. Here, however, senior lessees cannot be disturbed. Once in possession, the mortgagee is held to the standard of care of a prudent owner. This standard applies to profits ME should make and expenses ME might reasonably incur.

Example 15d

Will MEE's remedies differ from ME's?

Explanation

A junior mortgagee like MEE may have a broader right to a receiver than ME does. MEE is more likely to be able to show insecurity. MEE's right is independent of ME's. It can be exercised even though ME has not petitioned for a receiver. At the same time, once MEE's receiver is in possession, he cannot just devote the rent roll just to repayment of MEE's debt. Why? Because if he does not first devote the rent receipts to the payment of real estate taxes, a resulting tax lien might trump ME's lien or otherwise render ME insecure, and if he does not reasonably repair and maintain the building, he may be liable in waste.

Example 15e

Is the authority of a receiver, pending foreclosure, generally broader or narrower in a lien jurisdiction than it is in a title jurisdiction?

Explanation

Broader. When the mortgagee files a foreclosure action, equity, regarding as done what should be done, will give the receiver broader powers while the action is pursued diligently and in good faith. Equity's doctrine of equitable conversion is at work here, regarding the appointment of a receiver as a mechanism for giving the mortgagee what he will be entitled to upon the completion of foreclosure—repayment of the debt; and the same can be said of the other pre-foreclosure remedies discussed in this chapter—a mortgagee's taking possession and an assignment of rents.

Example 15f

If during foreclosure either ME or MEE has a receiver appointed, how long does the receivership last?

Explanation

Until the period of statutory redemption ends, or any decree in foreclosure is absolute.

Example 15g

If MEE petitions for a receiver to hold Officeacres, and the building generates more proceeds than necessary to satisfy MEE's debt (payments), is ME entitled to the surplus? If not, to whom does the surplus go?

Explanation

No. ME would get more than ME's bargain if such were the case. The surplus goes to MR. *See Sullivan v. Rosson*, 119 N.E. 405, 4 A.L.R. 1400 (N.Y. 1918). The junior mortgagee should be rewarded for its diligence, but not given a windfall.

Example 15h

If after MR's default in mortgage payments ME, MEE, and MR work out an agreement on future payments, should the title insurer be a party to the agreement?

Explanation

Yes, when each holds a title policy, because the agreement affects the lien priority of each.

Example 15i

If MR is in possession of one of the offices in the building when the mortgage was given, does MR have to surrender that office to a receiver?

Explanation

No. Even though mortgagor's partial possession of the secured property decreases the security offered the mortgagee for the debt, a mortgagee who takes the security on that basis is entitled to no more security than was bargained for. *See Holmes v. Gravenhorst*, 188 N.E. 285 (N.Y. 1933) (holding that the mortgagor-occupant need not pay a reasonable rent to a receiver). Furthermore, even if the occupying mortgagor agrees to pay rent to any receiver appointed under the mortgage covenants, that agreement may not authorize the mortgagor's eviction for nonpayment of the rent—eviction must await foreclosure. *Id. And see Carlin Trading Co. v. Bennett*, 264 N.Y.S.2d 43 (N.Y. App. Div. 1965), noted in 17 Syracuse L. Rev. 774 (1966).

Following is a covenant that might be included in a mortgage governing the mortgagee's right to a receiver.

Upon Borrower's breach of any covenant in this Mortgage or Borrower's breach of any material covenant of Borrower as lessor under any lease, Lender shall be entitled to the appointment of a receiver for the Property, without further notice to Borrower. This appointment shall be by agent or court-appointed receiver and may be made regardless of the adequacy of Lender's security or waste of the Property. Upon appointment, the receiver or agent shall enter and take control of the Property in order to operate and maintain it and shall have the right to cancel, modify, or execute leases and occupancy and use agreements for the Property, collect all its rents and revenues, enforce or carry out any provision of any lease, repair the Property, and maintain, terminate, or execute agreements providing for its management or maintenance, all on such terms and provisions as are best to protect the security of this Mortgage. Borrower hereby expressly consents to such receiver or agent's appointment. The receiver or agent shall be entitled to a reasonable fee for so managing the Property.

Example 16

When, as in this covenant, the receiver is given "the right to . . . enforce or carry out any provision of any lease," is the mortgagee liable as a landlord and the receiver's principal, for any duties imposed under applicable state landlord tenant law?

Explanation

Yes. So it might be wise to add to the foregoing: "Lender shall not be liable to perform or discharge any obligation to be performed or discharged by Borrower under said leases of the Property and Borrower shall indemnify Lender in the event Lender, its agent or receiver performs or discharges such obligations."

FEDERAL BANK RECEIVERS—THE SUPER RECEIVER

Normally a receiver is a person stepping into the shoes of the mortgagee and, as such, he is bound by the agreements that bind the mortgagee, whether or not they are documented. Not so for the federal receiver. Most commercial institutional mortgage lenders have deposits insured by the Federal Deposit Insurance Corporation (FDIC). When a bank fails, that federal agency has two roles. First, it takes over the bank and manages the bank's assets as a receiver, and second, it acts in its corporate capacity to continue its insurance on the bank's deposits as before.

As a receiver, the FDIC has two options. First, it can liquidate the assets of the bank and pay the insured depositors. Second, it can sell the bank's healthy assets (e.g., the mortgage loans not in default) to another bank. This sale is subject to two interrelated conditions: that (1) the purchasing bank assume the obligation to pay the depositors and (2) the purchasing bank receive from the agency a sum sufficient to cover the difference between the value of the assets sold and its future obligation to the depositors. The second condition is met by the agency's purchase, in its corporate, insuring capacity, of the failed bank's bad loans for an amount sufficient to meet that second condition. Thus the agency (acting as a receiver) sells the bad loans to itself (in its second, insuring capacity) for a sum to be paid over to the purchaser of the failed bank to cover the latter's obligations to depositors.

As a receiver, the federal agency takes the loan assets of a bank free of any undocumented secret agreements to which the documented loan is subject. This doctrine is called the *D'Oench* doctrine. *See D'Oench, Duhme & Co. v. FDIC*, 315 U.S. 447 (1942). If a note was either designed to deceive the bank's regulators or would have that effect, the note's written terms control and its maker is estopped to deny the effectiveness of those terms. No intent to defraud need be shown. "Rather, the doctrine prohibits all secret agreements that tend to make the [federal agency] susceptible to fraudulent arrangements." *See Timberland Design, Inc. v. First Serv. Bank for Sav.*, 932 F.2d 46, 48 (1st Cir. 1991). It also protects and expresses a preference for depositors who cannot otherwise protect themselves, over borrowers who can.

The *D'Oench* doctrine's status as a matter of federal common law is rooted in policy and estoppel principles, but nonetheless the doctrine has a statutory basis as well. 12 U.S.C.A. §1823(e) ("No agreement which tends to diminish or defeat the interest of the Corporation (the FDIC) in any asset acquired . . . shall be valid against the Corporation unless such agreement . . . is in writing"). Any agreement not so tending must still be executed and approved by the board of directors or loan committee of the failed institution and be part of its official records. *Id.*, §1823(e)(1)(A)-(D). The doctrine may be invoked only by an insolvent bank.

As a receiver, the FDIC can "disaffirm or repudiate any contract or lease—(A) to which the institution is a party; (B) the performance of which the . . . receiver, in the . . . receiver's discretion, determines to be burdensome; and (C) the disaffirmance or repudiation of which . . . the receiver determines . . . will promote the orderly administration of the institution's affairs." 12 U.S.C.A. §1821(e). A rule of reasonable business judgment and prudence is imposed on the receiver by this statute.

Examples

Example 17

When the FDIC takes over the assets of Assets Bank, a loan file contains a written agreement that the bank will retain a percentage of the loan proceeds and pay them to C. The agreement is executed by the mortgagor MR, but not by Assets. On the date of the takeover, C is litigating the enforceability of the agreement against both Assets and MR. Is the agreement enforceable against the FDIC as a receiver?

Explanation

No. At the time the FDIC acquires the loan as a receiver, the requirements of §1823(e) cannot be satisfied. In addition, whether Assets accepted the agreement cannot be ascertained from the loan file, and so the agreement is a secret one for the purpose of this doctrine. The purpose of the *D'Oench* doctrine is to prevent the regulator taking over a bank from being misled, and an unclear document in a loan file does so. Any actual or constructive knowledge of C's rights gained by the FDIC from reading the file is irrelevant to the doctrine and its codification in §1823(e). Otherwise, every unclear loan file in an insolvent bank's possession might have to be litigated.

SUBORDINATION, NONDISTURBANCE, AND ATTORNMENT AGREEMENTS

In a commercial mortgage transaction, a subordination, nondisturbance and attornment agreement (SNDA) is an agreement reorienting the priorities of mortgages and leases, typically first making a lease executed before a mortgage subordinate in priority to the mortgage. At the same time, second, it assures the subordinating lessee that the now-senior mortgagee will not disturb the possession of the lessee. A nondisturbance agreement thus prohibits any cause of action to evict so long as the lessee is not in default under the lease. Third and finally, it further assures the mortgagee that (1) if it forecloses on the property, the lessee will accept the foreclosure sale purchaser as its landlord and (2) if the mortgagee buys the property at its own foreclosure sale, it will not assume the past liabilities of the lessor/mortgagor of the property. (Both subordination and attornment covenants can be, and typically are, inserted in commercial leases for major or signature tenants, as it is easier and cheaper to negotiate these ahead of time, at the execution of the lease, rather than negotiate an SNDA as a lease amendment later.)

Thus, an SNDA is best seen as a three-party agreement made between mortgagees, lessees, and mortgagors/owners of a commercial property, although the owner is not strictly a necessary party if the document is merely a subordination

Although the mortgagee may agree to correct conditions that exist as of the date of attornment and abide by the economic terms of the lease, it is not customarily liable for damage or other lease claims arising before the date of attornment. For example, the mortgagee purchasing at foreclosure will not wish liability for pre-attornment unfinished construction liabilities, and the SNDA will typically expressly say so. Further, such a mortgagee will not want to be bound by lease modifications, and the SNDA will say this too.

Further, a mortgagee may require the attorning lessee to waive the right to any credit for prepaid rent, the right to demand completion of unbuilt-out construction work or unfinished common area improvements, any or all lease warranties, any abated or free rent, any right to exercise an option to buy, expand, or relocate the lease premises, or the right to assert some foreclosure defenses.

So SNDAs adjust priorities and make a lease subordinate to a mortgage. They are particularly important (1) when leases are vital to the business conducted on the secured property, as with shopping centers (where anchor tenant leases are crucial to cash flow), or (2) when governmental regulations require that the mortgagee hold a senior mortgage lien. (3) They put the mortgagee and the lessee into privity of contract, so the mortgagee can demand things directly from the lessee after default. (4) They provide the mortgagee with an express covenant that the tenant will perform for the lender after foreclosure. (5) To the extent that the lease and the mortgage are found to have conflicting provisions, they bring the parties to the table to resolve them.

Before a mortgagee negotiates an SNDA agreement, it should examine the lease to make sure that a landlord's duties are not onerous. If it finds onerous duties, it will want to negotiate a covenant providing that a mortgagee in possession or a foreclosure sale purchaser is not subject to them.

Absent an SNDA agreement, if the lease remains senior, its provisions (on insurance proceeds, condemnation payments, etc.) trump the mortgage's provisions on the same subject. So if the lease provides that insurance proceeds will be used to rebuild, but the mortgage provides that the lender can use the proceeds to pay down the loan, the SNDA's nondisturbance covenant does not alone make the mortgage senior to the lease, but the subordination covenant will.

EXAMPLES

Examples

Example 18

Will a lease covenant of quiet enjoyment alone keep the subordinating lessee in possession after foreclosure?

Explanation

No. Only an SNDA agreement to which the mortgagee is a party will do that.

Example 19

Once the mortgage is senior under an SNDA, there is a conflict between the now-junior lease and the mortgage: The lease requires the landlord to rebuild after a fire, the mortgage provides that the proceeds of the insurance can, at the lender's option, be used to pay down the loan, and the SNDA provides that the mortgagee will honor the lease provision. When the mortgagee forecloses, bids, and buys at the foreclosure sale, can it still argue that it doesn't have to honor this lease covenant and rebuild?

Explanation

Yes. It will argue that its interest at foreclosure was in its business of lending money, so it did not foreclose on the property for investment purposes; rather, it did so to recoup its loan losses. Thus any improvements to be made must recoup those losses. The SNDA agreement is only made to prevent the impairment of its security. When the agreement provides that the "lease continues in full force and effect," that is only as to real covenants and the covenant to insure in a lease is not a real covenant.

Example 20

The SNDA states that post-foreclosure "the lender is not liable for the pre-foreclosure acts or omissions" of the mortgagor/landlord. How might the mortgagee justify such a provision?

Explanation

The justifications number three at least: (1) these acts or omissions are liabilities the mortgagee did not cause, had no control over, and did not contribute to; (2) lessees are free to fashion other remedies within their landlord-tenant relationship: for example, a letter of credit, a guaranty, or a bond covering such acts; (3) the mortgagee is no guarantor of its mortgagor's obligations. Lessees sometimes propose that the mortgagee post-foreclosure be liable for conditions of which tenant gives the mortgagee actual notice, but this does not address the lender's concerns that it be liable only for conditions after the date of the attornment—that is, once the lessee has performed its obligation to attorn.

Example 21

The SNDA states that the mortgagee "is not bound by any amendments to" the subordinated lease. What are the parties' negotiating points with regard to this provision?

Explanation

A lessee may think such a provision is better put in the lease, not the SNDA, and so may resist it. A mortgagee's reply is that the SNDA's silence invites litigation on the point and that it made its bargain for the mortgage loan on the basis of the original lease (which format it typically approved), not the amended one, and that a later foreclosure takes place when the mortgagor's business judgment is clouded, and the mortgagor desperate and prone to "sweetheart" amendments.

Example 22

The subordination covenant in an SNDA states that the subordinating lessee is "subordinate to all present and future mortgages." Is this provision prudent? Is this subject to attack?

Explanation

No and yes, it may be subject to attack as an executory agreement. As such, courts might require that the future replacement mortgage be reasonably like the present one to be subject to the SNDA agreement. So the future mortgage should be described with reasonable specificity; otherwise, it might be too indefinite to perform or become an unreasonable restraint on alienation.

CHAPTER 18

Foreclosures

When mortgage payments remain unpaid after they are due, the mortgagor is in default on the note. Whenever that repayment is unlikely, the mortgagee's principal remedy is foreclosure. Foreclosure is an *in rem* action against the property that provided the security for the mortgage debt. A judgment *in rem* creates no personal liability. It operates only on the property securing the lien of the mortgage. The purpose of foreclosure is generally to give the mortgagee or other foreclosure purchaser the same title to the secured property possessed by the mortgagor when the foreclosed mortgage was executed—that is, a title subject to any liens, encumbrances, or interests existing at that time, but free of any such interests executed after the execution of the foreclosed mortgage. *See Littlebrook Airpark Condo. Ass'n v. Sweet Peas, LLC*, 199 A.3d 627, 680 (Me. 2019). Its object is the perfection of the lien of the mortgage. It is everywhere the subject of very detailed state statutes prescribing the procedures that the mortgagee must use. The use of such statutes is mandatory for mortgages and deeds of trust. Notwithstanding the statutory basis of this action, the cause of action is generally regarded as an equitable one. Foreclosure law lies at the intersection of the equitable remedies provided by the courts and the mandatory statutory remedies provided by the legislature. *See JP Morgan Chase Bank, N.A. v. Essaghof*, 249 A.3d 327, 334 (Conn. 2020).

Examples

Example 1

A mortgagee brings a foreclosure action against its mortgagor. The latter raises a defense based on a violation of the federal Truth in Lending Act. Mortgagee objects. Will the defense succeed?

Explanation

No. The defense is unavailable to the mortgagor: Foreclosure is not an action to collect a debt, and a judgment in foreclosure is not an action for money damages. It is an *in rem* proceeding. Its purpose is not to impose personal liability but to determine the status of the secured property. *See Green Tree Consumer Discount Co. v. Newton*, 909 A.2d 811, 815 (Pa. Super. Ct. 2006). If the mortgagee brought an action on the note, the answer would be otherwise. The action would then be *in personam*, meaning that the personal assets of the mortgagor/debtor would be liable for any judgment the mortgagee/creditor obtains. A mortgagee has the choice, either to sue on the mortgage in foreclosure, or on the note, to collect the outstanding debt.

ACCELERATION

The mortgagee's filing a foreclosure action is typically preceded by attempts to collect the amounts in default, first by letters and then by more personal means. Collection procedures are followed by a notice to the mortgagor accelerating the debt if that is permitted by the mortgage covenants. This acceleration is authorized by a covenant in the note permitting the mortgagee, upon a default in payment, to declare the whole sum of accrued interest plus unpaid principal due and payable. It permits the mortgagee to sue for the whole debt at one time or to collect any part of the debt at once by a judgment against the mortgagor.

Such acceleration clauses were inserted in mortgage documents first in the 1930s to avoid, absent agreement otherwise, two rules of law about mortgage agreements: first, that the mortgagor has no right to prepay. The mortgagee bargained for an investment of a certain length, and he's to have it. The second rule is that the mortgagee has no right to accelerate the debt, absent evidence of anticipatory repudiation. Neither of these presumptions about the mortgagor and mortgagee's agreement makes sense today. Such clauses were at first intended to lay a basis for an action by the mortgagee in equity to prevent multiple suits; this action was for the issuance of the equitable writ of *quia timet* (literally, "he who fears").

Examples

Example 2

Acceleration covenants are typically upheld. Why?

Explanation

First, because the alternative is onerous, involving multiple suits. Second, because they are not a penalty: They merely set an alternate and earlier date for repayment after a default.

Example 3

The exercise of the typical acceleration covenant is optional on the part of the mortgagee. *Webster Bank v. Oakley*, 830 A.2d 139 (Conn. 2003). However, when the covenant requires that a notice of acceleration be given to the mortgagor, there must be strict compliance with the notice provision. *See Woel v. Christiana Trust*, 228 A.3d 339 (R.I. 2020). Would a mandatory covenant be valid?

Explanation

Yes. No public policy stands in the way.

The no prepayment and no acceleration rules of law are default rules; they are repudiated today only because the documentation for a residential mortgage universally declares otherwise. As to the acceleration right, when an acceleration covenant is today not express in the mortgage, it might be implied.

Foreclosure is an expensive process. The mortgagee would rather spend some money on collection procedures before resorting to it. Thus acceleration is typically used after collection procedures are tried, and by that time, the mortgagor may be six months to a year in arrears on payments. Acceleration is typically used only against the chronic defaulter and when a basis for anticipatory repudiation of the whole debt is established by the mortgagee. Standard FNMA-FHLMC mortgage forms often require that a 30-day notice be given by letter before an acceleration. The case law of many jurisdictions, which provides the legal background for these forms, denies the mortgagor the right to reinstate the debt after the mortgagee accelerates it. However, FNMA-FHLMC standard mortgages permit the mortgagee to recoup the reasonable costs of collection upon reinstatement of the outstanding debt and lien.

Many jurisdictions by statute provide that a mortgagee must give a mortgagor notice before accelerating. Sometimes this notice applies to accelerations preceding a mortgage foreclosure, but not to accelerations preceding a suit on the personal liability in the note. *See Certified Realty Co. v. Smith*, 597 P.2d 1043 (Colo. 1979), noted at 52 U. Colo. L. Rev. 301 (1981). This is a reason why acceleration covenants are often included in both the note and the mortgage. The Uniform Commercial Code provides that inclusion in the note does not prevent its negotiability. UCC §3-105(c). More generally, defenses raised in a foreclosure may alternatively also be raised in a later suit on the note when the foreclosure does not make the mortgagee whole.

Absent a statute, an acceleration is effective when a mortgagee does an overt act indicating an intent to accelerate, either in a letter indicating such an intent or indicating that acceleration has occurred, or by commencing foreclosure. Considering due process concerns, the better rule is to require both a notice to accelerate and to foreclose.

Examples

Example 4

What if the mortgagee accepts payment from a mortgagor in default after giving notice that it intends to accelerate because of nonpayment?

Explanation

The general rule is that a mortgagee does not have to be otherwise insecure to accelerate. So the foreclosure action may proceed. On the other hand, when a mortgagor negotiates a repayment plan agreed to by the mortgagee, whose counsel has meanwhile accelerated and commenced foreclosure, the mortgagor may have the action dismissed on a motion for summary judgment. *See Peoples Heritage Bank v. Pease*, 838 A.2d 354 (Me. 2003).

GRAF v. HOPE BUILDING CORP.

An acceleration will be enforced according to its terms, absent equitable defenses to its use. The leading case is *Graf v. Hope Building Corp.*, 171 N.E. 884 (N.Y. 1930). The majority in this case set a standard of strict enforcement, over the vigorous dissent of Judge Benjamin Cardozo.

Graf involved a loan regularly and fully repaid up to the time a slight miscalculation of a quarterly payment's amount due was made. The slightly deficient payments were tendered on time, with a letter stating that when the one person authorized to sign checks for the mortgagor corporation was again available, the deficiency would be made up. The note provided for acceleration of the total unpaid debt 20 days after a default in any payment. Twenty-two days after default, the mortgagee began foreclosure.

The majority in *Graf* thought that the acceleration clause was good for all purposes. They said: "We feel that the interests of certainty and security in real estate transactions forbid us, in the absence of fraud, bad faith, or unconscionable conduct, to recede from the [well-recognized effect of an acceleration covenant] doctrine that is so deeply imbedded in equity."

Judge Cardozo thought otherwise, that it was good only to protect the mortgagee against insecurity. He insisted that "[e]quity declines to treat a mortgage upon realty as a conveyance subject to a condition, but views it as a lien irrespective of its form." Then, citing cases when liquidated damage clauses have been struck down, Cardozo states that "a like dispensing power . . . runs through the whole rubric of accident and mistake." When "the default is limited to a trifling balance," "the failure to pay the balance is the product of mistake," and "where the mortgagee indicates by his conduct that he appreciates the mistake and has attempted by silence and inaction to turn it to his own advantage," equity should reinstate the debt and the lien. The mortgagee, in Cardozo's view, was evading payment, which he must have known he could have for the asking. What profit, after all, did the mortgagee derive from the foreclosure? If the answer is none, or one disproportionate to the injury to the mortgagor, then the acceleration works a penalty on the mortgagor, and the parties to the loan agreements have made a mutual mistake of fact in forecasting the consequences of their agreement.

Cardozo's dissent has been influential in many states, but not in New York. Most FNMA/FHLMC standard mortgage forms today invoke the *Graf* majority's strict acceleration rule indirectly by providing that the lender waives no rights or remedies by accepting tender of a payment. If the mortgagor is to avoid acceleration, it will be by a motion for summary judgment, to the effect that the mortgagee has expressly waived its right; is evading payment or failed to notify the mortgagor of the assignment of the note to another; is estopped to assert its right; has accelerated in a fraudulent, oppressive, or unconscionable way; or has exercised the right to declare a default in bad faith. Animus by the mortgagee's loan committee would be grounds for a bad faith claim.

An occasional case, decided in New York and elsewhere, ameliorates the harshness of the *Graf* holding. For an antidote to *Graf*, *see Bisno v. Sax*, 346 P.2d 814 (Cal. App. 1959) (an opinion weighing the benefit to the accelerating mortgagee against the injury to the mortgage and relieving the mortgagor of acceleration after a one-day default); *See Kerin v. Udoft*, 334 A.2d 434 (Conn. 1973); *Beal v. Mars Larson Ranch Corp.*, 586 P.2d 1378 (Idaho 1987). The last two cases find an equitable right to reinstate both the debt and the lien, implying a rejection of the majority in *Graf* whether the acceleration covenant is in the note or the mortgage.

The *Graf* majority's strict acceleration rule is also qualified in some states by statutory reinstatement rights, as explained later in this chapter.

Examples

Example 5

Mortgagor's (MR's) loan committee (ME's committee) has a rule that when any mortgage loan collateral's fair market value drops by more than 20 percent in a single year, acceleration will be declared at the next opportunity. MR then delivers a required appraisal of the mortgaged property a day late. Is the resulting exercise of ME's otherwise valid right to accelerate in bad faith?

Explanation

There are two issues. First, should the strict acceleration rule in *Graf* be used when the default is a nonmonetary one? The *Graf* majority's rule raises no distinction between monetary and nonmonetary covenants in a mortgage, so that silence, and the freedom of contract rationale supporting it, suggests that the answer is yes. The second issue is whether when ME accelerates for reasons based on its business need to protect its portfolio of mortgages, ME is violating MR and ME's expectations at the time of the execution of the mortgage. ME's implied obligation to deal in good faith with MR does not mean that the portfolio-based reason for acceleration is in bad faith, but that term deals with the relationship between the parties, not the economic climate in which the loan was made. Since neither party has control over that climate, it can hardly be a matter of good or bad faith. Just the opposite, actually: Finding a rationale for an action in the economic climate shows that the parties' relationship is not involved, unless MR is treated differently from other mortgagors. Thus the term "bad faith" will likely only evaluate the way the parties treat each other. For example, if the loan committee had a faulty appraisal put in front of it, no bad faith would be present. Nor would it be if acceleration was due to a change in its lending policies and the change was not directed at MR specifically. So long as the committee is responding to valid economic concerns, no bad faith will be found.

Example 6

Acceleration covenants in commercial mortgages often provide that they may be exercised when the financial condition of the mortgagor deteriorates. Is such a covenant valid?

Explanation

Yes. No public policy condemns it. A freedom of contract rationale supports it. Just as a mortgagee is interested in receiving the same title in foreclosure as the mortgagor had when the mortgage was executed, so also it might be interested in the mortgagor's financial condition remaining stable over the course of the loan's repayment. A further issue is whether, when the nonmonetary acceleration is involved, a mortgage may avoid foreclosure and cure the breach by providing further assurance of repayment, such as a letter of credit or the pledge of other security for the loan's repayment. Some courts recognize that a mortgagee need not be insecure to accelerate but permit such a cure, citing a disparity of treatment by courts permitting either strict or curable accelerations for nonpayment of taxes and insurance premiums on the secured property or for breach of the mortgage covenant against waste. Mortgagors typically have to present proof that the secured property is insured on a periodic basis. *See Barrows v. Crossroads Bank*, 163 N.E.3d 281 (Ind. Ct. App. 2020).

Example 7

A mortgagor protests an acceleration, citing her delicate health. Does this protest provide a defense in foreclosure?

Explanation

No. A sympathetic condition, even judicial sympathy, is no defense to a foreclosure action, even when it is treated as equitable in nature. Judicial sympathy is not a recognized defense to foreclosure in a broad reading of the majority opinion in *Graf*. To quote that opinion one more time: "Rejection of the [mortgagee's] legal right could rest only on compassion. . . . Such a tender emotion must be exerted, if at all, by the parties rather than the court. Our guide must be the precedents prevailing since courts of equity were established by the state." Any inequity must involve the actions of the mortgagee—for example, its fraud or harassment of the mortgagor in attempting to collect the debt. (Harassment may also violate a "fair debt collection" statute in some jurisdictions.)

Example 8

What is the underlying assumption for the argument that the acceleration covenant may only be exercised if the mortgagee is insecure?

Explanation

It begins typically with the optional nature of the covenant (that it is exercised only at the mortgagee's option). If it is exercisable only at will, then it must be used in good faith, recognizing that this means that the court should balance the hardship on the mortgagor against the benefits given the mortgagee by the covenant and that the hardships on the mortgagee should be balanced against the benefits the covenant conferred on the mortgagee.

DEACCELERATION IN BANKRUPTCY

Chapter 13 of the Bankruptcy Code (11 U.S.C. §1301 et seq.) provides an insolvent debtor with an opportunity to reorganize her debts, rather than have her assets sold or liquidated (under Chapter 7) to satisfy them. When an acceleration precedes the bankrupt's filing, the filing automatically stays any pending foreclosure and, at least when the mortgage secures the debtor's principal residence, the debtor bankrupt's reorganization plan may cure the default and reinstate the mortgage debt. *See in re Taddeo*, 685 F.2d 24 (2d Cir. 1982). *Taddeo* has been widely accepted by other federal circuits and bankruptcy courts. The most prominent issue in many cases is when the deacceleration right ends. With acceleration but no foreclosure, deacceleration occurs; when foreclosure has proceeded to judgment, but no sale has taken place, most courts deaccelerate the debt. Even if there is a sale but the price has not yet been paid, the right exists. After a sale is complete, the acceleration is curable, but only when statutory redemption is available and the purchaser at the sale is paid off in a lump sum. If the mortgagee is the sale purchaser, the mortgage debt is reorganized along with the bankrupt's other debts.

REINSTATEMENT RIGHTS

Many FNMA/FHLMC uniform mortgages and some state statutes provide that up to a certain number of days after the complaint is served or before the foreclosure sale, a mortgagor may cure the default(s) by paying the amount due. *See Associated Bank v. Pufall*, 650 N.W.2d 560 (Wis. App. Ct. 2002); Ill. Comp. Stat. Ann. 735 ILCS 5/15-1602 (2010) (a 90-day right running from the date of service). Exercising this right short-circuits the foreclosure and deaccelerates the whole debt; its procedural effect is to dismiss the complaint and reinstate the amount of the debt outstanding prior to default. In some states, this right may be exercised only once in so many (say, three to five) years. Once a reinstatement right is not exercised, the mortgagee may immediately move for a summary judgment: The decree or order thus sought will state that the mortgage documents are valid, the foreclosing mortgagee may enforce them, the reinstatement period (as well as the fees and costs incurred) has expired, and fix the time, place, method, and notices of sale, including the bidding procedure to be used.

METHODS OF FORECLOSURE

Judicial Foreclosure

The most common method of foreclosure is *judicial foreclosure*. It is the only method of foreclosure in about 20 states but is available in all states. It requires a public sale of the secured property. The sale is organized by a public official, often the county sheriff, "crying the property from the steps of the courthouse." It is conducted like an auction, at which the foreclosing mortgagee is permitted to bid. (This is not uniformly so when the sale is conducted using other methods.) Its purpose is both to protect the equity of the mortgagor in the property and to liquidate the mortgagee's security by the sale, inviting competitive bidding intended to obtain the highest possible price for the mortgagor's benefit. How well it accomplishes that last objective is a subject of debate today. It is more consistent with the lien, rather than the title, theory of mortgages. It "forecloses" the equity of redemption and enforces the lien, meaning that it wipes out interests in the secured property junior to it and by operation of law takes the title from the mortgagor and transfers it to the purchaser at the sale.

The procedural steps in a judicial foreclosure are as follows:

1. the filing of a summons, a complaint showing proof of ownership of the note and mortgage, and a *lis pendens*, followed by an answer and other pleadings as necessary, and a motion for summary judgment and a trial;
2. the appointment of a master or referee to compute the debt outstanding (and sometimes to have the secured property appraised) and to search the title so that the proceeds of the upcoming sale can be allocated among the claimants for it;
3. the report of the referee;
4. a judicial order, judgment, or decree authorizing the sale (sometimes this is a *decree nisi*, ordering the transfer of title to the purchaser at the sale, unless the sale is for some reason upset);
5. notice or advertisement of the sale;
6. the sale; and
7. a judgment confirming the sale and the distribution of the proceeds.

When there are timelines attached to the last four steps, the opening of a judicial order, judgment, or decree of foreclosure to modify the date of the sale, its terms and conditions, the modified judgment is likely to be considered a new judgment, requiring the running of a new timeline. *See Bank of N.Y. Mellon v. Tope*, 286 A.3d 891, 901 (Conn. 2022).

There are three times during this process when agreed-to numbers are necessary: The first is when the amount of the outstanding debt is determined and the sale ordered; the second is when the purchase price at the sale is determined and the sale is confirmed; and the third is upon the distribution of the proceeds of the whole proceeding. Failing to agree at each of these points is likely to produce an appealable issue because a failure at each point will unsettle the next number. *See Saunders v. KDFBS, LLC*, 239 A.3d 1162, 1167 (Conn. 2020).

Examples

Example 9

A mortgagee files for foreclosure. The defendant mortgagor answers that the mortgagee must produce the note and mortgage. The mortgagee cannot. Upon the defendant's motion to dismiss, the judge dismisses the action. Will the dismissal be upheld?

Explanation

Yes, unless the mortgagee produces some substitute proving ownership of these documents or shows that he was transferred the note by the party in possession of it when it was lost, the mortgagee lacks standing to bring the suit.[1] The court dismissing the suit at this point is protecting the integrity of the judicial process because foreclosure is an action to satisfy the debt, in whole or part: If foreclosure is the equivalent of a final payment, the mortgagor is entitled to have the note cancelled so that the mortgage lien is extinguished.

There are UCC provisions that mortgagees and others use to overcome the "lost note or instrument" problem of proving their entitlement and standing to foreclose. Both are versions of UCC §3-309. Under a 1990 version of §309 in effect in about 35 jurisdictions, the plaintiff must prove

---

1. This proof becomes more difficult when several transfers have occurred in the secondary market for mortgages. The note upon each transfer will be endorsed, and when the spaces for endorsing on the note are filled, an *allonge* will be attached to the note. An allonge is a piece of paper attached to a negotiable instrument such as a note, in order to annotate further endorsements when the original note is filled with endorsements. Endorsements are needed when the note and mortgage are purchased by new investors, when a lender sells a mortgage portfolio, or when a bank is merged or acquired by another institution. Many notes were lost as a result of the reorganization of the mortgage market during the 2002-2008 financial recession, in which mortgage lending played a major part.

that it "was in possession of the instrument and entitled to enforce it when loss of possession occurred." *See Dennis Joslin Co. v. Robinson Broad. Corp.*, 977 F. Supp. 491 (D.D.C. 1997). A later, 2002 version of §309 requires proof identical to that required by the earlier version (§309(A)), but §309(B) also permits enforcement when a party "as directly or indirectly acquired ownership of the instrument from a person who was entitled to enforce" it when loss of possession occurred. *See Lawyers Title Ins. Co. v. Novastar Mortgage, Inc.*, 862 So. 2d 793 (Fla. Dist. Ct. App. 2003). About 15 jurisdictions use this early version of §309. Thus the mortgagee is more likely to obtain standing to foreclose under the 2002 version of §309 than under the earlier version. Section 309's other requirements for obtaining standing, applicable in every jurisdiction adopting the UCC, are that the note was not lost as the result of its "transfer or lawful seizure" and that the plaintiff "cannot reasonably obtain possession" because "the instrument was destroyed, its whereabouts cannot be determined, or it is in the wrongful possession of an unknown person or one not amenable to service of process."

Preparation for this sale includes a search of the title, in order to establish the persons to whom the proceeds of the sale are to be paid and the order in which they will be paid. Thus judicial foreclosure is particularly useful as a remedy when there is some dispute about priority of liens that the searcher and the court can help to resolve.

At the foreclosure sale, equity of redemption is wiped out. The interest being sold is twofold: It includes both the interest of the mortgagor and the interest of the mortgagee—both borrower's and lender's interests are sold. The purchaser is not necessarily buying a fee simple absolute; rather, the title to be sold is subject to any liens superior to that of the foreclosing mortgagee.

A bid at the sale is an offer to purchase. It is binding upon acceptance by the official conducting the sale. The successful bidder cannot withdraw her bid after the fall of the auctioneer's hammer; that is, the point at which the bid is considered accepted, although a few cases hold that a judicial confirmation is the point of acceptance. Few cases permit a successful bidder to withdraw the bid. Were it otherwise, a sale that may be routinely undone is unlikely to bring out serious bidders or fetch a high price. So generally even a mistake of fact is insufficient to permit withdrawal of the successful bid. Moreover, even if a court does order a resale after acceptance of the successful bid, any deficiency in the price brought by the later judicial sale may be assessed against the bidder at the first, as damages.

When the mortgagee bids, she is a privileged bidder at a judicial sale; she has a "credit bid," for which no cash need be raised and no certified check presented, up to the amount of the mortgagor's outstanding debt. By this point in the proceedings, this amount will be either certified by the court or incorporated into its presale judgment. Thus the mortgagee does not have to pay cash up to the amount of her lien. Her status as a credit bidder has in practice dampened competitive bidding at judicial sales.

The decree in foreclosure confirms the lien and title priority of various lienholders. Sometimes, however, it is a *decree nisi*, issued before the sale. This type of decree becomes absolute after the sale, unless some objection is raised to the conduct or the results of the sale. On the other hand, sometimes the decree is granted after the sale, and in this instance it confirms the sale.

The proceeds of the sale are distributed, first, to pay the expenses of the foreclosure, including court costs, the costs incurred by the sheriff, and the attorneys' fees and other costs incurred by the foreclosing mortgagee; second, to pay the foreclosing mortgagee the outstanding debt; third, to pay other liens that would otherwise be extinguished by the proceeding, in the order of priority established in the order for the sale; and, fourth, to the extent there is a surplus, to pay the mortgagor. If the sale proceeds are insufficient to pay the outstanding liens and encumbrances subject to the action, then the mortgagor is liable for the amount of the insufficiency in what is known as an action for a deficiency judgment.

The advantages of a judicial foreclosure are several. First, because the sale is conducted under the supervision of a court, it is less susceptible to abuse and is beyond suspicion. Second, if the sale does not fetch enough to satisfy the amount of the debt, a deficiency judgment is possible in most jurisdictions. Third, as noted previously, this method of foreclosure will resolve conflicts involving the priority of various liens; so, if a title problem is known beforehand, judicial foreclosure is often the preferred method of foreclosure. Fourth, where the mortgagee has made optional advances, the status of the foreclosing mortgagee's lien may be "split" and the portion with the higher priority may be foreclosed. Thus, when there are title problems, junior liens, disputes over the amount of the outstanding debt, or a need for an appraisal to evidence the value of the secured property for deficiency judgment purposes, this method of foreclosure will likely be used.

EXAMPLES

Examples

Example 10

Should the holders of interests existing at the time the mortgage was executed and recorded be notified of the foreclosure and made parties to it?

Explanation

No. The holders of these "senior" interests are not affected by the foreclosure. They are not necessary parties to it.

Example 11

Who should receive notice and be joined?

Explanation

The original mortgagor and the current owner of the secured property (when not the mortgagor) should be. Being an estate in land, the equity is alienable and is thus transferred to the current owner, whether or not the transfer is express (the equity is an implied, not an express right). The original mortgagor and the current owner are both holders of the equity of redemption, are thus necessary parties, and, if not joined, will not have that right foreclosed by the action. Persons who guaranteed the debt secured may also be served, but need not be. They are proper but not necessary parties: In the foreclosure action their liability on their guarantee is contingent, often on the enforcement of any later deficiency judgment. All persons who might exercise the equity of redemption should receive notice and be joined: That includes junior mortgagees, on the theory that on the mortgagor's conveyance of a junior lien, the interests and estates remaining with the mortgagor after executing the senior mortgage include the right to exercise the equity of redemption if the mortgagor does not do so. When the mortgagor fails to exercise the equity, the junior is, by the doctrine of equitable subrogation, permitted to step into the mortgagor's shoes.

Example 12

Once the action is commenced and all necessary parties are served, can the mortgagor transfer the equity of redemption?

Explanation

Theoretically yes, but as a practical matter, the answer is no. Why? Because the effect of the *lis pendens* is that once the action is commenced, all persons with actual or constructive notice of it are bound by it and may not thereafter become bona fide purchasers of the equity; thus, in effect everyone is on notice of the pending foreclosure action. This explains why a foreclosure is an *in rem* action.

Power of Sale Foreclosure

There is an alternative to judicial foreclosure in many states. The next most widely available method of foreclosure is a *power of sale foreclosure*. It is available in 35 states and the District of Columbia. The sale here is conducted under a mortgage with a power of sale, or a deed of trust (today a common form of security instrument).

The sale conducted under a power of sale or a trust deed is a private sale; the person conducting it is a private party, not a public official. Otherwise, the sale will look like that conducted in the course of a judicial foreclosure;

it will often be an auction sale, advertised in advance as required by state statute. Because this private sale is typically authorized in a deed of trust, rather than a mortgage, the person conducting the sale will often also be the trustee authorized to do so in the deed. It is cheaper than judicial foreclosure and takes substantially less time.

The first step after the debt has been accelerated is a notice of default to the trustee, which is often recorded on the public records. When and if the trustee orders the sale in response to the notice, that order may be recorded as well. Thus at various crucial steps, the public records will reflect the exercise of this power.

While preparing for the sale, the trustee will typically order a title search and obtain a title insurance policy. Searching the title is required in a judicial foreclosure, but not in a power of sale foreclosure. Nonetheless, obtaining a title search and insurance is a widespread practice that harmonizes a power of sale with a judicial foreclosure.

Three typical statutory requirements for a power of sale foreclosure are (1) that the property be appraised and a floor bid set, (2) that the sale, privately conducted, not be firm until confirmed by a court decree, and (3) that the mortgagee not be permitted to bid at the sale. In one state, Colorado, power of sale foreclosures must be conducted by a public trustee, who is a county employee with jurisdiction over all private power foreclosures in that county.

Why has power of sale foreclosure proven so popular? Its cheapness, informality, and relative speed are definite advantages, but there are some procedural advantages as well. The deed of trust empowers the trustee to hold the lien and foreclose it when given notice of a default by the mortgagee (here known as the beneficiary of the trust). Thus the deed of trust looks like a return to the title theory of mortgages. With a mortgage, the mortgagee must initiate the action in foreclosure to perfect her lien; she has the burden of litigation. With the deed of trust, the burden of bringing litigation shifts to the "mortgagor" (known as the settlor of the trust), who must initiate litigation to enjoin the sale from taking place or to exercise the equity of redemption. The shift in the burden of litigation also signals a shift (to the borrower) in the burden of proof. Finally, the trust lasts as long as its purpose—collection of the debt—and no statute of limitations runs against it from the due dates of the loan.

Typically, too, the trustee will be an officer of the lender or lending institution. She is nominally the mutual agent of both the beneficiary and the settlor. Generally, a court will not interfere with the exercise of a power of sale absent fraud, chilled bidding, or other conduct by the mortgagee exercising the power shocking to the court and working irreparable injury to the mortgagor. *See Wansley v. First Natl. Bk. of Vicksburg*, 566 So. 2d 1218, 1224 (Miss. 1990) (noting that the trustee conducting a sale is more akin to an agent than a fiduciary). In some states, there is no right of statutory redemption following a sale under a private power by a trustee.

The constitutionality of power of sale foreclosures has been litigated extensively. Most of the cases have found that there is no state action and so the Due Process Clause of the Fourteenth Amendment is inapplicable. *See Charmicor v. Deaner*, 572 F.2d 694 (9th Cir. 1978); *Northrip v. Federal Natl. Mortgage Assn.*, 527 F.2d 23, 27 (6th Cir. 1975); *Kottcamp v. Fleet Real Estate Funding Corp.*, 783 P.2d 170, 172 (Wyo. 1989). Most of the theories of state action have been argued and rejected in the context of a power of sale foreclosure. However, the question of state action and that of the due process requirements for a hearing are distinct. *See FDIC v. Morrison*, 568 F. Supp. 1240 (N.D. Ala. 1983) (finding the lack of personal or *Mullane* notice to be a violation of due process), rev'd, 747 F.2d 610 (11th Cir. 1984) (finding that the mortgagor was not deprived of any property interest because Alabama is a title state).

Strict Foreclosure

The third method, *strict foreclosure*, once common, is today an ancillary method. We have already discussed this method in Chapter 11, in its common law form. The passage of "law day," the day when the accelerated debt is due, extinguishes the mortgagor's equity of redemption. *See U.S. Nat'l Bank v. Rothermel*, 260 A.3d 1187,1193 (Conn. 2021) (extinguishment upheld for payment one day after law day). This early extinguishment is peculiar to strict foreclosure. Moreover, there is often no sale in a strict foreclosure, and (even if there is a sale) traditionally no request for a deficiency judgment, since its purpose is to make the defeasible title of the mortgagee absolute and terminate the equity of redemption. At common law, the risk that the property proves insufficient to satisfy the debt in full is on the mortgagee. Strict foreclosure is used regularly today in only two states, Connecticut and Vermont. *See JP Morgan Chase v. Essaghof*, 249 A.3d 327,333-334 (Conn. 2020) and *Prue v. Royer*, 67 A.3d 895, 913 (Vt. 2013). "Historically, a foreclosure proceeding was an absolute bar to further action on the mortgage debt. *** Starting in 1835, a succession of statutes established the mortgagee's right to a judgment for the deficiency when the value of the property proves inadequate to satisfy the mortgage debt in full." *Esaaghof*, *op. cit*, 249 A.3d at 334. There is also a considerable body of case law on its use in Illinois as well. In this latter state it is hedged with statutory restrictions on its use. About ten states have abolished it by statute. In most of the 19 states that permit it today, it is reserved for residual use in three types of situations: (1) when the mortgagor is insolvent (and thus impervious to a deficiency judgment); (2) when she has little or no built-up equity in the secured property (which equity could be protected or turned into cash by a sale), or where the mortgage being foreclosed was given for the entire purchase price of the property; and (3) when she has abandoned the property or does not appear in the course of the foreclosure action. Thus it is used when the property is worth less than the debt. In addition, it can be used where the mortgagee waives the right to any deficiency. *See Great Lakes Mortgage Corp. v. Collymore*, 302 N.E.2d 248 (Ill. App. Ct. 1973).

Today, strict foreclosure law has sometimes abandoned its sole reliance on the property as security and (as in Connecticut) extends the right to a deficiency judgment to foreclosing mortgagees. "It has long been the law in Maine that strict foreclosure of a mortgage satisfies the mortgage debt only to the extent of the value of the property at the time of foreclosure. Accordingly, actions were allowed for deficiencies following strict foreclosure." *See Hammond v. Stiles*, 567 A.2d 444, 445 (Me. 1989). By the same token, if there is a surplus over the debt when the mortgagee sells the property gained through strict foreclosure, the mortgagee does not have to disgorge it. *See Oceanic Kampgrounds, Inc. v. Camden Natl. Bank*, 473 A.2d 884 (Me. 1984). It does not, after all, involve a sale of the mortgagor and mortgagee's interest.

As we shall see, strict foreclosure is also used to fix up improperly performed foreclosures of other types, particularly to extinguish the interests of omitted junior lienholders, when justice requires it. *See Ellis v. M & I Bank*, 960 N.E.2d 187, 191 (Ind. App. 2011).

DEFENSES TO FORECLOSURE

In a judicial foreclosure, defenses are raised in the answer to the complaint, but in a nonjudicial, power of sale foreclosure, the mortgagor must obtain an injunction against proceeding with the sale, when raising matters such as the following:

1. No notice of acceleration of the debt was given.
2. No default in repayment occurred.
3. The amount of the debt is misstated.
4. Notice was not given to all necessary or indispensable parties.
5. The mortgage loan transaction was fraudulent and the mortgagee should have discovered the fraud.
6. The mortgagee agreed to modify the loan and then began foreclosure. *U.S. Bank Assn. v. Blowers*, 212 A.3d 226 (Conn. 2019).
7. The foreclosing mortgagee did not originate the mortgage and note and has not shown a chain of ownership of the note leading to itself.

The last defense listed, the "show me the note" defense, has given rise to much litigation in the decade after the financial recession of 2007-2008. Then an increasing number of jurisdictions, by statute or judicial decision, required the foreclosing party to show a chain of note assignments from the originating mortgagee to itself. Because of mergers and acquisition among mortgage lenders, producing the note is harder than it might seem: Mortgage loan files may be either lost or irretrievable as one lender succeeds another. *See J.E. Roberts Co. v. Signature Properties, LLC*, 71 A.3d 492 (Conn. 2013) and *United States Bank Natl. Assn. v. Ibanez*, 941 N.E.2d 40, 652-653 (Mass. 2011) (noting that in some jurisdictions, the assignment of the note carries with it the assignment of the mortgage, but that this is not so in Massachusetts: There the mortgage holder remains unchanged when the note is assigned).

Defenses must be raised before the sale, and often sooner, before the order or decree setting the terms of the sale is handed down. *See Carrington Mortgage Servs., LLC v. Moore*, 234 A.3d 293 (N.J. Super. Ct. 2020) (no defense to foreclosure that house was destroyed in a super-storm or hurricane).

Foreclosure is an equitable action. Equity acts *in personam*. Thus it is possible to sue in foreclosure in the jurisdiction in which the mortgagor can be found, even when her mortgaged property is located in another jurisdiction. It's possible, but as a prudential matter, a court in the jurisdiction where the mortgagor is will most likely decline to take up the matter. Why? Because its ruling on any defense would not have precedential value in the jurisdiction where the property is located, because it lacks the power to put the purchaser at the sale into possession, and because its *lis pendens* notice would have little value.

Examples

Example 13

A mortgagee sues mortgagor in foreclosure. Mortgagor raises the defense that the mortgagee did not comply with the jurisdiction's usury laws when the mortgage loan was originated. Will this defense succeed?

Explanation

No. Foreclosure is not an action to collect a debt; it is an *in rem* action against the security for the debt. So a judgment in foreclosure is not a judgment for money. This is the better argument, but the argument to the contrary is that if usury is present, the amount of the debt is misstated. See defense number 3, *supra*.

Example 14

In its foreclosure action, the mortgagee proves that it holds the note as an assignee from the originating mortgage lender. In answering the complaint, the mortgagor alleges fraud in the originating mortgage transaction. Will this defense succeed?

Explanation

No. The fraud defense is good against the originating mortgagee, but not against its assignee. It is a personal defense. The holder in due course doctrine limits the mortgagor's defenses to non-personal ones. Kurt Eggert, Held Up in Due Course, 35 Creighton L. Rev. 503, 536-544 (2002).

THE PROBLEM OF THE OMITTED JUNIOR LIEN

The previous discussion of the status of a junior mortgagee defined her as a necessary party to the foreclosure of the senior lien. In the properly conducted senior judicial foreclosure, her interest is wiped out. *See Crosskey v. Phillips*, 608 N.W.2d 475 (Iowa 2000); *U.S. Dept. of Hsg. & Urb. Dev. v. Union Mtge. Co.*, 661 A.2d 163 (Me. 1995); *Miami-Dade County v. Imagine Properties, Inc.*, 752 So. 2d 129 (Fla. App. 2000) (three cases involving judicial foreclosure). In these cases, a junior mortgagee was omitted from the foreclosure proceedings. These proceedings are not nullified by the omission, but at their completion, the junior's interest would be wiped out. The proceedings are not, however, *res judicata* as to her: A person not made a party to an action cannot be bound by its judgment or decree. So the omitted junior must be given an opportunity to exercise whatever rights she would have had in it had it proceeded with her participation. Chief among her rights was the right to exercise the equity of redemption if the mortgagor did not. Thus if the applicable statutes and rules would permit her to join the proceedings while her equity of redemption was still exercisable, she should be permitted to do so, restoring the opportunity she missed.

In about half the states using power of sale foreclosure, foreclosing mortgagees do not have to notify junior lienors. No such duty, no problem when they are omitted from the proceedings. Grant Nelson & Dale Whitman, Reforming Foreclosure: The Uniform Nonjudicial Foreclosure Act, 53 Duke L.J. 1399, 1470-1476 (2004). However, in the other states when the foreclosure sale is nonjudicial, and when judicial foreclosure is used, what can be done for the omitted junior (aka OJ) consistent with the prior proceedings?

When an OJ has been excluded from a senior foreclosure sale, she has several remedies. First, the OJ might bring an action to annul the prior foreclosure, forcing the foreclosing senior lienholder to reforeclose. The expense of doing this might force the senior—or the purchaser at the sale—to buy the OJ's lien. Second, the OJ may foreclose her lien. Bringing this action forces a revival of the senior lien, taking it out of the hands of the sale purchaser (who in effect bought it at the sale), but giving that purchaser the right to a credit or certified bid in the amount of that successful bid so long as it is no higher than the amount owed the senior. This ceiling on the purchaser's bid leads to a third remedy; that is, the OJ might "redeem"—buy and be assigned the senior lien. The omitted junior "redeems from the mortgage, not from the foreclosure sale to which he was not a party." *See Quinn Plumbing Co. v. New Miami Shores Corp.*, 129 So. 690, 693 (Fla. 1930). This third remedy gives the omitted junior the right to satisfy the senior mortgage by payment of the debt it secures. It requires the most cash—and on that account is the least used. *See Abdoney v. York*, 903 So. 2d 981 (Fla. App. Ct. 2005).

An OJ has narrower remedies as well. For example, if the foreclosure sale produced more than enough to satisfy the foreclosing senior lien, that surplus might be claimed by the OJ when it might otherwise go to the mortgagor. The OJ's claim in this instance seeks the imposition of an equitable or constructive trust on the surplus. *See Caito v. United California Bank*, 576 P.2d 466 (Cal. 1978). A further example, available in states having statutory reinstatement rights, is to roll back the prior proceedings so as to reinstate the senior debt by paying the senior the amount necessary to cure the default(s).

When the OJ discovers the senior foreclosure after the sale, what are the successful purchaser's rights? *See Murphy v. Farwell*, 9 Wis. 102 (1859). The purchaser at the foreclosure sale of the senior mortgage has an election to make. He has three remedies. First, he can pay off the junior lien and take title free of the omitted lien. This is the most commonly used remedy and is likely to be used if the property is appreciating in value. Second, he can reforeclose, this time including the OJ or the person holding her rights. In this reforeclosure, the purchaser will become the holder of a revived senior lien—the same lien with which the senior lienholder began the first foreclosure action. Third, he can petition for strict foreclosure against the OJ. In this strict foreclosure action, the decree will issue if the court finds that the junior lienor is not prejudiced by being omitted from the foreclosure.

This third remedy (strict foreclosure) by the purchaser against the OJ may be useful when it is unlikely that another sale would result in bids higher than were submitted in the original (defective) foreclosure or in bids sufficient to satisfy the OJ's debt, making a second foreclosure a futile act. So when the mortgagor has no built-up equity in the property, or when the property is 100 percent leveraged by the senior mortgage, strict foreclosure of the OJ's lien is appropriate: Decreeing it in these situations is akin to an equity court determining that the omission did not prejudice the OJ's rights. No harm, no foul. In addition, the OJ may have a cause of action on the note against the mortgagor, or against a negligent title searcher performing the title search for the prior proceedings.

An OJ's actual knowledge of the senior foreclosure might be another occasion for decreeing strict foreclosure against him. But what about the other remedies—reforeclosure or reinstatement? The OJ could have asserted a reinstatement right or attended the sale and bid. In this situation, he is estopped from foreclosing subject to the revived first mortgage and should be limited to his redemption rights. *Put up or shut up* should be the judicial response to someone who created this legal mess!

Examples

Example 15

ME forecloses on MR's home for good cause. ME purchases at the judicial sale. After the foreclosure decree is confirmed, an OJ appears and petitions to reopen the decree. ME responds that before the decree can be reopened, the OJ should deposit with the court the amount of the senior's (ME's) mortgage debt. Is ME correct?

Explanation

No. The omitted junior has an election to make. She can elect one of two remedies. First, she can foreclose her lien; in that foreclosure, she takes the title as she bargained for it (with the senior lien attached to it). However, because the senior lienholder's rights have been transferred by the foreclosure sale to the purchaser at that sale, that lien is revived for the purpose of the junior foreclosure, and the purchaser at the senior's sale becomes the holder of a revived senior lien. Second, the OJ can buy out the senior lien rights, now held by the purchaser at the senior sale. The forced deposit requested by ME here would turn the foreclosure remedy into a forced redemption before the election is made.

Example 16

P purchases at ME's foreclosure sale. P goes into possession and improves the property. OJ, an omitted junior mortgagee, petitions to open the judgment and elects to foreclose. Can P become a revived mortgagee at OJ's foreclosure sale for the amount of the senior debt, plus the value of her improvements?

Explanation

Yes, if the improvements were made in good faith and without the knowledge of OJ. In addition, P's revived lien can recover the cost of necessary repairs, taxes, and insurance, as well as the costs of the OJ's foreclosure (but not the costs of the original foreclosure from which OJ was excluded), with a setoff for the rents and profits that P received from the property. If OJ were to redeem, the same values would be added and offset in computing the redemption price.

Example 17

Would your answers to the previous examples change if for the OJ you were to substitute an omitted mechanic's lienor or lessee of the secured property?

Explanation

No. Those who either have improved the property, like the mechanic's lienor, or are entitled to possession, like the lessee, are entitled to at least as much deference as the purchaser at the sale. The problem of the omitted party is a generic one—indeed, a classic one in the law of mortgages.

Omitted interest holders The holder of a recorded easement or other less-than-fee interest created and recorded after the mortgage and subject to extinguishment in the senior foreclosure may also be entitled to notice of the foreclosure, and be similarly omitted from the proceedings. That omitted holder is then also entitled to exercise an equity of redemption and any other rights that he would have had in the proceedings, and is subject to strict foreclosure. The less-than-fee interest does not mean that the redemption may be partial. The extent of the borrower's right, given when unexercised to the omitted holder, determines the extent of any later redemptioner's right. *See Diamond Benefits Life Ins. Co. v. Troll*, 77 Cal. Rptr. 581 (Cal. App. 1998) (collecting cases). Other types of less-than-fee holders entitled to omitted junior rights have included contingent remaindermen and co-tenants (although the cases split as to the latter). *See Williams v. Kimes*, 25 S.W.3d 150 (Mo. 2000). Omitted parties may also have their rights limited by power of sale foreclosure codes casting a heavy burden of proof on them when asserting their remedies. State statutes that create a rebuttable presumption of the trustee's compliance with statutory duties are examples. *See Perez v. 222 Sutter Street Partners*, 272 Cal. Rptr. 119 (Cal. App. 1990).

PURCHASE MONEY MORTGAGES

A vendor might agree to waive a portion of the purchase price in exchange for a mortgage or deed of trust secured by the property. This "take-back" financing is also known as a purchase money mortgage; that is, the vendor takes back a mortgage from the purchaser for the balance of the purchase unpaid in cash at the closing. Even if a take-back vendor knows that the purchaser will also finance his purchase from a third-party mortgagee and the latter mortgagee records his mortgage first, the purchase money mortgage has priority over the third-party mortgage lien. *ALH Holding Co. v. Bank of Telluride*, 18 P.3d 742 (Colo. 2000). The execution of the purchaser's deed and the purchase money mortgage are considered simultaneous acts, so the purchaser's title is never unencumbered by the vendor's mortgage, and the purchaser is never in a position to assign rights in the property not subject to the preexisting take-back lien. Restatement (Third) of Property, Mortgages, §7.2 (1997), at 458. This purchase money mortgage doctrine rests on the same equities as a vendor's lien and sometimes on the expectation that the purchaser will use the property to satisfy the debt. This vendor's lien also takes priority over liens attached to the property by the purchaser preceding the execution of the third-party mortgage. This generous priority was also extended to a third person (other than the vendor) extending a loan for the purchase price, and in addition meant priority over any homestead, dower, community property claim, or any judgment docketed before the purchase money mortgage is executed.

Examples

Example 18

T loans P money for a 20 percent down payment, on the basis of which P agrees to purchase Blackacre from V in a brief but enforceable contract of sale. V agrees to loan P 10 percent of Blackacre's purchase price and P arranges for a mortgage loan for the rest of the purchase price from Big Bank. After P's sales contract for Blackacre is closed, what is the priority of the three mortgage liens?

Explanation

V, T, and Big Bank's lien have priority in that order. Both Y's and V's loans qualify as purchase money mortgages. Both of their resulting liens have priority over Bank's mortgage lien on the theory of instantaneous *seisin*. The purchase money mortgage status of both T's and V's liens is not destroyed either by the presence of Bank's lien or by the presence of multiple purchase money mortgage liens. Multiple purchase money mortgage liens, being creatures of the common law, are governed by a rule of first in time, first in right. Because T's mortgage lien attaches at the closing, however, and V's attaches earlier as the result of the vendor's lien attaching to the contract of sale, V's lien has priority over T's. The subsequent recordation of Bank's lien will not change this result. *See Insight LLC v. Gunter*, 302 P.3d 1052 (Idaho 2013).

DEFECTS IN THE FORECLOSURE SALE

A foreclosure sale is an "as is" conveyance of both the mortgagor's and the mortgagee's interest in the secured property. Submission of the high bid at the sale is in effect an offer to purchase, subject to judicial acceptance or an intervening objection that will delay the effect of any preexisting decree.

Moreover, the conduct of the sale itself may also create a defect in the title of the purchaser. *See BCGS, LLC v. Jaster*, 700 N.E.2d 1075 (Ill. App. Ct. 1998) (a judicial foreclosure).

With power of sale foreclosures, a substantial defect in the sale can render the purchaser's interest void. Examples involve the forgery of the mortgage being foreclosed, the foreclosure by a person not the holder of the note, or a sale without the mortgagee's authorization. Similarly, a failure of the foreclosure statute to meet the requirements of the constitution renders the purchaser's interest void. *See Turner v. Blackburn*, 389 F. Supp. 1250 (W.D. N.C. 1975). Other defects render the purchaser's interest voidable—that is, subject to redemption by the mortgagor unless the purchaser's interest comes into the hands of a bona fide purchaser. Examples of situations giving rise to a voidable interest in the purchaser are a defect in the authority of a trustee to conduct a private sale, a confusing description of the property subject to foreclosure, the conduct of the sale at the wrong door of the courthouse (per the notice or the deed of trust), and defective (rather than no) notice. These examples draw distinctions similar to the use of the void-voidable distinction elsewhere—for example, in the case of defective deeds. Most defects make the sale voidable, rather than void.

When the foreclosure is conducted under the authority of a power of sale, the trustee is a fiduciary of both the beneficiary and the trustor-mortgagor. As such, she may not "chill the sale": She may not inhibit or suppress the bidding. For example, announcing that the mortgagee will bid the full value of the property while knowing that the bid will actually be much less is in effect a scheme hatched with the mortgagee to prevent others from bidding. *See Sullivan v. Federal Farm Mortgage Corp.*, 8 S.E.2d 126 (Ga. App. 1940). And while she may announce the bids of prospective, but absent, purchasers, she steps closer to breaching the fiduciary's required fidelity to her principals by financing the purchase of the property with a loan to the successful bidder. Not requiring the cash or certified check announced as part of the terms of sale from a bidder, and later financing that bid with a loan, steps over that line. Finally, when she secretly buys at the sale, she is in breach of her duty: She has acquired an interest in the outcome of the sale and put herself in conflict with the mortgagor. *See Boatman's Bank v. Community Interiors, Inc.*, 721 S.W.2d 72 (Mo. App. 1986), noted in 53 Mo. L. Rev. 151 (1988).

Statutes also protect the purchaser's title after a power of sale foreclosure. In a dozen or so states, statutes provide that a notice of the sale, with recitals about its conduct, create a rebuttable presumption that the sale was in fact properly conducted. Other state statutes (including one in California) create an irrebuttable presumption to the same effect, but only with regard to the service of the notice.

In some 14 other states, the trustee conducting the sale is required to give the purchaser a deed that states that the sale was properly conducted; this statement renders the purchaser *prima facie* a bona fide purchaser.

Examples

Example 19

A state statute authorizes upsetting a power of sale foreclosure when the bidding has been chilled by the trustee. The property is purchased at the sale by someone paying less than one-fifth of its fair market value. The mortgagor protests. Will the sale be upset?

Explanation

Yes. At a certain point in every state a winning bid is so low when compared to the value of the property that the bidder can be denied the status of a bona fide purchaser, being presumed to know of the disparity. *See Krohn v. Sweetheart Properties, Ltd.*, 52 P.3d 774 (Ariz. 2002). Upsetting the sale on this basis is an exercise of an equitable function of the court and needs no statutory authority. (You may be surprised, however, at how low the price must be before a sale may be upset: A finding that the property sold for 20-25 percent of value is necessary.)

DISTRIBUTION OF SALE PROCEEDS

The purpose of foreclosure sale procedures is to ensure that the proceeds of the sale are applied to the outstanding debt. First, however, the costs of foreclosure (including the mortgagee's attorney's fees) must be paid; then the foreclosing mortgagee's debt is paid and, after that, junior mortgages and other liens and interests in the secured property (such as easement holders and lessees who would otherwise be wiped out by the foreclosure) are paid so that the sale purchaser obtains a marketable title; and finally the excess proceeds (should there be any) go to the mortgagor, the rationale being the first stated—that the overall purpose of the foreclosure is to pay the outstanding lien debt(s).

Examples

Example 20

MR owns Blackacre, subject to ME's mortgage lien. The property doubles in value. ME's lien is validly foreclosed. P1 is the successful high bidder at the foreclosure auction. P1 pays the deposit required by statute, but does not complete the sale and receive a deed to Blackacre. The auctioneer conveys Blackacre to the next highest bidder, P2. After all costs and liens, including ME's, are paid in full, P1 claims the excess. Will P1's claim succeed?

Explanation

No. P1 had no interest in the resale to P2 so long as she did not complete the sale, even if she improved the property in the interim. No equitable interest attaches to a sale bidder who does not perform as promised according to the terms of the sale. *See Simard v. White*, 831 A.2d 517 (Md. App. 2003), aff'd on other grounds, 859 A.2d 168 (Md. 2004). It is often said that winning bidders have an equitable interest in the secured property before the sale is confirmed and they receive a deed. However, that equity is a right to compel the issuance of the deed in specific performance and that right is lost if P1 does not perform according the terms of the sale. Bidders are not parties protected by the sale; the mortgagor is. The excess goes to MR.

Example 21

A foreclosure sale proceeds properly and the senior mortgagee is paid in full, leaving surplus proceeds. The mortgagor claims the surplus. A junior mortgagee successfully objects. Why is the objection sustained?

Explanation

The surplus is the remnant of—and substituted property for—the mortgagor's equity of redemption, and that is what was conveyed to the junior mortgagee when the junior mortgage was executed, so the mortgagor's claim to the surplus is reduced in priority accordingly. *See Bank of America NA v. B.A. Mortgage LLC*, 111 P.3d 226 (N.M. App. Ct. 2005). When might the junior mortgagee lose this priority? When she has additional security for the same debt in other property sufficient to satisfy her claim, a court *might* as a matter of equity vary the priority.

Example 22

In a junior mortgagee's foreclosure, the senior mortgagee claims the surplus. Will the claim succeed?

Explanation

No. The senior mortgage's lien is left intact after the junior's foreclosure. Even if the mortgagor is bankrupt, courts deny the claim.

Example 23

May a mortgagor waive his right to surplus proceeds?

Explanation

Probably, if a separate consideration is given for the waiver (of the equity of redemption) in the negotiation over the conditions of the sale. Bidders lose nothing by the waiver and it may also protect the process of bidding, preventing the mortgagor from bidding when he is without the means to buy and intends to default on his bid.

THE MERGER DOCTRINE AND DEEDS IN LIEU OF FORECLOSURE

When a holder of a less-than-fee interest, such as a mortgagee, acquires the fee, the lesser interest is extinguished by operation of law—that is, extinguished by the common law. Thus in litigation based on the common law actions, the lesser interest is merged into the greater. In contrast, in equity merger is a matter of intent. *See Licursi v. Sweeney*, 594 A.2d 396 (Vt. 1991).

Examples

EXAMPLES

Example 24

Suppose that a mortgagee ME holds both the junior and senior liens. If she forecloses the junior and a third party buys at the sale, is the senior lien extinguished?

Explanation

No. Foreclosure is an equitable action. Merger is a matter of intent in an equitable action like foreclosure. A purchaser at the sale presumptively made allowances for the amount of the senior lien when formulating the bid made at the sale. After this calculation is made, the purchaser takes title subject to the senior lien, which is not merged.

Example 25

Suppose the same facts as in the preceding example, except that ME buys at the junior sale.

Explanation

Now the senior lien is extinguished and merged into the fee. ME is presumed to have made the same calculation as would a third-party purchaser, but the effect of her purchase is that she is presumed to agree that the land stands for the total debt and the senior lien is extinguished. A second approach to this problem is to ask what ME bought at the sale. It is the mortgagor's right of equitable redemption. This being so, ME becomes both a borrower and a lender, which, Polonius advised, one should never be. The law takes Polonius's advice and merges the senior lien with the fee simple title. A third approach to this problem involves a principle of judicial economy: ME is in effect forced to foreclose both the junior and the senior liens at the same time. *See Licursi v. Sweeney*, 594 A.2d 396 (Vt. 1991); Belleville Sav. Bank v. Reis, 26 N.E. 646 (Ill. 1891). However, if there was an intervening lien at the time of the purchase by the foreclosing junior, her senior lien would not be destroyed. To extinguish the senior lien in this situation would give the intervening lienor a priority that she did not expect and mean that the foreclosing junior would lose a valuable priority, so no merger. *See Tom Riley Law Firm, P.C. v. Padzensky*, 430 N.W.2d 416 (Iowa 1988).

Example 26

Suppose that MR, a mortgagor, acquires both the note and the mortgage of ME, MR's lender. What is the state of MR's title?

Explanation

MR holds the fee simple absolute. The doctrine of merger extinguishes the mortgage lien by fusing it (a less-than-fee interest) into a greater—the fee simple. Neither can MR be both a borrower and a lender at one and the same time. MR's presumptive intent is to extinguish the note and the mortgage. This presumption has a title-cleansing effect; it frees the fee for further alienation.

Example 27

ME and MR execute a brief but enforceable note and mortgage. MR conveys her interest to GE, who takes title subject to ME's mortgage but does not assume the personal obligation to pay the note. Later GE acquires the note and the mortgage from ME. Are the note and the mortgage merged into GE's fee simple?

Explanation

Not completely. Merger is only partial in this instance. In a falling market, the amount of the debt purchased by GE may be greater than the fair market value of the land that GE earlier purchased. In such a case, GE has rights against MR for the difference between the outstanding debt purchased and the fair market value of the land. In taking title, GE calculated the worth of the land and so the doctrine of merger might extinguish the mortgage up to the amount of the purchase price, but GE would still have the benefit of her bargain with ME and so have ME's rights against MR up to the amount of the difference money. This protects ME's right to assign her investment in a falling market.

Example 28

Suppose the same facts as in the preceding example, but GE buys the note and mortgage at the same time as she takes title subject to. Merger?

Explanation

Probably. GE makes her deal when closing the transaction and takes without further rights against MR. GE is presumed to have made the calculations outlined in the preceding paragraphs at the closing table and adjusted (down) the price paid MR accordingly. It is also presumed that MR bargained less vigorously, knowing that merger would occur. Suppose in addition that GE assumes the obligation to pay the note. Then the answer is a clear yes.

Example 29

Now consider the other side of the chain of title. Suppose that ME acquires the title from a grantee (GE) of the mortgagor (MR). Is ME's mortgage lien merged into her title acquired from GE?

Explanation

It depends. Remember the problems about transfers from the mortgagor. The intervening grantees could either be assuming grantees (ASGs) or non-assuming grantees (NAGs). If ME becomes a NAG, no merger results, but if she becomes an ASG, then there is a merger. Mortgagees must be careful in this situation: Their counsel should explain to them that they should only take subject to if they wish to maintain their rights against MR in the future.

Example 30

ME begins foreclosure against MR, but settles the action before a decree by accepting a deed to the secured property in lieu of foreclosure from MR. What does that deed convey?

Explanation

MR's right of equitable redemption, as well as the fee title. MR could not give up the right of equitable redemption at the outset of the ME-MR mortgage transaction. Such redemption rights cannot be waived at the execution of the mortgage. To allow such a waiver would be a clog on the equity of redemption. Later, however, for good consideration, MR can bargain it away. (Courts look closely at this bargain.) MR exchanges it here for the extinguishment of the mortgage lien. But what about the debt? This is not a case of merger, but rather is an instance of a debt discharged by payment (substitute performance) or accord and satisfaction. ME has substituted the land for the debt. In accepting the deed in lieu, a mortgagee must realize that, because the foreclosure on the lien has not gone forward to a decree, any junior liens are not extinguished. Rather, they move up in priority. Thus, the mortgagee accepting a deed in lieu should be careful about forgoing foreclosure, and particularly careful about filing a deed of release for their lien, before searching the title to find out whether there are junior liens. *See Janus Properties, Inc. v. First Florida Bank*, N.A., 546 So. 2d 785 (Fla. App. Ct. 1989).

Example 31

MR is in default and negotiates with ME over the transfer by MR of a deed in lieu of foreclosure. MR wants one of the following three covenants in the deed: (1) a covenant that MR will receive one-half of the proceeds of any later sale of the property by ME; or (2) a covenant that ME will not sell the property for a year and will sell it back to MR if the latter finds a purchaser of whom ME approves and to whom ME will lend. As MR's attorney, which of these options would you advise?

Explanation

The first option would result in a shared appreciation mortgage, a SAM. *See* Chapter 13 for further discussion on alternative mortgage instruments. ME would not agree to this unless the appreciation can be realized within a short time. However, if MR agrees not to file for bankruptcy, he may obtain the mortgagee's agreement to share the proceeds on any resale. Because a mortgagor might later assert that this agreement was an equitable mortgage, MR may have to agree not to do this in order to obtain ME's consent. Several remaining problems also make this first option problematic. Does MR get to review the terms of the sale when it is finally made? How will one-half be calculated—as half the capital appreciation since the deed was given, half the purchase price, half the cash received at closing, subject to deductions for closing costs, and so on? It might be better, if ME is initially interested, to redo the deal as a fully thought-out SAM. The second covenant makes the deed look more like an equitable mortgage and so is unlikely to gain any mortgagee's approval. Better to refinance with a new mortgage.

STATUTORY REDEMPTION

Statutory, as distinguished from equitable, redemption is a post-sale right. Several New England states provide for it, as do all but four of the states west of the Mississippi River. In all, it is available to mortgagors in 33 states. Many of the major commercial states do not provide for statutory redemption, and some states do not provide this right in a power of sale foreclosure. While equitable redemption redeems the mortgage (paying the outstanding amount of the secured debt), statutory redemption redeems the title from the sale, paying the sale price.

Statutory redemption rights begin at the sale, when the right to equitable redemption ends. It provides a period of time, varying from state to state—usually six months but sometimes as long as two years—in which the person eligible to redeem can pay the sale price and redeem the title. It is intended to act as a check on low bidding at the foreclosure sale and to allow a mortgagor additional time to obtain refinancing of the property while having its use; the mortgagor is typically assumed to be the most likely redemptioner. Its effect, however, may be to depress the bids, because would-be purchasers know that they cannot possibly obtain a marketable title until the right expires.

The mortgagor has the right of possession during the redemption period.[1] The right is alienable by the mortgagor, but the mortgagee cannot levy on it. It often applies to both judicial and power of sale foreclosures.

The effect of the mortgagor's exercise of this right is to terminate the title acquired by the purchaser at the foreclosure sale. The mortgagor's title is restored ("redeemed") to its status just before the sale, not transferred from the purchaser. The next issue is the extent to which other liens are revived. Some courts hold that all junior liens are revived; some in addition take the position that not only are junior liens revived, but so are senior liens to the extent that they remain unsatisfied by the proceeds of the sale. Still others attach the foreclosing mortgagee's lien, but only to the extent of a deficiency judgment. (The third position differs from the second because many states limit the right to a deficiency.) Finally, a few courts hold that the grantee or transferee of a mortgagor has a redemption right that when exercised does not revive junior liens. This fourth position has been roundly criticized as a violation of the rule that no grantee can obtain more than her

1. So the mortgagor also has the ability to work the property for rents and profits and so perhaps to eventually refinance the defaulted mortgage. While this possession may be of some benefit to the mortgagor, studies show that very few persons holding these rights actually exercise them. Even assuming that they increase the costs of doing business for mortgagees, legislators like statutory redemption nonetheless: The lenders are in a better position to spread the costs over all mortgagors for the benefit of those mortgagors who can and do redeem.

grantor has to convey. It is, however, an incentive to mortgagees who foreclose to bid up the foreclosure sale price. On the other hand, the California Civil Code, §729, takes the position that liens extinguished by the sale are not reattached after redemption. Thus junior liens are extinguished and the accompanying note cannot be used to levy a judgment in order to satisfy the debt that note represents.

Junior mortgagees and lienors are often authorized to redeem as well. Often their redemption rights are limited in time (to a period, following a time during which the mortgagor alone is entitled to redeem). Moreover, they are typically permitted to redeem one at a time, in accordance with their original priority of title. Thus senior redeemers can preempt the rights of juniors. Less frequently, juniors can redeem in any order and the priority of liens is relevant only to the extent that it determines what amount the junior must pay for the privilege—that is, all interests and liens senior to the redemptioner's must be paid in the process.

When redeeming, a junior mortgagee or lienor acquires the rights of the purchaser at the sale. The latter is regarded as the successor to the mortgagor for this purpose. Because the junior may herself be subject to a prior right to redeem, the title she gets upon redemption is more akin to the purchaser's than the revived mortgagor's title because, during the remainder of the redemption period, it ripens into an absolute title. Absent special statutory language, this ripening accords with the spirit of the statute, provides the full period of redemption to all eligible to redeem, and encourages a foreclosing mortgagee to bid up the sale price. Regarding the redemptioner as taking the purchaser's right is also a matter of judicial economy: Since the purchaser has all the rights gathered into the foreclosure proceedings, further judicial action is not needed to confirm the redemptioner's title.

Often only those joined in the foreclosure action can assert a statutory redemption right. Or. Rev. Stat. §23.560 (2010). Thus omitted juniors do not have this right. *See Portland Mortgage Co. v. Creditors Protective Assn.*, 262 P.2d 918 (Or. 1953).

This right is a creation of statute, and determining who has it requires close attention to the statute at issue.[2] The following examples reflect the types of statutory analysis you might encounter.

---

2. These rights are limited in various ways. Minnesota extends the redemption period when the foreclosure sale price is low. Minn. Stat. §580.23 (2010). Missouri limits the right to foreclosures that result in the mortgagee purchasing at the sale (as well as to power of sale/deed of trust foreclosures). Mo. Rev. Stat. §443.410 (2010). Kentucky permits redemption only when the foreclosure sale price is two-thirds of fair market value. Ky. Rev. Stat. Ann. §426.220 (2010). In some states the right may be waived; in others it may not. Kan. Stat. Ann. §60-2414 (2010). Some Midwestern states have longer statutory redemption periods for agricultural land and permit redemption at the fair market value, not the sale price as is usual. Others require the mortgagee purchasing at the sale of agricultural land to offer the mortgagor a right of first refusal before reselling.

Examples

Example 32

P purchases land at a properly conducted foreclosure sale. During the statutory redemption period, T trespasses on the land. May P sue T in trespass?

Explanation

It depends. Ask yourself what P bought. Some statutes have been interpreted to provide P with a determinable fee simple—that is, one subject to termination upon the exercise of the statutory redemption right. Others say that, up to the end of the redemption period, P has the right to get his purchase price back—a right to money, but not the title nor any interest in it—and thereafter has title in fee simple absolute. If P has a determinable title during the redemption, he has the right to sue trespassers, but if he has only a right to money, he has no right to sue.

Example 33a

MR and ME execute a brief but enforceable mortgage, upon which ME begins foreclosure for good cause. The title of the purchaser at the sale is subject to a one-year statutory redemption right. Before the sale, MR conveys her interest in Blackacre to GE, who assumes MR's obligation on the mortgage debt. Can GE exercise MR's statutory redemption right?

Explanation

Yes. Unless the statute provides otherwise, even a statutory right is freely alienable. Such a right is often an opportunity to attempt to refinance the property, and the mortgagor can be expected to transfer the right to a creditworthy person. Unless the transaction is a fraudulent one, the right to transfer is implied from the statute and the redemption right is now GE's.

Example 33b

Assume the same facts as in the preceding example, except that GE takes a title subject to the mortgage but does not assume the debt. Does your answer change?

Explanation

GE is not able to exercise MR's statutory redemption right because GE has not fully stepped into MR's shoes, and only by doing so is she extended the right to redeem. Only when GE assumes the debt is the object of the transfer assumed to be refinancing, MR here retains the right to refinance and MR has not fully stepped into the MR's position. MR retains the right to refinance and should seek refinancing assumable by GE.

Example 33c

Now assume that GE takes title after the foreclosure sale. Does this make a difference?

Explanation

GE has no statutory redemption rights. They normally arise at the sale. Why don't we extend statutory redemption rights to GEs who take before the final decree, rather than the sale? We probably should.

Example 33d

What if GE conveys her interest in Blackacre to VE under an installment land sale contract, and both GE as the vendor under the contract and VE wish to exercise the statutory redemption right? Who has priority?

Explanation

GE, as the vendor under the installment land sale contract, has priority of redemption as against her vendee VE. Where two persons both hold the statutory redemption right, the person closest to MR has the prior right.

Example 33e

If ME purchases at the foreclosure sale, can she exercise a redemption right?

Explanation

No. Otherwise, the lender would be encouraged to submit a very low bid at the foreclosure sale, sue out a deficiency judgment, and then exercise the statutory redemption right, obtain the title to the property, and resell it. Likely the mortgagee would be made more than whole by this panoply of remedies. The purpose of statutory redemption is to put a check on such low bids, so giving the lender statutory redemption rights would defeat the purpose of the statute.

Example 33f

MR (the defaulting mortgagor) successfully exercises the right of statutory redemption in a timely manner. How does she then hold the title?

Explanation

When MR redeems, absent a statutory scheme to the contrary, all the liens preexisting the foreclosure (except the foreclosed lien) are revived.

Sometimes, the lien being foreclosed is also revived, but only to the extent of a deficiency. Other courts do not revive the deficiency lien, reasoning that the foreclosing mortgagee has an independent remedy for a deficiency. Not reviving liens would result in a windfall to MR, but on the other hand, nonrevival of liens would encourage full credit bids by mortgagees and junior lienors at the sale. Revived liens are the result of winding the state of the title backward to the time of the sale. If the redemption right is exercised by a subsequent, presale purchaser of the property such as GE in Example 33a, some courts hold that junior liens are not revived as they would be against the redeeming mortgagor; nonrevived junior lienors may then sue on their notes and reduce their judgments to new liens on the property.

MORATORIA ON FORECLOSURES

During the 1930s, several states enacted moratoria on the foreclosure of mortgages and deeds of trust. These statutes were enacted on an emergency basis, for limited amounts of time, and in the hope that after the moratoria period had passed, the value of the property as security for the debt would have been restored by the return of good times. Meanwhile, they permitted mortgagors to remain in possession of the secured property. Such statutes were found constitutional in *Home Building & Loan Assn. v. Blaisdell*, 290 U.S. 398 (1934) (finding no taking or impairment of contract). During the 1980s, as regions of the country experienced economic hard times in the Farm Belt and the Rust Belt, more limited moratoria were enacted, often for residential or farm mortgages, allowing (say) a six-month postponement of foreclosure in order to obtain refinancing or restructure the terms of a mortgage. Iowa and Minnesota enacted such statutes. A court considering a postponement petition was to take account of the relative financial strengths of the mortgagor and mortgagee, the mortgagor's other assets, credit history, employment prospects, equity in the secured property, and the prospect that a postponement or restructuring of the debt would eliminate the default. Similar moratoria have been enacted during the COVID-19 pandemic.

ANTIDEFICIENCY LEGISLATION

Many jurisdictions impose some type of control on deficiency judgments, even if they are only procedural, with special notice and time limits placed on the action to enforce them. A deficiency judgment is a judgment for the unpaid amount of the outstanding debt, sought after foreclosure fails to recoup it. A cause of action for a deficiency judgment is an ancillary action on the note and may be executed on the personal assets of the mortgagor to the extent that the debt in the note has not been satisfied by the proceeds of the foreclosure of the mortgage lien. In fact, deficiency judgments are not often sought after a foreclosure, but mortgagees like the threat they pose.

Typically the petition in foreclosure seeks a deficiency judgment in the alternative. If it does not make this request, then the deficiency must be sought within the statute of limitations or within the time after which such an action is barred by laches, unless there is ongoing, related litigation interfering with the computation of the deficient amount or reopening the foreclosure decree.

State statutes prohibiting or limiting the amount of deficiency judgments are of two types. The first type prohibits such judgments when (1) the mortgage is for purchase money when the vendor either takes back a mortgage for a portion of the purchase price (usually its balance), or (2) the purpose of the loan is the acquisition of title (the loan being extended either by a third party or the vendor), or (3) the property is foreclosed under a power of sale as opposed to judicial foreclosure or other method subject to judicial supervision, or finally (4) the foreclosure is not subject to statutory redemption (as power of sale mortgages sometimes are not). Such statutes must be closely examined as to their scope. The first two prohibitions are often known as restrictions on purchase money mortgages. These "purpose and procedure" statutes can seldom be waived at the time of the execution of a mortgage.

The second type of antideficiency statute requires that the foreclosure sale price be for "fair value." This is not just the property's fair market value. These statutes provide that a deficiency judgment shall be for no more than a foreclosure court finds would be the excess of the debt over the property's fair value, assuming that is what would be bid at the foreclosure sale and sometimes considering not just the current fair market value but also the use value of property whose current fair market value is depressed or for which there is no market in the very worst of times. They recognize that foreclosures often occur in hard times and affect property that would fetch more if the economy were better. Sometimes these statutes permit a lender to recover only the amount by which the unpaid debt exceeds the fair market value—assuming that no matter what the sale fetches, the lender shouldn't bid less than that value. *See Jackson Lumber & Millwork Co., Inc. v. Rockwell Homes, LLC*, 266 A.3d 288 (Me. 2022). These statutes require that an appraisal be built into the foreclosure process—something lenders will do anyway if they intend to bid at the sale. When the appraised value is determined in preparation for the sale, the mortgagee using it to bid at the sale should remember that, when a court will be asked to confirm the sale, it will be the value at the time of the sale that is determinative of the amount of the deficiency judgment. *See New England Phoenix Co., Inc. v. Grand Isle Veterinary Hospital, Inc.*, 275 A.3d 134, 142 (Vt. 2021). If the foreclosure is of a junior mortgage, the amount of the deficiency permitted will be the fair value minus the amount of any senior liens. Fair value statutes are not subject to waiver.

Both types of statutes were enacted during the Great Depression in the 1930s. They (1) assume that there is no sense in attempting to redo the sale to force a higher bid; furthermore, their objectives are to (2) prevent the foreclosed mortgagors from not only losing their property, but becoming debtors to boot—in a depression or recession, to prevent the continuation of such hard times—and (3) force mortgagees to bear the risk of a downturn in property prices.

Examples

EXAMPLES

Example 34a

Your jurisdiction enacts the following statute: "In all sales of real property by mortgagees and/or trustees under powers of sale contained in any mortgage or deed of trust . . . or where judgment or decree is given to secure the payment of the balance of the purchase price of real property, the mortgagee or trustee or holder of the notes secured by such . . . shall not be entitled to a deficiency judgment." Will this statute apply to commercial transactions as well as residential ones? How will we know the statute applies to a mortgage?

Explanation

As to the second question, the face of the mortgage should tell you, and if the mortgage does not state that it secures the purchase price, then the statute does not apply and it may be presumed that the mortgagor has waived its benefit. This statute is a highly edited version of N.C. Gen. Stat. §45-21.38 (1986), patterned after Or. Rev. Stat. §88.070 (1986). As to the first question, this statute applies to both types of transactions on its face. Mortgagees will suggest that commercial transactions will be hindered as a result, but unless there is support in the legislative history, this argument asks for a measurement of the number of deals that did not take place and is speculative.

Example 34b

What if after default, a purchase money mortgagee executes and records a deed of release for the mortgage lien and sues on the note? Does the statute in the prior example apply to that suit?

Explanation

Yes. Once a mortgage, always a mortgage. The lender cannot escape the reach of the statute by the release, even if it is executed before a default. *See Barnaby v. Boardman*, 330 S.E.2d 600 (N.C. 1985).

Example 34c

Does the statute apply to installment land sale contracts?

Explanation

An installment land sale contract is by definition a purchase money instrument, so the answer is yes, if the case law in the jurisdiction is sufficiently clear that these contracts function as mortgages and so require foreclosure in place of the enforcement of the forfeiture clauses often contained in them. By the same token, the statute should apply to a suit based on a vendor's lien, unless there is some equitable basis for not applying it: Such liens are creations of equity and so not clearly controlled by the statute's terms.

Example 34d

A vendor takes back a junior mortgage in the course of a land transaction. The senior mortgagee forecloses and the junior mortgage is wiped out by the decree. The proceeds of the foreclosure sale are insufficient to satisfy the debt secured by the junior mortgage. Does the statute apply to the junior mortgagees in this situation?

Explanation

In such a situation, the junior mortgagee will be permitted to release the mortgage lien and sue for a deficiency judgment, because if she can't, she lacks an effective remedy and the statute may unintentionally encourage mortgagor fraud. The statute does not on its face distinguish between senior and junior liens, and if this distinction were made, an unsecured junior lender might be better off than the secured one. A junior lender might in this situation ask for a negative pledge and an agreement not to further encumber the land. *See* Chapter 12, *supra*.

Example 34e

A vendor gives a land acquisition purchase money mortgage, but later agrees to subordinate its first lien position to a mortgage given for further development of the land in a brief but enforceable subordination agreement. Does the statute apply to this now-junior mortgagee?

Explanation

Yes. The subordinating junior executed a purchase money mortgagee, for whom the prohibition on deficiency judgments is express. The statute denying a deficiency judgment defines that term as of the time the mortgage is executed, and the rule should be: Once denied such a judgment, always denied, unless the statutory purpose can be advanced by recharacterizing the transaction after the fact. *See Barnaby v. Boardman*, 330 S.E.2d 600, 603 (N.C. 1985). But there is a split of authority on this issue. *See Spangler v. Memel*, 498 P.2d 1055, 1062 (Cal. 1972). The issue here is whether to assign purchase money mortgage status at the time the mortgage is executed or later, when the deficiency judgment is sought.

Example 34f

A purchase money mortgagee properly begins foreclosure, but settles the action by taking a deed to the secured property in lieu of foreclosure. Does the statute apply?

Explanation

Yes. Unless there is some agreement otherwise, the mortgagee in this instance has substituted the property for the debt that would be collected in a deficiency judgment, just as might occur if the mortgagee bought a cause of action in strict foreclosure.

Fair Value Statutes. Twenty-two jurisdictions have this second type of antideficiency statute. The determination of "fair value" requires a judicial hearing and must be proven by a preponderance of the evidence. In this matter, the mortgagee has the burden of proof. Either the judge or a jury may determine fair value. This determination is made not at the time the mortgage was executed, but at the time of the foreclosure sale. The use of the phrase "fair value" and not fair market value is deliberate, intended to protect mortgagors in a falling market. Thus "fair value" might mean the secured property's investment value, its use or asset value, or some combination of these, along with its fair market value, giving courts discretion to use some combination of all these values. *See West Pleasant-CPGT, Inc. v. U.S. Home Corp.*, 233 A.3d 463 (N.J. 2020).

Example 35a

Consider a fair value statute providing that within a short time after the foreclosure judgment, "an action may be commenced to recover the balance due upon the debt for which the deed of trust was given as security" with a complaint setting forth the entire amount of such debt outstanding and the amount for which the property sold. Before rendering judgment, the court shall find the property's fair value at the date of sale: It "may not render judgment for more than the amount by which the amount of the indebtedness with interest, costs, and expenses of sale, including trustees and attorneys fees, exceeds the fair market value of the property as of the date of the sale." Is a junior mortgagee washed out in a power of sale foreclosure subject to the fair value provision of this statute?

Explanation

Not expressly, and because such a junior mortgagee as a plaintiff is not seeking to collect any deficiency from the preceding foreclosure, the answer is no: She is not limited by the fair value provision. Utah Code §57-1-32 (2005) (on which the provision in this example is based).

Example 35b

After a power of sale foreclosure, is a suit against a guarantor of the debt subject to the provision?

Explanation

It depends. The statute is not specific as to who may be sued. So, construed liberally as a debtor protection statute, guarantors of the debtor might also have the protection of the statute. A guarantee ensures a debt's payment, not its collectibility—and so is readily seen as performing the same function as a deficiency judgment. However, in many states with antideficiency statutes, courts are reluctant to cover them so long as the guarantor is not also the debtor otherwise protected by the statute. After all, the guarantee is a separate transaction whose form the courts often respect, and courts dealing with statutes not expressly covering them often await legislative action on the matter, allowing the common law right to sue on a contract to control in the interim. Second, guarantees are most used in states having antideficiency statutes, where they provide an alternative to a deficiency judgment for mortgagees and are relied on by them.

Example 35c

In a jurisdiction with a fair value statute, the fair market value at the time of the mortgage's execution is $125,000. The outstanding mortgage debt at the time of the foreclosure is $100,000. The mortgagee's winning bid at the foreclosure is $75,000, and the fair value of the property at the time of the sale is $90,000. What is the amount of the deficiency permitted the mortgagee?

Explanation

Ten thousand dollars ($10,000), that amount being the difference between the mortgage debt of $100,000 and the $90,000 fair value of the secured property. The foreclosing mortgagee is assumed to have obtained the difference between its bid of $75,000 and the fair value of $90,000 through the sale. The objective of the statute is to encourage the mortgagee to bid the fair value of the property. Here it did not. The mortgagee may sue for a $10,000 deficiency, add it to the $75,000 it bid at the sale, and the difference between that $85,000 total and its debt of $100,000 is lost to the mortgagee.

Example 35d

In the prior Example, if the cost and expenses of the foreclosure were $1,000, should that amount be added to the allowable deficiency?

Explanation

Yes, because those expenses will have first priority when the proceeds of the sale are distributed, so the foreclosing mortgagee will pay them and then recover them in the suit for the deficiency. They are not part of the fair value calculation.

Example 35e

In a jurisdiction with a fair value statute, a senior mortgagee forecloses on secured property whose fair value is $50,000 and submits a winning full credit bid of $30,000 at the foreclosure sale, extinguishing a $30,000 junior mortgage lien. The junior mortgagee moves for a deficiency judgment. The mortgagor opposes the motion. What is the mortgagor's best argument?

Explanation

It is that the junior mortgagee could have bid at the sale and wiping out his lien is the price he pays for not bidding. That argument is a good one when the proceeding is a judicial foreclosure, but weakens when a power of sale foreclosure is used because junior mortgagees are not often entitled to notice of the sale, as they are in a judicial foreclosure. More generally stated, the issue is whether fair value statutes are intended to protect mortgagors from wiped out juniors. Maybe not. Their objective is to protect mortgagors from foreclosing mortgagees who bid low at the sale, resell the secured property, and then sue for a deficiency, becoming unjustly enriched in the process. That being the objective, the statute should not shield the mortgagor from the junior's suit on his note. Moreover, he's not the foreclosing mortgagee and his suit is, strictly speaking, based on his note and is not for a "deficiency" but is instead a suit in assumpsit on the debt.

Example 35f

In the foreclosure of a junior mortgage in a fair value jurisdiction, what is the fair value of the secured property?

Explanation

Its fair value minus the amount of the senior lien(s).

Example 35g

In the prior Examples involving fair value statutes, does it matter that the purchaser at the foreclosure sale is a third party, as opposed to the foreclosing mortgagee?

Explanation

No. In either situation, the person protected by the statute is the mortgagor. Any purchaser is charged with knowledge that the jurisdiction has a fair value statute and will bid accordingly. In fair value jurisdictions, foreclosures are more expensive, and so mortgagees may be more inclined to modify the mortgage loan in default or accept deeds in lieu of foreclosure.

Example 36

If the mortgagee forecloses and then brings a suit based on a fraud in the mortgage loan application misrepresenting the value of the land, does an antideficiency statute apply to such a suit?

Explanation

Not if the misrepresentation amounts to fraud, because the statute is meant to bar secondary actions on the loan agreement or contract, not actions based in tort. *See Kass v. Weber*, 67 Cal. Rptr. 876, 879 (Cal. App. 1968). A fraud-based cause of action is not one based on the original loan agreement and debt. Bad faith waste of the property would similarly be beyond the reach of an antideficiency statute. *See Cornelison v. Kornbluth*, 542 P.2d 981 (Cal. 1975) (also holding that good faith waste, brought on by general market decline, is within the reach of the statute).

Example 37

A junior mortgagee subject to an antideficiency statute files a judicial foreclosure. She then learns that the senior is planning to file as well. The senior then files its own, more rapid, power of sale foreclosure that will extinguish the junior's lien. After the senior foreclosure is final, may the junior sue on its note as before?

Explanation

Yes, the junior's right to sue on the note is unaffected. The junior's rights shouldn't be affected by the statute just because the senior has chosen a more rapid method of enforcing its security interest. *See Bank of America Natl. Trust & Savings Assn. v. Graves*, 59 Cal. Rptr. 2d 288 (Cal. App. 1996).

Example 38

V sells property to P. V receives 20 percent of the purchase price and takes a note, but not a mortgage, for the balance. P then obtains a loan for the amount of that balance from ME, and in exchange gives him a note and mortgage. ME's mortgage loan goes into default, and at ME's foreclosure, V appears and claims priority for his vendor's lien. Does the statute apply? As between ME's mortgage and V's lien, which has priority?

Explanation

No, and ME's mortgage has priority. V took back no mortgage, so V does not have the benefit of the purchase money mortgage doctrine. While V has avoided the antideficiency judgment statute, V is left with only an equitable vendor's lien, reducible to judgment but not yet executed. ME's legal mortgage trumps V's equitable lien.

Example 39

O takes title to his home, giving a purchase money note and mortgage subject to a purchase money antideficiency statute to L1. O transfers the title to A, who assumes the mortgage, but later defaults. L1 files for foreclosure, buys at the sale for 70 percent of L1's outstanding debt, receives the deed, and transfers the title to O. O repurchases with loan money secured by L2's note and mortgage. It's a rule of law in the jurisdiction (as in many jurisdictions) that any purchase by O at the sale revives preexisting liens to the extent they then remain unpaid. Does L2 have lien priority over L1?

Explanation

Yes. The L2 lien has priority over the revived L1 lien. L1 is barred by the statute from obtaining a deficiency judgment, and L2 supplied the money for the purchase, thus energizing it. Then, using the stated rule and following the purchase money mortgage doctrine, it is fair that the L1 lien revive and reattach to the title, but that it be second to L2's. If L2 had not supplied the mortgage loan proceeds, L1's lien would have had no chance at revival and L1 would have no lien. *See DMC, Inc. v. Downey S&L Assn.*, 129 Cal. Rptr. 761 (Cal. App. 2002).

OTHER ANTIDEFICIENCY STATUTES

Other types of antideficiency statutes have the property appraised and require that the foreclosure sale bring that amount, or some stated fraction, say two-thirds, of the appraised value. W. Va. Code §38-4-23 (requiring two-thirds or an upset price established by the court). These statutes have a civil law origin, the first one being enacted in Louisiana. New York's statute, enacted in the 1930s, provided that a property bringing less than two-thirds of the appraised fair market value was subject to the statute, permitting the court to reset the amount of the deficiency permitted the mortgagee (again) as the difference between the outstanding mortgage debt and the fair value. The New York statute became a model for 11 other jurisdictions during the Great Depression.

Still another variety of statutes, available in only a few jurisdictions, provides that the mortgagee must elect either to sue on the note or to foreclose the mortgage lien, but not both. Such "election statutes" are also known as one action statutes. A related type of statute, found in seven jurisdictions, requires that a mortgagee sue first to foreclose the mortgage and only afterward to enforce the note—a so-called foreclose first statute. Like all other antideficiency statutes, they may not be waived. Often "one action" and "foreclose first" statutes are found in jurisdictions also having a fair value statute.

Example 40a

A mortgagee entitled to file foreclosure brings suit on the mortgage note before foreclosing. Has it violated the one action statute?

Explanation

No. The "action" here is not the filing of the suit, but obtaining a judgment either on the note or in the foreclosure action. The election to pursue one or the other must be made before recovering the debt in either action, or else the statute is violated. The objective of the statute is the prevention of a mortgagee's double recovery. When that happens, either the note or the mortgage becomes void.

Example 40b

Instead of suing either on the note or to foreclose, a mortgagee sues a third-party guarantor of the debt. Has the mortgagee elected an "action"?

Explanation

No. Why? Because the guarantor is not directly involved in the mortgage transaction and the mortgagor is unaffected by this suit. Thus a mortgagee may typically petition for the appointment of a receiver for the secured property, take action in the mortgagor's bankruptcy proceedings, or sue a guarantor, and not violate a "one action" statute.

Example 40c

In a "foreclosure first" jurisdiction, when the secured property is contaminated by pollution, a mortgagee entitled to foreclosure wishes to waive its lien and sue on the mortgage note. May it do this?

Explanation

Yes, if it can prove that in fact the secured property is worthless in foreclosure. Then the statute will not apply.

UPSETTING THE FORECLOSURE SALE

It is difficult for a mortgagor to upset the sale. In order to upset it, the mortgagor must show fraud or a gross irregularity in its conduct. In most jurisdictions, the inadequacy of the sale price standing alone is insufficient. *See McNeill Family Trust v. Centura Bank*, 60 P.3d 1277 (Wyo. 2003). Inadequacy coupled with fraud, however, is a basis for upsetting the sale. In these cases, the inadequate price is usually less than 40 percent of the property's fair market value. In some jurisdictions, a *gross* inadequacy of price, one shocking to the conscience of the court, is also a sufficient basis, even when standing alone: Here an inadequate price is a sufficient basis for upsetting a sale when the inadequacy is extreme, (say) less than 25 percent of value. *See Holt v. Citizens Cent. Bank*, 688 S.W.2d 414 (Tenn. 1984). Even when the price is grossly inadequate, the mortgagor must also convince the court that a second sale will bring a different, fairer result. Were it otherwise, the second sale would add to the amount of the deficiency judgment, doing the mortgagor no good.

One state imposes a fiduciary duty on mortgagees to conduct the sale to achieve a "commercially reasonable" result, akin to that imposed in UCC foreclosure sales of goods. See *First NH Mortgage Corp. v. Greene*, 653 A.2d 1076 (N.H. 1995), noted 40 St. Louis L.J. (1996). Most states considering the matter have rejected the imposition of such a fiduciary duty on mortgagees. *See Warner v. Clementson*, 492 S.E.2d 655 (Va. 1997); *Dreyfuss v. Union Bank of California*, 11 P.3d 383 (Cal. 2000) (also holding that a mortgagee has no duty of good faith and fair dealing to make a foreclosure bid in any particular amount).

Examples

Example 41a

A mortgagor (MR) purchased a house ten years ago for $100,000 and paid $20,000 down. The rest of the money came from a third-party, institutional mortgage lender, who took an $80,000 note and mortgage in exchange. MR lost her job three years ago, went into default on the note payments, and the mortgagee foreclosed a year ago when the outstanding debt on the note was $60,000. The foreclosure results in a high bid of $50,000, made by the mortgagee in a properly conducted sale. The fair market value of the house was $150,000 a year ago. Would you advise the mortgagor to use her still-available right of statutory redemption? How likely is it that the mortgagor will obtain the financing to permit her to do so?

Explanation

The statutory redemption right is worth exercising because it only requires that the mortgagor come up with $50,000, the foreclosure sale price, but the prospects of a defaulting mortgagor getting a new loan are dim. Still, she may qualify for a consumer loan, and getting a $150,000 home for $50,000 may be worth the higher interest rates on such loans.

Example 41b

Assuming that MR in the prior example does not exercise a right of statutory redemption and that she knows the mortgagee is offering the house for sale for $220,000, what would you advise MR to do?

Explanation

The fact that the price is a small fraction of the property's fair market value is insufficient, standing alone, to upset the sale. Here there is no suggestion of fraud and the chances of overturning the sale are (again) low. The mortgagee bargained for the use of the property as security and got what she bargained for in the foreclosure. Where price alone suffices to overturn the sale, the price is often lower than the price here. A very low price may raise a presumption of fraud in a few jurisdictions, but this is not the general rule. *See Danbury Sav. & Loan Assn., Inc. v. Hovi*, 569 A.2d 1143 (Conn. App. Ct. 1990). Although equitable redemption is unlikely once statutory redemption is available, it is not unheard of. *See State ex rel. LeFevre v. Stubbs*, 643 S.W.2d 103 (Mo. 1982); *Blades v. Ossenfort*, 481 S.W.2d 531 (Mo. App. Ct. 1972). The fact that the house is not yet sold weighs in the mortgagor's favor: No innocent purchaser is present, with equities outside the mortgagor-mortgagee relationship. So MR might be able to enjoin the sale.

Example 41c

Assume the facts in the previous two examples, but in addition assume that the bank is seeking a deficiency judgment against the mortgagor for \$10,000 (\$60,000 – \$50,000). What advice can you now give the mortgagor? If the deficiency is assessed, is MR paying twice?

Explanation

Yes. Resisting the deficiency judgment is possible. *See Suring State Bank v. Giese*, 246 N.W. 556 (Wis. 1933). The mortgagor has surrendered her equity in the house, and paying a deficiency would now unjustly enrich the foreclosing mortgagee.

CHAPTER 19

Real Estate in Trouble

WORKOUT PRELIMINARIES

A workout or loan modification is a term used by real property professionals to mean negotiations aimed at restructuring a mortgage loan for a borrower who is in default or having financial difficulties. With large mortgage lenders, these negotiations are typically conducted by persons who did not participate in the underwriting of a loan. A successful workout, like any negotiation, proceeds in stages. From the mortgagee's perspective, the first stage is to clear away some of the legal underbrush in order to understand the parameters of the discussion. An initial agreement on four items is needed: (1) the validity of the debt (aimed to flush out any defenses to it), (2) the facts constituting the default by the mortgagor, (3) the writings constituting the agreement about the loan (aimed at flushing out whether there are oral agreements extrinsic to these documents), and (4) any reservation of rights by either party surviving the present negotiations. Thus, this initial agreement is required by the mortgagee and would conclude that the debt is valid and subject to no defenses; that there is a default based on recited facts; that the documents incorporated by reference are the complete agreement between the parties and that these documents are not subject to parol evidence; and that the lender reserves all other rights under the documents agreed to be that complete agreement. How should a debtor-mortgagor, or his counsel, respond to a lender's request to execute such a four-part agreement before entering into further workout discussions?

As to the default, a mortgagee intending to enter into loan modification discussions must exercise caution. While a default may entitle the mortgagee to certain remedies, the mortgagee must not threaten to invoke these remedies as such threat can trigger a later charge of negotiating the workout in bad faith. *See K.M.C. Co. v. Irving Trust Co.*, 757 F.2d 752 (6th Cir. 1985). The mortgagee must clearly forgo the use of such remedies as long as workout discussions are ongoing. At the same time, mortgagees realize that a mortgagor may have ample incentive to drag out such discussions: All the while, the mortgagor remains in possession for the property, collecting its rents and profits, and perhaps milking the property by reducing maintenance costs. To prevent this, a mortgagee may at the same time it enters into workout negotiations, file for foreclosure, if for no other reason than to set a time limit on such negotiations.

As to defenses, if the parties cannot agree that there are no defenses, they might at least agree that any litigation resulting from their disagreement be limited in various ways—by agreeing that the resulting litigation (if any) be governed by the law of a particular jurisdiction, that a particular choice of law rule be used, that a trial by jury be waived, that special or consequential damages are waived, or that arbitration be used.

If there is any disagreement as to what the "complete agreement" between the parties is and what oral agreements exist, the parties still might agree, as a fallback, that there are no oral promises on enumerated subjects (and so on).

THE TERMS OF THE WORKOUT: MODIFYING THE REPAYMENT SCHEDULE

Workouts often involve rearranging the payment terms of the loan. This is because the mortgagee realizes that if the mortgagor files for bankruptcy, a court could order the mortgagor to do the same. The mortgagee, for instance, might agree to forgo missed payments of principal and interest and postpone their due date until the end of the mortgage's term (when they in effect will become a balloon payment) or whenever the property is sold, if that occurs earlier than the end of the term.

In the alternative, the mortgagor may agree to pay whatever he can afford, and the difference between the amount he pays and the amount he owes is added to the principal or else is repayable at an agreed-to date in the future. Or the interest rate of the existing note can be lowered, but the term is extended for a compensating amount. For example, a 12 percent rate, 15-year loan can become a 9 percent, 30-year loan.

If the debtor has other properties free of debt, the missed payments can become a lien against those assets and, with the passage of each due date for a payment, the amount of the lien increased by the payment missed. The combinations of these suggestions are many, but several may also involve bringing other parties to the table—junior mortgagees, for example, if a modification of a senior mortgage might be a default under their own documents.

DEED IN LIEU OF FORECLOSURE

Often, in its simplest form, the goal of the workout is the conveyance of a deed in lieu of foreclosure. This is the least complicated form of workout. In form, a deed in lieu of foreclosure, given by a borrower-mortgagor to avoid foreclosure, looks like any deed. It has the same components of granting clause, habendum, warranties, testimonium, and attestation provisions. Its special purpose, however, is to memorialize an agreement by the mortgagor to avoid a foreclosure action. It is a friendly foreclosure—one achieved by contract. This special purpose, however, raises several problems. Preliminary recitals for a deed in lieu of foreclosure might be as follow:

1. The default should be specified. (Specifying the late charges due, accrued but unpaid interest, prepayment penalties, and unpaid mortgage escrow amounts should suffice, as well as the assumption by the mortgagee of any unpaid property taxes.)
2. The consideration should be recited. (A low consideration gives rise to a charge of duress.)
3. The deed is not an equitable mortgage.
4. The deed is freely given.
5. The transfer is made in lieu of foreclosure.
6. Acknowledgment is made that the transfer is made at the request of the mortgagor (if this is the case).
7. Attached and incorporated by reference is a current appraisal.
8. Disclosure is made of the results of the title search and (if true) a statement that no junior liens exist.
9. The parties intend by this transfer to terminate the mortgagor-mortgagee relationship.
10. The parties to the transfer do not intend to merge the lien of the mortgage with the fee simple absolute.
11. The parties intend to effect mutual releases of all liability on the debt by means of the transfer.

12. The parties have been represented in the course of the transfer by independent legal counsel.
13. The parties do not intend to benefit third parties and expressly reserve their rights against third parties.

The advantages of a deed in lieu are several. The mortgagee avoids the high costs of a foreclosure action. The deed can provide a resolution of disputes flowing out of the foreclosure action as well: actions for a deficiency judgment, attacks on the foreclosure sale, allegations of fraud, duress, and so forth. The potential for time-consuming squabbles between the parties is considerable in a foreclosure action. In contrast, successful negotiation over such a deed can provide an amicable solution to the mortgagor-mortgagee relationship, and when that relationship was long-standing, the deed serves to keep it alive for the future. For a real estate developer and his lender, this may be important. Equally important may be keeping the details of the transaction as confidential as possible so that as little damage as possible is done to the business reputations of the parties. Embarrassment and an impaired credit rating might otherwise result. Finally, the deed may remove the secured property from the bankruptcy estate of the mortgagor. (As we will see, it is necessary to emphasize the "may" in the preceding sentence.)

The disadvantages of using such deeds are also numerous. A foreclosure of a senior lien will wipe out the lien of a properly joined junior mortgagee, but the transfer of a deed in lieu has no such effect. Not only that, the mortgagee may also be giving up rights ancillary to the mortgage transaction—rights to a deficiency judgment, to guarantees of the debt, and so forth. Moreover, the mortgagor may later have a change of mind and seek to attack the transfer for any one of a number of reasons or to avoid the transfer by filing for bankruptcy. From the mortgagor's perspective, a bankruptcy liquidation is a second bite of the apple and moreover may be perceived as bringing more money for the property than a foreclosure sale of any type. Further, the purpose of bankruptcy may not be liquidation of the assets of the bankrupt, but the reorganization of debts as well, depending on which chapters of the Bankruptcy Code are utilized.

An alternative to the voluntary deed in lieu is abandonment of the property by the mortgagor. Abandonment requires an intent to abandon and acts evidencing that intent, such as a failure to perform vital maintenance, to pay property taxes, insurance premiums, or utility charges—or, of course, giving a deed in lieu. However, the tax consequences of abandonment are severe: The abandonment is treated just like a sale or other disposition by deed. *See Arkin v. Commissioner*, 76 T.C. 1048 (1981).

Examples

Example 1

An owner of a commercial office building is in default on his mortgage, and listens to his attorney as she recites the advantages and disadvantages of a deed in lieu. Then he asks: "Why don't I just mail the mortgagee the keys to the building?" How would you respond?

Explanation

You might say don't do it: Mailing the keys is not the equivalent of a delivery of the deed. Delivery requires acceptance by the mortgagee. That's not present here. Nor is it proof that the mortgagor abandoned the property. Further, the mortgagee will want to avoid becoming a mortgagee in possession, with the ensuing liabilities that status brings for the carrying costs of the property. The mortgagee will likely return the keys or reply that he is holding them for the mortgagor. So mailing the keys achieves nothing. The mortgagee who accepts a deed in lieu not only avoids the high transaction costs associated with any type of foreclosure but also, when the fair market value of the property exceeds the debt, acquires the equity of the mortgagor as well. At the time of the mortgage closing, however, recall that the deed in lieu could not be placed in escrow for the benefit of the mortgagee because the establishment of the escrow, with delivery of the deed conditional upon the mortgagor's default in payment of the mortgage debt, would be a clog on the mortgagor's equity of redemption and the deed itself might be found to be an equitable mortgage. Escrows generally should not be used for a deed in lieu.

Thus, there must be a consideration for the granting of the deed in lieu that is separate from that realized in the original mortgage transaction—otherwise, the equity is clogged. A mortgagor cannot release or waive the equity as a part of the original transaction, but that is no bar (of course) to its subsequent release. Thus, a deed in lieu cannot be executed at the time of the original mortgage transaction, and even a provision for one in the original loan documents is likely to invalidate the later deed.

Because this equity of redemption is in fact a right of late payment, it does not arise, and so cannot be released, until there is a default that gives rise to the mortgagee's right to foreclose. What is the drafting consequence for a deed in lieu? It is the inclusion, in such a deed, of a recital concerning the prior default.

As to including a recitation in the deed of the consideration, that is also advisable but does present a problem of its own. Remember the rule that "mere inadequacy of consideration is insufficient to avoid a foreclosure sale, unless coupled with evidence of fraud; gross inadequacy of price is needed to avoid a sale, often coupled with evidence of fraud." Some consideration must be given. Not stating a consideration leaves a court free, later, to infer that factors involving fraud and duress induced the transfer. So it is better to state some consideration, even though a conveyance (of any type) does not require such a statement.

A conveyance made "in full satisfaction and release of the debt evidenced in the note and mortgage" is, from the mortgagor's standpoint, the best that can be obtained. Perhaps the word "satisfaction" is better than "cancellation," unless the mortgagee produces the cancelled note and mortgage, or those two documents are attached to the deed and referred to there. And, when the mortgagee knows of junior liens on the same property, the word "cancellation" should be avoided to prevent a merger of the lien and the fee that would promote the junior's status to senior lienholder. On the other hand, for the mortgagee, taking the deed is the equivalent of collecting the debt, but only to the extent of the fair market value of the property at the time of the deed's execution. This may or may not make the mortgagee whole. Thus, an appraisal of the property at the time the deed is delivered should establish that value and determine the extent to which the note might remain enforceable.

However, what if the mortgagor is not liable on the note? In other words, if the note is nonrecourse, how should the consideration be recited? Here the mortgage lien is granted by one not liable for the debt. Consideration other than the release of the debt will have to be found; that consideration might be the monetary value of avoiding a foreclosure

From an income tax perspective, when the sole consideration is stated as the discharge of some portion of the debt, the conveyance by deed in lieu will be treated as a sale to the mortgagee for the amount of the debt released. Assigning a monetary value to the consideration is thus important for documenting the tax consequences of the sale, for often the consideration will have other elements besides whole or partial release from the debt. *See Comm'r v. Spreckels*, 120 F.2d 517 (9th Cir. 1941). When title to mortgaged property is transferred by a deed in lieu, any accompanying debt forgiveness by the mortgagee will result in a concomitant realization of income by the mortgagor. The underlying premise for this is that since the execution of the mortgage loan was not a tax event for the mortgagor when receiving the proceeds of the loan, the Treasury recoups that loss of tax revenue when the debt is forgiven. Thus mortgagors with loans with a high loan-to-value ratio, who have steeply depreciated mortgaged property, should beware the federal income tax consequences of a deed in lieu.

The deed in lieu should also have, as its purpose, the termination of the mortgagor-mortgagee relationship. Ending that relationship is the reason for reciting that the deed satisfies and releases the debt. Further, the rationale for any continuing relationship between the parties should be closely scrutinized. The mortgagor's continued possession of the property, his option to buy the property, or his lease of the premises after giving the deed all increase the risk that the transaction may be recharacterized as an attempt of the parties to continue their preexisting relationship.

Junior liens on the property transferred by a deed in lieu complicate terminating the mortgagor-mortgagee relationship. A junior mortgagee will argue that, so long as there are no intervening liens, the senior mortgagee's acceptance of the deed merges the senior's mortgage lien into the fee transferred in the deed. This merger of a lessor interest into a grant interest is an example of the merger doctrine. Thus the junior mortgagee might argue that the acceptance of a deed in lieu by a senior mortgagee moves him up, giving him senior status. Most courts reject such an argument; they permit the senior to revive and foreclose its mortgage lien if and when the junior forecloses. Anticipating a later junior foreclosure, the senior will want to head off the junior's argument in advance. But how? An anti-merger clause in the deed might provide that all of the senior's loan documents remain in force, the deed might be given to a subsidiary or third-party nominee of the senior (not to the senior mortgagee itself), or the senior might retain the mortgagor's note, thus not extinguishing the debt itself and at the same time executing a covenant not to sue the mortgagor. Because merger is a matter of intent, an anti-merger clause in the deed provides evidence that no merger is intended. Preserving the loan documents' effectiveness gives the mortgagee a continuing right to (say) enforce the assignment of rents covenant in the mortgage and oversee leasing without abrogating an SNDA agreement the senior made with tenants. Likewise, retaining the loan documents, and giving a covenant not to sue the mortgagor allows the senior mortgagee to participate in a later junior foreclosure. *See Miller v. Martineau*, 983 P.2d 1107, 1113-1114 (Utah Ct. App. 1999). A more sweeping solution would be for a court to adopt the position of the Restatement (Third), Property (Mortgages), §8.5 (1997); it abolishes the merger doctrine for mortgages.

Examples

Example 2

What are the remedies of a junior mortgagee against the property that has been conveyed to a senior mortgagee by means of a deed in lieu of foreclosure?

Explanation

Its remedies are the same as those of a junior mortgagee omitted from the foreclosure of the senior lien. *See* Chapter 18, "Foreclosures." These remedies are twofold. First, the junior can foreclose his own mortgage, and second, the junior can redeem the senior mortgage by paying the amount of the outstanding mortgage. Because the second remedy may involve a large cash outlay, it is seldom employed. The first remedy, of foreclosure, is more likely, but if the junior mortgagee seeks foreclosure, the priority of the junior lien may move up to senior lien status. It could do so if the senior lien is merged with the mortgagor's title. The doctrine of merger provides that when a mortgagee's lien and the underlying fee come into the same hands, the lien is merged with the fee and is extinguished. To avoid merger, a senior mortgagee accepting a deed in lieu should release the mortgagor from personal liability on the note but not cancel the note, thus preserving the mortgage lien too.

Example 3

Considering that one advantage of a deed in lieu is often its confidentiality, one might want to avoid a recital of the details of the underlying transaction on the deed itself because the grantee will want to record the deed in the public records. How should this matter be handled?

Explanation

By inclusion of the recitals in an affidavit accompanying the deed, but retained by the title insurance company or legal counsel, rather than on the face of the deed itself.

Example 4a

Ben Devon develops commercial properties. One of them is the Big Ben Building. It is 60 percent leased two years after its completion. The loan for its construction costs was provided by Builder's Bank, but hard times made the large insurance company once committed to the building's long-term financing walk away. Builder's Bank then provided a long-term note and mortgage, for 20 years, at a variable rate of interest 3 points over its prime rate, for 75 percent of the fair market value. The mortgage contains a covenant authorizing the use, upon default, of a power of sale foreclosure. Ben's four most recent payments have been late, and he has been assessed late payments on these in the amount of 5 percent of the late payment amounts of principal and interest due. Ben would like to continue to attempt to lease the building until it is 90 percent leased. He is willing to deposit the deed into an escrow pending completion of this last effort. If he fails, he would like to continue to manage the property, perhaps giving a deed with an option to buy the property back, but Builder's resists this idea. Ben and the bank's attorneys are negotiating the terms of a deed in lieu of foreclosure. Ben has other real property interests that are not in distress. The following standard form deed will need modification. How should you use or modify it?

DEED IN LIEU OF FORECLOSURE

By this deed, the grantor(s), __________, do convey, grant, and release, to the grantee(s), __________, for the consideration of __________, the following interest: __________, in the following described property:
TO HAVE AND TO HOLD, with all appurtenant rights,
The grantor(s) covenant(s) that they have the right to make this conveyance, that they are seised of the property in fee simple absolute, that it is subject to no encumbrances and defects undisclosed at the time of the conveyance, and that they will warrant the grantees the right of quiet enjoyment of the interests conveyed and make such further assurances to them as become necessary to continue such enjoyment.

Given this __________ day of __________date, __________year

____
Grantor

____
Grantor

Attestation: Executed voluntarily, on ____________, before the undersigned.

____
Notary Public
My Commission expires: ______

Explanation

Your first concern might be whether there are any outstanding junior mortgages or mechanic's liens filed against the property. Will the junior lien get senior status when the mortgagee of the senior lien takes a deed in lieu? Will a mechanic's lien do the same under similar circumstances? May a quitclaim deed be used as a deed in lieu? If you don't have ready answers to such questions, consult your local title insurer about continuing the lender's coverage (if the latter has a policy) as a mortgagee in possession. This might be a good case for giving the lender a deed if Ben has 25 percent equity in the building, its rental market's vacancy rate is low, and there are no junior liens. Perhaps the developer can continue to manage the property after the deed is given, with an option to buy back the property before the end of the maximum amount of time that the bank can hold real property in its own name.

Example 4b

Title insurance loan policies provide continuing coverage for insured mortgagees who accept a deed in lieu, but only for recorded liens and encumbrances in existence as of the date of policy. Should that policy be updated to the date of acceptance of the deed? And should a new policy be issued?

Explanation

Yes, both times, in order to insure against liens recorded after the date of policy and encumbrances created by the mortgagor during the term of the loan, as well as to procure an endorsement against any attack on the deed as an equitable mortgage, a clog on the mortgagor's equity of redemption, and a fraudulent or preferential transfer setting aside the deed in bankruptcy. Such endorsements are expensive, require back-stopping guarantees in favor of the insurer fending off or litigating such attacks, but the mortgagor will likely pay for the new protection. The mortgagee will likely retain the old policy as well as procure a new one.

Example 4c

Suppose Builder's Bank is willing to accept a deed in lieu, but is unwilling to release the note. How would you advise Ben to respond?

Explanation

Ben might ask the bank for a covenant or agreement not to sue on the retained note, subject to exceptions ("carve-outs") for fraud and other bad acts. Rather than a release of the debt, the bank might want to preserve the right to a deficiency judgment if the fair market value of the property drops or has been misrepresented in the negotiation for the deed.

FEDERAL TAX LIENS

The federal government is entitled to a lien "upon all property and rights to property, whether real or personal, belonging to [a delinquent taxpayer]" who "neglects or refuses to pay any federal tax imposed by the Code." IRC §6321, 26 U.S.C. §6321. Even an installment land sale contract purchaser or a lessee is subject to this lien. It comes into existence at the time the IRS "assesses" the lien: "the lien imposed by section 6321 shall arise at the time the assessment is made." IRC §6322. Further, it "shall not be valid as against any purchaser, holder of a security interest, mechanic's lienor, or judgment lien creditor until notice thereof . . . has been filed." IRC §6323. So if, when the lien is assessed, a valid mortgage in a taxpayer's property is recorded before the lien is filed, the intervening mortgage lien is not in most cases subordinated to the federal tax lien. *See Streule v. Gulf Fin. Corp.*, 265 A.2d 298 (D.C. App. 1970) (holding that the lien attaches upon assessment and that creditors protected by §6323 would have to have notice of the lien to lose their priority over it). No actual or constructive knowledge of the IRS's agents of other private liens will defeat the federal lien. Even if the property changes hands by adverse possession, the adverse possessor has been held to acquire the title subject to the lien. A purchaser at a power of sale foreclosure takes subject to the lien, unless the IRS has notice of the foreclosure. IRC §7425(b)(1). Problems involving this lien's priority are matters of federal law, except that the courts, to the extent permitted by statute, may look to state rules of lien priority when there is no need for a uniform federal rule.

In bankruptcy proceedings, an IRS tax penalty may be avoided by the trustee, but a federal tax lien may not: Unless the IRS consents to a reorganization or payment plan by the debtor in bankruptcy, the lien need not be discharged by the bankruptcy proceeding.

Examples

Example 5

MR, a mortgagor, negotiates for delivery of a deed in lieu to the mortgagee ME. G, a guarantor of MR's debt, offers to pay off a federal tax lien on the property, but only in exchange for a lien on the property with the same priority as the lien has. How would you respond?

Explanation

Lien priority might be negotiated, but when a person other than a debtor pays off the lien, that person does not gain the IRS's priority position by subrogation. The IRC makes no provision for such subrogation.

MORE WORKOUTS

In addition to deeds in lieu, workouts may involve (1) forbearance by the mortgagee, (2) restructuring or modification of the terms of the mortgage and note, (3) a (short) sale of the mortgaged property, or (4) a foreclosure or bankruptcy agreed to in advance.

The cast of characters sitting around the workout table and participating in crafting the terms of the workout includes borrowers, mortgage lenders, and guarantors. For a senior mortgagee, undertaking the negotiations for a workout may be preferable to writing off the loan or suing for a deficiency. For junior mortgagees, participating in a workout might offer hope of not being wiped out in a foreclosure of the senior lien. Moreover, all of the guarantors and insurers[1] must agree to the workout agreement; otherwise,

1. In March 2010, the American Land Title Association temporarily withdrew its creditors' rights endorsement for loan policies, making coverage against the assertion of creditors' rights under fraudulent conveyance statutes and the Bankruptcy Code unavailable. The association asserted that in hard economic times such as 2007-2010, such coverage was not a title matter against which insurers might protect themselves.

they will claim that they are prejudiced by it and thereby released from their obligations. This possibility may limit the extent to which a loan can be restructured in the course of a workout. In addition to the forgoing parties, general and subcontractors (for finishing any partially completed improvements on the secured property), sureties (providing bonds for completion of and payment for construction), and fixturizers (when personal property, such as furniture, on the property is separately financed) may be participants as well. The guarantors and sureties must be included lest the terms of the workout prejudice them so substantially that their guarantees and bonds are totally or partially annulled.

The workout agreement emerging from the process must be binding for a reasonable length of time, one sufficient to give the borrower time to work out of the financial hole. Attorneys for all involved will be busy documenting agreements as they are made—no agreement should go unmemorialized—and obtaining releases based on prior, possibly inconsistent, conduct: "In exchange for and in consideration of the accommodations and agreements contained herein, the borrower, its sureties, insurers, and guarantors, hereby release the lender for any actions taken to date and all claims arising out of such actions." In some circumstances, such a blanket release may be too broad. It may be preferable to waive statutory rights specifically by reference to the statutory citation; if antideficiency statutes are available to the borrower, then those rights should be specifically, voluntarily, and knowingly waived, after the borrower has had the benefit of counsel's advice and with a lender's right forgone in exchange.

Forbearance Mortgagee concessions in this type of workout might include (a) forbearing to accelerate the loan, (b) waiving nonmonetary covenant and capital requirement defaults, (c) suspending principal amortization, (d) forgiving default interest (often much higher than the interest rate on the nondefaulted loan), partially releasing security or collateral, (e) releasing guarantors, (f) providing an opportunity to repay the debt at a discount, and (g) changing debt into equity in the secured property. The mortgagor's objective is to maintain possession of the secured property and protect whatever equity the mortgagor has in it.

Any of these concessions might be exchanged for (a) additional security, (b) acquisition of new loans from other lenders, (c) new guarantors, (d) requiring budget planning and financial reporting, (e) maintaining lockboxes and cash management for project revenues, (f) waiving defenses to foreclosure, counterclaims for lender liability, and consenting to remedies such as a receivership, a pre-negotiated foreclosure decree, a confession of judgment against mortgagors and new guarantors, and a waiver of automatic stay protection in bankruptcy. In general, any useful forbearance will give the mortgagee quick and cheap remedies if the workout does not prove to be the basis for the successful operation of the secured property.

Meanwhile, a mortgagor's frankness and truthfulness is key to a mortgagee's confidence in the workout.

Residential loan restructuring and modification From the 1990s until 2008, residential mortgages were sold into the secondary market ("securitized") to an extent unknown previously; demand for secondary market, mortgage-backed securities was intense. When this market collapsed in 2008, the foreclosure rate surged. Why? The market had been fueled by a historic increase in subprime mortgage lending, as much as 20 percent of all residential mortgage lending by 2006.

Subprime lending involves mortgages given to uncreditworthy mortgagors, with high loan-to-value ratios and closing costs, on harsh terms, and marketed in an aggressive, sometimes deceptive, and typically commission-driven manner.[2] When such a loan goes into default, the result is an insecure mortgagee. Existing federal statutes cope with such mortgages. The Truth in Lending Act (TILA, 15 U.S.C. §1635, et seq.) provides a rescission right when the annual percentage rate (APR) on the loan is misstated. The Home Ownership and Equity Protection Act [15 U.S.C. §1602(a)(a)] provides further rescission rights when the loan has fees more than 8 percent of the principal or an APR that is more than 8-10 percent higher than a rate for U.S. Treasury bonds, and a special notice cautioning the mortgagor of the financial risks he undertakes. The Real Estate Settlement Procedures Act (12 U.S.C. §2607) requires an estimate of closing costs before closing, and places limitations on referrals and kickbacks among settlement service providers like real estate brokers and title insurers. In addition, state Unfair and Deceptive Trade Practices Acts provide protection against mortgage brokers and originators generating inflated income statements for mortgagors, with and without their knowledge. Finally, some states have Predatory Lending Acts designed to police subprime mortgage lending by regulating or prohibiting harsh mortgage and note provisions and practices. *See HSBC Bk. USA, N.A. v. Morris*, 190 N.E.3d 485 (Mass. 2022).

Large lender modification programs, sometimes encouraged but sometimes required by state and federal governments, have met with very limited success (e.g., 12 U.S.C. §1715z-23 (Hope for Homeowners Program)). These programs are very time-consuming because they require borrowers to get information from mortgage servicers before even applying, and mortgagees often delay action on completed applications. Moreover, lenders that modify the term of the loan and the interest rate often find that the modified loans

2. ". . . [Courts] have uniformly held that absent some statutorily imposed obligation, lenders have 'no duty to refrain from making a loan if the lender knows or should have known that the borrower cannot repay.'. . ." *See Anderson v. First Franklin*, 2010 U.S. Dist. LEXIS 17285, *22 (E.D. Mich., Jan. 29, 2010) (quoting *Northern Tr. Co. v. VIII South Michigan Assocs.*, 657 N.E.2d 1095, 1102 (Ill. App. Ct. 1995), and collecting similar cases).

are subject to recidivist defaults. Modifying the principal of the debt might help, but lenders have been most unwilling to do this. Up to the beginning of 2010, about 1 million mortgage loans had been modified on a trial basis, and fewer than 200,000 had been permanently modified in some way; all the while, the foreclosure rates on mortgage loans climbed higher.

A short sale In the years 2004-2010, many residential properties lost 30 percent of their previous fair market value. This loss meant that many mortgagors had recently incurred mortgage debt that exceeded the value of their properties. In the jargon, such loans were "under water": If mortgagors needed to sell, the proceeds of the sale would not wholly repay the debt. In the context, sales of underwater properties are known as "short sales." They are an alternative to a prearranged foreclosure or other workout, allowing the mortgagor to avoid the impact on his credit rating that foreclosure would have. Some real estate brokers, however, refuse to handle them. One reason for this refusal stems from the fact that they are time-consuming, requiring 3 to 18 months, and require mortgagee approval at both the beginning and the end; it is a sale in which the mortgagee calls the shots, making decisions on the deposit, the price, the costs and commissions, and the terms of the contract of sale. Some mortgagees have been swamped with requests for approvals, and some mortgagees approve them when they are the only alternative to foreclosure. In any event, the underwater vendor will have to present the mortgagee with an appraisal of the property in order to prove the worthiness of any proposed short sale and an executed contract with a substantial down payment. The purchaser will meanwhile need a locked-in mortgage loan commitment with several extension rights. The contract's purchase price is typically below market, but not so far below to make the mortgagee object, so that the vendor typically walks away from the closing with nothing.

Examples

EXAMPLES

Example 6

B, a real estate broker accepting the listing of a property involved in a short sale, is asked by a potential purchaser whether the property is being "sold in a short sale." What would you advise B to say?

Explanation

The broker is put in a difficult and legally uncertain position in many states. Does he violate a fiduciary duty of loyalty to his client, the listing vendor, or does he become liable in tort to the purchaser for misrepresenting a material fact of the transaction if he is silent? Some brokers will not accept short sale listings on this account.

During the years 2008-2010, the federal government encouraged short sales through its Foreclosure Alternatives Program, administered by its Department of Housing and Urban Development. This program has produced standard forms for use in short sales.

If the short sale is successfully completed, the mortgagee releases the mortgage lien at the closing. The lien's release does not release the debt at the same time. Absent antideficiency statute limitations, the mortgagee may still pursue a deficiency judgment.

CURRENT OBSTACLES TO WORKOUTS

The secondary mortgage market's use, over the last 40 years, of mortgage-backed securities (MBSs) complicates many[3] mortgagor-mortgagee relationships when a mortgage is in default, benefiting neither the original mortgagor nor subsequent security holders. Instead, the structure of MBSs delays and prevents loan workouts and modifications, frustrating workouts that would typically make economic sense for the parties.

In the secondary market, the note and mortgage have been sold or passed on by several parties. The ultimate purchaser is the trustee of the pool of secured mortgages. The trustee of the loan holds the legal title to the note and mortgage. The servicer of the loan is the trust's collection agent (an assignee of a debt for collection); it receives monthly payments and deals directly with the mortgagor. Its agency is broad, collecting the payments and rendering them (minus a fee) to the trust. The servicer can sue in its own name, but for purposes of bringing foreclosure, it is often unclear whether the servicer, as the holder of an equitable interest in the debt, is also an assignee of the cause of action. The trustee in turn is responsible to several types (or "tranches") of security holders. Each tranche represents a different level of equity and risk and has a concomitantly different rate of return on the security it holds: The higher the risk, the greater the return. In effect, a cash flow waterfall is created, flowing first to a high-risk tranche, then to other tranches in turn. Each security holder has, in turn, an equitable right to payment from the pool. *See CW Capital Asset Management LLC v. Chicago Properties LLC*, 610 F.3d 497 (7th Cir. 2010).

This tiered structure impedes workouts because (1) the mortgagor is often unaware of who holds the note and mortgage; (2) the servicer, trustee, and MBS holders often do not know when a workout makes economic sense; (3) the servicer who deals directly with the mortgagor has little incentive to pursue loan modifications without clear direction from the

---

3. In 1970, $500 million worth of mortgages were securitized, whereas in 2003, $432 billion were, and this pace continued up to the financial crisis of 2008.

trustee; (4) the trustee—the party responsible for safeguarding the yield of the secured mortgage pool—has a fiduciary duty to many parties and tranches with divergent interests within the pool of investors, discouraging the trustee from modifying mortgages for fear of favoring one tranche over another; (5) the "true sale" transaction[4] to the trustee blurs the lines between contract and traditional real estate law, eschewing the latter's protections from clogs on a mortgagor's equitable rights; (6) as a result, the difficulty in characterizing the MBS security confuses the MBS purchaser's legal rights in relation to both the trustee and borrower.

The basic mechanics of the market The typical MBS begins with a borrower and lender forming a traditional mortgagor-mortgagee relationship. After originating the mortgage, the lender will then add the loan to a pool of similar mortgages. This pool is then often sold to a Special Purpose Vehicle/Entity (SPE) constituting a "true sale," and rendering the SPV bankruptcy remote from the lender originating the loan. This pool held by the SPV is rated by a national rating agency, such as Moody's, and tranches are created with varying elements of risk. Servicers, typically a Master Servicer for performing loan and a Special Servicer for troubled mortgages, are under contract (aka a Pooling and Servicing Agreement, a PSA) to service the loan. Early in the history of the modern market, in the 1970s and 1980s, the lender who originated the loan was its servicer, but gradually, servicing was recognized as valuable employment on its own.

Past real estate recessions affected far fewer mortgagors. In the 1980s, Savings and Loan Associations became insolvent by dealing in various types of commercial mortgages. During the crisis that ensued, the federal government created the Resolution Trust Corporation (RTC). The RTC was designed as a vehicle to manage the fallout from the Savings and Loans, solving the problem of what to do with the glut of failing banks' assets. In dealing with these assets, the RTC created pools of mortgage loans, and sold mortgage-backed securities from the pools. The RTC is often credited with creating the current paradigm for MBSs. However, an MBS market based on residential as well as commercial mortgages was ripe for securitization because loan documentation for residential mortgages is fairly uniform, the collateralized land is comparable, and residential mortgages have comparable amortization tables. The more money is attracted to MBSs, the more money is available for future mortgage loans. The market thus fed on itself, creating a housing bubble. The more money, the more securitization occurs. This forces mortgage lenders to compete more fiercely, lowering their underwriting standards while doing so and attracting new mortgagors to the housing market,

4. Trusts are organized as Real Estate Master Investment Conduits (REMICs) that, under IRC §860, are required to take and hold (meaning not trade) title to a "static" pool or portfolio of mortgages.

so that eventually subprime mortgagors are closing mortgage loans, taking on debt they cannot afford when the economy and the job market turn down. Thus, in the real estate downturn of 2006-2010, many residential and commercial mortgagors were caught in the web of interests previously described. Today, because of the legal uncertainties in this web, it is unclear who has the standing to bring foreclosure; it may even be difficult to locate the note that must be presented to the court with the pleadings.

Before today's MBS structure, during default an originator would have an incentive to work out with a borrower for fear the asset on their balance sheet would lose value. With the mortgage no longer on the bank's books, this incentive disappeared. As the mortgage is moved through the secondary market, it becomes increasingly difficult to determine who had any such incentive, and further what party actually had authority to initiate a workout. Moreover, neither the servicers nor the trustees today have any incentive to participate in a workout before the loan is actually in default or in imminent danger of default: This is so because adding new mortgages to the trustee's pool is generally prohibited after the start-up period for the trust and a substantially modified loan is viewed as "new" mortgage. Thus, securitized mortgages in trouble are seldom worked out while in the hands of the Master Servicer and, once in the hands of the Special Servicer, the most common workout involves an extension (shorter than two years) of the term of the loan, or its reamortization with a balloon payment, rather than a change in the interest rate or the principal amount. Special Servicers also tend to accept a deed in lieu as opposed to pursuing foreclosing, but once property is taken, within a short time it must be professionally managed and disposed of within three years. As the transaction costs attending these requirements rise, Special Servicers lose any incentive to make quick decisions.

Tranche warfare A trustee of the mortgages backing MBSs owes fiduciary duties to all holders of those securities. The creation of the different tranches places the trustee in the awkward position of catering to beneficiaries who all hold different interests. As a result, where debt workouts were once handled in bilateral negotiations (lender-mortgagor), any debt workout undertaken by the trust would have to balance the interests of a wide array of security holders, all with different goals. The potential for a trustee to conduct such a workout without favoring one tranche over another becomes nigh impossible. This conflict of interest occurs because those holding the highest risk, subordinated securities (i.e., first loss purchasers) will more than likely lose their investment in the event of a decrease in the value of the property and attendant defaults. "Subordinate" in this sense means the lowest on the cash flow waterfall. This tranche will be the most willing to modify the mortgages upon default, because it has the most to lose. However, other tranches, typically holding the controlling majority of securities in the trust, will likely seek to limit the Special Servicer from modifying contracts because they have more to gain in the foreclosure or liquidation of the asset.

Because the most subordinate tranche is also the most likely to be wiped out, typical PSAs confer on its members the power to approve or reject some acts of, or even to terminate or replace, the Special Servicer. This places that Servicer in a difficult position and subjects it to the same conflicts of interest that apply to its principal, the Trustee. For example, the Servicer may not begin foreclosure or modify the monetary covenants of a mortgage without approval. Moreover, a first-loss tranche loses these powers if and when the value of the pool declines below prearranged benchmarks, but then another tranche takes its place, with the same powers conferred upon it.

Examples

Example 7

Ben Builder is the developer/mortgagor of the largest, most sought-after office building in town. The first mortgage was part of a securitized MBS pool divided into ten tranches. Junior to this mortgage was securitized mezzanine debt divided into five tranches. The value of the building declined to only about 75 percent of the value underwritten at the building's completion. The building ran into cash flow problems and, although Ben attempted to work out the loans, the conflicts of interests among the trustees proved intractable: Trustees were unwilling to reduce the principal of the loans, fearful that if the market returned, they would have wiped out the riskier tranches' payments and be liable for violating their fiduciary duties. As a result, foreclosure seemed to be the only option. The senior loan was put into the hands of a Special Servicer. However, with the bursting of the housing bubble and the drought of capital for real estate, the trustees wondered who would show and bid at the foreclosure sale and whether the trust could finance the winning bidder's purchase. How would you advise the trustees to proceed?

Explanation

The typical PSA does not address the trustee's authority to finance the purchasers at a foreclosure sale. If it had, the "true sale" of the mortgage loan to the trustee might have been called into question. Modification of the mortgage looks too much like trading mortgages, an activity that might destroy the conduit status of the trust as a REMIC. If the alternative to modification is a wipeout and (1) IRS regulations permitting modifications can be relaxed, (2) a mortgagor's cancellation of indebtedness (COD) income can be avoided, and (3) the trustees' and the PSA's authority of the servicers under the PSA can be determined and clarified, then offering the purchaser a participating mortgage might prove useful. In a participating mortgage, discussed *supra*, Chapter 13, the mortgagee accepts a below-market rate of interest and the mortgagor gets to "participate" in the cash flow, receiving a fixed percentage of it (say, 20-30 percent) and so participating in any future appreciated cash flow. This is the closest thing to holding an equity interest in a property without actually having one. This might be particularly appealing to the holders of the mezzanine MBSs, since it most closely resembles their original bargain.

Foreclosure or bankruptcy agreed to in advance These are often described as "friendly foreclosure" or bankruptcy, and involve prearranging the issues and questions to be settled in the proceeding. If a foreclosure, the aim is to end the proceedings at the summary judgment stage. If a Chapter 11 bankruptcy, the aim is to draft the reorganization plan ahead of time. Both types of proceedings are most useful when many parties hold liens and interests in the secured property, or the title to the property is held by a multiperson limited partnership or limited liability company.

BANKRUPTCY

Bankruptcy is a last resort and a federal matter. 11 U.S.C. §§1 et seq. (the Bankruptcy Code of 1978). Bankruptcies come in three forms, each with a separate chapter within the code.

A *Chapter 7* bankruptcy liquidates the debtor's assets for the benefit of her creditors. The debtor may be either corporate or individual. A court-appointed trustee receives the petition and conducts the liquidation, but the debtor must be actively involved and continuously review her efforts and actions. In a Chapter 7 bankruptcy, the trustee has the benefit of any defense available to a debtor-mortgagor and can become a bona fide purchaser against any mortgage unrecorded at the date of the filing.

Chapter 11 is a reorganization of assets for commercial debtors. Under this chapter, the appointment of a trustee is unusual, and the debtor generally remains in possession of the assets of the bankruptcy estate (as all assets subject to the jurisdiction of the court are called). It also provides a timetable for presenting a reorganization plan. The debtor must produce the plan within 120 days of the filing of the petition unless the court grants the debtor an extension of time, but after 180 days, any creditor can file a plan too. So the debtor usually will take first crack at producing a plan but is under time pressure to do so. In the plan, creditors are placed in classes, each with similar types of debts—secured and unsecured, for instance. Within each class, the debts are restructured in a similar manner, with extensions in maturity dates, changes in payment schedules, or reductions in the interest rate or principal amounts all possible. In addition, the reasonableness of fees and charges involved in all debt instruments will be reviewed. Each class of creditors with impaired claims then votes on the reorganization plan, which must be approved not only by one-half of the creditors in the class, but also by creditors holding two-thirds of the debt in the class. If approved in this way, the plan is then confirmed by the court. 11 U.S.C. §1129(a). A plan approved by at least one, but not all, classes is subject to further court review, after which the court may override the objections of the dissenting classes if it finds that the plan is fair and does not discriminate unfairly against the dissenters. 11 U.S.C. §1129(b)(1). This is often called the "cramdown" provision of the chapter. 11 U.S.C. §1129(b)(2) details the criteria for judging the fairness of the plan.

Chapter 13 is a reorganization for an individual debtor. She must have regular income, unsecured debts below $100,000, and secured debts under $350,000. These three requirements mean that, for many middle-class debtors, the principal asset of the bankruptcy estate will be a residence. The debtor-mortgagor stays in possession of the property after the stay, and the Chapter 13 reorganization plan must be implemented and completed within three to five years of the filing. After a mortgagee has accelerated the debt under a mortgage covenant, this plan can deaccelerate any mortgage default and reinstate the debt upon the payment of the arrearages in payments, although the authorities and cases split on when the right to deaccelerate is cut off. There is some reluctance to extend it after a foreclosure judgment, but so long as the debtor is still in possession, there is some authority for extending the right.

In general, any chapter of the Bankruptcy Code has two goals. The first is the rehabilitation of the debtor; bankruptcy has a redemptive quality, providing a financial fresh start for the debtor. Achieving this involves some risk on the part of creditors. In the case of a Chapter 11 reorganization, this risk is a continuous one because a Chapter 11 reorganization plan requires creditors to exchange their old debts for new ones. *See United Sav. Ass'n. of Texas v. Timbers of Inwood Forrest Assocs., Ltd.*, 484 U.S. 365 (1988). The second goal is equality of treatment for all creditors: Similar claims should be treated similarly, but the pre-bankruptcy status of creditors should be respected as well: This respect typically results in a court's dividing creditors into secured and unsecured classes and utilizes code provisions annulling preferences. 11 U.S.C. §§547, 548. Preferences are creditor actions collecting the debtor's assets a short time before bankruptcy; annulling such preferences encourages collective action by creditors in order to maximize the totality of interests held by the creditors as a group. In short, the creditors must strike a bargain among themselves. If the creditors do not reach agreement, the court will strike a bargain for them. In this forced bargain lies the core of the idea of a cramdown: The idea is that even a secured creditor's bargain with the debtor can be restructured. 11 U.S.C. §§1122, 1129(b), and 1322. Cramdowns, moreover, can divide a secured mortgage lender's debt into secured and unsecured portions.

The stay The effect of filing a petition in bankruptcy is an automatic stay of any state and federal nonbankruptcy remedies, including any pending mortgage foreclosure. 11 U.S.C. §362(a). Violation of the stay is contempt of court, and any action taken to violate or avoid it is void. It is effective even without any actual notice of the filing for bankruptcy and is continued for an indeterminate time until it is lifted or modified by the court. The mortgagee may have taken the property as security for the debt, presumably to avoid the effect of the mortgagor's insolvency; nevertheless, her pending foreclosure action can be stopped in its tracks. No future notice of default can be sent, no foreclosure sale conducted or, if already held, confirmed—and even the running of a statutory redemption period is halted and the mortgagee's claim thrown into a pool along with those of other creditors. Her secured status will put her into a line with other secured creditors, ahead of unsecured ones, but the remedy for which she bargained—foreclosure—is denied her.

Relief from the stay To obtain relief from the stay, a mortgagee may request a hearing before the bankruptcy court to show "cause, including the lack of adequate protection, why the stay should be lifted, or to show that the debtor has no further equity in the property or that it is unnecessary to an effective reorganization of the debtor's assets." 11 U.S.C. §362(d)(1)-(2). The Bankruptcy Code, §361, provides some illustrations of what adequate protection is; periodic cash payments or additional liens may be provided by the court. Thus, the difficulty with alleging inadequate protection is that the court can decree relief that is less than a lifting of the stay but sufficient to provide §361 protection. Mortgagee creditors wanting the stay lifted generally argue that the debtor has no equity in the property or that the stay is not necessary to formulate a reorganization plan. If relief is granted by lifting the stay, the mortgagee can proceed to foreclose or to finish foreclosure actions stopped by the stay. So the stay may be lifted when the mortgagee creditor is not given a remedy in bankruptcy equivalent to foreclosure. Additionally, the stay does not apply to the commencement or continuance of a criminal proceeding against the debtor, the collection of alimony, maintenance or support payments, or a governmental action involving the government's police or regulatory powers or the enforcement of a judgment arising out of any such action. 11 U.S.C. §362(b)(1), (2), (4)-(5).

Assignment of rents and profits One covenant in a mortgage on commercial property readily distinguishes it from a residential mortgage. It generally provides

> in consideration for the indebtedness extended by the Note, Borrower hereby absolutely and unconditionally assigns and transfers to the Lender all of the

> rents, profits, and revenues of whatever type, including those now due, past due, or to become due, without regard to any rights under any lease, license, or other agreement concerning the occupancy or use of all or any portion of the secured property.

The "absolute and unconditional" language of the assignment is intended to render the transfer nonexecutory and complete ("choate") under state law. In this way, the mortgagee hopes to gain priority over any later appointed trustee in bankruptcy having the power to avoid executory agreements made by the debtor. This avoidance power is most used in Chapter 11 reorganizations of the debtor's assets.

The Bankruptcy Code's §552(b)(2) (enacted 1994) federalized the law on this matter. It provides that when a mortgage lender records an absolute assignment of rents before a default in the mortgage, the assignment is effective to create a security interest in those rents after the filing of a bankruptcy petition, without regard to whether the enforcement requirements of state law are met.

The special case of hotel bankruptcies Hotel room revenues are often held to be accounts receivable, rather than rent, and so the assignment of rents does not apply here. A majority of bankruptcy and other courts considering this issue have so characterized them. The majority of courts reason that a hotel guest is a licensee, rather than a tenant, under state law. Hence the language in the assignment applies it to any "lease, license, or other agreement." 11 U.S.C. §363(a). The effect is twofold: First, the hotel operator may use the cash flowing from the accounts receivable to run the hotel during the bankruptcy; and second, a UCC Art. 9 filing by the mortgagee is necessary if the assignment is to be effective as to room revenues. 11 U.S.C. §552(b).

The special case of shopping center bankruptcies Upon the shopping center tenant's bankruptcy, the unexpired lease is subject to the automatic stay (11 U.S.C. §362) imposed upon any proceeding against the tenant. Assuming that the stay is not lifted, it is treated as an asset of the bankrupt's estate, and the trustee in bankruptcy is then entitled to either assume or reject the lease. 11 U.S.C. §365(a). Neither an anti-assignment covenant nor a covenant stating that the lease is forfeited upon the tenant's bankruptcy will prevent the trustee from exercising this §365 right. The trustee has the right to reject a lease when, in the exercise of business judgment, it is prudent to do so. An assumption must be made by express court order, within the statutory time frame, or rejection is presumed. 11 U.S.C. §365(d)(4). A trustee may also assign the lease. 11 U.S.C. §365(f). When a trustee assumes, or assumes and assigns, a shopping center lease in default, she must beforehand provide the landlord with adequate assurance of future performance. This expressly includes (1) a showing of the source of future rent, and, in the case of an assignment, a showing that the financial condition of the assignee is similar to that of the lessee at the time of the execution of the lease; (2) assurance that the percentage rent will not substantially decline; (3) assurance that the assumption or assignment will not cause a default in "any other lease, financing agreement, or master agreement relating to the shopping center"; and (4) an assurance that the assumption or assignment "will not disrupt any tenant mix or balance" in the center. 11 U.S.C. §365(b)(3)(A)-(D). To invoke this special protection, a shopping center landlord must establish that indeed a "shopping center" is involved, a term not defined in the code. A master lease and covenants, fixed hours of operation, common areas, and joint advertising are elements of such a showing. Contractual interdependence is required among tenants. The landlord's common ownership, joint parking facilities, even the existence of an anchor tenant are insufficient.

Single asset entity bankruptcies Commercial real estate projects are routinely conducted through a legal entity whose major if not sole asset is the property being developed. The term "single asset real estate," defined in 11 U.S.C. §101(51B), is nonresidential "real property constituting a single property or project . . .which generated all of the gross income of the debtor and on which no substantial business is being conducted by the debtor other than the business of operating the real property and activities incidental thereto. . . ." Courts have struggled over the scope of this definition. Raw land has been found to qualify, but hotels have not. The code seeks to expedite single asset bankruptcy proceedings by providing that the court shall grant relief to creditors unless within 90 days of filing the debtor files a reasonably confirmable plan of reorganization and begins making market interest rate payments to mortgagees. 11 U.S.C. §362(d)(3).

A COLLAPSING LENDER

Upon the collapse of a lender, the status of the workout agreement when the lender is taken over by federal or state regulators is uncertain. The regulators often have the authority to "disaffirm or repudiate any contract or lease" to which the lender is a party and is in the opinion of the federal conservator "burdensome," all in order to "promote the orderly administration of the institution's affairs." 12 U.S.C.A. §1821(e) (authorizing FDIC conservators for failed lenders); *See Union Bank v. Federal Sav. & Loan Assn.*, 724 F. Supp. 468, 471 (E.D. Ky. 1989) ("burdensome" means unprofitable, undesirable, or failing to conserve the assets of the lender). Absent an abuse of discretion on the conservator's part, a repudiation of a workout agreement would be hard to overturn in court. Federal conservators take free of many defenses that the borrower might otherwise have against the lender. *See Mery v. Universal Sav. Assn.*, 737 F. Supp. 1000, 1004 (S.D. Tex. 1990) (listing fraudulent inducement, fraud, misrepresentation, failure of consideration, duress, defenses based on secret side agreements, duties of good faith and fair dealing, breaches of fiduciary duty, usury, negligence, gross negligence, unfair trade practices violations, and unjust enrichment as defenses of which the conservators are freed). They are in effect super bona fide purchasers. 12 U.S.C.A. §1823(e).

Index

www.ingramcontent.com/pod-product-compliance
Lightning Source LLC
LaVergne TN
LVHW082026200926
848481LV00010B/2930
9798894101583